MW01117985

THE UNIVERSITY UNDER PRESSURE

RESEARCH IN THE SOCIOLOGY OF ORGANIZATIONS

Series Editor: Michael Lounsbury

Recent Volumes:

RESEARCH IN THE SOCIOLOGY OF ORGANIZATIONS
VOLUME 46

THE UNIVERSITY UNDER PRESSURE

EDITED BY

ELIZABETH POPP BERMAN
University at Albany, SUNY, USA

CATHERINE PARADEISE
Université Paris-Est-Laboratoire Interdisciplinaire Sciences Innovations Sociétés, France

United Kingdom – North America – Japan
India – Malaysia – China

Emerald Group Publishing Limited
Howard House, Wagon Lane, Bingley BD16 1WA, UK

First edition 2016

Copyright © 2016 Emerald Group Publishing Limited

Reprints and permissions service
Contact: permissions@emeraldinsight.com

No part of this book may be reproduced, stored in a retrieval system, transmitted in
any form or by any means electronic, mechanical, photocopying, recording or
otherwise without either the prior written permission of the publisher or a licence
permitting restricted copying issued in the UK by The Copyright Licensing Agency
and in the USA by The Copyright Clearance Center. Any opinions expressed in the
chapters are those of the authors. Whilst Emerald makes every effort to ensure the
quality and accuracy of its content, Emerald makes no representation implied or
otherwise, as to the chapters' suitability and application and disclaims any warranties,
express or implied, to their use.

British Library Cataloguing in Publication Data
A catalogue record for this book is available from the British Library

ISBN: 978-1-78560-831-5
ISSN: 0733-558X (Series)

ISOQAR certified
Management System,
awarded to Emerald
for adherence to
Environmental
standard
ISO 14001:2004.

Certificate Number 1985
ISO 14001

INVESTOR IN PEOPLE

CONTENTS

PART III
IMPACTS ON THE ORGANIZATION

LIST OF CONTRIBUTORS

Mikaila Mariel Lemonik Arthur	Department of Sociology, Rhode Island College, Providence, RI, USA
Julien Barrier	French Institute of Education & Triangle–CNRS Research Unit, Ecole Normale Supérieure de Lyon, Lyon, France
Sondra N. Barringer	Institute of Higher Education, University of Georgia, Athens, GA, USA
Elizabeth Popp Berman	Department of Sociology, University at Albany, SUNY, Albany, NY, USA
Manuelito Biag	John W. Gardner Center for Youth and Their Communities, Graduate School of Education, Stanford University, Stanford, CA, USA
Amy Binder	Department of Sociology, University of California, San Diego, CA, USA
George W. Breslauer	Department of Political Science, University of California, Berkeley, Berkeley, CA, USA
Daniel Davis	Department of Sociology, University of California, San Diego, CA, USA
James A. Evans	Department of Sociology, University of Chicago, Chicago, IL, USA
Irwin Feller	American Association for the Advancement of Science, Washington, DC, USA; Pennsylvania State University, State College, PA, USA
Ghislaine Filliatreau	Observatoire des Sciences et Techniques du HCERES, Paris, France

Joseph C. Hermanowicz	Department of Sociology, University of Georgia, Athens, GA, USA
Otto Hüther	Faculty of Social Sciences, University of Kassel, Kassel, Germany
Daniel Lee Kleinman	Department of Community and Environmental Sociology, University of Wisconsin-Madison, Madison, WI, USA
Georg Krücken	International Centre for Higher Education Research Kassel (INCHER-Kassel), University of Kassel, Kassel, Germany
Séverine Louvel	Sciences Po Grenoble, PACTE, Grenoble, France
Christine Musselin	Sciences Po, Center for the Sociology of Organizations, CNRS, Paris, France
Robert Osley-Thomas	Department of Sociology, University of Wisconsin-Madison, Madison, WI, USA
Catherine Paradeise	Université Paris-Est-Laboratoire Interdisciplinaire Sciences Innovations Sociétés, Paris, France
W. Richard Scott	Department of Sociology, Stanford University, Stanford, CA, USA
Abby Stivers	Department of Sociology, University at Albany, SUNY, Albany, NY, USA
Pedro Teixeira	CIPES Centro de Investigação de Políticas do Ensino Superior, Universidade do Porto, Porto, Portugal
Craig Tutterow	Booth School of Business, Department of Organizations & Markets, University of Chicago, Chicago, IL, USA

EDITORIAL ADVISORY BOARD

SERIES EDITORS

Michael Lounsbury
Associate Dean of Research

Thornton A. Graham Chair
University of Alberta School of Business, Alberta, Canada

ADVISORY BOARD MEMBERS

Howard E. Aldrich
*University of North Carolina,
USA*

Stephen R. Barley
Stanford University, USA

Nicole Biggart
*University of California at Davis,
USA*

Elisabeth S. Clemens
University of Chicago, USA

Jeannette Colyvas
Northwestern University, USA

Barbara Czarniawska
Göteborg University, Sweden

Gerald F. Davis
University of Michigan, USA

Marie-Laure Djelic
ESSEC Business School, France

Frank R. Dobbin
Harvard University, USA

Royston Greenwood
University of Alberta, Canada

Mauro Guillen
*The Wharton School, University of
Pennsylvania, USA*

Paul M. Hirsch
Northwestern University, USA

Brayden G. King
Northwestern University, USA

Renate Meyer
*Vienna University of Economics and
Business Administration, Austria*

EDITORIAL ADVISORY BOARD

Mark Mizruchi
University of Michigan, USA

Walter W. Powell
Stanford University, USA

Hayagreeva Rao
Stanford University, USA

Marc Schneiberg
Reed College, USA

W. Richard Scott
Stanford University, USA

Haridimos Tsoukas
ALBA, Greece

INTRODUCTION: THE UNIVERSITY UNDER PRESSURE

Elizabeth Popp Berman and Catherine Paradeise

ABSTRACT

Universities in both North America and Europe are under substantial pressure. We draw on the papers in this volume to describe those pressures and explore their consequences from an organizational standpoint. Building on the institutional logics perspective, field theories, world society theory, resource dependence, and organizational design scholarship, these papers show how the changing relationship between the state and higher education, cultural shifts, and broad trends toward globalization have led to financial pressures on universities and intensified competition among them. Universities have responded to these pressures by cutting costs, becoming more entrepreneurial, increasing administrative control, and expanding the use of rationalized tools for management. Collectively, these reactions are reshaping the field(s) of higher education and increasing stratification within and across institutions. While universities have thus far proven remarkably adaptive to these pressures, they may be reaching the limits of how much they can adapt without seriously compromising their underlying missions.

Keywords: Universities; organizations; higher education; organization theory; resources; organizational change

The University under Pressure
Research in the Sociology of Organizations, Volume 46, 1–22
Copyright © 2016 by Emerald Group Publishing Limited
All rights of reproduction in any form reserved
ISSN: 0733-558X/doi:10.1108/S0733-558X20160000046001

Claims of a university under pressure and in crisis go back for decades (e.g., Ridgeway, 1968) and regularly renew themselves. Yet universities as organizations have, so far, proven remarkably adaptable. Nevertheless, the cumulative effects of economic, political, and cultural change lead us to suspect, with Irwin Feller (2016), that "this time it really may be different." Whether the future brings a steady but meaningful evolution or the organizational collapse that is sometimes predicted, the time is ripe for evaluating the pressures universities are under and how they, as organizations, are reacting.

This volume explores these topics from an organizational perspective, and one that is explicitly comparative of Europe and the United States. The comparative angle helps in distinguishing between global pressures (of which there are many) and locally specific ones (which also proliferate). American and European institutions share a sense of being under threat. But many of their problems are quite different. The cross-national variation across European higher education systems adds to the complexity of the comparison. Nevertheless, broader trends — rising costs and tight state budgets, managerialism and rationalization, internationalization, and a changing sense of the appropriate relationship between government and university systems — affect both continents. They are refracted through different national institutions and regional circumstances, but they originate in shared patterns of change.

Fears about the present situation vary by type of stakeholder, as well as across continents. In the United States, students and their families worry about the cost of college, which is ever-increasing, and whether a degree will be a ticket to the middle class, or leave them with a low-paying job and lots of debt. For more privileged or savvy families, this can mean an escalating competition for admission to a handful of elite schools on the assumption that *they*, at least, can provide a degree that will guarantee security. The families of first-generation college students may share a sense that college has become a necessity, but lack knowledge about how to navigate the system as low-cost options become harder to access and for-profit institutions seek to fill the void.

American faculty see their own role diminishing and becoming less secure, as non-tenure-track positions proliferate and shared governance erodes. They worry about budget pressures that encourage universities to focus single-mindedly on obtaining revenue, sometimes in ways that are incompatible with traditional academic values. And they observe increasing stratification: between tenure-track and non-tenure-track faculty, between the sciences and the humanities, between faculty and administrators, between publics and privates, and most of all between "have" and "have-not" institutions. These insecurities are amplified by a growing sense that a substantial part of the electorate sees universities (and professors) not just as expensive or irrelevant, but as actively harmful to the national fabric.

U.S. policymakers, too, have their concerns – largely economic ones. How can the ever-increasing costs of higher education be borne when state governments have less and less room for discretionary spending? What is the public getting for its money? Are students learning? Are they graduating? And do they find good jobs once they graduate? These questions are particularly resonant given that U.S. college graduation rates, once highest in the world, are now 19th among 29 OECD countries (OECD, 2014).

Concerns in Europe are somewhat different. Young people in Europe share with their American counterparts fears about their future employability. But costs are less uniformly a major issue for European students and their families, particularly in countries like Germany and France where tuition is still nearly free. The situation is different in places like England, where many universities now charge tuition of £9,000 a year, and where student loans play an increasingly central role in financing higher education.

European faculty, like their American colleagues, also worry about ever-present budget pressures and the rapid expansion of temporary positions. But government efforts to promote a subset of universities to "world-class" status over the last decade give Europeans a distinctive set of concerns. For some, this means pressure to focus their attention on the international stage, and to judge their work based on international (read: American) standards, or risk its being deemed low in value. For others, new metrics for rewarding performance or schemes for encouraging competition reduce the cherished self-directedness of an academic career. Either way, the selection of a handful of institutions for greater investment has produced a sense of bifurcation into "haves" and "have-nots" that echoes that felt in the United States.

Finally, for European policymakers, the place of European universities on the world stage is a central fear. Relatively few European universities show up on the global rankings, due to the continent's history of broadly distributing resources, rather than concentrating them in a few elite institutions. Policymakers are very actively trying to change this. Cost, too, is always on the horizon for policymakers in Europe, as is also the case in the United States.

Concerns about the future of the university may vary by stakeholder. While some may be shared across continents, others are nationally specific. But they nevertheless emerge from a common set of pressures, and lead to some common organizational responses. Some of the 15 papers in this volume attempt to diagnose these pressures, and others to understand their effects on universities as organizations or on the organizational fields of higher education. In this introduction, we synthesize some of their findings. We begin with a quick review of the organizational frameworks our authors draw upon to understand universities and highlight some of their theoretical contributions, then identify several broad trends creating pressure on universities in the United States and Europe. Next, we examine how universities are responding to those pressures, before turning to field-level effects: how do those reactions cumulate into broader change? Finally, we conclude with a discussion of work yet to be done given the uncertainties of the present moment.

THINKING ABOUT THE UNIVERSITY AS AN ORGANIZATION

While the papers in this volume are all broadly organizational, they vary in the extent to which they draw explicitly on organizational theory and seek to develop it further. Collectively, however, they contribute to recent theoretical work in organizational sociology, as well as applying established theories to the particular context of the university. At the end of the 1990s, organization theory, reacting to the dominance of neoinstitutionalism and isomorphism arguments, shifted toward explaining change in organizations and organizational fields rather than stability. But more recent years have seen work flourish on the relationship between the two − whether that means understanding how local actors hybridize institutional logics in new ways, or examining how isomorphism and differentiation can sometimes coexist − and calls have been made for more work in this direction (Greenwood, Hinings, & Whetten, 2014). The proliferation of scholarship on these questions, and in particular research on organizational practices, institutional logics, and strategic action fields, are particularly important for thinking about universities, which are experiencing global pressures toward rationalization and managerialism, along with internal competitions between market and professional logics, and which exist in a wide variety of national organizational fields that channel these developments in particular directions. In this section, we briefly discuss some of the concepts and frameworks that authors in this volume use to understand the pressures on universities − moving roughly from macro to micro levels of analysis − as well as their own contributions to theory-building within organizational sociology.

Global Changes and World Society Theory

The most global of the trends we observe – trends toward rationalization, managerialism, and quantification – can be viewed through the lens of world society theory, which suggests not only that such processes create isomorphism, but also that they can explain the expansion of higher education itself (Meyer, Ramirez, Frank, & Schofer, 2008; Schofer & Meyer, 2005). While earlier versions emphasized the decoupling of organizational practices from environmental demands for rationalization (Meyer & Rowan, 1977), critiques that emphasized the extent to which higher education organizations varied from such predictions and looked for sources of that variation (Kraatz & Moore, 2002; Kraatz & Zajac, 1996) pushed some scholars working in the Meyer tradition to address the local instantiation of global trends. More recent work has, for example, emphasized the increasing formal demands of "accountings and countings" (Meyer & Bromley, 2013), such as that produced by university rankings, which in turn suggests a greater attention to the tumultuous process of recoupling (Hallett, 2010). Other research assumes that global pressures on higher education are real, but explores the cross-national variation that nevertheless persists (Drori, Delmestri, & Oberg, 2013; Paradeise, Reale, Bleiklie, & Ferlie, 2009). And work looking at world-society pressures on universities to become "complete organizations" (Krücken & Meier, 2006) takes a similar turn in this volume with Otto Hüther and Georg Krücken's (2016) paper on how such pressures can result in simultaneous isomorphism (in the European field of higher education) and differentiation (in national fields) (Paradeise & Thoenig, 2015). More generally, themes around global change and local variation and on the ways that rankings and metrics link organizations and their environments – as can be found in papers by Craig Tutterow and James Evans (2016), and Catherine Paradeise and Ghislaine Filliatreau (2016) – more tightly echo these developments, whether or not they explicitly engage with them.

Field-Level Analysis

Field theory has been reinvigorated in recent years with Fligstein and McAdam's (2012) attempt to link organizational and Bourdieusian field theories while also incorporating politics and insights from the social movements literature. Interest in understanding the relationships between fields, not only stability and change within them, has increased. For example, within higher education Berman (2012a) has explored how changes in one field (science policy) enabled changes in another, dependent field (research universities) by changing the rules governing the latter field and the resources available to it. Within a single field, Wooten (2015) has shown how the structure of the higher education field drove organizational adaptation by historically black colleges. In the present volume, W. Richard Scott and Manuelito Biag (2016) argue more generally for the value of a field-level perspective on higher education, emphasizing its importance for understanding the full range of higher education organizations (not just universities), for drawing attention to the role of governance organizations, and for understanding how competitive, as well as isomorphic, dynamics play out within it. Mikaila Mariel Lemonik Arthur develops new methods for describing the underlying network structure of fields, with an eye toward better understanding the diffusion of new practices. In their paper on the rise of student loans, Elizabeth Popp Berman and Abby Stivers continue to explore the link between higher education and policy fields, with an examination of why student loans expanded and with what likely effects on higher education organizations. And Paradeise and Filliatreau describe the emergence of a global field of rankings and metrics producers that is increasingly setting the rules of the game for higher education across a range of countries.

Hüther and Krücken, in particular, make a significant theoretical contribution to field theory in their paper on nested organizational fields. Building from their observations about the changes experienced by European universities, in which a subset of universities are becoming more isomorphic with one another while the population as a whole is differentiating, they argue for a theory of nested fields. Universities are simultaneously located in national and European fields, and understanding their actions as responding to pressures in both fields can explain what superficially appear to be contradictory patterns. By demonstrating how organizations' location in multiple nested fields shapes their adaptive processes, Hüther and Krücken identify dynamics that should apply to arenas well beyond higher education.

Institutional Logics and the Linking of Levels

The institutional logics research program (Thornton, Ocasio, & Lounsbury, 2012) has been one of the most vibrant areas of organizational research in recent years. Within it, focus has shifted from explaining how one logic replaces another within an organization or field to an emphasis on ongoing contestation between logics, the hybridization of logics, and the connection between logics and organizational practices (Battilana & Dorado, 2010; Lounsbury, 2007; Reay & Hinings, 2009). Such research provides a different path toward understanding global change and local variation, with the potential to link broad institutional orders, field-level dynamics, and local instantiations of institutional logics within organizations and in specific practices. Universities are exemplars of organizations in which multiple logics compete and coexist (Dunn & Jones, 2010; Murray, 2010), and past work has shown, for example, how environmental changes can favor the growth of innovative practices based on one logic rather than another (Berman, 2012b). In contrast with a field theoretic approach focused primarily on intentional projects of change, such an analytical strategy highlights the ways in which such local variations can cumulate into field-level change (Berman, 2014).

In this volume, Berman and Stivers link institutional logics and field theoretic approaches by extending Berman's earlier argument about how changes in policy fields − in this case, the field of student aid policy − can provide resources for the spread of market-logic practices − for example, enrollment management practices, which focus on the economic value of students to higher education organizations. Joseph C. Hermanowicz (2016) does not explicitly use the term "institutional logics," but his paper examining the connection between a field-level shift toward the "valorization of shiny things" − universities coming to value activities based on their economic contribution − and decreasing career satisfaction among science faculty − is quite consonant with work looking at the links between institutional logics and local practices. Daniel Lee Kleinman and Robert Osley-Thomas, while using the language of codes rather than logics, characterize the coevolution of two prominent such codes within the university over several decades. And Daniel Davis and Amy Binder, taking an inhabited institutionalism approach (Binder, 2007; Hallett & Ventresca, 2006), make multiple contributions, showing both how practices based on a market logic can spread from one part of the university to another, as well as how professional communities with allegiances to particular logics and practices compete for dominance at the ground level of the organization.

Resource Dependence

Since financial challenges are a central pressure for universities, it is no surprise that resource dependence arguments (Pfeffer & Salancik, 1978) underlie several papers in this volume – perhaps even less so given that universities were one of the types of organizations that originally inspired resource dependence theory (Pfeffer & Salancik, 1974; Salancik & Pfeffer, 1974). While Sondra N. Barringer (2016) finds in this volume that new patterns of resource flows to U.S. public universities have not been associated with similar changes in spending patterns, George W. Breslauer describes (in a less theoretical vein) specific actions that Berkeley has taken to replace diminishing appropriations from the state of California with other revenue streams, actions which appear to fit the expectations of resource dependence theory. While resource dependence arguments do have the potential to be purely metaphorical (Pfeffer, 2003), Wry, Cobb, and Aldrich (2013) have suggested that they may also be productively linked with work on institutional logics. This position is echoed in Berman and Stivers' paper on student loans, which points to potential links between the increasing financial importance of federal student aid to universities and the spread of market-logic-based practices designed to better capture such flows.

Organizational Design

Finally, organization theory has seen recent calls for greater attention to questions of organizational design (Greenwood & Miller, 2010), a call which it appears scholars are heeding. Organizational design scholarship on universities, however, is almost nonexistent (though see Simon, 1967), perhaps because one does not usually think of "designing" universities. The spate of university mergers in Europe, however, along with the emergence of new higher education models (e.g., large for-profit colleges) in the United States, suggest that this is a significant oversight. Séverine Louvel (2016) tackles this topic in the present volume by comparing how pressures for universities to become interdisciplinary – common across France and the United States, the two nations she studies – lead to design strategies that are similar in many regards, but that are more strongly shaped by state preferences in France. Julien Barrier and Christine Musselin (2016) also help to fill this gap with an interview-based study of two university mergers in France. Building on the tradition of Selznick (1957) and Simon (1953), they examine rational, political, and cultural factors that shaped how these mergers were structured. Going beyond that, however, they identify new elements that shaped the design process: for example, the sense of time pressure around executing the mergers meant that many decisions were made because they would avoid creating conflict that could potentially derail the process. These insights extend our understanding of changing universities, but are also likely to apply to other types of organizational mergers.

SOURCES OF PRESSURE ON THE UNIVERSITY

The authors in this volume draw on these frameworks to think about pressures on the university at a variety of scales. In this section, we discuss how broad social changes have reshaped universities' environment, and then review the pressures universities find themselves under as a result.

It is ironic that universities are experiencing this turmoil even as they have become more important social institutions. As Hüther and Krücken point out, the shift toward a knowledge society increases the centrality of both their educational and knowledge-producing roles. Rising social inequality and declining social mobility also give individuals a greater economic stake in their own pursuit of higher education. Finally, the "massification" of higher education means that any fiscal challenges experienced by the university will be taking place on a very large scale.

In the context of these broad societal trends, universities' relationship with the state has rapidly evolved (see Stevens & Gebre-Medhin, 2016 for a U.S.-focused review). Welfare states in developed countries have become fiscally constrained, as the ever-expanding costs of healthcare, pensions, unemployment, incarceration, and national defense, along with a rising proportion of retirees to workers, has made austerity the watchword of the day. In the United States, as Breslauer notes, the expensive expansion of the prison system has placed additional pressure on state budgets. These widespread changes have limited governments' ability to invest in higher education.

At the same time, assumptions about what the government role in higher education should be are evolving as well. A focus on the economic payoff to a degree has made it seem reasonable for individuals to bear more of the costs of their education, as Pedro Teixeira (2016) observes. This shift has gone furthest in the United States, where even public universities have moved toward a high-tuition/high-aid model, and average student loans are sizable. But English universities have imposed significant tuitions as well, and several countries in Continental Europe have also introduced controversial fees, though at much lower levels.[1]

Even as commitment to state-provided access to tuition-free higher education has eroded, the idea that government should hold universities accountable for their performance has gained ground. This has been most visible in Europe, where "new public management" policies designed to encourage competition and provide incentives for excellence are widespread. These are most extensive in the United Kingdom, where the Research Excellence Framework requires universities to collect a great deal of data on faculty output, and results have significant financial consequences for universities as well as for faculty. The United States has, to date, seen only weak state performance measures implemented (Dougherty & Natow, 2015), though more serious conversations about accountability have begun at the federal level, and Berman and Stivers suggest are likely to continue.

The impact of changing government—university relations is exacerbated by difficulties controlling costs in universities. Observers frequently point to "Baumol's cost disease" (Baumol & Bowen, 1966) to explain rising educational costs: it still takes a professor roughly the same time to teach a class of students as it did 50 years ago, so given productivity gains in other areas, education has become relatively more expensive. The cost of research increases, too, with more technological sophistication. Other cost contributors, each of them hard to limit, include administrative expansion, greater information technology needs, higher student expectations for facilities and services, and lower teaching loads among faculty.

Finally, all these developments take place against a wider backdrop of internationalization and globalization. In Europe, the intergovernmental Bologna process has worked to improve compatibility between national higher education systems, and Erasmus schemes have made it easier for students from one E.U. country to study in another. Both the E.U. and individual countries have used their governing capacity to introduce or reinforce competitive funding schemes to strengthen research. More generally, the market for higher education is becoming increasingly global, and while only a small proportion of students leave their country to study, students from Asia and especially China are having a growing impact on North American, European, and Australian universities. The emergence of global rankings and metrics, as Paradeise and Filliatreau discuss, has drawn further attention to universities' places not only in national systems of higher education, but also in a global field.

These broad trends combine to place two major kinds of pressure on universities, and the fears sketched at the beginning of this essay can generally be linked to one or both of these. First, rising expenses combined with a contractionary mood in government lead to strong financial pressures. Second, intensified competition among universities produces stresses of its own. Some competition is a secondary effect of budget challenges, as universities scramble to secure new sources of funding or to attract high-paying students. But it also results from globalization, as institutions must vie with international peers for faculty, students, money, and prestige. And governments are, in many cases, explicitly encouraging more competition between colleges, whether through competitive research funding schemes, as in Continental Europe, or by channeling more government aid through students, as in the United States and United Kingdom.

UNIVERSITY RESPONSES TO PRESSURE

Universities respond in several ways to these broad changes in society, economy, and government. First, they react to financial pressures — the tension between ever-rising costs and constrained government funding — by looking to cut expenses themselves and to raise money however they can. Since paying faculty is still universities' largest expense, limiting the hiring of new faculty is one effective means of controlling costs. Both Europe and the United States have seen university teaching rapidly casualized, with a growing fraction — most, in the United States — of higher education instructors in short-term, generally low-paid positions (Curtis, 2014; Paradeise, 2011).

Other changes are less consistently effective. In countries where professors' salaries are not tightly bound by civil service rules, the salaries of those in less competitive fields can also be controlled, and the budgets of less favored disciplines, like many of the humanities, can be allowed to erode. Sometimes clerical functions are centralized to save money, as Breslauer (2016) describes in this volume, though the savings are often less than anticipated (e.g., Rivard, 2013). Universities have hoped that technologies like online education would save money by allowing each teacher to reach more students, but so far online classes have introduced costs of their own without reducing the need for labor very dramatically. At moments of budgetary crisis, more drastic measures are sometimes taken, such as the closing of entire departments — often in the humanities — at least in countries where that is possible (Hutner & Mohamed, 2013).

Even more than by cutting costs, though, universities have sought out new sources of revenue. Breslauer identifies four main strategies universities use. Tuition-paying students are, of course, an important potential source of income. If governments allow, tuitions can be raised, and/or higher-paying students can be admitted. In Europe, this strategy is hotly debated, and countries like France, Switzerland, Norway, and Germany have not instituted significant tuitions for regular undergraduates. But others, including England and Wales, have turned sharply in this direction, and even countries with free undergraduate tuition may charge fees for graduate programs or non-European students. In the United States, private universities can set their own tuition levels, which have been rising above the rate of inflation for years (College Board, 2014). Another response among public institutions is to focus on attracting higher-paying students (out-of-state or international), or on expanding fee-generating master's programs. Major public universities in the United States and a growing number of European countries have increasingly taken this tack.

Beyond tuitions, universities have also intensified their search for research grants, a strategy which may prove successful for some but which is a game that not all universities can win in an era of flat budgets. It does, however, induce redistribution of resources among universities and contributes to more stratification across both the United States and Europe. Private fundraising efforts are a third option that schools pursue with varying degrees of success. Here, elite private U.S. universities have been wildly successful, while public flagships' results have been more moderate but still significant. European universities, as Teixeira notes, are working actively to build fundraising capacity but at present raise limited funds from private donors.

Finally, the search for revenues results in the general encouragement of what Breslauer calls "unit-level entrepreneurialism." Berman (2012a, 2012b) has shown how entrepreneurial activity began to expand among academic scientists as early as the late 1970s as more resources to support such activity became available. More recently such developments have intensified and spread beyond the research enterprise. Davis and Binder's corporate partnership programs, in which campus career centers sell access to their students to large companies, provide one example of the entrepreneurship that administrators welcome in an era of tight budgets. So, too, do the entrepreneurial nanomedical scientists that Louvel studies in both France and the United States. Joseph C. Hermanowicz draws a line between universities' increased valuing of "shiny things" — activities that can bring in revenue — and the declining career satisfaction he finds among American physicists.

Universities have also responded to pressure by increasing administrative control, which has in turn encouraged the expansion of corporate logics in the organization. As Meyer and Bromley (2013; see also Drori, Meyer, & Hwang, 2009) would predict, as universities became larger and more multifaceted and also faced an increasingly complex regulatory environment, they became more centrally organized. In the United States, this took the form of a gradual drift toward managerialism, as was also the case in Europe till 2000. After that, however, European governments began to demand greater accountability and introduced new public management reforms. This actively pushed European universities – once extremely internally decentralized – to become "complete organizations" (Brunsson & Sahlin-Andersson, 2000), with internal and external accountability, defined goals, formal structures, and professional managers (Krücken & Meier, 2006). The pursuit of mergers, as Barrier and Musselin describe, is one strategy that has been used in Europe to respond to government demands for "world-class" universities while also increasing the power of university leadership.

This change has increased the influence of administration relative to faculty. In the United States, faculty perceive that their role in governance is greatly eroded. European universities, however, were once notably under-managed, so that this shift can be seen as rebalancing at least as much as subordinating academic power. More generally, an increasingly managerial, rather than academic, orientation among administrators helps corporate logics and practices to flourish elsewhere in the university. Such practices include those that focus on the economic value of students, like enrollment management (as discussed by Tutterow & Evans, 2016; also see Kraatz, Ventresca, & Deng, 2010), or on branding and marketing the university (Drori et al., 2013). This shift has generally gone further in the United States than Europe, though it can certainly be seen on both continents (Paradeise et al., 2009).

A final response at the organizational level to these pressures involves the introduction and expansion of various kinds of rationalized tools for organizational management. These may be linked to a greater focus on the bottom line, though not all such devices are. They also require a certain degree of administrative centralization to implement, and can be powerful management tools when successfully implemented. Some rationalized tools, like enrollment management (again, see Tutterow & Evans, 2016), which calculates which students will bring the most value (financial or academic) to the university, have expanded mostly in response to economic pressures (Ort, 2000). Others, like the extensive and highly quantified system for evaluating research output found in the United Kingdom, are the outcomes of explicit government demands. Still others, like the trend in many countries toward rewarding researchers for performance on particular metrics, are implemented in reaction to global competition.

FIELD-LEVEL EFFECTS OF UNIVERSITY RESPONSES

The sources of pressure experienced by universities result from societal trends (e.g., globalization), economic realities (e.g., the challenge of cost control), and government changes (e.g., the renegotiation of the state-higher education relationship). Adaptations to these developments take place mostly at the organizational level, as individual universities seek to compensate for budget cuts, respond to government demands, and survive in an increasingly competitive environment.

Collectively, though, these organizational adaptations can accumulate into field-level changes. In the field of European higher education, Hüther and Krücken note (and Teixeira confirms) two simultaneous, and apparently contradictory, trends: greater isomorphism across countries, along with greater stratification both across and within them. Historically, national higher education systems in Europe have not been highly stratified, and have varied considerably from country to country. But the European focus on creating "world-class universities" has encouraged individual countries to invest heavily in a handful of institutions with the potential for global recognition, and to look to international, not national, models of excellence. This intersection of an emerging European field of higher education with existing national fields can thus produce both (international) isomorphism and (national) stratification. It also produces new forms of stratification between countries, as only a subset of European nations have universities that are real contenders for global recognition.

The U.S. field of higher education – by virtue of its size, its decentralization, and its dominance of world rankings – is less focused on its place in a global system, though this is gradually changing. The pressures and organizational adaptations noted here, however, are driving increased stratification in the United States as well, though as a result of different dynamics. Public universities have become increasingly strapped as state appropriations have been reduced, elite private universities have rapidly built their endowments, and more marginal private institutions struggle to remain solvent. Among publics themselves, a gulf widens between relatively wealthy, sometimes semi-privatized, flagship institutions (e.g., Berkeley, Michigan, Virginia) and their less notable peers, for whom strategies of fundraising, grant-getting, and international recruiting are typically less successful, leaving a reliance on cost-cutting.

As we look to the future of the field as a whole, one question stands out. Will it be one in which current trends simply continue? Or will something more dramatic happen? Some observers have predicted that "disruptive innovation" — whether in the form of MOOCs (massive open online courses) or alternative educational models, like competency-based certifications — will lead to a massive shakeout in coming decades in which many institutions close their doors (e.g., Learning New Lessons, 2012; Selinger & Phelps, 2014).

Feller, however, suggests two alternative scenarios, both of which seem to us more likely possibilities. In one, universities will become (or continue to be) "marvelous invalids": despite their apparent illness, they will somehow continue to perform without much obvious deterioration. To date, universities have been quite adaptable to the environmental pressures they have faced. While the pain of budget cuts has been real, universities have been resourceful in reacting to them. So long as budgetary conditions do not worsen, universities may continue to evolve in ways that do not fundamentally weaken the institution.

However, Feller acknowledges that such adaptation can only work up to a point, and it is not clear what that point is. Should budget cuts continue, eventually they will do serious damage to the institution. In this case, he argues, what we are most likely to see is not massive university closures, but higher education behaving like a "sick industry," to borrow a term from industrial organization — one in which performance gradually erodes, and contraction gradually takes place, but through a slow, incremental, painful process, rather than a dramatic episode of change.

CONCLUSION

At first glance, our review of the broad pressures on the university — of budget struggles, a changing relationship with the state, and globalization as sources of stress; and a turn to resource management, managerialism, and rationalized tools as organizational responses — may seem distant from specific fears about the future of tenure or runaway student loans sketched at the beginning of this introduction. And the papers in this volume, which do not focus on topics ripped from the headlines, may on the surface appear remote from practical concerns, and perhaps a bit sanguine, at a time when a cherished institution is under threat.

But we believe that direct lines can in fact be drawn between the findings presented in these chapters and the day-to-day concerns of students, faculty, and policymakers. Stories about administrators trying to silence faculty members who fail to toe the line (e.g., at the University of British Columbia and the University of Saskatchewan, see MacQueen, 2015;

University of Saskatchewan Fires, 2014; or at the University of Warwick, see Morgan, 2014) make sense in the context of an organization in which the balance of power between faculty and administrators has shifted. We might see them as reflecting a university leadership that identifies with corporate logics, which would suggest an employee who spoke publicly against an organizational decision should be silenced and perhaps punished, more than academic logics, in which the right to speak out is among the most fundamental.[2] Similarly, public controversy over whether the United Kingdom will introduce a Teaching Excellence Framework that rewards schools for producing high-earning graduates (e.g., Adams, 2015) can be understood in the context of a changing relationship between government and higher education in the context of ongoing budget pressures and the expansion of rationalized tools. While the dots must be connected, the connections are not hard to make.

Not everything is covered in this volume, of course. We note particularly the decided absence of students and their experiences. Even those papers that touch on issues of relevance to students (e.g., Berman & Stivers, 2016; Davis & Binder, 2016; Kleinman & Osley-Thomas, 2016) are remote both from student experience and from the educational process. Perhaps it is understandable that faculty are more interested in changes that affect themselves, and that organizational scholars emphasize organizational effects. This is nevertheless a major lacuna, particularly since scholarship can clearly take a student-focused approach while remaining quite organizational in approach (e.g., Armstrong & Hamilton, 2013; Binder & Wood, 2013; Stevens, 2007). We hope that the future will see more organizational research that begins with students and emphasizes the educational mission of universities.

The papers in this volume also focus, as does most academic writing, primarily on research universities, which make up only a very small fraction of higher education organizations. To some extent this is governed by our volume theme: the *university* under pressure. And a few of our papers — particularly those by Scott and Biag (2016) and by Arthur (2016), both of which emphasize the entire universe of higher education organizations — do take a wider angle. Recent work (e.g., Kirst & Stevens, 2015) suggests a resurgence of interest in other types of institutions, which we commend, and would like to see spread. But despite the present volume's focus on research universities, many of the insights collected here — particularly those about new government demands and increased stratification — nevertheless have implications for a wide range of colleges, even though pressures and responses may play out differently in other types of higher education organizations. For example, the growing resource gap between research universities and teaching-focused institutions could produce a scenario in which the former became "marvelous invalids" while the latter become a "sick industry."

Finally, while we see the Europe—U.S. comparison as a particular strength of this volume, there is of course a whole world beyond those places. Nations like China and South Korea are investing an enormous amount of money in their university systems and Asian countries are beginning to show up on global rankings. One can imagine a future in which the flow of students no longer moves (mostly) unidirectionally from Asia to North America and Europe, but is bidirectional or even reverses. Serious competition from Chinese universities for global leadership might also make other countries look to China for a new organizational model of how to produce knowledge and educate students successfully. Yet at the same time, any global adoption of a Chinese model would have to address aspects of that model — like its severe lack of academic freedom — that most academics would not like to see exported. Though moving beyond Europe and North America makes it still harder to generalize about developments in higher education, we look forward to a truly global sociology of higher education organizations in the future.

One volume cannot do everything. The papers here make a real contribution, individually and collectively, to an organizational sociology of higher education that has been emerging for some time but is finally beginning to consolidate. The collective insights they provide not only map out important topics for future research — on the restructuring of the field of higher education, on the organizational effects of metrics, on organizational design within universities, on the dynamics of nested fields — but also point toward a coherent explanation of why, in fact, the university is under so much pressure and how, to date, it has reacted. Will this time really be different? Only time will tell. But the contributions of organizational sociology can help us think through the situation in which universities find themselves today, and understand the range of possibilities that are likely for the future.

NOTES

1. Universities in England, Wales, and Northern Ireland now charge tuition up to £9,000; fees in Scotland remain substantially lower.
2. It is worth noting, however, that the Saskatchewan case ultimately resulted in administrators losing their jobs due to campus outcry.

REFERENCES

Adams, R. (2015). 'Lamentable teaching' is damaging higher education, Minister warns. *The Guardian*, September 9. Retrieved from http://www.theguardian.com/education/2015/sep/09/lamentable-teaching-damaging-higher-education-jo-johnson-minister-warns

Armstrong, E., & Hamilton, L. T. (2013). *Paying for the party*. Cambridge, MA: Harvard University Press.

Arthur, M. M. L. (2016). Mapping the network of North American colleges and universities: A new approach to empirically-derived classifications. In E. P. Berman & C. Paradeise (Eds.), *The university under pressure* (Vol. 46). Research in the Sociology of Organizations. Bingley, UK: Emerald Group Publishing Limited.

Barrier, J., & Musselin, C. (2016). Draw me a university: Organizational design processes in university mergers. In E. P. Berman & C. Paradeise (Eds.), *The university under pressure* (Vol. 46). Research in the Sociology of Organizations. Bingley, UK: Emerald Group Publishing Limited.

Barringer, S. N. (2016). The changing finances of public higher education organizations: Diversity, change, and discontinuity. In E. P. Berman & C. Paradeise (Eds.), *The university under pressure* (Vol. 46). Research in the Sociology of Organizations. Bingley, UK: Emerald Group Publishing Limited.

Battilana, J., & Dorado, S. (2010). Building sustainable hybrid organizations: The case of commercial microfinance organizations. *Academy of Management Journal, 53*, 1419–1440.

Baumol, W., & Bowen, W. (1966). *Performing arts, the economic dilemma: A study of problems common to theater, opera, music, and dance*. New York, NY: Twentieth Century Fund.

Berman, E. P. (2012a). *Creating the market university: How academic science became an economic engine*. Princeton, NJ: Princeton University Press.

Berman, E. P. (2012b). Explaining the move toward the market in U.S. academic science: How institutional logics can change without institutional entrepreneurs. *Theory and Society, 41*(3), 261–299.

Berman, E. P. (2014). Field theories and the move toward the market in U.S. academic science. *Political Power and Social Theory, 27*, 193–221.

Berman, E. P., & Stivers, A. (2016). Student loans as a pressure on U.S. higher education. In E. P. Berman & C. Paradeise (Eds.), *The university under pressure* (Vol. 46). Research in the Sociology of Organizations. Bingley, UK: Emerald Group Publishing Limited.

Binder, A. J. (2007). For love and money: Organizations' creative responses to multiple environmental logics. *Theory and Society, 36*, 547–571.

Binder, A. J., & Wood, K. (2013). *Becoming right: How campuses shape young conservatives*. Princeton, NJ: Princeton University Press.

Breslauer, G. W. (2016). UC Berkeley's adaptations to the crisis of public higher education in the U.S.: Privatization? Commercialization? Or hybridization? In E. P. Berman & C. Paradeise (Eds.), *The university under pressure* (Vol. 46). Research in the Sociology of Organizations. Bingley, UK: Emerald Group Publishing Limited.

Brunsson, N., & Sahlin-Andersson, K. (2000). Constructing organizations: The example of public sector reform. *Organization Studies, 21*(4), 721–746.

College Board. (2014). *Trends in college pricing*. Retrieved from http://trends.collegeboard.org/sites/default/files/2014-trends-college-pricing-final-web.pdf

Curtis, J. W. (2014). *The employment status of instructional staff members in higher education, Fall 2011*. Washington, DC: American Association of University Professors.

Davis, D., & Binder, A. (2016). Selling students: The rise of corporate partnership programs in university career centers. In E. P. Berman & C. Paradeise (Eds.), *The university under pressure* (Vol. 46). Research in the Sociology of Organizations. Bingley, UK: Emerald Group Publishing Limited.

Dougherty, K. J., & Natow, R. S. (2015). *The politics of performance funding for higher education: Origins, discontinuations, and transformations.* Baltimore, MD: Johns Hopkins University Press.

Drori, G., Meyer, J. W., & Hwang, H. (2009). Global organization: Rationalization and actorhood as dominant scripts. *Research in the Sociology of Organizations, 27,* 17–43.

Drori, G. S., Delmestri, G., & Oberg, A. (2013). Branding the university: Relational strategy of identity construction in a competitive field. In L. Engwall & P. Scott (Eds.), *Trust in higher education institutions* (pp. 134–147). London: Portland Press.

Dunn, M. B., & Jones, C. (2010). Institutional logics and institutional pluralism: The contestation of care and science logics in medical education, 1967–2005. *Administrative Science Quarterly, 55,* 114–149.

Feller, I. (2016). This time it really may be different. In E. P. Berman & C. Paradeise (Eds.), *The university under pressure* (Vol. 46). Research in the Sociology of Organizations. Bingley, UK: Emerald Group Publishing Limited.

Fligstein, N., & McAdam, D. (2012). *A theory of fields.* Oxford: Oxford University Press.

Greenwood, R., Hinings, C. R., & Whetten, D. (2014). Rethinking institutions and organizations. *Journal of Management Studies, 51,* 1206–1220.

Greenwood, R., & Miller, D. (2010). Tackling design anew: Getting back to the heart of organizational theory. *Academy of Management Perspectives, 24*(4), 78–88.

Hallett, T. (2010). The myth incarnate: Recoupling processes, turmoil, and inhabited institutions in an urban elementary school. *American Sociological Review, 75,* 52–74.

Hallett, T., & Ventresca, M. J. (2006). Inhabited institutions: Social interactions and organizational forms in Gouldner's *patterns of industrial bureaucracy. Theory and Society, 35,* 213–236.

Hermanowicz, J. C. (2016). Universities, academic careers, and the valorization of "shiny things". In E. P. Berman & C. Paradeise (Eds.), *The university under pressure* (Vol. 46). Research in the Sociology of Organizations. Bingley, UK: Emerald Group Publishing Limited.

Hüther, O., & Krücken, G. (2016). Nested organizational fields: Isomorphism and differentiation among European universities. In E. P. Berman & C. Paradeise (Eds.), *The university under pressure* (Vol. 46). Research in the Sociology of Organizations. Bingley, UK: Emerald Group Publishing Limited.

Hutner, G., & Mohamed, F. G. (2013). The real humanities crisis is happening at public universities. *New Republic,* September 6. Retrieved from http://www.newrepublic.com/article/114616/public-universities-hurt-humanities-crisis

Kirst, M. W., & Stevens, M. L. (Eds.). (2015). *Remaking college: The changing ecology of higher education.* Stanford, CA: Stanford University Press.

Kleinman, D. L., & Osley-Thomas, R. (2016). Codes of commerce and codes of citizenship: A historical look at students as consumers within US higher education. In E. P. Berman & C. Paradeise (Eds.), *The university under pressure* (Vol. 46). Research in the Sociology of Organizations. Bingley, UK: Emerald Group Publishing Limited.

Kraatz, M. S., & Moore, J. H. (2002). Executive migration and institutional change. *Academy of Management Journal, 45*(1), 120–143.

Kraatz, M. S., Ventresca, M. J., & Deng, L. (2010). Precarious values and mundane innovations: Enrollment management in American liberal arts colleges. *Academy of Management Journal, 53*, 1521–1545.

Kraatz, M. S., & Zajac, E. J. (1996). Exploring the limits of the new institutionalism: The causes and consequences of illegitimate organizational change. *American Sociological Review, 61*(5), 812–836.

Krücken, G., & Meier, F. (2006). Turning the university into an organizational actor. In G. Drori, J. Meyer, & H. Hwang (Eds.), *Globalization and organization: World society and organizational change* (pp. 241–257). Oxford: Oxford University Press.

Learning New Lessons. (2012). *The Economist*, December 22. Retrieved from http://www.economist.com/news/international/21568738-online-courses-are-transforming-higher-education-creating-new-opportunities-best

Lounsbury, M. (2007). A tale of two cities: Competing logics and practice variation in the professionalizing of mutual funds. *Academy of Management Journal, 50*, 289–307.

Louvel, S. (2016). Going interdisciplinary in French and US universities: Organizational change and university policies. In E. P. Berman & C. Paradeise (Eds.), *The university under pressure* (Vol. 46). Research in the Sociology of Organizations. Bingley, UK: Emerald Group Publishing Limited.

MacQueen, K. (2015). The acrimony and enigma of Arvind Gupta's exit from UBC. *Maclean's*, August 18. Retrieved from http://www.macleans.ca/education/university/the-acrimony-and-enigma-of-arvind-guptas-exit-from-ubc/

Meyer, J. W., & Bromley, P. (2013). The worldwide expansion of 'organization'. *Sociological Theory, 31*(4), 366–389.

Meyer, J. W., Ramirez, F. O., Frank, D. J., & Schofer, E. (2008). Higher education as an institution. In P. J. Gumport (Ed.), *Sociology of higher education: Contributions and their contexts* (pp. 187–221). Baltimore, MD: Johns Hopkins University Press.

Meyer, J. W., & Rowan, B. (1977). Institutionalized organizations: Formal structure as myth and ceremony. *American Journal of Sociology, 83*, 340–363.

Morgan, J. (2014). Warwick suspends prominent critic of higher education policy. *Times Higher Education*. Retrieved from https://www.timeshighereducation.co.uk/news/warwick-suspends-prominent-critic-of-higher-education-policy/2012013.article

Murray, F. (2010). The oncomouse that roared: Hybrid exchange strategies as a source of distinction at the boundary of overlapping institutions. *American Journal of Sociology, 116*, 341–388.

OECD. (2014). *Education at a glance 2014: OECD indicators*. Paris: OECD Publishing.

Ort, S. A. (2000). Federal and state aid in the 1990s: A policy context for enrollment management. *New Directions for Student Services, 89*, 19–32.

Paradeise, C. (2011). Higher education careers in the French public sector. In S. Avveduto (Ed.), *Convergence or differentiation: Human resources for research in a changing European scenario* (pp. 159–184). Naples: ScriptaWeb.

Paradeise, C., & Filliatreau, G. (2016). The emergent action field of metrics: From rankings to altmetrics. In E. P. Berman & C. Paradeise (Eds.), *The university under pressure* (Vol. 46). Research in the Sociology of Organizations. Bingley, UK: Emerald Group Publishing Limited.

Paradeise, C., Reale, E., Bleiklie, I., & Ferlie, E. (Eds.). (2009). *University governance: Western European comparative perspectives*. Dordrecht: Springer Netherlands.

Paradeise, C., & Thoenig, J.-C. (2015). *In search of academic quality*. New York, NY: Palgrave Macmillan.

Pfeffer, J. (2003). Introduction to the classic edition. In J. Pfeffer & G. Salancik (Eds.), *The external control of organizations: A resource dependence perspective* (pp. xi–xxix). Stanford, CA: Stanford University Press.

Pfeffer, J., & Salancik, G. R. (1974). Organizational decision making as a political process: The case of a university budget. *Administrative Science Quarterly, 19*, 135–151.

Pfeffer, J., & Salancik, G. R. (1978). *The external control of organizations: A resource dependence perspective*. New York, NY: Harper and Row.

Reay, T., & Hinings, C. R. (2009). Managing the rivalry of competing institutional logics. *Organization Studies, 30*, 629–652.

Ridgeway, J. (1968). *The closed corporation: American universities in crisis*. New York, NY: Random House.

Rivard, R. (2013). Shared services backlash. *Inside Higher Ed*, November 21. Retrieved from https://www.insidehighered.com/news/2013/11/21/u-michigan-tries-save-money-staff-costs-meets-faculty-opposition

Salancik, G. R., & Pfeffer, J. (1974). The bases and use of power in organizational decision making: The case of a university. *Administrative Science Quarterly, 19*, 453–498.

Schofer, E., & Meyer, J. W. (2005). The worldwide expansion of higher education in the twentieth century. *American Sociological Review, 70*, 898–920.

Scott, W. R., & Biag, M. (2016). The changing ecology of U.S. higher education: An organization field perspective. In E. P. Berman & C. Paradeise (Eds.), *The university under pressure* (Vol. 46). Research in the Sociology of Organizations. Bingley, UK: Emerald Group Publishing Limited.

Selinger, E., & Phelps, A. (2014). Colleges need to act like startups—or risk becoming obsolete. *Wired*, March 5. Retrieved from http://www.wired.com/2014/03/universities-moocs-need-consider-culture/

Selznick, P. (1957). *Leadership in administration*. New York, NY: Harper & Row.

Simon, H. A. (1953). Birth of an organization: The economic cooperation administration. *Public Administration Review, 13*(4), 227–236.

Simon, H. A. (1967). The business school: A problem in organizational design. *Journal of Management Studies, 4*(1), 1–16.

Stevens, M. (2007). *Creating a class*. Cambridge, MA: Harvard University Press.

Stevens, M., & Gebre-Medhin, B. (2016). Change in U.S. higher education. *Annual Review of Sociology, 42* (forthcoming).

Teixeira, P. (2016). Two continents divided by the same trends? Reflections about marketization, competition and inequality in European higher education. In E. P. Berman & C. Paradeise (Eds.), *The university under pressure* (Vol. 46). Research in the Sociology of Organizations. Bingley, UK: Emerald Group Publishing Limited.

Thornton, P. H., Ocasio, W., & Lounsbury, M. (2012). *The institutional logics perspective: A new approach to culture, structure, and process*. Oxford: Oxford University Press.

Tutterow, C., & Evans, J. (2016). Reconciling the small effect of rankings on university performance with the transformational cost of conformity. In E. P. Berman & C. Paradeise (Eds.), *The university under pressure* (Vol. 46). Research in the Sociology of Organizations. Bingley, UK: Emerald Group Publishing Limited.

University of Saskatchewan Fires President Ilene Busch-Vishniac Amid Controversy over Professor's Dismissal. (2014). *National Post*, May 22. Retrieved from http://news.

nationalpost.com/news/canada/university-of-saskatchewan-fires-president-ilene-busch-vishniac-amid-controversy-over-professors-dismissal

Wooten, M. E. (2015). *In the face of inequality: How black colleges adapt.* Albany, NY: SUNY Press.

Wry, T., Cobb, J. A., & Aldrich, H. E. (2013). More than a metaphor: Assessing the historical legacy of resource dependence and its contemporary promise as a theory of environmental complexity. *Academy of Management Annals, 7*(1), 441–488.

PART I
THE UNIVERSITY UNDER
PRESSURE – AN OVERVIEW

THE CHANGING ECOLOGY OF U.S. HIGHER EDUCATION: AN ORGANIZATION FIELD PERSPECTIVE

W. Richard Scott and Manuelito Biag

ABSTRACT

Media characterizations of the state of higher education in America often seem bipolar. They emphasize either the accomplishments of the most successful elite schools or the failures of colleges that are beset by problems and falling behind the performance of schools in other developed societies. A more complete understanding of higher education is obtained by embracing an organization field perspective, which recognizes the multiplicity of schools that exist — their varying origins, missions, structures, and performance metrics. This diversity is concretized by focusing on the evolving characteristics of colleges in one metropolitan region: the San Francisco Bay Area. The field perspective also calls attention to the support and governance systems that surround colleges and account for much of the stability of the field.

Organization fields are shaped by both isomorphic and competitive processes. Isomorphic processes have been dominant for many years, but

The University under Pressure
Research in the Sociology of Organizations, Volume 46, 25−51
Copyright © 2016 by Emerald Group Publishing Limited
All rights of reproduction in any form reserved
ISSN: 0733-558X/doi:10.1108/S0733-558X20160000046002

now competitive processes are in ascendance. All fields are embedded in wider societal structures, and the field of higher education is richly connected in modern societies with the economic, stratification, and political spheres. Some of these interdependences reinforce within-field processes, some recast them, and still others disrupt them. The appearance of new technologies, new types of students, and changing work requirements have begun to unsettle traditional field structures and processes and encourage the development of new modes of organizing. Over time, the dominant professional mode of organizing higher education is being undercut and, in many types of colleges, supplanted by one based on market forces and managerial logics.

Keywords: Higher education; institutional fields; economic regions; broad access colleges

How are we to make sense of all the recent reports on the state of higher education in the United States? Some commentators regard higher education in the country as among the most successful "industries." The much cited Shanghai rankings of world universities reported in 2014 that of the top 100 universities, more than half were in the United States; of the top 25, 18 were also in the United States (OECD, 2014). By contrast, college completion rates in the United States now rank 12th among 36 developed countries (Lewin, 2010), and student college loan debt currently exceeds that of credit cards. While public affection for higher education remains high, tax support from states for public colleges has sharply declined in the past 50 years.

Can these contradictory pictures of the current state of higher education in the United States be reconciled? We believe that they can if we embrace an *organizational field* perspective — an approach that begins by stipulating that higher education is a highly complex and differentiated field (or industry or sector) that embraces multiple types of colleges and their supporting/ constraining partners. These college populations serve different types of students, pursue diverse missions, assume various structures, and experience diverse outcomes. Descriptive or evaluative comments do a disservice unless they take into account the diversity of this sector.

The field perspective can be applied at multiple levels: from international to national to regional. We limit attention to the United States, and while we report some data at the national level, we concentrate our empirical focus on the field of colleges within one region, the San Francisco Bay Area during the period 1970–2012.

A field approach emphasizes the forces that are generated as organizations of varying types relate to one another, attempting both to learn from and imitate one another as well as to differentiate themselves. The former involve *isomorphic* forces operating primarily within the higher education field, as organizations of the same or related types experience regulative, normative, and cultural pressures to conform to legitimated models (Meyer & Rowan, 1977; Scott, 2013). In U.S. higher education, these forces dominated well into the 20th century. The latter *competitive* forces are produced by within-field forces but amplified and fueled by pressures stemming from the wider environment, as educational organizations struggle to respond to varying demands from external constituencies. These forces have been in ascendance since the 1970s and have produced a more dynamic and conflicted arena for all colleges.

The first section of our discussion describes the emergence of several differentiated populations of educational organizations that currently coexist and emphasizes the regulative, normative, and cultural forces that together have induced stability and inertial processes that have dominated higher education under recent decades. The second section highlights within-field competitive processes as well as wider societal forces that have begun to reshape and disrupt the field.

HIGHER EDUCATION AS AN ORGANIZATION FIELD

Fields are arenas of organized social activities: "small worlds" in which related and interdependent actions take place within bounded networks of relations, guided by shared beliefs and associated practices ("institutional logics"), and overseen by various types of governance structures (DiMaggio & Powell, 1983; Scott, 2013). Higher education in the United States (or in any society) is such an arena, emerging from European origins but evolving over two centuries into an established social system with distinctive players, capacities, strengths, and problems. Fields are also contested arenas in which multiple types of players pursue their interests and defend their turf (Bourdieu, 1971; Fligstein & McAdam, 2012).

Fields are typically constructed around *focal organizational populations*, collections of organizations that share a common mission, structure, and identity. In higher education, the focal organizations encompass those entities that provide direct educational services to students. In addition to these core providers, a field conception incorporates other types of organizations directly linked to them including their exchange partners, supporting associations, and governance bodies. Beginning with the focal organizations, while there are many useful classifications, we adopt the Carnegie classification to identify six types of providers (see http://carnegieclassifications.iu.edu/).

College Populations[1]

We differentiate colleges into six categories, identifying distinctive *populations of organizations*:

1. baccalaureate colleges (liberal arts colleges)
2. comprehensive colleges (baccalaureate and advanced degrees)
3. research universities (focused on more advanced degrees and knowledge creation)
4. associate degree colleges (community colleges)
5. special-focus institutions (e.g., theology, medicine, law, art)
6. for-profit entities (special-focus, baccalaureate, associate, and advanced degrees)

Emerging in particular historical periods, each of these college types serves differing missions and exhibits a distinctive structure.

Baccalaureate Colleges

These colleges were the first to be established in the United States and were closely modeled on their European counterparts. Some have served as the center for the creation of a comprehensive or research university (e.g., Harvard, Yale), but many have retained their original mission, providing liberal education leading to a baccalaureate degree (e.g., Oberlin, Reed). Such colleges are typically small, organized as nonprofit entities, exhibit high ratios of teachers to students, and emphasize individualized instruction. They serve full-time students who live in college residences, so that, to a considerable extent, students are enveloped in a "total institution" (Goffman, 1961). The mission of these colleges has primarily been to provide a basic liberal arts education with some specialized work in a subfield or "major." However, in recent decades these schools have given increasing attention to career preparation (Brint, 2002). Successful completion results in a Bachelor of Arts (B.A.) degree.

Comprehensive Colleges

These colleges began to emerge in the late 19th century as vocational and professional programs were attached to baccalaureate colleges. The majority of these colleges are public, supported by states or large cities. They experienced rapid growth with the passage of the Morrill Land Grant Act – enacted in 1862 and expanded in 1890 – whereby the federal government partnered with the states to "promote the liberal and practical education of the industrial classes in the several pursuits and professions in life" (see http://www.law.cornell.edu/us/code/text/7/304). The growth of comprehensive colleges was also driven by the efforts of professional associations to connect their training programs to a college or university (Bledstein, 1976). These colleges pursue a more diverse mission which includes baccalaureate as well as advanced professional training.

Research Universities

Modeled after the German universities developed during the latter years of the 19th century, these universities adopt as their principal mission the role of knowledge creation and research training. Although the emphasis is placed on advanced graduate and professional training, in the United States, as noted, they are often spawned by or linked to baccalaureate colleges. Research universities expanded in size and influence during the middle of the 20th century by partnering with the federal government to conduct basic and applied research, principally in the military and medical arenas, and to provide research training (Lowen, 1997).

Associate Degree Colleges

Most often taking the form of community colleges, associate degree colleges emerged early in the 20th century, but experienced its most rapid growth after the 1960s in response to a public sector agenda to expand educational opportunity by increasing college capacity (Fischer & Hout, 2006). Today, these two-year programs enroll roughly 45 percent of all college students (Rosenbaum, Deil-Amen, & Person, 2006). Unlike traditional educational programs, community colleges serve a broad array of missions including preparing students for transfer to four-year programs, career training, and remedial and adult education. Students in Associate (AA) degree colleges also differ from those served by conventional colleges, exhibiting greater racial/ethnic diversity and lower academic preparation. Community college students are also more likely to be older, married, employed, and attend on a part-time basis (Deil-Amen, 2015). Many take a few courses to upgrade their basic skills or improve their employment prospects. Faculty in these colleges experience less autonomy and are more likely to be unionized. Increasingly, many faculty are employed part-time, working as adjunct faculty and teaching at more than one college.

Special-Focus Institutions

These institutions date from the mid-19th century and continue to thrive. They concentrate on specialized, skill-based, vocational technical, or professional training in multiple areas; however, the bulk of these programs are concentrated in personal services (e.g., cosmetology), business, law, health services, languages, and the arts. They range from less than two-year to professional post-graduate degree programs.

For-Profit Enterprises

These programs have operated for many years on the margins of the field providing specialized training. The great majority of them continue to operate in this niche; however, during the 1980s a number of for-profit institutions began to provide generalized college training at the two- and four-year level as well as offering advanced degrees. These proprietary institutions are not defined by their academic programs so much as by their distinctive rationale and structure. Shareholder concerns are prominent: these colleges attempt to maximize profits either by growing as rapidly as possible or by cutting costs. Tuition in these programs are considerably higher than in comparable two- and four-year public colleges. Some of the stronger programs also emphasize student services including academic counseling, coaching, and placement. For-profit institutions have also adopted the corporate model of organizing. Curricular decisions are highly centralized, most teaching staff are employed part-time, and much emphasis is placed on marketing. This centralized model not only affords more efficiency in the creation, approval, and implementation of programs, it gives for-profit colleges more latitude in removing under-performing instructors.

In short, while all colleges share common features and beliefs, they vary considerably in their *organizational archetypes* − structural elements that embody different vocabularies of action (Greenwood & Hinings, 1993) − and *institutional logics* − a set of "material practices and symbolic constructions" that provide the models and rationale for a specific type of organization (Friedland & Alford, 1991, p. 248). Moreover, given their wide and diverse range of missions, it is myopic and inappropriate to evaluate college performance by a single metric such as degree completion.

A Regional Example: The San Francisco Bay Area

A better sense of the complexity and changing ecology of higher education in the United States may be obtained by describing changes over time in the numbers and characteristics of colleges in one metropolitan region — the seven-county San Francisco Bay Area, which includes the cities of Oakland, San Francisco, San Jose, and Santa Cruz, California.[2] This is a region containing in 2010 a population of just over 7.1 million residents, and is not intended to be representative of all such regions in this country. Indeed, as the home of Silicon Valley, it reflects effects associated with operating in a more technologically advanced area, and so perhaps can offer clues to future patterns.

To our surprise, this region was home in 2012 to over 350 postsecondary institutions (see Table 1).[3] Table 1 compares the portrait of higher education obtained from utilizing multiple sources — including the Bureau for Private Postsecondary Education, California Association of Private Postsecondary Schools, and college websites — with the results reported in "official" education statistics, specifically the Integrated Postsecondary Education System (IPEDS), which is restricted to colleges that are degree-granting, accredited, and qualify for federally sponsored student loans.

Table 1. Number of Colleges in the San Francisco Bay Area in 2012, by Highest Degree Conferred and Data Availability.

	Multiple Data Sources	IPEDS
Public		
Research-1	4	4
Four-year and above	3	3
Two-year	23	23
Nonprofit		
Research-1	3	3
Four-year or above	78	37
Less than two-year	38	4
For-profit		
Four-year or above	36	13
Two-year	15	10
Less than two-year	176	22

Notes: Research-1 universities include Stanford University, Mills College, Santa Clara University, University of California Berkeley, University of California Santa Cruz, University of California San Francisco, and University of California Hastings. Data retrieved from IPEDS, California Postsecondary Education Commission, Bureau for Private Postsecondary Education, college websites, and other sources.

While the reports correspond exactly in their tally of public systems, they diverge in the information they report on nonprofit and, especially for-profit colleges.[4] The IPEDS data fail to report about half of the nonprofit four-year colleges and miss almost all of the nonprofit programs operating less than two-year programs. Likewise, IPEDS omits about 75 percent of the four-year for-profits, 60 percent of the two-year programs, and about 90 percent of the less than two-year programs. Omitted colleges include a wide variety of programs, such as divinity and Bible colleges, graphic/computer design programs, alternative medicine (e.g., acupuncture, massage), culinary arts, and cosmetology programs.

The public four-year colleges are comprehensive state colleges, three serving the San Francisco Bay Area. The public two-year colleges are all community colleges. About half of the nonprofit four-year programs are operated by religious organizations, while the remaining programs are independent. Both nonprofit and for-profit programs that are shorter than two years are specialized vocational programs in areas as varied as aviation maintenance, criminal justice, restaurant management, digital training, dental support/assistance, travel and hospitality, and fashion. None of these programs granted degrees, but offer certificates of completion or diplomas. They do not appear in the "official" statistics tracked by federal agencies so the time trends data we report below reflect only the more established, conventional subset of the population of postsecondary programs. Most of the colleges operating less than two-year programs and many of the two-year programs serve "nontraditional" students: older adults who are working full- or part-time.

Fig. 1 presents changes occurring over time between 1970 and 2012 in the numbers of degree-granting postsecondary institutions in the San Francisco Bay Area. Note that the population of public comprehensive colleges has remained relatively stable during this period, while community colleges steadily increased up to 2000 and then leveled off. By contrast, the number of four-year nonprofit colleges increased up to 2000, and then have substantially declined, while two-year nonprofit colleges grew slowly up to 1990 and since have declined. For-profit colleges, both two- and four-year, have increased in numbers since 1990. In organization population terms, the 40-year trend in the Bay Area is one of relative stability in the numbers of the two- and four-year public colleges, a decline in the numbers of two- and four-year nonprofit programs, and an increase in the numbers of two- and four-year for-profit schools.

Fig. 2 presents data on changes in enrollment in the five types of college populations. The elephant in the room is clearly the two-year publics

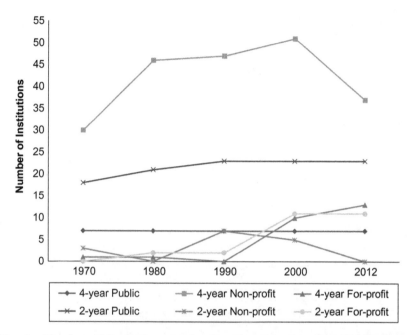

Fig. 1. Number of Institutions in the San Francisco Bay Area by Level and Control, 1970–2012. *Source*: Higher Education General Information Survey (1970–1985) and Integrated Postsecondary Education Data System (1986–2012).

("community colleges"), where enrollments surged between 1970 and 1980 and have remained at high levels ever since. Enrollments in four-year public colleges have slightly increased, especially between 2000 and 2012, and would have been even higher had state funding kept pace with enrollment pressures (Callan, 2014). Space is often unavailable for qualified transfer students, and many of the most popular programs are "impacted" — unable to accept new enrollees. Enrollments in four-year for-profit enrollments have also increased slightly since 1990 even though the number of these schools has declined. It appears that the remaining, more successful nonprofits have found ways to increase their student numbers, typically by emphasizing more career oriented programs such as business or health care training.

While every region will vary somewhat in its specific make-up and dynamics, we believe that our descriptive data are indicative of some of the more general trends in the ecology of the field of higher education in the United States. The field contains a large number of very diverse providers.

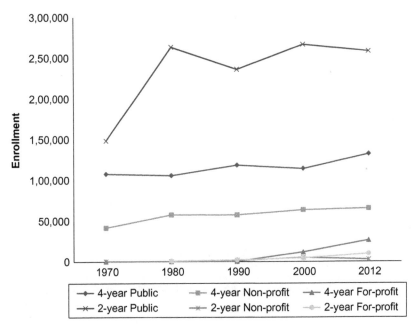

Fig. 2. Enrollment in the San Francisco Bay Area by Level and Control, 1970−2012. *Source*: Higher Education General Information Survey (1970−1985) and Integrated Postsecondary Education Data System (1986−2012). *Notes*: We are missing data for the year 1990 for the four-year for-profit and the two-year for-profit sectors; thus, the figure reflects 1989 data for these sectors. We are also missing data for the 1980 and 2012 years for the two-year for-profit sector, so the figure represents enrollment for 1981 and 2006.

Public programs continue to be dominant, not in number of organizations but in the number of students served. Two-year community colleges have grown to the point where they enroll half of all college students. Nonprofit programs − both two- and four-year − have diminished in numbers while for-profit programs in these areas have increased their market share.

Isomorphic Pressures

As discussed, an organization field approach typically focuses on the providers of goods and services, but also directs attention to many other organizations that emerge to assist or control them. A staggering number and variety of these organizations exist in the United States, a clear sign that higher education is a highly developed, "mature" industry or field. A core proposition guiding organizational field analysis is that pressures develop — both competitive and symbolic — that encourage organizations of the same type to adopt the same structures and processes (Meyer & Rowan, 1977). Within an organization field, these pressures include legal and regulatory frameworks which guide and constrain actors and actions, normative pressures conveyed through interpersonal and inter-organizational networks, and cultural-cognitive frames that provide scripts for actors and schemas for organizing (DiMaggio & Powell, 1983; Scott, 2013). Being similar to other organizations providing the same set of services is fundamental to winning acceptance and approval, and obtaining legitimacy from one's peers and clients.

Regulatory Systems

Whereas many Western democracies operate their higher education systems under a single public system, from its origins, the United States has opted for a mixture of public and private control arrangements. The Federal government funds and oversees a few military academies (e.g., West Point), but exercises little to no direct control over rank-and-file colleges. Agencies such as the Department of Education, while active in standard setting and funding of some aspects of Kindergarten-high school (K-12) programs, provide primarily staff services to higher education programs, overseeing student loan and accreditation programs. The federal courts weigh in on many issues confronting higher education including: diversity, both in student admissions and the hiring of faculty and staff; equal protection issues, for example, financial support for women athletes; protection of free speech; separation of church and state; and freedom of information, including student and personnel records.

Most field-level administrative and regulatory controls occur at the state government level. Each of the 50 state systems contains a mixture of public universities, four-year colleges, and community colleges. States vary in mode of organization, but most operate under some type of state board of education with higher education overseen by one or more specialized boards (Richardson, Reeves-Bracco, Callan, & Finney, 1999).[5] Community colleges are often supported by local or regional funds, and create local control systems. Most states also establish some sort of regulatory system to oversee private postsecondary and vocational schools. In California, for example, weak oversight is carried out by the Department of Consumer Affairs.

In addition to these public controls, private colleges are subsumed under broader administrative frameworks. In the early years, most private colleges were operated under religious auspices, both protestant and Catholic. The former varied in degrees of hierarchy (e.g., Episcopal vs. Methodist), and Catholic systems vary depending on whether the college is operated by a separate order (e.g., Jesuit) or by diocesan authorities. Some for-profit colleges are independent, but most operate as part of a network or chain of colleges owned by a corporation (e.g., the Apollo Education Group owns the University of Phoenix). The typical for-profit system is highly centralized with curriculum, financing, staffing, and organizing patterns planned and directed from the central office (Tierney & Hentschke, 2007).

Normative Systems
Normative controls "introduce a prescriptive, evaluative, and obligatory dimension into social life" (Scott, 2013, p. 64). They typically operate through informal networks, communal ties, and occupational/professional connections. In modern societies, professional associations are particularly powerful sources of normative influence as these groups set standards for their members and the wider public (Brunsson & Jacobsson, 2000; Scott, 2008).

The disciplinary associations play a governance function unique to the field of higher education. As Clark (1983, p. 29) has pointed out, in addition to being a network of varying enterprises, "a national system of higher education is also a set of disciplines and professions." These disciplinary systems are increasingly transnational in structure and operation (Djelic & Sahlin-Andersson, 2006). They are especially salient for colleges in the upper tiers of the field − research universities, comprehensive and elite colleges, and professional schools. For faculty members in these settings, discipline trumps enterprise.

Abbott argues that the resilience of the academic disciplines within higher education rests on their "dual institutionalization":

> On the one hand, the disciplines constitute the macrostructure of the labor market for faculty. Careers remain within discipline much more than within university. On the other hand, the system constitutes the microstructure of each individual university. All arts and sciences faculties contain more or less the same list of departments. (Abbott, 2001, pp. 208−209)

Whereas in most countries, educational accreditation is carried out by a governmental agency, in the United States, until quite recently, the function of quality assurance has been performed entirely by private membership associations staffed by academics. In the mid-1990s, the U.S. Office of Education began to provide some coordination and oversight of these bodies (Glidden, 1996). Six regional associations serving specified geographic areas (e.g., Western Association of Schools and Colleges) routinely review the structures, routines, and performance of the vast majority of public and nonprofit as well as many for-profit institutions of higher education, primarily those seeking to qualify to serve students with federally backed loans.

Cultural-Cognitive Controls

Cultural and cognitive controls stress the "shared conceptions that constitute the nature of social reality and create the frames through which meaning is made" by participants within an organization field (Scott, 2013, p. 67). Educational systems are highly institutionalized in the sense that there is high consensus among practitioners and the public about the basic nature of schools and colleges – the centrality of "teachers" and "students," the shared conception of "curriculum," "course," and "credit hour," the value of being a "college graduate" (Meyer, 1977). Although knowledge and learning are amorphous concepts, there is remarkable uniformity within the United States and increasingly around the world in what constitutes the set of disciplines to be included in a college curriculum, and the broad requirements for graduation (Ramirez & Boli, 1987). The same professional associations that determine the content and organization of curricula also define the roles, qualifications, and training for specific actors, and oversee their ongoing socialization over their lifetimes. Similarly, thousands of professional associations help to define and guide the performance of a multitude of specialized administrative roles: registrars, admissions officers, personnel directors, development specialists, and college presidents.

Moreover, the field of higher education is the only one in which all of its core participants have been trained and socialized by an organization that is the same or similar in many ways to the one in which they are employed. While this assertion has rung true for most of the 20th century, it is beginning to change. More and more college faculty members find themselves working in a different setting than that in which were trained. For example, while virtually all faculty participants are trained in a research university or comprehensive college, a large number of them find employment in community colleges or more specialized systems. As a consequence, many attempt to reproduce their training environment, putting emphasis on the liberal arts transfer function, and resisting attempts to develop programs aimed at providing terminal vocational training (Brint & Karabel, 1991). In addition, as discussed below, for-profit structures and processes depart substantially from those of the traditional college.

To an unusual extent among all the various types of organization fields extant in modern society, the field of higher education, particularly its top tiers — research universities, comprehensive and baccalaureate colleges, and professional schools — have been controlled by normative and cultural-cognitive forces rather than regulatory or market mechanisms. These forces dominated for many years and have created a system of tiered colleges within which individual schools have been pressured to adhere closely to a limited set of legitimate models. Expansion has occurred within this differentiated framework, and the field, up to the 1970s, exhibited relative stability and harmony. More recently, however, competitive forces have come to dominate and the field has become more turbulent.

Competitive Pressures

Even though isomorphic pressures for conformity and uniformity remain strong, a counter set of institutional pressures is increasingly disrupting the reigning consensus on what colleges are and how they should operate. These forces stem from the widely shared belief in modern societies that organizations (including colleges) are constituted to be "rational actors": agents having a defined set of interests that govern their organizing processes and work activities (Meyer & Jepperson, 2000). Embracing this conception, Fligstein and McAdam (2012) argue that while actors in fields share a general understanding of "what is going on" in the field — who the players are and what is the nature of the game — most fields are more usefully viewed as arenas for competition, contestation, and strategic behavior.

From the beginning of their existence in the United States, colleges have been more subject to the play of market forces than their European counterparts. Confronted with higher levels of geographical mobility among the states, colleges have long competed with one another for financial resources, student enrollments, athletes, faculty, and coaching talent. Beginning during the mid-20th century, colleges and universities began to embrace a conception of themselves as strategic actors, competing for federal funds that grew as a consequence of the military needs of World War II and then the continuing Cold War. To construct and implement their strategies, managers exercised more control as decision making became more centralized, faculty governance was replaced or augmented by administrative controls, and the ratio of administrators to faculty increased. Colleges and universities began to develop mission statements and engage in "branding" activities to highlight their distinctive features and programs (Hasse & Krücken, 2013).

Rating Systems

The competition for distinction and resources became increasingly global in the early 1980s, as *U.S. News and World Report* launched its rankings of colleges and universities. Today, multiple ranking systems exist. Based on a wide variety of data concerning faculty and student characteristics and experiences, variety of programs, and quality of facilities and student amenities, these rankings have become more differentiated and informative over time, comparing colleges of the same types, disciplines and schools within colleges and universities, and specialized professional programs. Research examining the effects of these rankings suggests that while they have affected the behavior of external audiences, such as student applicants and resource providers, their largest effects have been on the decisions and behavior of college administrators and faculty members. Many participants appear to have largely internalized the judgments reported by the external ratings and increased their efforts to improve the scores awarded by these agencies (Bastedo & Bowman, 2009; Wedlin, 2006).

Rising Costs

One of the most prominent features of higher education in recent years is the increasing cost to students and their families of obtaining a college degree. For more than two decades, the cost of a college education in the United States has risen by 1.6 percentage points more than inflation every year (Economist, 2014). Three important changes related to costs are directly associated with increased competitive pressures. Two of these occurred in 1972 when a set of amendments to the Higher Education Act (1) determined that federal aid should be distributed to students rather than directly to institutions; and (2) expanded the conception of the field from "higher education" to "postsecondary education." The first change compelled colleges to compete for students receiving aid, and the second made degree-granting proprietary schools, such as the University of Phoenix, eligible to admit such students. From this time, nonprofits were forced to compete not only with other nonprofits but also with for-profits for students (Carnegie Commission, 1973, Peterson, 2007).

The third change has occurred as a result of declining fiscal support from the federal government and the states for public education. With the end of the Cold War and greater attention to rising deficits, the federal government has cut back significantly on research grants and contracts to higher education. These changes, however, have primarily impacted research universities. Of more importance for mainstream public colleges, funding from the states has dropped from averaging over 50 percent of public college revenues in the 1970s to under 30 percent in 2012 (National Center for Educational statistics, 2012). Colleges attempt to make up these differences by increasing tuition and fees and competing for students – including out-of-state and foreign students – to be able to meet these higher costs. Increasing competition for students also indirectly contributes to rising costs as colleges attempt to attract students by expanding their offerings or providing more attractive facilities and amenities, engaging in an "arms race" to attract the best students.

SOCIETAL FORCES SHAPING THE FIELD OF HIGHER EDUCATION

As Friedland and Alford (1991) have pointed out, all organization fields are subsystems of wider societal structures, which contain differentiated and sometimes conflicting objectives and follow diverse institutional logics. Stevens and colleagues (Stevens, Armstrong, & Arum, 2008) point out that colleges have become a central "hub" of modern societies – interdependent with and shaped by other vital sectors including the economy, government, and the stratification system.

Reinforcing and Recasting Forces

Economic and Stratification Connections
In earlier days, colleges and universities were viewed as "ivory towers," separated and protected from business, commerce, and the practical demands of living. To be sure, colleges have long served as primary levers of upward mobility, having become the mechanisms through families could deploy their resources to insure the success of their children (Fischer & Hout, 2006). Early routes led to destinations such as the ministry, law, and the healing professions, but more recently careers in business and engineering are favored. As the world has become more dependent on the development of scientific knowledge and technological know-how, educational

institutions are increasingly viewed as engines of economic development (Berman, 2012). This conception arose out of and reinforces a broader conception of the university as the seat of and champion for modernization and rationalization forces in the modern world (Meyer, Ramirez, Frank, & Schofer, 2007). Accompanying this change in macro framing of the functions of higher education, at the micro level, driven by the popularity of neo-liberal beliefs, popular opinion in most societies now views education as primarily serving private interests rather than public purposes. College institutional logics which for many years emphasized the centrality of the liberal arts are being reframed to stress the importance of the practical arts. Research by Brint (2002) on changing curricular choices by students in four-year liberal arts and colleges reports that since the 1970s students are increasingly choosing programs that emphasize occupational and professional skills. Most colleges still contribute to a person's "cultural capital" – cultivating their tastes and broader intellectual and civic knowledge – but give the lion's share of attention to increasing their "human capital" – their value in the labor market.

Our studies of degree-granting colleges in the San Francisco Bay Area reveal substantial change since 1970 in the curriculum and internal structuring of instruction in colleges. Across all types of colleges, occupational and professional versus liberal arts programs have grown to the point where they account for a majority of degrees conferred. Programs such as business, engineering, computer science, and health care are attracting students to the point where many of these courses in state colleges are "impacted" – unable to admit new students. By contrast, humanities courses such as history and English are declining in enrollments, as are many social science programs. The proportion of tenure-track faculty has also declined throughout the period in all types of college populations, and in many of the community colleges, tenured faculty members are asked to carry the administrative burdens of curricular planning and report preparation, as well as to oversee the growing number of part-time instructors and adjunct faculty. Many of the "adjuncts" are recruited from industry and are expected to bring to their teaching expertise in their current work as well as contacts with companies for students.

As predicted by resource dependency theory (Pfeffer & Salancik, 1978; see also, Weisbrod, Ballou, & Asch, 2008), all colleges are engaging in "boundary-spanning" activities to better connect to sources of support. In recent decades, many colleges in the Bay Area have worked to develop a variety of ties with local industry to, for example, create industry advisory boards to assist colleges in developing "relevant" career and technical course offerings, develop internships opportunities for students, and jointly arranged internship or placement programs. As expected, the extent of these efforts varied across the region, colleges in the southern (San Jose) area and the northern (San Francisco) area, being much more active in creating these programs than those in the East Bay (Oakland). Micro regions create varying pressures as well as opportunities for developing partnerships with local employers.

Governmental Connections
In addition to federal grants and contracts to research universities, the earliest support at the national level for colleges and universities began at the end of World War II with the creation of the G.I. program to support, among other benefits, the continuing education of returning veterans. By 1956, roughly 2.2 million veterans had used these funds to attend colleges or universities. Through a series of continuing revisions, the program provided support for successive cohorts of veterans from the Korean to the Vietnamese conflicts (Keane, 2001). In addition to aiding individual students, these monies were indirectly instrumental in shoring up the financial support for both public and private colleges during the post-war period. Currently, the largest source of federal support for higher education is the "Title Four" program under the Department of Education, which provides low-interest loans to students.

However, the larger governmental thrust in support of higher education has taken place at the state level. California led the way in expanding the number and types of public postsecondary institutions available to serve its rapidly growing population. Beginning early in the 1920s, this state became the first in the nation to create a system of public community colleges to provide two years of college to students seeking transfer and terminal degrees as well as educational opportunities for part-time adult students. By 1930, roughly 20 percent of California's college-age populations were in an institution of higher education, compared to 10 percent in the other states (Douglass, 2010). This progress was notably advanced in the 1960s with the passage of the state's "Master Plan" for higher education, which created three tiers of programs: community colleges, state comprehensive colleges, and research universities (Rothblatt, 1992). These policy changes were coupled with expanded financial support for all tiers, especially community colleges, which by 1975 enrolled some 60 percent of all California undergraduate students and, by 2006, 70 percent (Douglass, 2010). However, as suggested by the graphs in Fig. 1, since 1980, funding for higher education has been volatile, reflecting the ups and downs of the business cycle and political priorities (Callan, 2014), so that enrollments have not kept pace with demand.

California was only the point of the arrow of change in this country:

> Over the course of the twentieth century, the United States built one of the largest and most comprehensive public educational systems in the world ... At the end of World War II, there was space enough in colleges and universities for only one-fifth of Americans age eighteen to twenty-two; by the early 1990s, there was space enough for about four-fifths of them. The expansion came about almost solely through the construction and subsidization of *public* higher education. (Fischer & Hout, 2006, p. 21, p. 251)

As Stevens (2007), points out, public policy in higher education has been the most important welfare program for the middle class during the second half of the 20th century.

Disruptive Forces

New Technologies

The new computer-based technologies have transformed virtually every industry sector within modern societies, and workers in many white- and blue-collar jobs are expected to regularly interface with them in the course of their daily work (Karoly & Paris, 2004). These same forces are just now beginning to penetrate higher education. They began to move into colleges in the late 1990s and early 2000s, as some public colleges incorporated a few online courses into their curriculum. For-profit colleges, however, were quickly out in front in terms of adoption rates during this early period. Online instruction was more compatible with their mode of operation, which was built on centralized controls, greatly reduced faculty discretion, emphasis on cost savings, and attracting large numbers of students (Tierney & Hentschke, 2007).

Somewhat unexpectedly, a new cadre of players — faculty within major research universities — began to take leadership in advancing online teaching technologies. The first Massive Open Online Courses (MOOCS) appeared in Canada in 2008, but were quickly followed by the efforts of faculty members at Harvard, MIT (Massachusetts Institute of Technology), and Stanford, who partnered with nonprofit providers (e.g., Coursera, Udacity), to develop and distribute materials featuring first-rate scholars teaching foundational courses available to students online at little or no cost (Economist, 2014).

MOOCS, however, have proved not to be a panacea. Although enrollments are often large, with enrollees in some courses numbering into the hundreds of thousands, completions have been disappointing, with more than 75–95 percent failing to finish the course. The current period is one of rethinking and improvisation. Content is being modified to emphasize more interactive, customized programs. Computers are being constructed to function more as tutors than as rote instructors. Additionally, courses are increasingly being "blended," combining online instruction with face-to-face interactive groups organized to reinforce and supplement the materials presented (Kamenetz, 2010, 2015).

New Types of Students and Work Requirements
During the last half century, important shifts have occurred in the markers associated with becoming an adult (leaving home, finishing school, finding work, getting married, having children), indicating a broader change in life course transitions (Berlin, Furstenberg, & Waters, 2010; Settersten & Ray, 2010). Schooling is no longer reserved primarily for those under 25 and, given changes in the world of work both in job requirements and the structuring of the labor market, adults are returning — more than once over the course of their work life — to schools for additional training. These developments are particularly prominent in regions hosting the new economy — such as the Bay Area. Workers in the newer industries, including computers, internet services, social media, and biotechnology, are expected to regularly upgrade their skills, advance by moving across organizations rather than being promoted by their employers, work as contract or temporary employees, and be responsible for their own medical and retirement benefits (Benner, 2002).

Because of the increased importance of education in obtaining desirable jobs, more and different types of students are seeking entrance to college. While the more conventional types of students continue to predominate in the more traditional, baccalaureate, residential colleges, "nontraditional" students — older, independent, married, part-time, off-campus, non-Caucasian, first-generation — are now in the majority in the newer types of colleges: community colleges and for-profit schools. Indeed, in 2007, these two school types accounted for almost three-fourths of first-year undergraduate enrollments in the United States (Deil-Amen, 2015).

New Forms
As first recognized by the institutional economist, Schumpeter (1961), when new disruptive technologies arise they unleash "the gales of creative

destruction," crippling existing industries and their component organizations, but giving rise to new ways of organizing: to new forms and reconfigured organizational fields. Community colleges arrived in response to two earlier developments – demographic (expanding numbers) and political (demands for increased access) – but in recent years have adapted their programs to accommodate the demands of "nontraditional" students and new industries. For-profit colleges, which had long operated on the sidelines of the higher education field, found themselves front-and-center and well positioned to take advantage of the demands posed by the new types of students.

Rather than reluctantly bending to the winds of the marketplace, as have public colleges, for-profits have actively embraced the challenge. Most of these schools operate within a corporate structure, featuring strong centralized controls exercised by managers who act as agents for stockholders. Faculty governance is nonexistent; virtually all faculty members are part-time. Curricular planning and faculty training are also centralized. Course selection is driven primarily by market demand not faculty preference. Students are treated as customers not as clients, and great importance is placed on student evaluations of courses and faculty. Faculty are assisted by novel types of staff such as marketing personnel and "success coaches" who provide advice and assistance to students. Academic terms such as semesters and quarters are abolished; most students take one or two courses at a time, each lasting a few weeks. Students are admitted the day they apply and frequently are granted academic credit for past experiences and skills acquired. In sum, for-profits follow a different organizing template than traditional colleges (Tierney & Hentschke, 2007).

While for-profits emphasize the role of technology and market processes in their image and promotional materials, they have benefitted greatly from legislation passed in the 1970s, described above, which allows them to qualify for public funding. The majority of current enrollees in these programs are students receiving federal loans.

Community colleges operate increasingly as hybrid structures, with tenured faculty overseeing and staffing more conventional degree programs while large number of part-time, adjunct faculty staff the more skills-oriented, practical programs. The latter programs are designed and governed by school and department administrators in programs such as engineering, computer design, and health care.[6] They are often conducted in close association with industry representatives and advisory boards. The extent to which schools and programs within community colleges embrace such entrepreneurial programs and processes varies substantially from program to program and from region to region, but most colleges are moving in this direction. Presiding over this type of hybrid enterprise presents unusual and demanding challenges for college leadership.

Our research on colleges in the San Francisco Bay Area suggests that while some public colleges and their leaders are engaged in heroic and imaginative efforts to enable their programs to be responsive to industry demands, the pace of change is such that it is very difficult for these more traditional programs to adapt quickly enough to meet the needs of companies. Long established isomorphic pressures create organizational inertia. Such conditions provide for-profits, which are better able to quickly respond to changing needs and demands, a competitive edge in this region.

Nevertheless, it is important to emphasize that the most important context confronting for-profit colleges is the extant field of higher education. For-profit colleges have been careful to adopt and exhibit many of the trappings widely associated with the taken-for-granted meaning of what a "college" is. They use much of the traditional vocabulary − for example, faculty, courses, credit hours − and in addition to awarding "certificates" signaling the possession of specific skills, they retain emphasis on providing "degrees," signifying broader and deeper knowledge and capabilities. In any mature field, it is good for a participant to emphasize distinguishing characteristics, but it is essential to exhibit generic features indicating you are an accepted member of the "college" category.

Moreover, while "organization inertia" often has negative connotations, many celebrate the capacity of colleges to resist market processes in order to retain their commitment to serving longer-term academic values and to continue to stress the importance of liberal arts programs for students as a means of promoting civic virtues and enabling quality lives.

CONCLUDING COMMENTS

The sector of higher education is usefully viewed as a differentiated organization field that encompasses diverse types of organization populations providing postsecondary educational services oriented around multiple missions and serving a wide range of students. These organizations are connected to − constrained and supported by − other organizations and associations which together constitute a complex ecological system. The several college populations arose at different times, exhibit varying structural characteristics, and have experienced diverse survival rates. Public programs, dominant throughout the 20th century, remain relatively resilient up to the present time, with community colleges experiencing strong growth. Private nonprofit programs have declined in numbers and size, while for-profits, although highly volatile, have experienced rapid growth.

Organizations are shaped by and respond to varying field-wide forces, including isomorphic and competitive pressures. Throughout most of their history, isomorphic pressures on colleges, carried and enforced by academic professional associations, have been strong. More recently, frames and norms associated with the modern conception of organizations have brought to the fore competitive forces encouraging each collage organization to cultivate its own distinctive mission and brand. These developments have been enhanced by the efforts of media to compare and rate colleges.

The field of higher education is embedded in wider society-wide economic, stratification, and political systems. As societal institutional logics change, these beliefs are incorporated into the fabric of colleges, so that increasingly colleges are assumed to serve private rather than public interests, and are expected to contribute not only to general cultural but to individual human capital. Some types of external pressures have been even more disruptive, giving rise to new kinds of organizations: to new types of colleges. Created early in the 20th century, community colleges have been better able to absorb and adapt to changes in information and communication technologies and provide the kinds of skills required in the new economy. Even more so, for-profits colleges have succeeded in shuffling off most of the traditional academic structures and routines to respond rapidly to changing job demands. Still, for-profit schools work to maintain their legitimacy as academic institutions and are constrained by the demands of being taken seriously by other organizations and governance bodies within the field.

In general, however, as in many other fields (see Scott, 2013, pp. 251−256), a professional organization model in which faculty members relied on collegial controls and exercised a large measure of self-governance is giving way to a more managerial model in which administrators exercise strategic control and increasingly respond to market forces. Even in upper tier programs, these changes are evident in, for example, the declining ratio of tenure-track faculty, and the growing numbers and influence of educational managers.

NOTES

1. This section draws extensively on Scott (2015).
2. For this study, we define the Bay Area as encompassing seven counties: Alameda, Contra Costa, Marin, San Francisco, San Mateo, Santa Clara, and Santa Cruz.
3. Even this number understates the presence of postsecondary programs in the San Francisco Bay Area. Excluded, for example, are a number of branch campuses from distant universities, such as Carnegie-Mellon, the operation of Extension Programs by state universities, such as the University of California Berkeley and Santa Cruz, and specialized training programs, both those internal to companies (e.g., Cisco Systems, Hewlett Packard) and free-standing (e.g., "boot camps" for computer training).
4. In virtually all publically available data sources, public organizations, as well as those receiving public funding are over-represented. These organizations are subject to more stringent transparency and reporting requirements than are private organizations (Dobbin, Edelman, Meyer, Scott, & Swidler, 1988).
5. In California, for example, public higher education is organized into three segments, the University of California (research universities), the California State Universities (comprehensive colleges), and the California Community Colleges. Each operates under a separate governing board whose autonomy and powers vary considerably. For example, there is much greater legislative intervention in and oversight for the community colleges than the other two segments (Richardson & Martinez, 2009).
6. In the San Francisco Bay Area, Stanford University in particular, and other research universities have provided important models for these programs. The Stanford School of Engineering has pioneered in partnering with industry and encouraging its faculty members to engage in entrepreneurial activities, such as founding start-up companies to follow innovations from ideas to products (Gibbons, 2000).

ACKNOWLEDGMENTS

This paper had its origins in work the senior author began as a part of the project, "Reform and Innovation in the Changing Ecology of U.S. Higher Education" funded by the Bill and Melinda Gates Foundation, Michael W. Kirst and Mitchell Stevens, Principal Investigators, Stanford University School of Education (Kirst & Stevens, 2015). It reports early findings from a follow-up study conducted by staff associated with the John W. Gardner Center for the Youth and Their Communities, Stanford University. This research is supported by the S. D. Bechtel, Jr. Foundation and LearningWorks, Michael W. Kirst, Principal Investigator. Brian Holzman and Bernardo Lara provided statistical support for the work reported.

REFERENCES

Abbott, A. (2001). *Chaos of disciplines*. Chicago, IL: University of Chicago Press.

Bastedo, M. N., & Bowman, N. A. (2009). *U.S. news & world report* college rankings: Modeling institutional effects on organizational reputation. *American Journal of Education, 116*, 163–183.

Benner, C. (2002). *Work in the new economy: Flexible labor markets in silicon valley*. Malden, MA: Blackwell.

Berlin, G. L., Furstenberg, F. F., Jr., & Waters, M. C. (2010). Transition to adulthood: Introducing the issue. *The Future of Children, 20*, 3–18.

Berman, E. P. (2012). *Creating the market university: How academic science became an economic engine*. Princeton, NJ: Princeton University Press.

Bledstein, B. J. (1976). *The culture of professionalism: The middle class and the development of higher education in America*. New York, NY: W.W. Norton.

Bourdieu, P. (1971). Systems of education and systems of thought. In M. K. D. Young (Ed.), *Knowledge and control: New directions for the sociology of education* (pp. 189–207). London: Collier Macmillan.

Brint, S. (2002). The rise of the 'practical arts'. In S. Brint (Ed.), *The future of the city of intellect* (pp. 231–259). Stanford, CA: Stanford University Press.

Brint, S., & Karabel, J. (1991). Institutional origins and transformations: The case of American community colleges. In W. W. Powell & P. J. DiMaggio (Eds.), *The new institutionalism in organizational analysis* (pp. 337–360). Chicago, IL: University of Chicago Press.

Brunsson, N., & Jacobsson, B. (Eds.). (2000). *A world of standards*. Oxford, UK: Oxford University Press.

Callan, P. M. (2014). Higher education in California: Rise and fall. In L. F. Goodchild, R. W. Jonsen, P. Limerick, & D. A. Longanecker (Eds.), *Higher education in the American west regional history and state contexts* (pp. 233–256). New York, NY: Palgrave Macmillan.

Carnegie Commission on Higher Education. (1973). *The purposes and performance of higher education in the United States*. New York, NY: McGraw Hill.

Clark, B. (1983). *The higher education system: Academic organization in cross-national perspective*. Berkeley, CA: University of California Press.

Deil-Amen, R. (2015). The "traditional" college student: A smaller and smaller minority and its implications for diversity and access institutions. In M. Stevens & M. W. Kirst (Eds.), *Remaking college: The changing ecology of higher education*. Stanford, CA: Stanford University Press.

DiMaggio, P. J., & Powell, W. W. (1983). The iron cage revisited: Institutional isomorphism and collective rationality in organizational fields. *American Sociological Review, 48*, 147–160.

Djelic, M.-L., & Sahlin-Andersson, K. (Eds.). (2006). *Transnational governance: Institutional dynamics of regulation*. Cambridge, UK: Cambridge University Press.

Dobbin, F. R., Edelman, L., Meyer, J. W., Scott, W. R., & Swidler, A. (1988). The expansion of due process in organizations. In L. G. Zucker (Ed.), *Institutional patterns and organizations: Culture and environment* (pp. 71–98). Cambridge, MA: Ballinger.

Douglass, J. A. (2010). *From chaos to order and back? A revisionist reflection on the California master plan for higher education @ 50 and thoughts about its future*. Berkeley, CA: Center for Studies in Higher Education, Research and Occasional Papers Series.

Economist. (2014). The digital degree. *Economist* June 28, pp. 11, 20−22.

Fischer, C. S., & Hout, M. (2006). *Century of difference: How America changed in the last one hundred years*. New York, NY: Russell Sage Foundation.

Fligstein, N., & McAdam, D. (2012). *A theory of fields*. Oxford, UK: Oxford University Press.

Friedland, R., & Alford, R. R. (1991). Bringing society back in: Symbols, practices and institutional contradictions. In W. W. Powell & P. J. DiMaggio (Eds.), *The new institutionalism in organizational analysis* (pp. 232−265). Chicago, IL: University of Chicago Press.

Gibbons, J. F. (2000). The role of Stanford university: A dean's reflections. In C.-M. Lee, W. F. Miller, M. G. Hancock, & H. S. Rowen (Eds.), *The Silicon Valley edge: A habitat for innovation and entrepreneurship* (pp. 200−217). Stanford: CA: Stanford University Press.

Glidden, R. B. (1996). Accreditation at a crossroads. *Educational Record, 66*(4), 22−24.

Goffman, I. (1961). *Asylums*. Garden City, NY: Doubleday.

Greenwood, R., & Hinings, C. R. (1993). Understanding strategic change: The contribution of archetypes. *Academy of Management Journal, 36*, 1052−1081.

Hasse, R., & Krücken, G. (2013). Competition and actorhood: A further expansion of the neo-institutional agenda. *Sociologia Internationalis, 51*, 181−205.

Kamenetz, A. (2010). *DIYU: Edupunks, edupreneurs, and the coming transformation of higher education*. White River Junction, VT: Chelsea Green Publishing.

Kamenetz, A. (2015). DIYU: Higher education goes hybrid. In M. Stevens & M. L. Kirst (Eds.), *Remaking college: The changing ecology of higher education* (pp. 39−60). Stanford, CA: Stanford University Press.

Karoly, L. A., & Paris, C. W. A. (2004). *The 21st century at work: Forces shaping the future workforce and workplace in the United States*. Santa Monica, CA: RAND Corporation.

Keane, J. (2001). *Doughboys: The great war and the remaking of America*. Baltimore, MD: The Johns Hopkins Press.

Kirst, M. W., & Stevens, M. L. (Eds.). (2015). *Remaking college: The changing ecology of higher education*. Stanford, CA: Stanford University Press.

Lewin, T. (2010). Once a leader, U.S. lags in college degrees. *New York Times*, July 7.

Lowen, R. S. (1997). *Creating the cold war university: The transformation of Stanford*. Berkeley, CA: University of California Press.

Meyer, J. W. (1977). The effects of education as an institution. *American Journal of Sociology, 85*, 55−77.

Meyer, J. W., & Jepperson, R. L. (2000). The "actors" of modern society: The cultural construction of social agency. *Sociological Theory, 18*, 100−120.

Meyer, J. W., Ramirez, F. O., Frank, D. J., & Schofer, E. (2007). Higher education as an institution. In P. J. Gumport (Ed.), *Sociology of higher education: Contributions and their contexts* (pp. 187−221). Baltimore, CA: The Johns Hopkins Press.

Meyer, J. W., & Rowan, B. (1977). Institutionalized organizations: Formal structure as myth and ceremony. *American Journal of Sociology, 83*, 55−77.

National Center for Educational statistics. (2012). *The condition of education, 2012*. Washington, DC: U.S. Department of Education.

OECD. (2014). *Academic rankings of world universities, center for world class universities of Shanghai Jiao Tong University*. Strasbourg, France: European Center for Higher Education of UNESCO.

Peterson, M. W. (2007). The study of colleges and universities as organizations. In P. J. Gumport (Ed.), *Sociology of higher education: Contributions and their contests* (pp. 147−184). Baltimore, MD: The Johns Hopkins University Press.

Pfeffer, J., & Salancik, G. R. (1978). *The external control of organizations: A resource dependence perspective.* New York, NY: Harper & Row.

Ramirez, F. O., & Boli, J. (1987). Global patterns of educational institutionalization. In G. Thomas, J. W. Meyer, F. O. Ramirez, & J. Boli (Eds.), *Institutional structure: Constituting state, society, and the individual* (pp. 150–172). Newbury Park, CA: Sage.

Richardson, R., & Martinez, M. (2009). *Policy and performance in American higher education: An examination of cases across state systems.* Baltimore, MD: The Johns Hopkins University Press.

Richardson, R. C., Reeves-Bracco, K., Callan, P. M., & Finney, J. E. (1999). *Designing state higher education systems for a new century.* Phoenix, AZ: American Council on Education.

Rosenbaum, J. E., Deil-Amen, R., & Person, A. E. (2006). *After admission: From college access to college success.* New York, NY: Russell Sage Foundation.

Rothblatt, S. (Ed.). (1992). *The OECD, the master plan and the California dream: A Berkeley conversation.* Berkeley, CA: Center for Studies in Higher Education, University of California, Berkeley.

Schumpeter, J. A. (1961). *The theory of economic development.* New York, NY: Oxford University Press (first published in 1926).

Scott, W. R. (2008). Lords of the dance: Professionals as institutional agents. *Organization Studies, 29,* 219–238.

Scott, W. R. (2013). *Institutions and organizations: Ideas, interests, and identities* (4th ed.), Los Angeles, CA: Sage.

Scott, W. R. (2015). Higher education in America: Multiple field perspectives. In M. Stevens & M. Kirst (Eds.), *Remaking college: Broad-access higher education for a new era* (pp. 19–38). Stanford, CA: Stanford University Press.

Settersten, R. A., Jr., & Ray, B. (2010). *Not quite adults: Why 20-somethings are choosing a slower path to adulthood, and why It's good for everyone.* New York, NY: Random House.

Stevens, M. L. (2007). *Creating A class: College admissions and the education of elites.* Cambridge, MA: Harvard University Press.

Stevens, M. L., Armstrong, E. A., & Arum, R. (2008). Sieve, incubator, temple, hub: Empirical and theoretical advances in the sociology of higher education. *Annual Review of Sociology, 34,* 127–151.

Tierney, W. G., & Hentschke, G. C. (2007). *New players, different game: Understanding the rise of for-profit colleges and universities.* Baltimore, MD: The Johns Hopkins University Press.

Wedlin, L. (2006). *Ranking business schools: Forming fields, identities and boundaries in international management education.* Cheltenham, UK: Edward Elgar.

Weisbrod, B. A., Ballou, J. P., & Asch, E. D. (2008). *Mission and money: Understanding the University.* Cambridge, UK: Cambridge University Press.

NESTED ORGANIZATIONAL FIELDS: ISOMORPHISM AND DIFFERENTIATION AMONG EUROPEAN UNIVERSITIES

Otto Hüther and Georg Krücken

ABSTRACT

European universities have changed dramatically over the last two to three decades. The two dominant frameworks to analyze these changes are "New Public Management" and the construction of "complete organizations." Both of these approaches highlight isomorphic processes leading to increased homogenization within European universities. However, empirical evidence suggests that European universities are differentiating from each other at the same time as they are becoming more isomorphic. To explain the simultaneity of homogenization and differentiation among European universities, we use the concept of nested organizational fields. We distinguish between a global field, a European field, and several national, state, and regional fields. Homogenization and differentiation are then the result of similar or different field embeddedness of European universities. The advantage of this approach lies in explaining homogenization and differentiation of universities within individual countries on

The University under Pressure
Research in the Sociology of Organizations, Volume 46, 53–83
Copyright © 2016 by Emerald Group Publishing Limited
All rights of reproduction in any form reserved
ISSN: 0733-558X/doi:10.1108/S0733-558X20160000046003

the one hand, as well as cross-national homogenization and differentiation of subgroups of universities on the other hand.

Keywords: Nested organizational fields; isomorphism; differentiation; European universities

INTRODUCTION

In this paper, we discuss fundamental changes affecting European universities over the last two to three decades. These changes are the result of substantial environmental pressure on universities and are by no means complete, but will continue to shape European universities in the years to come. We expect to see even more changes in the future since universities are deeply embedded in ongoing changes within society as a whole (Hüther & Krücken, 2016, p. 46). For example, the trends toward a knowledge society (Bell, 1973), blurring national and sectorial boundaries (Bauman, 2000; Castells, 2011; Gibbons et al., 1994; Latour, 1988; Nowotny, Scott, & Gibbons, 2001; Stevens, Armstrong, & Arum, 2008) and the rise of an audit society (Power, 1999) are increasing the relevance of universities within European societies, but at the same time putting them under pressure to reposition themselves.

Two dominant analytical approaches are used in the literature to describe the changes at European universities. First, "New Public Management" (NPM) (Braun & Merrien, 1999; de Boer, Enders, & Schimank, 2007; Dobbins & Knill, 2014; Kehm & Lanzendorf, 2006b; Schimank, 2005); second, the concept of the construction of "complete organizations" (Brunsson & Sahlin-Andersson, 2000; de Boer, Enders, & Leisyte, 2007; Krücken & Meier, 2006; Seeber et al., 2015).

NPM describes a certain governance structure of universities and university systems. NPM encompasses strong external guidance of universities by the state or intermediaries such as university boards or accreditation agencies. This kind of steering is replacing tightly state-regulated bureaucratic guidelines, previously common in the European system. At the same time, NPM describes a strengthening of decision-making competences of university and faculty heads. In the traditional system, the decision-making center of universities was a collegial body of professors; this collegial decision mode is now increasingly being replaced by the hierarchical decision mode. In addition, competition, both between universities and between units within universities, is being instigated or strengthened.

The second approach describes the development of universities from an arena to a complete organization. In the organizational form of the arena, "members perform their tasks relatively free from control by the local leadership" and are instead "controlled by external parties" (Brunsson & Sahlin-Andersson, 2000, p. 734). This highly functional organizational form is losing legitimacy in its broader sociopolitical environments and, therefore, what Brunsson and Sahlin-Andersson (2000) call the complete organization is gaining importance within universities. Complete organizations are characterized by identity (autonomy, collective resources, boundaries, being an organization and being special), hierarchy (co-ordination and control, internal management), and rationality (setting objectives, measuring results, and allocating responsibility).

In recent years, research on NPM and complete organizations has produced central and important insights with regard to the changes occurring in European universities. Nevertheless, there seems to be an unresolved puzzle. Both of these approaches highlight isomorphic processes leading to increased homogenization. However, empirical evidence suggests that European universities are differentiating from each other at the same time as they are becoming more isomorphic. Traditional differences between European universities remain and new differences are arising (Paradeise & Thoenig, 2013).

The processes and structures underlying the observed simultaneous homogenization and differentiation between European universities have, until now, not been well understood. The main aim of this paper is therefore to discuss the unresolved puzzle by starting from the idea that universities as organizations are embedded in nested organizational fields. The advantage we find in such an approach is to explain homogenization and differentiation of universities within individual countries on the one hand, as well as cross-national homogenization and differentiation of subgroups of universities on the other hand.

The paper is structured as follows. First, we describe some important changes occurring in European universities. The main finding here is that we simultaneously see homogenization and differentiation between European universities. In the following sections, we discuss nested organizational fields as a possible explanation for this finding. Initially, we describe the concept and discuss the implications for European universities in an abstract way. In the following section, we apply the concept to European universities to make more sense of the simultaneous homogenization and differentiation among them. In the concluding section, we summarize our findings and discuss some further research questions.

ON THE WAY TO A NEW EUROPEAN UNIVERSITY
MODEL?

Before we turn our attention to current changes occurring in European universities, we will briefly describe in a simplified, archetypical way the starting point of the Western European university landscape based on Clark (1983). This allows us to depict these changes in comparative European perspective. We draw on Clark because his was the first and most influential attempt to systematically compare university systems and universities in different countries. On the one hand, Clark elaborated the differences between the university models in France, Germany, and the United Kingdom; on the other hand, he also focused on overarching similarities among these national systems. To put it simply, the inner organization of European universities has been dominated by professors, and the autonomy of teaching and research was primarily the autonomy of professors and − in clear distinction to the more recent NPM ideas on universities or the concept of the university as a complete organization − not the autonomy of the university as an organization. Within universities, internal hierarchies were widely absent; instead collegial decision-making arenas were predominant. In addition, a strong influence of the state on universities as organizations − at least in the German and the French model − was to be found. Steering via competitive structures at the organizational level − be it in terms of research funding, or in relation to students − was, according to Clark (1983), broadly absent in Europe, with the exception of the United Kingdom. Market and competitive mechanisms were almost exclusively located at the level of individual academics who competed for reputation and associated career opportunities.

But from the 1980s onwards, traditional European university structures have been facing significant changes. The starting point was changes in the British university system (Leisyte, de Boer, & Enders, 2006; Risser, 2003) that quickly spread to the Scandinavian countries and the Netherlands (de Boer & Huisman, 1999; de Boer, Leisyte, & Enders, 2006). Later we find reforms in France (Mignot Gerard, 2003; Musselin, 2014), Italy (Capano, 2008), Germany (Hüther & Krücken, 2013, 2015; Kehm & Lanzendorf, 2006a), and Eastern European countries (Dobbins & Knill, 2009; Dobbins & Leisyte, 2014).

In recent years, research has shown a move in nearly all European countries toward the directions indicated by the approaches mentioned in the introduction: NPM and the construction of complete organizations in universities.

At the formal level within Europe, a significant move toward NPM as well as toward the construction of complete organizations can be observed (de Boer et al., 2007; Kehm & Lanzendorf, 2006b; Krücken, Kosmützky, & Torka, 2007; Paradeise, Reale, Bleiklie, & Ferlie, 2009; Seeber et al., 2015). These changes are mainly due to state regulation. A strengthening of the position of university management and a changeover in state steering toward a "state supervising model" can be found nearly everywhere at the formal level. Furthermore, in nearly all European countries the importance of intermediary units, like university boards, and accreditation and evaluation agencies, has increased (Kretek, Dragšić, & Kehm, 2013; Schwarz & Westerheijden, 2004). Competition between and within universities has also increased. One example is the introduction of performance-based research funding systems in a number of European countries, with the English Research Assessment Exercise (RAE) from 1986 being the forerunner (Geuna & Martin, 2003; Hicks, 2012). Within the framework of these models of resource allocation, universities compete on the one hand for funding and, on the other hand, for the reputation that goes with it.

Despite these common trends at the formal level of European universities, it is also clear that only a limited homogenization is evident (Paradeise, Reale, Bleiklie, et al., 2009; Paradeise & Thoenig, 2013). Rather, a differentiated "translating" and "editing" process (Czarniawska-Joerges & Sevón, 2005; Sahlin & Wedlin, 2008) is taking place in individual countries. They have taken over certain features of NPM but rejected others. Significant differences can also be found in the adopted features because they had to be adapted to national circumstances.

The redistributive impact of funds, for example, brought about by the introduction of performance-based research funding systems, varies greatly. In some countries, the unit of performance analysis is the department or subfields within the universities (England, Italy, Poland), in others the individual researcher (Spain). Additionally, the methods of measuring performance differ. Some countries use foremost peer review (England, Spain, Portugal), others bibliometric information (Norway, Denmark, Sweden) such as paper counts or citation information. In addition, the share of performance-based funding is rather low in some countries (Italy, Norway 2%), in others considerably higher (Slovak Republic 15% of total funding, UK 25% of research support) (Hicks, 2012).

A further example of different translating and editing processes at the national level is the precise meaning of the generally assumed strengthening of university leaders and deans (Öquist & Benner, 2015; Paradeise, Reale, Bleiklie, et al., 2009). In some countries, deans are now appointed by the university leaders (Netherlands, Denmark, Norway, the United Kingdom), in others, they are still elected by collegial bodies (France, Germany, Italy). Another example of differentiation is the formal power potentials of university leaders and deans vis-à-vis the academics. Formal power potentials constitute an important precondition for hierarchical decision making. As Hüther and Krücken (2013) show, there is strong evidence that this formal power varies between European universities. This can be seen by the example of the strongly varying opportunities that university leaders in European universities have to dominate academics by promoting or preventing academic careers. This strategy of managerial domination in "soft bureaucracies" is described particularly by Courpasson (2000). The basis of this strategy of domination is that "decisions of promotion or demotion, (...) are often centralized in the hands of senior management" and that "decisions of promotion or demotion (...) depend more and more on senior managers" (Courpasson, 2000, p. 153). However, since the career systems for academics still vary greatly between national systems (Enders, 2000; Huisman, de Weert, & Bartelse, 2002; Musselin, 2005, 2010; Öquist & Benner, 2015), the extent to which higher education management (here: university leaders and deans) can make use of this strategy varies too. Recourse to this strategy is only possible if, for example, internal organizational career tracks or internal career markets exist in the university. This is not the case in all European states, rather great heterogeneity exists. Therefore, the actual potential of university leaders and deans for hierarchical decision making differs enormously.

Not only at the formal level, but also at the level of actual work practices we find huge heterogeneity among European universities. Studies show that formal decision-making rules within universities are bypassed informally, that the state has not fully withdrawn to an output steering position, and that competition within universities is partly undermined by collegial mechanisms of resource allocation (Braun, Benninghoff, Ramuz, & Gorga, 2015; Enders, de Boer, & Weyer, 2013; Enders & Westerheijden, 2014). Research also shows significantly different practices at the level of individual universities, even if the same formal frameworks are in place (Kodeih & Greenwood, 2014; Paradeise & Thoenig, 2013; Seeber et al., 2015). At the organizational level, therefore, a differentiated translation and editing process of NPM and of the components of the idea of constructing a complete organization are occurring in practice. A decisive factor for the question of homogenization and differentiation of European universities is therefore the organizational level.

To sum up, the changes at European universities simultaneously show homogenization and differentiation. Whereas in the 1990s and the early 2000s, there was an emphasis on homogenization tendencies, recent years have seen a focus on the differential developments of European universities. This more realistic view of homogenization can be primarily explained by the fact that the analytical level has shifted over time. Whereas early research focused particularly on the formal level, in recent years the practice level has shifted to the center of attention and this is where the differences are more pronounced. Due to the increasing emphasis on differences, research now is concerned with how these differences come about and what they depend upon. It should be noted that previous research mainly looked for causes at the state or national level (an exception is Paradeise & Thoenig, 2013). Thus, the political and administrative structures of the respective countries (Bleiklie & Michelsen, 2013), the different national traditions of university systems (Ramirez & Christensen, 2013), the use of different reform narratives in European countries (Ferlie, Musselin, & Andresani, 2008), and the timing of political reforms (Dobbins & Knill, 2009, p. 425) have all been used as explanatory factors.

As important as these research results are, we see two major problems. First, there are few explanations for why we observe isomorphism and differentiation between universities in one country if the state is the central environmental force in the field of higher education. This problem can be solved by the traditional organizational field approach as developed by DiMaggio and Powell (1983). Based on their approach, the state is only one source of institutional pressure in organizational fields. State pressure via coercion is accompanied by mimetic and normative pressures. One must also include more recent discussions of DiMaggio and Powell's concept. Recent neo-institutional research on organizational fields has increasingly focused on "dynamics that allow for heterogeneity, variation, and change" (Wooten & Hoffman, 2008, p. 143). Dynamic concepts are to be found with regard to the organizational field (Fligstein & McAdam, 2012; Kodeih & Greenwood, 2014; McPherson & Sauder, 2013; Meyer, Gaba, & Colwell, 2005; Reay & Hinings, 2005; Thornton & Ocasio, 1999; Thornton, Ocasio, & Lounsbury, 2012), but also concerning the way organizations in a field cope with different institutional demands (Goodrick & Salancik, 1996; Oliver, 1991). Isomorphism and homogenization of organizations in an organizational field are only one possibility: the other is differentiation (Boxenbaum & Jonsson, 2008). We believe that such dynamics are of great analytical importance for the case of European universities. By making use of such concepts one can better explain why universities within one country show isomorphic tendencies, but also those toward differentiation.

The second problem we see is that current research can hardly explain isomorphism and differentiation with regard to subgroups of universities that cross-cut national boundaries. Paradeise and Thoenig (2013) identify such cross-national isomorphic processes; likewise Marginson (2006) focuses on national and global competition in higher education. Tackling this problem transcends the traditional concept of the organizational field and more recent developments. Therefore, we propose employing the relatively new concept of nested organizational fields. Such an approach is able to explain cross-national homogenization and differentiation of subgroups of universities as well as homogenization and differentiation of universities within individual countries by referring to universities' embeddedness in different, nested and partially overlapping organizational fields.

THE NESTED ORGANIZATIONAL FIELD STRUCTURE OF EUROPEAN UNIVERSITIES

To apply the concept of nested organizational fields to European universities, we have to abandon the common assumption that organizations are only embedded in one organizational field. Instead, the idea here is that organizations are embedded in different nested organizational fields. For example, Scott (2013, p. 233) describes three interrelated fields for global infrastructure construction projects in which a project company could be embedded. First, there is a field of global infrastructure players, second, a starting field of the host community of a specific project, and third, a new organizational field created by the project. In analyzing the adaptation of the "Cities for Climate Protection" program in US American, Canadian, and Australian cities, Vasi (2007) distinguished between three nested organizational fields in which municipalities are embedded: a global, a national, and a local field.[1] Fligstein and McAdam (2012, p. 9) describe fields as a "Russian doll: with any number of smaller fields nested inside larger ones."

With regard to European universities, we assume that a global field, a European field, and several national fields have to be taken into account. In federal countries like Germany and Switzerland, state fields are additionally nested in the national fields. Furthermore, separate or overlapping regional fields should be considered. Regional fields are able to encompass universities from different federal states or even countries. For instance, the German Rhine-Main Region integrates universities from three different federal states (Hesse, Baden-Württemberg, and Rhineland-Palatinate). One of many examples for the integration of universities in different countries in a regional field can be found between Germany and Denmark, with extensive cooperation between the University of Southern Denmark and the University of Flensburg.[2] Fig. 1 shows this field structure in a schematic way.

We do not think that the different fields are similarly developed, structured, and stable. In some fields, coercive pressure via formal regulations is absent (e.g., in the global field). In these fields, "soft power" (Hedmo & Wedlin, 2008) like rankings or evaluations are of paramount importance for the field structure (Wedlin, 2007). Also, the composition of actors is in some fields more fluid than in others. For instance, the composition of universities embedded in the global field would be less stable than that of universities embedded in national fields. Likewise, one should not assume sharp field boundaries with regard to all field characteristics, like actors, logics or governance structures (Scott, 2013, p. 225). We would, for example, expect a great deal of overlapping in institutional logics or systems of

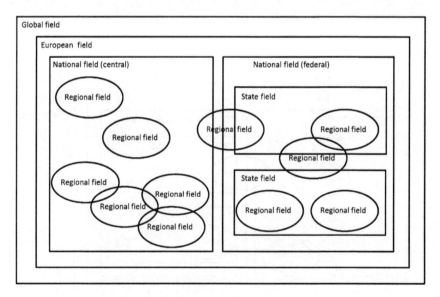

Fig. 1. Nested and Partially Overlapping Organizational Fields with Regard to European Universities.

meanings between all fields because for all universities research and teaching are important goals.

Let us try to illustrate the analytical potential of the nested organizational field approach with a schematic, simplified, and hypothetical example using four universities in two different countries (see Fig. 2).

In our example, university A is relatively strongly embedded in the global and the national fields but relatively weakly in the European and regional fields. In contrast, university B is strongly anchored in the national field and several overlapping regional fields but not in the global field and only weakly in the European field. If we assume that the universities A and B are both in the same country, then their different embeddings lead to partially overlapping institutional pressures but also to differences. The embeddings in the nested and overlapping fields are associated with different institutional environmental pressures and thereby can explain both isomorphism (via shared embeddings) but also differentiation (via the different or differently strong embeddings).

In contrast, universities C and D are in the same national context and share the embedding in a regional field. However, both universities are embedded in different fields at the state level and whereas the global field is important for university C, university D is embedded in the European rather than the global field. In this case too, we would expect similarities

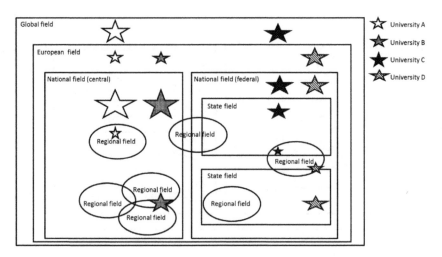

Fig. 2. Nested and Partially Overlapping Organizational Fields − Schematic Example.

and differences within one country due to the similar and differing embeddings.

The concept of nested organizational fields can also explain homogenization and differentiation across national borders through shared and different environmental embeddings. Universities A and B share an embedding in the global field and are thus exposed here to the same environmental expectations that in certain areas can lead to isomorphism. In contrast, universities A, B, and D are all embedded in the European field, which in turn could lead to isomorphism between these universities with regard to the important areas in this field.

Consequently, by using the concept of nested fields, we find evidence of factors that can lead to homogenization and differentiation of universities within single countries but also to homogenization and differentiation of subgroups of universities across national borders. In the following, we substantiate these rather abstract concepts with specific examples of European universities.

ISOMORPHISM AND DIFFERENTIATION AMONG EUROPEAN UNIVERSITIES

For analyzing the effects of universities' embeddedness in nested organizational fields, we employ the three mechanisms for isomorphism as described by DiMaggio and Powell (1983). In their now classic paper, DiMaggio and Powell (1983) offer an explanation for why organizations within an organizational field become more and more similar. They describe three analytically separate isomorphic processes or mechanisms (coercive, mimetic, normative) and use these to explain homogenization processes between organizations. These mechanisms allow us to systematize our description of nested organizational fields in European higher education and relate this description to a well-established concept in organizational sociology. However, we do not assume that the three mechanisms necessarily lead to isomorphism, but rather trigger differentiation at the same time (Boxenbaum & Jonsson, 2008; Wooten & Hoffman, 2008).

When discussing the three mechanisms we will bring one question to the forefront. How do these mechanisms relate to the embeddedness of universities in nested organizational fields and therefore produce homogenization and differentiation among European universities?

COERCIVE ISOMORPHISM

Coercive isomorphism describes homogenizing processes based on "formal and informal pressures exerted on organizations" (DiMaggio & Powell, 1983, p. 150). In the following, we will mainly discuss the coercive pressure via formal regulation and via resources. At first sight, both kinds of coercive pressure seem to be mostly relevant for the national fields, and only in federal states does an additional layer of coercive pressure seem to be existent. However, the European Union (EU) is increasingly exercising pressure on universities through resources, though formal regulation hardly plays a role. At the global field level, there is neither direct pressure through formal regulation nor through resources. Nevertheless, we will show that the embeddedness in the global field is related to coercive pressure through formal regulation and resources at the national level. Therefore, the relations between fields and mechanisms are more complex than they seem at first sight.

Coercive Pressure via Formal Regulation

In most European countries, formal regulations are one key force to embed universities and hold them in separate national fields. Therefore, in nested fields formal regulation is not only an isomorphism mechanism, but also a strong mechanism to embed organizations in certain fields and limit their possibilities to fully change toward other fields.

Coercive pressure via formal regulation produces homogenization and differentiation within European universities because there are both similarities, due to state formal pressure on European universities, but also differences. At the formal level of universities in the individual European states, we certainly do find isomorphic tendencies due to similar orientations regarding NPM and the construction of complete organizations. At the same time, it is also true that the concept of how a university should look varies between the nation states, and therefore differentiation arises simultaneously. These processes have been well researched over recent years and the insights on them were presented above. Therefore, this is nothing new.

One might assume that the EU is exercising formal pressure on European universities. In particular, the Bologna process, leading to the introduction of Bachelor and Master degrees in Europe, could indicate this (Reinalda & Kulesza-Mietkowski, 2005). Nevertheless, formal pressure from the EU via the Bologna process is only indirect, because national bodies in individual countries have the authority to implement the Bachelor and Master system. Here again we find different translating and editing processes in each country, and the national authorities exercise pressure on their universities, not the EU.

In federal countries like Germany, the picture is even more complex. The most important source of formal regulation here is the federal state level; therefore formal regulation is pushing German universities in different state fields. Hüther (2010) showed for Germany that the individual states translated and edited NPM differently. Therefore, different hybrid models of NPM and the traditional German governance model have evolved. For example, in some states the university boards are weak advisory bodies, while in others they are powerful steering actors. Also, the decision-making power of university presidents, the election rules of presidents and deans, and the formal grounds for state ministries to overrule decisions made by universities are very different in the individual states. Consequently, in federal countries the different translating and editing processes at the state level are an additional source of differentiation. Nonetheless, some formal regulations in Germany are at the national level. A prominent example is the formal regulation of fixed-term employment arrangements below the professorship. Another one, with even more consequences, is the protection of the freedom of teaching and research in the German constitution.

But formal regulation, in part in combination with financial incentives, is employed in some countries to foster university mergers in order to create the so-called "world class universities" (Harman & Harman, 2008; Salmi, 2009, p. 43). We find this, for example, in France, where the attempt is being made at "merging universities, research organisations and grandes écoles to enhance capacity and visibility" (Hazelkorn & Ryan, 2013, p. 88). Also Denmark could be mentioned in this regard, where mergers led to the existence of only four larger universities (Öquist & Benner, 2015, p. 248). Another example is the merger between the Technical University of Karlsruhe and the Karlsruhe Research Centre in Germany. These examples show that some universities are being pushed by national formal pressure into the global organizational field. On the one hand, that leads to an increased differentiation at the national level as not all universities are targeted here. On the other hand, there is a stronger cross-national isomorphism among those universities that are becoming part of the global organizational field.

In some countries, one can see that universities are being pushed in the opposite direction as the regional organizational field is being strengthened by national laws (Ferlie, Musselin, & Andresani, 2009, p. 10). Different countries employ different instruments for strengthening regional ties. Some, such as France, Italy, and the Netherlands, integrate representatives of local organizations in steering committees (e.g., boards of trustees) (Paradeise, Reale, Goastellec, & Bleiklie, 2009, p. 234). Since the late 1990s, French regions have played an additional role in financing universities. Consequently, "local authorities have become non-escapable partners because of their role as 'funding bodies'" (Musselin & Paradeise, 2009, p. 27). During the 2000s in the United Kingdom, it came to a move "away from the classic UK Unitary State" (Ferlie & Andresani, 2009, p. 183) and a strengthening of regions (Wales, Scotland). The regions could directly influence their universities, resulting in a "growing importance of local assemblies and politicians" (Ferlie & Andresani, 2009, p. 187). The question of whether and how countries formally regulate a strengthening of the regional level is a further source of homogenization but also differentiation between European universities.

Coercive Pressure via Resources

Most European universities are foremost publicly funded and higher education is seen as a public good. Hence, coercive pressure via resources is again first of all a national field pressure. Like formal regulations, funding is also an important mechanism to embed and hold universities in the national fields.

The fact that many European countries are changing the funding of universities toward a more competitive approach is again a source for homogenization. Universities all over Europe must compete for their resources and funding is more and more performance-oriented, whereas two decades ago the funding was demand-oriented. The introduction of the above described performance-based research funding systems in many countries is in fact an important trigger for homogenization. However, in regard to coercive pressure via resources there are also translating und editing processes in each country, leading to differentiation. For example, in the English system we see competition for research funding and for the tuition fees of students (Brown & Carasso, 2013). In other countries, like Sweden, Finland, Austria, or Germany, tuition fees are absent. Moreover, as we described above the competition criteria and the share of the total funding which is distributed via competition differ considerably.

In Germany as a federal country, the picture is again different. Similar to the coercive pressure of formal regulation, the coercive pressure of resources embeds German universities in different federal state fields and the national field.

Resource pressure also has another interesting consequence. Whereas resource competition mostly takes place between universities in a country or a state, some countries have introduced special competition programs between their universities based on excellence. The goal of these competitions is to embed or to push some universities into the global field and to compete with the existing world class universities. Examples of this are the German excellence initiative (Kehm & Pasternack, 2009), the French programs "Operation Campus" or "Investments for the Future" (Hazelkorn & Ryan, 2013) or the "launch of specific strategic excellence funding programs" (Hallonsten & Silander, 2012, p. 367) in Sweden. Here, we can see another source for differentiation between the universities of a country; but at the same time, a source for isomorphic tendencies between a subset of European universities from different countries.

The EU is another source of coercive pressure via resources. The influence of the EU on universities has increased in recent years (e.g., Hedmo & Wedlin, 2008; Keeling, 2006; Magalhães, Veiga, Ribeiro, Sousa, & Santiago, 2013) and its greater importance is evidenced, for example, in increasing third-party funds allocated by the EU and the establishment of the "European Research Council" (Hedmo & Wedlin, 2008, p. 118; Slaughter & Cantwell, 2012, p. 587). In contrast to the above-mentioned Bologna process, and far more interesting for us, the EU pressure via funding is direct, because European universities are competing directly for funds — without mediation at the national or state level.

When we consider the EU as an important actor exerting resource pressure on European universities, we also find reasons for both isomorphic tendencies and for differentiation. First of all, the EU is pushing universities toward the European field and therefore the coercive pressure of the EU strongly favors cross-national isomorphism through the creation of a "European Research Area" (Hazelkorn & Ryan, 2013, p. 85). In addition, collaborative European research projects must be composed of members from different countries, leading to an increased network-structure across Europe. Such structures favor the stability of the European organizational field in higher education.

However, there should be a varying relevance of EU pressure for university practices. For universities from small and/or financially weak countries, research funding from the EU is far more important than for those in larger and/or richer countries. In other words, the resource dependency (Pfeffer & Salancik, 1978) of universities in smaller and/or financially weak countries is much higher and the pressure to adjust to institutional pressure of the EU is therefore much stronger. For example, universities from smaller/financially weaker countries like the Netherlands or Portugal are often keener to join EU funded research consortiums compared to universities from the larger/richer countries like Germany or France. A possible research hypothesis here would be that in countries where pressure from the EU is stronger, greater isomorphism between universities exists.

At the country level, there is one more source of coercive differentiation of European universities. Differentiation arises because countries mix formal and resource pressure in different ways. Some countries use mostly formal pressure, others mostly resource pressures, and still others mix both pressures. We can assume that pressure is higher if the flow of resources is fundamentally changed (England, Sweden), whereas pressure should be less if the main impetus is changing formal organizational decision-making structures (Germany). In the latter case, it is much easier for universities to decouple the activity structure from the formal structure (Meyer & Rowan, 1977).

To sum up, we see, on the one hand, how the coercive mechanism relates to the embeddedness of universities in nested organizational fields and, on the other hand, how both isomorphism and differentiation among European universities are produced.

MIMETIC ISOMORPHISM

Homogenization by means of mimetic processes occurs because an organization mimics structures and processes of another organization which is perceived as successful or better adapted to its institutional environment. The probability of mimetic homogenization processes increases in organizations first, when other organizations are perceived as superior or more successful; and second, "when goals are ambiguous, or when the environment creates symbolic uncertainty" (DiMaggio & Powell, 1983, p. 151). Both causes for mimetic processes are relevant for our case. As with the first isomorphic mechanism, we can assume that a certain university model is to be realized.

Contrary to the first mechanism though, homogenization stems from the university as an organization and it is more likely that not only the organization's formal structures but also its activity structures will be included in the homogenization process.

Can we assume that European universities want to mimic the same university model, leading to homogenization?

We do not think that is the case. Successful organizations in the global field, the European field, the national fields, the state fields and the regional fields are different and therefore we find different successful organizational models to emulate. Which of these models are seen worthy of emulation by European universities not only depends on their embeddedness in the organizational fields but also on how important each field is for the legitimacy of each university. This conceptualization of different models also explains the obvious observation that many European universities neither want to nor can imitate the model of the US research university because for structural reasons the university is not capable of realizing or even emulating the model (Kodeih & Greenwood, 2014; Paradeise & Thoenig, 2013). However, all organizational models which are perceived as successful in the different fields share some common features, like a connection of research and teaching, some autonomy of professors and universities, and the importance of discipline structures. So there is a source of isomorphism in the common features of the "archetype" university or shared features of institutional logics in the relevant organizational fields.

For European universities embedded in the global field, it could be argued that the US research university serves as a leading model that is well worth emulating and therefore that mimetic processes strengthen isomorphism among universities embedded in the global field. This means that at least among a subset of European universities, we should find imitation of the same model, reinforcing the isomorphism of these universities.

For universities that are more strongly embedded in national fields, alternative national models are also perceived as successful and legitimate. For France this is the case for the model of the Grande École. Kodeih and Greenwood (2014) show with the example of four French business schools that the model of the international business school is of ever increasing importance. At the same time, central elements of the French model of the Grande École are retained as this model is a major source of legitimacy for French business schools. The two models differ, for example, with regard to core values (vocational and teaching orientation vs. academic orientation) and the recruitment of faculty (mostly, French professors with a French doctorate vs. international professors with international PhDs).

With this example, we see that at the national level alternative university models play a role, also due to their embeddedness in different organizational fields.

The same holds true for Germany, where the historically highly successful model of Wilhelm von Humboldt is still seen as a concept worth emulating. And, of course, there are overlaps between the US research university model and the Humboldtian model. Both models share some features, because historically the US universities emulated the German Humboldtian universities in the 19th century (Kerr, 1963, p. 18). At the same time, there are differences. One example is that the strong independence of the professor in the German university model was never adapted by the US universities. US universities rather translated and edited the German model on the basis of their own traditions of stronger departments and collegial structures (Perkin, 1991; Shils, 1992). To this day, these differences remain and in Germany we find a chair model, but in the United States a department model (see Neave & Rhoades, 1987 for a description of both models).

A contemporary example of how German universities do not fully emulate the US research university model is the scientific career system. In some countries, like the United States and United Kingdom, we traditionally find tenure track systems; in others, like Germany, a formal and informal ban on internal promotion to a professorship ("Hausberufungsverbot") (Hüther & Krücken, 2013). In recent years some countries, like Finland (Pietilä, 2015), have introduced tenure track systems, emulating the US and UK model. So there is some isomorphism, partly promoted by formal coercive pressure. However, with regard to the German junior professorship one can see an interesting point. Since 2002 most universities in Germany can offer junior professors[3] a tenure track option and therefore emulate the US research university career system. But all data show that the vast majority of Germany universities do not use this option. Only 15% of the junior professors in Germany have a tenure track option (Rathmann, 2014, p. 18). Here, one can see that most German universities do not emulate the US research university career model, but rather the traditional German model.

Not only are different organizational models perceived as successful at the global and national field levels, but models perceived as successful in regional organizational fields also partly differ. For many universities, embeddedness in regional fields is of special importance and they draw their legitimacy and resources from their anchoring in the region, expressed in spatially limited research and teaching activities. At the regional level, the strength of the connection to local employers, local schools, and regional innovation systems seems far more important for a successful university. Universities emulating this regional organizational model should be different in many aspect from universities that are foremost embedded in the global, European, and/or national field. At the same time, universities from different countries that are emulating the regional organizational model should have similar features and thereby a tendency toward transnational isomorphism, highlighting in particular "third mission activities", that is, direct contributions to their immediate sociopolitical and socioeconomic environments that go beyond the traditional twin missions of teaching and research (Göransson, Maharajh, & Schmoch, 2009).

A further interesting point with regard to the European field level is the European ranking "U-Multirank" (Van Vught & Ziegele, 2012). This ranking fosters mimetic processes by making particularly successful European universities visible. U-Multirank is multidimensional and identifies universities that are successful in research involvement, knowledge exchange, international orientation, or regional engagement. This implies that within different organizational fields different models may be pursued. In distinction from global rankings, where US American research universities dominate the field, the measurement goes beyond a pure research orientation.

Our examples show that with regard to mimetic processes there are different models in different fields which can be seen as successful and legitimate options for European universities. The importance of these different models can vary greatly from university to university, depending on their embeddedness in nested organizational fields. Thus it becomes apparent that we can find isomorphism not only between the universities within individual different countries, but also in relation to specific subgroups of universities in Europe with similar field embeddedness. The choice of different models leads to both isomorphism and differentiation among European universities.

NORMATIVE ISOMORPHISM

Due to supra-organizational professionalization processes, normative processes lead to increasing homogenization among organizations. If the organizations in a field draw on members of a profession in a certain area then homogenization occurs in this area because the professionals "tend to view problems in a similar fashion, see the same policies, procedures and structures as normatively sanctioned and legitimated, and approach decisions in much the same way" (DiMaggio & Powell, 1983, p. 153). Here it is the norms, values and procedures of a profession that lead to homogenization. On the one hand, the homogenization mechanism is located among a prominent subgroup of the organization's members, and on the other hand it is also outside the organization in the professional context. The application of normative isomorphism to universities requires, however, that not only one but at least two[4] professions should be considered. These are the academic profession and the professional higher education leaders (e.g., Presidents, Vice Presidents).

Here too we ask how embeddedness in nested organizational fields is related to normative pressure from professions and through this we address how normative pressure leads to isomorphism and differentiation among European universities.

The Academic Profession

There are good reasons to assume that the academic profession was and is a central driver of the high degree of isomorphism in research structures and processes among universities worldwide. Academics do not just orient themselves toward scientific values described by Merton (1973), but are also trained to apply certain questions, methods, and solutions in their various disciplines. Furthermore, most scientific communities are structured as worldwide networks of communication, connecting universities from around the world via individual scientists. Therefore, the academic profession is a central factor embedding universities in a global organizational field. In addition, in many disciplines the competition for reputation takes place at the global level.

Though what we described above is of overall importance for academic institutions and their academic staff, we nevertheless expect differences concerning concrete embeddedness in organizational fields. Academics with a particularly strong orientation toward the global competition for reputation push their universities toward the global organizational level. Conversely, universities in which academics with a particularly strong orientation toward to the regional or national level are to be found also shape the field embeddedness of their universities. The embeddedness in fields and their relevance for academics as carriers of normative pressure should lead to reinforcing effects concerning the field embeddedness of universities, leading to very different outcomes based on the composition of "locals" and "cosmopolitans" (Gouldner, 1957, 1958) in European universities.

For the academic profession, different ideas of how a university should look are also related to academics' different disciplinary backgrounds. There are no doubt commonalities in the university model preferred by the academic profession whose ideal model consists primarily of the combination of high individual autonomy and academic self-organization. Nevertheless, we still find differences here. In engineering and the life sciences, for example, there is a higher affinity for the ideas of NPM compared to the humanities (Schmid & Wilkesmann, 2015). Depending on the different disciplines and departmental structures, a university encompasses, these different attitudes toward NPM could also well be found in the preferred university model of the local academic profession. This can be viewed as a further factor limiting the homogenization of universities within one country. At the same time, we could conjecture that universities with the same disciplinary specialization across all countries show stronger isomorphic tendencies because in these universities the preferred university models of the local academic profession overlap more.

University Leaders

The second profession in European universities we take into consideration here is the leaders. At first sight it would seem that this profession also contributes to isomorphism among European universities. Over the last 30 years, the influence of leaders on universities has grown in all European countries (de Boer et al., 2007; Dobbins & Knill, 2014; Paradeise, Reale, Bleiklie, et al., 2009; Schimank, 2005; Shattock, 2013; Smith & Adams, 2008; Whitley & Gläser, 2014). We can safely say that this profession encounters similar problems in all countries (they have to lead/manage a professional organization), develops similar views, and then prefers similar solutions. We can also assume that the concept of the complete organization is of particular importance. Although we can find evidence indicating that isomorphic tendencies exist there is also some evidence of differentiation.

Let us again begin with the embeddedness of universities in different and nested organizational fields. Depending on the field and its relevance, we assume that universities select different kinds of leaders. Goodall (2006, p. 388) shows that world class universities "appoint top researchers as their vice chancellors and presidents". For Sweden, Engwall (2014) finds changes in recruitment practices for vice chancellors since the 1960s in all universities but also differences in recruitment practices between old research-oriented and young practice-oriented universities. Additionally, Breakwell and Tytherleigh (2010) find systematic differences in presidents' characteristics between the old (pre-92 universities) and new universities (post-92 universities) in the United Kingdom. They conclude that "institutions seek out individuals to become their VC [vice chancellors] that match the aspirations and identity of the institution" (Breakwell & Tytherleigh, 2010, p. 503).

A further aspect concerning normative pressure in nested organizational fields is that the "markets" for university leaders are first and foremost national ones. It is very rare among European universities that university leaders are recruited from other national systems. This reinforces the embeddedness of universities in the national field. However, there seems to be an exception from the rule as the study by Breakwell and Tytherleigh (2010, p. 502) demonstrates that in old, traditional universities in the United Kingdom, 9% of the vice chancellors had previously been employed at an "oversea" university. This finding could indicate that transnational recruitment takes place in particular among and between universities with a very high reputation, and that these recruitment practices in turn reinforce the embeddedness in the global organizational field.

A further question is whether university leaders should be considered a profession. In most European countries, there is no established separate career track for university leaders. Rather, they are recruited in the traditional way from the academic profession for a fixed term and then return to their previous duties (Breakwell & Tytherleigh, 2010, p. 498; Engwall, 2014, p. 338; Röbken, 2006; Smith & Adams, 2008). In many universities in Europe, the primary socialization of the Presidents and Deans occurs "on the job." The lower the degree of professionalization, the less consistent the preferred university model within the leaders of higher education is likely to be, which would be more likely to promote differentiation among European universities. DiMaggio and Powell describe this situation: "To the extent that organizations in a field differ and primary socialization occurs on the job, socialization could reinforce, not erode, differences among organizations" (DiMaggio & Powell, 1983, p. 153). This implies that in countries where we find strong professionalization of university leaders, we can expect stronger isomorphic tendencies concerning the overall and preferred idea of how the university should look. In addition, we expect that in individual countries subgroups of universities prefer professionalized university leaders. Such universities might also form specific cross-national subgroups of European universities, among which related isomorphic tendencies might be seen.

The interplay of the carriers of normative pressure, academics, and university leaders, and their at times conflicting images of how a university should look could be a further source of differentiation among European universities. The power relations between academics and higher education leaders within universities vary considerably between countries (de Boer et al., 2007; Paradeise, Reale, Bleiklie, et al., 2009; Teichler, Arimoto, & Cummings, 2013) and even between universities in the same country. Examples for the latter are the atypical cases of Cambridge and Oxford in the United Kingdom or the Grandes Écoles in the French system. It can easily be imagined that, depending on the power relations between academics and leaders, some university models are more likely to be promoted than others. Especially if academics can exert a high degree of influence on the choice of the university model, then the choice of an NPM model or a complete organization in the way we described both models in the introduction is unlikely.

Like the discussion of the other two mechanisms as put forward by DiMaggio and Powell (1983), our discussion of the normative mechanism has shown how this mechanism affects the embeddedness of European universities within nested organizational fields. Through this, some reasons for both isomorphism and differentiation among European universities have become visible.

CONCLUSION AND DISCUSSION

To recapitulate our main results, it could be shown that European universities have been affected by NPM reforms and a trend toward constructing universities as complete organizations. Whereas both analytical approaches highlight isomorphic tendencies, recent research shows simultaneous processes of homogenization and differentiation among European universities. So far, comparative higher education research has mainly looked for causes at the national level to explain these two processes.

The concept of nested organizational fields we employed allows for extending this state-centered perspective on "European universities under pressure" without neglecting the crucial role nation states still play in shaping the field of higher education. Within that analytical framework, we were able to show how isomorphic mechanisms contribute to embedding universities in different and nested organizational fields. These processes can not only explain homogenization, but also differentiation among European universities. In contrast to a state-centered perspective, however, the nested organizational field perspective not only focuses on processes of homogenization and differentiation within and between national systems, but also among cross-national subgroups of universities. This is where we see a great advantage in order to transcend the hitherto state-centered perspective in comparative higher education research. The concurrence of homogenization and differentiation among European universities can thus be explained by the complex interplay between different and nested organizational fields, related translating and editing processes as well as strategic behavior at the level of universities. Such a perspective proves to be fruitful in comparative higher education research, but we contend that comparative research on other areas where global, European, national and regional influences on organizations (firms, hospitals, schools, etc.) play a role, might also benefit from such an approach.

As we have shown, the nested field framework is well suited to identifying structural and systematic factors for homogenization and differentiation. However, the framework is certainly not conceived to provide a complete and comprehensive explanation of every single case. Factors specific to the individual case can certainly counteract systematic and structural factors. As an example, we can consider two university presidents who, in spite of comparable field embeddings, chose different strategies and therefore produce differentiation. The nested field approach is no substitute for empirical research, which is the only mean for discovering case-specific factors. The approach can, however, change research questions because we must now try to find out why – in spite of comparable field embeddings – different strategies are both possible and implemented.

Based on our analysis of nested organizational fields in the end, we would like to briefly discuss two further directions for studying "European universities under pressure" in more depth. On the one hand, one could focus more systematically and empirically on the organizational fields we took as relevant units for the analysis of changes among European universities. In our paper, we did not deal with questions concerning the rise and evolution of such fields, their internal structure in terms of broader cultural accounts, institutional logics, governance structures and actors, the stability and dynamics of their structure, their relations to other fields, including overlapping, but also contracting characteristics as well as mechanisms for coupling and decoupling nested organizational fields in higher education. Addressing these questions is a major challenge for future research. On the other hand, one could also address more thoroughly how universities as organizations react to the pressure arising from the different fields we described in the paper. European universities are indeed under pressure. But simply seeing them as being under pressure does not suffice. They are embedded in different and nested organizational fields whose demands and expectations are by no means homogeneous, and at times they can even change field embeddedness and the pressure that comes with it. This allows for an increase in agency and strategic choices that is worthwhile studying.

NOTES

1. Here, we also see a parallel to recent multidimensional conceptualizations of "glocalization" within neo-institutional research (Drori, Höllerer, & Walgenbach, 2013, 2014).

2. In order not to overcomplicate our basic argument in this article, we only consider geographical fields. However, we do think that field structures are far more complex than we can illustrate here. We could consider further nested and overlapping functional fields that may well cross-cut geographical fields. We can imagine, for example, fields encompassing and differentiating different types of universities and higher education institutions (such as Grand Écoles vs. universities in France, universities vs. universities of applied science in Germany, or research universities vs. community colleges in the United States).

3. A junior professorship has a fixed term of six years and is similar to an assistant professorship in the United States. Usually an evaluation takes place after three years to decide whether the professor should continue for the remaining three years. The junior professorship was introduced in Germany in 2002 and offers an alternative path to the habilitation to attaining a full professorship.

4. We do not consider administrative management here, only the academic profession and academic leadership, but see on administrative management (Gornitzka & Larsen, 2004; Krücken, Blümel, & Kloke, 2013; Slaughter & Rhoades, 2004; Whitchurch, 2006).

ACKNOWLEDGMENT

We are very grateful to the two editors, one anonymous reviewer, and Stefan Kirchner for their comments that have greatly improved the paper.

REFERENCES

Bauman, Z. (2000). *Liquid modernity*. Cambridge: Polity Press.

Bell, D. (1973). *The coming of post industrial society: A venture in social forecasting.* New York, NY: Basic Books.

Bleiklie, I., & Michelsen, S. (2013). Comparing HE Policies in Europe. *Higher Education,* *65*(1), 113−133.

Boxenbaum, E., & Jonsson, S. (2008). Isomorphism, diffusion and decoupling. In R. Greenwood, C. Oliver, R. Suddaby, & K. Sahlin (Eds.), *The SAGE handbook of organizational institutionalism* (pp. 78–98). London: Sage.

Braun, D., Benninghoff, M., Ramuz, R., & Gorga, A. (2015). Interdependency management in universities: A case study. *Studies in Higher Education, 40*(10), 1829–1843.

Braun, D., & Merrien, F.-X. (Eds.). (1999). *Towards a new model of governance for universities? A comparative view.* Philadelphia, PA: Jessica Kingsley Publishers.

Breakwell, G. M., & Tytherleigh, M. Y. (2010). University leaders and university performance in the United Kingdom: Is it 'who' leads, or 'where' they lead that matters most? *Higher Education, 60*(5), 491–506.

Brown, R., & Carasso, H. (2013). *Everything for sale? The marketisation of UK higher education.* New York, NY: Routledge.

Brunsson, N., & Sahlin-Andersson, K. (2000). Constructing organizations: The example of public sector reform. *Organization Studies, 21*(4), 721–746.

Capano, G. (2008). Looking for serendipity: The problematical reform of government within Italy's universities. *Higher Education, 55*(4), 481–504.

Castells, M. (2011). *The rise of the network society: The information age: Economy, society, and culture.* Chichester John Wiley.

Clark, B. R. (1983). *The higher education system. Academic organization in cross-national perspective.* Berkeley, CA: University of California Press.

Courpasson, D. (2000). Managerial strategies of domination. Power in soft bureaucracies. *Organization Studies, 21*(1), 141–161.

Czarniawska-Joerges, B., & Sevón, G. (2005). *Global ideas: How ideas, objects and practices travel in a global economy.* Copenhagen: Copenhagen Business School Press.

de Boer, H., Enders, J., & Leisyte, L. (2007). Public sector reform in Dutch higher education: The organizational transformation of the university. *Public Administration, 85*(1), 27–46.

de Boer, H., Enders, J., & Schimank, U. (2007). On the way towards new public management? The governance of university systems in England, the Netherlands, Austria, and Germany. In D. Jansen (Ed.), *New forms of governance in research organizations. Disciplinary approaches, interfaces and integration* (pp. 137–152). Dordrecht: Springer.

de Boer, H., & Huisman, J. (1999). The new public management in Dutch universities. In D., Braun & F.-X., Merrien (Eds.), *Towards a new model of governance for universities? A comparative view* (pp. 100–118). Philadelphia, PA: Jessica Kingsley Publishers.

de Boer, H., Leisyte, L., & Enders, J. (2006). The Netherlands — "Steering from a distance". In B. M. Kehm & U. Lanzendorf (Eds.), *Reforming university governance. Changing conditions for research in four European countries* (pp. 59–96). Bonn: Lemmens.

DiMaggio, P. J., & Powell, W. W. (1983). The iron cage revisited: Institutional isomorphism and the collective rationality in organizational fields. *American Sociological Review, 48*(2), 147–160.

Dobbins, M., & Knill, C. (2009). Higher education policies in Central and Eastern Europe: Convergence towards a common model? *Governance, 22*(3), 397–430.

Dobbins, M., & Knill, C. (2014). *Higher education governance and policy change in Western Europe: International challenges to historical institutions.* New York, NY: Palgrave Macmillan.

Dobbins, M., & Leisyte, L. (2014). Analysing the transformation of higher education governance in Bulgaria and Lithuania. *Public Management Review, 16*(7), 987–1010.

Drori, G. S., Höllerer, M. A., & Walgenbach, P. (2013). *Global themes and local variations in organization and management: Perspectives on glocalization.* New York, NY: Routledge.

Drori, G. S., Höllerer, M. A., & Walgenbach, P. (2014). Unpacking the glocalization of organization: From term, to theory, to analysis. *European Journal of Cultural and Political Sociology, 1*(1), 85–99.

Enders, J. (Ed.). (2000). *Employment and working conditions of academic staff in Europe.* Frankfurt/M.: GEW.

Enders, J., de Boer, H., & Weyer, E. (2013). Regulatory autonomy and performance: The reform of higher education revisited. *Higher Education, 65*(1), 5–23.

Enders, J., & Westerheijden, D. F. (2014). The Dutch way of new public management: A critical perspective on quality assurance in higher education. *Policy and Society, 33*(3), 189–198.

Engwall, L. (2014). The recruitment of university top leaders: Politics, communities and markets in interaction. *Scandinavian Journal of Management, 30*(3), 332–343.

Ferlie, E., & Andresani, G. (2009). United Kingdom from bureau professionalism to new public management? In C. Paradeise, E. Reale, I. Bleiklie, & E. Ferlie (Eds.), *University governance. Western European comparative perspectives* (pp. 177–195). Dordrecht: Springer.

Ferlie, E., Musselin, C., & Andresani, G. (2008). The steering of higher education systems: A public management perspective. *Higher Education, 56*(3), 325–348.

Ferlie, E., Musselin, C., & Andresani, G. (2009). The governance of higher education systems: A public management perspective. In C. Paradeise, E. Reale, I. Bleiklie, & E. Ferlie (Eds.), *University governance. Western European comparative perspectives* (pp. 1–19). Dordrecht: Springer.

Fligstein, N., & McAdam, D. (2012). *A theory of fields.* Oxford: Oxford University Press.

Geuna, A., & Martin, B. (2003). University research evaluation and funding: An international comparison. *Minerva, 41*(4), 277–304.

Gibbons, M., Limoges, C., Nowotny, H., Schwartzman, S., Scott, P., & Trow, M. (1994). *The new production of knowledge. The dynamics of science and research in contemporary societies.* London: Sage.

Goodall, A. H. (2006). Should top universities be led by top researchers and are they? A citations analysis. *Journal of Documentation, 62*(3), 388–411.

Goodrick, E., & Salancik, G. R. (1996). Organizational discretion in responding to institutional practices: Hospitals and cesarean births. *Administrative Science Quarterly, 41*(1), 1–28.

Göransson, B., Maharajh, R., & Schmoch, U. (2009). New activities of universities in transfer and extension: Multiple requirements and manifold solutions. *Science and Public Policy, 36*(2), 157–164.

Gornitzka, Å., & Larsen, I. M. (2004). Towards professionalisation? Restructuring of administrative work force in universities. *Higher Education, 47*(4), 455–471.

Gouldner, A. W. (1957). Cosmopolitans and locals: Toward an analysis of latent social roles I. *Administrative Science Quarterly, 2*(3), 281–306.

Gouldner, A. W. (1958). Cosmopolitans and locals: Toward an analysis of latent social roles II. *Administrative Science Quarterly, 2*(4), 444–480.

Hallonsten, O., & Silander, C. (2012). Commissioning the university of excellence: Swedish research policy and new public research funding programmes. *Quality in Higher Education, 18*(3), 367–381.

Harman, G., & Harman, K. (2008). Strategic mergers of strong institutions to enhance compe-
    titive advantage. *Higher Education Policy*, *21*(1), 99–121.
Hazelkorn, E., & Ryan, M. (2013). The impact of university rankings on higher education pol-
    icy in Europe: A challenge to perceived wisdom and a stimulus for change. In P. Zgaga,
    U. Teichler, & J. Brennan (Eds.), *The globalisation challenge for European higher educa-
    tion: Convergence and diversity, centres and peripheries* (pp. 79–99). Frankfurt/M.:
    Lang.
Hedmo, T., & Wedlin, L. (2008). New modes of governance: The re-regulation of European
    higher education and research. In C. Mazza, P. Quattrone, & A. Riccaboni (Eds.),
    European universities in transition: Issues, models and cases (pp. 113–132).
    Northampton, MA: Edward Elgar Pub.
Hicks, D. (2012). Performance-based university research funding systems. *Research Policy*,
    41(2), 251–261.
Huisman, J., de Weert, E., & Bartelse, J. (2002). Academic careers from a European perspec-
    tive: The declining desirability of the faculty position. *The Journal of Higher Education*,
    73(1), 141–160.
Hüther, O. (2010). *Von der Kollegialität zur Hierarchie? Eine Analyse des New Managerialism
    in den Landeshochschulgesetzen*. Wiesbaden: VS Verlag.
Hüther, O., & Krücken, G. (2013). Hierarchy and power: A conceptual analysis with particu-
    lar reference to new public management reforms in German universities. *European
    Journal of Higher Education*, *3*(4), 307–323.
Hüther, O., & Krücken, G. (2015). Incentives and power: An organizational perspective. In
    I. M. Welpe, J. Wollersheim, S. Ringelhan, & M. Osterloh (Eds.), *Incentives and perfor-
    mance* (pp. 69–86). Heidelberg: Springer.
Hüther, O., & Krücken, G. (2016). *Hochschulen. Fragestellungen, Ergebnisse und Perspektiven
    der sozialwissenschaftlichen Hochschulforschung*. Wiesbaden: Springer.
Keeling, R. (2006). The Bologna process and the Lisbon research agenda: The European
    Commission's expanding role in higher education discourse. *European Journal of
    Education*, *41*(2), 203–223.
Kehm, B. M., & Lanzendorf, U. (2006a). Germany – 16 länder approaches to reform. In
    B. M. Kehm & U. Lanzendorf (Eds.), *Reforming university governance. Changing condi-
    tions for research in four European countries* (pp. 135–185). Bonn: Lemmens.
Kehm, B. M., & Lanzendorf, U. (Eds.). (2006b). *Reforming university governance. Changing
    conditions for research in four European countries*. Bonn: Lemmens.
Kehm, B. M., & Pasternack, P. (2009). The German "Excellence Initiative" and its role in
    restructuring the national higher education landscape. In D. Palfreyman & T. Tapper
    (Eds.), *Structuring mass higher education: The role of elite institutions* (pp. 113–127).
    New York, NY: Routledge.
Kerr, C. (1963). *The uses of the university*. Cambridge, MA: Harvard University Press.
Kodeih, F., & Greenwood, R. (2014). Responding to institutional complexity: The role of
    identity. *Organization Studies*, *35*(1), 7–39.
Kretek, P., Dragšić, Ž., & Kehm, B. M. (2013). Transformation of university governance: On
    the role of university board members. *Higher Education*, *65*(1), 39–58.
Krücken, G., Blümel, A., & Kloke, K. (2013). The managerial turn in higher education? On
    the interplay of organizational and occupational change in German academia. *Minerva*,
    51(4), 417–442.

Krücken, G., Kosmützky, A., & Torka, M. (Eds.). (2007). *Towards a multiversity? Universities between global trends and national traditions.* Bielefeld: transcript.

Krücken, G., & Meier, F. (2006). Turning the university into an organizational actor. In G. S. Drori, J. W. Meyer, & H. Hwang (Eds.), *Globalization and organization. World society and organizational change* (pp. 241–257). Oxford: Oxford University Press.

Latour, B. (1988). *The pasteurization of France.* Cambridge, MA: Harvard University Press.

Leisyte, L., de Boer, H., & Enders, J. (2006). England – Prototype of the "Evaluative State". In B. M. Kehm & U. Lanzendorf (Eds.), *Reforming university governance. Changing conditions for research in four European countries* (pp. 21–56). Bonn: Lemmens.

Magalhães, A., Veiga, A., Ribeiro, F. M., Sousa, S., & Santiago, R. (2013). Creating a common grammar for European higher education governance. *Higher Education, 65*(1), 95–112.

Marginson, S. (2006). Dynamics of national and global competition in higher education. *Higher Education, 52*(1), 1–39.

McPherson, C. M., & Sauder, M. (2013). Logics in action: Managing institutional complexity in a drug court. *Administrative Science Quarterly, 58*(2), 165–196.

Merton, R. K. (1973). *The sociology of science, theoretical and empirical investigations.* Chicago, IL: University of Chicago Press.

Meyer, A. D., Gaba, V., & Colwell, K. A. (2005). Organizing far from equilibrium: Nonlinear change in organizational fields. *Organization Science, 16*(5), 456–473.

Meyer, J. W., & Rowan, B. (1977). Institutionalized organizations: Formal structure as myth and ceremony. *American Journal of Sociology, 83*(2), 340–363.

Mignot Gerard, S. (2003). Who are the actors in the government of French universities? The paradoxal victory of deliberative leadership. *Higher Education, 45*(1), 71–89.

Musselin, C. (2005). European academic labor markets in transition. *Higher Education, 49*(1–2), 135–154.

Musselin, C. (2010). *The market for academics.* New York, NY: Routledge.

Musselin, C. (2014). Empowerment of French universities by funding and evaluation agencies. In R. Whitley & J. Gläser (Eds.), *Organizational transformation and scientific change: The impact of institutional restructuring on universities and intellectual innovation* (pp. 51–76). Bingley: Emerald.

Musselin, C., & Paradeise, C. (2009). France: From incremental transitions to institutional change. In C. Paradeise, E. Reale, I. Bleiklie, & E. Ferlie (Eds.), *University governance. Western European comparative perspectives* (pp. 21–49). Dordrecht: Springer.

Neave, G., & Rhoades, G. (1987). The academic estate in Western Europe. In B. R. Clark (Ed.), *The academic profession. National, disciplinary and institutional settings* (pp. 211–270). Berkeley, CA: University of California Press.

Nowotny, H., Scott, P., & Gibbons, M. (2001). *Re-thinking science – Knowledge and the public in an age of uncertainty.* Cambridge: Polity Press.

Oliver, C. (1991). Strategic responses to institutional processes. *Academy of Management Review, 16*(1), 145–179.

Öquist, G., & Benner, M. (2015). Why are some nations more successful than others in research impact? A comparison between Denmark and Sweden. In I. M. Welpe, J. Wollersheim, S. Ringelhan, & M. Osterloh (Eds.), *Incentives and performance* (pp. 241–257). Heidelberg: Springer.

Paradeise, C., Reale, E., Bleiklie, I., & Ferlie, E. (Eds.). (2009). *University governance: Western European comparative perspectives.* Dordrecht: Springer.

Paradeise, C., Reale, E., Goastellec, G., & Bleiklie, I. (2009). Universities steering between stories and history. In C. Paradeise, E. Reale, I. Bleiklie, & E. Ferlie (Eds.), *University governance: Western European comparative perspectives* (pp. 227–290). Dordrecht: Springer.

Paradeise, C., & Thoenig, J.-C. (2013). Academic institutions in search of quality: Local orders and global standards. *Organization Studies, 34*(2), 189–218.

Perkin, H. (1991). History of universities. In P. G. Altbach (Ed.), *International higher education. An encyclopedia* (Vol. 1, pp. 169–204). New York, NY: Garland Publishing.

Pfeffer, J., & Salancik, G. R. (1978). *The external control of organizations: A resource dependence perspective.* New York, NY: Harper & Row.

Pietilä, M. (2015). Tenure track career system as a strategic instrument for academic leaders. *European Journal of Higher Education, 5*(4), 371–387.

Power, M. (1999). *The audit society: Rituals of verification.* Oxford: Oxford University Press.

Ramirez, F. O., & Christensen, T. (2013). The formalization of the university: Rules, roots, and routes. *Higher Education, 65*(6), 695–708.

Rathmann, A. (2014). *Die Juniorprofessur im Vergleich zu traditionellen wissenschaftlichen Karrierewegen I: Die Sicht von Nachwuchswissenschaftler(inne)n.* Retrieved from http://www.che.de/downloads/Veranstaltungen/CHE_Vortrag_Praesentation_Rathmann140929_PK433.pdf. Accessed on December 19, 2014.

Reay, T., & Hinings, C. R. (2005). The recomposition of an organizational field: Health care in Alberta. *Organization Studies, 26*(3), 351–384.

Reinalda, B., & Kulesza-Mietkowski, E. (2005). *The Bologna process: Harmonizing Europe's higher education.* Bloomfield Hills, MI: Barbara Budrich Publishers.

Risser, D. (2003). Governance and functioning of British universities. *Beiträge zur Hochschulforschung, 25*(1), 84–101.

Röbken, H. (2006). Profile deutscher Universitätsleitungen. *Beiträge zur Hochschulforschung, 28*(4), 6–29.

Sahlin, K., & Wedlin, L. (2008). Circulating ideas: Imitation, translation and editing. In R. Greenwood, C. Oliver, R. Suddaby, & K. Sahlin (Eds.), *The sage handbook of organizational institutionalism* (pp. 218–242). London: Sage.

Salmi, J. (2009). *The challenge of establishing world-class universities.* Washington, DC: World Bank Publications.

Schimank, U. (2005). "New public management" and the academic profession: Reflections on the German situation. *Minerva, 43*(4), 361–376.

Schmid, C. J., & Wilkesmann, U. (2015). Ansichtssache Managerialismus an deutschen Hochschulen – Ein empirisches Stimmungsbild und Erklärungen. *Beiträge zur Hochschulforschung, 37*(2), 56–87.

Schwarz, S., & Westerheijden, D. F. (Eds.). (2004). *Accreditation and evaluation in the European higher education area.* Dordrecht: Springer.

Scott, W. R. (2013). *Institutions and organizations: Ideas, interests, and identities.* London: Sage.

Seeber, M., Lepori, B., Montauti, M., Enders, J., de Boer, H., Weyer, E., … Reale, E. (2015). European universities as complete organizations? Understanding identity, hierarchy and rationality in public organizations. *Public Management Review, 17*(10), 1444–1474.

Shattock, M. (2013). University governance, leadership and management in a decade of diversification and uncertainty. *Higher Education Quarterly, 67*(3), 217–233.

Shils, E. (1992). Universities — Since 1900. In B. R. Clark & G. Neave (Eds.), *Encyclopedia of higher education. Analytical perspectives* (Vol. 2, pp. 1259–1275). Oxford: Pergamon.

Slaughter, S., & Cantwell, B. (2012). Transatlantic moves to the market: The United States and the European Union. *Higher Education, 63*(5), 583–606.

Slaughter, S., & Rhoades, G. (2004). *Academic capitalism and the new economy: Markets, state, and higher education.* Baltimore, MD: Johns Hopkins University Press.

Smith, D., & Adams, J. (2008). Academics or executives? Continuity and change in the roles of pro-vice-chancellors. *Higher Education Quarterly, 62*(4), 340–357.

Stevens, M. L., Armstrong, E. A., & Arum, R. (2008). Sieve, incubator, temple, hub: Empirical and theoretical advances in the sociology of higher education. *Annual Review of Sociology, 34*, 127–151.

Teichler, U., Arimoto, A., & Cummings, W. K. (Eds.). (2013). *The changing academic profession: Major findings of a comparative survey.* Dordrecht: Springer.

Thornton, P. H., & Ocasio, W. (1999). Institutional logics and the historical contingency of power in organizations: Executive succession in the higher education publishing industry, 1958–1990. *American Journal of Sociology, 105*(3), 801–843.

Thornton, P. H., Ocasio, W., & Lounsbury, M. (2012). *The institutional logics perspective: A new approach to culture, structure, and process.* Oxford: Oxford University Press.

Van Vught, F. A., & Ziegele, F. (Eds.). (2012). *Multidimensional ranking: The design and development of U-multirank.* Dordrecht: Springer.

Vasi, I. B. (2007). Thinking globally, planning nationally and acting locally: Nested organizational fields and the adoption of environmental practices. *Social Forces, 86*(1), 113–136.

Wedlin, L. (2007). The role of rankings in codifying a business school template: Classifications, diffusion and mediated isomorphism in organizational fields. *European Management Review, 4*(1), 24–39.

Whitchurch, C. (2006). Who do they think they are? The changing identities of professional administrators and managers in UK higher education. *Journal of Higher Education Policy and Management, 28*(2), 159–171.

Whitley, R., & Gläser, J. (Eds.). (2014). *Organizational transformation and scientific change: The impact of institutional restructuring on universities and intellectual innovation.* Bingley: Emerald.

Wooten, M., & Hoffman, A. J. (2008). Organizational fields: Past, present and future. In R. Greenwood, C. Oliver, R. Suddaby, & K. Sahlin (Eds.), *The SAGE handbook of organizational institutionalism* (pp. 130–147). London: Sage.

PART II
PRESSURES AT THE FIELD LEVEL

THE EMERGENT ACTION FIELD OF METRICS: FROM RANKINGS TO ALTMETRICS

Catherine Paradeise and Ghislaine Filliatreau

ABSTRACT

Much has been analyzed regarding the origins and the impact of rankings and metrics on policies, behaviors, and missions of universities. Surprisingly, little attention has been allocated to describing and analyzing the emergence of metrics as a new action field. This industry, fueled by the "new public management" policy perspectives that operate at the backstage of the contemporary pervasive "regime of excellence," still remains a black box worth exploring in depth. This paper intends to fill this loophole. It first sets the stage for this new action field by stressing the differences between the policy fields of higher education in the United States and Europe, as a way to understand the specificities of the use of metrics and rankings on both continents. The second part describes the actors of the field, which productive organizations they build, what skills they combine, which products they put on the market, and their shared norms and audiences.

Keywords: Rankings; metrics; new public management; regime of excellence; Europe; United States

The University under Pressure
Research in the Sociology of Organizations, Volume 46, 87–128
Copyright © 2016 by Emerald Group Publishing Limited
All rights of reproduction in any form reserved
ISSN: 0733-558X/doi:10.1108/S0733-558X20160000046004

INTRODUCTION

The practice of ranking universities has a long history. Indeed, national rankings have existed for over a century in the United States. The first ones were set up by scholars who were interested in obtaining a better view of how the best departments were distributed across a large national territory. A second step was when media such as *US News and World Report* (USNWR) released its well-known American colleges ranking in 1983. Since the 1980s, major media outlets have also developed rankings all over Europe. The ranking fever reached Asian countries in the 1990s, where media and government played an important role in their development. The first international rankings of business schools were set up during the same period of time. The first world league – the Academic Ranking of World Universities (ARWU) – was issued by an academic research center at Jiao Tong University in 2003. By 2005, it was hailed as "the most widely used annual ranking of the world's research universities" (The Economist, 2005), making it a leading benchmark in a highly competitive market that contains top players including the media, specialized research centers of universities and their spin-offs, ministry departments, and accreditation agencies, which have grown rapidly in recent years. An impressive number of national and international rankings have been and are still being issued by various organizations, among which the UK *Times Higher Education World University Ranking* (THE), and the QS World University Rankings (*Quacquarelli Symonds*) are the most cited. While many rankings were set up, relatively few have survived.

Building metrics, some of which are used in developing rankings, is an equally long story. Traditional R&D metrics were developed and enriched after World War II in order to assess the research and innovation potential of nations. Such metrics were based on a variety of indicators such as R&D budgets, number of scientists in the public and private sector, patents, etc. Indicators covering OECD member countries were set up in 1962 by experts and registered in the so-called "*Frascati Manual*," which has been constantly updated since then. They progressively became the standard for data collection in R&D in the OECD and in the European Union, but also in many non-member economies (Godin, 2006).

At the turn of the millennium, R&D metrics were enhanced by the development of bibliometric indicators, which originated after World War II in the field that is now called "science of science policy" (Lane, Largent, & Rosen, 2014; Wouters, 1999) and were popularized by library management (Garfield, 1998; Gingras, 2014). They started being used as tools for assessment, not only of national performance in publications, but also of institutional, disciplinary, and individual performance. Technically speaking, scientometrics at large flourished due to the joint expansion of numerous national and institutional collections of data at the university and national level – notably bibliometric ones – and of ingenious software, which were able to process the data and build all sorts of indicators. But the "fever of evaluation" (Gingras, 2014) that started in the 1990s and blossomed after 2000 in the wake of new public management (NPM) policy was the main driver that stimulated developments of both various indicators and rankings exercises.

Besides using available metrics, rankings have themselves generated a proliferation of indicator-based products, paving the way for a convergence of interests between two communities of providers – rankers and scientometricians. These products range from off-the-shelves rankings that are customizable by discipline, region, and type of institution to for-profit tailor-made visualization, profiling of specific institutions (THE, QS, Leiden, etc.), and customizable open-source altmetrics (Reimsbach-Kounatze, 2015) available online (*SIRIS*, etc.). Such products were set up by university research centers (such as the *Center for World-Class Universities* at Shanghai Jiao Tong – CWCU – or *Center for Science and Technology Studies* – CWTS – at Leiden) or their spin-offs (such as the Scimago Lab at the Spanish public research organization *Consejo Superior de Investigaciones Científicas* (CSIC)), by media (such as THE) and by information companies (such as QS). Alternative multidimensional rankings have differentiated themselves from typical classifications by providing customizable information but no ranking (e.g., U-Multirank, promoted by the European Commission).

Much has been analyzed regarding the origins and impacts of rankings and metrics on policies, behaviors and missions of universities, at national (Hazelkorn, 2015), local (Paradeise & Thoenig, 2015), and individual levels (Tutterow & Evans, 2016). Much has been written on how rankings have reinforced a mindset change among policy-makers, scientists, and the public. Much has been debated about their methodological correctness or fairness. Yet most stakeholders – from governmental policy-makers and agencies to donors and students – keep appropriating rankings as a way to orient themselves, or to justify their orientation, in the all too large and unknown world born out of globalization (Marginson, 2001). In this open space populated by thousands of universities, "notation agencies" are required (Pusser & Marginson, 2013). These notation agencies testify the value of universities to "fully inform" their many audiences in civil society and provide accessible data that can become part of university management toolboxes.

Surprisingly, little attention has been allocated to describing and analyzing the emergence of metrics as a new action field. The industry fueled by the "new public management" policy perspectives that operate at the backstage of the contemporary pervasive "regime of excellence" still remains a black box worth exploring in depth (Dodier, 2009; Miller & O'Leary, 1987; Rose, 1991).

One way to study this move in the field of metrics is to examine the emergence and subsequent proliferation of rankings and associated metrics. Metrics were fostered at the very end of the 20th century by the development of evidence-based national policies in higher education (HE) and research. Their influence grew dramatically when global rankings erupted at the turn of the 21st century, and the fever of new evidence-based methods of government became widespread. Policy-makers suddenly had to face "evidence of excellence" for their country provided by international rankings, and eventually used these as a set of arguments and tools to back their policies. In other words, rankings have operated as catalysts for the emergence of a larger field of metrics that has subsumed national policies. They dramatically publicize universities' level of performance in the international arena. Today, no country can avoid the fact that their universities will be globally benchmarked, without having any form of control over rankers. To face this new reality built by numbers, they are encouraged to turn to producers of more and more sophisticated metrics that become major strategic tools to improve their positioning within overall rankings.

The origins, development, and impact of the action field of metrics on decision-making processes nevertheless vary depending on individual stakeholders, universities as institutions, and countries, according to the specificities of national policy fields of HE.

This section sets the stage for this new action field by first shaping a theoretical framework to understand the reasons for its emergence. Next, we discuss the differences between the policy fields of higher education in the United States and Europe, including the specificities of its expansion on both continents. Following Fligstein and McAdam's (2012) guidelines, the next section approaches the field by describing the development of its actors, skills, products, norms, and audiences.

SETTING THE SCENE: THE NEW REGIME OF GOVERNMENTALITY AND THE DEVELOPMENT OF THE ACTION FIELD OF METRICS IN EUROPE AND THE UNITED STATES

Truth, Governmentality, and Action Field of Metrics

From a Regime of Truth to a New Regime of Governmentality
Indicators are naturalized proxies for a reality that they actually help create by institutionalizing categories (Desrosières, 1993). They qualify

the properties of an institution or a person in a simplified manner, usually along an ordinal scale. "Excellence indicators," which score performance, are supposed to supply the best quality proxies, which are both feasible given existing data and plausible for various audiences. The use of indicators to define quality progressively imposes a new language of numbers based on the notion that the essential value of action can be equated with its measurable outputs (see e.g., the Lisbon agenda, 2000). This "commensuration" process (Espeland & Stevens, 1998) reconfigures judgments on the relevance and value of the university, the research center, and the scholar's activity (Dodier, 2009). It impacts expectations and behaviors of actors, it alters their cognitions as to what is the value of various activities (Espeland & Sauder, 2007), and it redistributes resources between them and modifies professional norms and standards (Paradeise, 2012).

By equating qualities into quantities, this regime opens the door to implementing policy objectives according to a decontextualized assessment of the "production of knowledge" by nations, organizations or individuals (Myers & Robe, 2009). As they become legitimate public choice criteria, metrics come to play a key role as tools kits for steering organizations and public policies. Trust in numbers as expressions of the "true value" of research and education activities becomes the basis of a new "regime of governmentality" (Foucault, 2010, 2011, 2012) that associates new individually internalized forms of knowledge with an evidence-based control technology of government. In large parts of the world, including Europe, this technology has been formalized to support new public management policies. They have redesigned universities as autonomous "agents" reporting to their "principals" — public authorities and other funders — and have reorganized the relationships between both, with the goal of monitoring agents' behavior and optimizing \resource allocation by referring to performance indicators, which are considered as quasi-prices adjusting performance and funding (Miller, 2001; Miller & O'Leary, 1987, 1994; Rose, 1991; Rose & Miller, 1992).

The Emerging Action Field of Metrics

Trusting numbers such as isolated indicators or rankings means delegating — if not subcontracting — trust to specific organizations, which are supposedly able to build them in a professional way. Exploring the history of the French national statistical system, Desrosières (1993) has shown how reliable and trustworthy statistical data were compiled for the use of policymakers, entrepreneurs, and citizens in the 19th and 20th centuries. These data were based on the combined development of international scientific communities that developed new knowledge, of national schools that trained civil servants in statistics, of national organizations that recruited these specialists and set up production routines and processes, and of rules that protected the objectivity of information at a distance from the pressures, prejudices, passions, and vested interests of their stakeholders (Porter, 1995).

The same types of dynamics are currently occurring at the global level in the field of metrics, involving various players linked by similar interests, values, and methodologies that progressively instill this faith in numbers as central to our understanding of value, thereby building a new global action field.

The development of evidence-based policies in the field of higher education calls for gathering, organizing, standardizing, and disseminating information in order to ensure the objectivity of the data based on the rigor of numbers (Paradeise, 2012; Porter, 1995). These numbers lie at the very core of knowledge required by new public management policies. It thus awakens the attention of new players. It opens the field to new specialists, technologies, and methods. It sets up new arenas to establish shared technical norms and social rules of good practice. In other words, it paves the way for a new action field, defined as "a constructed meso-level social order in which actors (who can be individual or collective) attend to and interact with one another on the basis of shared (which is not to say consensual) understandings about the purposes of the field, relationships to others in the field (including who has power and why), and the rules governing legitimate action in the field" (Fligstein & McAdam, 2012).

As far as indicator building and processing is concerned, key factors include scientometricians and rankers, who both design metrics. The relationships between the two communities are ambiguous. Rankers either build on existing metrics and data or design specific ones for their own purpose. To gain respectability, they are pushed to make their measures more sophisticated, either by building new metrics that may be made public, or by inserting well-established indicators into the computation of rankings scores. Scientometricians reassert their scientific legitimacy by highlighting the methodological quality of their data, the epistemological rigor of the rankings they build, and their range of validity. They define themselves as the warrants of scientific correctness in face of uncontrolled fabrication and use of rankings. They thus create a competition around methodological standards. As a consequence, it becomes increasingly difficult for lay users to disentangle the relative positioning of the two communities of players. Although they do not target the same audiences, they increasingly design competing products that can be used for similar purposes. Bibliometricians consider

rankers to be dangerously simplistic, whereas rankers suspect that bibliometricians may not be that helpful for users. Yet, whether they like it or not,
rankers and scientometricians have become more and more interdependent.
They face similar problems. Both are exposed to cost issues. They have to
defend the scientific and methodological rigor of their products. Building
user-friendly and attractive interfaces that make intuitive understanding of
information possible also becomes a key issue. And they all know that establishing one's legitimacy in a world of competition between standards requires
being widely used and acknowledged by a credible third-party.

A Comparative Approach to Policy Fields of Higher Education

Rankings could have remained information that no one − neither policy-
makers nor students nor universities − paid much attention to. Why did
they become so pervasive, opening up the way for new players? And how
did they change the field of metrics? Who are these new players, their distinctive products and audiences? Do they share common norms and values?
How interdependent are they?

Let us recall the release of the first ARWU ranking. Without any specific
marketing effort made by its designers, who barely looked for or even considered that their initiative could become a major success, the ranking
quasi-instantly erupted on the international scene. When Prof. Liu at Jiao
Tong of Shanghai University created "the Shanghai ranking" in 2003, he
had no other ambition than to create a tool that would help position
Chinese universities among world players and locate future possible
alliances.

The surprise was that rankings have quite suddenly become a fundamental focus of stakeholders all over the world. Clearly, their sudden and rapid
influence relates to changes in the ways university resources are allocated
by performance-based policies. These changes can be seen across the globe,
both in countries characterized by decentralized funding, which is linked to
individual stakeholders' choices, and countries where it is more common to
have a centralized mode of funding by public authority. Yet they did not
impact each region of the world to the same extent nor through the same
mechanisms.

The United States: A Consumer-Driven Market
As mentioned earlier, rankings have existed for over a century in the
United States. But it is only since the turn of the millennium that they have

become a concern of university presidents. In 2002, 20% of US university presidents claimed they ignored rankings (Levin, 2002 cited in Hazelkorn, 2009). But by 2007, 80% of them were worried enough to refuse to answer the reputational portion of the US News and World Report ranking survey. They suspected that its data were not "collected in accord with clear, shared professional standards." They argued that such rankings "imply a false precision and authority that is not warranted by the data they use; obscure important differences in educational mission in aligning institutions on a single scale; say nothing or very little about whether students are actually learning at particular colleges or universities; encourage wasteful spending and gamesmanship in institutions' pursuing improved rankings; overlook the importance of a student in making education happen and overweight the importance of a university's prestige in that process; and degrade for students the educational value of the college search process" (Presidents' Letter, 2007).

As of today, the attention allocated by decision-makers and politicians to world rankings remains rather low in the United States. One of the reasons is that the nation is the global winner that monopolizes the top positions. It is overrepresented among the top 500 and even more among the top 100 universities in the Shanghai ranking. Nevertheless, the reason why the national USNWR college ranking is targeted by the above-cited presidents' letter is that they fear the direct impact of rankings on their stakeholders' behaviors.

For one thing, students' higher education choices are highly influenced by increasing costs of universities, which is associated with changes in federal aid policy. These changes in policy in turn impact applications and thus influence universities' revenue expectations. Between 2007 and 2012, fees increased by 27% at public universities, rising 1.6% more than inflation each year. At the same time, government funding per student fell by 27%. Berman and Stivers (2016) explain why and how student aid was progressively centralized at the federal government level and allocated in the form of loans. The 37 million student loan borrowers (with over seven million debtors in default) have an average of $24,301 in student debt, bringing the overall loan debt to over $1.2 trillion (with around $864 billion in federal student loan debt).

While loans now outnumber grants, and students have experienced the dramatic rise of tuition and fees, "massification" of higher education brought students' enrollment from 15.2 million in 1999 to 20.4 million in 2011, increasing the share of medium or lower-income students in universities. More families behave as poorly informed consumers who are increasingly sensitive to signals of universities' "value for money." Enrollment regressed by 2% in 2012. Although most observed variations in rank order are without any statistical significance, the attention universities allocated to rankings rose. They started developing marketing and communication campaigns. They reallocated internal resources to upgrade their standing according to rankings' scores (Davis & Binder, 2016; Tutterow & Evans, 2016). They also began to learn how to cheat numbers. Magazines are full of dreadful stories about schools, faculty heads, and university presidents shivering while awaiting the new issue of USNWR yearly rankings. Espeland and Sauder (2007) show how law school deans feel trapped each year by the necessity to at least keep or at best improve their rank, as "moving onto the front page of the USNWR college rankings increases applications by 4%, and among universities in the top 25, moving up a spot increases applications by 1%" (Berman & Stivers, 2016, this volume, following Bowman & Bastedo, 2009).

Such rankings provide relatively simple criteria that directly matter to students, especially undergraduates. For example, USNWR ranking of colleges pays no attention to research, but stresses mainly academic reputation, work conditions, student selectivity, retention, and graduation by disciplinary field. World rankings of universities by magazines, including USNWR, devote 60% or less of their overall mark to research (instead of 90–100% in academic rankings, see Table 1). A large percentage of their total rank is computed from indicators related to teaching, international openness, or industrial relations. They rely heavily on reputation surveys (25–50%) which academic rankings dismiss. Rankings are more and more customizable for free or for a small fee by region of the world, by degree and by large fields. Students are indeed at least as much interested in the status of the discipline in which they wish to graduate at a given university as by the overall rank of the university itself. Rankings such as THE also make it possible to customize rankings according to individual preferences, from the relative importance of research and teaching to the relative proportion of international and domestic students. But whatever the enrichment of data they provide, their conception and design remains altogether quite simple.

Other stakeholders also are impacted by rankings, which generate a Matthew effect. The increasing concentration of donations in fewer higher education institutions shows how much rankings contribute to the transformation of universities' reputations into brands, thereby encouraging donors to more often consider their score and to subsequently adjust their contributions.

Table 1. The Major Products and Services Offered by Seven Ranking Producers.

Use	Rankings							
	THE (Times Higher Education)	QS (Quacquarelli Symonds)	US News and World Report	CWTS Leiden B.V.	Shanghai Ranking Consultancy	CWTS Leiden B.V.	ScimagoLab	NTUR (National Taiwan University)
1 Evaluation: Institutional rating	No	P	P	P	No	P	P	No
2 Evaluation/strategy: Institutional benchmark	No	P	P	P	F	P	P	No
3 Monitoring: Institutional follow-up	No	P	–	P	No	P	P	No
4 Online access to the data	P	No	P	NA	NA	NA	NA	No
5 Online access to customized ranking	P	P	P	–	F	–	P	No
6 Featured products: compass, guides, etc.	F	P	P	No	F	No	–	No
7 Promotion, advertisement	P	P	P	No	No	No	No	No
8 Commercial fairs, conferences, events	P	P	–	No		No	No	No
9 Training courses	No	No	No	P	No	P	P	No
10 On request consultancy	No	P	No	P	–	P	P	No

F: free of charge; P: paying; NA: not applicable; –: unknown.

The growth of the policy field around higher education does not only relate to the increasing share of federal aid to students, but also to the rise of the share of research money allocated through federal grants. Altogether, the concentration of resources in the federal policy field of higher education (Graham & Diamond, 1997) fosters the rise of accountability control from the federal government as is the case in traditionally more centralized countries. Such a requirement was clearly expressed by President Obama in 2013. He proposed building a national scorecard to better adjust the distribution of federal aid to colleges based on their performance in terms of access, a hot issue on the policy agenda. Already in 2005, the Washington Monthly had anticipated such a shift in orientation by "rating schools based on their contribution to the public good," not only "by producing top research and education but also by recruiting and graduating low-income students and encouraging students to give something back to their country" (Washington Monthly, 2014).

Europe and the Rest of the World: A Policy-Makers-Driven Market
In countries where universities are centrally funded and steered, the target of rankers is not students but decision-makers. In many of the most advanced countries outside the United States – Europe and the Commonwealth countries, but also Latin America and most parts of Asia – universities have been and still are in most cases public, with access being restricted to only a fringe of young people. At the same time, they aimed at providing an increasing proportion of them with the same free educational service regardless of their origins or location. Hence, in many countries universities and their staff are ruled by an identical public status, and steered by central national or regional ministries. National or regional public budgets were in charge of funding them based on the number of students they served. As a consequence, students had no reason to behave as consumers. Fees still remain low in universities and they essentially deliver the same service and equivalent grades to all. This situation explains why national rankings, which were issued by many newspapers during the 1980s, did not really catch public interest in Europe as they did in the United States during the same time period.

It is thus a completely different context that explains why world rankings were immediately considered relevant by policy-makers in Europe, the Commonwealth countries, and Japan, but also in emerging countries. For at the time, NPM-style reforms were sweeping across the globe based on the national ambitions to become important players on the global stage. They were also pushed by international organizations such as UNESCO,

OECD, the World Bank and the European Commission, which converged to encourage national higher education systems to reform.

Such policies call for metrics, including rankings, which legitimate decision-making that relies on indicators and on centralized bureaucratic control (for Europe, see Paradeise, Reale, Bleiklie, & Ferlie, 2009). Metrics are used as quasi-prices, linking incentives, performance and allocation of resources. Here, two joint issues are at stake. The first issue is the need to address the rising costs of HE and research, which can be a burden on national budgets. These rising costs are linked to massification and the use of increasingly expensive technologies. Policy-makers must provide good reasons for their allocation choices. The second issue involves (re)configuring HE systems in order to fit the requirements of the so-called "knowledge-based economy," by favoring concentration of public research funding in "world class" universities, while sustaining appropriate educational programs for a larger fraction of citizens, thereby fostering differentiation of homogenous university systems.

The ARWU ranking itself complied with an ambition of the Chinese government to position national universities in the world landscape, as it aimed to catch up with the rest of the world. The purpose was to compile information to help operate the nation's "excellence program," the first of its kind, which was to become a very successful policy tool throughout the world, and to help China position itself in the new international struggle for influence in HE (Cheng, Wang, & Liu, 2014). Such an international ranking system thus supports a vision that serves a project of "excellence." Its indicators encapsulate norms of excellence and competition, summarized into the concept of the "world class university" promoted by the Chinese government, which all ambitious countries in higher education would work toward.

The impact of university world leagues has been instantaneous. The mediocre scores of their universities were felt as a real trauma by old European countries. Willing or not, they were now submitted to global assessments that were out of their control. While sometimes rebelling against the inescapable rise of Chinese ambitions, they entered an era in which they had to deal with international comparisons that carried along a new challenge for national decision-makers; they had to make their universities "visible from Shanghai" by promoting policies more clearly turned toward visible performance.

In spite of the "nostalgia for a world without numbers" (Weingart, 2015), rankings are here to stay. An international 2006 survey conducted in Germany, Australia and Japan reported that 63% of presidents say that they have taken action in response to rankings, compared to only 8% who have not (Hazelkorn, 2007). A recent survey by the European Universities Association (Hazelkorn, Loukkola, & Zhang, 2014) confirms several relevant impacts of rankings on major university decisions, including mergers, salaries of top university officials, claims on resources, and monitoring of international rankings' results. Sixty percent of responding universities now include staff dedicated to such a mission.

Governments and university leadership certainly overestimate the information delivered by rankings when complying with the new government by numbers. Such an attitude not only expresses naïve pragmatism. It also contributes to the rationale for the liberal or neo-liberal turn of national systems of HE observed all over the world, well described in Europe by Krücken and Meier (2006), and largely accounted for in the different context of the United States (for instance, Slaughter & Rhoades, 2004). Strikingly, since the 1980s, and especially since the 2000s, national steering systems are experiencing extensive organizational and governance reforms. They rebuild legal frames and economic incentives with two complementary targets. First, they aim at agentifying universities as autonomous, accountable and internally rationalized institutions. Second, they try to reconfigure their national systems by fostering more stratification. This is accomplished by concentrating resources on the best-performing HE institutions in research, which is based on assessment and public competitive grants (Aghion, Dewatripont, Hoxby, Mas-Colell, & Sapir, 2009; Paradeise et al., 2009). Both dimensions of these reforms call for developing indicators to help assess and incentivize autonomous universities.

Assessing the outcomes of individual universities and their components has become a big deal in countries where higher education is steered by public authorities at the national or regional levels, and where historically public budgets have been allocated on the basis of the number of registered students. Assessment of "excellence" provides a framework to reconsider the devolution of a proportion of universities' budgets, which varies across countries (Rauhvargers, 2013) and is based on ex-post evaluation of performance. The make-up of the UK Research Assessment Exercise (later the Research Excellence Framework), of evaluation agencies (such as in the French AERES – Agence d'évaluation de la recherche et de l'enseignement supérieur – which would become the HCERES), as well as many accreditation or quality assessment agencies (Enders, De Boer, & Westerheijden, 2015; Reale, Inzelt, Lepori, & Van den besselaar, 2012) serves this purpose.

Performance orientation has also been encouraged by the development of competitive funding programs. Many "programs of excellence" have been launched in established Western or Eastern countries, such as the French and German "Initiatives of Excellence" operating since the beginning of the 2010s, or the Japanese 21st Century Center of Excellence (COE), which was established in 2002. It is also the case in emergent Asian countries, with programs such as the Chinese 211 and 985 Projects, or in Korea the 1999 Brain Korea 21 (BK21), followed by the 2004 New University for Regional Innovation (NURI) program and the 2008 World Class University (WCU) program.

Thus the proliferation of global rankings converges with the ambition to steer higher education and research organizations (as well as schools, medical services, local police offices, etc.) using numbers, bringing about policies that have already inspired many public reforms since the 1980s. It reinforces the new vision of how good performance should be identified and rewarded, impacting not only the focus of policy-makers, but also of universities, faculty, and students. It thus strengthens the rationale for reforms that had been going on quite silently since the 1990s, at first as a way to face the squeeze between a rise in demand for higher education and a decrease in the supply of resources, given fiercer competition for public resources in welfare states (Paradeise et al., 2009), and later to improve higher education performance in so-called knowledge-based societies. It contributes to this new way of considering the value added by universities to their countries and to their students and legitimizes the (re)allocation of resources toward those identified as best-performing.

Global rankings are appropriated by emerging countries which are building their higher education systems, as well as by established ones that wish to redesign their own and look for "good reasons" (Boudon, 1993) to oppose conservative views. By reinforcing the good reasons for national policies, rankings fueled some organizational isomorphism (DiMaggio & Powell, 1983) at the world level, not without allowing for much differentiation between and within countries bearing different organizational heritage (Hüther & Krücken, 2016; Paradeise & Thoenig, 2015; Paradeise et al., 2009; Texeira, 2016). Rankings such as ARWU instantly gained influence among national systems and with individual universities. Both were facing rising competition for financial resources and talents, and were increasingly sensitive to signals of economic returns on educational investments. Unlike the USNWR college ranking, ARWU is of little interest for students, apart from a very small (but growing) fringe with a high potential for mobility. The ranking does not take into consideration all aspects of an institution. It does not consider work conditions or the environment at large. It does not say anything about education. It is totally research-focused. Purposely, it does not involve opinion surveys as UNSWR, THE, or QS do. It confines itself to factual information, even if restricting its number of indicators. It was not built to facilitate students' choices, but to orient a national policy, and it has ended up playing a major role in many national policies. It has become inescapable for national and local decision-makers who aim to capture prestige and resources by improving their rank. Within barely 12 years, it has become an obvious and non-debated part of our mental landscape. While common knowledge of reputation is bound to a territory, a discipline, or a social group, ARWU provides scores that formally pretends to differentiate the better from the worse.

Today, policy-makers consider global rankings as flagships of a quantitative, evidence-based toolbox required to govern a "well-driven" economy. Not all rankings are as internally well-controlled and replicable as ARWU. Nevertheless, all legitimize the belief that the relative "excellence" of universities, with the "world class" ones at the top, can be unambiguously expressed by ranks on such scales. Rankings are thus supposed to subsume any other form of valuation and provide indisputable bases for judgment and decision-making by assimilating "value" to "value for money." By retroaction, service provision is equated with the provision of a commodity, and valuated by quasi-prices on quasi-markets (Paradeise & Thoenig, 2013). Due to their simplicity and self-sustaining character, they are particularly attractive to policy-makers, especially when they possess the joint property of providing a rationale for decision-making and tracing lines for its implementation.

FROM CHANGES IN THE POLICY FIELD OF HIGHER EDUCATION TO THE EMERGENCE OF A NEW ORGANIZATIONAL FIELD OF RANKINGS[1]

Developing Productive Organizations

Rankings and metrics are not suspended in mid-air. As far as rankings are concerned, three global leagues dominate the field in terms of global media impact: the Chinese Shanghai Academic Ranking of World Universities, the British Times Higher Education Ranking, and the QS World University Ranking. Three others come next: the Dutch Leiden Ranking (which became global after having been European), the Spanish Scimago

Ranking of World Universities, and the Taiwanese Performance Ranking of Scientific Papers for World Universities.

This limited group suggests that operators are quite different in terms of nationality, legal status, business models, and purposes. Two broad categories of actors structure the field: businesses on one side and academic research centers (and their possible spin-offs) and public agencies on the other. The Chinese ARWU, Dutch Leiden, Spanish Scimago, and *higher education evaluation and accreditation council of Taiwan* (HEEACT) rankings are tightly linked with academic institutions. Three other world leagues are issued by private companies, two in the media business (THE and the recent USNWR) and the other in "intelligence, communications and events organization in international higher education" (QS).

Commercial Rankings

Whether national or international, many rankings originate with a magazine or a communication agency. They are often set up in service of a general magazine readership, addressing students and the public at large. The press has been involved in this business since quite early on. The well-known THE world ranking was first released in 2004 — only one year after ARWU — by *Times Higher Education*, a magazine established in 1971 as the late heir of the *Times Educational Supplement*, itself dating back to 1910. THE, like other business companies, widely advertises its ranking, but remains rather silent about the way it is produced. Opacity is the name of the game. The THE world ranking is just one product among the many offered by its parent company, TES Global, a "global digital education business dedicated to supporting and enabling the world's teachers with a portfolio of tailored services, tools and technology" (TES Global Limited, linkedin.com). TES Global Marketplace also includes specific websites providing recruitment and educational services in various countries.

Communication firms also operate rankings. Such is the case of QSIU, founded by Quacquarelli Symonds (QS) in 2008 as a distinct and autonomous unit to "meet the increasing public interest for comparative data on universities and organizations, and the growing demand for institutions to develop deeper insight into their competitive environment." THE first associated with QS to build a joint world ranking in 2004 but separated in 2009 due to a divergence over methodology. In 2010, it chose to associate with Thomson Reuters, which helped counterbalance biases in global reputational surveys (Vidal & Filliatreau, 2014) by adding well-balanced bibliometric indicators, while QS kept working on its own, extending its reputational exercises and partnering with another big database provider, Scopus, to enrich its scientometrics data.

In a few cases, such as at USNWR, a media organization handles the entire job of building its own rankings. In this case, the company went so far as to give up its paper newsmagazine to focus only on the rankings business. But more often, such organizations release rankings that are pro-duced by or derived from foundations, university research centers, and think tanks. *Die Zeit* issues data collected by a think tank, the *Centrum für Hochschulentwicklung* (CHE), that does not produce a league-table ranking, but rather a multifactorial classification of German, and more recently Austrian, Dutch, and Swiss universities in certain fields of knowledge. In the association with *Die Zeit*, CHE is responsible for con-ception, data collection, and analysis, while the newspaper takes care of editorial conception, web diffusion, publication, sales, and marketing. In the same way, *El Pais* releases the ranking developed by the *Instituto de Análisis Industrial y Financiero* of the *Universidad Complutense* of Madrid. French newspapers also often draw rankings from official publications of the state ministry in charge of higher education.

Public Rankings

Rankings are often operated by some public service or research center of a public or not-for-profit organization, such as the statistical department of a ministry, an assessment agency, a university lab, or a think tank or founda-tion, all of which are usually more or less loosely linked to public decision-making. The well-known ARWU ranking originates at the *Center for World-Class Universities*, which is very close to the Graduate School of Education at the Shanghai Jiao Tong University. The Dutch Leiden rank-ing, which develops a more comprehensive and complex description of the research performance of universities – first European then global – is pro-duced by the *Centre of Science and Technology Studies* (CWTS) research center at the eponymous university. The Taiwanese Performance Ranking of Scientific Papers for World Universities, which was first developed by the Taiwanese Higher Education Evaluation & Accreditation Council, moved to the National Taiwan University to gain more independence. Similarly, the Polish Perspektywy Education Foundation has operated at the national level since 1998. Another institution of importance in Europe, the German *Centrum für Hochschulentwicklung*/Center for Higher Education (CHE), was founded in 1994 by the Bertelsmann Foundation to enhance transparency and "promote reforms to modernize German higher education based on international comparisons." In collaboration with the German Rector Conference (HRK), in 1998 it established a ranking of German higher education institutions that is now considered to be paradigmatic for field-based, multidimensional, interactive ranking utilizing a grouping approach rather than league tables, and that is oriented toward students but has no impact on university funding. CHE performs various follow-ups for the German government. It acts as a think tank for the government and various institutions through its CHE Consult division, which provides consultancy support to universities and other stakeholders on a private basis.

Public ranking operators may also be flanked by spin-offs. Examples of these can be seen at the University of Leiden with the CWTS B.V., or the Spanish Scimago Lab founded by a professor at the CSIC *Instituto de Políticas y Bienes Públicos*. Such spin-offs are suited to consulting opportunities. Part of their know-how is derived from their related research centers, which they reciprocally feed with new methods, data and experience. Their for-profit status provides them with commercial and scientific independence from their mother-institution. Scimago Lab, for instance, works closely with publishers and scientific information suppliers such as Elsevier, universities, and government. It defines itself as strictly client-oriented: "we are a technologically-based company offering innovative solutions to improve the scientific visibility and online reputation (and designing) ... science, technology and innovation analytics solutions ... (to) help our clients to boost their communication and publication channels" (scimagolab.com).

Spin-offs may perform other functions as well. While the Shanghai research center at Jiao Tong University only gets academic funds and does not intend to market itself for any paying services, Shanghai Ranking Consulting was probably built to escape the bureaucratic burden of a university or a state agency. Similarly, NTUR moved its affiliation from the Taiwanese accreditation agency to the National Taiwan University.

Bibliometric Data Providers
Rankings are based on processing primary data that most of the rankers do not compile themselves, except when they use their own surveys. They collect their data from administrative files or they buy access to one of two rather expensive big databases, Scopus and the Web of Science produced by a duopoly Elsevier and Thomson Reuters. Elsevier is a wealthy, global academic publishing company. Thomson Reuters is a powerful provider of professional information and news.

These companies leverage information they already have to set up global databases. Elsevier established Scopus as a by-product of its core business as an academic publisher. This process was made all the easier by rising concentration in the publishing industry, which has allowed Elsevier to considerably enlarge its coverage to nearly 22,000 titles from over 5,000 publishers in 2014. Enriching such databases becomes a motive for even more concentration in the publishing business, as suggested in 2015 by recent acquisitions made by Springer or Elsevier.

With its news agencies, its newspapers, its broadcast media and a limited and late involvement in publishing, Thomson Reuters has long specialized in information processing and delivery of highly specialized information created by others, providing services such as customizable, high volume and real time data mining solutions. In 1992, it bought the Institute for Scientific Information (ISI), a small company dedicated to scientific information that built the ISI Web of Knowledge. Basing itself on the classical Zipf's law (1949), the company subscribes to a "core set" of journals that represent the scientific activity in each field of research (Garfield, 1990, 1996) and builds its own database, including in 2014 12,000 journals, 50,000 scholarly books, and 160,000 conference proceedings in all academic fields.

Both companies are now extending their supply of indicators by exploiting more and more deeply the primary data that each has accumulated to become a "one stop shop for scientific information." Thomson Reuters has started to develop various services such as integrated scientific profiles based on bibliometrics as well as new products like *InCites* to be sold to client universities. Elsevier does the same with Scopus, notably with its sophisticated and expanding *SciVal* services for evaluation.

Open-Source Players
Diversification of rankers also occurs with the rising sophistication of tools and the availability of all sorts of databases. More and more often, new producers release rankings, which include various indicators beyond the standard research and educational excellence. The list of unexplored types of excellence is endless. From the *Washington Monthly* ranking of US universities, which combines access with more traditional research indicators, to *GreenMetric WUR*, developed by an Indonesian academic team to emphasize campus sustainability and environmentally friendly university management, they generally rely on a few specific indicators. The number and variety of promoters, and the diversity of themes and methodologies of such rankings, is rapidly growing. Promoters range from MeltyCampus, which selects the top three universities according to safest sex rates in the United States, to the Free Speech University Ranking (FSUR), which is

sponsored by various reformist movements and ranks British universities according to democratic freedom and liberty of speech practices.

The open-source movement has also reached database production, a good example being 4ICU (4icu.org), an open-source network of academic engineers who built a search engine that can identify the names of organizations. They maintain a directory of "all" world higher education institutions, which works like an open directory to which anyone can contribute by updating it to include any missing institution and providing information on how to check its existence. It thus is permanently updated and enriched based on open cooperation. The list is available to anyone who wishes to use it. The availability of web portals working as sophisticated directories will probably increase in the future, opening the way to new types of data processing and new and sophisticated services. The University of Texas system launched such a tool in 2015. Named *Influent* (influent.utsystem.edu) and jointly developed with Elsevier, it is based on exploitation of the Scopus database and allows private sector and government agencies to easily identify the "expertise profile" of 15,000 UT System researchers in science, medicine, engineering, energy, transportation and business, according to their publications in Scopus.

Fabricating Rankings

Assembling Competencies

The fabrication of rankings requires the combination of various competencies in engineering, informatics, social studies of science and communication. It mixes several job qualifications. On the one hand, low-skill employees are required to select and standardize data according to specific rules. On the other hand, highly specialized skills are needed, such as defining meaningful and feasible indicators, developing and implementing informatics applications, data mining, and organizing and processing the rapidly increasing amount of available and exploitable data. The development of rankings brings together people from different backgrounds who previously worked in administration, consulting firms, and research centers. The rankings community hybridizes existing specialists of various kinds into a new configuration. In this new configuration, practitioners, social scientists and computer scientists select, build, feed and make sense of indicators. Specialists in communications frame the products in a way that is able to meet the expectations of media and enroll stakeholders. The emerging professional community recruits applied scientists who are familiar with providing numbers-based scientific evidence – computer and information scientists, physicists of complex systems, experimental physicists, econometricians, etc. Rankings provide them with a unique opportunity to value their competencies in the manipulation of data and the creation of algorithms for calculation. Rankers also hire applied social scientists who contribute by documenting higher education players' strategies and policies. Most are specialized in media and know how to format information for various stakeholders. Building, operating and improving rankings usually involves small teams of around 10 full-time employees (and possibly several advanced students in university research centers), including experts in bibliometrics, database development, software development, information visualization, specialists in new methodologies and sources, specialists in the use of indicators in assessment and marketing, as well as collaborators who proceed according to routinized procedures to look for data, clean them up, harmonize names of institutions, and implement them according to standards developed in-house.

Selecting Institutions and Indicators
Rankings are computed based on a set of indicators applied to a set of higher education institutions. Two operations are thus required: categorizing and selecting eligible institutions, and selecting and informing indicators. For rankings that are organized as league tables, a third operation is needed: weighting the indicators and combining them to create a single rank number.

Selecting eligible institutions might be difficult due to their number (the International University Association identifies about 15,000 of them in the world) and the high variability of national higher education systems, including comprehensive and specialized universities, schools, and colleges, etc. In fact, rankers who do not rely on bibliometrics must base their selection on ready-made lists, the largest one (4icu) providing a list of 11,000 institutions. Others use a time-consuming and costly method that requires concentrating only on a limited number of universities, thereby giving a premium to research-productive institutions. They use Web of Science (WoS) or Scopus, the two major multidisciplinary databases, to sort out the most productive publishers, harmonize denominations, crosscheck with other available lists so that no one is missing, and then select the "most productive" institutions (the top 500, for instance).

Selecting the indicators is a second key methodological task. The cost and feasibility of collecting data encourages the use of bibliometric data as a main source. Patent data may also be used (e.g., PATSTAT, a huge database that compiles patents of most patent offices), as well as costly reputational surveys conducted among academics, universities and employers, and surveys on the return of educational investment as measured by alumni salaries.

Each type of quantitative indicator has to be considered carefully as it carries with it a potential for specific biases (see for instance Geisler, 2000), such as insisting on research rather than on other university missions, overweighting the role of the disciplinary fields best-represented in the journals of the database, subordinating evaluation to ill-informed subjectivities, and confusing the impact of institutional reputation on career with education value-added in terms of content.

Pre-packaged, ready-to-use data usually do not exist. For instance, national statistics require international harmonization, possibly facilitated by the availability of supranational resources such as those provided by the OECD, UNESCO, or the Bologna process for Europe at large. More generally, rough data have to be processed. For instance, it may be necessary to credit publications to the multiple institutions mentioned by a single author or by co-authors of the same paper, taking note of the rules of authorship specific to each academic community, or making decisions about the final selection of indicators and their respective weights.

Each data set requires a homogenization process at the world/global level. Data other than the bibliometric type are prone to difficulties in complying with this requirement. For instance, ARWU uses only factual indicators, based on reference data originated by third parties and that can be checked by anybody for their quality. It is one of the reasons why it has such significant influence. But it uses only six indicators, because such worldwide data are scarce. Therefore it generates only a very limited number of useful indicators, which hardly meet the rising demand for comparing global universities from various perspectives. This is still a problem, even though the multiplication of data required by the rise of managerialism and the accumulation of data linked to the very exercise of building rankings increases the quantity of available data.

Building indicators also involves a time-consuming and costly job of understanding how supposedly identical data have been produced in different countries, to understand their local meaning, and to aggregate them in a global database. This often requires either a partnership or local recruitment. The obstacle may be financial. How much money does it cost and is it worth spending that much? It may also be a matter of difficulty in access to supranational, national or local bureaucracies. Are data available online or are they classified as state secrets? How difficult is it to climb up the chain of authorizations, and is it possible to gain the support of local or national bureaucrats to get access to such data? At the end of the day, rankers do their best with the data that are available, and cope with their limitations rather than dream of ideal but unattainable measures.

In opposition to commercial rankings, academic ones do not use survey-based data. The reasoning behind this is that they raise issues of cost, feasibility, and trustworthiness. Cost of administration depends on the size, scope, and method of the survey. And, though internet opinion surveys such as those used by Quacquarelli Symonds or Thomson Reuters are alternatives that reduce costs massively, they inevitably overvalue Harvard and the respondents' universities. It may have made sense to ask the opinions of well-informed American academic leaders earlier in the 20th century, when the first US reputation surveys were conducted, but it has now become sheer nonsense to expect any single academic to have the synoptic vision to rank universities comprehensively at the world level.

The feasibility of getting good data from surveys depends on universities' ability to collect them and make them available to others. Simultaneously, universities are increasingly under pressure to complete compulsory surveys by national, regional, and international authorities due to accountability requirements. This has led Germany, for instance, to try building single frameworks able once and for all to answer all bureaucratic questions (Hinze, 2014) or the United Kingdom to provide open-source high-level data and statistics in a shared repository. Feasibility is also tied to universities' willingness to provide data, and many are feeling increasingly threatened by rankings.

Developing Technologies
Rankings are built by productive organizations that play the role of "centers of calculation." They act as nodes that commensurate by standardizing heterogeneous sources of information, which they unify into a common language (Desrosières, 2014, p. 49). Each organization develops specific competencies that vary with the audiences it targets, the type of indicators it selects, and the methodology it uses.

Yet even customizable rankings developed by media and accessible on a smartphone use ready-made tools. They remain rather poor and opaque in methodological terms, so it is difficult for scientists to check their transparency and reproducibility. Only academic rankings can really claim to be innovative. Many examples are available. Scimago, for instance, targets institutional policy-makers and research managers with a new line of bibliometrics based on a recursive and sophisticated algorithm, counting not only how many citations a publication gets, but also the weight of these citations based on the visibility of the publication in which they originate (Falagas, Kouranos, Arencibia-Jorge, & Karageorgopoulos, 2008). Interestingly, Scimago warns that people who do not belong to these institutions may use such ranking exercises out of context.

In sum, fabricating rankings is very costly. Much money is needed to get access to databases or to build surveys when data are missing. Recruiting, developing, and managing experts who are able to decide which indicators to select, gather, check, process, and harmonize data is time-consuming and costly. Expenditures and time are also needed to enroll data owners or gatekeepers, such as governments, public administrations, or university departments, in order to access existing resources.

Building a Professional Community

Rankings would not be so successful without involving scientifically responsible and reasonable scholars.

Socializing rankers to norms and controls is a real issue. While control over transparency and reproducibility remains low, especially for commercial rankings, five still-fragile mechanisms consolidate the action field of metrics, including rankings. These arrangements link data, technical skills and persons, and allow for circulation of ideas, norms, and methods. Commercial and academic rankers must be singled out for their specific roles in the field.

First, they incorporate marginal secant individuals (Crozier & Friedberg, 1980) who simultaneously belong to various academic and professional fields. University research centers are led by scholars affiliated with the various fields of engineering (Scimago), higher education (ARWU and CHE), and scientometrics (CWTS), who may also be active as consultants. Such scholars bridge the action systems of university, administration, and business that they are part of as researchers, experts, or consultants. Thus, they play a major role in building up the scientific legitimacy of their organizations, the trust in their ability to conduct business, and the acceptability of the rankings and derived metrics that they present to decision-makers. By publicizing their products − mostly rankings − through media and open-source access, they maintain the interest of large audiences − and policy-makers − for such evidence.

Second, academic ranking research centers enroll distinguished scholars and professionals as strategic counselors or members of a scientific board who (considered to be "experts" by the academic community) advise, legitimate and promote their products.

Third, rankers, and more broadly metrics builders, pay great attention to their scientific respectability. They are plugged into the current growing research on metrics. Journals such as *Scientometrics, Journal of the American Society for Information Science* (JASIS), and *Research Evaluation* have been in place for a long time and publish papers on rankings. New associations have emerged, such as *The European Network of Indicators Designers* (ENID), an open network aimed to "facilitate and promote the cooperation between institutions and individuals actively engaged in designing, constructing, producing as well as using, and interpreting Science and Technology Indicators (S&T Indicators)." As for improvements in accessing data, programs have been created, such as the *Research Infrastructure for Research and Innovation Policy Studies* (RISIS), which links 13 public research and higher education partners from 10 European countries, and aims at consolidating, integrating and building databases, and at developing and coordinating data-processing facilities in open access for European researchers.

Some conferences deal with rankings, such as the Shanghai conference held every second year under the auspices of the ARWU team. Its main purpose is to observe the development of "world-class universities" and the higher education policies at various levels in which WCUs are flagships. Such a conference attracts an increasing number of participants from all over the world, including the United States. Other meetings are organized by the *International Ranking Expert Group*. Events are sponsored by international organizations such as the OECD, UNESCO, the World Bank or the IMF, which present showcases of rankings and their impacts, contribute to the migration of concepts and methods, and also bestow reputation and status throughout what is becoming a community.

For private rankers, it is a must to be visible at these scientific conferences. They also display abundant details on their websites on the ways they gather, build and combine data. But not all of them give enough information to ensure that they are respectful of scientific norms and their results are reproducible, which would directly plug their legitimacy into the scientific sphere. The ARWU team (Docampo, 2013), along with the CWTS and NUTR groups, certainly best exhibits what should be a scientific approach to rankings.

Fourth, the organizational field builds its legitimacy through its attempts to regulate competition between rankings, formalizing common scientific, and ethical norms. International organizations focus on promoting good practices, considering rankings – if comparative – as a potential vehicle for increasing the accountability level of higher education institutions in Eastern and developing countries. Such was the mission endorsed by the *European Centre for Higher Education* of UNESCO (UNESCO-CEPES) and the *Institute for Higher Education Policy* in Washington, DC when they initiated the *International Ranking Expert Group* (IREG) in 2002 as an informal group gathering ranking teams, universities, and other bodies, as well as individual experts from academia and high-level administrative staff in the higher education sphere (Merisotis, 2002). In 2006, IREG published the *Berlin Principles on Ranking of Higher Education Institutions*, which can be considered sort of a manifesto for the emerging community, with the ambition to "set a framework for the elaboration and dissemination of rankings." The Berlin declaration carefully qualifies a list of items, with the ambition to promote a frame shared by all rankers. However, most of them still do not comply with such demanding principles. In particular, since the accessibility of data is severely hampered at the international level, rankers who try to differentiate themselves by using unusual data are prone to accommodate them at the expense of quality.

In 2009 IREG was transformed into a not-for-profit organization, the *IREG Observatory on Academic Ranking and Excellence*. Bringing together around 50 members from all over the world, including a large number of countries from Eastern Europe, from the "Russian influence area" and from the Gulf and Far East countries, its membership is still reminiscent of the UNESCO-CEPES mission. In 2013, the IREG Observatory performed its first audits, referring to the standard set of detailed rules prepared under the guidance of the Berlin Principles, in order to assess the accountability of rankings. Yet, as a guild open to rankers, normative agencies and universities, the Observatory accepts the affiliation of second-tier players who seek to benefit from its legitimacy. For Eastern European countries, membership in IREG appears to help promote policies that improve their own visibility, but is also a way to defend themselves against governmental bureaucracy. More broadly, university managers in charge of international relations today more often refer to the IREG rules and label when deciding which rankings they can trust to evaluate their environment.

Indeed, UNESCO never acted as a third-party guarantor institution, providing labels that could be trusted by all parties (Brunsson & Jacobsson, 2000; Hedmo, K Sahlin, & Wedlin, 2001). Thus while the Berlin principles provide a good basis for evaluation, the mixed institutional composition of IREG has probably kept stakeholders from entrusting unconditional confidence to the organization. Illustrative of this situation is the fact that, up to now, only a few global and regional rankings from QS and from the Poland's Perspektywy foundation have been audited and approved. Nevertheless, things seem to be evolving. After having conferred its two first labels, IREG bestowed a third one in 2014 to the CHE multi-criteria typology. Maybe in order to prevent the suspicion generated by its hybrid membership, some of IREG's members proposed to incorporate economic information into the information requested for audit.

Fifth, in addition to efforts by this international network to push rankers to establish the methodological value of their products, rankers themselves repeatedly try to establish their legitimacy by providing recommendations to users and warning them not to make rankings mean what they are not able to say. Many methodological notices flank each ranking. Commercial rankers try to join this conversation. For instance, QS devotes a blog, *University Ranking Watch*, to the analysis and discussion of university rankings and other topics related to the quality of higher education, which does not yet have a real scientific impact. On the same note, Elsevier publishes an online journal dealing with methodological questions about metrics use, *Research Trends*, which is also not yet considered to be of much scientific interest.

More recently, five leading academic scientometricians in the field, located in the United States, the Netherlands, and Spain, have issued the so-called *Leiden manifesto for research metrics* in *Nature* (2015). It urges research evaluation to respect principles[2] that could be seen as applying to all cases of scientometric assessments, including rankings. Basically, it suggests that users let quantitative evaluation assist indispensable expert qualitative assessments; confer more respect for the mission, research, and disciplines of the specific institution under evaluation; and recognize the systemic impact of assessment and indicators. Nevertheless, much like the Berlin Principles, these statements remain recommendations. In the same way, some Guidelines for Stakeholders of Academic Rankings were proposed at the June 2015 Aalborg IREG forum to inform various audiences on the appropriate use of rankings.

Leveraging Up Audiences

Rankings and many metrics, if not whole databases, are available for free on the web. Anyone possessing a personal laptop, tablet, or a smartphone with an internet connection has access to graphical representations, statistics, lists, and tables. Yet producing these metrics costs money: to buy or build databases, elaborate methodologies, recruit a skilled labor force, and sort out results. What makes it worth it to develop them? This raises at least two questions. First, what demands does the supply of rankings match or generate? Second, what is the economic rationale that sustains such a costly activity?

The Demand Side

It has become common to assert that rankings are here to stay, based on the implicit assumption that they sustainably address and satisfy the interests of various stakeholders of higher education.

First, alleging the major contribution of research to knowledge-based societies, national policy-makers, or supranational actors such as the OECD use metrics to account for research performance. Rankings are newcomers but they are by far the easiest for benchmarking the relative value of universities or countries. They also support policies that encourage the international research trajectory of universities. What is true at the national level is also true at the local level for individual universities. Because they impact public policies as well as donors' behavior, rankings push university presidents to build strategies or tactics to upgrade their performance on indicators that impact their global rank. Cheating the rules – for instance by investing important sums in buying citations, by recruiting prestigious academics just before evaluation, or by manipulating data – has become an extensive and well-documented practice in the "arms race" between universities (Franck & Cook, 1995). As analyzed by Porter (1995), rankings actually benefit challengers more than universities whose reputations are long-established. It allows the former to oppose their objectively assessed excellence to more subjectively established reputations. The latter may arrogantly pretend to be absolved from monitoring rankings ... but they carefully keep an eye on them, because they might feel threatened if reputation came to exceed performance as defined by such metrics (Paradeise & Thoenig, 2015).

Conversely, low or unranked universities may reject rankings as they narrow the definition of excellence to research-based competition, which comes at the expense of other university missions. They highlight their negative impacts: they could deepen the gap between research universities and others, and disqualify academic activities apart from cutting-edge research. Additionally, many academics fear that they provide a justification for organizational rationalization that could jeopardize the benefits of collegiality (Tuchman, 2009).

Because of their impact on students' choices, rankings are often rejected by university decision-makers in the United States. They are disdained by top universities, who view them as inadequate, and are considered detrimental by others. In turn, European and Latin America university presidents point out their elitism and focus on excellence in research. Over 70% of European and Latin American University presidents are concerned about ranking-based policies because they push toward the American model of the research university without considering the need for diversity in higher education. They stress that the concentration of resources increasingly favors a few private institutions. This disadvantages local and public universities, downgrades the major role they play in the democratization of society, and jeopardizes access for all (Courrier International, 2012; Ordorika & Lloyd, 2013). While university presidents complain about the impact of rankings on policy-making, policy-makers themselves are caught between a rock and a hard place. On the one hand, world leagues are helpful as legitimizing tools for their policies, fostering more stratification in their previously homogeneous higher education systems. On the other hand, rankings do not do justice to the quality of their higher education and research. Thus, while keeping their eyes on world rankings, European governments have encouraged building alternative classifications. On the other hand, rankings are supposedly improving the information available to students "about what it is they are purchasing." As shown by Berman and Stivers (2016), this is true to a certain extent in the United States, especially at the graduate level and notably for culturally ill (under)-informed lower-middle and lower class students. Yet, students − especially undergraduates and underprivileged − eventually register at the closest higher education institution to their family home, to minimize costs.

In European countries, where universities largely remain a free public good designed to provide equal opportunities, identifying the very best places in the world to study does not make much sense except for elites who can culturally and economically afford it, or for decision-makers who allocate scholarships to study abroad. Like most social innovation, rankings more rapidly reach upper and upper-middle class students and families, who use them as tools to orient themselves among world elite universities at the graduate level. This is especially true for internationally mobile students and decision-makers from emerging countries, stimulating a fierce competition for rankings between universities and countries looking to recruit well-paying out-of-state (or non-European) students. Despite rankings, this situation has remained largely unchanged, although anyone connected to media can now easily detect hidden hierarchies among world universities. Rankings may induce alternative behaviors, but also increase the relative frustration of students who discover that their degrees are not worth what they had believed.

For the same reasons that European students are not obsessed with rankings in general, students are not of central interest in public rankings. For example, though it is supposed to first serve students' needs, U-Multirank has the same conflict of orientation and appears to drift away from the one it originally intended. While students argue that this multidimensional tool is much too complicated to be useful for their needs, policymakers ask for more discriminating information. This is the path followed by the authors, who decided to distinguish five performance groups of universities instead of the three which they first identified.

Third, the scientific community itself shows interest in rankings, either because they feed a positive image back to a discipline or an individual scholar, or because of the reverse effect. This image evidently depends on the field's coverage in journal databases and on the number of individual publications in the journals that are selected. Individual scientists and their communities' receptivity to rankings and other metrics co-varies with various factors (Weingart, 2015): the weight of research in their university or field, the importance of publishing in international journals in a field, etc. In that way, by delegating judgment to out-of-context experts who do their best with the databases they have (Gingras, 2014), rankings redistribute power inside and across disciplines and among members of this broad category of academics (Withley, Glaeser, & Engwall, 2010).

The Supply Side
Motivation for, costs of, and returns to ranking exercises vary according to whether rankers are public research centers or private media companies.

The very motivation of the small teams of skilled staff inside public research centers is to launch innovative exercises, and rankings oftentimes showcase their competencies or are developed as side products of their main activities. The Shanghai team fully illustrates this latter case. It first developed the ARWU rankings as a tool to be used in China to position Chinese universities in the world competition of major research institutions. Similarly, the CWTS team stresses the purpose of developing rankings as pedagogic tools for the community, and expects to stimulate refinement of other rankings that bibliometric approaches consider too rough and possibly misleading. The motivations of the Scimago team appear similar. The sophisticated tools developed by its engineers and applied to higher education rankings exhibit new ways to compute and visualize classical bibliometric data, and incidentally apply them to universities. Such exercises provide opportunities for researchers to gain respected reputations as applied social and information scientists.

As said above, if assessed at full cost, developing such methodologies is quite expensive. But the costs allocated by such academic teams to specifically develop rankings are marginal. They are funded for the expertise and technical means involved − including bibliometric databases which they can also use for other purposes. Data-providers such as Thomson Reuters, Elsevier, and also public institutions may sponsor various promotional events.

Additionally, public research centers often allow for lucrative consultancy by their spin-offs or through individual researchers acting as experts. These by-products may also contribute to funding.

Activities developed in research centers and their spin-offs are usually so intimately linked that it is not easy to disentangle them. The relationships between CWTS and CWTS B.V. showcase this phenomenon. As a profitable self-sustaining business, CWTS B.V. employs researchers − all affiliated with CWTS − under the authority of a chaired university professor, offering a wide range of tailor-made products and consultancy activities derived from methodologies and data in part provided by the CWTS research network. The spin-off helps secure new recruits, contributing both to the research center and developing new sophisticated tools. As a center assessed on its research performance, CWTS uses classical academic channels such as top journals and presentations at conferences to disseminate research results in the field of scientometrics, remaining very cautious not to get too deeply involved in ranking games, which remain scientifically and politically controversial.

Developing rankings is also costly for private media. They have to hire specialized permanent staff, or at least consultants. Their journalists must learn by doing as they collaborate with various service providers. They also have to buy or create their own data, including costly reputation surveys.

Investing quite significant amounts of money to develop rankings makes sense, as it gives the media ways of signaling themselves as serious experts and owners of data who are able and willing to inform their readers and the citizens about the "true value" of universities, so as to become legitimate actors and powerful players in the higher education system. Ben Sowter, head of the intelligence unit that compiles the QS ranking, recently declared that its rankings have been a huge boost for the company rather than a revenue source.

By gaining attention from public authorities and university staff, media may expect two types of returns. They may anticipate that rankings will strongly contribute to both increasing the visibility of their newspaper's brand and gaining readership for their products at large. Additionally, they may use rankings as a marketing tool to encourage targeted audiences to advertise in their dedicated spaces. Communication agencies may also use them to give visibility to the services they supply. Thus, the national (and now international) *US News and World Report* rankings are very effective at catching the attention of universities, which extensively use the magazine to publicize such and such a program. *QS* uses rankings as a way to promote the students' fairs it organizes as "the leading global provider of specialist higher education and careers information and solutions."

In sum, media companies expect relevant returns from rankings in terms of image, influence, and sales. They feel that displaying a ranking is one of the "core services" they owe to their customers. Along with selling their newspapers, companies become platforms for specialized advertisement by universities, offer specialized products such event organization, and sell by-products of rankings such as profiles, which can expand into a very profitable business. This exemplifies the circular benefits of the ranking business for private companies: the profiling of a well-ranked university provides fresh data that − if the university agrees − can in turn be used by rankers to complement (at no cost) the information provided in its web-diffused ranking. Rankings elaborate numbers that are coherently designed, thus providing coherent quantitative information fit for multi-level uses.

The situation is somewhat different with public research groups. For instance, CWTS did not depend on rankings and was cautious about rankings from the very beginning, including the first ones that they set up for pedagogic purposes. The irony of its story is that it was overwhelmed by their success and so-to-speak was cornered by the market to develop them further.

Competition between Rankings and the Differentiation of Products
Rankers must compete with one another, since they exist only if they attract users. By improving and diversifying their rankings and making them more sophisticated, they use them as marketing showcases of their know-how, in a constant effort to impose their own standards as the best one-stop shop for identifying excellence. Even if they are free, they draw the attention of consumers to the paying services they provide in consultancy, information and communication. In order to catch their audience's attention, each ranking must differentiate on a variety of characteristics, but all must also conform to the same generic principles as stated by

the 2006 Berlin declaration, triggering the endless game of ranking the rankings (The Economist, 2014): their philosophy of action, the audiences they want to inform, the data they use, their computation methods for calculating indicators and the equation used to create ranks, the type of interface they offer to display results, their partnerships, and their funding for dissemination. The six major rankings presented above clearly differentiate as to how they weigh each of these six characteristics. The academic ones clearly emphasize how serious they are in terms of methodology and respect for scientific principles. They stress their independence and eventually take steps to improve it, as ARWU did by creating its spin-off Shanghai Ranking. The *Higher education evaluation and accreditation council of Taiwan* (HEEACT) ranking took a similar step by moving its affiliation from an assessment agency to a university and changing its name to *National Taiwanese University ranking* (NTUR). All academic centers insist that their rankings' validity is contained within certain limits. They restrict their choice of indicators to the most reliable ones. They highlight the quality of their data processing. Shanghai puts much effort into its ongoing and incremental improvement. Leiden underscores the limitations of bibliometric approaches to enhance its own data and methods. Due to its distinctive technological specialization, Scimago relies on friendly interfaces and sophisticated display of the rankings results.

The two major private providers, THE and QS, strongly care for the usability of their interfaces and their partnerships for dissemination purposes. They serve their readership and try to extend it. They are professionals of dissemination, who must balance their efforts between caring about the technical quality of their rankings and making them user-friendly. Such rankings try their best to remain top references for their audience by continuously evolving in terms of technical sophistication, and by including new variables, new customization possibilities, new visualization tools, etc. As for their data, they set up costly surveys to sort out specific reputational data, a potential advantage mitigated by severe methodological limitations, especially when operating at the international level. To expand their resources, they lobby the various actors – universities, governments, supranational organizations such as OECD – who can influence the stabilization of methodological standards. They also apply and lobby for labels, as QS successfully did with IREG for some of its products in 2014.

At the same time, rankers differentiate their products along two lines (Table 2). On the one side, they move from the "unidimensional league table" to multiple specific rankings for classifying or mapping. On the other side, they multiply ranking criteria.

Table 2. Actors, Tools, Norms, and Rankings in the New Action Field of
Metrics.

Rankings and Metrics Producers	
Research groups, think tanks, and spin-offs	
CWCU	Center for World-Class Universities at Shanghai Jiao Tong University, public status, China
Shanghai Ranking	Spin-off of the CWCU, private status, China
CWTS	Center for Science and Technology Studies, public status, the Netherlands
CWTS-BV	University subsidy organization, private status, the Netherlands
CHE	German Center for Higher Education development, public status, Germany
Magazines	
THE	Times Higher Education, England
USNWR	US News and World Report, USA
Others	
Quacquarelli Symonds Ltd.	Leading global provider of information for students and their families, private status, England
Altmetrics producers	
Scimago Lab	Small company funded by scientists of the Consejo Superior de Investigaciones Científicas, private status, Spain
Cybermetrics Lab	Research lab of the Consejo Superior de Investigaciones Científicas, public status, Spain
Data Providers	
Thomson Reuters	Global broker for specialized professional information, private status, Canada
Elsevier	Major scientific publisher, private status, the Netherlands
Norms Makers	
IREG observatory	International network of experts, universities and companies organized in not-for-profit association
Databases	
WoS, Web of Science	Thomson Reuters' bibliographic database
Scopus	Elsevier's bibliographic database
Norms and Guidelines	
Frascati Manual	OECD manual for collection of data on R&D
Berlin principles on ranking of higher education	Guidelines for ranking producers, issued by IREG
The Leiden Manifesto for research metrics	Guidelines for use of indicators in scientific evaluation issued by scholars in the field …
Rankings	
ARWU	Academic Ranking of World Universities, known as "the Shanghai Ranking," China
CWTS	Leiden Ranking
NTUR	National Taiwan University Ranking, by a university team

Table 2. *(Continued)*

Rankings and Metrics Producers	
Webometrics	Ranking based the web visibility of world institutions, by the Cybermetrics lab, Spain
U-Multirank	Multidimensional Ranking of World Universities, European Commission
U-Map	Classification of European Universities, European Commission by public-private consortium
QS Ranking	Quacquarelli Symonds world university rankings, England
THE Global ranking	Times Higher Education World University Ranking, England
USNWR	US News and World Report Rankings, USA

The new generation of international rankings intends to overcome their initial limitations and pitfalls by introducing more sophisticated data and data-organization techniques and strategies. Following and extending the CHE approach and the U-Map classification, U-MultiRank exemplifies the first trend. It is fostered and funded with seed money by the European Commission, as a counter-offensive against the disqualification of European universities by world leagues. The key goal is to continue attracting internationally mobile students. It promotes the diversity of the European supply of higher education as a resource to better serve the diversity of students' needs, instead of underscoring, as world leagues do, its weakness with regard to the very normative model of "university excellence," which focuses on research competition rather than service to students.

As stated by the European Commission, it aims at protecting the "diversity of excellences": it is possible that no institution gets an excellent score on each of the 31 criteria displayed at the disciplinary level, but each can demonstrate excellence in one or several of them. It thus offers "to compare universities … seeing what each is best at." U-MultiRank combines two approaches: on one side, the UMap Carnegie-style approach for classifying universities (McCormick, 2006); on the other side, a disciplinary approach inspired by the German University Ranking tool built by CHE at the beginning of the 2000s to inform student choice of programs. The structuration of available data discourage any effort at globalized ranking. It offers the possibility of customizing comparisons between institutions included in the database on various and multiple aspects of their activities.

These new innovative entrepreneurs, who enter the competition by exploiting opportunities linked to new technological resources, increase its intensity. They bring about new differentiation based on open-source and cooperative tools that track down, normalize, and accumulate information in repositories, directories, or peer networks, based on free cooperation of members of the community. Ranking is not the intended purpose of such tools. Nevertheless, as they grow, they become increasingly relevant sources for building innumerable indicators and benchmarks for individuals and institutions, and eventually they could surpass traditional rankings.

As rankings diversify, the network of academics inspiring the new *Altmetrics movement* (Priem, Taraborelli, Groth, & Neylon, 2010) foster "new metrics based on the Social Web for analyzing and informing scholarship." Based on open-source data, scripts, and algorithms, the movement aims at tracking the actual impact of articles on audiences at large, including those published in not peer-reviewed journals nor cited inside the academy. Other tools of the sort could develop from initiatives such as *Impact Story*, *PLoS*, *ReaderMeter*, *Academia.edu*, *Mendeley*, *VIVO*, *PNoSPL*, *Article Level Metrics*, or the *Social Sciences Research Network* repository.

Only two of these tools, Webometrics and Scimago (partially), have designed stable rankings based on altmetrics indicators. Webometrics is the largest academic ranking about the web performance of institutions. It includes universities from all over the world, and is based on their web presence and impact, measured by the academics of the *Cybermetrics Lab* at the Spanish CSIC.

In conclusion, the rising competition substitutes the original unidimensional rankings with more and more sophisticated tools aimed at better capturing complexity and fairly accounting for the true value of the multiple activities of specific institutions, disciplines and individuals located in a specific context. Such an ambition requires that multidimensional and customizable rankings or classifications as well as sophisticated measures of impact get built. Such new data nevertheless run the risk of losing in visibility what they gain in adequacy. The dream of recreating the complexity of the real world using numbers and rankings is a major dilemma faced by whomever undertakes the immense project of classifying the objects of the real world.

CONCLUSION

Over the last decade, many players have entered the academic and commercial business of ranking higher education institutions. They are clearly segmented by their status, public or private, and their primary targets:

policy-makers and university staff for the former, and students and economic stakeholders for the latter. New open-source inspired producers have entered the game. The accumulation of data, the sophistication of methods, and the search for new applications, users and clients increasingly blur the lines between rankings and metrics at large, and the production of both is becoming increasingly interlinked. Even if they are run by different business models, definitions of excellence, and main targets, all rankers compete with each other to attract the attention of users. Since they are essentially available for free, they do not delineate a market. Rather, they relate to various commodity and reputation markets that they promote. Some external parties, such as international organizations, and internal parties, such as influential scholars, try to impose shared soft law principles. Because no external guarantee outside the weak IREG label has yet imposed itself to regulate the domain, these principles remain recommendations. The ranking industry is nevertheless in the process of institutionalizing itself as an emergent action field.

This paper provides a better understanding of the backstage of the cognitive turn involved in the development of rankings and associated metrics. It describes the traits of this emergent action field that link various players to users or clients, using the language of numbers. It recalls the spectacular installation and success of world rankings. It describes how organizations produce them, the division of labor between them, the competencies they gather and format, the process of fabricating rankings, their expansion and their diversity, the blurring of frontiers between all sorts of metrics, and the growth of the audiences of rankings as free showcases for other paying services.

A new regime of truth, based on numbers, has imposed itself in the field of higher education. Global rankings are a flagship of this new regime, fueled both by the request for "more transparency for the citizen" and the requirements of "more value for money" that are addressed to the various actors of the higher education field who are both pushing up and solidifying the new landscape. They are a symptom as well as a vector of the expansion of this regime.

This paper describes the endless cycles of supply-and-demand for numbers taking place that push forward this soft technology. Trust in numbers means that numbers can only be challenged by "better" numbers (based on more diverse data, created by more complex calculations, classifying before ranking, make groups rather than ranks, being more inclusive, etc.) or "new" numbers (measuring other values, performances, behaviors, etc.). Building better or new numbers also implies developing productive capacity and social control to discipline the battle over standards occurring between rankers. Indeed, confidence in rankings calls for confidence in rankers.

Rankings are here to stay because they are establishing an action field that crystallizes a shared language of excellence and evidence, appropriated by true believers or strategic actors among national policy-makers, universities leaderships, disciplines, and individual faculty. Rankings provide tools that can impact their national system, their own university, their own discipline, and their individual choices. Thus they put individual universities, disciplines and scholars under strong pressure by encouraging them, whatever their context, to conform to those benchmarks of excellence they have contributed to build.

NOTES

1. Unless specified, our knowledge is drawn from two sources: first, participant observation during institutional events such as scientific board sessions, expert group meetings, debates, and conferences and second, websites of the various institutions mentioned.

2. Quantitative evaluation should (1) support qualitative, expert assessment; (2) measure performance against the research missions of the institution, group or researcher; (3) protect excellence in locally relevant research; (4) keep data collection and analytical processes open, transparent, and simple; (5) allow those evaluated to verify data and analysis; (6) account for variation by field in publication and citation practices; (7) base assessment of individual researchers on a qualitative judgement of their portfolio; (8) avoid misplaced concreteness and false precision; (9) recognize the systemic effects of assessment and indicators; (10) scrutinize indicators regularly and update them (Hicks, Wouters, Waltman, de Rijcke, & Rafols, 2015).

REFERENCES

Aghion, P., Dewatripont, M., Hoxby, C. M., Mas-Colell, A., & Sapir, A. (2009). The governance and performance of research universities: Evidence from Europe and the U.S. Working Paper No. 1485. National Bureau of Economic Research, Boston, MA.

Berman, E. P., & Stivers, A. (2016). Student loans as a pressure on U.S. higher education. In E. P. Berman & C. Paradeise (Eds.), *The university under pressure* (Vol. 46). Research in the Sociology of Organizations. Bingley, UK: Emerald Group Publishing Limited.

Boudon, R. (1993). Toward a synthetic theory of rationality. *International Studies in the Philosophy of Science*, 7(1), 5−19.

Bowman, N. A., & Bastedo, M. N. (2009). Getting on the front page: Organizational reputation, status signals, and the impact of US news and world report on student decisions. *Research in Higher Education*, 50(5), 415−436.

Brunsson, N., & Jacobsson, B. (2000). *A world of standards*. Oxford: Oxford University Press.

Cheng, Y., Wang, Q., & Liu, N. C. (Eds.). (2014). *How world class universities affect global higher education. Influences and responses*. Rotterdam: Sense Publishers.

Courrier International. (2012, May). Amérique latine. Haro sur les classements universitaires internationaux/Rectores de Latinoamérica contra los 'rankings'. *Courrier International*. Retrieved from http://www.elespectador.com/noticias/educacion/rectores-de-latino america-contra-los-rankings-articulo-348025

Crozier, M., & Friedberg, E. (1980). *Actors and systems. The politics of collective action*. Chicago, IL: University of Chicago Press. (1st ed. Paris: Seuil, 1977).

Davis, D., & Binder, A. (2016). Selling students: The rise of corporate partnership programs in university career centers. In E. P. Berman & C. Paradeise (Eds.), *The university under pressure* (Vol. 46). Research in the Sociology of Organizations. Bingley, UK: Emerald Group Publishing Limited.

Desrosières, A. (1993). *La politique des grands nombres. Histoire de la raison statistique*. Paris: La Découverte.

Desrosières, A. (2014). *Prouver et gouverner. Une analyse politique des statistiques publiques*. Paris: La Découverte.

DiMaggio, P., & Powell, W. W. (1983). The iron cage revisited: Institutional isomorphism and collective rationality in organizational fields. *American Sociological Review, 48*, 148–149.

Docampo, D. (2013). Reproducibility of the Shanghai academic ranking of world universities results. *Scientometrics, 94*(2), 567–587.

Dodier, N. (2009). *Penser un régime d'évaluation de la recherche scientifique*. Paris: INSERM.

Enders, J., De Boer, H. F., & Westerheijden, D. F. (2015). *Reform of higher education in Europe*. Rotterdam: Sense Publishers.

Espeland, W. N., & Sauder, M. (2007). Rankings and reactivity: How public measures recreate social worlds. *American Journal of Sociology, 113*(1), 1–40.

Espeland, W. N., & Stevens, M. L. (1998). Commensuration as a social process. *Annual Review of Sociology, 24*, 313–343.

Falagas, M. E., Kouranos, V. D., Arencibia-Jorge, R., & Karageorgopoulos., D. E. (2008). Comparison of SCImago journal rank indicator with journal impact factor. *The FASEB Journal, 22*, 2623–2628.

Fligstein, N., & McAdam, D. (2012). *A theory of fields*. Oxford: Oxford University Press.

Foucault, M. (2010). *The government of self and others: Lectures at the Collège de France 1982–1983*. London: Palgrave Macmillan.

Foucault, M. (2011). *The courage of truth: Lectures at the Collège de France 1983–1984*. London: Palgrave Macmillan.

Foucault, M. (2012). *The birth of biopolitics: Lectures at the Collège de France 1978–1979*. London: Palgrave Macmillan.

Franck, R. H., & Cook, P. J. (1995). *The winner-take-all society. Why a few at the top get so much more than the rest of us*. New York, NY: The Free Press.

Garfield, E. (1990). How ISI selects journals for coverage: Quantitative and qualitative considerations. *Current Contents*, May 28.

Garfield, E. (1996). The significant scientific literature appears in a small core of journals. *The Scientist*, September 2.

Garfield, E. (1998). From citation indexes to infometrics: Is the tail now wagging the dog? *Libri, 48*, 67–80.

Geisler, E. (2000). *The metrics of science and technology*. Westport, CT: Qurum Books.

Gingras, Y. (2014). *Les dérives de l'évaluation de la recherche. Du bon usage de la bibliométrie.* Paris: Raisons d'agir Éditions.

Godin, B. (2006). The knowledge-based economy: Conceptual framework or buzzword? *The Journal of Technology Transfer, 31*(1), 17–30.

Graham, H. D., & Diamond, N. (1997). *The rise of American research universities: Elites and challengers in the postwar era.* Baltimore, MD: Johns Hopkins University Press.

Hazelkorn, E. (2007). The impact of league tables and ranking systems on higher education decision-making. *Higher Education Management and Policy, 19*(2), 87–110.

Hazelkorn, E. (2009). *Impact of global rankings on higher education research and the production of knowledge.* Forum on Higher Education, Research and Knowledge, UNESCO Occasional Paper No. 15.

Hazelkorn, E. (2015). *Rankings and the reshaping of higher education the battle for world-class excellence* (2nd ed.). London: Palgrave Macmillan.

Hazelkorn, E., Loukkola, T., & T. Zhang. (2014). *Rankings in institutional strategies and processes: Impact or illusion?* EUA reports. Retrieved from http://www.eua.be/Libraries/Publications_homepage_list/EUA_RISP_Publication.sflb.ashx

Hedmo, T., Sahlin, K., & Wedlin, L. (2001). *The emergence of a European regulatory field of management education: Standardizing through accreditation, ranking and guidelines.* Stockholm Center for Organizational Research.

Hicks, D., Wouters, P., Waltman, L., de Rijcke, S., & Rafols, I. (2015). The Leiden manifesto for research metrics. *Nature, 520*, 429–431.

Hinze, S. (2014). *Standardisation of research information − A basic requirement for measuring and assessing research performance: The German perspective.* CRUS, Bern, June 5.

Hüther, O., & Krücken, G. (2016). Nested organizational fields: Isomorphism and differentiation among European universities. In E. P. Berman & C. Paradeise (Eds.), *The university under pressure* (Vol. 46). Research in the Sociology of Organizations. Bingley, UK: Emerald Group Publishing Limited.

IREG Guidelines for Stakeholders of Academic Rankings. (2015). Draft version. Retrieved from http://ireg-observatory.org/en/forum-aalborg-invitation

Krücken, G., & Meier, F. (2006). Turning the university into an organizational actor. In G. S. Drori, J. W. Meyer, & H. Hwang (Eds.), *Globalization and organization: World society and organizational change* (pp. 241–257). Oxford: Oxford University Press.

Lane, J., Largent, M., & Rosen, R. (2014). Science metrics and science policy. In B. Cronin & C. Sugimoto (Eds.), *Next generation metrics: Harnessing multidimensional indicators of scholarly performance.* Cambridge, MA: MIT Press.

Lisbon Agenda. (2000). Lisbon European Council. Presidency. Conclusion. European Union Parliament Website. March 23–24. Retrieved from www.europarl.europa.eu/summits/lis1_fr.htm. Accessed on September 2015.

Marginson, S. (2001). Strategizing and ordering the global. In R. King, S. Marginson, & R. Naidoo (Eds.), *Handbook on globalization and higher education.* Cheltenham: Elgar Publishing.

McCormick, A. (2006). The Carnegie classification of institutions of higher education the Carnegie foundation for the advancement of teaching. OECD Workshop on Institutional Diversity, December 4.

Merisotis, J. P. (2002). Summary report of the invitational roundtable on statistical indicators for the quality assessment of higher/tertiary education institutions: Ranking and league table methodologies. Higher Education in Europe, XXVII(27), 475–480. UNESCO-CEPES.

Miller, P. (2001). Governing by numbers: Why calculative practices matter. *Social Research*, 68(2), 379–396.

Miller, P., & O'Leary, T. (1987). Accounting and the construction of the governable person. *Accounting, Organizations and Society*, 12(3), 235–265.

Miller, P., & O'Leary, T. (1994). Governing the calculable person. In A. G. Hopwood & P. Miller (Eds.), *Accounting as social and institutional practice* (pp. 98–115). Cambridge: Cambridge University Press.

Myers, L., & Robe, S. (2009). *College rankings. History, criticism and reforms*. Report for the Center for College Affordability and Productivity. Retrieved from http://eric.ed.gov/?id=ED536277. Accessed on September 2015.

Ordorika, I., & Lloyd, M. (2013). A decade of international university rankings: A critical perspective from Latin America. In P. T. M. Marope, P. J. Wells, & E. Hazelkorn (Eds.), *Rankings and accountability in higher education*. Paris: UNESCO Publishing.

Paradeise, C. (2012). How much is enough? World annual conference of the Agence française de développement, translated in English as How much is enough? Does indicators-based management guarantee effectiveness? In evaluation and its discontents: Do we learn from experience, in development? Proceedings of the 9th AFD-EUDN Conference, pp. 63–91, published in *Revue d'Economie du Développement*, no. 4, December, pp. 67–94.

Paradeise, C., Reale, E., Bleiklie, I., & Ferlie, E. (Eds.). (2009). *University governance: Western European comparative perspectives*. Dordrecht: Springer.

Paradeise, C., & Thoenig, J. C. (2013). Academic institutions in search of quality: Local orders and global standards. *Organization studies*, 34(2), 189–218.

Paradeise, C., & Thoenig, J.-C. (2015). *In search of academic quality*. London: Palgrave Macmillan.

Porter, T. M. (1995). *Trust in numbers. The pursuit of objectivity in science and public life*. Princeton, NJ: Princeton University Press.

Presidents' Letter. (2007). The education conservancy, May 10.

Pusser, B., & Marginson, S. (2013). University rankings in critical perspective. *The Journal of Higher Education*, 84(4), 544–568.

Priem, J., Taraborelli, D., Groth, P., & Neylon, C. (2010). *Altmetrics: A manifesto. (v.1.0)*, October 26. Retrieved from http://altmetrics.org/manifesto-.

Rauhvargers, A. (2013). Global university rankings and their impact – Report II. EUA.

Reale, E., Inzelt, A. M., Lepori, B., & Van den Besselaar, P. (2012). The social construction of indicators for evaluation: Internationalization of funding agencies. *Research Evaluation*, 21(4), 245–256.

Reimsbach-Kounatze, C. (2015). *The proliferation of "Big Data" and implications for official statistics and statistical agencies: A preliminary analysis*. OECD Digital Economy Papers No. 245. OECD Publishing. Retrieved from http://dx.doi.org/10.1787/5js7t9wqzvg8-en

Rose, N. (1991). Governing by numbers: Figuring out democracy. *Accounting, Organizations and Society*, 16(7), 673–692.

Rose, N., & Miller, P. (1992). Political power beyond the state: Problematics of government. *British Journal of Sociology*, 43(2), 173–205.

Slaughter, S., & Rhoades, G. (2004). *Academic capitalism and the new economy: Markets, state, and higher education*. Baltimore: Johns Hopkins University Press.

Teixeira, P. N. (2016). Two continents divided by the same trends? Reflections about marketization, competition and inequality in European higher education. In E. P. Berman & C. Paradeise (Eds.), *The university under pressure* (Vol. 46). Research in the Sociology of Organizations. Bingley, UK: Emerald Group Publishing Limited.

The Economist. (2005). The brains business. A survey of higher education. *The Economist*. Retrieved from http://www.utsystem.edu/ipa/planning/Economist-TheBrainsBusiness-091005.pdf. Accessed on September 10, 2005.

The Economist. (2014). Ranking the rankings. *The Economist*, November 8.

Tuchman, G. (2009). *Wannabe U: Inside the corporate university*. Chicago, IL: University of Chicago Press.

Tutterow, C., & Evans, J. (2016). Reconciling the small effect of rankings on university performance with the transformational cost of conformity. In E. P. Berman & C. Paradeise (Eds.), *The university under pressure* (Vol. 46). Research in the Sociology of Organizations. Bingley, UK: Emerald Group Publishing Limited.

Vidal, P., & Filliatreau, G. (2014). Graphical comparison of world university rankings. *Higher Education Evaluation and Development*, *8*, 1–14.

Washington Monthly. (2014). *Introduction to the 2014 September/October issue: A different kind of college ranking*. Retrieved from http://www.washingtonmonthly.com/magazine/septemberoctober_2014/features/introduction_a_different_kind_1051749.php?page=all

Weingart, P. (2015). Nostalgia for the world without numbers. *Soziale Welt*, 66. Jg., Heft 3, Themenheft (special issue) Der Impact des impact Factors.

Withley, R., Glaeser, J., & Engwall, L. (Eds.). (2010). *Reconfiguring knowledge production: Changing authority relationships in the sciences and their consequences for intellectual innovation*. Oxford: Oxford University Press.

Wouters, P. (1999). *The citation culture*. PhD thesis, FNWI. Retrieved from http://hdl.handle.net/11245/1.163066

Zipf, G. K. (1949). *Human behavior and the principle of least effort*. Boston, MA: Addison-Wesley.

STUDENT LOANS AS A PRESSURE ON U.S. HIGHER EDUCATION

Elizabeth Popp Berman and Abby Stivers

ABSTRACT

The United States has been at the forefront of a global shift away from direct state funding of higher education and toward student loans, and student debt has become an issue of growing social concern. Why did student loans expand so much in the United States in the 1990s and 2000s? And how does organization theory suggest their expansion, and the growth of federal student aid more generally, might affect higher education as a field? In the 1960s and 1970s, policy actors worked to solve what was then a central problem around student loans: banks' disinterest in lending to students. They did this so well that by 1990, a new field of financial aid policy emerged, in which all major actors had an interest in expanding loans. This, along with a favorable environment outside the field, set the stage for two decades of rapid growth. Organization theory suggests two likely consequences of this expansion of federal student loans and financial aid more generally. First, while (public) colleges have become less dependent on state governments and more dependent on tuition, the expansion of aid means colleges are simultaneously becoming more dependent on the federal government, which should make them more susceptible to federal demands for

The University under Pressure
Research in the Sociology of Organizations, Volume 46, 129–160
Copyright © 2016 by Emerald Group Publishing Limited
All rights of reproduction in any form reserved
ISSN: 0733-558X/doi:10.1108/S0733-558X20160000046005

*accountability. Second, the expansion of federal student aid should
encourage the spread of forms and practices grounded in a logic focused
on students' financial value to the organization, such as publicly traded
for-profit colleges and enrollment management practices.*

Keywords: Higher education; student loans; financial aid; resource
dependence; field theory; institutional logics

The last decade has seen a global shift in how higher education is financed.
The cost of providing it is rising, and government budgets are under pressure
from a variety of directions. Increasingly, college is seen as an investment
individuals make to increase their future income, which encourages policy-
makers to ask them to bear a significant portion of the cost. At the same
time, policymakers are also interested in encouraging competition for funding among colleges in the hopes of improving their performance, and one
way to do that is to make them more dependent on student decisions about
where to enroll. These factors have combined to lead, in many nations, to
higher tuitions and more reliance on student loans to finance higher education. England and Australia have moved particularly aggressively in this
direction (Chapman & Ryan, 2002; McGettigan, 2010), but the trend is
global (Chapman, Higgins, & Stiglitz, 2014; Charles, 2012; Johnstone &
Marcucci, 2010; Teixeira, Johnstone, Rosa, & Vossensteijn, 2008).

While these same pressures also affect the United States, here student
loans have expanded for a distinctive set of reasons. The U.S. history with
federal student loans dates back to 1958. But the expansion of federal loans
in the United States has been incremental (Lindblom, 1959), not more-
or-less rationally planned as in some other countries. The size and global
importance of the U.S. system of higher education, as well as the scope of
its outstanding student debt (currently $1.3 trillion; see FinAid, 2015),
make its unique trajectory worth exploring. Why did U.S. student loan
debt grow so much after 1992, more than tripling on a real per-student
basis? And what does organization theory suggest this growing reliance on
federal student aid might mean for U.S. colleges and universities? This
paper provides provisional answers to both questions in the hope that they
will interest not only American observers of higher education, but those
from other countries as well.

To do so, we take a broadly organizational perspective. A large majority of U.S. student loans are made or guaranteed by the federal government, and without federal backing, the student loan system would
collapse. Thus, we begin by considering federal financial aid policy as a
strategic action field (Fligstein & McAdam, 2012) that has made this
expansion possible. Federal aid policy began to emerge as an organized
social space in the 1960s, but was originally small and diffuse. For several
decades, its central problem with respect to student loans was how to get
banks to make them, since policymakers did not want government itself to
provide loans on a large scale. Over time, policymakers solved this
problem by creating financial incentives for banks to lend and a government-sponsored enterprise (Sallie Mae) to provide a secondary market for
student loans.[1]

By about 1990, this strategy had proven so successful that Sallie Mae
had grown large, and banks no longer threatened to walk away from the
student loan business. Instead, banks and especially Sallie Mae had become
major actors in the field of financial aid policy. They shared an interest in
the expansion of federal loans, which higher education organizations did
not oppose. With other factors like financialization and rising college
costs also favoring more lending, the stage was set for rapid growth of
government-backed student loans during the 1990s and 2000s.[2] This
growth only leveled off with post-financial-crisis legislation that ended government guaranteed and subsidized lending by banks and shifted to direct
government lending. In the classic formulation, policy created politics
(Schattschneider, 1963): efforts to solve an initial problem created new
actors, and new interests for existing actors, that set student loan policy on
a decades-long expansionary path.

Although both scholars and the media have paid considerable attention
to the growth of student loans in the United States, they have mostly
focused − reasonably enough − on their effects on students themselves
(Gicheva, 2011; Houle & Berger, 2013; Rothstein & Rouse, 2011; Shao,
2014), rather than on higher education organizations.[3] Organizational
sociology, however, suggests that the rise of student loans and the expansion of federal financial aid are likely to affect colleges and universities as
organizations as well.

In the second part of this paper, we discuss two ways organization theory might predict that the rise of student loans would affect higher education organizations. First, resource dependence arguments (Pfeffer &
Salancik, 1978) suggest that organizations are responsive to the sources of
their main revenue streams. Trends in U.S. higher education finance,

particularly for public institutions, are often described as shifting from reliance on state funding to tuition dollars (e.g., Barr & Turner, 2013), a narrative that aligns well with both the reality of reductions in state appropriations and the (also real, but somewhat misleading due to widespread discounting) increase in the sticker price of college in recent years. From a resource dependence perspective, however, this overlooks the extent to which colleges and universities are simultaneously becoming more dependent on the federal government, as the guarantor and/or provider of student loans and other forms of aid. We would expect, then, that higher education organizations would become increasingly responsive to student preferences (in ways that might have both positive and negative consequences), but also more susceptible to federal demands for accountability in exchange for increased levels of aid.

Second, field theory has suggested that changes in a superordinate field can affect a dependent field by encouraging the spread of organizational forms and practices grounded in a secondary logic. For example, as federal science policy became more focused on trying to use science to drive economic growth, more resources became available for university practices focused on the economic value of science (Berman, 2012a, 2012b). Similarly, as federal aid policy has made more money available to schools that can attract students with financial aid dollars, the environment should favor the growth of forms and practices that can leverage such resource potential. The rapid growth of for-profit colleges, for example, and rationalized practices around enrollment management are both consistent with such a prediction. The paper concludes by suggesting that both the political economy of financial aid and its organizational role in higher education are likely to be high payoff areas for future research.

FEDERAL FINANCIAL AID POLICY AS A STRATEGIC ACTION FIELD AND THE RISE OF STUDENT LOANS

Student loans would, essentially, not exist in the United States had they not been actively developed by the federal government, and changes in federal student aid policy have repeatedly transformed the landscape in which they are made. While we do not mean to suggest that federal policy is the only factor explaining the rapid growth in student loans in recent decades (and we briefly discuss other contributors in this section), it is a central part of the story. Given the limited extent to which it has been written about elsewhere, we make it our focal point. In this section, we draw on primary and secondary sources to present a stylized history of the development of a strategic action field (Fligstein & McAdam, 2012) around federal student aid policy. Efforts to solve a central problem in that field — banks' reluctance to make student loans — created new actors and interests that aligned major groups in the field around support for student loans, and set them on a growth trajectory that continued from about 1992 to 2010, when post-financial-crisis legislation put at least a temporary cap on that growth.

We divide this story into two main parts: one covering the period from 1958, when the first federal student loan program was created, to 1990, when the Federal Credit Reform Act changed the terms of debate around student loans; and a second part, during which loans rapidly expanded, that began in 1990 and ended in 2010 with the passage of the Health Care and Education Reconciliation Act. The first period saw a strategic action field emerge around federal student aid policy. For most of this period, direct government lending to students on a significant scale was not a politically viable option. Instead, the central problem actors within the field were trying to solve was how to get banks to lend to students.

By 1990, this question had largely been answered, in large part through the creation and expansion of Sallie Mae, but also through generous guarantees and subsidies for private lenders. The Federal Credit Reform Act, however, changed accounting standards in a way that opened a political door to direct government lending. The central question of the 1990–2010 period would be whether the old system, dominated by privately made student loans subsidized and guaranteed by the federal government, would continue, or whether a new system of direct loans from the government to students would replace it.

Had this door to direct lending been opened 20 years earlier, the result might have been a rapid shift in that direction and less expansion of student loans. But by the early 1990s, Sallie Mae had become an influential political actor, and banks had come to value their federally subsidized student loan business. When some politicians tried to shift toward a system of direct government lending, these actors resisted in ways that encouraged the general expansion of student loans. With other actors in the field (like higher education organizations) either neutral or supporting such expansion, and broader developments like financialization and rising college costs also favoring it, federal student loan volume tripled on a per-student basis between 1993 and 2010 (Fig. 1).

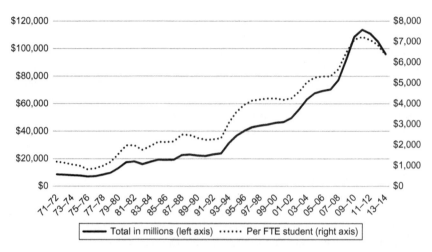

Fig. 1.   Annual Volume Federal Student Loans (Guaranteed + Direct), 1971–2014
            (in 2013 dollars). *Source*: College Board (2014b, Tables 1, 3).

1958–1990: Convincing Banks to Make Student Loans

Federal student lending began in the United States in 1958, with the
National Defense Student Education Act, passed in response to Sputnik.
These loans were made directly by the federal government to needy, academically superior students who planned to teach or had promise in science,
math, engineering, or foreign languages, and reached only about 25,000
students.[4]

By the mid-1960s, though, interest was growing in expanding access to
higher education more generally. As part of this effort, a group of actors
who were beginning to form a strategic action field, including various policymakers, the banking industry, colleges and universities, and state and
nonprofit groups that were then facilitating student loans, hammered out a
larger and broader federal loan program. The Higher Education Act of
1965 established, among other provisions, the Guaranteed Student Loan
(GSL) program, targeted at middle-income students (Cervantes et al.,
2005).

The federal government could have continued to lend money directly to
students in its new program, as it had with National Defense Student
Loans. But accounting rules meant that direct government loans showed
up as an upfront cost that would gradually be recovered in subsequent
years (U.S. Library of Congress, 1991a, pp. 2–3). If the government

instead provided guarantees of repayment to private lenders, the loans would not impact the budget until any guarantees had to be made good (Cuny, 1991, p. 19). Thus, guaranteed loans were politically preferable to direct loans, and larger direct loan programs were not seriously considered until accounting rules were changed in 1990.

It quickly became clear, though, that despite the guarantees and subsidies the GSL program provided, banks were not lending at the rates policymakers hoped for − partly because banks opposed government involvement in lending, and partly because they didn't think student loans would be profitable (Cervantes et al., 2005). Congress repeatedly acted to sweeten the deal, but by the early 1970s lenders were "increasingly reluctant to commit additional funds for GSLs because of their relative lack of liquidity, long repayment schedules and relatively high servicing costs" (U. S. Library of Congress, 1982, p. 1). With direct loans off the table, this problem − how to get banks to lend − would remain central to the field for two decades.

Congress's biggest step in solving this problem was to create the Student Loan Marketing Association, or Sallie Mae. Almost an afterthought to the 1972 reauthorization of the Higher Education Act (Gladieux & Wolanin, 1976, p. 197), Sallie Mae was a government-sponsored enterprise (GSE) − a financial corporation created by, but officially independent of, the U.S. government. Modeled after Fannie Mae, the Federal National Mortgage Association, Sallie Mae would not make student loans itself, but would "provide liquidity to GSL lenders through two secondary market activities: (1) through purchases of GSLs from lenders' portfolios, and (2) through 'warehousing advances' (loans) to lenders, with lenders using GSLs as collateral to obtain funds from Sallie Mae to make additional student loans" (U.S. Library of Congress, 1982, p. 1). By making it easier for banks to lend to students, and providing them a way to sell off loans they did not want to hold, Sallie Mae made student lending more desirable for banks.

Student lending grew after the creation of Sallie Mae, but the rapid expansion of federal grant aid in the 1970s limited demand for loans.[5] This changed after 1978, when Congress removed the income cap from the GSL program. Since the GSL interest rate was set at 7% − with no interest accruing until graduation − and inflation was at double digits, this was better-than-free money. The volume of GSLs issued nearly tripled in the next three years, until an income cap was reinstated in 1981 (Cervantes et al., 2005, pp. 36−38; College Board, 2014b, Table 1).

But despite this growth in the program, as late as 1980, many banks were still reluctant to make student loans despite their high yield rates, due to their large servicing costs and difficult collections (U.S. Congress, 1980, pp. 1–2). And while Sallie Mae was firmly established, it was still a small organization, holding only about $1.2 billion in student loans it had purchased from banks (U.S. Library of Congress, 1982, p. 19). After 1981, growth in the annual volume of new loans being issued became much more moderate, increasing only another 25% over the rest of the decade – and only about half that after accounting for rising enrollments (College Board, 2014b, Tables 1, 3). But two things were changing over the course of the decade that would set the stage for a larger shift after 1990.

First, Sallie Mae became much larger, financially innovative, politically savvy actor which, by the end of the decade, was beginning to play an outsized role in the field of financial aid policy. In the 1970s, the GSE had supported its activities by borrowing from the Federal Financing Bank. But the rapid expansion of lending between 1978 and 1981, along with the encouragement of the Reagan administration, led it to turn to the financial markets for money after 1981, and it began to wind down its government borrowing (U.S. Library of Congress, 1982, pp. 18–19).

Its intense need for capital to support its growth – the organization was nearly doubling in size each year – led Sallie Mae to become very financially innovative: it was the first U.S. corporation to conduct interest rate swaps, among other instruments it pioneered (Forde, 1982; Office of Sallie Mae Oversight, 2006, p. 69, Appendix 3-A). It also began issuing common stock in 1983, and in the second half of the decade became a hot stock on Wall Street (Lawrence, 1989; McCue, 1983, Appendix 3-A; Office of Sallie Mae Oversight, 2006). By 1990, Sallie Mae had more than $40 billion in assets, up from $5 billion in 1981, and held half of all federally insured student loans (Office of Sallie Mae Oversight, 2006, p. 62; U.S. Congress, 1991, p. 247).[6]

Second, while new loans were increasing at a modest pace, the total volume of loans was accumulating, gradually increasing banks' stake in federal student loan programs. Outstanding guaranteed loans increased from $23 billion to $53 billion in current dollars – some 70% in real terms – between 1982 and 1990 (U.S. Department of Treasury, 1991, A-47).[7] Figures prior to 1982 are difficult to find, but given that the annual volume of new federal loans tripled in real terms between 1978 and 1981 (College Board, 2014b, Table 1), it seems likely that outstanding loan volume was under $10 billion in at the beginning of that period – meaning that it, too, roughly tripled in real terms between 1978 and 1990.

As banks' financial stake in student loans increased, their attitude toward the field of financial aid policy evolved as well. As suggested above, the central problem of the field was, until late in this period, how to get banks to lend to students. Historically, "the banks had threatened to walk away from the program whenever lawmakers tried to change it" (Congressional Quarterly, 1992). By the mid-1980s however, the banking industry had the most active lobbyists around the GSL program (Wilson, 1987). When the program was challenged in the early 1990s, they would react aggressively, "indicat[ing] just how important student loans had become to them" (Congressional Quarterly, 1992).

If banks' stake in the policy field was increasing, Sallie Mae's was even greater. For banks, student lending was but one modest slice of their business. For Sallie Mae, it was its raison d'être. It, too, was actively invested in lobbying (Office of Sallie Mae Oversight, 2006, Appendix 3-A), and had a large stake in maintenance and expansion of the GSL program. Banks and Sallie Mae's interests in the field were in many ways opposed, with banks "see[ing] Sallie as a competitor" (Zigas, 1986). But they now shared a commitment to guaranteed student loans.

Higher education organizations themselves were, of course, the other major player in the student aid policy field. In general, colleges preferred direct institutional support to student aid, and within the category of student aid, preferred grants to loans. The most active lobbying on loans came from the for-profit trade schools, which were heavily reliant on federal grants and loans for their survival, and, unsurprisingly, favored their expansion. But despite their preference for other forms of aid, colleges rarely objected to the expansion of student loans, nor did they have a large stake in whether government or banks made them, as long as they were made by someone.

1990–2010: Aligning around Growth

By 1990, then, the major actors in the field of student aid policy had either developed an interest in maintaining and expanding the GSL program (after 1988, renamed Stafford Loans) or did not strongly oppose it. But the volume of student loans was increasing at a relatively moderate pace. The passage of the Federal Credit Reform Act that year disrupted the status quo, however, and helped set student loans on a growth trajectory that, facilitated by the favorable alignment of external factors, would last for two decades.

Prior to 1990, federal accounting standards made direct loans look more costly (at least in the short run) than guaranteed loans. The Federal Credit

Reform Act changed those accounting standards, requiring federal lending programs to be accounted for in terms of their net present value. The cost of direct loans, rather than all showing up in year one then gradually being repaid, were presented from the outset in terms of disbursements minus expected repayments, greatly reducing their short-term budget impact. By contrast, the expected cost of guaranteed loans now showed up immediately on the budget, making them much more comparable to direct loans (U.S. Library of Congress, 1991a, pp. 2–3).

While the student loan program did not motivate the credit reform legislation (Cuny, 1991), the new accounting standards immediately changed the politics of the field. By 1991, legislators were introducing bills that would create a direct student loan program to supplement or replace the guaranteed loans program. Because it would eliminate subsidies to lenders, it was estimated that such a change could save about $1 billion a year (U.S. Library of Congress, 1991a, p. 3). These proposals, immediately divisive, set forth a new organizing question for the field: not how to get banks to lend to students, but whether loans should come directly from the federal government, or from private lenders backed by government guarantees. This question would not be fully resolved until 2010.

In response to these new proposals to end the guaranteed loan system – which for Sallie Mae was an existential threat – "financial-service companies mounted a ferocious lobbying campaign to preserve the current system," with Sallie Mae "[l]eading the charge" (Boot, 1993). They ran advertisements in the *Wall Street Journal*, organized letter-writing campaigns, and won the support of some college representatives who were concerned about how changes would be implemented (Boot, 1993). In general, colleges' role in the debate was limited: they were outspent by the banks and not unified in their support of direct loans (DeLoughry, 1992). Though direct lending proposals were popular (Jaschik, 1993), the lending industry was able to partially, though not entirely, beat them back (Parsons, 1997). Congress created a pilot direct loan program in 1992 (McCormick, 1994), and the following year authorized government to provide an increasing percentage of loans directly, with the intent of reaching 60% or more by 1998 (Congressional Quarterly, 1994).

This intense battle, new in the field of financial aid policy, had at least three consequences that contributed to the acceleration of student loan growth. First, and most immediately, it set up a competition between the direct and guaranteed loan programs. This was intentional, and seen by Congress as a test of which system would work better (Congressional Quarterly, 1994). The battle for student lending between banks, Sallie Mae, and government was expected to be "fierce" (Henry, 1993), as indeed it turned out to be. Over the next five years, lenders moved aggressively to retain the market, channeling their government subsidies into lower costs for students in an effort to undercut the Education Department (Burd, 1999).

As a result, direct lending never reached the expected 60% of loan volume, instead peaking at 34% in 1998 before starting to decline (College Board, 2014b, Table 1). An increase that year in banks' student loan subsidy, the product of "bitter" political fighting (Congressional Quarterly, 1999), put the direct loan program in what one journalist called "a fight for its survival" (Burd, 1999). While many had expected direct loans to displace guaranteed loans entirely by the end of the decade, instead, by 2002, direct loans would account for less than 30% of the total, and by 2004, less than a quarter (College Board, 2014b, Table 1). Thus during the 1990s, the new competition between guaranteed and direct loans forced banks to work to retain and expand their student loan business rather than coasting along, taking it for granted.

Second, it helped achieve the creation of unsubsidized Stafford loans. As of 1992, eligibility for traditional, subsidized Stafford loans was subject to a cap on family income of about $50,000 (in 2015 dollars). While the cap was raised that year, the new unsubsidized Stafford would have no such income limit. Unsubsidized Stafford loans would still be made by private lenders and guaranteed by the federal government, but interest would not be deferred while students were in school (Congressional Quarterly, 1993).[8] These loans to higher-income families would prove to be an area of rapid growth in the student loan system (Fuller, 2014, pp. 56–57). Within five years, unsubsidized Staffords would account for a third of all federal student lending, and for three-quarters of the increase in student loan volume during that time (College Board, 2014b, Table 1).

Third, the fight over direct lending led Sallie Mae to push for its own privatization. Sallie Mae had been interested in privatizing as early as the 1980s, and the idea was floated during the Reagan administration (Hill, 1986; Office of Sallie Mae Oversight, 2006, Appendix 3-A). But direct lending "called into question [Sallie Mae's] existence," and its stock lost more than half its value in from 1993 to 1994 (McLean, 2005). Though banks opposed it, in 1996 Congress began the process of privatizing Sallie Mae, with the GSE's strong support. This move would allow Sallie Mae to originate loans for the first time and give it greater flexibility to aggressively pursue new markets, like private – that is, not government guaranteed or subsidized – student loans (Office of Sallie Mae Oversight, 2006), which would become increasingly important in the following decade.

While the political effects of the new pro-lending alignment in the field of federal aid policy played a considerable role in encouraging the growth of student loans, factors outside the field encouraged the growth of lending as well. The ever-rising cost of college is the most obvious of these, even if some portion of the cost increase was an effect, rather than a cause, of expanding loan availability (see note 2). Nevertheless, college costs increased rapidly in the 1980s, a period that saw only modest growth in student loan volume, so tuition increases cannot be the only factor driving student loan expansion (College Board, 2014a, Table 2). Beyond the pressure of rising tuitions, two other trends also facilitated student loan growth during the 1990s: financialization, and the emergence of a new model of for-profit college.

Many of the developments that encouraged the expansion of mortgage lending during the 1990s and especially 2000s also applied to student loans. The first student loan asset-backed securities (SLABS) were issued in 1993 (New Securities Debut with Student Loans Used for Collateral, 1993), and Sallie Mae, as mentioned earlier a financially sophisticated actor, began securitizing the loans it held in 1995. This move was quite successful, and the GSE largely financed its privatization by securitizing more than $100 billion of student loans over the next decade (Office of Sallie Mae Oversight, 2006, pp. 25, 107).

As a market for SLABS became established, it created a new demand for student debt that increased banks' options for selling off the student loans they made. This helped support the expansion not only of federal student loans, but also, for the first time, a significant number of fully private student loans. As was the case in the mortgage market, the ability to securitize and sell off student loans made banks willing to make riskier loans, even without government guarantees. The private student loan market grew from essentially nothing in 1995 to $21 billion, representing 23% of all student loans, in 2008 (College Board, 2014b, Table 2). SLABS were, in fact, one of the hottest asset categories in the mid-2000s, emerging as a "core asset class" in 2003 (Feldheim, 2004), and growing "five times as fast as the $1.97 trillion asset-backed bond market" in 2005 (Richard, 2006).

Finally, while for-profit colleges had long played a role in the student aid field, and indeed were at the center of a modest student loan default crisis in the late 1980s (Best & Best, 2014), until the 1990s these were typically small trade schools. After a shakeout in the early 1990s, a new model of for-profit college emerged — one that was publicly traded, aimed at working adult students, heavily reliant on online education, and rapidly growing (Mettler, 2014). Enrollment in the sector increased from less than a quarter million in 1995 to over two million in 2010 – a time when enrollment in other colleges grew only by a third (NCES, 2014, Table 303.10). With a large majority of its revenues coming from federal student aid (U.S. Senate, 2012), the rapid growth of this sector also created a new demand for student loans – as well as an interest on the part of the sector in making sure of their continued availability.

Thus by the year 2000, with the existential threat of direct loans pushed back if not eliminated, major actors in the field of financial aid policy remained aligned around the expansion of student loans, and factors outside the field similarly supported their growth. The 2000s saw a rapid increase in student loan volume, even as the fraction coming directly from the federal government steadily decreased. From the time the era of growth began in 1993, to its end in 2010, the annual volume of federal student loans nearly quintupled in real terms; if private loans are included, the rate of increase is even larger. This period transformed the importance of student loans in the U.S. higher education system.

2010 to Present: Eliminating the Middleman

It took an external shock of the size of the 2007–2008 financial crisis to disrupt this steady growth in the field of federal aid policy and to resolve the question of whether loans should be made by banks (and guaranteed by government), or made directly by government. Most critically, the freezing up of credit markets in 2008 led banks to pull out of student lending for the coming year, leading to the real possibility students might simply lose access to loans. In the short run, Congress acted to backstop loans (Congressional Quarterly, 2009). In the slightly longer run, the realization that a guaranteed loan program could fall apart under such circumstances, along with a general shift in public sentiment toward financial institutions, proved to be just the disruption that could limit opposition to direct loans. In 2010, with the financial sector, including Sallie Mae, still crippled, a new law completely eliminated the guaranteed program and replaced it with direct government loans, mostly ending a two-decade debate (Congressional Quarterly, 2011).

Since then, the dynamics of the field have changed considerably. With the question of whether loans should be direct or guaranteed resolved for now, a new question has taken center stage: how much student debt is too much? Actors and their interests have evolved as well. Banks are no longer invested in the student loan program as lenders. The behemoth Sallie Mae is now two smaller players. One (Sallie Mae) provides private loans and other education-related banking products and is less dependent on the federal government. The other (Navient) exemplifies an important new type of actor in the field: it services existing loans, especially through profitable contracts with the U.S. Department of Education. The for-profit higher education industry has received bad publicity, resulting in a decline in enrollments of perhaps 20% (Bidwell, 2015a). Finally, a small but vocal social movement has emerged around opposition to student loans, with the result that anti-loan sentiments have had more voice in the last five years than they did in the previous 20.

These factors and others – including a general enrollment decline after a post-recession peak (NCES, 2014, Table 303.10), the failure of securitization markets to reemerge after the financial crisis, and the related failure of a thriving market in private student loans to reappear (College Board, 2014b, Table 1) – have meant that as of 2014, the annual volume of student loans remains, in real terms, 13% below its 2011 peak. It remains to be seen whether the present leveling of loan volume is a long-term change or a temporary blip, as increased spending at private colleges (College Board, 2014a), decreasing state support for public colleges, and strong pro-loan arguments among economists (e.g., Akers & Chingos, 2014; Avery & Turner, 2012) certainly suggest the possibility for renewed growth. Even if student aid levels remain at present levels, though, their large size, which reflects a historically unusual level of federal involvement in higher education, has the potential to impact colleges and universities as organizations. It is to the possible organizational effects that we next turn.

HOW CHANGES IN THE FIELD OF FEDERAL AID POLICY MIGHT AFFECT THE FIELD OF HIGHER EDUCATION

Both academic and public debate over the rise of student loans in the United States have focused primarily on their impact on students (e.g., in sociology, see Dwyer, Hodson, & McCloud, 2013; Dwyer, McCloud, & Hodson, 2012; Houle, 2013, 2014; Jackson & Reynolds, 2013; Quadlin & Rudel, 2015). Conversations about the pressures on higher education, on the other hand, tend to focus on a different set of issues: for example, budget problems, the role and treatment of contingent faculty, and the potential for "disruption" from the educational technology sector.

Considering U.S. higher education as an organizational field, however, as suggested by Scott and Biag (2016), highlights a different set of issues around the effects of federal student loans. In the rest of this paper, we draw on the insights of organization theory to suggest two consequences we should expect to follow this expansion of federal student loans and federal financial aid more generally.

First, while public institutions have become less dependent on state government and more dependent on tuition, the expansion of aid means colleges are simultaneously becoming more dependent on the federal government, which should make them more susceptible to federal demands. At the moment, increased accountability requirements seem to be the most likely demands to intensify. Second, the expansion of federal student aid should encourage the spread of organizational forms and practices that are consistent with a logic focused on students' financial value to colleges. These would include forms like for-profit colleges, but also practices like enrollment management, which have come to play a much greater role in higher education institutions as rapid student loan growth has taken place. In the sections that follow, we discuss each of these predictions in turn.

The Effects of Changing Resource Dependencies

While the sociological literature on student loans does not offer many insights regarding their likely effects on higher education organizations, the resource dependence literature (Pfeffer & Salancik, 1978) does suggest predictions. Resource dependence theory was built partly upon the study of universities (e.g., Pfeffer & Salancik, 1974; Salancik & Pfeffer, 1974), and its central insights — that organizations respond to satisfy external actors that control resources on which they depend, and that they will work to manage those dependencies in order to maximize their autonomy — have been shown to apply to higher education (Kraatz & Zajac, 2001; Tolbert, 1985; Zajac & Kraatz, 1993). While some evidence suggests that the behavior of higher education organizations may be only loosely coupled to their sources of revenue (Barringer, 2016), resource dependence theory is nevertheless a useful starting point for thinking about how higher education organizations might react to environments in which their revenue sources are rapidly changing.

The conventional wisdom about budgetary trends at U.S. colleges focuses on increasing dependence on tuition — to keep up with rising spending, in the case of private colleges (Desrochers & Hurlburt, 2014); or to counteract state budget cuts, in the case of public ones (Barr & Turner, 2013; Breslauer, 2016). This would suggest colleges might increase their responsiveness to student (and parent) preferences, a reaction with potentially complex organizational consequences. While we will return to this possibility below, the history of student loan policy presented in this paper also suggests a second and less obvious reading of how the resource dependencies of higher education organizations are changing. Even as universities are becoming more dependent on student decisions about where to take their (growing) tuition payments, they are simultaneously increasing their dependence on the federal government, which makes much of that money available in the form of grants and loans.

Both the sticker price (i.e., the published price) and the net price (i.e., what students actually pay) of college tuition have increased dramatically in the United States in recent decades (College Board, 2014a, Table 2). Indeed, net tuition has recently overtaken state appropriations − traditionally the dominant source of funding for public institutions − as a source of revenue for public universities (Desrochers & Hurlburt, 2014, Table 2).[9] But looking at net tuition as a fraction of all revenues, or comparing its volume to that of state appropriations, understates the ongoing government role in providing funds to higher education.

Net tuition figures typically exclude institutional grants to students − that is, discounts provided by the college itself. But they include some forms of federal support. Government grants (like Pell Grants) may or may not be counted as part of net tuition, depending on who is doing the calculating.[10] And student loans, whether direct, guaranteed, or fully private, are generally included in net tuition figures (e.g., College Board, 2014a, p. 8; Delta Cost Project Database, 2015).

The decision to include student loans as part of net tuition makes sense if one is interested in the financial burden of college on students and their families, since it is them who have to repay such loans. Including government grants to students can be justified as well, since students decide where such dollars will go. But such figures hide the extent to which colleges and universities depend on financial aid that, while channeled through students, is ultimately made available by the federal government.

If, instead of comparing state appropriations to net tuition, we compare state appropriations to federal student aid, we see a different picture.[11] The higher education sector cannot solely be characterized by a shift in dependence from public to private funds. It is also characterized by a shift from state to federal − or at least federally enabled − funds (Fig. 2).

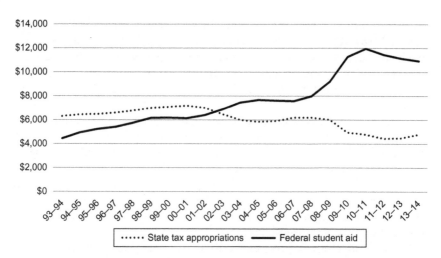

Fig. 2. Annual Federal Student Aid and State Tax Appropriations per FTE Student, 1993–2014 (in 2013 dollars). *Source*: College Board (2014b, Tables 1, 3); Grapevine (various years); U.S. Bureau of Labor Statistics.

We only gesture here toward what a serious analysis of changing dependence on federal student aid would entail. For starters, such an analysis would require breaking down the fractions of aid going to public, private, and for-profit institutions; the latter two types absorb a disproportionately large share of student aid relative to their enrollments (College Board, 2014b, Table 7; Deming, Goldin, & Katz, 2012; NCES, 2014, Table 303.10). Nevertheless, at a minimum these figures suggest that as a whole, the field is becoming more dependent on federal student aid relative to state appropriations, and thus on the field of federal aid policy to ensure its continued availability, even as it also depends more on students' decisions about where to enroll in order to receive those aid dollars. Resource dependence arguments, then, would make two sets of predictions about how colleges should respond to the expansion of federal student aid: one set based on the increasing financial importance of student enrollment decisions, and another based on their growing dependence on federal aid policy.

In the first case, there are clear signs that colleges have already put more focus on attracting students. For example, marketing spending at midsized colleges nearly doubled in real terms between 2001 and 2010 (Lipman Hearne, 2010). Enrollment management, a topic we return to below, came of age as a profession in the 1990s and 2000s and helped rationalize student recruitment and financial aid decisions (Tutterow & Evans, 2016). And while the climbing walls and lazy rivers that receive so much media attention may not reflect the experience of most students, the fraction of spending going to student services did in fact increase across institution type in the 2000s (Desrochers & Hurlburt, 2014, Figure 6).

If the expansion of federal aid does make colleges more responsive to student preferences, the effects are likely to be complex. On the one hand, the position that support for higher education should be tied to students, not institutions, dates at least back to the 1950s, and has been made by economists from a variety of political positions (Archibald & Feldman, 2004; Friedman, 1955; U.S. DHEW, 1969). Colleges will serve students better, the argument goes, if they compete for their attendance rather than following their own organizational imperatives.

Relying on student preferences to encourage good behavior among colleges has problems of its own, though. Despite the proliferation of rankings (Paradeise & Filliatreau, 2016), students have limited information about what they will actually get from a particular college, and transaction costs associated with changing colleges are high (Monaghan & Attewell, 2014, p. 14). Nor are student decisions about whether or how much to borrow for school particularly rational (Avery & Turner, 2012; FDR Group, 2015).

Moreover, what students want only partially aligns with colleges' educational mission. If colleges are interested in attracting students, but students value lifestyle over education, colleges may, for example, create easy majors to appeal to the wealthy but academically disinclined (Armstrong & Hamilton, 2013). Students have, in fact, been shown to respond to amenity spending on activities, sports, and dormitories. Only high-achieving students, by contrast, demonstrate a taste for academic quality (Jacob, McCall, & Stange, 2013). Thus, while resource dependence theory would suggest the expanding importance of student aid should result in greater attention to student preferences, this is not necessarily the same as attention to educational quality.

If federal financial aid is making up a bigger part of colleges' revenue stream, however, colleges are also becoming more dependent on the federal government as the ultimate source of those dollars. Here, we might expect to see increased investment in lobbying, for example. There is some evidence, at least, that this is the case. Such spending more than doubled in real terms between 1998 and 2010, though it has declined about 30% since then (Center for Responsive Politics, 2015).[12]

We also should expect to see colleges become more susceptible to federal demands as they become more dependent on federal support. While research universities have long relied on federal R&D spending for a substantial part of their budget, they have also (consistent with resource dependence theory) worked to buffer their dependence by ensuring that scientists control how such money is distributed (Guston, 2000).

Dependence on financial aid, though, means dependence on a different set of government organizations and decision-makers. Such new dependencies may not yet have affected higher education organizations substantially. But they certainly have the potential to, and colleges might have trouble buffering themselves against new demands. For example, in 2014 gainful employment regulations were put into place that threaten colleges' federal aid access if graduates' loan payments represent too high a percentage of their income (Bidwell, 2015b).

While gainful employment rules will likely affect for-profit colleges almost exclusively, the last few years have also seen the emergence of broader policy conversations about accountability, often in close conjunction with discussions of federal aid, across the whole spectrum of higher education organizations. These have included serious consideration of federal college rankings based on affordability, job outcomes, and loan repayment rates — a proposal ferociously opposed by colleges (Bidwell, 2014). Proposals to implement a unit-records database, which would track individual students through and potentially beyond college, have also received attention, though they are politically controversial (Nelson, 2013; Stratford, 2014). Should such proposals come to pass, they would open the door to much more aggressive federal management of higher education based on student outcomes. While colleges would no doubt resist such a push, their growing dependence on federal aid makes them increasingly vulnerable should policymakers decide such measures are desirable.

Facilitating the Spread of New Forms and Practices

Beyond the resource dependence literature, recent work on strategic action fields (Fligstein & McAdam, 2011, 2012) suggests further predictions about how the expansion of student loans might affect colleges and universities. Fligstein and McAdam's version of field theory points to the importance not only of dynamics within fields, but also of the relationship between them, in understanding how fields like higher education change (see also Hüther & Krücken, 2016).

More generally, institutionalists have argued that changes in fields' external environments can facilitate the spread of new logics within them by selecting for practices consistent with those logics. For example, when U.S. policymakers started trying to promote science in order to achieve economic goals, preexisting university practices that focused on the economic value of science began to spread, largely because new resources became available to support those practices (Berman, 2012b). This is also broadly consistent with organizational ecology arguments that emphasize environmental resources, particularly more evolutionary versions, which would also expect that new organizational forms might emerge and spread (Aldrich & Ruef, 2006; Hannan & Freeman, 1976).

In the present case, decisions made in the field of federal financial aid policy substantially affect the resource environment of higher education organizations. In particular, we might expect that the post-1990 alignment of the field around support for the expansion of student loans would encourage the spread of forms and practices, and associated logics, that were able to help organizations secure the newly available resources implied by greater loan volume.

Specifically, regardless of whether the expansion of student loans *caused* colleges to charge more, they certainly made it *possible* for colleges to charge more; were loans not available, many students simply would not have been able to pay for an education of equivalent cost. Thus, an expansionary loan policy in the federal aid field makes students, and the tuition they bring (including that part of tuition paid for by federal aid), an increasingly important revenue stream for the university. This should encourage the spread of forms and practices that can take advantage of that new revenue stream. In particular, forms and practices based on logics that focus on the financial value of students to higher education organizations should thrive.

Obviously, other factors besides the expansion of loans might also encourage such financial logics. For example, a reduction in state funds might make tuition more important (and thus a financial view of students more prevalent), even in the absence of more federal student aid. But the expansion of federal aid is at least one potential inducement for such a logic to spread. We would suggest that at least two major developments in the field of higher education since 1990 might have been facilitated through such a process. One is the rapid expansion of a new for-profit organizational model. The other is the spread of enrollment management practices.

There has long been a close relationship between for-profit higher education and federal student aid. Proprietary schools were included in federal loan programs from the outset, and 40-year-old critiques of their participation ("A new breed of proprietary school has evolved – schools at which nearly every student, and thus the school itself, is dependent upon government aid") sound remarkably prescient (Kronstadt, 1973, p. 9, cited in Best & Best, 2014, p. 56).

But the proprietary schools of the 1970s and 1980s were generally trade schools, and smaller in size (U.S. Library of Congress, 1991b, p. 2). From the mid-1990s, a new kind of actor came to dominate the sector. The University of Phoenix, founded in 1976, had a different business model, focused not on career training but college degrees for working adults. It grew modestly its first decade, began offering online classes as early as 1989, and in 1994 went public. By 1999, it enrolled 100,000 students (Hanford, 2012b). Other schools – institutions like DeVry Inc. and Strayer College – emulated the same model, and soon became "glamour stocks on NASDAQ, rivaling internet companies" (Hanford, 2012a, p. 13; Winston, 1999).

The old-model proprietary schools had been criticized for their heavy use of federal aid. At the end of the 1980s they were consuming 28% of subsidized, guaranteed loans, despite enrolling a much smaller fraction of students, and about half their students were eventually defaulting (College Board, 2014b, Table 7; NCES, 2014, p. 60; U.S. Library of Congress, 1991b, p. 3).[13] This led to a government crackdown – modest restrictions on the fraction of school income that could come from student loans and default thresholds above which schools might lose eligibility for aid (Best & Best, 2014, p. 58). By 1996, the fraction of Stafford Loans going to for-profit schools was down to a mere 7% (College Board, 2014b, Table 7).

The newly expansionary environment for student loans, however, allowed the new-model for-profits to grow massively from the late 1990s. A greater focus on advertising, marketing, and recruiting; the possibilities for scale offered by the internet; and a substantial influx of capital from Wall Street all led to rapid growth. From 1995 to 2001 enrollment in for-profit institutions doubled; by 2007 it had doubled again, and by its 2010 peak, it was more than eight times 1995 levels, representing growth from 1.7% to 9.6% of all postsecondary enrollments (NCES, 2014, p. 303.10). In tandem with this, the sector had come to absorb 25% of Pell Grants and subsidized loans, as well as 28% of unsubsidized loans – percentages comparable to those of 1989, but on a base nearly five times as large in real terms (College Board, 2014b, Tables 1, 7).[14]

This highly successful new organizational form was based explicitly on a market logic; in 2009, 42% of revenues at a group of publicly traded for-profits went to marketing and advertising or profit, compared to 17% on instruction (U.S. Senate, 2012, p. 6). Yet it was heavily reliant on federal aid for its growth; the same group of organizations received 86% of its revenue from government grants and loans (U.S. Senate, 2012, p. 25). While an expansionary federal aid environment was not the only factor enabling the sector's massive expansion, it was likely a necessary one.

Enrollment management (see also Tutterow & Evans, 2016) provides a second example of how the expansion of federal aid facilitates the growth of practices focused on the financial value of students to the organization. Enrollment management uses data to rationally analyze the behavior of prospective and current students as a means to achieve institutional goals. Like the proprietary school, enrollment management predates the post-1992 expansion in federal student loans. It originated among private universities in the 1970s, at a time when baby boom enrollment growth was ending and admissions officers were looking nervously to the future (Coomes, 2000).

But enrollment management remained small in scale until the 1990s, when "[u]niversities, beset by their own fiscal problems and by intense competition for highly qualified, fee-paying students ... ceased to think of their financial aid efforts principally as a noble charitable operation and ... instead [came] to focus on the financial aid operation as a key strategic weapon in both recruiting students and in maximizing institutional revenues" (McPherson & Schapiro, 1998, p. 1). By the end of the decade, three-quarters of colleges in one large survey had established an enrollment management unit (Ort, 2000). While in the 1990s enrollment management was seen mostly within private institutions, it has since expanded to public colleges and universities as well (Hossler & Kalsbeek, 2013).

Enrollment management is simply a rationalized set of techniques that can in theory be used to achieve a variety of goals, whether those are financial, educational, equity-focused, or status-improving. They do, however, necessarily see students as collections of certain qualities (SAT scores, demographic traits, likelihood of attendance and completion, etc.) tied to a particular quantity of revenue (full-price or discounted rates, in-state or out-of-state tuition, etc.). While enrollment management is not solely focused on revenue maximization, it nevertheless relies on a financial logic. The calculated expansion of out-of-state and international enrollments at public institutions (see, e.g., Breslauer, 2016), for example, reflects enrollment management practices. By expanding such enrollments, the university seeks to balance political pressures and status maintenance with revenue raising, but is fundamentally (and arguably necessarily) focused on the bottom line.

As is the case for for-profit colleges, multiple factors have encouraged the spread of enrollment management practices. But we would expect that an expansionary federal aid environment would encourage their growth and spread. If revenues are only indirectly tied to what students are willing to pay, as was historically the case for public institutions funded primarily through state appropriations, there is less to be gained from careful calculation of how much financial aid will attract a particular type of student. But as the expansion of federal aid increases the amount of money an additional student can bring, such practices gain remunerative potential. Thus, a policy shift originally intended to improve access (as well as to bring profits to financial institutions) might have the unintended effect of expanding the "culture-bearing," "value-subverting" innovation of enrollment management (Kraatz, Ventresca, & Deng, 2010, pp. 1521, 1527) more broadly throughout higher education.

CONCLUSION

This paper has provided partial and provisional answers to the question of why student loans have expanded so much in the United States over the last 25 years, and what effects we might expect such expansion to have on higher education organizations. Multiple factors have contributed to the rise of student loans, and in particular demand-side factors like the rise of tuition costs and the temporary appeal of student loan asset-backed securities are likely to play an important role. We focus, however, on the development of the field of federal aid policy that has made student loans possible in the first place. A strategic action field emerged around student aid policy in the 1960s and 1970s that focused on the problem of how to get banks to lend to students. It solved this problem so successfully, in part by creating the government-sponsored enterprise of Sallie Mae, that by 1990 all major interest groups in the field favored the expansion of student loans, a situation that persisted until 2010. With political interests so well aligned, a series of policy decisions were made that allowed the annual volume of federal student loans to quintuple over that 20-year period.

While scholars have paid increasing attention to the effects of this expansion on students, less notice has been given to its potential effects on higher education organizations. But organization theory points to several expected results of this growth in federal grants and loans. First, as colleges increase their relative dependence on federal aid, they should become more responsive to student preferences, which might have both positive and negative effects from an educational perspective. At the same time, colleges will also be more susceptible to federal demands, although they will likely try to insulate themselves from these to the extent possible. Second, as expanded federal aid (whether in the form of grants or loans) means that each student can potentially bring more dollars to a college, organizational forms and practices that follow a financial logic — that see students at least in part as revenue streams — should flourish. The spread of for-profit colleges and enrollment management practices that has taken place over the last two decades are both consistent with such a prediction.

More generally, we suggest that the issues raised here point to a broad research agenda around student loans that might be opened up in organizational and economic sociology. Certainly there is much work to be done on student loan debt from an access and stratification perspective. But other sets of questions about this major development are also begging for answers: from its relationship to a broader culture of finance that was simultaneously emerging in the United States (Fligstein & Goldstein, 2015; Goldstein, 2013), to the role of securitization in driving the growth of student loans, to more explicitly organizational questions about how higher education organizations respond to evolving resource dependencies associated with an increase in federal student aid.

The 2010 reconfiguration of the field of federal aid policy points to yet another set of questions. The Department of Education has replaced banks as a lender to students, and in the process has gained a more direct financial stake in the terms of those loans and whether they are repaid. At the same time, while financial institutions are no longer in the business of making government-guaranteed loans, a number of them have turned to the business of servicing government-made loans through contracts with the Education Department, with relatively unexplored consequences. In the context of global shift toward individually financed higher education, such questions are likely to remain important and interesting for the foreseeable future.

NOTES

1. Sallie Mae both bought student loans from banks and loaned money to them that they in turn would provide to students.
2. The "Bennett hypothesis" suggests that colleges raise costs in response to the availability of federal aid — that is, they are an effect, rather than cause, of student

loan availability. While tests of the Bennett hypothesis have shown mixed results (Cellini & Goldin, 2012; Epple, Romano, Sarpça, & Sieg, 2014; Turner, 2010, 2014), they generally suggest that even if colleges are capturing a portion of increased aid, they are not capturing all of it. It is very unlikely that the availability of financial aid alone explains tuition increases in recent decades.

3. Partial exceptions are the modest literature in economics that looks at how financial aid policy affects college tuitions, some of which is cited above; the relatively atheoretical literature on comparative higher education finance (e.g., Heller & Callender, 2013; Johnstone & Marcucci, 2010); and some work on the politics of higher education policy (e.g., Best & Best, 2014; Mettler, 2011, 2014).

4. Public Law 85-864 §204.

5. The Basic Educational Opportunity Grant, later renamed the Pell Grant, was also created in 1972, and returning Vietnam veterans were eligible for grants through the G.I. Bill. Federal grant aid more than doubled in real terms between 1972 and 1976, at which point federal grant dollars outnumbered federal loan dollars four to one, a historical high point (College Board, 2014b, Table 1).

6. A contemporaneous Treasury report suggests that Sallie Mae held 31% of outstanding guaranteed loans in 1990 (U.S. Department of Treasury, 1991, p. 47), but the reason for the discrepancy is not clear to us.

7. Inflation adjustments throughout the paper are made using U.S. Department of Labor figures at http://data.bls.gov/cgi-bin/cpicalc.pl

8. When the full direct loan program was introduced, it would include both subsidized and unsubsidized Stafford loans (College Board, 2014b, Table 1).

9. As of 2012, net tuition exceeded state and local revenues for research and master's granting public institutions, the two revenue streams were roughly equal for public bachelor's institutions, and state and local revenues still substantially exceeded net tuition at two-year public colleges. See the Delta Cost Project's Trends in College Spending (http://tcs-online.org/Home.aspx) for the latest figures.

10. For example, the College Board excludes Pell Grants from its calculation of net prices; the Delta Cost Project includes Pell Grants, though it makes both sets of numbers available.

11. Though the first half of this paper focuses on the expansion of student loans in particular, the volume of Pell Grants also tripled during the 2000s after remaining flat in the 1990s; about 30% of federal financial aid now comes in the form of grants (College Board, 2014b, Table 1). For purposes of discussing resource dependence, it makes sense to include these along with federal loans.

12. Though the industry category here is simply "education," the top 25 spenders in the category all represent higher education interests.

13. According to the National Center for Education Statistics, only 1.7% of students were enrolled in for-profit institutions in 1990. This figure seems unlikely, however, given the fraction of loans those institutions absorbed. In their study of the San Francisco Bay Area, Scott and Biag (2016) find that the Integrated Postsecondary Educational Data System (IPEDS, the source of these numbers) "omits about 75% of the four-year for-profits, 60% of the two-year programs, and about 90% of the less than two-year programs." The Congressional Research Service suggested in 1991 that 1.5–2 million students were enrolled in

the proprietary sector, which would imply a more believable 10–15% of all postsecondary students (U.S. Library of Congress, 1991b, p. 2).

14. Again, given the limitations of enrollment figures pointed out in the previous footnote, this may reflect enrollment growth in large for-profit colleges, and fail to count enrollments in small proprietary trade schools. This would not change the underlying point, however. Figures on the proportion of federal aid going to for-profits are likely to be more accurate than enrollment figures.

ACKNOWLEDGMENTS

The authors would like to acknowledge helpful feedback from Dan Hirschman, Catherine Paradeise, and an anonymous reviewer. A previous version of this paper was presented at the Peking University–University of Wisconsin workshop, "Lessons Learned: International Collaboration and Competition in Higher Education, Science, and Technology," in Beijing in May 2015. All remaining errors are our own.

REFERENCES

Akers, B., & Chingos, M. M. (2014). *Is a student loan crisis on the horizon?* Washington, DC: Brown Center on Education Policy at Brookings.

Aldrich, H. E., & Ruef, M. (2006). *Organizations evolving* (2nd ed.). Thousand Oaks, CA: Sage.

Archibald, R. B., & Feldman, D. H. (2004). Funding students instead of institutions. *Business Officer Magazine*, October.

Armstrong, E., & Hamilton, L. T. (2013). *Paying for the party*. Cambridge, MA: Harvard University Press.

Avery, C., & Turner, S. (2012). Student loans: Do college students borrow too much—or not enough? *Journal of Economic Perspectives*, *26*(1), 165–192.

Barr, A., & Turner, S. E. (2013). Expanding enrollments and contracting state budgets: The effect of the great recession on higher education. *Annals of the American Academy of Political and Social Science*, *650*, 168–193.

Barringer, S. N. (2016). The changing finances of public higher education organizations: Diversity, change, and discontinuity. In E. P. Berman & C. Paradeise (Eds.), *The University under Pressure* (Vol. 46). Research in the Sociology of Organizations. Bingley, UK: Emerald Group Publishing Limited.

Berman, E. P. (2012a). *Creating the market university: How academic science became an economic engine*. Princeton, NJ: Princeton University Press.

Berman, E. P. (2012b). Explaining the move toward the market in U.S. academic science: How institutional logics can change without institutional entrepreneurs. *Theory and Society*, *41*(3), 261–299.

Best, J., & Best, E. (2014). *The student loan mess: How good intentions created a trillion-dollar problem.* Berkeley, CA: University of California Press.

Bidwell, A. (2014). Obama administration seeks input on college ratings draft. *U.S. News & World Report,* December 19. Retrieved from http://www.usnews.com/news/articles/2014/12/19/obama-administration-seeks-public-input-on-college-ratings-draft-proposal

Bidwell, A. (2015a). For-profits and community colleges hit hard by falling enrollment. *U.S. News & World Report,* May 14. Retrieved from http://www.usnews.com/news/blogs/data-mine/2015/05/14/for-profits-and-community-colleges-hit-hard-by-falling-enrollment

Bidwell, A. (2015b). Gainful employment survives for-profit challenge. *U.S. News & World Report,* June 24. Retrieved from http://www.usnews.com/news/articles/2015/06/24/federal-court-sides-with-education-department-on-gainful-employment-rule

Boot, M. (1993). Behind the student-loan deal. *Christian Science Monitor,* August 5, p. 3.

Breslauer, G. W. (2016). UC Berkeley's adaptations to the crisis of public higher education in the U.S.: Privatization? Commercialization? Or Hybridization? In E. P. Berman & C. Paradeise (Eds.), *The University under Pressure* (Vol. 46). Research in the Sociology of Organizations. Bingley, UK: Emerald Group Publishing Limited.

Burd, S. (1999). Showdown looms on student loans. *Chronicle of Higher Education,* June 18, p. 3.

Cellini, S. R., & Goldin, C. (2012). *Does federal student aid raise tuition? New evidence on for-profit colleges.* Cambridge, MA: National Bureau of Economic Research. Retrieved from http://www.nber.org/papers/w17827

Center for Responsive Politics. (2015). *Education industry profile.* Retrieved from https://www.opensecrets.org/lobby/indusclient.php?id=W04

Cervantes, A., Creusere, M., McMillion, R., McQueen, C., Short, M., Steiner, M., & Webster, J. (2005). *Opening the doors to higher education: Perspectives on the higher education act forty years later.* Round Rock, TX: TG Research.

Chapman, B., Higgins, T., & Stiglitz, J. E. (Eds.). (2014). *Income contingent loans: Theory, practice and prospects.* New York, NY: Palgrave Macmillan.

Chapman, B., & Ryan, C. (2002). *Income-contingent financing of student charges for higher education: Assessing the Australian innovation.* Canberra: Centre for Economic Policy Research, Australian National University. Retrieved from https://digitalcollections.anu.edu.au/handle/1885/40577

Charles, N. (2012). Income-contingent student loan repayment: A higher education payment system importable into France? *Revue Française de Sociologie, 53*(2), 193–233.

College Board. (2014a). *Trends in college pricing.* Retrieved from https://secure-media.collegeboard.org/digitalServices/misc/trends/2014-trends-college-pricing-report-final.pdf

College Board. (2014b). *Trends in student aid.* Retrieved from https://secure-media.collegeboard.org/digitalServices/misc/trends/2014-trends-student-aid-report-final.pdf

Congressional Quarterly. (1992). Education bills advanced in committees. In *CQ Almanac 1991.* Washington, DC: Congressional Quarterly.

Congressional Quarterly. (1993). Congress expands college loan eligibility. In *CQ Almanac 1992.* Washington, DC: Congressional Quarterly.

Congressional Quarterly. (1994). The direct approach to student loans. In *CQ Almanac 1992.* Washington, DC: Congressional Quarterly.

Congressional Quarterly. (1999). Higher education act reduces interest rates, increases grants. In *CQ Almanac 1998* (54th ed.). Washington, DC: Congressional Quarterly.

Congressional Quarterly. (2009). Legislation shores up student loans. In *CQ Almanac 2008*. Washington, DC: Congressional Quarterly.

Congressional Quarterly. (2011). Student loan measure moves quietly. In *CQ Almanac 2010*. Washington, DC: CQ-Roll Call Group.

Coomes, M. D. (2000). The historical roots of enrollment management. *New Directions for Student Services, 89*, 5–18.

Cuny, T. J. (1991). Federal credit reform. *Public Budgeting and Finance, 11*(2), 19–32.

DeLoughry, T. J. (1992). Banks and trade schools increase their campaign gifts as congress reauthorizes the higher-education act. *Chronicle of Higher Education*, May 20, pp. A19–A21.

Delta Cost Project Database. (2015). *Data dictionary*, August 17. Retrieved from https://nces.ed.gov/ipeds/deltacostproject/download/Delta_Data_Dictionary_1987_2012.xls

Deming, D. J., Goldin, C., & Katz, L. F. (2012). The for-profit postsecondary school sector: Nimble Critters or Agile Predators. *Journal of Economic Perspectives, 26*(1), 139–164.

Desrochers, D. M., & Hurlburt, S. (2014). *Trends in college spending: 2001–2011*. Washington, DC: American Institutes for Research.

Dwyer, R. E., Hodson, R., & McCloud, L. (2013). Gender, debt, and dropping out of college. *Gender and Society, 27*(1), 30–55.

Dwyer, R. E., McCloud, L., & Hodson, R. (2012). Debt and graduation from American universities. *Social Forces, 90*(4), 1133–1155.

Epple, D., Romano, R., Sarpça, S., & Sieg, H. (2014). *The U.S. market for higher education: A general equilibrium analysis of state and private colleges and public funding policies*. Cambridge, MA: National Bureau of Economic Research. Retrieved from http://www.nber.org/papers/w19298

FDR Group. (2015). *Taking out and repaying student loans: A report on focus groups with struggling student loan borrowers*. Retrieved from https://static.newamerica.org/attachments/2358-why-student-loans-are-different/FDR_Group_Updated.dc7218a-b247a4650902f7afd52d6cae1.pdf

Feldheim, D. (2004). Student loans grow as a class among securities. *Wall Street Journal*, January 7, p. 4C.

FinAid. (2015). *Student loan debt clock*, August 30. Retrieved from http://www.finaid.org/loans/studentloandebtclock.phtml

Fligstein, N., & Goldstein, A. (2015). The emergence of a finance culture in American households, 1989–2007. *Socio-Economic Review*, Online before print. doi:10.1093/ser/mwu035

Fligstein, N., & McAdam, D. (2011). Toward a general theory of strategic action fields. *Sociological Theory, 29*(1), 1–26.

Fligstein, N., & McAdam, D. (2012). *A theory of fields*. Oxford: Oxford University Press.

Forde, J. P. (1982). Sallie Mae, ITT unit set 'rate swap'. *American Banker*, September 3, p. 3.

Friedman, M. (1955). The role of government in education. In R. A. Solo (Ed.), *Economics and the public interest*. New Brunswick, NJ: Rutgers University Press.

Fuller, M. B. (2014). A history of financial aid to students. *Journal of Student Financial Aid, 44*(1), 42–68.

Gicheva, D. (2011). *Does the student-loan burden weigh into the decision to start a family?* Greensboro, North Carolina: Department of Economics, University of North Carolina at Greensboro. Retrieved from http://www.uncg.edu/bae/people/gicheva/Student_loans_marriageAug11.pdf

Gladieux, L. E., & Wolanin, T. R. (1976). *Congress and the colleges: The national politics of higher education*. Lexington, MA: Lexington Books.

Goldstein, A. (2013). *Inequality, financialization, and the growth of household debt in the U.S., 1989–2007*. Working Paper. University of California, Berkeley.

Guston, D. H. (2000). *Between politics and science: Assuring the integrity and productivity of research*. Cambridge, MA: MIT Press.

Hanford, E. (2012a). *The case against for-profit colleges and universities*. Retrieved from http://americanradioworks.publicradio.org/features/tomorrows-college/phoenix/case-against-for-profit-schools.html

Hanford, E. (2012b). *The story of the university of Phoenix*. Retrieved from http://american radioworks.publicradio.org/features/tomorrows-college/phoenix/story-of-university-of-phoenix.html

Hannan, M., & Freeman, J. (1976). The population ecology of organizations. *American Journal of Sociology, 82*, 929–964.

Heller, D. E., & Callender, C. (Eds.). (2013). *Student financing of higher education: A comparative perspective*. New York, NY: Routledge.

Henry, S. (1993). Fierce competition seen in student loan arena. *American Banker*, December 16, p. 10.

Hill, P. (1986). Sallie Mae 'privatization' proposed. *American Banker*, January 24, p. 1.

Hossler, D., & Kalsbeek, D. (2013). Enrollment managment and managing enrollments: Revisiting the context for institutional strategy. *Strategic Enrollment Management Quarterly, 1*(1), 5–25.

Houle, J. N. (2013). Disparities in debt: Parents' socioeconomic resources and young adult student loan debt. *Sociology of Education, 87*(1), 53–69.

Houle, J. N. (2014). A generation indebted: Young adult debt across three cohorts. *Social Problems, 61*(3), 448–465.

Houle, J. N., & Berger, L. (2013). *Is student loan debt discouraging home buying among young adults?* Presented at the Association for Public Policy Analysis and Management. Retrieved from http://www.appam.org/assets/1/7/Is_Student_Loan_Debt_Discouraging_Home_Buying_Among_Young_Adults.pdf

Hüther, O., & Krücken, G. (2016). Nested organizational fields: Isomorphism and differentiation among European universities. In E. P. Berman & C. Paradeise (Eds.), *The University under Pressure* (Vol. 46). Research in the Sociology of Organizations. Bingley, UK: Emerald Group Publishing Limited.

Jackson, B. A., & Reynolds, J. R. (2013). The price of opportunity: Race, student loan debt, and college achievement. *Sociological Inquiry, 83*(3), 335–368.

Jacob, B., McCall, B., & Stange, K. M. (2013). *College as country club: Do colleges cater to students' preferences for consumption?* Cambridge, MA: National Bureau of Economic Research. Retrieved from http://www.nber.org/papers/w18745

Jaschik, S. (1993). Popularity of direct-lending proposal blunts banking lobby's assault on capitol hill. *Chronicle of Higher Education*, March 10, p. A28.

Johnstone, D. B., & Marcucci, P. N. (2010). *Financing higher education worldwide: Who pays? Who should pay?* Baltimore, MD: Johns Hopkins University Press.

Kraatz, M. S., Ventresca, M. J., & Deng, L. (2010). Precarious values and mundane innovations: Enrollment management in American liberal arts colleges. *Academy of Management Journal, 53*, 1521–1545.

Kraatz, M. S., & Zajac, E. J. (2001). How organizational resources affect strategic change and performance in turbulent environments: Theory and evidence. *Organization Science*, *12*(5), 632−657.

Kronstadt, S. (1973). Student loans: How the government takes the work out of fraud. *Washington Monthly*, pp. 5−12.

Lawrence, J. C. (1989). Sallie Mae: Wall street's new love. *USA Today*, March 14, p. 3B.

Lindblom, C. E. (1959). The science of "muddling through". *Public Administration Review*, *19*(2), 79−88.

Lipman Hearne. (2010). Wondering what works? The changing marketing mix in higher education. Retrieved from http://lhi-cdn-dev.lipmanhearne-services.com.s3.amazonaws.com/wp-content/uploads/2010/07/2010_LHI-CASE_Marketing_Spend_Report.pdf

McCormick, J. L. (1994). *The direct loan demonstration program: An analysis of the legislative process involving federal student loan policy*. PhD thesis in Public Administration, University of Texas, Austin.

McCue, L. J. (1983). Sallie Mae agrees to underwrite uninsured loans. *American Banker*, September 15, p. 3.

McGettigan, A. (2010). *The great university gamble: Money, markets and the future of higher education*. London: Pluto Press.

McLean, B. (2005). When Sallie Mae met wall street. *Fortune*, December 26. Retrieved from http://archive.fortune.com/magazines/fortune/fortune_archive/2005/12/26/8364649/index.htm

McPherson, M. S., & Schapiro, M. O. (1998). *The student aid game: Meeting need and rewarding talent in American higher education*. Princeton, NJ: Princeton University Press.

Mettler, S. (2011). *The submerged state: How invisible government policies undermine American democracy*. Chicago, IL: University of Chicago Press.

Mettler, S. (2014). *Degrees of inequality: How the politics of higher education sabotaged the American dream*. Ithaca, NY: Cornell University Press.

Monaghan, D. B., & Attewell, P. (2014). The community college route to the bachelor's degree. *Educational Evaluation and Policy Analysis*, *37*(1), 70−91.

National Center for Education Statistics [NCES]. (2014). *Digest of education statistics 2013*. Washington, DC: U.S. Department of Education. Retrieved from https://nces.ed.gov/programs/digest/

Nelson, L. A. (2013). Idea whose time has come? *Inside Higher Ed*, May 13. Retrieved from https://www.insidehighered.com/news/2013/05/13/political-winds-shift-federal-unit-records-database-how-much

New Securities Debut with Student Loans Used for Collateral. (1993). *Wall Street Journal*, June 23, p. C17.

Office of Sallie Mae Oversight, U.S. Department of the Treasury. (2006). *Lessons learned from the privatization of Sallie Mae*. Washington, DC: U.S. Government Printing Office.

Ort, S. A. (2000). Federal and state aid in the 1990s: A policy context for enrollment management. *New Directions for Student Services*, *89*, 19−32.

Paradeise, C., & Filliatreau, G. (2016). The emergent action field of metrics: From rankings to altmetrics. In E. P. Berman & C. Paradeise (Eds.), *The University under Pressure* (Vol. 46). Research in the Sociology of Organizations. Bingley, UK: Emerald Group Publishing Limited.

Parsons, M. D. (1997). *Power and politics: Federal higher education policy making in the 1990s*. Albany, NY: SUNY Press.

Pfeffer, J., & Salancik, G. R. (1974). Organizational decision making as a political process: The case of a university budget. *Administrative Science Quarterly, 19*, 135–151.

Pfeffer, J., & Salancik, G. R. (1978). *The external control of organizations: A resource dependence perspective.* New York, NY: Harper and Row.

Quadlin, N. Y., & Rudel, D. (2015). Responsibility or liability? Student loan debt and time use in college. *Social Forces, 93*(4), 589–614.

Richard, C. (2006). Tuition costs create a boom in bonds. *International Herald Tribune*, July 12, p. 14.

Rothstein, J., & Rouse, C. E. (2011). Constrained after college: Student loans and early-career occupational choices. *Journal of Public Economics, 95*(1–2), 149–163.

Salancik, G. R., & Pfeffer, J. (1974). The bases and use of power in organizational decision making: The case of a university. *Administrative Science Quarterly, 19*, 453–498.

Schattschneider, E. E. (1963). *Politics, pressures, and the tariff.* New Haven, CT: Archon Books.

Scott, W. R., & Biag, M. (2016). The changing ecology of U.S. higher education: An organization field perspective. In E. P. Berman & C. Paradeise (Eds.), *The University under Pressure* (Vol. 46). Research in the Sociology of Organizations. Bingley, UK: Emerald Group Publishing Limited.

Shao, L. (2014). *Debt, marriage, and children: The impact of student loans on marriage and fertility.* San Diego, CA: Department of Economics, University of California. Retrieved from http://iacs5.ucsd.edu/~lshao/pdfs/shao_jmp.pdf

Stratford, M. (2014). One dupont and unit records. *Inside Higher Ed*, March 11. Retrieved from https://www.insidehighered.com/news/2014/03/11/new-america-report-takes-aim-private-college-lobby-student-unit-record-system

Teixeira, P. N., Johnstone, D. B., Rosa, M. J., & Vossensteijn, J. J. (Eds.). (2008). *Cost-sharing and accessibility in higher education: A fairer deal?* Dordrecht: Springer.

Tolbert, P. S. (1985). Institutional environments and resource dependence: Sources of administrative structure in institutions of higher education. *Administrative Science Quarterly, 30*(1), 1–13.

Turner, L. J. (2014). *The road to pell is paved with good intentions: The economic incidence of federal student grant aid.* College Park, MD: Department of Economics, University of Maryland. Retrieved from http://econweb.umd.edu/~turner/Turner_FedAidIncidence.pdf

Turner, N. (2010). *Who benefits from student aid? The economic incidence of tax-based federal student aid.* San Diego, CA: Department of Economics, University of California. Retrieved from http://escholarship.org/uc/item/7g0888mj

Tutterow, C., & Evans, J. (2016). Reconciling the small effect of rankings on university performance with the transformational cost of conformity. In E. P. Berman & C. Paradeise (Eds.), *The University under Pressure* (Vol. 46). Research in the Sociology of Organizations. Bingley, UK: Emerald Group Publishing Limited.

U.S. Congress, Congressional Budget Office. (1980). *State profits on tax-exempt student loan bonds: Analysis and options.* Washington, DC: U.S. Government Printing Office.

U.S. Congress, Congressional Budget Office. (1991). *Controlling the risks of government-sponsored enterprises.* Washington, DC: U.S. Government Printing Office.

U.S. Department of Health, Education, and Welfare (DHEW), Office of the Assistant Secretary for Planning and Evaluation. (1969). *Toward a long-range plan for federal financial support for higher education: A report to the President (Rivlin report).* Washington, DC: U.S. Government Printing Office.

U.S. Department of Treasury. (1991). *Report of the secretary of the treasury on government sponsored enterprises.* Washington, DC: U.S. Government Printing Office.

U.S. Library of Congress, Congressional Research Service. (1982). *Legislative history of the student loan marketing association.* Washington, DC.

U.S. Library of Congress, Congressional Research Service. (1991a). *Direct student loans: A pro and con analysis.* Washington, DC: U.S. Government Printing Office.

U.S. Library of Congress, Congressional Research Service. (1991b). *Proprietary schools.* Washington, DC: U.S. Government Printing Office.

U.S. Senate, Health, Education, Labor and Pensions Committee. (2012). *For profit higher education: The failure to safeguard the federal investment and ensure student success.* Washington, DC: U.S. Government Printing Office.

Wilson, R. (1987). Two banking industry representatives play key lobbying role on student loans. *Chronicle of Higher Education*, April 15, p. 26.

Winston, G. C. (1999, January–February). For-profit higher education: Godzilla or Chicken Little? *Change, 31*, 13–19.

Zajac, E. J., & Kraatz, M. S. (1993). A diametric forces model of strategic change: Assessing the antecedents and consequences of restructuring in the higher education industry. *Strategic Management Journal, 14*(S1), 83–102.

Zigas, D. (1986). Tax reform casts dark shadow on student loan bond market. *American Banker*, May 30, p. 6.

MAPPING THE NETWORK OF NORTH AMERICAN COLLEGES AND UNIVERSITIES: A NEW APPROACH TO EMPIRICALLY DERIVED CLASSIFICATIONS

Mikaila Mariel Lemonik Arthur

ABSTRACT

This research paper aims to better understand the network structure of higher education in North America. It draws on a relationally networked dataset of 1,292 degree-granting colleges and universities in North America to develop a modularity class approach to categorizing colleges and universities based on their own self-defined peer networks and assesses the utility of the modularity class approach as well as several measures of network centrality for predicting offerings of new curricular fields. Results show that not all measures of network centrality equally predict organizational change outcomes, with hub/authority position being most important. Additionally, results show that an empirically derived modularity class approach to categorizing organizations has important strengths in relation to more typical approaches based on

The University under Pressure
Research in the Sociology of Organizations, Volume 46, 161–195
Copyright © 2016 by Emerald Group Publishing Limited
All rights of reproduction in any form reserved
ISSN: 0733-558X/doi:10.1108/S0733-558X20160000046006

prestige or perceived organizational characteristics. The approaches detailed in this paper will be useful for future analysts seeking to explain the spread of innovations and behavior across the higher education institutional field, as well as those seeking to understand clustering and organizational divergence.

Keywords: Network analysis; higher education; organizations; classification; curricular change; colleges

Higher education in North America, as in many other parts of the world, is currently facing a set of pressures and challenges that have the potential to reshape colleges and universities in various ways. According to neoinstitutional theorists, such environmental uncertainty is supposed to increase mimetic isomorphism (DiMaggio & Powell, 1983). In other words, where organizations face political ambiguity, financial contingency, and other sorts of unpredictability, they are expected to be more likely to imitate the behaviors and characteristics of other organizations which are generally seen as successful. Such a perspective would suggest that colleges and universities are coming to look more and more alike, as they all imitate some common model, whether that be the for-profit or the flagship research university. But there is another perspective.

Perhaps rather than simply conforming to one general model, colleges and universities in different organizational contexts might experience different sorts of pressures that lead to further organizational divergence (Oliver, 1988; Scott & Biag, 2016). For instance, private colleges and universities, especially those without extensive endowments and dedicated alumni fundraising machines, are more likely to face concerns about basic survival (Office of Federal Student Aid, 2015), while public colleges and universities instead must readjust to shrinking budgets, increased political control, and consolidation of branch campuses. More specific examples can be drawn from the current political context. As faculty at the flagship campus of the University of Wisconsin face fears over the erosion of faculty governance and tenure protections, many others have long served without the protections of tenure. In Fall 2010, just 26.8% of instructional faculty at postsecondary educational institutions (excluding medical schools) in the United States were in full-time tenured or tenure-track positions; 7.5% of full-time faculty worked at colleges or universities with no tenure system at all (Knapp, Kelly-Reid, & Ginder, 2011). To take another example, a proposal in Spring 2015 to require all faculty across the public colleges and universities in North Carolina to teach at least eight course sections per academic year ignored both the fact that the institutional mission of a research university differs from that of a teaching-focused college and that faculty at several four-year campuses were already teaching more than four courses per semester (Dean, 2015). Indeed,

> ... classification systems like the Carnegie system embrace a hierarchical imagery that overemphasizes the role of the top-tier institutions, ignoring both the contribution of broad-access colleges that educate more than 85 percent of all postsecondary students and their diversity .... A focus on isomorphism masks this diversity in mission and clientele. (Scott, 2015, p. 29)

Classifications and rankings themselves can increase isomorphism, as they provide a framework in which colleges and universities make decisions about which other organizations they might best imitate. Yet alongside such dynamics exist many other mechanisms of diffusion and organizational change, including the reinforcement of professional associations (Scott & Biag, 2016) and peer networks. Research relying on existing classification and prestige ranking systems can thus reinforce status quo expectations and fail to uncover interesting mechanisms of organizational change. In contrast, this paper seeks to understand relations between colleges and universities in North America through an exploration of self-defined relational peer networks, and thus to understand where and how transmission of new organizational behaviors might actually be occurring. It applies network analysis techniques to empirically derive a new type of classification scheme for categorizing colleges and universities based on modularity classes, and the utility of that scheme is tested by comparing it to the 2000 Carnegie Classifications in order to assess each scheme's ability to explain a set of curricular outcomes. The paper further utilizes network analysis methods in order to enhance our understanding of the structure and shape of the network of colleges and universities and to develop a better sense of which particular colleges and universities we should see as most central to the overall institutional field. The findings provide a useful corrective to analyses which take prestige or various ranking systems' top institutions for granted as the driving force behind organizational change in higher education.

CATEGORIZING COLLEGES AND UNIVERSITIES

The higher education system in the United States is vast and complex. As of the 2011–2012 academic year, there were 4,706 postsecondary degree-granting institutions in the United States, including branch campuses; 2,968 of these granted four-year degrees while the remainder granted two-year degrees (National Center for Education Statistics, 2013; table 306). In the 2010−2011 academic year, these institutions collectively granted almost one million associate's degrees, 1.7 million bachelor's degrees, and over 890,000 graduate degrees (table 310). And within this vast system there are multitudes of variations − colleges and universities in the United States range from small, rural colleges to vast multicampus systems enrolling tens of thousands of students, from publicly funded and state-controlled institutions to those run for profit or by religious orders, from those offering a single degree in a single specialized field of study to "multiversities" fulfilling Ezra Cornell's dream of offering instruction in "any study" (Rudolph, 1989). These details become even more complex if one expands the geographical scope of the analysis to include neighboring countries such as Canada.

How do we get a handle on such a complex and ever-changing system? Over the past several decades, scholars, commentators, and higher education professionals have sought − with varying degrees of success − a variety of methods and approaches for classifying, categorizing, and clarifying the United States system of higher education. These approaches have included "a priori" schemes for making sense of the varied missions, goals, organizational types, and organizational characteristics of colleges and universities as well as procedures for empirically deriving taxonomies based on surveys, algorithms for clustering similar institutions, or other quantitative techniques (Brint, 2013; Ruef & Nag, 2011, 2015).

The National Center for Education Statistics uses categories such as control (public, private not-for-profit, or private for-profit) and highest degree level awarded (Prescott, 2011), while the Carnegie Classification are based on a more complex assessment of degree program offerings and organizational characteristics such as size (Carnegie Foundation for the Advancement of Teaching, 2001; Prescott, 2011). Within this set of basic parameters, operative since the first Carnegie Classifications were developed in 1973 (Ruef & Nag, 2015), the Carnegie Classification system has been revised three times in the past 15 years. Indeed, the Carnegie Foundation itself made the first attempt to define what it meant to be a college, which initially required institutions to be nonreligious in nature, offer a curriculum lasting at least four years, have an endowment and at least six faculty members, and require high school diplomas for admission (Rudolph, 1989); of course these parameters have expanded enormously over the years (Stevens, Armstrong, & Arum, 2008). Researchers continue to draw on the Carnegie Classifications as the basis for taxonomies of higher education institutions, as Scott and Biag (2016) do in their analysis of higher education in the San Francisco Bay area. As Brint (2013) argues, these sorts of "a priori" classifications have considerable power in shaping subsequent organizational behaviors and identities, thus constructing the institutional field after their own image.

Many other classification schemes emphasize prestige, eliteness (Ruef & Nag, 2015), and selectivity (Zemsky, Shaman, & Iannozzi, 1997), as do rankings, which are in some ways just another type of classification scheme (Brint, 2013) that concretizes understandings of the system of higher education (Smelser, 2013). Prestige and selectivity have real impacts on organizational behavior — colleges and universities differ in terms of their responsiveness to donors, student preferences, and labor market demands depending on prestige and selectivity (Brint, Proctor, Murphy, & Hanneman, 2012), and middle-status organizations may be more likely to conform to behavioral norms than organizations with either high or low prestige (Phillips & Zuckerman, 2001).

Yet despite the taken-for-grantedness of both the Carnegie Classifications and prestige-based classification schemes, many scholars, administrators, and commentators have called for alternative systems that they feel would more accurately reflect the real distinctions between organizational types in higher education. For example, perhaps the type of student served (traditionally aged residential students vs. older commuters; wealthy students vs. low-income first-generation students; etc.) or the primary modalities (online, in-person, low residency/hybrid) utilized for delivering course content might better reflect the distinctions observed in today's higher education field (Prescott, 2011). Or perhaps drawing on new theoretical and methodological tools developed in organization studies might produce more empirically valid and relevant taxonomic schemes (Ruef & Nag, 2015). A proper understanding of the institutional field of higher education might also benefit from a consideration of organizational niches (Rawlings & Bourgeois, 2004), both in terms of organizational identities and in terms of specific organizational practices, as the current classification systems under-explain at least some types of institutions (Ruef & Nag, 2015). Such approaches entail building empirically grounded taxonomic schemes (Brint, 2013).

In part to respond to concerns about the best way of categorizing colleges and universities, an analysis of network structure based on surveys of college presidents at 275 colleges and universities in the United States empirically derived seven organizational clusters (Brint, Riddle, & Hanneman, 2006): elite private colleges and universities (including both selective Liberal Arts Colleges and private research universities); large, mostly public research universities; other doctoral-granting institutions; public master's granting institutions; private master's granting institutions; selective baccalaureate institutions (mostly religious); and nonselective baccalaureate institutions (also mostly religious). Specialized, for-profit, and associate's level institutions were not incorporated into this analysis, which, in combination with the small sample size, means that the results are not representative of the entire spectrum of higher education in the United States. However, it is instructive that even with these exclusions, the clusters Brint, Riddle, and Hanneman derived "correspond only loosely to the Carnegie Classification" (Ruef & Nag, 2015, p. 90).

In another attempt to empirically derive a classification system for colleges and universities, Ruef and Nag (2011, 2015) use Latent Dirichlet Allocation, a process of inferring membership in unobserved categories based on Bayesian modeling of observed organizational characteristics, in order to estimate a set of organizational categories drawing on a series of relevant variables, including organizational characteristics (institutional control, degrees offered, acceptance of transfer credits, and availability of particular types of learning opportunities); student demographics (including gender, race, age, and geographical distribution); and subjective identity (extracted from official mission statements). The results of this analysis produced three distinct sets of 18 categories, all of which include fewer types of research and graduate institutions and many more types of community and technical colleges than are typical of classification systems. These results highlight the elite bias of prior taxonomic schemes, which tend to collapse almost all sub-baccalaureate colleges into no more than two organizational categories (associate's colleges and specialized vocational institutions) — but they also highlight the complexities of attempting to empirically derive classification schemes based on observed organizational characteristics.

However, the present analysis goes beyond the approaches developed by both Brint et al. (2006) and Ruef and Nag (2011, 2015) by using a much larger dataset than the former but a methodology attuned to relational connections rather than the organizational characteristics central to the latter. It does so by building a relational network based on colleges' and universities' own self-determined lists of peer institutions. Almost all institutions of higher education have such lists, as peer analysis is an important part of the self-study process for accreditation and is useful for other types of institutional research functions. Colleges and universities have wide latitude in how to develop such lists, which may include those institutions which are competitors for the same prospective students, part of the same consortium or athletic conference, with similar political and lobbying interests, with similar organizational or demographic features, or in close geographical proximity. Some colleges and universities fill their peer lists with institutions that seem quite similar to their own, while others add aspirational peers (Brint et al., 2006) designed to highlight their plans and goals for future accomplishments.

This diversity of types of peer lists may at first make them seem an odd feature upon which to base a taxonomic scheme, but in fact it provides a unique benefit: it allows us to categorize institutions based on what they think they do or hope to do in the future. Indeed, the very purpose of peer institution lists is so that colleges and universities have a reference group to which they can compare themselves for analytical and benchmarking purposes, and the internal literature and self-study documents of most colleges and universities are littered with references to how they compare to peers. In a study of the lists of peer institutions selected by colleges and universities seeking to move up in the prestige hierarchy, Brint et al. find that private institutions select aspirational peers that are more selective and often more expensive, while public institutions select aspirational peers with greater commitments to graduate education and research productivity (Brint et al., 2006). Where colleges and universities do not select aspirational peers at a higher prestige level, this may indicate a different type of organizational strategy, one that focuses on serving students rather than building selectivity (Brewer, Gates, & Goldman, 2002). More specific examples of how organizational actors use peer institution lists include the following: faculty groups may argue for pay raises by comparing typical salaries to those at peer institutions; facilities planning groups may visit the student union or athletics buildings at peer institutions to determine how renovations or new building projects ought to proceed; and National Survey of Student Engagement (NSSE) scores, retention and graduation rates, and similar figures are compared to peers to guide student life and academic administrators in setting policies and procedures to ensure organizational success.

In this paper, these peer institution lists are used to conduct a network analysis of the organizational field of North American higher education. For scholars of higher education, network approaches have become increasingly common in studies of student behaviors and pre- and post-college transitions, but these approaches have tended to focus on networks of individuals rather than networks of organizations. Organizational scholars have applied network analysis approaches to a wide variety of institutional fields, such as businesses and nonprofits, but studies of higher education have been slower to adopt these techniques (Stevens, Armstrong, & Arum, 2006). Even when network analysis techniques are applied to higher education organizations, they are more likely to rely on assumptions of structural equivalence, sometimes called positional networks (Moody & Leahey, 2006; Oliver, 1988), for example, the proposition that colleges and universities with similar prestige levels or in the same Carnegie Classification would adopt similar practices (see, for instance, Hashem, 2002; Kraatz & Zajac, 1996; Lounsbury, 2001; Rojas, 2007; Wood, 1979). Much less common are studies of higher education that focus on relational networks, sometimes called contagion effects, which are networks created by direct ties between actors (Moody & Leahey, 2006; Oliver, 1988). While positional networks can be useful (Burt, 1987), the focus on positional networks limits the potential for fully understanding network dynamics in higher education.

Analyses of network effects on organizational behavior also draw on neoinstitutional theory (DiMaggio & Powell, 1983, 1991), which would suggest that the organizations within these sectors would come to express similar behaviors and features through the processes of institutional isomorphism, whether due to normative, coercive, or mimetic pressures. Scholars have argued that neoinstitutional forces have profoundly shaped the global patterns of higher education, causing increasing isomorphism in educational systems around the world and even stronger isomorphism within specific national contexts (Meyer, Ramirez, Frank, & Schofer, 2005). Yet neoinstitutional analysts examining higher education have found that innovations may result in increasing organizational divergence, perhaps because of the important role played by local conditions and contexts (Kraatz & Zajac, 1996). Such research suggests that higher education may not be best understood as a single sector or institutional field, as different "sub-sectors" might exhibit different adaptive responses (Brewer et al., 2002; Lounsbury, 2001; Scott & Biag, 2016). These sub-sectors certainly have many distinct features and lead to distinctive experiences and outcomes for students (Armstrong & Hamilton, 2013). Furthermore, as Smelser (2013, p. 7) argues, "… even at the most fundamental level institutions of higher education … exhibit notable levels of ambiguity, nonspecificity, and taken-for-grantedness … [that] have been great institutional advantages for colleges and universities, essential for their freedom, autonomy, and adaptability." In consequence, colleges and universities need not all follow the same framework or behave in the same way, and even individual colleges and universities may not follow the same framework or behave in the same way when examined over time. Thus, we as analysts need to attend closely to the variations within the field in order to develop analytical approaches with sufficient specificity to be useful.

METHODS

The data included in this analysis come from an ongoing project examining curricular change in higher education in the United States (specifically, the emergence of tertiary-level academic programs in women's studies, Asian American studies, and queer/LGBT studies). In particular, network data are important to this study because they allow for the possibility of testing whether diffusion, mimetic effects, and/or institutional isomorphism shape the curricular change decisions of particular colleges and universities. Prior research in this area has tended to focus on diffusion across categories of institutions — looking, for instance, at whether colleges and universities in the same locality or who meet certain structural criteria will have similar curricular offerings. Therefore, this particular study was designed instead to explore the effects of higher education institutions' own self-defined peers (here referred to as "relational peers"), as discussed above.

To develop the network data, first a random sample of 60 colleges and universities in the United States was drawn. To be included in the sampling frame for this sample, a college or university must have received at least one dollar of federal research funding (Lombardi, Craig, Capaldi, & Gater, 2002) in the period 1997 through 2003 and it must have awarded four-year undergraduate degrees in the liberal arts and sciences. Each of the 60 colleges and universities was contacted directly and asked for a list of its own self-defined peers; the resulting list contained 525 colleges and universities. Each of these colleges and universities was then contacted and asked for a list of its own self-defined peers.[1] While the original sampling frame included only colleges and universities in the 50 U.S. states and Washington, DC, the final sample includes colleges and universities in Canada and in U.S. territories which were named as peer institutions. Some U.S. colleges and universities additionally provide their peer lists to the Department of Education's Integrated Post-Secondary Data Analysis System (IPEDS) as part of their annual reporting process; these lists were obtained where possible for those colleges and universities which did not respond to direct contacts. Between direct contacts and the IPEDS system, peer lists were not obtained for 12 colleges and universities. Instances in which a college or university indicated a peer ambiguously (for instance, listing "University of California" instead of a specific campus in the UC

System) are excluded from the analysis, as are institutions offering only graduate or specialized study (such as divinity schools). Therefore, *nodes* in this dataset represent individual colleges and universities who qualified for inclusion either by being part of the initial random sample of 60 colleges and universities or by being included on one or more lists of peer institutions. *Edges* represent self-defined peer relationships; they are directional, as peer relationships are not necessarily reciprocated. To provide a specific example, at the time at which the data were collected, the University of Wisconsin Madison listed 13 peer institutions.[2] These 13 universities were those that administrators and/or institutional research staff at the University of Wisconsin Madison had determined were either sufficiently similar to their university so as to be a suitable basis for comparison or were universities that they would aspire to be more like. Each university then became a node in the dataset, and a directional line *from* the University of Wisconsin Madison *to* each of its self-selected peers became an edge in the dataset.

The resulting dataset contains 1,292 colleges and universities in North America. Data on institutional and curricular characteristics were obtained from existing data sources, including the IPEDS system, the Carnegie Corporation, and CollegeSource (an online database of college and university course catalogs). In this analysis, only a small subset of the variables in the dataset were used. First of all, colleges' and universities' self-defined peer institutions as of the mid-2000s were used to develop a network graph. An edited and condensed version of the 2000 Carnegie Classifications (Carnegie Foundation for the Advancement of Teaching, 2001), with the following categories: Doctoral/Research Extensive, Doctoral/Research Intensive, Master's College I, Master's College II, Baccalaureate Liberal Arts, Baccalaureate General, Baccalaureate/Associate's, Associates, and Specialized, was used to develop comparisons between empirically derived and theoretically derived organizational classifications. A set of five curricular outcome variables measure the presence of curricular programs in women's and/or gender studies, Asian American studies, and queer/LGBT studies as of 2005, including whether a particular college or university offers a major (for women's studies and Asian American studies only) or any other curricular program in that area (such as a minor, certificate, or concentration). Data for these outcome variables were collected from the CollegeSource archive and summary statistics are available in Table 1. Finally, a measure of the percentage of a given college or university's self-defined peers that offered each particular program a decade earlier, in 1995, was computed. Colleges or universities which were designated as peer

Table 1. Frequency of Curricular Program Offerings, 2005.

	Women's Studies (%)	Asian American Studies (%)	Queer/LGBT Studies
Major program	19.5	4.0	N/A
Non-major program	34.8	2.5	N/A
Any program	54.3	6.5	3.5%
No program	45.7	93.6	96.5%

institutions, but which were not fully operational in 2005, are excluded from this analysis.

To visualize the network data included in this paper, a networked dataset was created in the Gephi network analysis software package (http://gephi.org/) using the ForceAtlas 2 visualization. Nodes represent individual colleges and universities; directed edges represent self-defined peer relationships, which may not be reciprocated (or even known about) by the connected college or university. The Gephi software allows for the calculation of network data such as modularity class and for the production of network graphs colored by variable, modularity class, or other factor. In Gephi, modularity class — a measure of the presence of distinct communities within the network (Blondel, Guillaume, Lambiotte, & Lefebvre, 2008) — is calculated using the Louvain Method (Blondel, 2011), an iterative algorithmic process that builds a "community of communities" in part by assessing the gain or loss in modularity by moving individual nodes between communities and producing a particular number of "meta-communities" (modularity classes) that best represents the organization of the network. The Louvain Method is an effective method of community detection that provides results in a more computationally efficient fashion than prior methods were able to (Blondel et al., 2008). Additional quantitative analysis supplements the Gephi network analysis.

The discussion below proceeds in three parts. First, various measures of organizational centrality are explored, with a discussion of the most-central colleges and universities according to several of these metrics. Second, the network structure, including in-degree and out-degree, is discussed, and organizational clustering is described via empirically derived modularity classes. Finally, the extent to which elements of network structure — including modularity class and structural position within the network — can predict the adoption of curricular innovations by colleges and universities is assessed.

ANALYSIS

One of the advantages of considering relational network data on higher education is that it allows for an analysis of revealed evidence of the centrality of particular colleges and universities to the network of colleges and universities as a whole. These measures may not correspond with received wisdom as to the most prestigious or elite colleges and universities. For example, not one of the top 10 national universities ranked by *U.S. News* or the top 10 American universities ranked by the Shanghai Academic Ranking of World Universities is a public institution or a small college; in contrast, the measures of network centrality in this dataset are largely topped by public research universities and smaller private colleges. These findings echo a network analysis of the law professoriate at 184 American Bar Association accredited law schools which found that a number of law schools are much more highly placed when revealed preferences (demonstrated by faculty hiring practices) are examined than they are in conventional rankings such as those produced by *U.S. News* (Katz et al., 2011). Such findings may give scholars of higher education pause, due to our confidence in the existing frameworks for describing the field of higher education. But the fact that this model has long been used does not necessarily mean it is the best model available.

To take an example from a quite different context, consider the issue of taxonomy in the biological sciences. Modern biological taxonomy is still largely governed by the schema Carl Linnaeus developed in the early 1700s. Linnaeus's approach was an obvious advance over prior systems, given its clarity, standardization, and objectivity (Paterlini, 2007), and Linnaeus worked carefully to construct "solutions using the best technologies available at the time" (Charles Godfrey, as quoted in Paterlini, 2007, p. 814). Due to the magnitude and persistence of Linnaeus's accomplishments, scientists are reluctant to abandon the old way of classifying life and thus only engage in limited tweaking of the Linnaean system. Yet his system of categories does not always conform to information discovered via more modern scientific techniques such as DNA analysis (Paterlini, 2007). While the classification of colleges and universities is obviously different from the classification of lifeforms, in both contexts there are risks to maintaining familiar frameworks with which the empirical data are beginning to conflict. This paper, therefore, argues for the utility of considering how new forms of empirical evidence and new analytical techniques can better inform our understanding of the organization and structure of the field of higher education.

Organizational Centrality

Closeness centrality is a measure of network centrality that assesses the ability of a given node to reach other nodes via the shortest paths, while *betweenness centrality* measures the extent to which given nodes are located between other nodes and thus are able to broker connections among otherwise-disconnected groups. Nodes high in betweenness centrality are more able to influence the network because they can bring ideas or innovations to multiple subgroups or cliques within the network (Burris, 2006), and this may result in reputational advantages for central organizations (Knoke, 2011). Both of these approaches offer advantages over simply considering organizations' number of ties to other organizations because they incorporate measures of nodes' indirect connections in order to determine the extent to which nodes are tied into overall networks, rather than only looking at the immediate neighborhoods in which nodes are situated (Hanneman & Riddle, 2005).

Authority is a measure of the degree to which a given node is treated as knowledgeable, relevant, or important by others in the network[3] (Cherven, 2015; Kleinberg, 1998). *Hubs*, in contrast, are nodes with network connections primarily to authorities. Hubs reinforce authorities' status without necessarily gaining status themselves and are able to glean knowledge from the authorities they are closely tied to. Thus, algorithms for computing hub and authority status use an iterative procedure to determine which nodes point to and are pointed to by which other nodes (Kleinberg, 1998). In this particular network, due to the limited number of potential ties between nodes, the positional ranking of nodes in terms of authority and hub measures is generally the same for the highest-ranked nodes, though the actual scores and the rankings of lower-ranked nodes are different. There are additional measures of network centrality, including the clustering coefficient, eccentricity, and Eigenvector centrality, but an analysis of these measures[4] adds little to the analysis presented here.

Table 2 details the top 10 colleges and universities in the network in terms of authority/hub status, closeness centrality, and betweenness centrality. These three measures are measuring very different network properties: the closeness centrality list does not share a single institution with either of the other lists, while the authority/hub list and the betweenness centrality list have only one common member (the University of Michigan). Furthermore, the different colleges and universities on these lists have little in common with one another. The closeness centrality list is divided between small colleges, large private universities, and less-elite

Table 2.   Top 10 Colleges and Universities by Various Measures of
Network Position.

Rank	Authority/Hub	Closeness Centrality	Betweenness Centrality
1	University of Illinois Urbana-Champaign	Jamestown College (ND)	Lee University
2	University of Michigan Ann Arbor	Montana Tech	Point Loma Nazarene University
3	Ohio State University	Mississippi College	Northwestern College (IA)
4	University of Wisconsin Madison	West Texas A&M University	Boston College
5	University of Minnesota Twin Cities	New York University	University of San Francisco
6	University of Texas Austin	Westmont College (CA)	Grinnell College
7	University of North Carolina Chapel Hill	Duke University	University of La Verne
8	Carleton College	West Virginia University	University of Michigan Ann Arbor
9	Oberlin College	Lincoln University (MO)	Florida A&M University
10	Texas A&M University	Lebanon Valley College (PA)	Catholic University of America

public universities, while the betweenness centrality list is primarily divided
between small colleges and large private universities with two public universities as well. These measures, then, provide a different sort of information
about the network. Rather than highlighting which colleges and universities
are closely connected to other well-positioned nodes, closeness centrality
and betweenness centrality tell us, respectively, the extent to which nodes
have structural positions in the network that facilitate their role in diffusion
processes, especially the extent to which nodes can facilitate or control the
flow of information across otherwise-disconnected sectors of the network
(van der Hulst, 2011).

Network Structure

The distributions of in-degree and out-degree are markedly different. In-
degree, in this analysis, is a representation of how many other colleges and
universities have selected a given college or university as a peer. There are,
of course, a variety of strategies undergirding peer selection, as discussed

above. This variation makes it more difficult to draw a clear conclusion about what it means to be a college or university with high in-degree, but we can assume that such institutions are generally regarded as successful and worth competing with or emulating. As shown in Fig. 1, the in-degree distribution roughly follows the pattern of an inverse exponential function, with many nodes having low in-degree; while only 6 have in-degree of 0, hundreds have in-degree of 1, and the median in-degree is 4. Just a few nodes have a high in-degree: eight institutions have in-degree of over 35; seven of these are flagship public universities,[5] and one is a selective Liberal Arts College.[6]

Of course, self-defined peers were only collected for the initial groups of colleges and universities in the dataset, meaning that out-degree is by definition 0 for 781 colleges and universities. But even when only looking at the colleges and universities for which self-defined peers are available, the out-degree distribution is much flatter than the in-degree distribution, as shown in Fig. 1. This may be due to normative procedures around the construction of peer lists: only 34 nodes had out-degree of between 1 and 5, while only 19 had out-degree of 35 or higher. The median out-degree is 14 for those nodes with any self-defined peers. While there are no specific and universal requirements for how many peers a college or university must select, there are costs and limitations to selecting too few or too many. For example, the selection of too few peers makes it difficult for institutional research offices to draw substantial or significant comparisons to practices

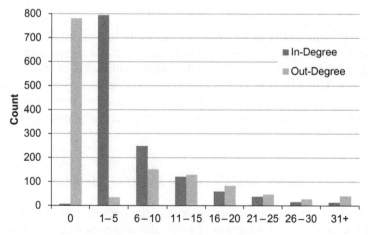

Fig. 1.   In-Degree and Out-Degree Counts.

elsewhere. On the other hand, with too many peers, data collection and analysis can become much more challenging; however, four institutions have 50 or more self-defined peers.[7]

Modularity measures the density of ties within clusters or communities in a given networked social space. To produce modularity classes in a given network, the algorithm compares the number of ties among clusters of nodes to the number of ties that would be expected in a randomly distributed network (Newman, 2006). Importantly, the algorithm does not require the analyst to specify the number of classes in advance — these are determined by the empirical structure of the network. The advantage of the modularity approach to community detection is that it incorporates nodes' degree heterogeneity, thus avoiding potential errors of categorization that would develop if community categories reflected in-degree and out-degree themselves (Porter, Onnela, & Mucha, 2009), while additionally being computationally efficient. A modularity analysis of the 1,292 colleges and universities in the network-linked dataset here produces eight modularity classes, ranging in size from 329 colleges and universities (25.5% of the dataset) to only 12. While the arrangement of nodes into modularity classes is a computational procedure, the determination of what these classes represent requires interpretation. A graph of the network colored by modularity class and labeled by college or university name can be found in Fig. A1 in the appendix, and Table 3 presents summary statistics on the modularity classes.

These modularity classes represent an empirically derived alternative to theoretically driven categories of colleges and universities, such as the Carnegie Classifications. As such, they provide a new way to think about the higher education field in the United States. A particular benefit of this approach is the ability to see how regional location and public/private control may matter more to colleges and universities' ties to one another than degree-granting and research productivity, hallmarks of the Carnegie approach. This new perspective, then, can provide a corrective to analyses of higher education that have become overly focused on prestige, especially in a political moment when renewed attention is being placed on undergraduate education.

Network Structure and the Spread of Innovation

Modularity class can be used as an empirically derived measure for considering the likelihood of adoption of particular innovations as an alternative to theoretically derived measures of organizational categorization such as

Table 3. Modularity Classes in Dataset, with Examples.

Description	Frequency	Percent
0: Private research universities	149	11.5
Harvard, NYU, Suffolk University		
1: Less-selective private colleges, Group I[a]	329	25.5
Seattle Pacific University, Mississippi College, Judson College		
2: Mostly public undergrad-focused colleges	328	25.4
CUNY Hunter College, Fort Valley State University, Morgan State University		
3: Public RII/RIII universities	157	12.2
University of Texas Dallas, Winona State University, San Jose State University		
4: Public RI universities	117	9.1
SUNY Albany, University of Connecticut, University of Wisconsin Madison		
5: Selective Liberal Arts Colleges	78	6.0
Mount Holyoke College, Reed College, Kenyon College		
6: Less-selective private colleges, Group II[a]	122	9.4
Drew University, Dana College, Arcadia University		
7: Missouri community colleges	12	0.9
Crowder College, Jefferson College, St. Louis Community College		

[a]At first, modularity classes 1 and 6 may seem to be referring to indistinguishable sets of colleges and universities. Both include almost entirely private not-for-profit institutions, with a handful of public and for-profit institutions. Both groups are broadly similar in terms of Carnegie Classifications, with a fifth of institutions classified as Master's I, about a tenth as Master's II, about a third as Baccalaureate General, and most of the remainder as Baccalaureate Liberal Arts. In both groups, about four fifths of the institutions have religious affiliations, with over half being affiliated with Protestant denominations, but more of the institutions in modularity class 6 are Catholic. Where a difference between the two groups does become clear is when looking at the regional locations of the institutions in each group. In modularity class 1, 50.7% of institutions are located in the South Atlantic or South Central regions, with another 14% in the Pacific region. Together, these regions make up only 7.4% of the institutions in modularity class 6. In contrast, 49% of the institutions in modularity class 6 are located in the West North Central region and 26.2% in the Mid-Atlantic region, which together account for only 14% of the institutions in modularity class 1.

Carnegie Classification. To test this approach, data on 2005 offerings of women's studies, Asian American studies, and queer/LGBT studies were crosstabulated with both the 2000 Carnegie Classifications (with all specialized institutions combined into one category) and the modularity classes derived above. All crosstabulations were significant at $p < 0.001$. As Table 4 shows, measures of association are quite similar when looking at the relationship between the outcomes and Carnegie Classification and when

Table 4. Comparison of Cramer's V Association Levels.

Outcome Variable	Association: Carnegie Classification	Association: Modularity Class
Women's studies	0.440	0.421
Asian American studies	0.235	0.230
Queer/LGBT studies	0.252	0.261

looking at the relationship between the outcomes and the empirically derived modularity classes. The Carnegie Classifications have a slightly stronger association with program offerings in women's studies and a slightly weaker association with queer/LGBT studies that do the modularity classes, while the Asian American studies association is almost the same for both measures. It is likely that the number of programs offered in each field is affecting these results: women's studies programs are considerably more common than Asian American studies and queer/LGBT studies programs.

While measures of association describe patterns of relationships in a crosstabulation as a whole, they are not as useful for understanding the ways in which specific categories may illuminate the social processes under consideration. Comparing crosstabulations of curricular outcomes with the empirically derived modularity classes and with the condensed 2000 Carnegie Classifications shows that the modularity classification provides a breakdown of institution type that more clearly matches the curricular outcomes (see Tables A1−A6 in the appendix). In the Carnegie Classification system, Doctoral Extensive and Baccalaureate Liberal Arts institutions are more likely to offer each of the three curricular programs examined here. In the modularity class system, we can see that the outcomes for Public RI universities are quite similar to the outcomes for Doctoral/Research Extensive universities. However, the modularity class system permits an examination of Selective Liberal Arts Colleges, a specific subset of the Baccalaureate Liberal Arts Carnegie Class. Selective Liberal Arts Colleges are much more likely to offer each of the curricular programs considered here than are Baccalaureate Liberal Arts institutions more generally, as few "true" liberal arts colleges remain in this group (Baker, Baldwin, & Makker, 2012; Brint, Riddle, Turk-Bicakci, & Levy, 2005). Thus, the modularity class system provides an additional level of specificity useful to these analytical purposes.

Logistic regressions comparing these two sets of categories as predictors of five curricular outcomes (presence of women's studies major or program, presence of Asian American studies major or program, and presence of queer/LGBT studies program), using Doctoral/Research Extensive and

Public RI as the excluded categories, resulted largely in pseudo-R^2 of similar strength. These regressions are based only on the 510 colleges and universities for which peer institution lists are available in the dataset, which also means that modularity class 7 (Missouri community colleges) is excluded from the analysis. Given the rareness of the outcomes of Asian American studies program/major offerings and queer studies program offerings, the standard errors for those regressions are inflated, thus severely reducing the reliability of the results (results on file with the author). However, a brief discussion is still warranted. Differences between the pseudo-R^2 figures for modularity class and Carnegie Classification for Asian American studies majors and queer studies programs were less than 0.04. For Asian American studies programs, the pseudo-R^2 was 0.08 larger using Carnegie Classifications than it was using modularity class. The same set of regressions was also run with the addition of a variable measuring the percentage of a given college or university's peers which offered that curricular program a decade previously. Adding this variable increased the strength of the pseudo-R^2 across all 10 regressions, with the same caveat about standard error, though the increase was negligible in the case of queer studies, which was also the only outcome for which the peers variable itself was not significant (results on file with the author). The findings in terms of the modularity classes themselves generally conform to what would be expected given the descriptive data in Tables A1–A6 in the appendix, except in that the Selective Liberal Arts College modularity class was not significantly different from the excluded Public RI category for any outcome other than Asian American studies programs.

The standard error is less of a concern for the regressions looking at women's studies outcomes, given their much greater prevalence in contemporary higher education. Inflated standard errors do remain for one Carnegie Class, baccalaureate/Associate's colleges, due to the fact that only three such colleges offer women's studies programs and only two offer women's studies majors, but standard errors are reasonable for all variables in the modularity class models. Common tests (VIF) for collinearity indicate no concerns in these models. Therefore, these regressions will be explored in more detail. Table 5 compares models predicting women's studies adoption based on modularity class and Carnegie Classification, with and without the peer variable. The results show that the inclusion of the peer variable considerably increases the goodness-of-fit of the regression and reduces the magnitude of the coefficients of both the modularity classes and the Carnegie Classifications. When peers are included in the Carnegie Classifications model, all of the categories become insignificant, while

Table 5. Logistic Regression Coefficients and Standard Errors, Comparing Modularity Class and Carnegie Classification as Predictors of Women's Studies Program Adoption.

Modularity Class	Model 1: Modularity Class without Peers	Model 2: Modularity Class with Peers	Carnegie Classification	Model 3: Carnegie Classification without Peers	Model 4: Carnegie Classification with Peers
Private research universities	-0.742 (0.518)	-0.138*** (0.554)	Doctoral/Research Intensive	-1.363** (0.442)	-0.033 (0.511)
Less-selective private colleges I	-3.969*** (0.518)	-0.956 (0.652)	Master's I	-2.031*** (0.382)	0.227 (0.473)
Mostly public undergrad-focused	-2.905*** (0.439)	-0.809 (0.532)	Master's II	-3.042*** (0.594)	-0.516 (0.790)
Public RII/RIII	-0.266 (0.538)	0.588 (0.577)	Baccalaureate/ Associate's	-23.793 (40192.970)	-21.066 (40192.970)
Selective Liberal Arts Colleges	1.341 (1.083)	1.305 (1.093)	Baccalaureate General	-3.459*** (0.478)	-0.285 (0.630)
Less-selective private colleges II	-2.772*** (0.545)	-0.733 (0.643)	Baccalaureate Liberal Arts	-0.041 (0.579)	1.129 (0.696)
Percent of peers offering program in 1995		5.113*** (0.690)	Associate's	-2.590 (1.456)	2.760 (1.551)
			Specialized	-4.382*** (1.134)	-2.606 (1.393)
			Percent of peers offering program in 1995		6.372*** (0.657)
Nagelkerke R^2	0.457	0.582	Nagelkerke R^2	0.297	0.586

$*p < 0.05$, $**p < 0.01$, $***p < 0.001$.

the inclusion of peers in the modularity class model renders all categories except for private research universities insignificant. Private research universities then become slightly less likely than the excluded public RI universities to offer women's studies programs. When comparing the models utilizing modularity class to the models utilizing Carnegie Classification, there is almost no difference in the goodness-of-fit for the models which include the peers variable, presumably because the peers variable accounts for such a large proportion of the variation in outcomes. However, when comparing the models without the peers variable, the modularity classes represent a considerably better fit for the outcome data than do the Carnegie Classifications (Table 6).

To explore the utility of different measures of network centrality, a series of bivariate logistic regressions were run using Gephi-computed network position scores as predictor variables and curricular outcomes as the dependent variable. Again, these regressions include only the 510 colleges and universities for which peer lists are available. As Table 7 shows, closeness centrality, authority, and hub significantly predict the likelihood of a college or university offering any of the given programs, while betweenness centrality does not, and the higher a college or university ranks on any of the significant centrality measures, the more likely it is to offer each of the five programs. It is possible that the lack of significance for betweenness centrality reflects a potential curvilinear relationship, in which middle-status organizations are most likely to conform to norms while both high- and low-status organizations are lower in conformity (Phillips & Zuckerman, 2001).

There are considerable data issues that constrain our ability to interpret the results of the logistic regressions, however. The range of values for the hub (0−0.0069) and authority (0−0.0045) variables is so constrained that an increase in score produces a quantitatively impossible increase in the odds of program offerings, and thus outsized coefficients and standard errors. Furthermore, given the fact that the range and units of the different network position statistics are quite different, the coefficient size cannot be compared between them. However, the pseudo-R^2 measures do provide the ability to compare the strength of different predictors. Of the significant variables, closeness centrality is the weakest predictor of all five outcomes. For women's studies programs, authority is the strongest predictor; for the remainder of the programs, hub status is the strongest predictor. However, hub and authority have pseudo-R^2 values within 0.004 of each other in all cases. The pseudo-R^2 for the regression with authority as the independent variable and women's studies programs as the dependent variable is the

Table 6. Logistic Regression Coefficients and Standard Errors, Comparing Modularity Class and Carnegie Classification as Predictors of Women's Studies Major Adoption.

Modularity Class	Model 1: Modularity Class without Peers	Model 2: Modularity Class with Peers	Carnegie Classification	Model 3: Carnegie Classification without Peers	Model 4: Carnegie Classification with Peers
Private research universities	-0.884** (0.309)	-0.532 (0.341)	Doctoral/Research Intensive	-1.469*** (0.313)	-0.571 (0.353)
Less-selective private colleges I	-3.750*** (0.749)	-2.071** (0.797)	Master's I	-2.313*** (0.284)	-0.955** (0.361)
Mostly public undergrad-focused	-2.349*** (0.352)	-0.904* (0.426)	Master's II	-2.670** (0.772)	-1.239 (0.818)
Public RII/RIII	-1.405*** (0.305)	-0.263 (0.362)	Baccalaureate/ Associate's	-21.793 (40192.970)	-20.188 (40192.970)
Selective Liberal Arts Colleges	0.020 (0.347)	-0.205 (0.365)	Baccalaureate General	-3.205*** (0.626)	-1.710* (0.679)
Less-selective private colleges II	-2.631*** (0.644)	-1.136 (0.695)	Baccalaureate Liberal Arts	-0.328 (0.305)	-0.068 (0.330)
			Associate's	-0.590 (1.426)	1.229 (1.457)
Percent of peers offering program in 1995		3.911*** (0.632)	Specialized	-2.382* (1.096)	-1.370 (1.225)
			Percent of peers offering program in 1995		3.643*** (0.602)
Nagelkerke R^2	0.281	0.369	Nagelkerke R^2	0.291	0.372

*$p < 0.05$, **$p < 0.01$, ***$p < 0.001$.

Table 7. Binary Logistic Regression of Network Position Variables on Program Outcomes.

	Predictor	B	Standard Error	Nagelkerke R^2
Women's studies programs	Closeness centrality	0.488	0.145	0.034***
	Betweenness centrality	0.000	0.000	0.004
	Authority	2074.206	244.271	0.311***
	Hub	1329.51	157.024	0.307***
Women's studies majors	Closeness centrality	0.585	0.170	0.037**
	Betweenness centrality	0.000	0.000	0.008
	Authority	1250.423	143.487	0.249***
	Hub	817.190	93.503	0.251***
Asian American studies programs	Closeness centrality	0.776	0.270	0.037**
	Betweenness centrality	0.000	0.000	0.008
	Authority	1143.572	161.731	0.211***
	Hub	745.914	105.294	0.212***
Asian American studies majors	Closeness centrality	1.398	0.464	0.073**
	Betweenness centrality	0.000	0.000	0.007
	Authority	1108.398	230.912	0.169***
	Hub	722.306	150.305	0.170***
Queer/LGBT studies programs	Closeness centrality	1.371	0.357	0.084***
	Betweenness centrality	0.000	0.000	0.003
	Authority	872.074	180.691	0.115***
	Hub	568.984	117.570	0.116***

$*p < 0.05$, $**p < 0.01$, $***p < 0.001$.

largest in this analysis, at 0.311, and many of the others are well over 0.2, suggesting that even as individual predictors these measures of network position have something to contribute to our understanding of the adoption of innovations.

However, as useful as these measures of network position may be, they are not as useful as direct measures of influence. A separate analysis (on file with the author) considers the role of network position variables in predicting curricular outcomes in logistic regressions that also incorporates the percentage of a given college or university's peers which offered that curricular program a decade previously. Incorporating the peer measure substantially increases the regression's strength over a model including just

184 MIKAILA MARIEL LEMONIK ARTHUR

the network position variables for all four outcomes except queer studies, which is also the only outcome for which the peer measure is not significant. Thus, it is likely that network position tells only a small part of the story, while isomorphism or diffusion among peer institutions is a more important explanation for the observed curricular outcomes.

CONCLUSION

This paper makes contributions in two areas: to the study of organizational change and diffusion across networks and to the study of higher education as an institutional field. In terms of the study of organizational change and diffusion, the results of the logistic regression analysis suggest that merely being located in a central position in a network may not be enough to influence your adoption of an innovation. Rather, being positioned as a hub or authority appears to be most highly correlated with adoption. What these results cannot determine, however, is whether organizations positioned as hubs or authorities are more likely to innovate or whether more innovative organizations begin to take on the characteristics of hubs and/or authorities. Additional analysis is also needed to further explore the extent to which different metrics of network position are useful in predicting adoption of innovations among organizations such as colleges and universities and the extent to which empirically derived measures of organizational categories (such as modularity class) may prove useful for analyzing organizational clustering and innovation. In particular, it would be valuable to apply this approach to the study of new natural science disciplines such as genetic toxicology (Frickel, 2004) in order to understand how patterns of adoption in such fields might differ from the patterns observed here.

In terms of the study of higher education as an institutional field, this paper describes the network of colleges and universities in North America, highlighting an empirically derived categorization of colleges and universities based on the computation of modularity class as well as the different ways in which network positions can be ranked within the higher education sphere. It presents a contribution to the expanding literature (Brint, 2013; Brint et al., 2006; Ruef & Nag, 2011, 2015) on empirically derived classification systems for colleges and universities. Furthermore, it shows that the colleges and universities we think of as most prestigious may not in fact be the most central or authoritative organizations in the contemporary higher education sphere. Researchers and policy makers can draw on these findings to encourage alternative measures of influence that go beyond the financial and popularity measures essential to rankings and selectivity, instead considering the influence that "authoritative" colleges and universities may have on innovations within higher education as well as what the revealed preferences of both prospective students (Avery, Glickman, Hoxby, & Metrick, 2013) and other colleges and universities tell us about the "real" hierarchies of colleges and universities. Indeed, the analysis presented here draws not on the measures of sameness so common in classifications of colleges and universities but rather on real measures of influence — colleges and universities actively compare themselves to, and often aspire to become more like, the peers they themselves have selected. Thus, policy makers seeking reform or innovation within the institutional field of higher education may also be better served by taking their proposals to central or authoritative colleges and universities rather than beginning with elite, wealthy, or otherwise convenient campuses.

These findings are especially relevant in our current historical moment, where colleges, universities, and higher education as a field are experiencing unprecedented pressures. Attacks on tenure, reductions in funding, the development of new evaluation metrics, and many other political trends have the potential to reshape what higher education does and how it functions. Commentary on these trends tends to focus on their impact on the most prestigious colleges and universities — in summer 2015 as this paper was being finalized, for example, the higher education media were focused on the impacts of legal changes in Wisconsin on tenure, shared governance, and funding, and many articles focused exclusively on how these changes would affect the flagship campus in Madison. As the findings above demonstrate, the University of Wisconsin Madison is indeed a central organization in the North American higher education field, and thus such a focus is undoubtedly warranted.

Yet the findings above also emphasize the importance of attending to many other organizational types and contexts. Research and commentary on higher education often suffers from what we might term a "bipolar" focus, primarily exploring elite sectors and, to a lesser extent, underperforming broad-access colleges (Scott & Biag, 2016; Stevens, 2015) — but ignores so many other organizational subfields that might elucidate the particular isomorphic — and political — pressures colleges and universities experience. These pressures can indeed encourage colleges and universities to be more and more alike. For example:

A state university official in Missouri observed: "There was a move on a lot of institutions in Missouri to expand and try to be like each other and compete with each other ... They were doing things like setting up satellite operations in each other's back yard; universities that ... grew out of normal school systems and then became regional universities were now wanting to be research universities ... [M]ostly there was expansion into areas that were more expensive for the institution as well as the state to support." (Dougherty & Natow, 2015, pp. 61–62, brackets and ellipses in original)

But changes in the political context can reverse such isomorphic pressures. Indeed, Dougherty and Natow argue that Missouri's performance funding initiative developed in part due to this over-duplication and inefficiency, and thus that performance funding can be used to encourage differentiation between public colleges and universities within a state. One way to examine such trends empirically is to consider peer institution lists: where the public colleges and universities in a given state are introspectively comparing themselves to one another, we might expect to see convergence; where they each develop unique peer lists speaking to their individual characteristics and aspirations, we might expect to see divergence.

Furthermore, there is evidence to suggest a high level of differentiation in strategic action between those institutions which have or are seeking prestige, on the one hand, and those which seek − instead of prestige − a strong reputation among the potential (often local) students they hope to enroll (Brewer et al., 2002). Among all undergraduate students, 40% attend two-year colleges (National Center for Education Statistics, 2015) and nearly three quarters begin their college careers in two-year or for-profit institutions (Deil-Amen, 2015). Viewed another way, only 18.5% of students who were high school sophomores in 2002 and subsequently enrolled in postsecondary education by 2006 first enrolled in a highly selective four-year institution[8] (Bozick et al., 2007, table 4). Colleges and universities that do not fit into the highly selective category experience different pressures and behavioral norms. A community college − or a public comprehensive college, for that matter − is unlikely to copy what Harvard or the University of Michigan are doing, except insofar as the community college needs to ensure that its credits are accepted in transfer, as the models employed by the elite sectors are not as relevant to the student bodies and institutional concerns of broader-access institutions. Such institutions do not, for instance, compete on a national scale for students, or worry about whether graduates of their non-existent Ph.D. programs will be able to secure tenure-track jobs. It may be worth contemplating how the concentration of research on higher education among researchers located in more elite universities might shape the assumptions researchers make about how prestige hierarchies and the diffusion of innovations work.

NOTES

1. Peer institution lists were collected between 2006 and 2010, with other data being collected to reflect the 2005 academic year.

2. The University of Wisconsin Madison's peer institutions were, in alphabetical order: Indiana University Bloomington, Michigan State University, Ohio State University, Purdue University, University of California Berkeley, University of California Los Angeles, University of Illinois Champaign-Urbana, University of Iowa, University of Michigan, University of Minnesota, University of Washington, University of North Carolina Chapel Hill, and University of Texas Austin.

3. The language for describing these network properties was developed in large part through studies of online (hyperlink) networks. In such networks, a network link, or hyperlink, demonstrates that the linker sees something of particular value or authority in the page s/he links to (Kleinberg, 1998). In the context of organizational networks, authority may work in a different fashion, but nodes with a high authority score remain those who are the most valued, in whatever sense, for connections. This may be because they are seen as authoritative − or it may be because other organizations compete with them for resources, or it may be for other reasons we do not have access to in a study of this kind.

4. Results on file with the author.

5. In order from lowest to highest in-degree, University of Minnesota Twin Cities, University of North Carolina Chapel Hill, University of Texas Austin, Ohio State University, University of Wisconsin Madison, University of Michigan Ann Arbor, and, at in-degree 41, University of Illinois Urbana-Champaign.

6. Carleton College, MN.

7. In order from lowest to highest out-degree, Kentucky Wesleyan College, University of the Pacific, Boston University, and, without-degree 60, the University of Missouri St. Louis.

8. "Highly selective" four-year institutions are defined here as those with "25th percentile ACT-equivalent scores of greater than 21" (Bozick, Lauff, & Wirt, 2007, p. A-13).

ACKNOWLEDGMENTS

The author thanks Elizabeth Popp Berman, Catherine Paradeise, and an anonymous reviewer for their comments on a prior draft of this paper, as well as Amanda DeLory, Christina DeSante, Lauren McGill, Tiana Pittman, and Ellen Rushman for their assistance with data collection and Michael Friedson for technical assistance. Data collection for this project was supported by NSF grant #0622299 and several Rhode Island College Faculty Research Grants.

REFERENCES

Armstrong, E. A., & Hamilton, L. T. (2013). *Paying for the party: How college maintains inequality*. Cambridge, MA: Harvard University Press.

Avery, C. N., Glickman, M. E., Hoxby, C. M., & Metrick, A. (2013). A revealed preference ranking of U.S. colleges and universities. *The Quarterly Journal of Economics, 128*(1), 425–467.

Baker, V. L., Baldwin, R. G., & Makker, S. (2012). Where are they now? Revisiting Breneman's study of liberal arts colleges. *Liberal Education, 98*(3), 48–53.

Blondel, V. D. (2011). *The Louvain method for community detection in large networks*. Louvain-la-Neuve: Université Catholique de Louvain. Retrieved from https://perso.uclouvain.be/vincent.blondel/research/louvain.html. Accessed on July 15, 2015.

Blondel, V. D., Guillaume, J.-L., Lambiotte, R., & Lefebvre, E. (2008). Fast unfolding of communities in large networks. *Journal of Statistical Mechanics, 2008*(October), P10008.

Bozick, R., Lauff, E., & Wirt, J. (2007). *Education Longitudinal Study of 2002 (ELS:2002): A first look at the initial postsecondary experiences of the high school sophomore class of 2002 (NCES 2008–308)*. Washington, DC: National Center for Education Statistics, Institute of Education Sciences, U.S. Department of Education.

Brewer, D. J., Gates, S. M., & Goldman, C. A. (2002). *In pursuit of prestige: Strategy and competition in U.S. higher education*. New Brunswick, NJ: Transaction Publishers.

Brint, S. (2013). A priori and empirical approaches to the classification of higher education institutions: The United States case. *Pensamiento Educativo. Revista de Investigación Educacional Latinoamericana, 50*(1), 96–114.

Brint, S., Proctor, K., Murphy, S. P., & Hanneman, R. A. (2012). The market model and the growth and decline of academic fields in U.S. four-year colleges and universities, 1980–2000. *Sociological Forum, 27*(2), 275–299.

Brint, S., Riddle, M., & Hanneman, R. A. (2006). Reference sets, identities, and aspirations in a complex organizational field: The case of American four-year colleges and universities. *Sociology of Education, 79*(3), 229–252.

Brint, S., Riddle, M., Turk-Bicakci, L., & Levy, C. S. (2005). From the liberal arts to the practical arts in American colleges and universities: Organizational analysis and curricular change. *The Journal of Higher Education, 76*(2), 151–180.

Burris, V. (2006). Network perspectives on the diffusion of innovation. In R. M. Spalter-Roth, N. L. Fortenberry, & B. Lovitts (Eds.), *What sociologists know about the acceptance and diffusion of innovation: The case of engineering education* (pp. 151–162). Washington, DC: American Sociological Association.

Burt, R. (1987). Social contagion and innovation: Cohesion versus structural equivalence. *American Journal of Sociology, 92*(6), 1287–1335.

Carnegie Foundation for the Advancement of Teaching. (2001). *The Carnegie classification of institutions of higher education* (2000 ed.). Menlo Park, CA: Carnegie Publications.

Cherven, K. (2015). *Mastering Gephi network visualization*. Birmingham, UK: Packt Publishing.

Dean, H. (2015). Proposal would require UNC professors to teach eight courses a year. *The Daily Tar Heel*. Retrieved from http://www.dailytarheel.com/article/2015/03/proposal-would-require-unc-professors-to-teach-eight-courses-a-year. Accessed on July 23, 2015.

Deil-Amen, R. (2015). The 'Traditional' college student: A smaller and smaller minority and its implications for diversity and access institutions. In M. W. Kirst & M. L. Stevens

(Eds.), *Remaking college: The changing ecology of higher education* (pp. 134–165). Stanford, CA: Stanford University Press.

DiMaggio, P. J., & Powell, W. W. (1983). The iron cage revisited: Institutional isomorphism and collective rationality in organizational fields. *American Sociological Review, 48*(2), 147–160.

DiMaggio, P. J., & Powell, W. W. (1991). The iron cage revisited: Institutional isomorphism and collective rationality in organizational fields. In W. W. Powell & P. J. DiMaggio (Eds.), *The new institutionalism in organizational analysis* (pp. 63–82). Chicago, IL: University of Chicago Press.

Dougherty, K. J., & Natow, R. S. (2015). *The politics of performance funding for higher education: Origins, discontinuations, and transformations.* Baltimore, MD: Johns Hopkins University Press.

Frickel, S. (2004). *Chemical consequences: Environmental mutagens, scientist activism, and the rise of genetic toxicology.* New Brunswick, NJ: Rutgers University Press.

Hanneman, R. A., & Riddle, M. (2005). *Introduction to social network methods.* Retrieved from http://faculty.ucr.edu/~hanneman/nettext/

Hashem, M. (2002). *Academic knowledge from elite closure to professional service: The rise of high-growth fields in American higher education.* Ph.D. dissertation, University of California Riverside, Riverside.

Katz, D. M., Gubler, J., Zelner, J., Bommarito, M., Provins, E., & Ingall, E. (2011). Reproduction of hierarchy? A social network analysis of the American law professoriate. *Journal of Legal Education, 61*(1), 76–103.

Kleinberg, J. M. (1998). Authoritative sources in a hyperlinked environment. Paper presented at the 9th ACM-SIAM symposium on Discrete Algorithms.

Knapp, L. G., Kelly-Reid, J. E., & Ginder, S. A. (2011). *Employees in postsecondary institutions, fall 2010, and salaries of full-time instructional staff, 2010–11.* Washington, DC: National Center for Education Statistics, U.S. Department of Education.

Knoke, D. (2011). Policy networks. In J. Scott & P. J. Carrington (Eds.), *The Sage handbook of social network analysis* (pp. 210–222). Thousand Oaks, CA: Sage.

Kraatz, M. S., & Zajac, E. J. (1996). Exploring the limits of the new institutionalism: The causes and consequences of illegitimate organizational change. *American Sociological Review, 61*(5), 812–836.

Lombardi, J. V., Craig, D. D., Capaldi, E. D., & Gater, D. S. (2002). *The top American research universities, 1999.* Gainesville, FL: TheCenter.

Lounsbury, M. (2001). Institutional sources of practice variation: Staffing college and university recycling programs. *Administrative Science Quarterly, 46*(1), 29–56.

Meyer, J. W., Ramirez, F. O., Frank, D. J., & Schofer, E. (2005). *Higher education as an institution.* Stanford, CA: Center on Democracy, Development, and the Rule of Law. Retrieved from http://iis-db.stanford.edu/pubs/21108/Meyer_No_57.pdf. Accessed on December 29, 2014.

Moody, J., & Leahey, E. (2006). Network foundations for the diffusion of innovations. In R. M. Spalter-Roth, N. L. Fortenberry, & B. Lovitts (Eds.), *What sociologists know about the acceptance and diffusion of innovation: The case of engineering education* (pp. 171–177). Washington, DC: American Sociological Association.

National Center for Education Statistics. (2013). *Digest of education statistics: 2012.* Retrieved from http://nces.ed.gov/programs/digest/d12/. Accessed on January 7, 2015.

National Center for Education Statistics. (2015). *The condition of education*. Retrieved from http://nces.ed.gov/programs/coe/. Accessed on June 2.

Newman, M. E. J. (2006). Modularity and community structure in networks. *Proceedings of the National Academy of Sciences, 103*(21), 8577–8582.

Office of Federal Student Aid. (2015). *Closed school monthly reports*. Retrieved from https://www2.ed.gov/offices/OSFAP/PEPS/closedschools.html. Accessed on July 23.

Oliver, C. (1988). The collective strategy framework: An application to competing predictions of isomorphism. *Administrative Science Quarterly, 33*(4), 543–561.

Paterlini, M. (2007). There shall be order: The legacy of Linnaeus in the age of molecular biology. *EMBO Reports, 9*(9), 814–816.

Phillips, D. J., & Zuckerman, E. W. (2001). Middle-status conformity: Theoretical restatement and empirical demonstration in two markets. *American Journal of Sociology, 107*(2), 379–429.

Porter, M. A., Onnela, J.-P., & Mucha, P. J. (2009). Communities in networks. *Notices of the American Mathematical Society, 56*(9), 1082–1097, 1164–1166.

Prescott, B. (2011). Thinking anew about institutional taxonomies. Paper presented at the Mapping Broad-Access Higher Education Convening, Stanford University.

Rawlings, C. M., & Bourgeois, M. D. (2004). The complexity of institutional niches: Credentials and organizational differentiation in a field of U.S. higher education. *Poetics, 32*(6), 411–437.

Rojas, F. (2007). *From black power to black studies: How a radical social movement became an academic discipline*. Baltimore, MD: Johns Hopkins University Press.

Rudolph, F. (1989). *Curriculum: A history of the American undergraduate course of study since 1636*. San Francisco, CA: Jossey-Bass Publishers.

Ruef, M., & Nag, M. (2011). Classifying organizational forms in the field of higher education. Paper presented at the Mapping Broad-Access Higher Education Convening, Stanford University.

Ruef, M., & Nag, M. (2015). The classification of organizational forms: Theory and application to the field of higher education. In M. W. Kirst & M. L. Stevens (Eds.), *Remaking college: The changing ecology of higher education* (pp. 84–109). Stanford, CA: Stanford University Press.

Scott, W. R. (2015). Higher education in America: Multiple field perspectives. In M. W. Kirst & M. L. Stevens (Eds.), *Remaking college: The changing ecology of higher education* (pp. 19–38). Stanford, CA: Stanford University Press.

Scott, W. R., & Biag, M. (2016). The changing ecology of U.S. higher education: An organization field perspective. In E. P. Berman & C. Paradeise (Eds.), *The university under pressure* (Vol. 40). Research in the Sociology of Organizations. Bingley, UK: Emerald Group Publishing Limited.

Smelser, N. J. (2013). *Dynamics of the contemporary university: Growth, accretion, and conflict*. Berkeley, CA: University of California Press.

Stevens, M. L. (2015). Introduction: The changing ecology of U.S. higher education. In M. W. Kirst & M. L. Stevens (Eds.), *Remaking college: The changing ecology of higher education* (pp. 1–18). Stanford, CA: Stanford University Press.

Stevens, M. L., Armstrong, E., & Arum, R. (2006). *A report to the American sociological association on the conference 'A new research agenda for the sociology of education'*. Unpublished manuscript.

Stevens, M. L., Armstrong, E. A., & Arum, R. (2008). Sieve, Incubator, Temple, Hub: Empirical and theoretical advances in the sociology of higher education. *Annual Review of Sociology, 34*, 127—152.

van der Hulst, R. C. (2011). Terrorist networks: The threat of connectivity. In J. Scott & P. J. Carrington (Eds.), *The Sage handbook of social network analysis* (pp. 256—270). Thousand Oaks, CA: Sage.

Wood, D. J. (1979). *Women's studies programs in American colleges and universities: A case of organizational innovation.* Ph.D. dissertation, Vanderbilt University, Nashville, TN.

Zemsky, R., Shaman, S., & Iannozzi, M. (1997). In search of strategic perspective: A tool for mapping the market in postsecondary education. *Change, 29*(November—December), 23—38.

APPENDIX: SUPPLEMENTAL TABLES AND FIGURES

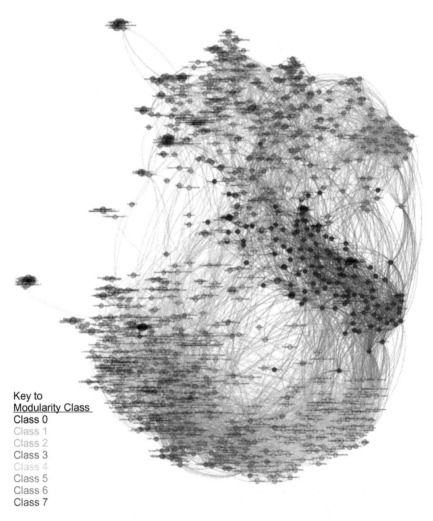

Key to
Modularity Class
Class 0
Class 1
Class 2
Class 3
Class 4
Class 5
Class 6
Class 7

Fig. A1.   Network Graph Colored by Modularity Class.

Table A1. Empirically Derived Modularity Classes and Women's Studies Offerings.

	Major Program (%)	Minor/Other Program (%)	No Program (%)
0: Private research universities	26.4	49.3	24.3
1: Less-selective private colleges I	4.6	23.4	72
2: Mostly public undergrad-focused	10.7	27.1	62.6
3: Public RII/RIII universities	26.8	59.9	13.4
4: Public RI universities	60.7	32.5	6.8
5: Selective Liberal Arts Colleges	55.1	37.2	7.7
6: Less-selective private colleges II	5.7	40.2	54.1
7: Missouri community colleges	0	0	100
Total	19.5	34.8	45.7

Table A2. Condensed 2000 Carnegie Classifications and Women's Studies Offerings.

	Major Program (%)	Minor/Other Program (%)	No Program (%)
Doctoral/Research Extensive	61.7	31.5	6.7
Doctoral/Research Intensive	26.5	41.8	31.6
Master's I	13.6	49.6	36.8
Master's II	6.8	36.5	56.8
Baccalaureate Liberal Arts	32.8	42.1	25.1
Baccalaureate General	3.7	23.4	72.9
Baccalaureate/Associate's	9.5	4.8	85.7
Associate's	3.8	5.1	91.1
Specialized	1.5	1.5	97.1
Total	19.5	34.8	45.7

Table A3.   Empirically Derived Modularity Classes and Asian American Studies Offerings.

	Major Program (%)	Minor/Other Program (%)	No Program (%)
0: Private research universities	3.4	8.8	87.8
1: Less-selective private colleges I	0.6	0.9	98.5
2: Mostly public undergrad-focused	0.3	1.2	98.5
3: Public RII/RIII universities	5.7	5.7	88.5
4: Public RI universities	12.8	11.1	76.1
5: Selective Liberal Arts Colleges	0	11.5	88.5
6: Less-selective private colleges II	0	0	100
7: Missouri community colleges	0	0	100
Total	2.5	4.0	93.6

Table A4.   Condensed 2000 Carnegie Classifications and Asian American Studies Offerings.

	Major Program (%)	Minor/Other Program (%)	No Program (%)
Doctoral/Research Extensive	13.4	12.8	73.8
Doctoral/Research Intensive	0	3.1	96.9
Master's I	2.5	3.7	93.8
Master's II	0	1.4	98.6
Baccalaureate Liberal Arts	1.1	6.6	92.3
Baccalaureate General	0	0	100
Baccalaureate/Associate's	0	0	100
Associate's	0	0	100
Specialized	1.5	0	98.5
Total	2.5	4	93.6

Table A5. Condensed 2000 Carnegie Classifications and Queer/LGBT Studies Offerings.

	Program (%)	No Program (%)
Doctoral/Research Extensive	15.4	84.6
Doctoral/Research Intensive	1	99
Master's I	1.5	98.5
Master's II	0	100
Baccalaureate Liberal Arts	5.5	94.5
Baccalaureate General	0.5	99.5
Baccalaureate/Associate's	0	100
Associate's	3.8	96.2
Specialized	1.5	98.5
Total	96.5	3.5

Table A6. Empirically Derived Modularity Classes and Queer/LGBT Studies Offerings.

	Major Program (%)	No Program (%)
0: Private research universities	4.1	95.9
1: Less-selective private colleges I	0	100
2: Mostly public undergrad-focused	1.5	98.5
3: Public RII/RIII universities	3.2	96.8
4: Public RI universities	15.4	84.6
5: Selective Liberal Arts Colleges	12.8	87.2
6: Less-selective private colleges II	0.8	99.2
7: Missouri community colleges	0	100
Total	96.5	3.5

CODES OF COMMERCE AND CODES OF CITIZENSHIP: A HISTORICAL LOOK AT STUDENTS AS CONSUMERS WITHIN US HIGHER EDUCATION

Daniel Lee Kleinman and Robert Osley-Thomas

ABSTRACT

Is the aim of the university to prepare citizens to contribute to civic and social life as well as to travel flexibly and successfully through a rapidly changing work world? Or is the purpose of higher education more narrowly to advance students' individual economic interests as they understand them? Should we think of students as citizens or consumers? Many analysts argue that, in recent years, the notion that higher education should serve to advance students' individual economic position has increasingly taken prominence over broader notions of the purpose of American higher education. In this paper, we examine whether and to what extent a shift from considering students-as-citizens to students-as-consumers has occurred in US higher education. We provide a longitudinal analysis of two separate and theoretically distinct discourse communities (Berg, 2003): higher education trustees and leaders of

The University under Pressure
Research in the Sociology of Organizations, Volume 46, 197–220
Copyright © 2016 by Emerald Group Publishing Limited
All rights of reproduction in any form reserved
ISSN: 0733-558X/doi:10.1108/S0733-558X20160000046007

*and advocates for liberal arts education. Our data suggest a highly
unsettled field in which commercial discourse as measured by the
student-as-consumer code has surely entered the US higher education
lexicon, but this code is not uncontested and the more traditional citizenship
code remains significant and viable.*

Keywords: Commercialization of higher education; higher education
as a public good; students as consumers; students as citizens

INTRODUCTION

What is higher education for? With colleges and universities under pressure
as a result of a slow-growing economy and budget crises at the state and
federal levels in the United States, politicians, university leaders, citizens,
and students are increasingly engaging in soul-searching and strategic
(re)thinking. One major divide is between those who see the role of universities as to broadly prepare students for adult life, including enabling them
to function successfully in the work world, but also providing them with
the skills and dispositions to be engaged citizens, and those who understand
the role of higher education more narrowly: to provide students with job-
ready skills. Advocates of the former see American universities as a unique
institution with multiple roles, which in addition to preparing students for
a life of engaged citizenship, also provide a space for unconstrained reflection on American society and an environment for the development of
socially relevant science and technology (see, e.g., Bok, 2007; Nussbaum,
2010). According to the latter logic, universities sell a commodity (education) much like any other good sold on the market. Here, students are consumers, whose individual interest is narrowly in workforce preparation and
whose demands educators should satisfy. Many argue that, in recent years,
the notion of higher education understood in the narrow sense has increasingly taken prominence over a broader, more socially robust notion of
American higher education (Bok, 2007; Geiger, 2004; Gumport, 2000;
Kirp, 2003; Readings, 1996; Slaughter & Rhoades, 2004; on students as
consumers in the United Kingdom see Woodall, Hiller, & Resnick, 2014).

Are we really seeing a transformation in the United States from a comprehensively oriented broadly social and civic institution to a more narrowly oriented consumer-focused one in the discursive realm? Discussions
about this supposed transformation have been hampered by the absence of
systematic empirical evidence. Focusing on one aspect of this issue, we set
out to examine whether and to what extent a shift from considering

students-as-citizens to students-as-consumers has occurred in US higher education. We do this by providing a longitudinal analysis of two separate and theoretically distinct discourse communities (Berg, 2003): higher education trustees and administrative leaders, on the one hand, and advocates of the liberal arts tradition, on the other. If a transition in recent years from an institution that aims to provide students with broad preparation to a more narrowly focused entity that meets student—consumer demands to provide them job-specific preparation has occurred, one might expect university trustees and administrators to increasingly see students as consumers and decreasingly think of them as citizens. Following a similar intuition, one might imagine that among liberal arts supporters, we would find resistance to the replacement of student-as-citizen by student-as-consumer.

To explore whether these expectations are correct, we examine discussions in these two discourse communities through an analysis of two trade publications, *Trusteeship* and *Liberal Education*.[1] We consider the period from 1960 to 2010. Our data suggest a more complex picture than we might expect. It is not a shock that we found that liberal arts advocates resist the idea that students are consumers and continue to think of students as citizens. The essential surprise in our data is that the notion of student-as-consumer has not replaced the idea of student-as-citizen among trustees and leaders in recent years as US universities have found themselves facing the pressures of state and federal budget cuts, a slowly growing economy and international competition. Trustees and university administrators do, indeed, increasingly refer to students as consumers but they also *increasingly* refer to students as citizens. Furthermore, criticism of the student as consumer label does not disappear from *Trusteeship* across our period either. In the pages that follow, we outline our empirical findings and consider their implications.

TWO CONCEPTIONS OF HIGHER EDUCATION

Perhaps since the early days of the republic, universities in the United States have been shaped by two very different notions of what higher education offers: an institution that has a broad public purpose and prepares students for a life of engaged citizenship and as an entity that prepares students to make their individual economic way and thereby aids the national economy. Although rarely seen in an ideal form, advocates of a broader notion of higher education see universities as serving the larger good of society. According to this view, universities should not reflect market demand, but should serve to supplement market weaknesses and failures. In doing so, the university should facilitate the free flow of information and provide research that can be shared by all members of society. Furthermore, from this perspective, university education is not primarily geared toward the benefit of students individually but toward the benefit of society at large (Bok, 2004; Nussbaum, 2010). Higher education develops citizen potential and human capital and fosters other legitimate pursuits of the nation-state (Gumport, 2000). In this context, when conflicts occur between the desires of individual students and the needs of society at large, the university supports what is best for the larger community. Consequently, higher education is something good for all members of society, the country's citizenry.

A more narrowly focused idea of the university is something completely different. Relying upon a corporate metaphor, advocates of this view see universities as a sector of the economy that produces and sells goods (Gumport, 2000; Kirp, 2003; Reading, 1995). Decisions about university change inevitably come down to questions of supply and demand (Gumport, 2000). Taken to its logical extreme, the university from this perspective chooses students and research projects that are most profitable. Rather than serving society at large, such universities seek to benefit individual clients, including students. Rather than serving citizens, universities serve consumers. Here, faculty members are seen as producers, research becomes a slew of products, and students are viewed as consumers.

Many have argued that the broader notion of the university in the United States has been overwhelmed by the narrower view in recent years (Bok, 2003; Geiger, 2004; Gumport, 2000; Kirp, 2003; Nussbaum, 2010; Reading, 1995; Slaughter & Rhoades, 2004). According to these analysts, universities increasingly orient to students as consumers and decreasingly think of them as citizens. Universities are no longer providing services to society at large, but are instead servicing individual consumers. Patricia Gumport, for example, suggests that, "the dominant legitimating idea of public higher education has been moving away from the idea of higher education as a social institution, and moving toward the idea of higher education as an industry" (2000, p. 70). Similarly, Martha Nussbaum suggests that "Pure models of education for economic growth are difficult to find in flourishing democracies ....However education systems all over the world are moving closer and closer to the growth model without much thought about how ill-suited it is to the goals of democracy" (2010, p. 24). Comparable concerns and arguments can be found among a wide range of other authors from former university presidents to historians and social scientists (see e.g., Bok, 2007; Geiger, 2004; Gumport, 2000; Kirp, 2003; Readings, 1996; Slaughter & Rhoades, 2004).[2]

If these authors are correct, we would expect to find a shift away from the discursive dominance of the notion of student as citizen over time as characterized in the stylized Fig. 1. As depicted in the solid black line, members of the broad US higher education community were theoretically more sympathetic to the notion of students as citizens in the 1960s and less so as we move toward the new millennium. Following this same line of anticipation, we would expect higher education community members to view students as consumers rather infrequently during the 1960s, but increasingly do so over time. In this framework, as time progresses, the notion of student as consumer overtakes the notion of student as citizen, such that those in the higher education field are more likely to refer to students as consumers in the 2000s.

This cultural shift from student-as-citizen to students-as-consumer appears to be common sense to many US higher education researchers and to many writers in such periodicals as the *Chronicle of Higher Education* (Hall, 2011) and *Inside Higher Ed* (Mora & Stern, 2013; Reed, 2013). But those who assert a transition from the dominance of the former to the prominence of the latter provide no longitudinal data to substantiate this shift. Authors who describe this trend largely rely upon case studies (Washburn, 2006), structural changes (Slaughter & Rhoades, 2004), or theoretical exposition (Gumport 2000; Nussbaum, 2010). Much of the historical work on the topic provides no specific evidence that the student-as-consumer

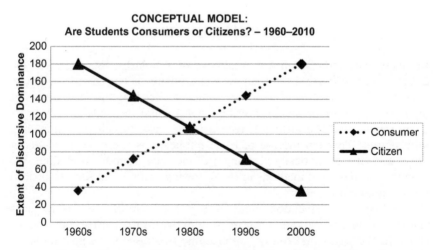

Fig. 1. Conceptual Model: Are Students Consumers or Citizens?

identity correlates with the mechanism they assert explains the growing trend toward a culture of student consumerism (see, e.g., Delucchi & Smith, 1997; Penn & Franks, 1982; Portfilio & Yu, 2006).

Beyond this, those writings on this topic have not systematically examined whether during a period in which they assert an increase in viewing students as consumers, advocates of this notion confront opposition or whether the spread of the student as consumer identity has occurred smoothly and straightforwardly. Nor have researchers considered how attitudes toward the notion of student-as-consumer might differ across different constituencies or discourse communities within the broader community of US higher education.

In the pages that follow, we take up one part of the asserted transformation of higher education in the United States from an institution with broad social purposes to an entity more narrowly focused on the needs of the immediate stakeholders (i.e., students) it serves. We explore how members of the broader university community think of students over an extended period (1960–2010) and consider whether, how, and to what extent members of the world of US higher education consider students consumers, rather than citizens. This issue is important since how we understand students' identities (citizens vs. consumers) and thus treat them is likely to reflect broader understandings of the purpose of higher education and thus shape a wide array of educational programs and practices.

RESEARCH QUESTIONS

In many ways, the empirical weakness of scholarly discussion on the asserted transition from the treatment of students as citizens to student as consumer is not surprising. How one would gather longitudinal data is not obvious. Appropriate panel surveys done at regular intervals over 50 years do not exist, and the historical record is not easy to cull for compelling information. Through the use of trade publications, we have developed a novel way of systematically gleaning attitudes and opinions over time. We describe our data and methods in the following section, but first we turn to our research questions.

The US higher education community is large and diverse and includes students, students' parents, professors, administrators, trustees, and politicians. In the pages that follow, we examine two discourse communities – components of the larger higher education world – that are likely to have very different opinions about how to think about students. We begin by looking at the one community that is most likely to demonstrate the greatest support for students as citizens: supporters of liberal arts education. Advocates of the liberal arts often speak forcefully about citizenship education, often criticize the notion of occupational training, and commonly support the notion of education for education's sake (see, e.g., Nussbaum, 2010). We would expect the liberal arts community to oppose treating education as a commodity and anticipate that they would not support the idea that students are consumers. Similarly, we expect that they would typically support the idea that students are citizens of a wider community.

We would anticipate finding the opposite set of understandings among university trustees, academic governing boards, campus chief executives, and high-level academic administrators. This is because such officials are typically most responsible for the financial stability of universities. They directly or indirectly confront the economic and related pressures their institutions face and confront students and parents concerned about getting "value for money," as student prepare for the world of work in uncertain economic times. Beyond this, trustees in US higher education institutions often come from the commercial world or interact with it regularly and thus are likely to be more amenable to notions consistent with the values central in that environment. Consequently, we would expect this discourse community to be much more supportive of the idea that students are consumers than liberal arts advocates would be and less supportive of the idea that students are citizens of a wider community.

To assess these expectations, we consider three basic questions about these two distinct discourse communities between 1960 and 2010:

- Within each discourse community, how much support is there for the notion that students are individual consumers?[3]
- Within each discourse community, how much skepticism can be found toward the notion that students are individual consumers?
- Within each discourse community, how much support is there for the notion that students should be seen as citizens of a larger society?

DATA AND METHODS

As we have noted, to explore these questions, we examined the conversations going on within two discourse communities: academic leaders, especially university trustees, on the one hand, and supporters of the liberal arts, on the other. We focused on discussions that either directly or indirectly consider the matters of whether we should think of students as consumers or as citizens. Doing so is important because the language actors use to frame practices captures the ways in which they understand their experiences and orient their behavior (Barley & Gideon, 1992; Hirsch, 1986; Kunda & Ailon-Souday, 2005). Thus, we can learn a great deal by studying the codes used by members of the academic world. As members of university and college communities go about their business, they employ various identities and metaphors that suggest how they are oriented toward the institutions of which they are a part, how they conceive of its goals, and how they envision its future. In this context, we ask whether there is an increasing trend, as some commentators argue, to view students as consumers within two different communities of American higher education.

To capture the US liberal arts community, we examined *Liberal Education*, a publication with an explicit commitment to advancing liberal arts education in the United States. *Liberal Education* is published by the American Association of Colleges and Universities (AAC&U), which is one of the oldest and largest organizations for degree-granting institutions of higher education. The AAC&U was founded in 1915 for college presidents, and there are currently more than 1,100 member institutions. Membership includes two- and four-year institutions as well as most major universities. Only accredited and degree-granting institutions are eligible for membership (http://www.aacu.org/liberaleducation/about.cfm. Accessed: May 20, 2011).

To explore the community of trustees and upper-level administrators, we examine *Trusteeship* (formerly *AGB Reports*), a publication that seeks to advance the interests of academic governing boards, campus chief executives, and high-level academic administrators. *Trusteeship* is published by the Association of Governing Boards (AGB). That organization was founded in 1921 and seeks to represent and serve the interests and needs of academic governing boards, related foundations, and campus leaders (http://agb.org/about-agb Accessed: May 20, 2011). AGB represents a similar large number of institutions (1,200), and these include a wide range of US colleges and universities and public college and university foundation boards.

We digitized all available issues of both periodicals from 1960 until 2010. We then searched our complete digital files for articles in which the terms "student," "consumer," and/or "citizen" were used. Our search produced 331 articles in which the word "consumer" was used in relationship to student and 591 that used the term "citizen." We read each of these articles and undertook several operations. First, taking the article as our unit of analysis, we undertook simple counts, considering how often each of our terms or codes is used and how this changes over time. Second, we assessed the use of the student-as-consumer code utilizing a three-point legitimacy scale: legitimate, uncertain, illegitimate.[4] The idea here was to capture the extent to which authors think that it is acceptable to view students as consumers. Such an assessment is relevant since many commentators essentially assert that calling students consumers is increasingly acceptable.

Our approach to the matter of legitimacy was inspired by critical discourse analysis (see Fairclough, 2003; Quinn, 2012) and by Latour and Woolgar's (1979) exploration of the publication careers of scientific facts. The category *legitimate* includes articles that identify students as consumers in an affirmative or uncritical matter. Such articles explicitly point to the virtues of calling students consumers, or they take for granted the appropriateness of doing so (we provide specific examples in the body of the analysis). We use the *uncertain* category when authors express skepticism or circumspection about a given identity (i.e., student, citizen, and consumer). We placed articles in the *illegitimate* category when an author explicitly challenges the equation of students and consumers, or asserts that doing so is inappropriate, bad, or problematic in a higher education context.

We also assessed whether the notion of student-as-consumer was utilized in qualified or unqualified way. *Qualified* uses are defined as those cases where authors must clarify who the consumers are. *Unqualified* uses simply employ the identity consumer without clarifying that the author is talking about students. This measure gives us some purchase on the extent to which the notion of student-as-consumer is taken for granted among authors and whether authors assume that characterizing students as consumers will make sense to readers. An increase in the unqualified use of student-as-consumer over time would suggest a change in the discursive terrain and how we think about students.

We apply these two analytic scales *only* to the notion of student-as-consumer because contemporary debates about whether students are citizens or consumers never question the legitimacy of treating students as citizens. In comparing the two, the question is whether consumer has become an increasingly prominent and legitimate way of characterizing students as against citizens. Authors may speak about students as citizens less frequently, but they never suggest that it is inappropriate to think of students as citizens.

Throughout our presentation and analysis of our data, we rely primarily on descriptive statistics. To flesh out the analysis, where appropriate, we undertake a small amount of qualitative textual analysis and provide significance tests. Broadly speaking, our main aim is to explore whether the notion of student as consumer has overtaken the notion of student as citizen within these two distinct discourse communities in the United States. To nuance the analysis, we explore whether authors decreasingly criticize the notion of student as consumer and ask whether authors are increasingly comfortable with using this identity.

ANALYSIS

Figs. 2 and 3 summarize our findings. The key question of this paper is whether the characterization of students as consumers is increasingly pervasive and legitimate among the authors of our two periodicals and has overtaken the description of students as citizens, between 1960 and 2010. Such a change would suggest that the role of higher education has become less consistent with the notion of universities as serving a broader social or civic purpose over our period. Fig. 2 is for *Liberal Education* only and demonstrates the number of articles employing the student as consumer using diamonds and dots and student as citizen using triangles and a dashed line. Those articles demonstrating a hesitation about the notion of student as consumer or suggesting explicit opposition to the idea are marked with a solid line punctuated with squares.

We discuss these findings in greater detail below but briefly speaking, this figure shows that the notion of consumer has not overtaken the notion of student as citizen within *Liberal Education*. Authors writing in this trade

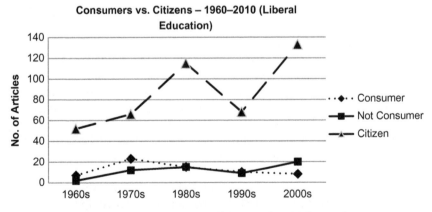

Fig. 2. Consumer versus Citizen (*Liberal Education*).

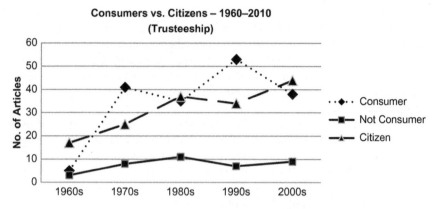

Fig. 3. Consumer versus Citizen (*Trusteeship*).

journal clearly refer to students as citizens more often than they do consumers across the 50-year period from 1960 through 2010. Also, authors criticize the notion of student as consumer roughly as frequently as they use it.

Fig. 3 provides the same data for *Trusteeship (AGB Reports)*. Briefly, here, we see that authors' writings in this periodical use the competing identities of citizen and consumer with relatively similar frequency. This finding suggests that the notion of student as consumer has not replaced the idea of student as citizen among the writers and readers of *Trusteeship*. Criticism of student as consumer label also does not disappear from *Trusteeship*, but the positive use of consumer occurs with more frequency than the occurrence of criticism. We explore these patterns in more detail below.

Student-as-Consumer: Positive Uses

In our more detailed analysis, we first consider the legitimate uses of the student-as-consumer code in our two periodicals. Here, we count articles in which authors identify students as consumers in an affirmative or uncritical manner. Take, for example, the following case from 2003 in *Trusteeship*:

> the bottom line is that it's hard to identify an industry other than higher education that has as many satisfied customers but is as reluctant to talk about outcomes in concrete terms. (Ward & Hartle, 2003, p. 11)

In this case, the author clearly refers to students as consumers. During a period when the notion of student-as-consumer is increasingly seen as legitimate, one would expect to find an increasing number of quotations like this in our periodicals. Of course, given that our two trade papers speak to different discourse communities, there would likely be variation across them. We might expect a less dramatic increase in the use of the student-as-consumer code in *Liberal Education* and perhaps more resistance than we would imagine in *Trusteeship*. Our data, however, suggest a more complicated situation.

Table 1 shows the number of positive instances of student as consumer per decade, the average number of articles per decade, and the percentage of articles per decade that invoked the student as consumer identity. For example, in the 1970s, 4.42% of articles in *Liberal Education* invoke the notion of student as consumer. This is in contrast to the frequency found in the 2000s when roughly 2.22% of articles did so.

With this table we can see that there is not a consistent increase in the characterization of students as consumers among authors writing in *Liberal Education* between 1970 and 2010. In fact, from 1970 forward the general trend is decline. Compared to the 1960s, in the decades following, authors in *Trusteeship* refer to students as consumer with greater frequency. That said, we do not see an even and linear increase. Instead, students are referred to as consumers most frequently during the 1970s and 1990s.[5] Finally, as we discuss in a subsequent section, the notion of student as consumer never overtakes the idea of student as citizen for either publication (compare Tables 1 and 2). In contrast to the assertions of many commentators, Table 1 does not suggest a simple move in public discussion away from treating higher education as playing a broad social and civic role and

Table 1.   Positive Uses of Student-as-Consumer by Decade.

	1960s	1970s	1980s	1990s	2000s
Liberal Education					
Raw counts	7	23	15	10	8
Average articles per decade	550	520	460	490	360
% of total # of articles[a]	1.27	4.42	3.26	2.04	2.22
AGB Reports					
Raw counts	5	41	35	53	38
Average articles per decade	270	430	640	690	850
% of total # of articles	1.85	9.53	5.47	7.68	4.47

[a]To calculate this metric, we first took three years of journal articles for each decade and averaged these three years. We then spread this average across the decade, and then used this average as the baseline of possible opportunities per decade to call students consumers, citizens, etc.

Table 2. Student-as-Citizen.

Citizen	1960s	1970s	1980s	1990s	2000s
Liberal Education					
Raw counts	52	66	115	68	133
Average articles per decade	550	520	460	490	360
% of total # of articles	9.5	12.7	25.0	13.9	36.9
AGB Reports					
Raw counts	17	25	37	34	44
Average articles per decade	270	430	640	690	850
% of total # of articles	6.3	5.8	5.8	4.9	5.2

toward students as consumers. What the table seems to point to is a field that is not homogeneous and is rather unsettled.

Student as Citizen

Next, we look at cases where authors refer to students as citizens. In doing so, we found articles that asked questions such as: "Is education to be primarily for citizenship or primarily for a career? Should it primarily introduce societal values and seek to expand social vision, or should it focus centrally on the development of skills and specific competencies (Joseph, 1982, p. 323)?" Similarly, we found that articles that spoke specifically to the idea that education is *about* citizenship preparation. Thus, one author in *Liberal Education* said:

> Since Thomas Jefferson, it has been central to the American experiment that education should serve as the means for preparing citizens for democratic participation. As we undertake the periodic process of rethinking the skills and knowledge we believe important for all undergraduates, we need to remind ourselves of the connection between the purposes of education and our democratic aspirations. (Hiley, 1996, p. 20)

Again, a perusing of news outlets such as *The Chronicle of Higher Education* and *Inside Higher Ed* suggests a commonsensical belief that in recent years US universities have moved away from serving broad social and civic purposes, and emblematic of this change students are increasingly viewed as consumers and less often as citizens. Interestingly, contrary to what one might expect if a discourse suggesting higher education oriented toward meeting the narrow employment needs of students were becoming increasingly taken for granted and dominant in the two discourse communities we are investigating, we see that *Trusteeship* authors use the citizenship identity at roughly the same rate through the years. Authors in *Liberal Education increasingly* use the student-as-citizen code across the full length of our period, with nearly 37% of articles in the 2000s invoking this identity (see Table 2).

Change within *Liberal Education* shows a statistically significant increase over time ($b = 0.005$; $p = 0.00$).[6] This is interesting in light of the fact that changes in the positive use of student-as-consumer were not statistically significant. While we have some evidence to suggest that authors increasingly orient to students as citizens, we have no evidence to suggest that they increasingly think of them as consumers. Certainly, at a minimum, the growing prevalence of the student-as-citizen code in both of our periodicals suggests that the discursive landscape in higher education has not been entirely overtaken by the language of higher education as narrowly focused on providing economic advantage to students. Students remain citizens even among those who lead US higher education and who are responsible for their institutions' financial well-being.

Resistance to Student as Consumer

In this section, we consider instances of articles that argue against the characterization of students as consumers or clearly indicate a negative reaction to use of this metaphor. Throughout the period covered by this paper, writers in each periodical pushback against the student-as-consumer formulation, again suggesting that the move to a narrowly oriented university in the United States is not broadly taken for granted. Thus, for example, an author writing in *Liberal Education* in 1964 contends that consumer is an inappropriate label for students:

> the slogan "the customer is always right" is absolutely inapplicable to the situation. Undergrads are not customers and colleges are not merchant markets. The student does not bring to the choice of an academic program the experience that guides a mature purchaser of material goods. The college catalog can give no precise analysis of its offerings and can furnish no guarantees. Education is not a commodity that can be measured out and bought by the pound or the yard. (Distler, 1964, p. 114)

A less direct rejection of the student-as-consumer code is presented by an author writing in the same periodical a decade later. According to Joseph McDermott, "We are afflicted with an educational consumerism which too often equates a credential or certificate with human worth and derogates the value of experience" (1975, p. 269).

It is clear that challenges to the student-as-consumer code never disappear in our periodicals. To the contrary, in *Liberal Education*, we see that the proportion of negative or critical uses of the student-as-consumer (as compared to affirmative instances) *increases* over time with a small reduction in the 1990s. When we look across decades, the ratio of positive to negative orientations toward student-as-consumer reverses (see Table 3). In the 1970s, 66% of *Liberal Education* authors invoking the identity consumer demonstrate a positive orientation toward this characterization, while 26% demonstrated a clearly negative orientation. By the 2000s, 29% of authors invoking the identity consumer demonstrate a positive orientation, while 61% demonstrated a negative orientation. When we compare trends across the entire period, we see a statistically significant increase in cases of negative orientation toward student-as-consumer ($b = 0.01$; $p = 0.001$).[7] This increase is admittedly small; however, it is interesting in light of the fact that we did not find a statistically significant increase in the *positive* use of student as consumer. In many ways, this is the opposite of what we would expect. Although we certainly would expect advocates of the liberal arts to continue to view students as citizens, if, as commentators assert, there has been a widespread increase in understanding students as consumers in higher education in general, we would expect this trend to affect liberal arts advocates as well as those less obviously committed to a broad social and civic orientation to higher education, and we might imagine that their opposition to the student-as-consumer formulation would decline. Here, we actually see the reverse.

Trusteeship has fewer instances of critical engagement with the student-as-consumer code, as we would expect given the audience for whom the periodical is written (see Table 4). The proportion of negative to positive orientations is fairly constant throughout the period of our study, except for in the 1980s, where we see that 20% of authors in *Trusteeship* invoking

Table 3.   Resistance to the Student-as-Consumer Code in *Liberal Education.*

Liberal Education	1960s	1970s	1980s	1990s	2000s
Legitimate	7	23	15	10	8
% Legitimate	78	66	50	53	29
Uncertain	1	3	2	3	3
% Uncertain	11	9	7	16	11
Illegitimate	1	9	13	6	17
% Illegitimate	11	26	43	32	61

Table 4.   Resistance to the Student-as-Consumer Code in *Trusteeship*.

AGB Reports	1960s	1970s	1980s	1990s	2000s
Legitimate	5	41	35	53	38
% Legitimate	63	84	76	88	81
Uncertain	2	7	2	4	5
% Uncertain	25	14	4	7	11
Illegitimate	1	1	9	3	4
% Illegitimate	13	2	20	5	9

student-as-consumer code demonstrate a negative orientation to this characterization. This jump might be explained by any of a number of factors, including a broadly negative reaction to neoliberalism (see, e.g., Portfilio & Yu, 2006; Readings, 1996, p. 11) or more narrowly to the marketing practices of institutions of higher education (see, e.g., Kirp, 2003; Slaughter & Rhoades, 2004). However, the numbers are too small to allow us to make any definitive causal claims. What we can certainly say is that while we do not have evidence of an increase in opposition to the student-as-consumer identity over time in *Trusteeship*, neither does opposition entirely disappear. And this is the periodical that we take to represent the discourse community most likely to embody a cultural transformation of higher education from an environment for citizenship preparation to a commodity for purchase by student consumers.

When a discourse becomes common sense, opposition declines. Our data in this case suggest a *contested field*. One might argue that the limited number of cases of criticism in *Trusteeship* means that this opposition is essentially marginalized and that for most authors, the student-as-consumer identity is common sense. But one cannot make this argument for *Liberal Education* where the rate of criticism of the student-as-consumer code has increased over time.

Qualify versus Unqualified

While our data suggest that the notion of student as consumer has not overtaken the notion of student as citizen, it is possible that the notion of student as consumer has become such a common part of the higher education landscape that authors are quite comfortable using it, and readers are not necessarily confused when they see it in print. One way to gauge such a change is to track whether authors in *Trusteeship* and *Liberal Education* employ qualification when identifying students as consumers. When a discourse or an identity is new, confusing, or contested, authors will often use qualifying terms to clarify what they are saying. In these cases, authors make a point to use clear and specific language. In effect, the prevalence of qualified uses suggests that an identity or discourse is less than straightforward and not a matter of common sense. On the other hand, when a discourse becomes substantially dominant and taken for granted, authors have little need to clarify what they are saying. In this situation, the identity in question is so widespread, common sense, and so well established that authors can be certain their audiences will know what they are describing. Here, we would expect the prevalence of unqualified uses, a condition that suggests that a given identity is clear and straightforward.

We define qualified uses of the student-as-consumer code as those in which the author must clarify who the consumers are. In other words, authors make a point to specify that they are talking about students, when they invoke the term "consumer." Thus, rather than, for example, saying "Consumers deserve good value for their tuition dollars," an author might say, "Student consumers deserve good value for their tuition dollars." Other qualifications might include "educational consumer" and "consumer (student)." In 1975, one author writing in *Liberal Education* deployed clearly qualified usage: "our colleges and universities, designed as market-places for ideas, have been reluctant to give their customers, the students, a realistic range of options. Students are thus forced to choose their priorities from a list of options that does not include all rational choices" (Veigel, 1975, p. 460). By contrast, an author writing in *Trusteeship* in 2003 used consumer in an unqualified fashion, commenting that "it's hard to identify an industry other than higher education that has as many satisfied consumers" (Ward & Hartle, 2003). Here, the authors suggest that higher education is just one of many consumer-oriented industries.

We examined the difference between qualified and unqualified usages in all cases where the student-as-consumer code was used affirmatively (see Table 5). Our results suggest that qualified use of student-as-consumer language has slowly declined relative to unqualified uses among those authors

Table 5. Qualified and Unqualified Uses of Student-as-Consumer.

	1970	1980	1990	2000
Unqualified	20	24	26	22
Qualified	20	14	7	5

who have a positive orientation toward this identity. This is true across both periodicals.

This table seems to suggest that those authors who have a positive orientation toward students-as-consumers feel less reason over time to clarify that they are talking about students when they use the term consumer. Since not all readers of articles using the term consumer as a substitute for student take for granted the equation of student and consumer, authors of these pieces must be able to assume that readers will at least know who the authors are talking about. There is, thus, some evidence, albeit not unambiguous given what we reported earlier in the paper, that the equation of student with consumer is becoming common sense over time. Or put less strongly, the authors with a positive orientation to the idea of students as consumers are increasingly using taken for granted rhetoric (or language that naturalizes their position). Thus, while it may not be naturalized or common sense among *all* writers in the field, the proponents see it as such, and increasingly see no reason to qualify their usage.

CONCLUSIONS

Many authors and activists in the United States worry that in the face of international economic competition, slower national economic growth, and fiscal constraints at state and national levels, higher education is increasingly understood to have the narrow role of preparing students for employment rather than having the broader purpose of setting the stage for students' lifelong civic engagement and learning capacities and that the array of involved stakeholders increasingly view students as consumers, not citizens. According to this analysis, the culture of colleges and universities in the United States is becoming isomorphic with those of the market and for-profit industry (see, e.g., Kirp, 2003; Tuchman, 2009). In this paper, we have sought to examine the extent to which a transition from thinking of students as citizens to understanding them as consumers has actually occurred within two distinct and central discourse communities within American higher education.

We examined two trade publications between 1960 and 2010 and asked whether support for the notion of student as consumer has increased, whether support for the idea of student as citizen has decreased, and whether criticism of students as consumers has decreased. Additionally, with the analysis of qualified versus unqualified statements, we asked whether supporters of the concept of students as consumers are more comfortable employing this identity for university students than they might have been in earlier periods. The existing scholarly and advocacy literatures seem to take for granted that the answer to these questions is "yes." Writers of this work are correct on the matter of qualified versus unqualified statements. Supporters of the idea that students are consumers do increasingly identify students as consumers with unqualified statements, a pattern which suggests that this identity is more familiar to both authors and readers.

The data become more complicated with our other measures, however. What we see is a highly unsettled field in which commercial discourse as measured by the student-as-consumer code has surely entered the US higher education lexicon, but this code is not uncontested and the more traditional citizenship code remains significant and viable. More specifically, first, in *Trusteeship*, we see that authors decreased their criticism and increased their use of the identity consumer over time. Surprisingly though, this increase was followed by an increased use of the notion of student as citizen, suggesting the idea of higher education as serving broad social and civic purposes has not disappeared from discussion. At the same time, the growing use of the unqualified form of the student-as-consumer code also suggests, at least among the authors in our periodicals, a move toward an orientation of viewing students as consumers and toward the commercialization of academic discourse becoming commonsensical. On the other hand, we see evidence of pushback against treating students as consumers with statistically significant increases in criticism of the student-as-consumer code and in statistically significant increases in the use of the student-as-citizen code. In sum, we appear to be at a moment of contest, not common sense and dominance.

Such findings lend support to an understanding of US university culture that highlights contradictions, hybrid logics, and the coexistence of opposing norms (Kleinman & Vallas, 2001; Kleinman & Osley-Thomas, 2014; Vallas & Kleinman, 2008). When it comes to the matter of student as consumer, we do not observe one culture replacing another. Instead, both identities persist side-by-side in an environment of contradictory coexistence. Conflicting pressures on the university appear to sustain this contradiction. US society places two conflicting demands on students and universities. On one hand, society asks universities to produce an educated populace prepared for positive social and citizenship engagement. On the other hand, society expects students to derive individual advantage from their education. Such conflicting demands make the identity of university students unstable and, consequently, stabilizes the coexistence of a citizen and a consumer understanding of students.

One thing our data do not allow us to explore is the factors that explain the rise and fall in the pervasiveness and legitimacy (see Colyvas & Jonsson, 2011) of the student-as-consumer and student-as-citizen identities. There is a substantial literature that provides speculation on these factors, but none of the work is grounded in rigorous empirical analysis and virtually all of it restricts its claims to the decade in which the given author is writing or about which she is speaking. Some authors writing in and/or about the 1960s and 1970s suggest the rise of the consumer movement played an important role in the rise in use and legitimacy of viewing students as consumers (see, e.g., Penn & Franks, 1982, p. 28, 29; Stark, 1976, p. 2; Stein, 1980, p. 8, 9). Elsewhere we have dissected this claim (Kleinman & Osley-Thomas, 2014), and it is fair to say that some of the rise in the legitimate use of the code student-as-consumer during this period is explained by the growing prominence of the consumer movement. Speaking of the 1980s and 1990s, many authors stress the spread of neoliberalism as an explanation for the rise in treatment of students as consumers (see, e.g., Portfilio & Yu, 2006). Why exactly a move away from government regulation and calls for increased entrepreneurialism and unregulated markets would prompt institutions of higher education and those attending them to increasingly emphasize the idea that students are consumers is not immediately obvious, and furthermore, the unevenness in our data suggests that this explanation is likely too simple. Of course, state and federal fiscal crises from the 1980s forward associated with massive tax cuts and the increased costs of entitlement programs and the related declines in state support for higher education have made universities more vulnerable to student demand, and this may conceivably have prompted some in higher education to view and respond to students as consumers, but, again, given the unevenness we see in our data, this cannot possibly be the entire story.

Certainly, without a better grasp of what to date has explained the rise and fall in the pervasiveness and legitimacy of our two identities, it is difficult to say with certainty what the future is likely to hold. In an increasingly commercialized culture, one can certainly imagine a time when the term student remains, but all users know it means consumer. Equally, one can imagine an era when the use of the student-as-citizen code plays an increasing part in discussions about the US university, but the term seems quaint and anachronistic in the face of larger changes in the culture and practices of higher education. Alternatively, the substantial pushback of social movements of various stripes and perhaps even data about the relationship between an increasingly narrowly instrumentally focused system of higher education and the negative experiences of college graduates could lead to a strengthening of a university culture in which the notion of students-as-citizens and all that goes with this orientation challenges the student-as-consumer identity.

Of course, our findings must be treated with some caution, since they only capture a limited swath of the US higher education landscape, and it is certainly possible to move beyond the two discourse communities on which we have focused. Still, our tentative findings of uncertainty and instability suggest the value of ongoing analysis to explore the extent and nature of change that may be underway. For those of us who wish to preserve a broadly socially- and civic-oriented realm for US higher education, we must understand what is happening, as we seek to develop successful strategies of resistance and affirmative plans for moving forward.

NOTES

1. A discourse community is simply any group of people with loosely shared roles, objectives and language (Berg, 2003). Although liberal arts advocates and university trustees share many values we think it is reasonable to assume that they also at times have differing goals, assumptions, and language.

2. Authors cite a variety of factors shaping the supposed rise of the equation of students and consumers. Among other things, they note that universities have begun to raise tuition, the federal government has shifted funding from universities to students, and neoliberalism has spread. Although we do not have space to go into these factors in greater detail, the following list summarizes the multiple factors authors have cited to explain the spread of the private goods university and rise of student as consumer identity:

> *Social Movements:* The Consumer Movement of the 1970s challenges universities (Penn & Franks, 1982; Stark, 1976; Stein, 1980).
> *Demographic changes:* Declining Enrollment growth of the 1970s (Geiger, 2004; Hartman, 1972, p. 246).
> *Government changes:* The federal government shifted higher education funding to students in 1972 (Slaughter & Rhoades, 2004, p. 35). The federal government also began to privilege loans over grants (Slaughter & Rhoades, 2004, p. 22).
> *University Decisions:* Business management practices entered the university in the early 1980s (Keller, 1983). Universities begin marketing to students in the late 1970s (Kirp, 2003; Slaughter & Rhoades, 2004). Universities begin raising tuition (Slaughter & Rhoades, 2004, p. 42) and using Total Quality Management (Schwartzman, 1995; Tuchman, 2009).

Broad Economic and Social Shifts: Neoliberalism and Globalization (Portfilio &
Yu, 2006; Readings, 1996, p. 11).

3. We treat the words "customer" and "consumer" as equivalent.

4. Important distinctions exist within the legitimate category and within the illegitimate category. Our original coding scheme reflected these distinctions and had
five categories instead of three. Thus, on the legitimacy side, for example, we distinguished between cases where authors called student consumers in a way that suggested
that the identity was common sense both to the author and the reader and where
authors explicitly advocated for the identity, suggesting that student-as-consumer was
legitimate to the author but not necessarily to the audience. We ultimately decided to
collapse these distinctions creating one legitimacy category. There were simply too few
cases to use these distinctions meaningfully.

5. The story of the student-as-consumer code is somewhat more complicated
than it would appear on the surface. It turns out that roughly one-quarter of all
uses of the student-as-consumer code in the 1970s are not what we might term standard business uses, but deploy the code in a way consistent with the rhetoric of the
US consumer movement of the time. Still, we would suggest that these uses of student-as-consumer are consistent with the more standard business uses and not consistent with the notion of student-as-citizen. This is because the use of consumer
movement flavored version of the student-as consumer code like other uses of the
code involves an incursion of commercial values into the university. Indeed, the
consumer movement typically accepted market logics and principles. For more on
this matter, see Kleinman and Osley-Thomas (2014).

6. To examine the relationship between time and uses of student as consumer, we
set student as consumer as the dependent variable. We calculated a simple regression equation with the independent variable of time set here as year of publication.

7. For this analysis, the number of negative uses of student as consumer was set
as the dependent variable. This was regressed over the independent variable of publication year.

ACKNOWLEDGMENTS

The authors would like to thank an anonymous reviewer and Elizabeth
Popp Berman, Catherine Paradeise, Clifton Conrad, Sara Goldrick-Rab,
Steve Hoffman, Michael Olneck, and Steve Vallas for their helpful sugges-
tions as we sought to strengthen this paper. Funding supporting this endea-
vor comes from the US National Science Foundation (SES-1026516), the
National Research Foundation of Korea (grant NRF-2013S1A3A2053087),
and the Wisconsin Alumni Research Foundation (through the Office of the
Vice Chancellor for Research and Graduate Education at the University of
Wisconsin-Madison). The opinions expressed in this paper are those of the
authors.

REFERENCES

Barley, S. R., & Gideon, K. (1992). Design and devotion: Surges of rational and normative ideologies of control in managerial discourse. *Administrative Science Quarterly, 47*, 363–399.

Berg, E. (2003). Discourse community. *ELT Journal, 57*(4), 398–400.

Bok, D. (2003). Perils of the entrepreneurial university. *Trusteeship, 11*(3), 9.

Bok, D. (2004). *Universities and the marketplace: The commercialization of higher education.* Princeton, NJ: Princeton University Press.

Bok, D. (2007). *Our underachieving colleges: A candid look at how much students learn and why they should be learning more.* Princeton, NJ: Princeton University Press.

Colyvas, J. A., & Jonsson, S. (2011). Ubiquity and legitimacy: Disentangling diffusion and institutionalization. *Sociological Theory, 29*, 27–53.

Delucchi, M., & Smith, W. L. (1997). A postmodern explanation of student consumerism in higher education. *Teaching Sociology, 25*(4), 322–327.

Distler, T. (1964). Report of the executive director. *Liberal Education, 50*, 112–118.

Fairclough, N. (2003). *Analysing discourse: Textual analysis for social research.* London: Routledge.

Geiger, R. (2004). *Knowledge and money: Research universities and the paradox of the marketplace.* Redwood City, CA: Stanford University Press.

Gumport, P. J. (2000). Academic restructuring: Organizational change and institutional imperatives. *Higher Education, 39*(1), 67–91.

Hall, B. (2011). Educating our 'customers'. Chronicle of Higher Education, March 30

Hartman, R. (1972). An alternative view. *AGB Reports, 14*, 18.

Hiley, D. (1996). The democratic purposes of general education. *Liberal Education, 82*, 20.

Hirsch, P. (1986). From ambushes to golden parachutes: Corporate takeovers as an instance of cultural framing and institutional integration. *American Journal of Sociology, 91*, 800–837.

Joseph, J. (1982). Education for citizenship: Excellence, equity, and employment. *Liberal Education, 68*, 323.

Keller, G. (1983). *Academic strategy: The management revolution in American higher education.* Baltimore, MD: Johns Hopkins University Press.

Kirp, D. L. (2003). *Shakespeare, Einstein, and the bottom line: The marketing of higher education.* Cambridge, MA: Harvard University Press.

Kleinman, D. L., & Osley-Thomas, R. (2014). Uneven commercialization: Contradiction and conflict in the identity and practices of American universities. *Minerva, 52*, 1–26.

Kleinman, D. L., & Vallas, S. P. (2001). Science, capitalism, and the rise of the 'knowledge worker: The changing structure of knowledge production in the United States. *Theory and Society, 30*, 451–492.

Kunda, G., & Ailon-Souday, G. (2005). Managers, markets and ideologies: Design and devotion revisited. In S. Ackroyd, R. Batt, P. Thompson, & P. S. Tolbert (Eds.), *The Oxford handbook of work and organization* (pp. 200–219). New York, NY: Oxford.

Latour, B., & Woolgar, S. (1979). *Laboratory life: The social construction of scientific facts.* Beverly Hills, CA: Sage Publications.

Mora, A., & Stern, A. M. (2013). Corporate values. *Inside Higher Ed*, November 25.

Nussbaum, M. C. (2010). *Not for profit: Why democracy needs the humanities.* Princeton, NJ: Princeton University Press.

Penn, J. R., & Franks, R. G. (1982). Student consumerism in an era of conservative politics. *NASPA Journal, 19*(3), 28–37.

Portfilio, B. J., & Yu, T. (2006). 'Student as consumer': A critical narrative of the commercialization of teacher education. *Journal for Critical Education Policy Studies, 4*, 1.

Quinn, L. (2012). Understanding resistance: An analysis of discourse in academic staff development. *Studies in Higher Education, 37*, 69–83.

Readings, B. (1996). *The university in ruins.* Cambridge, MA: Harvard University Press.

Reed, M. (2013). Who's the customer? *Inside Higher Ed*, October 16.

Schwartzman, R. (1995). Are students consumers? The metaphoric mismatch between management and education. *Education, 116*, 215–222.

Slaughter, S., & Rhoades, G. (2004). *Academic capitalism and the new economy: Markets, state, and higher education.* Baltimore, MD: Johns Hopkins University Press.

Stark, J. (1976). The emerging consumer movement in education. *New Directions in Higher Education, 1976*(13), 1–8.

Stein, R. H. (1980). The consumer movement in higher education: Past, present and future. *NASPA Journal, 18*, 8–14.

Tuchman, G. (2009). *Wannabe U: Inside the corporate university.* Chicago, IL: University of Chicago Press.

Vallas, S. P., & Kleinman, D. L. (2008). Contradiction, convergence, and the knowledge economy: The co-evolution of academic and commercial biotechnology. *Socio-Economic Review, 6*, 283–311.

Veigel, J. (1975). An interdisciplinary environmental program for undergraduates. *Liberal Education, 62*, 460.

Ward, D., & Hartle, T. (2003). The trouble with measuring quality. *Trusteeship, 11*, 1.

Washburn, J. (2006). *University, Inc.: The corporate corruption of higher education.* New York, NY: Basic Books.

Woodall, T., Hiller, A., & Resnick, S. (2014). Making sense of higher education: Students as consumers and the value of the university experience. *Studies in Higher Education, 39*, 48–67.

PART III
IMPACTS ON THE ORGANIZATION

THE CHANGING FINANCES OF PUBLIC HIGHER EDUCATION ORGANIZATIONS: DIVERSITY, CHANGE, AND DISCONTINUITY

Sondra N. Barringer

ABSTRACT

The environment surrounding U.S. higher education has changed sub-stantially over the past 40 years. However, we have a limited understand-ing of what these changes mean for the higher education organizations (HEOs) that occupy this organizational field. In this paper, I use descriptive statistics and multilevel latent class analysis (MLCA) to analyze the financial behaviors of public four-year HEOs from 1986 to 2010 to evaluate how HEOs adapt financially to their changing environ-ments. I advance the current conceptual and empirical understanding of public HEO behaviors by evaluating how public HEOs utilize combina-tions of revenue and spending streams to accomplish their mission and the extent to which the revenues and spending patterns of these institu-tions are related. Descriptive results confirm the shift away from state funding toward tuition revenues and the relative stability in spending patterns. MLCA results, which allow for the investigation of how

The University under Pressure
Research in the Sociology of Organizations, Volume 46, 223–263
Copyright © 2016 by Emerald Group Publishing Limited
All rights of reproduction in any form reserved
ISSN: 0733-558X/doi:10.1108/S0733-558X20160000046008

combinations of revenue and spending streams work together, indicate that public HEOs are changing the combinations of revenues they rely on in different ways, revealing multiple specific pathways for how public HEOs adapt to their changing environments. The spending profiles, in contrast, remain stable with only a few HEOs changing their profile over time. I argue that the loose coupling between revenues and spending and discontinuity in their patterns of change over time suggests that public HEOs are able to establish a buffer between their environment and spending or activities that allows them to continue engaging in the same broad set of activities despite environmental changes.

Keywords: Higher education organizations; higher education finance; organizational change; multilevel latent class analysis

INTRODUCTION

The environment surrounding higher education organizations (HEOs) in the United States has changed substantially over the last 40 years. State funding has declined (Rizzo, 2006) and the line between public and private nonprofit HEOs has blurred (Gumport & Snydman, 2006; Morphew & Eckel, 2009). The boundary between industry and HEOs is also increasingly hazy as these institutions commercialize research and other knowledge activities (Just & Huffman, 2009; Mathies & Slaughter, 2013; Smith, 2000). Competition has increased for a variety of resources as state funding has declined, the number of for-profit institutions has grown, and the number of schools seeking external research funding has grown (Bennett, Lucchesi, & Vedder, 2010; Geiger, 2004a; Kaplan, 2009; Weisbrod, Ballou, & Asch, 2008). There is also pressure to maintain and increase prestige which only continues to grow as ranking metrics proliferate (Cantwell & Taylor, 2013) and which, in combination with the changes in the nature of federal financial aid, has resulted in more market like relationships with undergraduate students (Geiger, 2004b; McPherson & Schapiro, 1998). Changes in the laws and norms governing university research (e.g., Berman, 2012; Powell & Smith, 1998) have also altered the nature of university research and knowledge production (Geiger, 2004a; Slaughter & Rhoades, 2004). Furthermore, there have been substantial changes in the enrollments at HEOs including, but not limited to, changes in the attendance status and demographic characteristics of the student population (Morphew, 2009).

A substantial body of work has looked at how these changes are affecting the stakeholders of HEOs including students, faculty, and staff (e.g., Bastedo & Gumport, 2003; Berman & Stivers, 2016; Schuster & Finkelstein, 2006). However, research on how the HEOs themselves are being affected by and responding to, these changes has been limited (Berman & Stivers, 2016). There has been some research on the changing governance, research, and knowledge production practices of HEOs, (e.g., Barringer & Slaughter, 2016; Just & Huffman, 2009; Popp Berman, 2008; Slaughter, Thomas, Johnson, & Barringer, 2014; Taylor, Cantwell, & Slaughter, 2013) but the majority has focused on the consequences of environmental changes for stakeholders. Despite the fact that many of these changes are financial in nature (e.g., declining state support and increased competition for these and other resource streams), and the calls for more research in this area, limited attention has been given to how these institutions are responding financially or how the revenues and spending patterns of HEOs are related (Blasdell, McPherson, & Schapiro, 1993; Fowles, 2014; McPherson & Schapiro, 1993; Toutkoushian, 2001).[1]

My goal in this paper is to address how HEOs are responding financially to their changing environments and thereby help to fill this gap. I have chosen to focus on public HEOs from 1986 to 2010, as opposed to public and private nonprofit HEOs, for three reasons. First, one of the largest, if not the largest, financial changes over the past 40 years is declining state support which primarily affects public HEOs. Second, public and private nonprofit HEOs reside in distinct, though overlapping, resource markets and have different missions and therefore will adapt differently (Belasco, Rosinger, & Hearn, 2015; Hearn & Rosinger, 2014; Morphew & Taylor, 2010). Third, as recent research by Taylor, Barringer, and Warshaw (2015) shows, universities in the two sectors have different mechanisms for strategic action adding further justification for the focus on public HEOs.

Two research questions are addressed in this paper. First, what are the different ways in which public HEOs alter their revenue and spending behaviors during this period of environmental change? We know that as these institutions have been forced to reduce their dependence on state funding they adopt new approaches to student recruitment, change their relationships with their home states (Brown & Clark, 2006; Turner, 2006), and take steps to diversify their revenue streams in response to their growing resource constraints (Hearn, 2003). However, we lack a clear large-scale empirical understanding of how public HEOs are changing in different ways and we do not know how these changes have translated to alterations in the combinations of revenue and spending streams these institutions rely on. For example, we do not know how the declines in state funding affected the relative prominence of other funding streams and if they did so in the same way for all public HEOs.

To that end, I use both descriptive statistics and multilevel latent class analysis (MLCA) to address this question. The use of descriptive statistics is consistent with existing research and allows for the investigation of trends in average levels of revenues and spending over time and the extent of variation across public HEOs and over time. However, public HEOs are multi-revenue/multiproduct organizations (Cohn, Rhine, & Santos, 1989; Leslie et al., 2012); therefore, their financial streams do not operate independently but rather work in combination to allow organizations to adapt and succeed under different conditions (Young, 2007). Consequently, I use MLCA to estimate the different revenue and spending profiles that public HEOs utilize between 1986 and 2010 to supplement the descriptive analysis. The profiles incorporate the funding sources or spending streams that HEOs draw on/spend *and* the proportion of total revenues/spending coming from/going to each source, and therefore allow for the evaluation of how public HEOs are capitalizing on different combinations of revenue and spending streams to survive and pursue their missions. Evaluating this question using both methods allows me to develop a more holistic understanding of how HEOs change their financial behaviors over time.

The second research question focuses on the relationship between the two aspects of public HEO financial behaviors and asks: how do the changing revenue patterns of public HEOs correspond to their spending patterns between 1986 and 2010? Generally speaking if a university alters its reliance on particular revenue streams then we would expect their spending patterns to also change (Froelich, 1999; Pfeffer & Salancik, 2003). Research to date has shown that public HEOs change some of their spending behaviors (Blasdell et al., 1993; Leslie et al., 2012; Weisbrod et al., 2008) as their revenue streams change, but a link between the two has yet to be fully examined for public HEOs (Toutkoushian, 2001). Two things are evaluated to answer this question. First, I look at the extent to which the two behaviors change together using both a descriptive analysis of the individual revenue and spending streams and their revenue and spending profiles. This allows me to assess if public HEOs change both aspects of their behavior in concert or if they protect their activities or spending patterns from the changes in their environments and specifically their dependencies. Second, I also evaluate the extent to which public HEOs that pursue the same revenue profile utilize the same spending profile to determine if certain revenue combinations are linked to certain spending profiles as the nonprofits and higher education literature suggest (Weisbrod et al., 2008). This also speaks more broadly to the nature of the tie(s) between the two aspects of financial behavior and sheds light on the costs and benefits of relying on particular funding streams and the potential consequences for the key constituencies of these institutions.

Answering these questions makes four contributions to the literature. First, it increases our empirical understanding of how public HEO finances change during a key period of transition within the field of higher education. Second, looking at the financial streams and profiles provides a more holistic picture of how public HEOs are changing financially by evaluating the combination of revenues and spending rather than individual streams which enhances both our conceptual and empirical understanding. Third, an evaluation of how the revenues and spending of public HEOs are related fills a notable gap in the literature (Fowles, 2014; Toutkoushian, 2001). Finally, this paper adds to the limited literature that evaluates the organizational level consequences of the environmental changes that have occurred in higher education over the last 40 years.

LITERATURE REVIEW

As noted earlier, there has been limited research into how public HEOs are responding to their altered environmental conditions at the organizational level generally and especially with regards to organizational finances (Berman & Stivers, 2016; Fowles, 2014; McPherson & Schapiro, 1993). The research that has been undertaken on financial adaptations of HEOs tends to focus on changes in revenues; there is less research on HEO spending (De Groot, McMahon, & Volkwein, 1991; McPherson & Schapiro, 1993; Shepherd, 2014). There is also a dearth of research on how revenues and spending are related (Toutkoushian, 2001). I summarize the existing research on these three aspects of HEO finances and the implications of research to date before turning to the data used and analyses undertaken here.

Revenue Streams of Public HEOs

There have been four key articles that focus on how public HEOs are changing their revenues over time. In a study of the finances of HEOs from

1979 to 1989, Blasdell et al. (1993) show that the majority of public HEO revenue streams were gradually increasing from 1979 to 1989, including state appropriations, when measured as inflation adjusted revenues per full time equivalent (FTE) student. However, the specific trends and magnitude of these increases differed across public HEOs. Gross tuition and fees was the fastest growing revenue stream for public universities exhibiting a 3.68% increase between 1979 and 1989. However, for public four-year colleges the 4.58% increase in state and local grants and contracts and the 5.14% decline in gifts and endowment income were the largest changes. The trends in the relative dependence on individual revenue streams, measured as a percentage of total revenues,[2] showed that public universities were becoming increasingly reliant on market-driven revenues (e.g., gifts and endowment and net tuition and fee revenues) and less reliant on government support (e.g., federal grants and contracts and state/local appropriations); however, the changes were all less than 5%. In contrast, public four-year colleges increased their reliance on state and local government funds *and* tuition while decreasing their dependence on federal government and gifts and endowment income. While changes were slightly larger than those of public universities (e.g., the 5.4% increase in tuition and 7.3% decline in gifts and endowment income) they were still relatively small.

Research looking at the 1990s and beyond showed evidence of both continuity *and* discontinuity with the earlier trends. Rizzo (2006) showed that average share of state general expenditures devoted to higher education has declined between 1982 and 2001. Toutkoushian (2001), when looking at public HEOs, confirmed this showing that the dependence of public HEOs on state appropriations declined from 57% of net education and general (E&G) revenues[3] in 1975 to 47% in 1995. In contrast, net tuition and fees increased from 13% to 21% of net E&G revenues. Increases in net tuition and fee revenues (3%) are also present when looking at changes in revenues per student, as are increases in state funding (3%) which declined as a percentage of net E&G revenues. However, Shepherd (2014) showed that the decline in state funding, measured as a percentage of total revenues, that occurs in the 1980s and 1990s persisted through 2011 with state appropriations dropping from 76.82% in 1986 to 56.85% in 2011 while tuition and fee revenues continued to rise. Fowles (2014) observed a similar trend for public four-year universities between 1987 and 2008 with a corresponding increase in net tuition revenue. So despite an increase in state funding dollars per student through 1995, the relative amount of state funding continued to decline as other revenue streams grew faster.

This work has established that generally state appropriations of public HEOs are declining, relative to other revenues, while tuition increases (Fowles, 2014; Wellman et al., 2009). However, despite this trend, the majority of public HEOs still rely heavily on state funding and it continues to be one of the largest revenue streams for these institutions (Fowles, 2014; Wellman et al., 2009). Research tells us less about how the other revenue streams of public HEOs have changed over the same period. This is unfortunate because, as research in both nonprofits and higher education has shown, changes in organizational revenue streams can have significant consequences for organizational structures, missions, policies, and behaviors (Ehrenberg, 2006; Froelich, 1999; Slaughter & Leslie, 1997; Weisbrod et al., 2008). There is also no discussion in this literature about if an how the overall combination of revenue profiles is changing which, along with our limited knowledge of the variability in these average trends, limits our understanding of how these institutions are adapting.

Public HEO Spending

Research on public HEO spending and resource allocation, like research on revenues, remains underdeveloped (Hasbrouck, 1997; James, 1990; Tuckman & Chang, 1990). This is unfortunate because spending provides insight into the priorities and activities of an organization (Hasbrouck, 1997; Weisbrod et al., 2008). As Hasbrouck states, "if one wishes to know what is valued by the organization, one should look to how the organization spends its money" (1997, p. 64).

As with revenue streams, looking at spending per student versus relative spending highlights different trends. Blasdell et al. (1993), in the same study discussed earlier, showed that spending at public universities, measured as constant dollars per FTE student, grew in all categories between 1979 and 1989. However, this increase was gradual with only two categories — restricted scholarships (5.99%) and plant additions (5.33%) — increasing by more than 5%. Public four-year colleges, for the most part, also saw growth but it was slower with restricted scholarships showing the only change exceeding 5% (5.48%) while libraries, operations and maintenance, and other spending declining over the period. Toutkoushian (2001), on the other hand, showed that there were substantial increases in per student net E&G expenditures with substantial growth in all categories and an overall increase of more than 30% in net E&G spending per student between 1975 and 1995, which is inconsistent with Blasdell et al. (1993).

Relative spending provides insight into the areas or activities that public HEOs are investing in and tells a story of overall stability between the late 1970s and mid-1990s. Blasdell et al. (1993) found that only three of the eight spending categories of public universities, measured as a percentage of total operating expenses, changed by more than 1%: instruction (−1.8%), research (+2.1%), and operations and maintenance (−1.3%). Public four-year colleges also only had three streams change by more than 1%: research (+2.0%), institutional support (+1.3%), and operations and maintenance (−2.1%). Toutkoushian's (2001) study of relative spending, measured as the percentage of net E&G expenditures, between 1975 and 1995 confirms this stability. Only four expenditure streams changed by more than 1% over the period: instruction (−5%), research (+2%), operations and maintenance (−2%), and transfers (+2%), but no change was sufficient to change the relative emphasis or the activities of public HEOs.

Overall, the story of public HEO spending is one of gradual growth that accelerates in the 1990s. However, since all spending streams are increasing at similar rates there is very little change in the relative emphasis on each of these activities over time; instructional spending remains dominant followed by research and both academic and institutional support spending from 1979 to 1995. Given the relative stability in spending, despite the significant changes in public HEO revenues, the conventional wisdom that "whoever pays the piper calls the tune" (McPherson, Schapiro, & Winston, 1993, p. 1) is called into question.

Revenue and Spending Relationships in Public HEOs

Despite both empirical and theoretical evidence that "shifts in revenue sources are significant to spending patterns because the source often dictates how the money can be spent" (Desrochers & Wellman, 2011, p. 12) there has been limited investigation of the relationships between university revenues and spending. Toutkoushian (2001) argues for further research on the relationship between revenues and spending while recognizing, like Wilsker and Young (2010), that spending can affect revenues just as much as revenues can affect spending. More recently Fowles (2014) notes that the existing literature on these relationships is largely cross-sectional and makes little attempt to connect the broad revenue shifts that are outlined earlier to changes in HEO behaviors including, but not limited to, HEO spending.

To date only a few studies within the higher education literature make a concerted effort to look at how HEO revenues affect HEO spending.

The four most relevant studies are summarized here. In the first, Hasbrouck (1997) focuses on how changes in the resource dependencies of public universities affect their resource allocations, which she argues are indicative of the priorities of public HEOs, in the 1980s and 1990s. She finds significant relationships between three key revenue streams and key mission-based expenditures. First, government appropriations and tuition and fee revenues were positively related to instructional spending. Second, gifts, grants, and contracts had a positive association with research and scholarship and fellowship spending. Finally, tuition and fees also had a positive relationships with scholarship and fellowships and student services.

Leslie et al. (2012) recently expanded on Hasbrouck's work by examining how variation in revenues affected spending at public *and* private nonprofit research universities and how those relationships changed between 1984 and 2007. The authors found that public university revenues were, in many cases, tightly tied to spending in the expected ways (e.g., tuition revenues were tied to instructional expenditures) and these relationships became stronger over time. Private universities, on the other hand, operated more strategically, using revenues from many categories to recruit students and engage in research. These analyses substantially increase our knowledge of university finances, but the emphasis is on understanding variation between public and private universities with less attention to changes over time and the different pathways of change within each sector.

Shepherd (2014) subsequently expanded on the work of Leslie et al. (2012) by evaluating the relationship between revenues and expenditures at all public colleges and universities as part of his dissertation which examined "institutional accountability and production processes" (Shepherd, 2014, p. 12). As a first step toward understanding these processes Shepherd looked at the relationships between revenues and expenditures per FTE student. He found that the shift toward tuition, rather than state money, occurring in public HEOs did not seem to negatively affect instruction and public services expenditures since tuition had a positive effect on all spending categories. State funding was also shown to have a positive association with the majority of spending streams (instruction, academic support, student services, institutional, and scholarship and fellowship expenditures). Federal grants and contracts funding, like state funding, had positive associations with instruction, academic support, and institutional spending but also had positive associations with research and public services spending. Shepherd's results for research universities were consistent with Leslie et al. (2012), however, he showed a broader range of effects between revenues and expenditures than either Leslie et al. (2012) or Hasbrouck (1997) which was likely a function of his focus on a larger set of public HEOs than the other two studies.

Fowles (2014) deviates somewhat from the other three in his evaluation of the relationship by using resource dependencies, measured as a percentage of total revenues, to predict only one outcome, relative spending on educational and related activities, rather than multiple spending categories. He finds a significant positive relationship between the share of total operating revenues from net tuition and the share of total spending devoted to education and related activities.

Despite the diversity of cases, time periods, and measures the overall story is similar across all four studies. The majority of revenue streams had positive associations with spending streams when revenues are measured as per FTE student. This is not surprising as more money equates to more spending. However, there is a consistent lack of specificity in the associations of revenue and spending streams. For example, both Shepherd (2014) and Leslie et al. (2012) find that tuition generally has a positive effect on all of the spending streams of public HEOs and public research universities respectively. For both of these analyses the majority of revenue streams are tied to a number, if not the majority, of the spending streams. The studies that look at how resource dependency affect spending still found significant positive effects but they were less widespread (Fowles, 2014; Hasbrouck, 1997). This, while not surprising given the propensity of these institutions to engage in cross-subsidization (James, 1983, 1990; Weisbrod et al., 2008), makes it difficult to understand the nature of the relationships between revenues and spending in much detail for public HEOs.

Limitations

Despite this literature on revenues, spending, and the relationships between the two; four issues remain underdeveloped. First, our understanding of trends in revenues is primarily focused in the trends of state appropriations and tuition revenues with only limited attention devoted to the other ways that public HEOs are adapting to their changing financial environments. Second, research on the spending patterns of public HEOs is dated, stopping in the mid-1990s (Fowles, 2014; Shepherd, 2014). Third, and perhaps most importantly for this paper, the research on both revenues and spending is focused on average trends in individual revenue or spending streams without attention to how these streams work together to sustain these institutions and to accomplish their mission respectively. This inattention to the full set of revenue and spending streams of these institutions and the focus on average trends not only obscures variation, as Fowles (2014) notes, but also limits our ability to understand the different ways that the sets of revenue and spending streams are used in combination and how the HEOs adapt in different ways. Finally, our understanding of the relationships between revenues and spending, despite the substantial contributions summarized earlier, remains underdeveloped because we lack a clear understanding of how changes in the combination of revenue streams public HEOs rely on affects their set of spending streams.

DATA

The analysis presented below proceeds in three stages, it: (1) evaluates how the revenue streams and revenue profiles of public HEOs have changed between 1986 and 2010, (2) evaluates how the spending streams and spending profiles of public HEOs have changed over time, and (3) evaluates the correspondence between these revenue and spending behaviors. To accomplish these goals, I used data on 516 four-year degree-granting public HEOs in the United States from 1986 to 2010 taken annually for a total of 12,588 HEO-years. The 516 public HEOs include all public four-year institutions granting undergraduate degrees that were classified as a Research, Doctoral, Master's and Baccalaureate institutions in the 2010 Carnegie Classification of Institutions and participated in, or applied for, the federal student financial aid program.

I chose to focus on public four-year undergraduate degree-granting institutions because these schools have broadly similar missions, share common environmental conditions, opportunities, and constraints and are therefore part of the same organizational field (Fligstein & Dauter, 2007; Fligstein & McAdam, 2011, 2012). Private nonprofit HEOs and two-year public institutions are excluded because of differences in resources, missions, and mechanisms of adaptation (Taylor et al., 2015). The time period of this analysis was chosen because it encompasses a period of substantial change within the field of U.S. higher education as state support declined (Rizzo, 2006), competition for resources increased (Weisbrod et al., 2008), and the privatization of public HEOs took hold (Morphew & Eckel, 2009). Therefore, it is ideal for evaluating how the financial behaviors of public HEOs change. The data were drawn from the Integrated Postsecondary Education Data System (IPEDS), which is compiled and maintained by

the National Center for Education Statistics. Because of changing governmental reporting standards for public HEOs during this period to ensure
consistent measurement of the revenue and spending streams over time. To
do this it was necessary to utilize a cross-walk that allowed for the creation
of consistent measures for the different revenue and spending streams over
time. I used the revenue and expenditure mapping file developed by the
Delta Cost Project to accomplish this for all the revenue and spending categories used here between 1986 and 2010.

The Revenue and Spending Streams of Public Universities

The same sets of revenue and spending streams that are used for the
descriptive analysis to evaluate trends are used in the MLCA analysis to
estimate the revenue and spending profiles. The six revenue streams used
are: tuition income; state government revenues; private gifts, grants and
contracts; federal government revenues; auxiliary enterprise; and miscellaneous revenues.[4] The first five are all established categories of spending
within IPEDS and are defined in Table A1 in the appendix. The miscellaneous revenues category is an aggregation of local government, endowment, independent operations, sales of educational activities, and hospital
revenues. These revenue streams were aggregated, rather than included
separately, for three reasons. First, the majority of public HEOs have little
or no funding coming from these revenue streams; the largest was hospital
revenues which, on average, accounts for 1.69% of total revenues in 2010.
Second, all five, measured as a percentage of total revenues, also changed
by less than 1.5% over the period. Third, all five of these revenue streams
were highly skewed due to the high occurrence of zero revenues for each of
these funding streams and therefore would have violated the assumption
that the observed variables are normally distributed within the clusters that
is necessary for the MLCA analysis (Hagenaars & McCutcheon, 2002).
Figs. 1 and 2 provide basic descriptive statistics for these six revenue
streams from 1986 to 2010.

Eight spending categories are used in both the descriptive analysis of
trends and MLCA analysis of spending profiles: instruction; research; student services; academic support; institutional support services; operation
and maintenance; auxiliary enterprises; and miscellaneous spending.[5] The
first seven are predetermined spending streams within the IPEDS data and
are defined in Table A1 in the appendix. Miscellaneous spending, like revenues, is not a predetermined expenditure category in IPEDS, but an

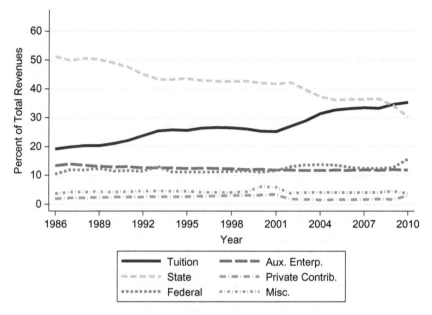

Fig. 1. Revenue Streams of Public HEOs, 1986–2010.

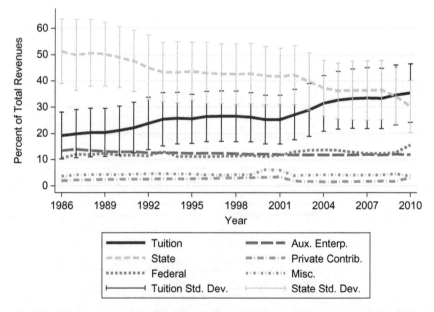

Fig. 2. Revenue Streams of Public HEOs plus Standard Deviations, 1986–2010.

aggregation of four spending streams: public service; scholarship and fellowship; hospital; and independent operations expenditures. These spending streams are aggregated into the miscellaneous category because their individual contribution to total spending is minimal,[6] some were not available for the full period (e.g., endowment income) and some are also not directly related to the provision on educational services (Toutkoushian, 2001). Further, like the aggregated revenue streams, these four expenditure streams were highly skewed and would therefore violate a necessary assumption for the MLCA analysis. Descriptive statistics for these spending streams are shown in Figs. 3 and 4.

To evaluate the changes in individual revenue and spending streams I look at the percentage of total revenues[7] and spending to evaluate trends in relative revenue and spending levels over time. I use relative levels of revenues and spending rather than the absolute levels of either because, while spending per FTE measures are valuable indicators of financial behaviors, relative amounts provide better indicators of the dependencies and emphases or activities of public HEOs respectively. This approach also parallels the revenue and spending profiles allowing for a comparison of the results.

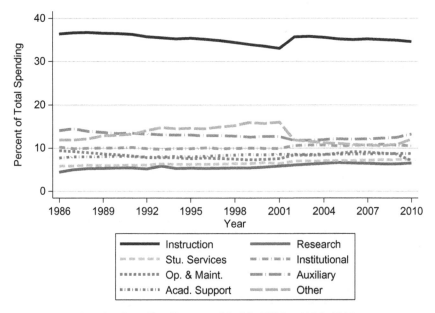

Fig. 3.   Spending Streams of Public HEOs, 1986–2010.

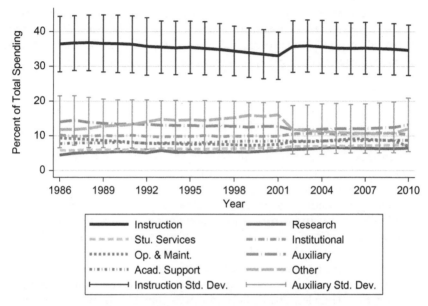

Fig. 4. Spending Streams of Public HEOs plus Standard Deviations, 1986–2010.

Defining the Revenue and Spending Profiles

Revenue and spending profiles, as noted earlier, refer to the *set* of revenue/spending streams utilized by a university at a given time. This incorporates the funding sources or spending streams that HEOs draw on/spend *and* the proportion of total revenues/spending coming from/going to each source. I estimated and evaluated the revenue and spending profiles, in addition to the individual revenue or spending streams for two reasons. First, evaluating the profiles in addition to the individual revenue and spending streams allows me to develop a better understanding of the ways in which HEO financial behaviors change over time (Young, 2007). Second, the revenue and spending profiles are also indicative of the dependencies of the organizations and their priorities, respectively (Hasbrouck, 1997; Weisbrod et al., 2008). The spending profiles, because they are measured using the percentages of total expenditures, provide a picture of their relative "outputs" indicating what they ultimately chose, after taking into account their priorities and constraints, to spend their resources on. For the revenue profiles using the percentage of total revenues provides a measure of their relative dependence on the key economic stakeholders of HEOs. To estimate the revenue profiles I used the percent of total revenues, net of investment and other revenues that come from six different revenue streams listed earlier. The spending profiles were estimated using the percentage of total spending allocated to each of the eight spending streams also outlined earlier.

METHODS

Two methods are used in the analysis of the revenue and spending behaviors of public HEOs from 1986 to 2010. First, I use descriptive statistics, primarily evaluations of average trends and standard deviations over time, to evaluate how individual revenue and spending streams change over the period. This is consistent with other examinations of how the revenue and spending behaviors of HEOs have changed over time (e.g., Blasdell et al., 1993; Toutkoushian, 2001). However, as noted earlier the evaluation of average trends in revenue and spending streams over time has two limitations. First, it can obscure variation across universities and within universities over time (Fowles, 2014). Second, given that HEOs are multiproduct multi-revenue organizations (Cohn et al., 1989; Leslie et al., 2012), their revenue and spending streams do not operate independently but rather in combination (Young, 2007). This descriptive approach does not allow the combination of revenue and spending streams to be taken into account.

Consequently, I use MLCA to estimate revenue and spending profiles of these institutions to supplement the descriptive statistics for two reasons. First, looking at the revenue and spending profiles of public HEOs allows for the examination of how the revenue and spending streams of these HEOs work in combination to allow them to pursue their missions which Young (2007) argues is necessary to understand the finances of multi-revenue and multiproduct organizations like nonprofits and HEOs. Second, evaluating how these different profiles change in prominence within the field over time allows for additional insight into the different ways in which public HEOs are changing over time as they adapt financially to their changing environments. It also speaks to the cross university variation that the descriptive analysis reveals in Figs. 2 and 4.

MLCA uses a series of fixed and random effects to capture variation or heterogeneity across and within HEOs over time to estimate clusters or groups of organizations that pursue the same financial profile (Hagenaars & McCutcheon, 2002).[8] It then allows HEOs to move in and out of the different groups or financial profiles as their observed behaviors change over time (Macmillian & Eliason, 2003; Vermut, 2003). MLCA, as specified here, capitalizes on all of the cases to estimate the groups of HEOs and the latent trajectories over time, and then allocates the HEO years into the groups at each point in time. In essence the latent classes or groups are static and the cases are mobile or dynamic (Hagenaars & McCutcheon, 2002) which allows me to examine the trends in both organizational (e.g., organizational change as expressed by HEOs switching profiles) and field-level behaviors over time (e.g., the changing prominence of profiles between 1986 and 2010).

MLCA was used, as opposed to a different clustering method, for two reasons. First, MLCA allows researchers to model variation across organizations and over time providing a more comprehensive understanding of the changing financial behaviors of public HEOs over time whereas other clustering methods are unable to account for both levels of variation (Macmillian & Eliason, 2003; Vermut, 2003). Second, MLCA allows researchers to evaluate the significance of each of the observed variables in the definition of the profiles which other clustering methods, such as cluster analysis, are unable to do. This allows researchers to evaluate the model specification and fit and to see if observed variables are contributing unique information to the definition of the clusters or if a single variable, or small set of variables, are the primary drivers of the latent class specifications.[9]

To generate the clusters of public HEOs based on their observed behaviors, I estimated two different MLCA measurement models, one for revenues and one for spending.[10] These measurement models used the observed behaviors or characteristics of the HEOs (relative funding and spending) to sort public HEOs into the specified number of latent classes based on how similar or different their observed behaviors are (Hagenaars & McCutcheon, 2002).[11] The number of latent classes for a given model is then determined after estimating a series of models where different numbers of latent classes or profiles were specified and comparing (1) the consistency of the model parameters, conditional means, log likelihood statistics, and profile characteristics; (2) model fit statistics; and (3) the proportion of cases in each profile (Hagenaars & McCutcheon, 2002).[12] The end result is that HEOs with very similar behaviors reside in the same latent class or profile while those with different behaviors are in different classes. The statistical model for MLCA model is a variation on a multinomial logistic regression model where the latent class variable is the categorical outcome while the observed behaviors, the time specification and the continuous random effects predict the likelihood of a particular university being in a particular latent group or cluster at a particular time point.

Limitations

There are a few limitations of the data and methods used here that should be noted. First, and foremost this analysis focused on 516 four-year undergraduate degree-granting public HEOs from 1986 to 2010. If a different set of institutions were used or a different time period the results will differ. The MLCA analysis is also dependent on the specification of the model; if different sets of revenue or spending streams were utilized it is possible that the results would look different. Though a notable limitation, this also points to potentially fruitful analyses of subgroups of institutions (e.g., research HEOs or HEOs within a particular state or region) to develop a more fine-grained understanding of university financial behaviors, trends within niches of the field of higher education, and more nuanced pathways of change over time. Looking at different behaviors (e.g., degree completions) would also allow for a different grouping of HEOs based on their similarities on different behaviors and allows for the development of a more refined understanding of how "peer" institutions vary across behaviors.

The nature of the revenue and spending categories within the IPEDS data is also a limitation. These categories, while useful, are also broad (see Table A1), which places limits on the substantive insights that can be gained from either the descriptive analysis or the profiles and their changing prominence over time and the implications of these changes for organizational behaviors. Two examples illustrate this point. First, it has been well established in the literature that HEOs, both public and private, are increasing their use of contingent faculty at the expense of tenure track faculty positions (American Federation of Teachers, 2009; Schuster & Finkelstein, 2006). However, since the salaries of both groups are included in instructional expenditures, looking at trends in the spending streams of public HEOs would not capture this shift in the employment practices of these institutions. Second, evaluating certain shifts in some financial behaviors are also difficult with this level of aggregation. For example, auxiliary enterprises revenues, a key category in the specification of the revenue profiles, include a wide range of activities (e.g., residence halls, food services, student health services, parking, and college bookstores). Some of these are key activities within which HEOs are diversifying to try to capture more revenues (Hearn, 2003); however, because these are all classified in a single category a detailed analysis of changes in these behaviors is prohibited.

Fourth, the role of federal support for public HEOs is partially obscured because federal financial aid is included in tuition revenues within the IPEDS data rather than as a separate category, which would be ideal, or in federal support. Given the growing dependence on tuition, and the increasing reliance of students on federal loans to pay that tuition (Berman & Stivers, 2016; College Board, 2014), this is an unfortunate limitation of all analyses of the revenues of HEOs generally, not just public HEOs.

Fifth, due to the changes in the reporting surveys for IPEDS, it is difficult to evaluate restricted and unrestricted revenue categories for the entire time period. The inability to take this into account limits potential insights about how public HEOs utilize restricted and unrestricted funds differently.

Finally, this analysis is primarily descriptive and does not evaluate causal relationships. The goal in this paper is to describe how revenue and spending behaviors of public HEOs change over time and evaluate the extent to which the changes in these two dimensions of university financial behavior correspond. As I argue earlier, this fills notable gaps in the literature. However, it does not evaluate specific explanations for organizational change.

ANALYSIS AND RESULTS[13]

Revenue Streams of Public HEOs

Fig. 1 shows the average levels of each of the six revenue streams across all HEOs between 1986 and 2010. The key shift in the revenues of HEOs, as this figure shows, is the decline in state funding and rise in tuition revenues. Specifically, state funding, as a percentage of total revenues net of other and investment income, declines from an average of 51.26% in 1986 to 30.30% in 2010. Tuition revenues, in contrast, rose from 19.17% in 1986 to 35.38% in 2010. The other revenue streams remained effectively constant as a percentage of total revenues between 1986. For example, the third largest revenue stream (on average), federal funding, only rose from 10.52% in 1986 to 15.62% in 2010, which while an increase, was minor compared to the changes in tuition and state funding. The other three revenue streams all changed by less than 2%.

Given the fact that average trends in university revenues and spending can obscure variation across universities and within universities over time (Fowles, 2014), I also looked at variation across universities. Fig. 2 builds on Fig. 1 to address this by incorporating cap lines that show plus/minus one standard deviation above and below the average trend lines for the two largest revenue streams on average for the whole period – tuition and state funding. These standard deviation ranges, which grow over time for tuition, encompass approximately 68.2% of all public HEOs in each year because both tuition and state funding are approximately normally distributed based on skewness statistics and histograms (Warner, 2008). As the cap bars in Fig. 2 indicate, there is a substantial variation across universities in these two revenue streams. Tuition revenues account for between 24.18% and 46.58% and state revenues account for between 20.35% and 40.25% of total revenues for public HEOs in 2010. This complicates the "simple" story that HEOs are simply replacing state funding with tuition revenues. Not everyone is becoming more dependent on tuition and those that are do so to different degrees. Looking at the revenue profiles of HEOs and how they change over time as schools move between them show how HEOs are changing the combination of revenue streams that they are relying on in different ways which allows for the examination of different pathways of change that Fig. 2 suggests are present.

The Revenues Profiles of Public HEOs

The revenue profiles of HEOs were estimated using the MLCA analysis described earlier. Based on model fit and consistency I determined that there are four latent revenue profiles that characterize HEO revenues between 1986 and 2010 which I labeled as: *state dependent, tuition + state, state enterprise, and diversified revenue profiles*. Fig. 1 displays the average spending levels of all of the HEOs in each of the four revenue profiles for the entire period to provide a sense of how the public HEOs in each profile are obtaining funds. As noted earlier, each of the revenue profiles is constant for the entire period and HEOs move in and out of them as their observed behaviors change.[14] I briefly describe each revenue profile and its changing prominence over time before turning to a more detailed discussion of how HEOs move in and out of these profiles as their behaviors change over time.

The HEOs in the *state dependent profile*, shown in the upper left of Fig. 5, are the HEOs most dependent on state funding (54% of total revenues on average). For example, a number of the California State University campuses[15] (e.g., Bakersfield and Fresno with 45.4% and 45.9% of total revenues from state funding in 2010), the University at Buffalo (46.6% in 2010), University of Hawaii-West Oahu (58.6% in 2010), and Eastern New

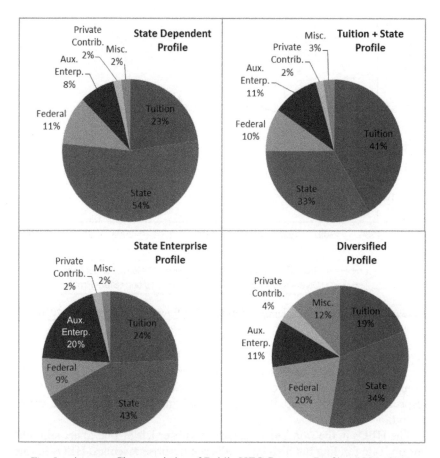

Fig. 5. Average Characteristics of Public HEO Revenue Profiles, 1986–2010.

Mexico University (50.0% in 2010) all reside in this profile for the entire period and are all heavily dependent on state funding. However, the majority of HEOs in this profile leave this profile between 1986 and 2010 resulting in a dramatic decline in the prominence of the *state dependent profile* from 49.40% in 1986 to 14.79% in 2010 (Fig. 6).

The *tuition + state profile*, upper right of Fig. 5, substantially increased in prominence between 1986 and 2010 growing from 5.78% to 48.72% of HEOs between 1986 and 2010 (Fig. 6). This profile contains those HEOs that were heavily dependent on both tuition and state government revenues on average. The University of Southern Maine drew 37.3% of total

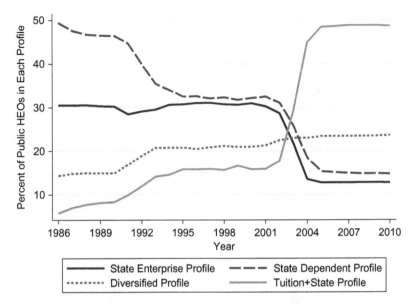

Fig. 6. Changing Prevalence of Public HEO Revenue Profiles, 1986–2010.

revenues from tuition and 32.4% from state funding in 2010 as did a number of the University of Wisconsin campuses (e.g., Green Bay with 37.4% from tuition and 31.8% from state and Parkside with 33.7% and 36.7% respectively in 2010) and therefore resided in this profile for the entire period.

The HEOs in the *state enterprise profile* (lower left of Fig. 5) are still reliant on state funding but also on auxiliary enterprise revenues. HEOs in this profile include: Western Illinois University (40.5% state revenues and 19.3% auxiliary in 2010), Appalachian State University (43.5% and 25.6% respectively in 2010), and a number of the SUNY colleges (e.g., Binghamton and Cortland). In contrast to the *tuition + state profile*, the *state enterprise profile* declined in prominence from 30.48% of HEOs in 1986 to 12.82% in 2010 (Fig. 6).

The *diversified revenue profile* (lower right of Fig. 5), was the most diverse of the four relying less on any single revenue stream. HEOs in this profile relied on state, federal and tuition funding to roughly the same extent. For example, the Universities of Arizona, Minnesota-Twin Cities, and California—Berkeley all drew on these three revenues streams by roughly equivalent amounts.[16] Fig. 6 shows that the *diversified profile* showed the smallest change in prominence over time but still increased from 14.34% of HEOs in 1986 to 23.67% in 2010.

Because the revenue profiles are consistent and HEOs move between them over time the different pathways of change become apparent. Clear shifts from state funding toward more market-driven revenues such as tuition, private contributions and federal funding are present between 1986 and 2010 providing evidence of privatization.

Those HEOs that initially resided in the *state dependent profile* exhibited three distinct pathways for change (Fig. 7a) which highlight three ways that HEOs were adapting to declining state funding. HEOs like the University of Florida and the University of Louisville all reduced their reliance on state funding (55.9−30.3% and 60.9−23.8%, respectively) and increased

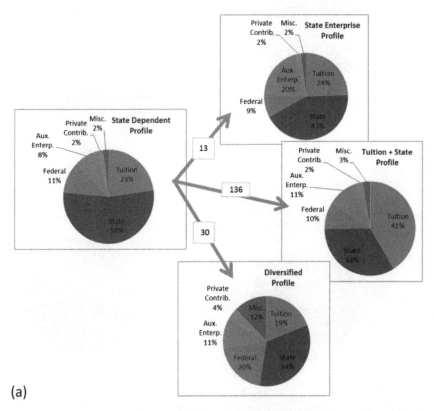

(a)

Fig. 7.   Movement of Public HEOs between Revenue Profiles, 1986−2010.

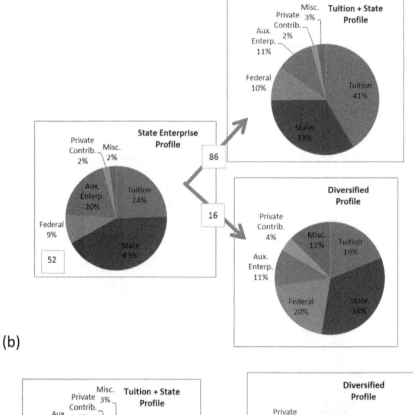

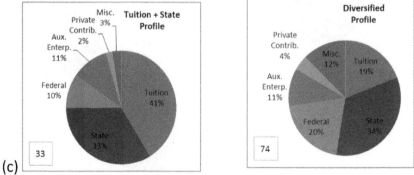

Fig. 7. (*Continued*)

their federal government (15.6–19.3% and 6.2–13.7%, respectively), miscellaneous (1.7–2.0% and 2–25%, respectively), and private revenues which resulted in them, along with 28 other HEOs, shifting into the *diversified profile*. An additional 136 HEOs increased their tuition revenues as they decreased their reliance on state funding with minimal changes in other revenue levels, like the University of Massachusetts-Boston which reduced its state funding from 68% to 27% and increased their reliance on tuition from 17% to 47%, and subsequently moved into the *tuition + state profile*. Only 13 HEOs decreased their reliance on state government revenues and substantially increased their reliance on auxiliary enterprise expenditures (e.g., Morgan State University 61.4–37.1% and 9.2–14.4%, respectively), shifting them into the *state enterprise profile*.

The *state enterprise profile* also declined over time as HEOs altered their revenue profiles in two different ways (Fig. 7b). The majority of these HEOs (86) shifted into the *tuition + state profile* as they reduced their reliance on state and auxiliary revenues and increased their reliance on state funding. However, 16 HEOs decreased their reliance on state funding, tuition income, and auxiliary enterprise revenues and increased their reliance on miscellaneous revenues and federal government revenues resulting in their movement from the *state enterprise profile* to the *diversified profile* (e.g., the Universities of Oklahoma, Montana, Southern Mississippi, and Kansas).

No schools moved out of the *tuition + state profile* or the *diversified profile* (Fig. 7c) indicating that once HEOs achieved either of these revenue profiles they maintained them for the remainder of the period. Overall these results are consistent with the trends in the revenue streams in Figs. 1 and 2 but also add additional nuance by showing how the combinations of revenues changed over time and illuminating the different pathways of change as they adapted to their changing environments.

Spending Streams of Public HEOs

In contrast to the shifts in revenue streams the relative prominence of the eight different spending streams remained effectively stable over time on average. The only changes exceeding 1% in the relative amount of spending in each of the eight areas were declines in instructional spending (−1.8%) and operations and maintenance (−2.3%) and increases in research (2.15%) and student services spending (1.5%) between 1986 and 2010 (Fig. 3).

As with revenues, the average trends in spending streams can obscure variation. Therefore, Fig. 4 incorporates cap lines for plus/minus one standard deviation around the average trend lines for instruction and auxiliary enterprise spending, the two largest spending streams in 1986 and 2010. The incorporation of these standard deviations shows that, even when accounting for the variation across universities, over 60% of HEOs spend a large plurality of their resources on instruction. However, it is also clear that there is a substantial overlap, and therefore potential for different levels of emphasis, across the other seven spending streams.

The Spending Profiles of Public HEOs

In contrast to the four revenue profiles described earlier there are only three latent spending profiles for HEOs from 1986 to 2010 based on model fit and profile consistency[17]: the *multiproduct, teaching intensive*, and *teaching plus spending profiles*. Fig. 8 displays the average levels of spending for

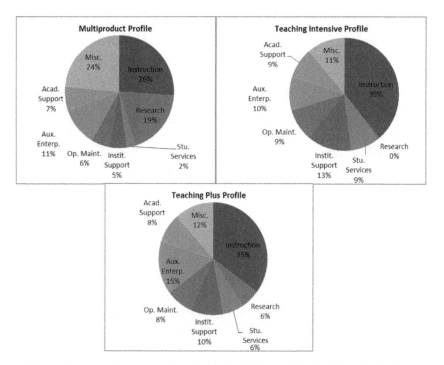

Fig. 8. Average Characteristics of Public HEO Spending Profiles, 1986–2010.

HEOs in each profile for the full period.[18] I will describe each in turn before discussing movement between them.

The *multiproduct profile*, in the upper left of Fig. 8, had no single dominant spending category. HEOs in this profile spent roughly the same relative amounts on instruction, research, and miscellaneous spending. In effect these HEOs (e.g., the University of Georgia, which spent 21.0% on instruction, 25.6% on research and 16.2% on miscellaneous spending in 2010), which were almost exclusively research/doctoral institutions, engaged almost equally in teaching and research while also dedicating substantial resources to public services and hospital expenditures, the two primary categories of miscellaneous spending for these HEOs.[19]

Unlike the revenue profiles outlined earlier, the spending profiles of HEOs did not change notably in prominence over time. The *multiproduct profile* was the least prominent of the three spending profiles including approximately 13% of HEOs for the entire period (Fig. 9).

The *teaching intensive profile*, upper right of Fig. 8, includes the HEOs that placed the greatest emphasis on instruction, including California State University-Long Beach, Dakota State University, and Governors State University, which devoted 44.9%, 40.7%, and 47.3% of total spending,

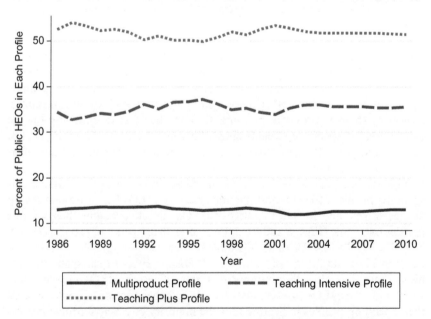

Fig. 9. Changing Prevalence of Public HEO Spending Profiles, 1986–2010.

respectively, to instruction in 2010. This profile increased marginally in prominence over time from 34.5% of HEOs in 1986 to 35.5% in 2010 (Fig. 9).

The final spending profile is the *teaching plus profile* which included those HEOs that heavily emphasized instruction but also spent money on research and auxiliary enterprise revenues, differentiating them from the HEOs in the *teaching intensive profile*. This profile was the most prominent in the field, accounting for 52.6% of HEOs in 1986 and 51.5% in 2010. HEOs in this profile include: Florida State University which spent 31.3% of resources on instruction, 14.1% on research, and 18.1% on auxiliary enterprises; and Texas Tech University which spent 27.9% of resources on instruction, 18.5% on research, and 17.5% on auxiliary enterprises in 2010.

The overriding characteristic of HEO spending profiles was the lack of mobility between the three profiles. Only 60 schools changed their profiles between 1986 and 2010 (Fig. 10) indicating that the mostly constant level of prominence for the three profiles across HEOs was due to the fact that the schools didn't change their spending behaviors over this period.

Revenue and Spending Trend and Profile Correspondence

To assess the extent to which revenue and spending behaviors coincide, I again look first at the revenue and spending streams before turning to the revenue and spending profiles. Figs. 1 and 2 show that the revenue streams on which HEOs were reliant on did change between 1986 and 2010, primarily in terms of a tradeoff between state funding and tuition revenues. However, there is no corresponding shift in the relative spending on the eight different spending streams shown in Figs. 3 and 4. So public HEOs, despite changes in their revenue streams, continued to pursue the same relative mix of spending.

This is consistent with the trends in the prominence of the revenue and spending profiles of HEOs and the movement of HEOs between them shown in Figs. 6, 7, 9, and 10. The majority of HEOs, despite changing their revenue profiles over time (Figs. 6 and 7), did not alter their spending profiles (Figs. 9 and 10). While 54.45% of HEOs altered their revenue profile (281 HEOs) between 1986 and 2010, only 11.63% (60 HEOs) altered their spending profiles. There was also discontinuity in terms of which HEOs moved. Only 15.30% of the HEOs (43 schools) that altered their revenue profiles altered their spending profiles indicating that the majority of revenue profile movers did not change their spending profile.

I also look explicitly at the correspondence between the public HEOs that reside in each combination of revenue and spending profiles to see if schools that pursue the same revenue profile pursue the same spending profile. Table 1 shows the percentage of HEOs from each revenue profile that were in each of the three spending profiles. The percentages are the percent of all HEO years in each revenue/spending profile combination

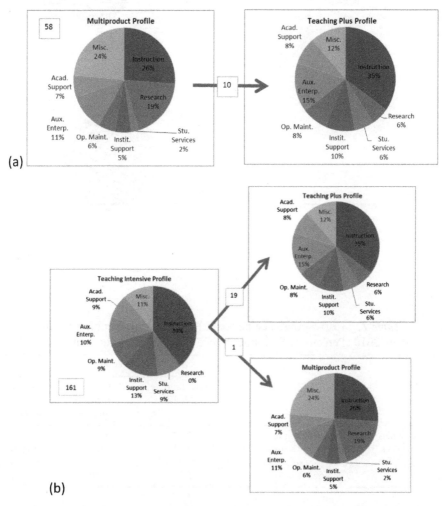

(a)

(b)

Fig. 10. Movement of Public HEOs between Spending Profiles, 1986–2010.

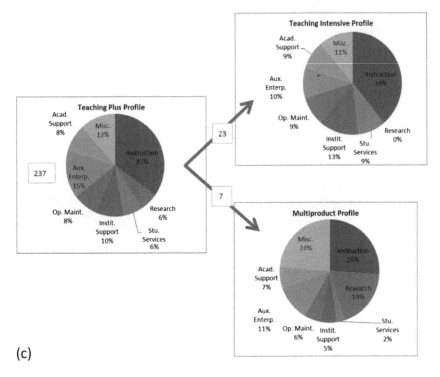

(c)

Fig. 10. (*Continued*)

Table 1. Correspondence between Revenue and Spending Profiles, 1986–2010 (Percent of Revenue Profile Cases in Each Spending Profile).

		Spending Profiles		
		Multiproduct profile	Teaching intensive profile	Teaching plus profile
Revenue profiles	State dependent profile	2.29%	52.56%	45.15%
	State enterprise profile	3.30%	22.55%	74.15%
	Tuition + state profile	0.92%	49.98%	49.10%
	Diversified profile	55.26%	7.07%	37.67%

for the entire period. For example, 2.29% of public HEOs in the *state dependent revenue profile* (in the entire period) were in the *multiproduct spending profile*, 52.56% were in the *teaching intensive profile*, and 45.15% were in the *teaching plus profile* in the corresponding HEO year. Table 1 shows that all of the revenue profiles are loosely coupled with all of the spending streams. There are no exclusive links between revenue profiles and spending profiles and only one strong tie (between the *state enterprise revenue profile* and the *teaching plus spending profile* which houses 74.15% of the HEOs in the *state enterprise profile*). This suggests one of two things. Either (1) revenue profiles are not strong predictors of spending profiles or (2) there are substantial mediating factors in the relationship between the revenue and spending profiles that dilute the strength of these ties. In effect, it could be indicative of a buffer between the revenue and spending profiles of HEOs.

DISCUSSION AND CONCLUSION

There are four key findings from this research. First, HEOs did substantially alter their revenues between 1986 and 2010 in terms of both revenue streams and revenue profiles. Second, the results of the MLCA analysis of revenue profiles, namely the multiple pathways of change in and out of the four revenue profiles, confirms the argument that public HEOs change their revenues in different ways over time. For example, there was an overall shift of public HEOs away from the *state dependent profile* and into the other three revenue profiles.

Third, contrary to expectations, there was no corresponding change in the average spending levels or movement of public HEOs between the spending profiles between 1986 and 2010. Only 11.82% of public HEOs changed their spending profiles during this period. Therefore, contrary to conventional wisdom and the expectations from the literature, the spending patterns of public HEOs do not change despite the fact that the external dependencies and stakeholders of these institutions changed over time.

Fourth, evidence here shows that there is a discontinuity or lack of correspondence between the revenue and spending profiles of public HEOs rather than the correspondence that the literature suggests should occur (e.g., Weisbrod et al., 2008). Though the revenue profiles changed substantially over time, corresponding changes in the spending profiles of public HEOs were not evident. Furthermore, with the possible exception of the tight tie between the *state enterprise revenue profile* and the *teaching plus spending profile* the revenue and spending profiles were all loosely coupled.

This suggests that while revenues are substantially influenced by the environment that the organization is situated in, their spending profiles are not affected by the environment surrounding HEOs. This implies that either (1) HEOs have created, or always had a barrier between their revenues and/or environment and stakeholders and their spending behaviors or (2) that the stakeholders who control the resources that these HEOs are utilizing agree with, or do not care, how the resources are spent. Given the increasing pressures for accountability and efficiency coming from state governments, students, and others (e.g., McLendon, Hearn, & Deaton, 2006), I would argue it is more likely that these institutions buffer their spending or activities from changes in their revenue profiles or environments. This buffer, I argue, is a function of the internal decision making, cross-subsidization, and mission of public HEOs. For example, the centrality of mission for these organizations could be constraining their spending profiles. The practice of cross-subsidization, which allows organizations to use profit generating activities to subsidize their unprofitable mission activities (James, 1983; Leslie et al., 2012; Weisbrod, 1998; Weisbrod et al., 2008), is a mode of resource allocation that is consistent with the importance of mission and would allow HEOs to sustain their spending profile despite changes to their revenue profiles. Despite the importance of cross-subsidization for HEOs, and nonprofits generally, empirical examinations of the extent and nature of cross-subsidization in HEOs has been limited. Regretfully, an in-depth examination of this practice is beyond the scope of the current analysis. Ongoing research by the author, however, has established that this process does occur in public and private nonprofit HEOs but follows different patterns in the two sectors and changes significantly over time.

Contributions and Policy Implications

This analysis has answered the questions of how public HEOs change their revenues and spending over time and the correspondence in these two dimensions of public HEO financial behaviors. These answers have a number of implications for policy makers, administrators, and researchers. For researchers, these results challenge our standard interpretation of key theories used to understand HEOs, specifically, resource dependency theory and the open systems perspective of organizational research. In effect, the results presented here suggest the need for scope conditions for resource dependency theory and open systems perspective of organizational behavior in the context of organizations like public HEOs that are multi-revenue/multiproduct organizations. The internal processes of an organization, such as the mission and cross-subsidization practices of HEOs, can mediate the effect(s) of resource dependencies and environmental conditions on some aspects of HEO behaviors. Resource dependency theory outlines a number of factors that should mediate the effects of dependence on behaviors such as the stakeholder's ability to control the allocation of the resources, the extent of the dependence, and the availability of alternative resources that could be used as possible mediating factors or scope conditions (Pfeffer & Salancik, 2003). However, an investigation of the extent to which the internal decision making processes, cross-subsidization practices, and mission constraints on the effect of dependence has yet to be undertaken and is beyond the scope of the current analysis.

For university administrators, this analysis provides insight into how their spending and revenue trends and profiles compare to those of other public HEOs. The more holistic picture of how the revenue and spending behaviors of public HEOs change, provided by the descriptive statistics and MLCA profiles, can help administrators gain insights about their peer institutions and knowledge of other revenue and spending profile options. This analysis also inductively derived groups of HEOs based on their behavior and uses movement between those groups to map out the nature of the field of public higher education. This approach could be applied to a variety of other HEO behaviors that administrators would find useful. For example, HEOs could be clustered based on their research output. The relationship between these research profiles and HEO success or economic contributions would be of substantial use to HEO administrators as well as state governments, research funding agencies, and policy makers.

For policy makers, this analysis has revealed key changes over time in one dimension of public HEO financial behavior, revenues, and stagnation or inertia in another dimension, HEO spending. By evaluating the revenue and spending profiles of public HEOs, in addition to the trends in individual revenue and spending streams, I have provided policy makers with a more detailed understanding of the nature of changes in HEO revenue profiles and the different ways in which these institutions are adapting to their changing resource environments. This is necessary to fully understand the implications of past policy changes and also to better anticipate the reactions of HEOs, and the field as a whole, to potential future policy changes. Furthermore, the lack of change in spending profiles highlights an area in which HEOs have not changed their behavior despite changes in policies, resource conditions, and other environmental forces that affect public HEOs. This is particularly relevant for policy makers in the context of evaluating the effectiveness of past changes to higher education policies. The multilevel nature of this analysis is also significant for policy makers. Because the analysis not only describes individual HEO-level changes, but also field-level trends for public higher education, it provides insight into how the different ways HEOs have adapted to past conditions and policies impacts the field of public higher education as a whole.

NOTES

1. Notable exceptions to this include Fowles (2014), Shepherd (2014), Hasbrouck (1997), and Leslie, Slaughter, Taylor, and Zhang (2012) all of which are discussed below.

2. Blasdell et al. (1993) included state, local, and federal government grants and contracts; state and local appropriations; gifts and endowment income; and net tuition in their calculation of total revenues.

3. Net E&G revenues refer to those revenues that are part of the mission-related activities of the HEO and therefore exclude non-mission-related revenues such as the sales and services of educational activities, auxiliary enterprises, hospitals, independent operations, and other sources (Toutkoushian, 2001).

4. In the MLCA analysis the square root transformation was used for private gifts, grant and contracts and federal government revenues which were skewed, but not irreparably so. A log transformation was used on miscellaneous revenues. These transformations ensured an approximately normal distribution based on their skewness statistics.

5. In the MLCA analysis the square root transformation was utilized for institutional support services, operation and maintenance, academic support, and miscellaneous expenditures to ensure an approximately normal distribution based on their skewness statistics.

6. The average levels in 2010 for each were 3.7%, 6.6%, 1.6%, and 0.11%, respectively, and the contribution to total spending for each stream changed by less than 1% on average between 1986 and 2010.

7. I used total current fund revenues net of investment income and other revenues because of the substantial number of negative values for these income streams in a number of years which made generating proportions problematic. Both investment income and other revenues are specific categories of revenues in the IPEDS data definitions of which are available, along with those for the other revenue and spending streams, at http://nces.ed.gov/ipeds/glossary/.

8. In this ability to account for the variation across organizations *and* over time MLCA is analogous to the two levels in a hierarchical linear model where one level accounts for the variation across cases and the other level accounts for the variation within cases over time (Macmillian & Eliason, 2003; Singer & Willett, 2003).

9. A discussion of the model parameters and their significance is included in the Methodological Appendix which is available upon request from the author.

10. When used with continuous indicators, as it is here, the measurement portion of the model can also be referred to as latent class cluster analysis or latent profile analysis (Hagenaars & McCutcheon, 2002).

11. This assignment is probabilistic because MLCA is a variation on a multinomial logistic regression model: it is predicting the probability of a HEO being in a particular group. Therefore, MLCA models, like many other types of latent class analysis, assign cases proportionally to the different latent classes. What this means is that a particular HEO can be 95% in latent class A and 5% in latent class B, for example. While this is possible, the majority of cases in this analysis are solidly in one class, that is, they are generally 99% or 100% in a single latent class at any particular point in time.

12. A more detailed discussion of the determination of the model specification, including log likelihood and BIC model fit statistics is available in a Methodological Appendix that is available upon request from the author.

13. HEOs throughout this section refer to public HEOs unless otherwise noted.

14. It should be noted that there are some fluctuations in the average levels of revenue dependence in each profile as HEOs move between them over time. The main change over time is that all of the revenue profiles are more dependent on tuition and less dependent on state funding in 2010 than they were in 1986. For example, the schools in the *tuition + state profile* drew 41% and 30% of total revenues from tuition and state funding, respectively, in 1986 and 44% and 28% in 2010. However, while there are fluctuations as the schools move in and out of the profiles, and as they experience shifts in revenues over time, the average characteristics of the schools in each profile are the same relative to each other. For example, the *state dependent profile* is the most dependent on state funding at the beginning and end of the period (58% in 1986 and 43% in 2010) and the *diversified profile* is the most diversified in 1986 and 2010 (tuition increased from 12% in 1986 to 25% in 2010 and state funding declined from 40% to 27% for the HEOs in this profile but the other revenue streams remained approximately the same for the period). Diagrams of the average revenue dependencies for the HEOs in each profile in 1986 and 2010 are available from the author upon request.

15. A full list of the HEOs in each profile is available upon request from the author.

16. For Arizona 29.2% of total revenues were from tuition, 23.6% from state, and 24.8% from federal; Minnesota had 23.3%, 24.9%, and 19.1% respectively; and UC Berkeley had 26.9%, 29.5%, and 19.4%, respectively, in 2010.

17. Further details on the justification of the three profile model are discussed in greater detail in the Methodological Appendix which is available upon request from the author.

18. As with the revenue profiles there are minor fluctuations in the average characteristics of each profile over time as a few HEOs switch between the profiles and make other slight alterations to their spending patterns. However, there were no changes to the average characteristics of these profiles that exceeded 2% between 1986 and 2010.

19. Miscellaneous spending for the HEOs in this profile were primarily hospital expenditures or public service expenditures (12.09% and 7.96%, respectively).

ACKNOWLEDGMENTS

This material is based upon work supported by the Association for Institutional Research, the National Science Foundation, the National Center for Education Statistics, and the National Postsecondary Education Cooperative under Association for Institutional Research Grant #DG12-44. The author would like to thank Joseph Galaskiewicz, Scott R. Eliason, Erin Leahey, Cindy L. Cain, Megan S. Wright, and Daniel Duerr for their helpful suggestions, guidance, and encouragement.

REFERENCES

American Federation of Teachers. (2009). *The American academic: The state of higher education workforce 1997–2007*. Washington, DC: American Federation of Teachers.

Barringer, S. N., & Slaughter, S. (2016). University trustees and the entrepreneurial university: Inner circles, interlocks, and exchanges. In S. Slaughter & B. J. Taylor (Eds.), *Higher education, stratification, and workforce development: Competitive advantage in Europe, the US, and Canada* (pp. 151–171). Berlin: Springer.

Bastedo, M. N., & Gumport, P. J. (2003). Access to what? Mission differentiation and academic stratification in U.S. public higher education. *Higher Education, 46*, 341–359.

Belasco, A., Rosinger, K. O., & Hearn, J. C. (2015). The test-optional movement at America's selective liberal arts colleges: A boon for equity or something else? *Educational Evaluation and Policy Analysis, 37*, 206–223. doi:10.3102/0162373714537350

Bennett, D. L., Lucchesi, A. R., & Vedder, R. K. (2010). *For-profit higher education: Growth, innovation and regulation*. Washington, DC: Center for College Affordability and Productivity.

Berman, E. P. (2012). *Creating the market university: How academic science became an economic engine*. Princeton, NJ: Princeton University Press.

Berman, E. P., & Stivers, A. (2016). Student loans as a pressure on U.S. higher education. In E. P. Berman & C. Paradeise (Eds.), *The university under pressure* (Vol. 46, pp. 129–160). Research in the Sociology of Organizations. Bingley, UK: Emerald Group Publishing Limited.

Blasdell, S. W., McPherson, M. S., & Schapiro, M. O. (1993). Trends in revenues and expenditures in U.S. higher education: Where does the money come from? Where does it go? In M. S. McPherson, M. O. Schapiro, & G. C. Winston (Eds.), *Paying the piper: Productivity, incentives, and financing in U.S. higher education* (pp. 15–34). Ann Arbor, MI: The University of Michigan Press.

Brown, B. E., & Clark, R. L. (2006). North Carolina's commitment to higher education: Access and affordability. In R. G. Ehrenberg (Ed.), *What's happening to public higher education: The shifting financial burden* (pp. 183–205). Baltimore, MD: The Johns Hopkins University Press.

Cantwell, B., & Taylor, B. J. (2013). Global status, intra-institutional stratification and organizational segmentation: A time-dynamic tobit analysis of ARWU position among U.S. universities. *Minerva, 51*(2), 195–223. doi:10.1007/s11024-013-9228-8

Cohn, E., Rhine, S. L. W., & Santos, M. C. (1989). Institutions of higher education as multi-product firms: Economies of scale and scope. *The Review of Economics and Statistics*, *71*(2), 284−290.

College Board. (2014). Trends in college pricing. In *Trends in higher education*. Washington, DC.

De Groot, H., McMahon, W. W., & Volkwein, J. F. (1991). The cost structure of American research universities. *Review of Economics and Statistics*, *73*, 424−431.

Desrochers, D. M., & Wellman, J. V. (2011). *Trends in college spending, 1999−2009: Where does the money come from? Where does it go? What does it buy?* Washington, DC: The Delta Cost Project.

Ehrenberg, R. G. (2006). *What's happening to public higher education? The shifting financial burden*. Baltimore, MD: Johns Hopkins University Press.

Fligstein, N., & Dauter, L. (2007). The sociology of markets. *Annual Review of Sociology*, *33*(1), 105−128. doi:10.1146/annurev.soc.33.040406.131736

Fligstein, N., & McAdam, D. (2011). Towards a theory of strategic action fields. *Sociological Theory*, *29*, 1−26.

Fligstein, N., & McAdam, D. (2012). *A theory of fields*. New York, NY: Oxford University Press.

Fowles, J. (2014). Funding and focus: Resource dependence in public higher education. *Research in Higher Education*, *55*(3), 272−287. doi:10.1007/s11162-013-9311-x

Froelich, K. A. (1999). Diversification of revenue strategies: Evolving resource dependence in nonprofit organizations. *Nonprofit and Voluntary Sector Quarterly*, *28*(3), 246−268.

Geiger, R. L. (2004a). *Knowledge and money: Research universities and the paradox of the marketplace*. Palo Alto, CA: Stanford University Press.

Geiger, R. L. (2004b). Market coordination in higher education: The United States. In P. Teixeira, B. Jongbloed, & D. D. Dill (Eds.), *Markets in higher education: Rhetoric or reality?* (pp. 161−184). Dordrecht: Kluwer.

Gumport, P. J., & Snydman, S. K. (2006). Higher education: Evolving forms and emerging markets. In W. W. Powell & R. Steinberg (Eds.), *The non-profit sector: A research handbook* (2nd ed., pp. 462−484). New Haven, CT: Yale University Press.

Hagenaars, J. A., & McCutcheon, A. L. (Eds.). (2002). *Applied latent class analysis*. Cambridge: Cambridge University Press.

Hasbrouck, N. (1997). *Implications of the changing funding base of public universities*. Ph.D. dissertation, University of Arizona, Tucson, AZ.

Hearn, J. C. (2003). Diversifying campus revenue streams: Opportunities and risks. In *Informed practice: Syntheses of higher education research for campus leaders*. Washington, DC: American Council on Education.

Hearn, J. C., & Rosinger, K. O. (2014). Socioeconomic diversity in selective private colleges: An organizational analysis. *The Review of Higher Education*, *38*(1), 71−104.

IPEDS Analytics. (2015). *Delta cost project database: Data mapping file*. Retrieved from https://nces.ed.gov/ipeds/deltacostproject/. Accessed on February 4, 2015.

James, E. (1983). How nonprofits grow: A model. *Journal of Policy Analysis and Management*, *2*(3), 350−365.

James, E. (1990). Decision processes and priorities in higher education. In S. A. Hoenack & E. L. Collins (Eds.), *The economics of American universities: Management, operations, and fiscal environment* (pp. 77−106). Albany, NY: SUNY Press.

Just, R. E., & Huffman, W. E. (2009). The economics of universities in a new age of funding options. *Research Policy*, *38*, 1102−1116.

Kaplan, G. (2009). Governing the privatized public research university. In C. C. Morphew & P. D. Eckel (Eds.), *Privatizing the public university: Perspectives from across the academy* (pp. 109–133). Baltimore, MD: The Johns Hopkins University Press.

Leslie, L. L., Slaughter, S., Taylor, B. J., & Zhang, L. (2012). How do revenue variations affect expenditures within U.S. research universities? *Research in Higher Education, 53*(6), 614–639.

Macmillian, R., & Eliason, S. R. (2003). Characterizing the life course as role configurations and pathways. In J. T. Mortimer & M. J. Shanahan (Eds.), *Handbook of the life course* (pp. 529–554). New York, NY: Kluwer Academic/Plenum Publishers.

Mathies, C., & Slaughter, S. (2013). University trustees as channels between academe and industry: Toward an understanding of the executive science network. *Research Policy, 42*(6–7), 1286–1300. doi:10.1016/j.respol.2013.03.003

McLendon, M. K., Hearn, J. C., & Deaton, R. (2006). Called to account: The origins and spread of state performance-accountability policies for higher education. *Educational Evaluation and Policy Analysis, 28*(1), 1–24.

McPherson, M. S., & Schapiro, M. O. (1993). The effect of government financing on the behavior of colleges and universities. In M. S. McPherson, M. O. Schapiro, & G. C. Winston (Eds.), *Paying the piper: Productivity, incentives, and financing in U.S. higher education* (pp. 235–250). Ann Arbor, MI: The University of Michigan Press.

McPherson, M. S., & Schapiro, M. O. (1998). *The student aid game: Meeting need and rewarding talent in American higher education.* Princeton, NJ: Princeton University Press.

McPherson, M. S., Schapiro, M. O., & Winston, G. C. (1993). *Paying the piper: Productivity, incentives and financing in U.S. higher education.* Ann Arbor, MI: University of Michigan Press.

Morphew, C. C. (2009). Conceptualizing change in the institutional diversity of U.S. colleges and universities. *The Journal of Higher Education, 80*(3), 243–269. doi:10.1353/jhe.0.0047

Morphew, C. C., & Eckel, P. D. (2009). *Privatizing the public university: Perspectives from across the academy.* Baltimore, MD: The Johns Hopkins University Press.

Morphew, C. C., & Taylor, B. J. (2010). Scholars as leaders? A review of Socrates in the Boardroom. *Higher Education, 61*(5), 617–619. doi:10.1007/s10734-010-9350-6

Pfeffer, J., & Salancik, G. R. (2003). *The external control of organization: A resource dependence perspective.* Stanford, CA: Stanford University Press.

Popp Berman, E. (2008). Why did universities start patenting? Institution-building and the road to the Bayh-Dole act. *Social Studies of Science, 38*(6), 835–871. doi:10.1177/0306312708098605

Powell, W. W., & Smith, J. O. (1998). Universities as creators and retailers of intellectual property: Life-sciences research and commercial development. In B. A. Weisbrod (Ed.), *To profit or not to profit: The commercial transformation of the nonprofit sector* (pp. 169–193). Cambridge: Cambridge University Press.

Rizzo, M. J. (2006). State preferences for higher education spending: A panel data analysis, 1977–2001. In R. G. Ehrenberg (Ed.), *What's happening to public higher education? The shifting financial burden* (pp. 3–35). Baltimore, MD: Johns Hopkins University Press.

Schuster, J. H., & Finkelstein, M. J. (2006). *American faculty: The restructuring of academic work and careers.* Baltimore, MD: Johns Hopkins University Press.

Shepherd, J. C. (2014). *Linking university expenses to performance outcomes: A look at departments, colleges and institutions.* Ph.D. dissertation, Vanderbilt University, Nashville, TN.

Singer, J. D., & Willett, J. B. (2003). *Applied longitudinal data analysis: Modeling change and event occurrence*. Oxford: Oxford University Press.

Slaughter, S., & Leslie, L. L. (1997). *Academic capitalism: Politics, policies, and the entrepreneurial university*. Baltimore, MD: Johns Hopkins University Press.

Slaughter, S., & Rhoades, G. (2004). *Academic capitalism and the new economy: Markets, state, and higher education*. Baltimore, MD: The Johns Hopkins University Press.

Slaughter, S., Thomas, S. L., Johnson, D., & Barringer, S. N. (2014). Institutional conflict of interest: The role of interlocking directorates in the scientific relationships between universities and the corporate sector. *The Journal of Higher Education, 85*(1), 1–35.

Smith, J. O. (2000). *Public science, private science: The causes and consequences of patenting by research one universities*. Doctorate of philosophy dissertation, University of Arizona, Tucson, AZ.

Taylor, B. J., Barringer, S. N., & Warshaw, J. B. (2015). *Affiliated nonprofit organizations: Strategic action and research universities*. University of North Texas and University of Georgia.

Taylor, B. J., Cantwell, B., & Slaughter, S. (2013). Quasi-markets in U.S. higher education: The humanities and institutional revenues. *The Journal of Higher Education, 84*(5), 675–707. doi:10.1353/jhe.2013.0030

Toutkoushian, R. K. (2001). Trends in revenues and expenditures for public and private higher education. In M. B. Paulsen & J. C. Smart (Eds.), *The finance of higher education: Theory, research, policy, and practice* (pp. 11–38). New York, NY: Agathon.

Tuckman, H. P., & Chang, C. F. (1990). Participant goals, institutional goals, and university resource allocation decisions. In S. A. Hoenack & E. L. Collins (Eds.), *The economics of American universities: Management, operations, and fiscal environment* (pp. 53–75). Albany, NY: SUNY Press.

Turner, S. (2006). Higher tuition, higher aid, and the quest to improve opportunities for low-income students: The case of Virginia. In R. G. Ehrenberg (Ed.), *What's happening to public higher education: The shifting financial burden* (pp. 251–274). Baltimore, MD: The Johns Hopkins University Press.

Vermut, J. K. (2003). Multilevel latent class models. *Sociological Methodology, 33*, 213–239.

Warner, R. M. (2008). *Applied statistics: From bivariate through multivariate techniques*. Los Angeles, CA: Sage.

Weisbrod, B. A. (Ed.). (1998). *To profit or not to profit: The commercial transformation of the nonprofit sector*. Cambridge: Cambridge University Press.

Weisbrod, B. A., Ballou, J. P., & Asch, E. D. (2008). *Mission and money: Understanding the university*. Cambridge: Cambridge University Press.

Wellman, J., Desrochers, D., Lenihan, C., Kirshstein, R., Hurlburt, S., & Honegger, S. (2009). *Trends in college spending: Where does the money come from? Where does it go?* Washington, DC: Delta Project on Postsecondary Education Costs, Productivity, and Accountability.

Wilsker, A. L., & Young, D. R. (2010). How does program composition affect the revenues of nonprofit organizations?: Investigating a benefits theory of nonprofit finance. *Public Finance Review, 38*(2), 193–216.

Young, D. R. (Ed.). (2007). *Financing nonprofits: Putting theory into practice*. New York, NY: AltaMira Press.

APPENDIX

Table A1.   Definitions of Key Expenditure and Revenue Streams.[a]

Expenditure Stream	Definition
Instruction expenditures	Expenses of the colleges, schools, departments, and other instructional divisions of the institution and expenses for departmental research and public service that are not separately budgeted. Also included are general academic instruction, occupational and vocational instruction, community education, preparatory and adult basic education, and regular, special, and extension sessions as well as expenses for both credit and non-credit activities.
Research expenditures	Expenses for activities specifically organized to produce research outcomes and commissioned by an agency either external to the institution or separately budgeted by an organizational unit within the institution (e.g., institutes and research centers, and individual and project research).
Academic support expenditures	Expenses for activities and services that support the institution's primary missions of instruction, research, and public service including: the retention, preservation, and display of educational materials (e.g., libraries and museums); organized activities that provide support services to the academic functions of the institution; media such as audiovisual services; academic administration; and formally organized and separately budgeted academic personnel development and course and curriculum development expenses.
Student services expenditures	Expenses for admissions, registrar activities, and activities whose primary purpose is to contribute to students emotional and physical well-being and to their intellectual, cultural, and social development outside the context of the formal instructional program. Examples include: student activities, cultural events, student newspapers, intramural athletics, student organizations, supplemental instruction, and student records. Intercollegiate athletics and student health services may also be included except when operated as self-supporting auxiliary enterprises.
Institutional support expenditures	Expenses for the day-to-day operational support of the institution such as general administrative services, central executive-level activities concerned with management and long range planning, legal and fiscal operations, space management, employee personnel and records, logistical services, and public relations and development.
Operation and maintenance expenditures	Expenses for operations established to provide service and maintenance related to campus grounds and facilities used for educational and general purposes. Examples: utilities, fire protection, property insurance, and similar items. Amounts charged to auxiliary enterprises, hospitals, and independent operations are not included.
Auxiliary enterprise expenditures	Expenses for self-supporting operations of the institution that exist to furnish a service to students, faculty, or staff, and that charge a fee that is directly related to, although not necessarily equal to, the cost of the service. Examples: residence halls, food services, student health services, intercollegiate athletics (only if essentially self-supporting), college stores, parking, and faculty housing.

Table A1. *(Continued)*

Revenue Stream	Definition
State funding	This includes (1) grants and contracts funding, that is, revenues from state government agencies that are for training programs and similar activities for which amounts are received or expenditures are reimbursable under the terms of a state government grant or contract and (2) appropriations, that is, revenues received by an institution through acts of a state legislative body, except grants and contracts.
Federal funding	This includes (1) grants and contracts funding, that is, revenues from federal governmental agencies that are for training programs, research, or public service activities for which expenditures are reimbursable under the terms of a government grant or contract and (2) appropriations, that is, revenues received by an institution through acts of the federal legislative body, except grants, and contracts.
Tuition and fees	Gross revenues from tuition and associated fees. This includes: federal student financial aid, institutional aid, state government financial aid, and scholarship income.
Private gifts, grants and contracts	Revenues from private donors for which no legal consideration is involved and from private contracts for specific goods and services provided to the funder as stipulation for receipt of the funds. Only those gifts, grants, and contracts that are directly related to instruction, research, public service, or other institutional purposes are included.
Auxiliary enterprise revenues	Revenues generated by or collected from the auxiliary enterprise operations of the institution that exist to furnish a service to students, faculty, or staff, and that charge a fee that is directly related to, although not necessarily equal to, the cost of the service. Auxiliary enterprises are managed as essentially self-supporting activities. Examples are residence halls, food services, student health services, intercollegiate athletics, college unions, college stores, and movie theaters.

[a]These definitions are from the IPEDS Glossary (http://nces.ed.gov/ipeds/glossary/) and the Survey forms (http://nces.ed.gov/ipeds/surveys/2010/pdf/f_1_2010.pdf).

RECONCILING THE SMALL EFFECT OF RANKINGS ON UNIVERSITY PERFORMANCE WITH THE TRANSFORMATIONAL COST OF CONFORMITY

Craig Tutterow and James A. Evans

ABSTRACT

University rankings and metrics have become an increasingly prominent basis of student decisions, generalized university reputation, and the resources university's attract. We review the history of metrics in higher education and scholarship about the influence of ranking on the position and strategic behavior of universities and students. Most quantitative analyses on this topic estimate the influence of change in university rank on performance. These studies consistently identify a small, short-lived influence of rank shift on selectivity (e.g., one rank position corresponds to ≤1% more student applicants), comparable to ranking effects documented in other domains. This understates the larger system-level impact of metrification on universities, students, and the professions that surround them. We explore one system-level transformation likely influenced by the rise of rankings. Recent years have witnessed the rise of enrollment

The University under Pressure
Research in the Sociology of Organizations, Volume 46, 265–301
Copyright © 2016 by Emerald Group Publishing Limited
All rights of reproduction in any form reserved
ISSN: 0733-558X/doi:10.1108/S0733-558X20160000046009

management and independent educational consultation. We illustrate a plausible pathway from ranking to this transformation: In an effort to improve rankings, universities solicit more applications from students to reduce their acceptance rate. Lower acceptance rates lead to more uncertainty for students about acceptance, leading them to apply to more schools, which decreases the probability that accepted students will attend. This leads to greater uncertainty about enrollment for students and universities and generates demand for new services to manage it. Because these and other system-level transformations are not as cleanly measured as rank position and performance, they have not received the same treatment or modeling attention in higher education scholarship, despite their importance for understanding and influencing education policy.

Keywords: Higher education; rankings; uncertainty; feedback effects; unintended consequences; yield rates

INTRODUCTION

University rankings have become a critical tool for students and their families to make decisions about where to attend college and graduate school. They also constitute the basis for generalized university reputation and bragging rights, which, in turn, have direct consequences for the sponsorship and research resources a university can attract. A growing literature in sociology and economics has considered the influence of these rankings on the system of higher education. Much quantitative work in this area focuses on the United States and identifies a statistically significant influence of shifts in these rankings on university-level performance, including number of student applications, yield rates, test scores, and financial aid. This *ranking effect*, however, is consistently *very* small and short-lived (Gnolek, Falciano, & Kuncl, 2014). An increase in one rank position generates less than 1% increase in applicants for most schools (Bowman & Bastedo, 2009). In this paper, we review the *ranking effect* as estimated across several recent studies, in higher education and other domains, all within the United States. Then we seek to reconcile the small size of the estimated effect with the massive attention university rankings have achieved from university administrators, students, policy makers, and scholars of higher education (Ehrenberg, 2000; Elsbach & Kramer, 1996; Espeland & Sauder, 2007; Grewal, Dearden, & Llilien, 2012; Luca & Smith, 2013, Sauder & Lancaster, 2006). Research focused on the university-level ranking effect cannot identify ranking's system-level consequences. We explore the range of ranking's influence by exploring a system-level transformation in higher education: the rise of the professions of enrollment management and independent education consultation. We document this historically, then use formal analysis and simulation to identify a plausible influence pathway from the increased importance of rankings to growth in the demand for these two professions. To inflate their ranking, universities now routinely solicit more applications in order to reject more students and appear more selective. This decreases the probability that a student will be accepted into any one school. Applicants respond by applying to more schools, but this increases the odds they will receive competing offers, leading to a lower likelihood that any given student will accept any particular offer of admission. We demonstrate that this process leads to greater uncertainty about enrollment for both students and universities, and is a possible mechanism to explain growth in demand for the third-party consultants who mitigate it. We believe that these and other consequences resulting from conformity to the criteria underlying rankings, although much less intensively studied than the ranking effect on university performance, justify the attention paid to ranking in higher education. Insofar as these consequences decrease the value proposition of higher education for students, we outline relevant policy considerations and suggest advances in research to rigorously investigate them.

What is the basis of modern university ranking schemes? Education is a multi-sided market in which both schools and students compete for affiliation with one another. Over the past two decades, increasing tuition costs and competition at entry-level labor markets in the US have led to more uncertainty about the financial return from a college degree. In this environment of increased uncertainty about the future, positional comparisons have become more salient. Publications that rank universities (e.g., *US News & World Report*) generate a prism through which students can make peer comparisons, and attention to these has led to positional competition between schools on observed criteria. While there is little evidence to suggest a substantial influence of school choice on educational or career outcomes at the undergraduate level (Dale & Krueger, 1999; Pascarella, Terenzini, & Feldman, 2005), rankings have been met with high demand from status-conscious high-school students and their parents. Furthermore, year-to-year changes in rank are shown to have only a small effect on application and matriculation decisions, but they are salient for administrators, leading to transformations in how resources are allocated within universities. The history of measuring and ranking universities, however, goes back much further.

A BRIEF (PRE)HISTORY OF UNIVERSITY METRICS AND RANKINGS

The origin of metrics in higher education may be dated to the rise of biblio-metric indicators and their use in assessing scientific institutions. Every written legal system, from ancient Rome to Late Medieval Britain had laws and cases that intensively referenced one another. These citations are most critical in systems of common law where precedence and "exemplar" cases shaped and constrained subsequent judgements. The first commercial "data-base" of linkages, however, was created at the end of the 19th century with Shephard's citation index (1873). References moved from initial "Adhesive Annotations" stuck with gum on pages of case law, to bound books of cita-tions indexed by different jurisdictions, to sets of CD ROMs, to a single web-accessible database. Citation analysis spilled beyond legal scholarship at the end of the 19th century. Early American psychologist James McKeen Catell, editor of *Science* magazine for nearly 50 years (1895–1944), was first to champion and create a systematic collection of statistics on quantity ("productivity") and quality ("reputation") of scientists by nation and field. His effort focused on tracking and boosting the research reputation of the United States and psychology as a science (Godin, 2006). Citation metrics on the system of science and scholarship emerged later with the pioneering work of physicist-turned-historian, Derek de Solla Price. Using publication and citation data, de Solla Price traced the historical exponential growth of science (1963), measured the half-life of reference age in the scientific litera-ture (1965), identified the long-tailed distribution of scientific contributions or "Price's Law" that a few contribute a lot, and most contribute very little, and demonstrated the existence of a popularity or preferential attachment process in citations (1976), whereby articles receive new citations propor-tional to their prior citations.

In the course of his work on scientific citation, de Solla Price consulted with Eugene Garfield, who created the Institute for Scientific Information (ISI) and constructed the first databases of scholarly citations, the Science Citation Index. Later, ISI generated companion products, the Social Science and Arts and Humanities Citation Indices. Garfield and the archi-tecture of these indices drew inspiration from Vannevar Bush's famous *Atlantic Monthly* article, "As We May Think," about building information machines to facilitate the logging and tuning of a scientist's cognitive research and reasoning paths (1945). "As We May Think" inspired the architecture of the World Wide Web, and Garfield's scholarly information resources and the citation metrics built upon them, served as inspiration for the HITS and Pagerank algorithms that have defined the ranking schemes of modern search engines (Gugliotta, 2009).[1] Garfield's resources also facilitated scholarly research, especially in the social sciences and humanities where scholarship itself is a legitimate research object. ISI later produced Journal Citation Reports atop their other information resources and designed the associated Impact Factor metric in 1975, which became the primarily basis of ranking scholarly journals. These journal rankings, in turn, have come to form the basis of productivity and reputation metrics for individual scholars, departments, and universities.

Soon afterwards, in 1983, *US News & World Report* published its first "America's Best Colleges" report, which they produced annually from 1988. This has become extremely influential (e.g., 10 million hits within the first week of online publication). Although citation and journal metrics do not enter these rankings directly, they rely on a fixed evaluation methodology: an annual survey sent to each school, the school's website, and opinion surveys of university faculty and administrators at competing schools. Bibliometric measures of productivity and impact are central to the U.S. National Academy of Sciences doctoral program rankings, as well as the influential Academic Ranking of World Universities (ARWU) compiled by the Shanghai Jiao Tong University (the "Shanghai Rankings") to rank universities globally and provide the Chinese government with a "global benchmark" against universities in China so they "could assess their progress" and "catch up" on "hard scientific research" (Marszal, 2012). Other global university rankings (e.g., from the *Times*) have followed. Rankings, bibliometrics, and surveys have also become central to some countries' research funding allocation process, like Great Britain's research assessment exercise.

STANDARDIZED METRICS IN CONTEMPORARY MARKETS

Intermediaries that provide standardized metrics on quality are increasingly prevalent in many contemporary markets beyond higher education. These metrics are used as heuristics, or compressed information about quality that substitutes for more costly primary research. Two factors that strongly influence the use of standardized metrics include (1) the population of institutions in question (i.e., the consideration set) and (2) the stakes associated with the decision. An increase in the size of the consideration set makes it more costly for an individual to collect a representative sample of the quality distribution in a given field. Small institutional fields, in which all participants are known to one another, demonstrate little demand for intermediaries. An increase in the economic, political, or moral stakes of a decision make it more important for an individual to minimize the margin of error regarding their sample, or tighten their "confidence interval." When both factors are present, the context is ripe for the entrance of specialized intermediaries that can perform research on the consideration set and provide guidance in the form of a recommendation or ranking to prospective consumers.

Both large market size and high stakes characterize the field of higher education in post-war United States. For example, the rise of information intermediaries in academic libraries − the shift from small, departmental libraries managed by the faculty to massive, centralized research libraries presided over by professional librarians and information scientists − tracks a global explosion in the number of researchers, research articles, and books published in all fields (Abbott, 2011). The increase in global research activity increased the burden of gaining adequate coverage of research in any area, and coincided with the emergence of professional librarians who managed the organization of complex research outputs. Similarly, growth in the number and increasing diversity of students from different international, ethnic and social class backgrounds has increased the demand for intermediating metrics to rank universities. These metrics and rankings facilitate a "view from Shanghai" − by anyone from anywhere − in the global field of higher education. As a result, students now consider a larger set of schools, less constrained by geographic location (Hoxby, 2009).

The stakes of research and education in the field of higher education have also grown. Larger government budgets associated with global research during and following World War II necessarily led to greater oversight than that which was afforded by basic accreditation and reputation alone. Sponsors likely wanted to fund the best work, which required the creation of intermediaries and metrics to provide higher resolution assessments of quality. A culture of civilian accountability for nonmilitary research investments also likely pushed a more defensible assessment of researcher quality. Similarly, for the student consumers of higher education, tuition costs have risen nearly three times the rate of inflation since 1978 (7.74% per annum vs. 2.67%) − outpacing even health care costs. These changes set the stage for the entrance of specialized intermediaries such as *US News & World Report* in the early 1980s.

The following sections will (a) discuss the empirical findings on the effect of rankings on student application and matriculation decisions, (b) compare the impact of rankings to other factors known to influence student decisions, and (c) compare the impact of college rankings to other mediated markets when standardized metrics are prominent.

EFFECT OF COLLEGE RANKINGS ON STUDENT PREFERENCES

The transformative impact of intermediaries and ranking in higher education has been frequently noted (Brewer, Gates, & Goldman, 2004; Ehrenberg, 2000, p. 61), but most empirical studies show very modest effect sizes for change in rank on decision making at the individual level. This section will survey what we know about standardized metrics and rankings in higher education and their effect on stakeholder decisions. Depending on the context and identification strategy, a one position change in rank can lead to a 0.2−2% increase in applications for a given school in the next academic year. This effect only holds for the top 25 national universities, however, for which prospective student demand is particularly elastic to status (Bowman & Bastedo, 2009). The perceived difference between the 1st and 10th schools is larger than that between the 40th and 50th.

Here, we focus on the effect of ranking for the performance of U.S. schools in the market for students, but we also compare effect sizes of rating and ranking across a range of contexts to provide a sense of their relative magnitude in higher education. While rigorous inferences cannot be made across studies due to a lack of standardization, there is suggestive evidence that students' educational choices respond to university ranks with a magnitude similar to that of consumer choices in other domains. Across contexts, there appears to be a consistently positive and statistically significant, but *very* modest effect of mediated ratings on institutional performance. Some of the most recent findings suggest that even the small positive effect of elevated status may be overestimated (Azoulay, Stuart, & Wang, 2014), and can even result in penalties under certain circumstances (Kovacs & Sharkey, 2014).

Together, the body of empirical evidence raises questions about the vast resources poured into rating improvements by large institutions. More comparative research is needed to generate robust inference on the effect of ratings in different contexts, and to expand knowledge beyond simple institution-level effects in order to empirically capture the size and mechanism by which intermediation effects the social system as a whole. It seems clear, however, that the vast majority of recent studies about ratings and rankings on institutional performance do not capture the experienced influence of imposed ratings and rankings on the system of higher education, where universities have conformed to measured criteria in order to advance in them (Sauder & Lancaster, 2006).

A number of studies have estimated the impact of rankings on student application and matriculation decisions. In law schools, Sauder and Lancaster (2006) estimate that a one place change in rank corresponds to a modest increase of 19 applications and only a 0.18% increase in matriculants the following year. To arrive at this finding, they use a conservative Prais-Winsten cross-sectional time-series regression technique with an autoregressive term for prior rank and fixed effects for school and year. By adding prior rank to their model, which controls for rank trajectory, this only allows identification of an *accelerating* change in rank, and so the effect is particularly small, but accumulates over time.

We know from other studies (Bowman & Bastedo, 2009) that top schools are particularly sensitive to changes in rank, so a stratified sample might show a larger effect for schools above a particular threshold. For top 25 national universities at the undergraduate level, Bowman and Bastedo (2009) show a 1% effect of a single place change in ranking on new applications in the subsequent admissions cycle. This effect does not hold for schools ranked 25–50, however, or for liberal arts colleges. Bowman & Bastedo also used fixed effects for school and year, but not an autoregressive term. Bowman & Bastedo show a much larger effect for movements between the first and second page of the *USNWR* rankings. Schools that move into the top 25 (and thus onto the first page of the rankings) experience a 9.6% increase in applications the following year. Although moving to the first page seems to be particularly salient, the schools that experienced this change are very small in number.

Lastly, Luca and Smith (2013) finds that when *US News* changed the presentation format of schools ranked 25–50 from alphabetical to ranked order, a one place increase in rank corresponded to a 0.55–0.71% increase in applications the following year. While the information comprising the ranking was available in both formats, the salience of the ordinal presentation was required for the effect. As expected, the effect was smaller than for top 25 schools. Collectively, this research shows a relatively minor effect of ranking improvements on the admissions selectivity of students. It also shows that prospective students may not be the most sophisticated information consumers and may be more influenced by salience of the presentation than the quality of information it conveys.

EFFECT OF OTHER FACTORS ON STUDENT PREFERENCES

The previously mentioned studies hold constant school-specific factors that also influence student application decisions, some of which have been shown to be more influential than ranking. Pope and Pope (2009) show that an appearance in the NCAA basketball tournament has roughly the same effect on applications as a one place increase in rank. Appearance in the NCAA basketball tournament leads to a 1% increase in applications, continuing to the "sweet 16" yields a 3% increase, making it to the "final four" a 4–5% increase, and winning the tournament a 7–8% bump in applications the following cycle. Smaller private schools are even more sensitive to this effect. In football, finishing in the top 20 yields a 2.5% increase in applications, the top 10 a 3% increase, and winning the championship yields a 7–8% rise. Like Bowman and Bastedo (2009), Pope & Pope use school and year fixed effects to control for unobserved heterogeneity. Schools outside the top 25 in *USNWR* would therefore receive a significantly larger bump from sports success than they would from marginally improving their position in the *US News* rankings.

Lifschitz, Sauder, and Stevens (2014) argue that much literature on status in higher education focuses solely on academic factors at the expense of nonacademic activities, which alumni and other external constituents find salient. In particular, they analyze how the football conference affiliations interact with a university's academic prestige. Schools tend to sort into conferences based on similar levels of academic prestige (with the Ivy league being the most prominent example). By affiliating and competing with schools of similar academic profile, games are made more salient for fans, such that something is at stake in winning or losing to a similarly ranked peer. In this way, athletic conferences constitute a space in which status dynamics are negotiated between schools. Lifschitz et al. also find that athletic affiliation feeds back into academic prestige, such that schools in the same conference converge on measures of academic status. This suggests that school status is a complex, multidimensional quality, contested across sectors with varying constituents.

Hoxby (2009) notes that decreasing travel and information costs led to a more integrated market for higher education in the second half of the 20th century. As such, student decisions are now less elastic with respect to location and more responsive to a school's resources and peer group. This has led to a stronger status sorting regime between schools. Providing evidence for this trend, Hoxby (1997) finds that the dispersion of student ability within schools has declined, while the dispersion of ability between schools has increased. School responses to this dynamic have been to increase prices as well as subsidies in order to compete for higher ability students. While lower status schools became less selective over this period, they also raised expenditures and subsidies for students.

Frank (1999) and Winston (2000) have argued that this empirical pattern can be described as an expenditure cascade. Expenditure cascades involve arms-race style competition for positional goods. In certain market contexts, excessive expenditures by high-status actors produce negative consequences for those further down the status hierarchy. In order to keep up, lower status institutions must adopt the same policies, and spend lavishly on other observables in order to signal resource-richness. While schools now compete on expenditures, they have not yet competed on price. This has led to student subsidies outpacing even the dramatic increase in tuition. While it is individually rational for each school to increase its student subsidy once the competitive dynamic is underway, all schools would be better off (from an institutional perspective) if they collectively agreed to regulate or tax extraneous expenditures on luxury goods.

We do not yet have reliable empirical estimates on the impact of status signals such as new dorms, athletic facilities, dining halls, and other amenities on student preferences, but colleges' increased competition in these areas suggest that they likely figure significantly into student choice. While resources are captured by most rankings, subsidies — signaled by lavish facilities or the marketing of other amenities (laundry services, haute cuisine) — are more observable on student visits and may have a significant effect on student college selections. To our knowledge, researchers have yet to estimate the relative impact of amenities and tangible wealth signals as compared to formal rankings on student decisions.

EFFECT OF METRICS IN OTHER INSTITUTIONAL DOMAINS

Comparing the effect of metrics in different domains is helpful for putting the effect of college rankings in perspective. Pope (2009) found that a one place increase in national rank corresponded to a 1% increase in nonemergency Medicare patient volume the following year. Hospitals are especially sensitive to within-state jumps in ranking. A one position increase in rank within a hospital's state corresponded to a 7% increase in Medicare patient volume. Since national rankings move five places on average each year,

Pope concludes that the *US News* rankings are responsible for about 5% of year-to-year change in patient volume. It appears that rankings have had a modestly greater effect in hospital settings compared with the college matriculation decision. While the top 25 national universities showed a similar effect size for ranking, the effect was smaller for schools outside of that category, and nonsignificant for some populations (liberal arts colleges). For hospitals, the aggregate effect was significant over all sub-populations. Furthermore, Pope's sample included 442 hospitals, much larger than the previously discussed studies, which typically restrict themselves to the "top 50." Moreover, from our analysis, university rankings vary much less year to year. Dating back to the inaugural 1983 *US News* issue, schools in the top 25 (and later the top 50 when rankings were expanded), move 1.92 places per year on average. The reason for this difference has yet to be explained, but could be attributed to either the higher stakes of the medical decision, or differences in the social organization and characteristics of the demographic groups.

In food service, Jin and Leslie (2003) analyze the impact of posted restaurant hygiene grades on the restaurant industry across municipalities in Los Angeles county. The public provision of hygiene grades leads to a small change in consumer behavior – restaurants moving from B to an A hygiene grade receive a 5% increase in revenue. The policy has larger effects on producer than consumer behavior, however, with average hygiene grades increasing from 75% to 90% over the two-year period of the study. This resulted in a 20% decrease in airborne illnesses in areas with the new policy in place. This empirical asymmetry, whereby the effect of a metric occurs more through supply-side anticipation than demand-side response, also appears to be the case in higher education's response to college rankings, though perhaps through a different pathway. This study also suggests that while ongoing rating/ranking changes may have little influence on school performance, their imposition as a whole may effect a much more dramatic influence on the standardization of universities and student applicants. Unlike Jin and Leslie (2003), most empirical studies estimate the impact of ratings or rankings on only one side of the market and therefore fail to identify second-order effects, or allude to them as implications in spite of relatively weak effect sizes.

In finance, researchers have found that investors respond rapidly to changes in ratings from securities analysts and bond rating agencies. For securities analysts, a categorical downgrade in recommendation (e.g., from buy to hold) yields an excess return of −2% for that share between the day preceding the announcement and the day following. Likewise, a categorical upgrade leads to a +0.75% excess return over the same period (Francis & Soffer, 1997). Hand, Holthausen, and Leftwich (1992) find that a Moody's or S&P bond downgrade across classes corresponded on average to a −1.27% excess return in the given bond on the day of and the day following the announcement. The median effect of the downgrade was −0.45%, indicating that it is partially driven by outliers. Likewise, firms' share prices are similarly affected by a bond downgrade (to the effect of −1.52% on average, −0.75% median). The larger impact on share price may be due to the fact that bondholders have priority over shareholders in bankruptcy proceedings. Nevertheless, downgrades do not have a monolithic effect and 40% of companies experience positive excess returns following the announcement. Notably, the financial market has a rather decentralized structure with competing intermediaries, although moreso in the securities than the bond market.

Two other relevant studies in consumer services are worth noting. First, in the Chinese hotel industry, Ye, Law, and Gu (2009) find that 10% higher ratings on an online review site correspond to a 5% rise in online bookings, though their analysis is not causal. Lastly, Luca (2011) contends that a one star increase in Yelp score corresponds to an 8% increase in revenue for Seattle area restaurants.

While making cross-domain inferences is impossible without standardized study designs and comparable units, it is clear that standardized metrics vary in their effects. Most appear in the anticipated direction to a greater or lesser degree. The higher education market does not appear to be the most responsive to standardized metrics. The lack of a more general framework for cross-context comparisons makes it difficult to make predictions about where these metrics should be more or less effective, much less to systematically and empirically test those predictions, though this is a promising avenue for future research.

To summarize effect sizes from the studies described above, we generated a graph (Fig. 1) that plots the coefficient and standard error of a one position increase in rank on the dependent variable in question. Here, an effect size of 1 indicates that a one place increase in the metric corresponds to a 1% increase in the performance metric, controlling for all other factors used in the model.

The central square is the point estimate of a one place movement in rank, rating, grade, etc. on the dependent variable in question from each study. The encompassing line represents the 95% confidence interval for that point estimate, as presented in the findings. In findings where the effect size was statistically significant, the confidence interval does not intersect with the dotted vertical line, which represents a 0 point estimate.

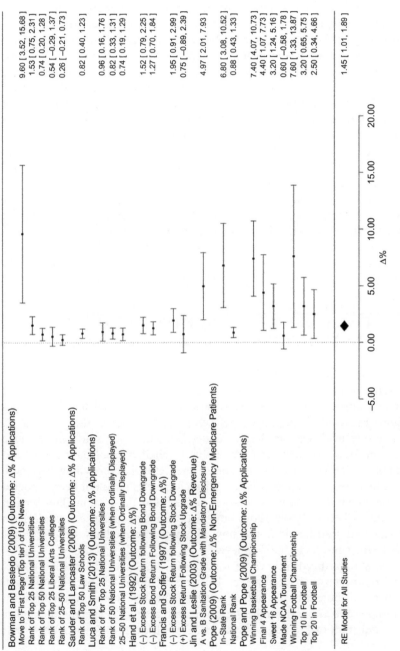

Fig. 1. Forest Plot of Effect Sizes by Study and Context.

The average effect size appears to be 1.45 with a standard error of 0.223. Noticeably, no studies produced a negative point estimate, or post a discount for rising up in the relevant metric. More recent studies, however, have discovered special cases where such a discount might occur (Kovacs & Sharkey, 2014). In another study, Azoulay et al. (2014) use a difference-in-difference estimator and show that the effect of academic prizes such as the Howard Hughes Medical Investigator awards are quite small and short-lived. Given these new findings, it is not clear that all intermediary-generated status boosts will produce a favorable result, or that the result will persist over time.

Fig. 1 does not standardize the effect size based on resolution of the explanatory variable. For instance, if a school moves up one place in the *USNWR* rankings, it passes one comparable peer. If a school moves from the second to first page of the rankings in years before schools 25–50 were ordinally ranked, it potentially moves past a set of 25 comparable peers. Likewise, a company whose bond is upgraded moves past potentially hundreds of comparable peers. In order to make more informative cross-context comparisons, one would need to standardize the effect size, scaling it by the number of comparative peers one would pass by moving up a unit in the metric.[2]

INCREASING RELIANCE ON METRICS BY INSTITUTIONS OF HIGHER EDUCATION

Like Jin & Leslie's finding for restaurants, there is an extensive body of qualitative evidence that producers are more responsive to metrification than consumers, and this responsiveness has produced substantial changes in how universities organize themselves and allocate their resources. Quantitative evidence on these broader, second-order shifts in resource allocation, however, has been scarce due to challenges of data access and an emphasis on causal identification of theoretically compelling variables. So far, the effects of intermediation through metrics have not been modeled at a systemic level, a topic we discuss in the following section. This section will review what we know about how institutions of higher education have responded to metrification, and how different intermediary structure produces distinct results at the field level.

What standardized metrics tie together in kind, they disperse in a one-dimensional metric space. The result is a focal point for peer comparison that has the potential to induce tournament-style competition between institutions. We know from the literature on reactivity (Espeland & Sauder, 2007), and multitasking agency theory (Dewatripont & Jewitt, 1999) that agents respond to observation by reallocating resources toward more observable activities.

Chambliss and Takacs (2014) suggest that schools may increase the number of small classes–a ranking criteria–by increasing the size of very large lecture classes. As a likely result, they show that students at some colleges do perceive a more intimate classroom experience even after the number of such classes at their institutions has risen. Espeland and Sauder (2007) discuss effects of the ranking such as increased expenditures on marketing to boost the number applications a school would receive to indirectly improve its selectivity score. Schools also spent more resources on career services to ensure that their students would count as being "employed" either at graduation, or nine months thereafter. Law school administrators also game the rankings, recently going so far as to sometimes falsify test-score data. Following the decline of the legal market in 2008, some schools established short-term internship programs funded by the law schools themselves, which served the latent function of counting their students as employed.

With the rise of rankings, law schools have dramatically shifted their admissions criteria toward factors of the ranking rather than taking a more holistic approach (Johnson, 2006). Prior to the *USNWR* law school rankings, soft factors such as work and life experience were sometimes taken into consideration in the admissions process. Following their introduction, however, admissions have tilted much more toward a student's GPA and LSAT score. This shift in policy at top law schools is well documented, Espeland and Sauder may overstate the ranking's self-fulfilling impact on external audiences, according to alternative studies. The subjective experience of rankings by law school administrators may be exaggerated relative to their empirical effect on student choice, considering the small effect of ranking on performance produced by Sauder and Lancaster (2006).

In an earlier study, Sauder and Espeland (2006) suggested that having multiple metrics or intermediaries may serve to protect against administrative cooptation by rankings. They compare law and business schools to demonstrate the effect of competition between ranking systems on the strategic response of administrators. Whereas law schools have a monolithic ranking system with no competition (*US News*), there have been multiple, prominent rankings of business school since the late 1980s (*Businessweek* and *US News*). More recent years have seen a number of additional periodicals add rankings to their portfolio as well (*Financial Times*, the *Economist*, etc.). The result is that: (1) multiple rankings produce ambiguity for readers, which forces them to arbitrate and reflect on the relative importance of factors related to quality; (2) weakens the effect of small differences between schools because of disagreement between rankings; (3) increases reputational control and flexibility by allowing administrators to play to multiple methodologies and emphasize distinct rankings in promotional materials; and (4) undermines the authority of rankings in general, safeguarding against the oversimplification of "quality." Together, these studies indicate that the publication of standardized metrics by an independent third party has had profound impacts on the allocation of resources by administrators in higher education, and that the structure and competition of intermediaries moderates the level of impact on institutional policies.

The best documented example of the introduction of a state-run rating system comes from the U.K.'s Research Assessment Exercise (RAE, which was replaced by the Research Excellence Framework in 2014). While there is an extensive body of literature on the impact of the RAE, we limit ourselves here to a few illustrative examples. Though he did not address them empirically, Elton (2000) considers a number of unintended consequences that could be attributed to the rating system. As one example, Elton suggests that the RAE methodology might cause researchers to overvalue publications in journals that "made the list" and therefore count toward faculty productivity scores. Because journals deemed to be of quality were tilted toward domestic publications, this might have favored parochial research programs that would appeal to an audience of domestic reviewers. While this could have favorable public consequences for the use of research funds by focusing research on domestic issues, it does little to enhance the quality of research beyond crudely measurable outcomes. Another unintended consequence of the RAE was that a rating system designed to produce stratification and efficiencies could have led to more equality in funding between schools. Funding was allocated in large part based on faculty productivity and this rating was initially assigned on a linear scale, with lower rated schools positively assessed relative to a nonstandardized or informal approach.

Other potential unintended consequences included the punishment of long-term research projects due to a four year review cycle. There could also be a penalty for interdisciplinary research in areas where field journals did not count toward faculty productivity scores, or in research requiring cooperation between peer institutions. This could induce less risk taking in novel or emerging research areas. Another possible consequence was the devaluation of teaching or the communication of research findings. While faculties might produce more research, they would spent less time passing that knowledge on to their students and the public. Importantly, the system could also increase competition between schools for faculty stars, and lead to bidding wars in which schools vie against each other for a faculty member's publications in the current period to attain public research funding in the next.

Elton also notes that the centralized system could potentially lead to more efficient management of research funds, as the return on investment for lower and middle-status researchers with substitutable skills might outperform the higher investments required by high-status researchers. Furthermore, departmental improvements in research productivity were observed at all levels. This resulted in RAE incentives having their intended consequence as less waste or "dead wood" remained in the faculty ranks. Nevertheless, it is not clear if more tacit dimensions of research quality have been benefited by centralized review.

Rolfe (2003) describes strategic administrative responses to the RAE. The system has led schools to leverage alternative forms of revenue to compete in the transfer market for research stars. In particular, they expanded part time programs, increased tuition and fees, and increased expenses on marketing and branding their universities to attract more students and attention. This has allowed them to compete more effectively for productive researchers in order to garner public research funds.

In general, it seems as though university responses to metrification have exceeded their effect on student preferences. This reciprocal effect, however, has not been formally modeled or measured due to its high dimensional and complex nature. Many have qualitatively documented that students and universities show increased attention and conformity to the criteria underlying ranking and scoring. We suggest that ranking and scoring likely influence system-level transformation even further afield. Recent years have witnessed the rapid growth of two new industries in the higher education sector: enrollment management and admissions consulting. Here, we document the rise of these fields, then argue and formally demonstrate how attenttion to rankings could drive large demand for these services and the transformation in higher education they portend. Due to the recent emergence of enrollment management and admissions consulting, very little has been written on them in the academic literature, and so our account is preliminary and leaves room for further research.

ENROLLMENT MANAGEMENT

Strategic enrollment management emerged as a specialized function within admissions offices in the mid-1970s, as the tidal wave of baby-boomer enrollments waned and tuition dollars became more scarce (Coomes, 2000).

This section will discuss recent work documenting the rise of the enrollment management profession, and its impact on the field of higher education.

While enrollment management has a more than 30 year history within universities following ebbing undergraduate enrollments in the early 1980s, it is clear that consulting firms play a larger role today in diffusing knowledge and competitive practices among universities. Historical work on universities reveals that increased competition over enrollments predates the introduction of rankings. Nevertheless, ranking amplified the competitive environment and applied greater pressure on admissions departments to inflate selectivity figures, leading to a greater need for specialized expertise in services like "application cultivation." Hossler (2011) suggests that while "most enrollment managers are not fond of rankings' they can 'ill afford to ignore them" (p. 77).

Today enrollment management services are increasingly provided by third-party consulting firms such as Ruffalo Noel Levitz, TargetX, and the Lawler Group. Of the 50 institutions interviewed by Schulz and Lucido (2011), 47 mentioned hiring or seeking "ideas from consultants, with most institutions having current or recent contracts with one or more external consultants" (p. 7). Over half of the enrollment professionals in their study used consultants to enhance their marketing efforts to more effectively influence student behavior, and over one third used consultants for student search and targeting (p. 9). Market size estimates are difficult to document, but Ruffalo Noel Levitz (formerly Ruffalo Cody), one of the largest specialized enrollment management consulting firms, has appeared on the Inc. 5,000 fastest growing companies list for the past eight years, last year reporting a staff of 5,265 employees and revenue of $92 million. In a 2013 Business Corridor article, the firm claimed over 900 clients in higher education, with an annual growth rate of 15–20% and plans to pursue aggressive acquisition and international growth strategies.

Historically, the role of admissions was performed by faculty and senior administrators. Growing enrollments in the early 20th century, however, created the need for a more specialized administrative function to coordinate student trajectories through the school. Following this period, a variety of tasks associated with student matriculation, retention and records were handled by the university registrar (Coomes, 2000). When enrollments began to surge following WWII with matriculation of the baby boom generation, the registrar's functions required further division, giving rise to specialized admissions departments. Enrollment management came into being following the ebbing of enrollments that occurred in the wake of baby-boomer graduations. Due to the expansion of higher education and student aid, schools became increasingly reliant on tuition revenue. As such, it became a matter of financial importance that schools meet enrollment targets in order to sustain operational spending levels (Coomes, 2000).

Hossler (2011) has noted that historically the work of admissions offices varied greatly across schools depending on their position in the status hierarchy. At higher status schools, admissions officers traditionally served more as "gatekeepers"; whereas at lower status schools, admissions officers served as "salespeople" for the university to generate demand (pp. 64–65). Still, these two functions overlap at all schools, vary in their importance across historical periods, and represent a general tension in the profession. Beginning in the 1970s, universities began to adopt for-profit business techniques to deal with budgetary pressures stemming from declining high-school student populations. In order to assist with strategic planning, admissions offices became tasked with developing and executing sophisticated marketing campaigns, which differentiated a school from its competitors (p. 68).[3] Later, in the 1990s, admissions departments coordinated with other university units and contracted with consulting agencies to develop optimal financial aid packages that selectively encouraged students to matriculate. Enrollment management grew to maturity in this era, developing models for predicting student application, matriculation, and completion. Enrollment management grew as a "systematic institutional response to issues related to student enrollment" (p. 70), which coordinated between various institutional units and managed a variety of objectives across the university. Increasingly, admissions offices are located within enrollment management divisions, and Henderson (2001) claims that enrollment management is "on the brink of a profession." While the task of enrollment managers is much broader and more complex than positioning the school in national rankings, they take ranking criteria into account as they prioritize their efforts (p. 89). Despite academic criticisms, this has led to spiraling competition to enroll students that rate highly on *USNWR* inputs via marketing efforts and tuition discounting (p. 89).

Kraatz, Ventresca, and Deng (2010) found that over 50% of "moderately selective," or middle-status, liberal arts colleges had adopted the enrollment management organizational structure, whereas none of the nine most selective schools had adopted it. They find that tuition dependence, competitor and field-level adoption, organizational propensity for professionalization, and prior implementation at another school by a sitting President play important roles in the adoption process. On the other hand, factors associated with academic purity and professional power, such as faculty salary, tenure-track faculty, and presidential tenure, were negatively correlated with adoption. This shift toward enrollment management structures appears to have slowed toward the end of the observation period. Kraatz et al. argue that strategic enrollment management poses a threat to the historically expressed value systems of higher education institutions through "its negative effect on equal access to higher education and its tendency to divert resources away from core educational purposes" (p. 1538). This process occurs as enrollment management constructs "mundane administrative arrangements" that allow "market values to unobtrusively penetrate a college and provides these values and their advocates with a structural and political foothold inside the organization" (p. 1523).

Kraatz et al.'s (2010) estimate of the impact of enrollment management on admissions practice is likely conservative. Their measure (the creation of a Vice President of Enrollment Management position) does not capture the impact of consulting firms on the practices of admissions departments, nor can it account for the informal influence of subordinate enrollment managers that work within established admissions departments. The American Association of College Registrars and Admissions Officers, founded in 1910, now claims itself as a nonprofit, voluntary, professional association encouraging best practices in such areas as enrollment management, information technology, instructional management, and student services. This mandate suggests the widespread effect that enrollment management practices now exert on higher education.

Schulz and Lucido (2011) also discuss the reasons university officials gave for hiring consultants, which include expertise (and cost savings), political expediency, a capacity for monitoring competitors and professional histories/personal relationships. The authors suggest that it is important for enrollment and admissions professionals within universities to reflect on the extent to which their institution's values align with those being promoted by consulting firms. Consulting firms are shown to import techniques from the business world, and draw inspiration from industries that more closely approximate the ideal of perfect competition than higher education.

While positional competition has likely enhanced demand for their services, many enrollment managers are critical of vertical competition on ranking criteria (Gnolek et al., 2014; Kalsbeek, 2009). The segmentation methods imported from corporate marketing are designed to deal with horizontal differentiation, or finding a good fit between student and school in the variegated higher education marketplace. For this reason, enrollment management as a field can ameliorate the effects of vertical competition amongst universities primarily through intensive marketing. Nevertheless, in a market with universally recognized quality standards, segmentation and direct marketing has limited influence, suggesting an uncertain and potentially changing role demand for enrollment management services in the future.

INDEPENDENT EDUCATIONAL CONSULTANTS

Another profession that has risen in prominence and impact are Independent Educational Consultants (IECs). The admissions consulting industry can be understood to contain a variety of services for students to improve their chances of acceptance. These services include: standardized test preparation, admissions coaching and essay editing. While a number of transactional services are individually available to students (e.g., test preparation, essay editing) and often offered by admissions offices (direct mailings, CRM software for targeted emails, etc.), here, we focus on full-service consultants. Given their smaller profile, and relatively recent rise, IECs have not received the same amount of scholarly attention as enrollment managers, but there is a growing body of literature identifying increased demand for their services, and their impact on the admissions landscape.

McDonough (1994) has called attention to "major changes in the field of college admissions from increased competition, higher admissions standards, and the phenomenal growth of non school-based admissions management services" (p. 443). In particular, she draws attention to the then new practice of admissions coaching, provided by Independent Educational Counselors (IECs), who help generally upper-middle class families to mitigate the uncertainty associated with the college admissions process. Smith (2014) has recently provided a detailed look at the business activities of IECs and the motivation of their clients. She describes how "IECs and parents spoke about how the admissions game has become more competitive due to demographic changes, marketing by schools, and media hype — especially the U.S. News and World Reports rankings" (p. 56).

As of 1989, independent educational consultants were small in number and generally treated with disdain by both school guidance counselors and admissions professionals (Sklaro, 2012, p. 69). Now, IECs have achieved a greater deal of legitimacy and are more tightly integrated into admissions institutions. Many admissions offices assign a staff member as point of contact for consultants and invite IECs for campus tours or special events (*ibid.*). Furthermore, many IECs participate in the professional body for admissions officers and vice-versa (Smith, pp. 39–40).

Demand for IECs grew exponentially over the past 25 years. In 1997, only 2.7% of college freshmen had worked with an IEC. More recent estimates put that figure closer to 22% (Smith, 2014, p. 41). In 2009, Lipman Hearne estimated that 26% of "high-achieving" high-school seniors, defined as those scoring above the 70th percentile on the SAT or ACT and receiving acceptances at three or more schools, were working with an Independent Educational Consultant (IEC) to help guide them through the admissions process.[4] In 2012, the IECA estimated domestic spending on IECs at around $400 million (Smith, 2014, p. 38)

The first national survey of IECs was carried out by McDonough, Yamasaki, and Korn (1997), and found that they charged an average of $87 per hour and had a caseload of 41 students per year. The overwhelming majority are white (98%), female (76%), highly educated (78% with a Master's or Doctoral degree), and located near large metropolitan areas. IECs reported that admissions management constitutes about three fourths of their work. McDonough et al. conclude that "under the privatization of college access, trusted public servants (high-school guidance counselors) are replaced by private entrepreneurs (independent educational consultants) who are driven by bottom-line financial considerations."

Stevens (2009) later noted a "growing market of private consultants", and described the approach of a former admissions officer, turned private consultant, who was able to charge families $7k to help students represent themselves in a way that "make(s) sense to admissions officers" (p. 214). Students at affluent private high schools were also known to have access to a cadre of guidance counselors "whose jobs revolve around getting kids into college" (p. 216).

Together with enrollment management services, admissions consulting appears to resolve increased uncertainty faced by students and universities. We will argue, and formally demonstrate in the following section, how increasingly slavish attention to rankings can explain the rise of this uncertainty. These effects cannot be captured by school-level year-to-year changes in performance, but rather accumulate and involve feedback between the behaviors of both sides of the higher education market.

THE DOUBLE BIND OF PRESTIGE-SEEKING

Our earlier review of the current literature indicates that year-to-year changes in university rank have a small but statistically significant effect on admissions outcomes at the school level, but these models understate the cumulative importance of rankings in reorienting resource allocation decisions of students and administrators. They cannot identify the conditions of transformation that give rise to new, uncertainty mitigating professions. While status order in higher education has been more or less conserved over time (Grewal et al., 2012), this has been accomplished at extraordinary expense via positional competition among schools and students, which saw the emergence of large outflows of capital to new consulting professions that resolve uncertainty for their respective counterparties.

Gnolek et al. (2014) show that most changes in university rank are attributable to small year-to-year changes in reporting or admissions policies, and positional gains erode as other schools adopt strategic policies. Gnolek et al. estimate that it would take an additional \$112 million in annual expenditures for a school ranked in the mid-30s to raise its level of faculty compensation and financial resources per student (two sub-factors) to the level of schools ranked in the top 20.

Table 1 shows the summary statistics of cumulative change in rank from 1996 to 2010 for national universities ranked within the top 50 in *USNWR*'s 1996 edition.

Over the 15 year window, schools ranked in the top 50 changed, on average, about 3.5 places. Because one school's gain comes at another's loss, the average change of the raw ranking is centered around zero. Fig. 2 traces a histogram of the raw change in *USNWR* rank from 1996 to 2010 for schools ranked in the top 50 in 1996. Gnolek et al. (2014) suggest that changes of two places should be interpreted as noise rather than signal for top 40 universities, and changes of up to four places can be interpreted as random variation for lower ranked schools. Only a few universities had larger confidence intervals that could be traced to institutional practices that "resulted in supplying notably different inputs to *U.S. News*" (p. 767).

In this section, we use an analytical approach to examine a stylized fact: the concurrent declines in both average acceptance rates and average yield rates at undergraduate universities. Yield rate is defined as the number of

Table 1. Summary Statistics of Cumulative Change in USNWR Rank from 1996 to 2010 for National Universities Ranked in the Top 50 in 1996.

Change in Rank	Mean	Median	Standard Deviation	Range
Absolute value	3.46	2.5	3.37	0, 17
Raw value	0.14	0	4.85	−15, 17[a]

[a]The two outliers here are University of Southern California, which moved up 17 places in the ranking, and Rutgers-New Brunswick, which moved down 15 places.

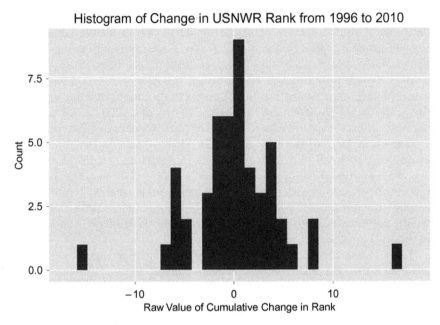

Fig. 2. Cumulative Change in *USNWR* Rank from 1996 to 2010 for Top 50
National Universities in 1996.

students that enroll, given an offer of admission. The National Association
for College Admission Counseling's (NACAC) 2012 report indicates a
drop in average acceptance rates from 69.6% to 63.8% from 2002 to 2011
(p. 16). The same report also shows a drop from 48.7% to 38% in the average yield rate for schools.

This dynamic creates additional uncertainty for both sides of the market.
For students, especially those at the top end of the status hierarchy, observing declines in acceptance rates creates uncertainty over their likelihood of
admission into any one school. Consulting industries such as standardized
test preparation, admissions coaches, and essay editors have benefited from
added uncertainty regarding admissions outcomes. For instance, a recent
Facebook advertisement from *Princeton Review*, shows a graph of declining
admissions rates with the text: "Ivy League Acceptance Rates Hit New
Lows! Think Your Child Can Get In?," together with a link to SAT preparation course offerings (http://on.fb.me/1NjJFyd).

For schools, declines in yield rates mean more unpredictability regarding
enrollment numbers. The 2012 NACAC report shows that the percent of

students submitting seven or more applications more than tripled, from 9% to 29%, between 1990 and 2011, while the number of students submitting more than three applications rose from 61% to 79% (p. 16). the report argues that this has made "the admission office's task of predicting yield rates and obtaining target enrollment numbers ... more complex" (p. 17). We show that this relationship is a formal one, resulting from an unstable equilibrium in which both sides of the market participate in behaviors that amplify their own uncertainty.

Evidence from recent years has pointed to changes in admissions policies to increase the number of applications a school receives so that it can reject more students and improve selectivity scores in *USNWR* rankings. Toor (2000, cited in Avery & Kane, 2004), writes that:

> The job of admissions officers is to recruit, to boost application numbers. The more applications, the lower the admit rate, the higher the institutional ranking. Increasing application numbers is usually the No. 1 mandate of the recruiting season. Partly, that means trying to get the very best students to apply. But it also means trying to persuade those regular, old Bright Well-Rounded Kids (B.W.R.K.'s, in admissionese) to apply — so that the college can reject them and bolster its selectivity rating.

In another account, Stevens (2009) describes a secondhand description of an admissions officer who:

> bragged ... about his school's exceptionally large numbers of applications from international students. The kids from abroad apparently were encouraged to apply online, for free. "And then you reject 'em all. But you have their applications...". (p. 50)

Schools have pursued a number of strategies to boost applications numbers in order to either improve selectivity or simply hit target enrollment numbers. These include application subsidies, direct mailings, television commercials, and generous financial aid policies. Schools began accepting the Common Applicationin larger numbers from the mid-1990s onward to reduce the time cost of application. Liu, Ehrenberg, and Mrdjenovic (2007) showed that adoption of the common application led to a one-time adoption shock that resulted in a 5.7–7% increase in applications and a 2.8–3.9% decrease in yield rate. These changes have persisted in the years after adoption. By rejecting more students and improving perceived selectivity at rates higher than peers, a school not only maintains its position in the ranking, but also enhances the signaling value of its degree. At the same time, it lowers its own and other schools' yield, making enrollment rates less predictable for all universities.

To illustrate this effect, we provide a simple formal analysis of this dynamic. Given some simplifying assumptions, the admissions system can be modeled as follows: Consider a fixed number of schools m, and a fixed number of students, n. Applicants submit b number of applications per student. All schools accept a total of a students in hopes of filling a class. Our first simulation of this system assumes that students apply to and enroll in schools at random, conditional on acceptance. It also assumes that schools randomly accept students that apply.

The average acceptance rate for schools can therefore be expressed as the number of schools times the number of students accepted per school, divided by the number of students times the number of applications submitted per student:

$$Average\ Acceptance\ Rate = \frac{ma}{nb} \tag{1}$$

Since applications per student lie in the denominator of this formula, average acceptance rate is inversely proportional to the number of applications per student. The ranking criteria incentivizes admissions offices to seek more applications in order to reject more students and improve perceived selectivity. Students, observing these trends, therefore have an incentive to diversify their application portfolio by applying to more schools. This leads to a feedback effect between increasing applications and decreasing acceptances.

Schools face a similar dilemma. In a system with a fixed number of students, an increase in applications per student will lead to more students receiving offers at competing schools. This results in a lower probability that any one student will accept an offer of admission into a given school. In particular, the probability that student i enrolls in school j can be expressed as:

$$P_{ij} = \left(App_{ij}\right)\left(Acc_{ij}\right)\left(C_{ij}\right) \tag{2}$$

where App_{ij} is the probability that student i applies to school j, Acc_{ij} is the probability that student i is accepted to school j, and C_{ij} is the sum of conditional probabilities that student i chooses school j, given offers of admission from competing schools. Given our simplifying assumption of random application choices by students, App_{ij} can be expressed as the number of applications per student divided by the number of schools:

$$App_{ij} = \frac{b}{m} \tag{3}$$

Similarly, since schools are assumed to randomly select students, Acc_{ij}, or the probability that any given student receives an offer of admission, can be expressed as the average acceptance rate (from formula (1)).

$$Acc_{ij} = \frac{ma}{nb} \quad (4)$$

C_{ij} is the sum of conditional probabilities that student i chooses school j, given offers of admission from competing schools. In this formula, y indexes the number of schools that student i is accepted into. This can be expressed as the sum of binomial probabilities of a student receiving y acceptances divided by y.

$$C_{ij} = \sum_{y \in \{1,...,b\}} \frac{1}{y} P(i \text{ accepted at } y-1 \text{ other } js) P(i \text{ rejected at } b-y \text{ other } js) \binom{b-1}{y-1} \quad (5)$$

Finally, in formula (6), we get the joint probability of all three of these terms:

$$P_{ij} = \frac{b}{m} \times \frac{ma}{nb} \times C_{ij} \quad (6)$$

Because b and m in the first two terms cancel out, this reduces to formula (7):

$$P_{ij} = \frac{a}{n} \sum_{y \in \{1,...,b\}} \frac{1}{y} P(i \text{ accepted at } y-1 \text{ other } js) P(i \text{ rejected at } b-y \text{ other } js) \binom{b-1}{y-1} \quad (7)$$

Given formula (7), the expected enrollment of school j can be expressed as the number of students, n, times the formula for P_{ij} (from Eq. (7)):

$$Enrollment_j = \sum_{i \in N} P_{ij} = n\frac{a}{n}(C_{ij}) = aC_{ij} \quad (8)$$

The total enrollment for all schools in the system can then be expressed as *Enrollment_j* (from Eq. (8)) multiplied by the number of schools

$$Total\ Enrollment = \sum_{j \in M} Enrollment_j = m(Enrollment_j) = maC_{ij} \qquad (9)$$

From formula (9), we get the average yield rate (or, the proportion of students that accept an offer of admission) for all schools in the system by dividing the total enrollment for schools in the system by the number of schools multiplied by the number of acceptances. This reduces to formula (5), or the sum of conditional probabilities that student i chooses school j, given competing offers of admission.

$$Average\ Yield = \frac{maC_{ij}}{ma} = C_{ij} \qquad (10)$$

Because b (number of applications) appears in the denominator of all formulas, we can say that a school's expected yield is inversely proportional to the number of applications submitted per student. As such, expected enrollment and average yield rates decline with an increase in the number of applications per student if a (number of acceptances) remains constant. Thus, schools face a conflict between encouraging more students to apply to improve selectivity, and resolving uncertainty about which students are more likely to attend, leading to policies such as early action/decision programs, enhanced student subsidies, and interviews, essays, and visits to screen for applicant interest.

Consider an arbitrary system with 100,000 students and 20 schools. Assume that each school accepts 10,000 students at random in hopes of enrolling a class of 4,800 students. Lastly, assume each student applies to only three schools. Plugging these constants into the above formulas, we get the following values for the average acceptance and yield rates at the 20 schools contained in the system. From formula (1), we get the average acceptance rate of schools in the system:

$$Average\ Acceptance\ Rate = \frac{20 \times 10,000}{100,000 \times 3} = \frac{2}{3} = 0.6667 \qquad (11)$$

and from formulas (10) and (5), we get the average yield rate:

$$Average\ Yield = \frac{12^0 1^2}{13\ 3}\binom{2}{0} + \frac{12^1 1^1}{23\ 3}\binom{2}{1} + \frac{12^2 1^0}{33\ 3}\binom{2}{2} = \frac{1}{9} + \frac{2}{9} + \frac{4}{27} = \frac{13}{27} = 0.481$$

(12)

Figs. 3 and 4 are charts depicting the average acceptance and yield rates of schools conditional on the number of applications per student.

As students apply to more schools, yield and acceptance rates both drop, such that schools have a harder time fielding a class due to more cross-admits. Students have a lower probability of being accepted into the schools to which they apply, but this is counterbalanced by the fact that they have more chances of getting in. Likewise, because competing schools are more selective, universities can expect a lower bound on declines in yield rates, as the students they select are less likely to get into other schools.

What if we were to remove the assumption of random application and admission choices by students and schools? If student and school preferences concerning the other side of the market became correlated, this would

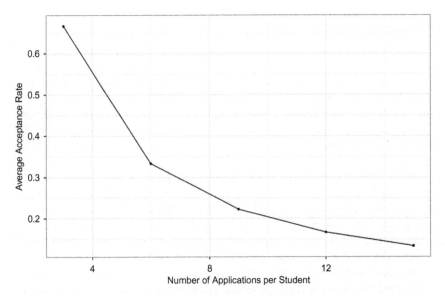

Fig. 3. Average Acceptance Rate by Number of Applications per Student.

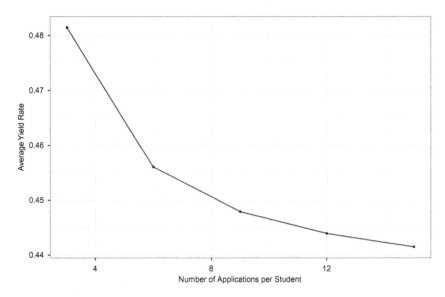

Fig. 4.   Average Yield Rate by Number of Applications per Student.

greatly exacerbate uncertainty for those at the lower end of the status hierarchy on both sides of the market. Because schools and students both wish
to find a match, however, we would expect admissions behavior to be
strongly correlated not only with others' opinions, but expectations for
reciprocity (Gould, 2002) and student–school fit. The result of this
dynamic is an unstable equilibrium, where schools seek more applications
and students submit more applications, further exacerbating uncertainty
about admission and enrollment. This dynamic has greatly increased the
problems that these professions seek to resolve, and so created enormous
demand for their services.

   There are a number of other forces that have also played a role in
increasing demand for enrollment management and independent educational consultation over the past two decades. These include a more professionalized managerial orientation among administrators, improvements in
technology and related expertise, and budgetary pressures on state universities, which have necessitated more accurate measurement of revenues and
costs associated with enrollment. Here, we have detailed one plausible, but
important mechanism through which rankings have likely contributed to
this growth.

DISCUSSION

Despite its meager influence on university performance, ranking and rating in higher education have had a profound effect on the experience of universities and applicants. The higher-order effects we demonstrate are one plausible mechanism contributing to rising demand for the Enrollment Management and Independent Education Consultation professions, who use specialized knowledge to mitigate uncertainty for each side of the market. Moreover, it appears that metrification resulted in a reduction of diversity or complexity among "elite" universities and students as they conform to and compete on measured criteria.

Nevertheless, this case does not exhaust the full range of system-level consequences from rankings on the system of higher education, and suggests a number of "open questions" that future research should explore. For example, what leads metrification to lead to more inequality in some contexts, but less in others? The RAE had unintended consequences, leading to greater parity between institutions in the allotment of research funds. This is attributed to the linear scale imposed on quality. Yet, the ordinal nature of *USNWR* rankings seems to be the most salient feature for U.S. universities and leads to greater inequality. What are other factors that lead to this contingent effect? Moreover, what leads metrification to have a more enduring effect in some contexts than others?

By suggesting the system-level costs that ranking and metrification have imposed on universities and students, without producing compensating benefits for those engaged in the transaction, our investigation also suggests the importance of considering implications for higher education policy that might ameliorate these effects. More specifically, if current investments in selectivity, facilities, amenities, sports, or other activities prove to be socially wasteful, what are policy interventions that could curb them?[5]

Schelling (1973) and Frank (2012) have noted that the competitive dynamics of zero-sum games can lead rational individual strategies to produce suboptimal social results. Frank suggests that status contests and the pursuit of positional goods leads to negative externalities for other members of the status hierarchy, which leads to an expenditure cascade for all involved. Under such circumstances, individual strategies of excessive expenditures are rational, but everyone would be better off if some agency, within or beyond the higher education system, would impose some sort of regulation prohibiting or punishing the behavior. Schelling's classic example involves hockey players wearing helmets. If one player opted to not wear a helmet, they would have more mobility and vision on the ice, thus conferring them an advantage. If this occurs, it could make sense for all other players to adopt a similar strategy, because they would be in a disadvantageous position if they did not, despite the safety hazard it imposes. The players are therefore all better off in a regulatory regime which mandates that all players wear a helmet. Multiple solutions exist for such a problem — a strict regulation, as is the case for hockey players, or a more relaxed one such as a consumption tax levied on noncooperating parties. In the higher education context, this could take the form of a luxury tax for institutions that excessively spend on peripheral activities. While these forms of regulation may be possible in centralized states, where universities are universally supported with public funds (e.g., Great Britain, France), they are more difficult to imagine in the disaggregated context of the United States, with its separate private and public universities. As a result, we expect that market corrections in higher education will play the largest role in the United States, even though such corrections could be disruptive for both universities and students if they resulted in a discount of the perceived value that students receive from expensive higher education.

Other approaches involve the design of market mechanisms that produce efficient matches between both sides of the market (Roth, 2002). Medical schools and some public school systems use this approach on a much smaller scale. It is unclear whether a modified version of these institutions could be implemented for such a heterogeneous environment as American higher education. It is important for policy makers, however, to consider the alignment between the goals of higher education and the efficiency of the admissions system in producing strong matches between schools and students.

CONCLUSION

In our review of scholarship regarding the influence of ranking/scoring on the position and the strategic behavior of universities, schools, and departments, we find that the estimated influence of rank on university performance is remarkably small (e.g., one rank position corresponds to 1% more applicants/students), considering the amount of attention that ranking has received in the popular and academic press. In our analysis, we found that it is comparable to the same effect in many other institutional domains, although slightly smaller than some, like medicine, where the stakes may be higher. We show from suggestive research in other domains, however, that this estimation exercise understates the larger effect of metrification on the experience of university administrators, as well as the institutional structure, strategy, behavior and quality of teaching and research outputs associated with science and scholarship in higher education. Because these high-dimensional, complex aspects are not as as cleanly measured as one-dimensional rank position, they have not received the same treatment or modeling attention in education scholarship, despite their clear importance for understanding and influencing higher education. This is ironic as rankings appear to have performed their magic on the producers of higher education data just as they did on the consumers of that data. By making one thing measurable and salient, ratings and rankings make it difficult for higher education researchers to estimate and publish about anything else just as they make it more difficult for consumers to consider other, unmeasured factors.

We hope that this paper inspires researchers to consider the limits of the current approach to the estimation of ranking effects, and to look beyond the most easily available metrics to assess the broader systemic influence of metrics on higher education. Research focused on university-level ranking effects simply cannot identify system-level consequences revealed in qualitative studies. In our analysis, we have used a formal example, simulation, and historical detail to identify a critical system-level consequence of increased focus on ranking and the framing of higher education as a positional good. To increase their rankings, universities now compete on selectivity by driving greater competition among applicants. Applicants respond by applying to more schools, which leads to greater uncertainty about enrollment for both students and universities. This feedback loop provides a plausible mechanism fueling the rise of enrollment management and independent education consultation professions. We believe that this process has strongly contributed to the conformity of both universities and students to ranking criteria, and so justifies the perceived importance and increased focus on rankings as substantial and consequential for higher education, far beyond the small size of estimated ranking effects. Insofar as the feedback sparked by ranking increases the costs without producing offsetting benefits for students and universities, we urgently encourage research on novel policy approaches to improve the efficiency of matching and resource allocation in higher education and increase the value of higher education for science and society.

NOTES

1. In the same way, that articles were deemed important if highly cited, webpages came to be deemed important if highly hyperlinked.

2. In lieu of standardized coefficients, we attempted to generate weights of the effect size and variance based on our estimate of the comparable "peers" one would pass by advancing one place in the relevant metric. Since detailed descriptive statistics of the various 'bins' were not published in a majority of the studies, the authors had to use their discretion in coming up with these estimates, so we do not include them here. As an exploratory exercise, however, it seemed to produce a more informative plot than the raw estimates. The scaling factor was computed as the natural log of the comparable peers one would expect to pass in the metric plus one (in order to rescale those metrics which are purely ordinal around one, i.e., one place corresponds to one peer). This procedure allowed for better cross-case comparisons of the salience for a given rating. This analysis suggested that more centralized tournament-style competition leads to larger standardized effects, especially at the top end of the distribution. In fields where there are multiple intermediaries and large 'bins' (stocks and bonds, for instance), the standardized effect size is smaller.

3. Marketing practices, however, predated admissions departments. Mass mailings were used as early as 1893, when "one state university had sufficient funds and political clout to send out brochures to every school superintendent in the state" and levy a $50 fine if they were not posted (Thelin, 1982, cited in Hossler, 2011, p. 66).

4. Lipman Hearne, a marketing agency specializing on non-profits, and National Research Center for College and University Admissions conducted the study.

5. The factors contributing to cost increases in higher education, and potential solutions have been discussed in more detail in Ehrenberg (2000) and Clotfelter (2014).

ACKNOWLEDGMENTS

We would like to thank Andrew Abbott for recommending that we develop the simulation detailed in the section on "The Double Bind of Prestige-Seeking", and Christopher Takacs for a number of insightful discussions on the state of affairs in higher education.

REFERENCES

Abbott, A. (2011). Library research infrastructure for humanistic and social scientific scholarship in the twentieth century. *Social knowledge in the making* (pp. 43–87). London: The University of Chicago Press.

Avery, C., & Kane, T. J. (2004). Student perceptions of college opportunities. The Boston COACH program. In C. M. Hoxby (Ed.), *College choices: The economics of where to go, when to go, and how to pay for it* (pp. 355–394). Chicago, IL: University of Chicago Press.

Azoulay, P., Stuart, T., & Wang, Y. (2014). Matthew: Effect or fable? *Management Science*, *60*(August), 92–109.

Bowman, N. A., & Bastedo, M. N. (2009). Getting on the front page: Organizational reputation, status signals, and the impact of U.S. news and world report on student decisions. *Research in Higher Education, 50*(5), 415–436.

Brewer, D. J., Gates, S. M., & Goldman, C. (2004). *In pursuit of prestige: Strategy and competition in US higher education.* Piscataway, NJ: Transaction Publishers.

Bush, V. (1945). As we may think. *The Atlantic Monthly, 176*(1), 101–108.

Chambliss, D. F., & Takacs, C. G. (2014). *How college works.* Cambridge, MA: Harvard University Press.

Clotfelter, C. T. (2014). *Buying the best: Cost escalation in elite higher education.* Princeton, NJ: Princeton University Press.

Coomes, M. D. (2000). The historical roots of enrollment management. *New Directions for Student Services, 2000*(89), 5–18.

Dale, S. B., & Krueger, A. B. (1999). *Estimating the payoff to attending a more selective college: An application of selection on observables and unobservables.* Technical Report. National Bureau of Economic Research.

de Solla Price, D. J. (1976). A general theory of bibliometric and other cumulative advantage processes. *Journal of the American Society for Information Science, 27,* 293.

Dewatripont, M., & Jewitt, I. (1999). The economics of career concerns, part II: Application to missions and accountability of government agencies. *Review of Economic Studies, 66*(1), 199–217.

Ehrenberg, R. G. (2000). *Tuition rising.* Cambridge, MA: Harvard University Press.

Elsbach, K. D., & Kramer, R. M. (1996). Members' responses to organizational identity threats: Encountering and countering the business week rankings. *Administrative Science Quarterly, 41*(3), 442–476.

Elton, L. (2000). The UK research assessment exercise: Unintended consequences. *Higher Education Quarterly, 54*(3), 274–283.

Espeland, W., & Sauder, M. (2007). Rankings and reactivity: How public measures recreate social worlds. *American Journal of Sociology, 113*(1), 1–40.

Francis, J., & Soffer, L. (1997). The relative informativeness of analysts' stock recommendations and earnings forecast revisions. *Journal of Accounting Research, 35*(2), 193–211.

Frank, R. H. (1999). *Higher education: The ultimate winner-take-all market?* Cornell Higher Education Research Institute Working Paper No. 2.

Frank, R. H. (2012). *The Darwin economy: Liberty, competition, and the common good.* Princeton, NJ: Princeton University Press.

Gnolek, S. L., Falciano, V. T., & Kuncl, R. W. (2014). Modeling change and variation in U.S. news and world report college rankings: What would it really take to be in the top 20? *Research in Higher Education, 55,* 761–779.

Godin, B. (2006). On the origins of bibliometrics. *Scientometrics, 68*(1), 109–133.

Gould, R. V. (2002). The origins of status hierarchies: A formal theory and empirical test. *American Journal of Sociology, 107*(5), 1143–1178.

Grewal, R., Dearden, J. A., & Llilien, G. L. (2012). The university rankings game: Modeling the competition among universities for ranking. *The American Statistician, 62,* 232–237.

Gugliotta, G. (2009). The genius index: One scientists crusade to rewrite reputation rules. *Wired Magazine, 17*(6), 92–95.

Hand, J., Holthausen, R., & Leftwich, R. (1992). The effect of bond rating agency announcements on bond and stock prices. *The Journal of Finance, 47*(2), 733–752.

Hearne, L. (2009). *Five great colleges want her. How will she decide?* Technical Report.

Henderson, S. (2001). On the brink of a profession: A history of enrollment management in higher education. In J. Black (Ed.), *The strategic enrollment management revolution* (pp. 3–36). Washington, DC: American Association of Collegiate Registrars and Admissions Officers.

Hossler, D. (2011). From admissions to enrollment management. *Student Affairs Practice in Higher Education* (pp. 63–95). Springfield, IL: Charles C. Thomas.

Hoxby, C. (2009). *The changing selectivity of American colleges.* NBER Working Paper No. 15446.

Hoxby, C. M. (1997). *How the changing market structure of us higher education explains college tuition.* Technical Report. National Bureau of Economic Research.

Jin, G., & Leslie, P. (2003). The effect of information on product quality: Evidence from restaurant hygiene grade cards. *The Quarterly Journal of Economics, 118*(2), 409–451.

Johnson, A. M. (2006). The destruction of the holistic approach to admissions: The pernicious effects of rankings. *Indiana Law Journal, 81*(1), 310–358.

Kalsbeek, D. H. (2009). Enrollment management: A market-centered perspective. *College and University, 84*(3), 2.

Kovacs, B., & Sharkey, A. J. (2014). The paradox of publicity how awards can negatively affect the evaluation of quality. *Administrative Science Quarterly, 59*(1), 1–33.

Kraatz, M. S., Ventresca, M. J., & Deng, L. (2010). Precarious values and mundane innovations: Enrollment management in American liberal arts colleges. *Academy of Management Journal, 53*(6), 1521–1545.

Lifschitz, A., Sauder, M., & Stevens, M. L. (2014). Football as a status system in us higher education. *Sociology of Education, 87*, 204–219.

Liu, A. Y.-H., Ehrenberg, R. G., & Mrdjenovic, J. (2007). *Diffusion of common application membership and admissions outcomes at American Colleges and Universities.* NBER Working Papers 13175. National Bureau of Economic Research.

Luca, M. (2011, September 16). *Reviews, reputation, and revenue: The case of yelp.com.* Harvard Business School NOM Unit Working Paper No. 12-016.

Luca, M., & Smith, J. (2013). Salience in quality disclosure: Evidence from the US news college rankings. *Journal of Economics & Management Strategy, 22*(1), 58–77.

Marszal, A. (2012). University rankings: Which world university rankings should we trust? *Telegraph.co.uk.* Retrieved from http://www.telegraph.co.uk/education/universityeducation/9584155/University-rankings-which-world-university-rankings-should-we-trust.html. Accessed on October 4.

McDonough, P. M. (1994). Buying and selling higher education: The social construction of the college applicant. *The Journal of Higher Education, 65*, 427–446.

McDonough, P. M., Yamasaki, E., & Korn, J. S. (1997). Access, equity, and the privatization of college counseling. *The Review of Higher Education, 20*(3), 297–317.

Pascarella, E. T., Terenzini, P. T., & Feldman, K. A. (2005). *How college affects students* (Vol. 2). San Francisco, CA: Jossey-Bass.

Pope, D. G. (2009). Reacting to rankings: Evidence from "America's Best Hospitals". *Journal of Health Economics, 28*(6), 1154–1165.

Pope, D. G., & Pope, J. C. (2009). The impact of college sports success on the quantity and quality of student applications. *Southern Economic Journal, 75*, 750–780.

Rolfe, H. (2003). University strategy in an age of uncertainty: The effect of higher education funding on old and new universities. *Higher Education Quarterly, 57*(1), 24–47.

Roth, A. (2002). The economist as engineer: Game theory, experimentation, and computation as tools for design economics. *Econometrica, 70*(4), 1341–1378.

Sauder, M., & Espeland, W. N. (2006). Strength in numbers? The advantages of multiple rankings. *Indiana Law Journal, 81*(1), 205–227.

Sauder, M., & Lancaster, R. (2006). Do rankings matter? The effects of US news & world report rankings on the admissions process of law schools. *Law & Society Review, 40*(1), 105–134.

Schelling, T. C. (1973). Hockey helmets, concealed weapons, and daylight saving: A study of binary choices with externalities. *Journal of Conflict Resolution, 17*(3), 381–428.

Schulz, S. A., & Lucido, J. A. (2011). *Enrollment management, inc.: External influences on our practice*. Center for Enrollment Research, Policy, and Practice.

Sklaro, M. H. (2012). Educational consulting: Justification to partnership. *Journal of College Admission, 2012*, (214), 69.

Smith, J. M. (2014). *The role of independent educational consultants in the college application process*. Ph.D. thesis, Brandeis University.

Stevens, M. L. (2009). *Creating a class: College admissions and the education of elites*. Cambridge, MA: Harvard University Press.

Thelin, J. R. (1982). *Higher education and its useful past. Applied history in research and planning*. Cambridge, MA: Schenkman Publishing Company.

Winston, G. C. (2000). *The positional arms race in higher education*. Technical Report. WPEHE discussion paper series/Williams College, Williams Project on the Economics of Higher Education.

Ye, Q., Law, R., & Gu, B. (2009). The impact of online user reviews on hotel room sales. *International Journal of Hospitality Management, 28*(1), 180–182.

UNIVERSITIES, ACADEMIC CAREERS, AND THE VALORIZATION OF 'SHINY THINGS'

Joseph C. Hermanowicz

ABSTRACT

What is associated with a rise in academic career expectations, and why have levels risen to such levels wherein prominent dissatisfaction is a sustainably generated outcome? This paper examines work satisfaction among faculty in U.S. research universities. At a micro level, I discuss the career patterns of work satisfaction as found in a set of universities, drawing on data from qualitative studies of academic careers. I present findings on four analytic dimensions: the overall modal career patterns of professors, their overall work satisfaction, their work attitudes, and whether they would again pursue an academic career. The data capture variation in careers over time and the type of university in which they work. A prominent and pervasive pattern is transparent: that of ill-content and ill-institutional regard. At a macro level, these patterns are suggestively situated in developments in the social-institutional environment of U.S. higher education. This environment consists of systemic trends in which neoliberalism enables academic capitalism to flourish with its

The University under Pressure
Research in the Sociology of Organizations, Volume 46, 303–328
Copyright © 2016 by Emerald Group Publishing Limited
All rights of reproduction in any form reserved
ISSN: 0733-558X/doi:10.1108/S0733-558X20160000046010

attendant effects in privatization and marketization. It is argued that a shift in organizational priority brought about by these conditions entails a "valorization of shiny things" — a valuing of market-related phenomena over knowledge of its own accord. This valorization, ritually supported by practices endemic of changed organizational culture, may weaken the ground on which the traditional scholarly role is played and may make precarious a basis for positive work sentiment.

Keywords: Careers; satisfaction; neoliberalism; academic capitalism; markets

I focus in this paper on work satisfaction among faculty in U.S. research universities. I take stock of the institutional environment in which academic careers are presently situated, and then turn to examining the career patterns of work satisfaction as found in a set of universities. Accordingly, we may glean the ways in which academic careers are experienced over time, how this might vary by organizational type, and how the patterns may be nestled in a constellation of forces at play with universities. As framed, a concern with satisfaction in academic careers informs an understanding of the social conditions of universities and the environment in which they operate. Thus conceived, careers serve as a proxy for organizational vitality and social-institutional well-being (Barley, 1989). As data and discussion will indicate, all is not well. Dramatic change in the institutional environment is suggestive of an alteration in the organizational culture of universities, and this by turn may express itself in how academics experience and interpret their work.

As a means to cast light on work satisfaction among academics, I draw upon materials generated from a national longitudinal study of scientists' careers. Data from the study are presented fully elsewhere (Hermanowicz, 1998, 2009a); my discussion here expands and develops a line from this work on the social psychology of organizations (Hermanowicz, 2009b, 2011). To set the stage, I begin by outlining the broader societal climate and institutional environment of universities.

MACRO CONDITIONS

The Social-Institutional Environment of Careers

Higher education literature provides ample indication that American universities in the late twentieth and early twenty-first centuries have not only changed but have done so dramatically. The changes are many and varied, but a major source involves the very way by which universities sustain themselves – how their existence is supported and maintained. This points to the repositioning and power of money.

The radical restructuring of American universities has entailed a concomitant shift in which education, faculty work, and the activities of universities, once viewed predominantly as public goods, become the principal matter of free enterprise. These changes, which became forceful especially in the 1980s and were reinforced by influential political figures such as Ronald Reagan and Margaret Thatcher and by influential policy such as the Bayh–Dole Act, which transferred ownership (and thus royalty) rights of inventions produced with federal funds from the government to universities, have been understood in terms of a philosophy of neoliberalism.

> Liberalism, or embedded liberalism, was a reaction to classic liberalism and sought to constrain capitalism to avoid depression, poverty, and social unrest. To achieve these ends, social and political oversight and regulatory planning functions were embedded in the state. The common goals of embedded liberal states were full employment, economic growth and the welfare of the citizenry. If necessary, the state would intervene in market processes to reach these goals ... In contrast, neoliberalism is a "theory of political economic practices that proposes that human well-being can best be advanced by liberating individual entrepreneurial freedoms and skills within an institutional framework characterized by strong private property rights, free markets and free trade ..." (Harvey, 2005, p. 2). While neoliberalism is presented as the key to freedoms of conscience, speech, meeting, association, and employment, this form of liberalism, as pointed out by Karl Polyani in 1944, also allows "the freedom to exploit one's fellows, or the freedom to make inordinate gains without commensurable service to the community, the freedom to keep technological inventions from being used for public benefit, or the freedom to profit from public calamities secretly engineered for private advantage," and generally confers freedom on those "whose income, leisure and security need no enhancing," leaving little for others (quoted in Harvey, 2005, p. 36) ... Generally, a neoliberal state shifts higher education from a public good knowledge/learning regime to ... an academic capitalist knowledge/learning regime. (Slaughter, 2011, p. 267)

"Academic capitalism," having itself ascended as a constitutive idea in the higher education lexicon, refers to market and market-like behaviors in universities and among faculty (Slaughter & Leslie, 1997; Slaughter & Rhoades, 2004). Such behavior includes institutional and faculty competition for monies, giving way to a "corporatization of higher education," in which actors, institutional and individual, are market-oriented (Slaughter & Leslie, 2001).

A broad and increasingly pervasive array of institutional and individual behaviors are indicative of the pattern: the search and competition for external grants and contracts, endowment funds, university–industry partnerships, spin-off companies, student tuition and fees, patenting and licensing agreements, and the sale of products and services enshrined in logos, sports paraphernalia, food facilities, and bookstores (Slaughter & Leslie, 2001). The search and competition has ancillary effects in which institutions spend monies in order to attract economic returns: in athletics programs, especially intercollegiate football and basketball; lavish sports, recreational, housing, and dining facilities; health centers and transit systems; study abroad programs in not a few but in numerous locations; technology, and the like. To oversee the enterprise, an administration of the contemporary American university has grown multi-faceted and complex, such that it is the source of the single greatest rise in higher education costs (Leslie & Rhoades, 1995).

In an academic-capitalist age, economic returns coupled with prestige are the central objects in which institutions and faculty members compete. The competition is fueled at a high degree by public-to-private shifts in revenue streams, but not exclusively so. It is fortified by the crystallization of rankings, particularly the *U.S. News and World Report* ranking of institutions and programs, whose origination in 1983 coincided with the onset of marketization and corporatist developments in U.S. higher education. It has been established that institutions alter their behavior to try to influence the rankings (Ehrenberg, 2002; Espeland & Sauder, 2007). "While some of the actions an institution may take to improve its rankings may also make sense educationally, others may not and, more importantly, may not be in the best interest of the American higher educational system as a whole" (Ehrenberg, 2002, p. 146). The practice in which institutions mis-report SAT and ACT scores of entering freshman (Ehrenberg, 2002), or in which law schools employ their own graduates to count them as employed (Espeland & Sauder, 2007), each in order to garner a higher rank and resource flows (human and fiscal), are but two of many cases in point. Rankings and the seriousness with which they are taken by higher education administrators (not to mention students and parents) have helped to create and reinforce a winning mentality in which academe consists of "haves" and "have-nots."

Grants, contracts, patents, licenses, logos, dining halls, dormitories, gyms, sports teams, quests for high ranking — and all the other interests of institutions that have come to revolve around money and revenue return — are what we may understand as "shiny things." The term sets up an implied contrast with the "real" thing; that is, an academic core of institutions, in which priority is assigned to faculty and students, their knowledge, discovery, and learning. These latter elements exist but have, as it were, become subordinate to the interests of academic capitalism. If it seems obvious and foolhardy to make the point that they exist, researchers remind us that over half of the U.S. professoriate now consists of non-tenure-line faculty members (Schuster & Finkelstein, 2006) and that actual learning on many campuses is adrift and limited (Armstrong & Hamilton, 2013; Arum & Roksa, 2011) − patterns that are themselves consequences of the ways in which institutions may be seen to be exploiting what were once key actors on behalf of financial interests.

One might also argue that clarity of the academic core has always been blurry. But this runs counter to the thesis of *The Academic Revolution* (Jencks & Riesman, 1968), among other historical treatments of U.S. higher education (e.g., Berman, 2012; Geiger, 2004; Kirp, 2003; Mirowski, 2011; Stephan, 2012; Thelin, 2004). Instead, some scholars have recently gone so far as to ask, "what ever happened to the faculty?" (Burgan, 2006). The evidence and magnitude of *contemporary* change in American higher education indicates a social-environmental shift of historical proportion (Chait, 2002); if the academic core was difficult to bring into view in the past, its sight appears clouded by still stronger counter-vailing systems today.

The "valorization of shiny things" constitutes a quintessential alteration of organizational priority. In universities it decenters priority from the intellectual to the market, from knowledge to money. This is not to say that money and intellectual pursuit never go hand in hand, but rather that the pursuit is more often for prestige, not a celebration of knowledge. Desire for recognition may always be seen as a precondition of science and scholarship (Merton, 1973). The point is that, increasingly, prestige operates as a function of market behavior in institutions as opposed to intellectual discovery. Sociologically, change in priority means that new and different behavior is valued, recognized, and sanctioned. Consequently, *valorization shapes culture.* If organizational culture is differently conditioned, the ground likely shifts for experience, attitude, and interpretation of work.

Some have argued that neoliberalism is "the most dangerous ideology of the current historical moment" because civil discourse is seen to give way "to the language of commercialization, privatization, and deregulation." Citizenship amounts to a privatized affair among self-interested individuals. As a result, such observers have reasoned, "the meaning and purpose of higher education" is thrown into question − words that further mark fundamental change (Giroux, 2002, p. 425).

MICRO CONDITIONS

Empirical Background

In 1994–1995, I interviewed 60 academics, physicists specifically, employed at universities across the United States about their careers and aspirations. In 2004–2005, I completed another series of interviews with the same people. I researched continuities and changes in careers, including what had developed as satisfactions and dissatisfactions for academics, and how they viewed their progress, or lack of it, toward what had been their professional goals. Fifty-five subjects from the original sample were interviewed as part of the longitudinal study, a response rate of 93 percent. (The response rate for the foundational study was 70 percent; for a discussion about academic fields and generalizability, see Hermanowicz, 2009a, pp. 252–260).

Individuals were originally sampled by departmental rank as measured by assessments of graduate programs conducted by the National Research Council (NRC – Goldberger, Maher, Flattau, 1995; Jones, Lindzey, Coggeshall, 1982). Top, middle, and tail-ranked departments were selected and built into the study design to permit a comparison of careers that are experienced under different structural and cultural conditions. A major goal of the study was to examine how people's careers are shaped by the academic organizations in which they work.

To aid comparison and contrast, the academics and their institutions were classified into three types. I call one type *elite* – those universities that place a high premium on research and whose departments ranked at or near the *top* of the NRC assessment. Examples include Cal Tech, Harvard, and Princeton. I call a second type *pluralist* – those universities that emphasize research as well as mass teaching and service and whose departments ranked in the *middle* of the NRC assessment. Examples include the University of Maryland, Florida State University, and the University of Oregon. I call the third type *communitarian* – those universities that primarily emphasize teaching and service, though not necessarily at the exclusion of research, and whose departments ranked at or near the *tail* of the NRC assessment. Examples include the University of Tulsa, University of Toledo, and the University of North Carolina – Charlotte.

Respondents in this work were also sampled by cohort, in order to include academics at a variety of career stages – early, middle, and late, generally speaking, at the time of the first study. These three cohorts were established by the year in which academics received their Ph.D.s, which is used as a proxy of their career stage. The eldest cohort consisted of academics who received their Ph.D.s prior to 1970. By the time of the longitudinal study, they were passing from late to post career stages. A middle cohort consisted of academics who received their Ph.D.s between 1970 and 1980. By the time of the longitudinal study, they were passing from middle to late career stages. The youngest cohort consisted of academics who received their Ph.D.s after 1980. By the time of the longitudinal study, they were passing from early to middle stages of their careers. The research design of the study is presented in Table 1.

Age and institutional location provide the structure to analyze individual, subjective careers through diachronic change. Longitudinal data add spatial and temporal dimensions to synchronic study, and we are consequently in a position to address the following questions about academic careers:

- How do academics account for the unfolding of their careers in light of the goals and aspirations that socially situate their profession?
- What continuities and changes − in aspiration, satisfaction, motivation, commitment, and identification with work − mark the careers of academics?
- What knowledge have academics acquired about themselves, their institutions, and the academic profession in 10 years?
- How does this knowledge vary by individual age and type of university?

Since I examined how members of a profession experience work and interpret the career, the interview constituted the primary method of data collection. Interview questions dealt with change and continuity in outlook (such as "What changes have you seen with regard to research?" and "What changes have you seen with regard to teaching?"). Interviews also consisted of questions about satisfaction and dissatisfaction ("What have

Table 1. Academics by Cohort and Organizational Type, Longitudinal Study.

| Organization | Cohort (by Year of Ph.D.) | | | |
	Pre-1970	1970−1980	Post-1980	Total
Elite	9	6	8	23
Pluralist	5	4	6	15
Communitarian	5	5	7	17
Total	19	15	21	55

developed as the three biggest joys about your job?" and "What have developed as your three biggest complaints about your job?" And, "Would you seek an academic career again, if you were starting all over?" "If so, what would you do differently?" "Have there been ways in which an academic career has been unrewarding?"). Interviewees were also asked about their current aspirations, where they see themselves having come, and where they see themselves headed professionally. In addition, academics who had retired were asked about the best and worst parts of retirement, about how they experienced the transition into retirement, and about what "retirement" means, in order to research how such meanings might vary from one organizational type to another.

Objective Career Patterns

There is little mistaking that the research role in the American academic profession has witnessed significant change as institutions themselves have changed in their favor of research. An indication consists in the normative expectations that govern research role performance in American universities.

Drawing upon data from the study of academic physicists, Table 2 presents publication productivity and promotion timing among scientists across the three types of academic organizations and across the cohorts. To obtain their first academic jobs, the eldest scientists, who would have entered the job market between the late 1950s and late 1960s, published an overall average of 4.0 articles. For the middle cohort of scientists, who entered the job market between 1970 and 1980, the number of articles was 11.1. By further contrast, the youngest cohort of scientists, who entered the job market after 1980, had published an overall average of 14.3 papers.

The number of papers published by the scientists at the time of tenure also varied significantly over time, further highlighting intensification of the research role. To obtain tenure, the eldest cohort of scientists had published an overall average of 11.2 papers, the middle cohort 23.0, and the youngest cohort, 32.0. At the time of their promotion to full professor, the eldest cohort of scientists had published an overall average of 21.1 papers, the middle cohort 41.5, and the youngest cohort, 44.0. Put differently, younger cohorts of scientists typically published at a rate wherein their productivity corresponded to an entire career stage occupied by older counterparts. Presumably academics did not engage in such a marked change in productivity out of a more intense love of science. The press for productivity

Table 2. Publication Productivity and Event Timing, by Cohort and Organizational Type.

	Elites	Pluralists	Communitarians	Overall Average
Pre-1970 Cohort				
No. Papers @ 1st Job	4.5	5.0	2.1	4.0
No. Papers @ Tenure	11.0	14.3	8.3	11.2
No. Papers @ Full Prof.	22.0	24.3	17.0	21.1
Time to Tenure (in years)	5.0	4.0	5.3	4.8
Time to Full Prof. (in years)	5.0	5.3	5.6	5.3
1970–1980 Cohort				
No. Papers @ 1st Job	15.0	11.3	7.0	11.1
No. Papers @ Tenure	29.0	24.3	14.4	23.0
No. Papers @ Full Prof.	52.4	46.0	26.0	41.5
Time to Tenure (in years)	3.4	4.5	5.2	4.4
Time to Full Prof. (in years)	7.0	5.3	5.0	5.8
Post-1980 Cohort				
No. Papers @ 1st Job	20.0	12.0	11.0	14.3
No. Papers @ Tenure	46.0	26.0	24.0	32.0
No. Papers @ Full Prof.	54.0	39.3	38.0	44.0
Time to Tenure (in years)	7.0	5.2	5.3	5.8
Time to Full Prof. (in years)	5.0	4.8	6.0	5.3

Source: Hermanowicz (2009a, tables 20, 23, and 26).

intensified across institutions, as apparent in the subgroup differences in Table 2. Individuals changed in their behavior.

What is more, these productivity changes occurred in only modest changes in the time to tenure and to promotion to full professor. It took the eldest cohort of scientists an overall average of 4.8 years to achieve tenure. It took the middle cohort 4.4, and the youngest cohort 5.8 years. Thus, comparing the cohorts on the outer ends, the younger scientists published an overall average of 20.8 more papers compared to their eldest counterparts, and did so in only a one year greater span of time. A similar pattern is observed in time to promotion to full professor. For the eldest cohort, it took an overall average of 5.3, for the middle 5.8, and for the youngest 5.3 years. Thus, at this juncture, strikingly different productivity patterns were established within roughly similar intervals of time. (It should be noted that the post-doctoral stage of scientific careers became institutionalized after the eldest cohort obtained their first academic positions. This also partly accounts for why one observes large productivity differences across the cohorts. However, it should also not be forgotten that while benefits may be derived from the stage, the stage itself points further to an additional set of hurdles on which subsequent career success is contingent.)

In light of these general conditions, how do academics perceive their careers and the quality of professional life in academe? Specific generalizations can be drawn about careers that represent the major distinctions across cohorts of academics in the three prototypical organizational contexts. Twenty dimensions of academic careers surfaced from data analysis and coding to ground these comparisons (see Hermanowicz, 2009a, 2009b). I focus here on four such dimensions because they are the most overarching and provide a general accounting of research findings. These include: overall modal career patterns, overall satisfaction, work attitudes, and whether professors would again pursue an academic career.

Subjective Career Patterns

Overall Modal Career

In passing from early to mid-career, elites stabilized and rededicated themselves to academe — to fulfilling the institutional goals of higher education by continuing in their research productivity. An individual put it in the following representative terms:

> The dream is to discover some fantastic new effect that knocks the socks off my friends and colleagues, that knocks the socks off the community, so that when I walk down the corridor, the young students know me and say, "There goes [Silverman], he invented the [Silverman] effect." That's what I want; I want my effect. I want to be the first person to predict such and such an event. (Hermanowicz, 2009a, pp. 86–89)

By contrast, pluralists experienced a reversal. They questioned their interest and commitment to the profession. They grew disillusioned with academic research, even projecting a disavowal, as illustrated by the following scientist:

> My attitudes about the job, about me, and about the university have undergone tremendous changes in the past ten years ... I'm not sure I want to even submit things to published journals anymore ... I'm disgusted by the whole thing ... I got tired of getting referee reports ... that spend a page talking about the bibliography; they were entirely concerned with whether I cited their work or their friends' work, and they hadn't read the paper ... I'm in a setting where the last thing people want is honesty ... You guys play your game; it's fine. There are more important things in life than getting grants from the National Science Foundation, getting Nobel Prizes even or any of that stuff. That's all just a game .... (Hermanowicz, 2009a, p. 105)

By mid-career, most communitarians ceased in research. For communitarians, cumulative disadvantages accrued to the point of shutting down interest and motivation to continue in scientific research. Their career pattern may best be described as succumbing to a stasis — there was no forward progress. An academic, just at mid-career, said:

> I certainly have had a lot of distractions around here, and I think I could have been much more successful ... I think there's a lack of support, actually obstacles. I think there's been an orchestration of people not wanting people to succeed, not wanting to succeed in the department because there are things they can't do. I see it happen to other people. (Hermanowicz, 2009a, p. 119)

In their mid to late career transitions, elites remained consistent in their identification with science and in their scientific productivity. Their publication productivity continued to accelerate. Pluralists either attempted to regenerate themselves following earlier fallow periods, or continued in the research that they had been doing. Communitarians entered into a demise; they decreasingly identified with research. In ways consistent with the last passage above, they became increasingly disaffected with their departments and universities, which they saw as having crippled their research aspirations.

In moving from late to post career phases, elites for the first time lessened their intensity and embrace of research. Pluralists characteristically withdrew from work. Communitarians separated themselves completely from it, usually severing all ties with work and their employing organizations. Overall modal career patterns of academics by career stage and institutional type are summarized in Table 3.

Overall Satisfaction
Patterns in modal careers are in turn associated with patterns in satisfaction and in attitudes about work. Among elites, satisfaction begins high and rises through the career. It then drops at the end. Among pluralists, satisfaction starts out on a high, drops, and levels off. Finally, it rises at the end, coinciding with a time at which they withdraw from work. Among

Table 3. Overall Modal Career Patterns of Academics.

Phases	Elites	Pluralists	Communitarians
Early to Mid	Stabilization and rededication	Reversal	Stasis
Mid to Late	Continuation	Regeneration or continuation	Demise
Late to Post	Attenuation	Withdrawal	Separation

Table 4.   Overall Satisfaction of Academics.

Phases	Elites	Pluralists	Communitarians
Early (1994–1995)	Medium	High	Low
Mid (2004–2005)	High	Low	Low
Mid (1994–1995)	High	Medium	Low
Late (2004–2005)	High	Medium	Low
Late (1994–1995)	High	Medium	Low
Post (2004–2005)	Medium-Low	High	Medium-High

communitarians, there is a low in satisfaction throughout their careers, until the end. At the end of their careers, for the first time, communitarians experience the greatest high. Coincidentally, it is a time at which they are separating themselves altogether from work. Patterns in overall satisfaction of academics by career stage and institutional type are summarized in Table 4.

Work Attitudes
Elites possessed positive attitudes toward their work throughout most of their careers. Only in the end do their attitudes turn ambivalent — about what they have done, how much they have achieved, and where they stand professionally. Unlike any previous period in their careers, there is a sense of disappointment and frustration about their efforts and what they have achieved. One academic put it in the following terms:

> Maybe there is some self-delusion in feeling that you're being a significant contributor to science. It's just [pause] you have been trained, you know this field, when you're an expert in something, you tend to take pride in it, and you tend to continue doing it. But I don't think it's always very significant in the grand scheme of things … I could have worked harder to become a better professional physicist … At some stages of my career, I could have easily done better. It would have made a difference. It might well have been a significant difference … If I had worked harder, it would have given me a little more status. I would have accomplished more in the field …. (Hermanowicz, 2009a, pp. 192–193)

Pluralists are, by turn, positive. Asked about a particular period in their careers thought to be the most positive, the following illustration was given:

> … Now. This is it. Yes, absolutely. There's no question about it … I'm a little older, and I've had the opportunity to look back and see how great it has been over the years, to see the whole career collectively and appreciate how lucky I've been to do all the

things I have done. That's a good feeling, and it's like, wow, this has been great. (Hermanowicz, 2009a, p. 200)

Communitarians feel detached from work and institution. Their attitudes are far from the negative ones that were most common among them at earlier points in their careers.

There really wasn't much else to look forward to. [Right now, I'm] not working as hard. I'm not doing research anymore. I had two or three pretty good ideas during the course of my career, and I haven't had any since. I really don't keep up with the literature … I think early on, even though I did some fairly decent work, both as a graduate student and in the beginning of my career, I never was satisfied. I always thought that I could have done better or sooner or more. In more recent years [near and in retirement], I have become content, not only with what I was doing, but also how much. I think this is a reflection of my coming to like myself more. (Hermanowicz, 2009a, p. 207)

Patterns in the work attitudes of academics by career stage and institutional type are summarized in Table 5.

Would Academics Pursue an Academic Career Again?

Many would not. The notable trend is not that many would, as is also the case: one might anticipate that long training and preparation for a profession would coincide with commitment and satisfaction, indicated by a strong desire to pursue the same profession were people given the chance to start over. By contrast, what is noteworthy is the large fraction of faculty members who say they would pursue another line of work, an indication of a profession's lack of vitality, conditioned by the circumstances that faculty members confront in their institutional environments.

Elites are most adamant in desiring an academic career again, despite the leveling in satisfaction they derive from their careers in late and post stages, as indicated above. Their sentiments evolve only slightly, and then only in late to post career stages, when positive adamancy turns into a milder "yes."

Table 5. Work Attitudes of Academics.

Phases	Elites	Pluralists	Communitarians
Early to Mid	Positive	Preponderantly negative	Preponderantly negative
Mid to Late	Positive	Ambivalent; Positive	Neutralized
Late to Post	Ambivalent	Positive	Detached

Table 6.   Would Academics Pursue an Academic Career Again?

Phases	Elites	Pluralists	Communitarians
Early to Mid	Definitely	No; Maybe; Yes	No
Mid to Late	Definitely	Maybe; Yes	No; Maybe
Late to Post	Yes	Maybe; Yes	No

Pluralists indicate a greater variation in attitudes. They are most variable in the transition from early to mid-career, but remain ambivalent throughout the duration of their careers.

Communitarians are the most in agreement about not again pursuing an academic career. Also notable is the pattern of this attitude emerging strongly in early stages of their careers. The pattern is slightly variable as communitarians pass from mid to late career stages, perhaps owing to greater career stability. Their attitudes about academic careers turn wholly negative in late to post stages. They perceive their institutions as blocking an ability to realize professional goals. Patterns in academics' attitudes toward pursuing an academic career again, by career stage and institutional type, are presented in Table 6.

Diachronic change across the three prototypical academic organizations evinces *reversals*: reversals of career orientation, outlook, attitude, and desire to pursue the career again. Elites may be most dedicated throughout their careers, but most devastated at the end. Communitarians may be less dedicated throughout their careers, but most satisfied and positive in their outlooks at the end. Pluralists exemplify the greatest variability in their careers; they may find a satisfaction in the end that overcomes previous ambivalence, but the timing is what may be taken as especially remarkable. As with communitarians, relief comes from exiting the career and letting it go. Why might these patterns take their specific shapes?

DISCUSSION

In taking stock of the micro patterns of how academics experience and view their contemporary careers, notable motifs are apparent and worthy of examination. They are the recurring sentiments of disappointment and frustration; at greater intensities they are bitterness and disavowal. In one light, these are particularly odd findings. To what other line of work could one turn and find the autonomy that characteristically marks academic labor? In this respect, it might seem surprising to see the patterns above, when one might otherwise expect to find more resolute satisfaction with academic work and the organizations that enable it. Even in the academic sciences, work may be viewed as artisanal and craft-based, providing further self-discretionary ground on which to build an apparently strong, positive occupational and organizational set of sentiments.

But this is not what the data suggest. Nor is this to claim that satisfactions do not exist or are not apparent. They are reported in the data. Faculty who work at elite institutions are more satisfied more of the time. *This suggests a stratification in the possible effects of macro forces.* Such stratification is magnified by the fact that most faculty work, not in elite institutions, but in pluralist and communitarian institutions. Thus, rather more remarkable and meritorious of attention are prevailing themes of ill-content. Put differently, sentiments of ill-regard have permeated the most concentrated quarters of the academic profession (cf. Paradeise & Thoenig, 2013). Given the scope of these sentiments, their occurrence does not seem to be random, but instead indicative of other social forces.

Social-psychological theory indicates strongly that recurrent and pervasive disappointment and frustration occur when expectations are high, and often so high as to be unachievable (Turner & Stets, 2006). An expectation can exist only if is communicable and socially understood. Thus, it is theoretically unsatisfying to conclude that individuals, embarked on their careers, have created high expectations on their own. It is likely that a relationship exists between the work attitudes of professors and the expectations in which they work, since evaluative assessments are but responses to socially established criteria of purpose and performance. *What is associated with a rise in academic career expectations, and why a rise to such levels where prominent dissatisfaction is a sustainably generated outcome?*

Sets of Considerations

There is more than one plausible set of conditions to address the question. One is that work expectations are, in fact, no higher, and work sentiments no more negative, than at any other historical time. That is, were I to have conducted my study in 1970 or 1950 or 1925, I would have found the same patterns. This argument holds that academic work is always arduous, that there is always inequity in the outcomes of work and in careers, and, consequently, that there is always disappointment and frustration in such work. The argument further holds that high expectations are a precondition for the advancement of knowledge in all times and, as such, ill-content will always be found among those who try to "move a frontier," because few prove able to do so in ways that are consonant with high expectations.

There are problems with the argument. If indicated only by objective career measures, expectations for research and publication productivity have increased, and they have done so across a spectrum of institutional types (Table 2). This indicates that a press for achievement has intensified, particularly (but not exclusively) achievement in research and scholarship. Expectations for research achievement may historically have been high at the most research-oriented institutions, but they are now higher even at those institutions and have arisen and intensified at other types of institutions over time.

What is more, the sheer number of U.S. institutions and individuals oriented to and working in research has increased over time. This also speaks of intensification of competition and a climate of expectation for performance institutionally and individually. As interest in research and publication productivity increased within and among a growing array of institutions, universities increasingly formalized policies governing advancement in academic careers. The institutionalization of "the dossier" arose, in which achievement in research, teaching, and service activities are elaborately documented; this usage has become commonplace at a broad array of institutions, including those that had made virtually no use of it prior to the 1980s (Hermanowicz, 1998).

The practice of soliciting external letters that assess candidates for promotion is now also widespread, but it was once confined (and carried out in a more ad hoc fashion) to a limited number of the most research-oriented institutions (Hermanowicz, 1998). External letters are unnecessary to evaluate teaching and service; these are local matters. Rather they are most directly concerned with research achievement. Desires to get "good letters" bespeaks a specific mindset in which high expectation is part and parcel of achievement.

Finally, while academic work may always be difficult, different historical periods evince varying conditions of professional opportunity (Geiger, 1999). Prior historical periods have occurred generally in a context of expansion, not only in the number of higher education institutions or of the funding to support them, but also in individual opportunity to realize professional goals (Thelin, 2011). This was a mark of the "academic revolution," raised previously, seen to be in place by the end of the 1960s. Supported by their institutions, professors ascended in their power from status secured through research achievement in specialized fields (Jencks &

Riesman, 1968). Everything else equal, would a physicist rather try to get a major grant in 1965 or in 2015? Would a Ph.D. in the field of English rather attempt to get an academic job in 1969 or in 2015? Would an assistant professor of sociology rather "go up" for tenure in 1972 or in 2020? The contemporary scene of American higher education involves greater competition among institutions and individuals. The stress is on adaptation to *greater scarcity* rather than to plenitude. These several patterns point to three interacting dynamics: a rise in expectation in careers, an intensified competitive climate in which these expectations circulate, and a greater difficulty in achieving goals.

A second set of considerations contends that contemporary academic career expectations are strikingly high because graduate school training at elite institutions — those universities that house the top programs in a field — inculcate in students aspirations for great achievement. It is an argument I have developed in prior examinations of academic careers (Hermanowicz, 1998, 2009a), and others have turned to schooling in order to account for a conditioning of orientations and outlooks on the future (cf. Becker, Geer, Hughes, & Strauss, 1961; Cookson & Persell, 1985; Miller, 1970; Willis, 1977). By a systemic view, if graduates of elite programs took jobs in departments that were comparable in stature, career expectations may be high in those settings but also concentrated and circumscribed by them. But this, to be sure, has not been the reality of the academic marketplace, especially in arts and sciences fields, since approximately the early- to mid-1980s (Bowen & Sosa, 1989). Instead, graduates of elite programs have taken academic jobs at an increasing variety of institutions. For example, regardless of where they eventually landed an academic job, the majority of respondents for the study described in this chapter earned their Ph.D.s from top 10 physics programs.

When graduates of elite programs are more widely dispersed among institutional types, taking with them strong scholarly commitment and identification with roles in research and publication, an environment of expectation is also wider-ranging, and can condition a more pervasive climate of competition for scarce rewards. More people playing the game at more places makes it more difficult for almost any given person to win.

What is more, not all places are the same; they vary in both the structures and cultures that shape scholarly and professional opportunity. Disappointment and frustration may be produced when individual ambitions exceed, or are significantly different from, institutional ways of life — a pattern conveyed by qualitative data discussed in the previous section.

Yet we have established that more institutions of varying kind have latched on to the research bandwagon. A greater array of institutions increasingly welcomes research achievement and the visibility that publication productivity and grants bring to their campuses. In this vein, advanced degree programs outside of the elite have increasingly assumed characteristics of the major graduate departments, not the least of which includes numerous faculty trained in touted programs and a press for research and publication that they in turn impart to students in these institutions. One need no longer go to only a limited number of programs to find a culture of research, the press for publication, and people − both faculty and graduate students − engaged in the rituals of these ways.

In a broad array of institutions, then, graduate education has itself undergone significant cultural shifts. It is not only that it is no longer concentrated among a relatively small set of elite departments, but that even in those programs and increasingly elsewhere, graduate education has become highly professionalized. Graduate education across the arts and sciences − and across institutions − is now set up as a means to maximize the likelihood of tenure in an assistant professorship (with or without a consequential post-doctoral appointment, depending on the field): by establishing a significant record of publication even before the degree; by collaborating with faculty members, even if at the expense of developing individual creative work; by learning how to apply for major grants, and possibly even being listed on one; by attending and often times presenting work, even if unfinished and underdeveloped, at national and international conferences; by trying to win awards for the "best graduate student paper" or the "best teaching assistant" or the "best graduate student instructor"; by becoming, in so many words, enamored of status and status distinctions. In these respects, the graduate education argument turns the originating question onto itself: why have expectations for academic careers risen, evidence of which now flourishes even in the graduate training for them?

The historical conditions of academic careers are not constant but have changed (by way of argument one); graduate education may be more consequence than cause of these changes (by way of argument two). As such, *macro conditions* have appeared to *raise ambitions* of aspiring and incumbent faculty members, and then *thwart them*, by a lack of opportunity: in the paucity of faculty positions combined with increased Ph.D. production, the expansion of the search for prestige to a broader range of institutions, and an intensified climate of competition.

How the Macro and Micro Communicate

What is the mechanism by which a macro environment of neoliberalist academic capitalism may condition the work attitudes and experiences of professors in a micro environment? I suggest that a key possibility, operating at a meso level that can link force and sentiment of the macro and micro, is the *operation of reward systems* in universities. Reward systems structure the allocation of resources and, in so doing, embody values of the principals who have the power to control both the terms and the ways in which people and their activities are sanctioned.

There are two principal domains in which the operation of reward systems likely conditions faculty attitudes. One consists of change in the allocation of resources among entities within universities. We may refer to this as *distribution by unit type*. The other domain consists of change in the allocation of resources in direct support of faculty work. We may refer to this as *distribution by work type*. In both domains, reward systems operate to reveal preferences and priorities in the types of activities that an organization most covets.

Examples of patterns indicative of the first domain include the de-funding of the humanities and the academic core of the arts and social sciences; a centering of programs that strengthen university–industry ties, such as biotechnology, engineering, pharmacy, law, medicine, and business fields; elaboration of development, patent, and intellectual property offices; heightened support and creation of a complex infrastructure for athletics; the building of well-appointed facilities for students and athletes, and; an expanded administrative structure to oversee institutional accretion. In all of these changes organizations are restructured such that the interests of money and revenue return are given greater priority to knowledge and intellectual discovery. Even the rhetoric of university presidents has been found to change, shifting from "fruits of research" narratives that emphasize the benefits of basic science to "orders of magnitude" narratives that celebrate technology and commercialization (Slaughter, 1993).

What is a scholar to make of a university that ostensibly assigns greater importance to money and money-making ventures than to knowledge? (cf. Hackett, 2001). It is possible that, for many, the answer is tied up in disfavorable, critical, and alienated sentiment. It is also possible that, for still others, detachment, disengagement, and apathy are apparent. These latter sentiments may be but the consequences at the extremes of an organizational condition. They are normally indicative of people having "given up."

The system appears so powerful and all-encompassing as to make resistance seem futile.

As for the second domain − the distribution of rewards by work type − compensation constitutes the central datum that informs how reward systems operate. Up until the 1970s, little differentiation within rank was evident in faculty salaries across fields (Slaughter & Rhoades, 2004). Full professors of English were roughly comparably paid to full professors of finance. What happened? Here again we confront marketization, beginning in the 1980s and intensifying thereafter. Fields, such as business and law, that supposedly have large alternative labor markets to which academics in these field could turn if not rewarded with comparatively high university salaries, create significant internal disparities. But a "star system" also emerged in which value on revenue generating activity assumed priority over quests for knowledge in and of themselves. Professors who publish, at one point in time the mark of notoriety, but who are not stars are thereby de-centered in the contemporary status system of American universities.

> During the past two decades … some professors have acquired a star status that enables them to bargain with universities for salary and other perks in the same way that major-league sports players bargain for multimillion dollar contracts … Popular conceptions about the market value of professors' expertise and societal endorsement of the intrinsic value of money help the relatively small number of star faculty to negotiate large salaries with their universities … Faculty who make commercially viable discoveries are not the only stars. Professors at research universities who bring in large amounts of federal funds are also treasured by administrations, many of which depend on these "million-dollar-a-year men" for a substantial proportion of their institutions' operating costs. Faculty members who achieve reputations through scholarship are similarly valued, particularly if they are courted by other universities. Professors who simply publish are less esteemed, because so many professors now publish, and journals proliferate. The power to generate external funds or command offers from other universities is what distinguishes stars from other professors. (Slaughter, 2001, p. 23)

The way in which a faculty reward system operates is undergirded by the rise of the institutional "audit." Universities now require faculty members to account for themselves by engaging in rituals of verification − documenting and recording their activities on an annual basis (Power, 1997). Administrators are charged with generating evaluations of how individuals and units are performing (Miller & O'Leary, 1987). This can create the sense that administrators govern faculty rather than govern *with* them (Tuchman, 2009). In addition, these practices encourage what has been called an "accountability regime," wherein academic work gets reconfigured in a metric reality (Hopwood, 1987; Tuchman, 2009). Professors become auditable commodities, and the system comprises a "new managerialism" that undercuts faculty authority by implementing change from the top down (Tuchman, 2009, p. 11). The practices create a new standard of economic rationality in university decision-making (Geiger, 2004). "Rather than universities being subordinated to the production and transmittal of knowledge, knowledge is now subordinated to the needs of universities for profit and recognition" (Tuchman, 2009, p. 11).

What is more, it is not only that knowledge is de-centered and displaced for money, but also that interest in and seriousness with knowledge is weakened in the culture of academic capitalism. This minimizes intellectual behavior in universities. Commensuration, the process of attributing meaning to measurement, "changes the form and circulation of information and how people attend to it" (Espeland & Sauder, 2007, p. 333). For instance, administrators might note that a professor published 100, 200, or 400 articles, but not explain why the articles mattered (Tuchman, 2010). Similarly, they elevate student evaluations of teaching, like citation counts and impact factors, among numerous other metrics, even if they do not know what they mean, or how to explain the difference between 3.8 and 4.2. The quest to be number 1, or in the top 10, or the top 25, or the top 50, or at least above average — instantiations of market behavior — can seem largely devoid of meaning; that is, unrelated to ideas, and hence repugnant to those who understand themselves as scholars and educators.

As in the first domain of change in the allocation of organizational resources, shift in the valuation of faculty work produces an institutional environment of haves and have-nots. Creative competition is supplanted by a celebration of money-making ventures. While these trends are evident throughout the U.S. system of higher education, they are intensified in the public sector, where institutions confront more stringent conditions to generate their own operating revenue. The inequality in higher education institutions, now pervasive, appears as but a microcosm of American society, where a neoliberalist orientation has likewise ascended in both policies and practices characterizing the distribution of rewards.

It stands to reason that such a conditioning of culture could adversely affect the attitudes and experiences of people attempting to engage in scholarly work. "The star system and academic entrepreneurship pit one group of professors against another in the struggle for resources. These skirmishes often create institutional climates of contention, bitterness, and cynicism, especially among the have-not segments of universities" (Slaughter, 2001, p. 24). The "have-not" segments of universities are highly populated; thus the consequences are wide-ranging. Among other segments, this consists of the liberal arts, once the scholarly backbone of academic organization, but now treated largely as an instructional service unit for the rest of the university.

In this regard, contemporary academe may ironically be viewed as a *culture without community*. Professors increasingly understand themselves and their work in terms of free agency, geared to a market, and interested especially if not exclusively in themselves. The idea of a *collegium*, once the organizing principle of the academic profession (Ben-David, 1972; Krause, 1996), is obliterated. One can thus realize a relationship between the ways of neoliberalism and the deprofessionalization of academic work.

CONCLUSION

If academic career expectations have grown significantly higher, and if this has rendered satisfaction in academic work more precarious, it seems reasonable to ask if larger conditions of universities have changed, since these are the organizations that structure academic careers. Have universities changed in ways to elevate expectation and thereby create unsteady ground for satisfaction in faculty work? Because expectation and satisfaction are fundamental components of careers, in the absence of which work is greatly compromised if not implausible, it seems equally reasonable to search for change in universities that is similarly fundamental, that is, which strikes at the core of how universities are constituted.

This paper has evaluated the micro conditions of faculty work satisfaction and the macro environment of universities. The micro conditions of faculty work, indicated by modal career patterns, overall work satisfaction, work attitudes, and whether professors would again pursue an academic career, evince permutations by career phase and the type of organization in which academics work. But this variation notwithstanding, the data expose prominent and pervasive attitudinal themes among contemporary academics: those of disappointment, frustration, bitterness, and disavowal.

A larger social-institutional environment consists of macro level trends wherein neoliberalism enables academic capitalism to flourish with its attendant effects in privatization and marketization. It has been suggested that the shift in organizational priority brought about by these conditions entails a "valorization of shiny things," that is, a valuing of market-related phenomena over knowledge of its own accord. This valorization, created and ritually supported by practices endemic of changed organizational culture, may weaken the ground on which the traditional scholarly role is played, and thereby throw into unsteadiness a basis for positive work sentiment and institutional regard.

The operation of reward systems in universities is presented as a messenger by which workers interpret and understand organizational culture. Two domains in which reward systems operate have been examined for the chief parts they play in communicating neoliberal values and priorities of universities. These include systems in which rewards are allocated differentially by types of units in institutions and those that allocate rewards differentially by the type of work performed by faculty members. In both cases, reward systems have come to sanction most affirmatively those activities that are thought to serve the financial interests of higher education institutions. This manner of operation makes reward systems structurally and symbolically consequential, a direct conduit for the valorization of shiny things.

The contemporary university has come to embody a deep chasm between money and knowledge, both now conferred as pursuable rights of institutions and individuals forging careers in them. It involves a contest that arguably many scholars, given their values and priorities, have had no interest in entertaining. For scholars the consequences are real, conveyed and constrained by an organizational culture that embeds actors, and felt tangibly by structural systems of reward. "Between two rights," Marx purported, "force decides" (1967 [1867], p. 225). "Obliged to live as appendages of the market and of capital accumulation rather than as expressive beings, the realm of freedom shrinks before the awful logic and the hollow intensity of market involvements" (Harvey, 2005, p. 185).

But the articulation of visions of what a university is or should be, as well as struggle and resistance, remain ways in which academics, through their collective organization and in the interests of their own work, help to constitute the values embodied by institutional culture. Critical reflection, engaged writing, and considered discussion of the "corporate university" are self-demonstrative. These possibilities will thus endure insofar as institutions subscribe to a belief in the advancement of knowledge, a component of their culture on which the future of the university is dependent.

REFERENCES

Armstrong, E. A., & Hamilton, L. T. (2013). *Paying for the party: How college maintains inequality*. Cambridge, MA: Harvard University Press.

Arum, R., & Roksa, J. (2011). *Academically adrift: Limited learning on college campuses.* Chicago, IL: University of Chicago Press.

Barley, S. R. (1989). Careers, identities, and institutions: The legacy of the Chicago school of sociology. In M. B. Arthur, D. T. Hall, & B. S. Lawrence (Eds.), *Handbook of career theory* (pp. 41–65). Cambridge: Cambridge University Press.

Becker, H. S., Geer, B., Hughes, E. C., & Strauss, A. L. (1961). *Boys in white: Student culture in medical school.* Chicago, IL: University of Chicago Press.

Ben-David, J. (1972). The profession of science and its powers. *Minerva, 10,* 351–383.

Berman, E. P. (2012). *Creating the market university: How academic science became an economic engine.* Princeton, NJ: Princeton University Press.

Bowen, W. G., & Sosa, J. A. (1989). *Prospects for faculty in the arts and sciences: A study of factors affecting demand and supply, 1987 to 2012.* Princeton, NJ: Princeton University Press.

Burgan, M. (2006). *What ever happened to the faculty? Drift and decision in higher Education.* Baltimore, MD: Johns Hopkins University Press.

Chait, R. (2002). The 'Academic Revolution' revisited. In S. Brint (Ed.), *The future of the city of intellect: The changing American university* (pp. 293–321). Stanford, CA: Stanford University Press.

Cookson, P. W., & Persell, C. H. (1985). *Preparing for power: America's elite boarding schools.* New York, NY: Basic.

Ehrenberg, R. G. (2002). Reaching for the brass ring: The *U.S. News & World Report* rankings and competition. *Review of Higher Education, 26*(2), 145–162.

Espeland, W. N., & Sauder, M. (2007). Rankings and reactivity: How public measures recreate social worlds. *American Journal of Sociology, 113*(1), 1–40.

Geiger, R. L. (1999). The ten generations of American higher education. In R. O. Berdahl, P. G. Altbach, & P. J. Gumport (Eds.), *Higher education in the twenty-first century* (pp. 38–69). Baltimore, MD: Johns Hopkins University Press.

Geiger, R. L. (2004). *Knowledge and money: Research universities and the paradox of the marketplace.* Stanford, CA: Stanford University Press.

Giroux, H. A. (2002). Neoliberalism, corporate culture, and the promise of higher education: The university as a democratic sphere. *Harvard Educational Review, 72*(4), 425–463.

Goldberger, M. L., Maher, B. A., & Flattau, P. E. (Eds.). (1995). *Research-doctorate programs in the United States: Continuity and change.* Washington, DC: National Academy Press.

Hackett, E. J. (2001). Science as a vocation in the 1990s: The changing organizational culture of academic science. In J. Croissant & S. Restivo (Eds.), *Degrees of compromise: Industrial interests and academic values* (pp. 101–137). Albany, NY: SUNY Press.

Harvey, D. (2005). *A brief history of neoliberalism.* Oxford: Oxford University Press.

Hermanowicz, J. C. (1998). *The stars are not enough: Scientists—their passions and professions.* Chicago, IL: University of Chicago Press.

Hermanowicz, J. C. (2009a). *Lives in science: How institutions affect academic careers.* Chicago, IL: University of Chicago Press.

Hermanowicz, J. C. (2009b). Faculty perceptions of work, the academic profession, and universities across careers. *Advancing Higher Education* (pp. 1–12). TIAA-CREF Institute.

Hermanowicz, J. C. (2011). Anomie in the American academic profession. In *The American academic profession: Transformation in contemporary higher education* (pp. 216–237). Baltimore, MD: Johns Hopkins University Press.

Hopwood, A. G. (1987). The archeology of accounting systems. *Accounting, Organizations and Society, 12*(3), 207–234.

Jencks, C., & Riesman, D. (1968). *The academic revolution.* Garden City, NY: Doubleday.

Jones, L. V., Lindzey, G., & Coggeshall, P. E. (Eds.). (1982). *An assessment of research-doctorate programs in the United States: Mathematical and physical sciences.* Washington, DC: National Academy Press.

Kirp, D. L. (2003). *Shakespeare, Einstein, and the bottom line: The marketing of higher education.* Cambridge, MA: Harvard University Press.

Krause, E. A. (1996). *Death of the guilds: Professions, states, and the advance of capitalism, 1930 to the present.* New Haven, CT: Yale University Press.

Leslie, L. L., & Rhoades, G. (1995). Rising administrative costs: Seeking explanations. *Journal of Higher Education, 66*(2), 187–212.

Marx, K. (1967 [1867]). *Capital* (Vol. 1). New York, NY: International Publishers.

Merton, R. K. (1973). Priorities in scientific discovery. In *The sociology of science: Theoretical and empirical investigations* (pp. 286–324). Edited and with an Introduction by N. W. Storer. Chicago, IL: University of Chicago Press. Article first published in 1957.

Miller, P., & O'Leary, T. (1987). Accounting and the construction of the governable person. *Accounting, Organizations and Society, 12*(3), 235–265.

Miller, S. J. (1970). *Prescription for leadership: Training for the medical elite.* Chicago, IL: Aldine.

Mirowski, P. (2011). *Science mart: Privatizing American science.* Cambridge, MA: Harvard University Press.

Paradeise, C., & Thoenig, J. (2013). Academic institutions in search of quality: Local orders and global standards. *Organization Sciences, 34*(2), 189–218.

Polyani, K. (1944). *The great transformation: The political and economic origins of our time.* Boston, MA: Beacon Press.

Power, M. (1997). *The audit society: Rituals of verification.* Oxford: Oxford University Press.

Schuster, J. H., & Finkelstein, M. J. (2006). *The American faculty: The restructuring of academic work and careers.* Baltimore, MD: Johns Hopkins University Press.

Slaughter, S. (1993). Beyond basic science: Research university presidents' narratives of science policy. *Science, Technology, and Human Values, 18*(3), 278–302.

Slaughter, S. (2001). Professional values and the allure of the market. *Academe, 87*(5), 22–26.

Slaughter, S. (2011). Academic freedom, professional autonomy, and the state. In J. C. Hermanowicz (Ed.), *The American academic profession: Transformation in higher education* (pp. 241–273). Baltimore, MD: Johns Hopkins University Press.

Slaughter, S., & Leslie, L. (1997). *Academic capitalism: Politics, policies, and the entrepreneurial state.* Baltimore, MD: Johns Hopkins University Press.

Slaughter, S., & Leslie, L. (2001). Expanding and elaborating the concept of academic capitalism. *Organization, 8*(2), 154–161.

Slaughter, S., & Rhoades, G. (2004). *Academic capitalism and the new economy: Markets, state, and higher education.* Baltimore, MD: Johns Hopkins University Press.

Stephan, P. (2012). *How economics shapes science.* Cambridge, MA: Harvard University Press.

Thelin, J. R. (2004). *A history of American higher education.* Baltimore, MD: Johns Hopkins University Press.

Thelin, J. R. (2011). All that glittered was not gold: Rethinking American higher education's golden age, 1945–1970. In J. C. Hermanowicz (Ed.), *The American academic*

profession: Transformation in contemporary higher education. Baltimore, MD: Johns
Hopkins University Press.

Tuchman, G. (2009). *Wannabe U: Inside the corporate university.* Chicago, IL: University of
Chicago Press.

Tuchman, G. (2010, October 22). The future of Wannabe U: How the accountability regime
leads us astray. *Chronicle of Higher Education,* Section B, B7.

Turner, J. H., & Stets, J. E. (2006). Sociological theories of human emotions. *Annual Review of
Sociology, 32,* 25–52.

Willis, P. (1977). *Learning to labour: How working class kids get working class jobs.* New York,
NY: Columbia University Press.

GOING INTERDISCIPLINARY IN FRENCH AND US UNIVERSITIES: ORGANIZATIONAL CHANGE AND UNIVERSITY POLICIES

Séverine Louvel

ABSTRACT

This paper analyses French and US universities' organizational responses to the more or less explicit pressures they face to go interdisciplinary. Defining universities as pluralistic organizations, I show that the implementation of interdisciplinary research does not result in well-integrated institutional strategies, but rather combines initiatives from the scientific community and from university leaders. Based on case studies conducted on the development of interdisciplinary nanomedicine in five leading French and US research universities, I identify three settings where the implementation of interdisciplinarity involves shifts in organizational structure — in principal investigator-based research teams and scientific networks, in departmental boundaries, and in institutional structures, and question issues of governance, leadership and resource allocation arising from those shifts. We see similarities between the two countries in terms of how initiatives by "entrepreneurial academics" — searching for funds

The University under Pressure
Research in the Sociology of Organizations, Volume 46, 329–359
Copyright © 2016 by Emerald Group Publishing Limited
All rights of reproduction in any form reserved
ISSN: 0733-558X/doi:10.1108/S0733-558X20160000046011

*for interdisciplinary research — and by the university leadership — also
searching for funds, and redefining institutional projects around interdisciplinarity — complement each other. We also identify one major difference — with French pro-interdisciplinary university policies being
strongly influenced by a political impetus from the French ministry of
higher education and research.*

Keywords: Interdisciplinarity; organizational change; university
policy; nanomedicine; French and US universities

INTRODUCTION

Interdisciplinarity finds continuing support, in both Europe and in the
United States, among policy makers (MESR, 2013, p. 10) and university
leaders (AAU, 2005; EUA, 2015, p. 97), as well as from funding agencies
(Global Research Council, 2013; Hackett, 2000; Zerhouni, 2003).[1] Its promoters present it as being essential to advancing fundamental knowledge,
for the social relevance of research, for business innovation and for
technology transfer, and for students' employability. The development of
interdisciplinary research and postgraduate education has resulted in a
growing body of literature analyzing interdisciplinary practices as well as
pro-interdisciplinary university policies, questioning their relevance and
examining the reasons behind their success or failure. Many studies are
dedicated to US universities and analyze either the management and
outcomes of the large interdisciplinary research centers funded mostly
by federal funding agencies (Boardman & Corley, 2008; Boardman &
Ponomariov, 2014; Ponomariov & Boardman, 2010; Sabharwal & Hu,
2013; Youtie, Libaers, & Bozeman, 2006) or pro-interdisciplinary university
policies (Brint, 2005; Holley, 2009; Hollingsworth & Hollingsworth, 2000;
Sá, 2008a).[2] These studies show that, in the US context, interdisciplinary
research initiatives are distributed among research teams, departments,
research centers, and universities — and often depend principally on the
ability of faculty and university leaders to seize and sustain funding opportunities for interdisciplinary research, rather than being integrated into
coherent institutional strategies.[3] However, to what extent these findings
are US-specific — notably because of the organization of research
funding — or are relevant for non-US (for instance, French) universities is
not clear. We assume the organizational changes accompanying university
interdisciplinarity in France to be (as in the United States), a joint product

of several types of actions from faculty members and/or in response to university policies. Indeed, such diverse efforts toward interdisciplinarity — as well as the resultant alliances and conflicts — reflect the definition of both countries' universities as pluralistic organizations with diffuse power, divergent objectives, and knowledge-based work (Denis, Langley, & Rouleau, 2007), as well as entrepreneurial universities where entrepreneurship is defined as an organizational effort to pursue opportunities via means beyond those that are currently available (Clark, 1998). In France, as in the United States, some university leaders (presidents, vice presidents, chancellors, and vice-chancellors) are crucial promoters of interdisciplinarity and initiate proactive policies in order to redraw university departments' boundaries. But faculty members' fund-raising activities also impact universities' disciplinary and/or interdisciplinary organizations. In particular, academics who succeed in attracting large grants for interdisciplinary research tend to be allowed increased autonomy by their disciplinary departments, and may also use their stronger positions as bargaining resources in their negotiations with other departments or with their universities' presidential teams (Paradeise, Noël, & Goastellec, 2015).

This paper seeks to compare the organizational changes brought about by the development of interdisciplinary research in French and US universities, as well as the university policies that initiate or support these changes. Our analysis is non-prescriptive (i.e., we are not looking to identify "best practices" to promote interdisciplinarity), but rather seeks to highlight issues of articulation and alignment between the different types of actions underlying the development of interdisciplinarity at individual universities. In which university settings does interdisciplinarity lead to organizational change? What roles do university policies play in these changes? How do interdisciplinary initiatives relate to each other and fit into universities' overall strategies? We address these issues via a qualitative approach, analyzing the implementation of interdisciplinary nanomedicine in five leading French and US research universities.[4] We focus on interdisciplinarity in research and in postgraduate education, and identify three situations where shift in organizational structure occur: in principal investigator-based research teams; in departmental boundaries; and in institutional structures. For each setting, we identify the key promoters of interdisciplinarity (university leaders, department heads, faculty members, funding agencies, policy makers, etc.) as well as their associated objectives and the organizational issues involved in their interdisciplinary endeavors (such as governance, leadership, and resource allocation). We conclude the paper by summarizing the major similarities and differences between the organizational shifts associated with the implementation of interdisciplinarity at the French and US universities we studied.

LITERATURE REVIEW

Many authors who have defined interdisciplinarity have differentiated it from other concepts, such as multidisciplinarity and transdisciplinarity. They usually agree that, while multidisciplinarity involves the simple juxtaposition of knowledge between disciplines, and transdisciplinarity implies the integration of knowledge across several disciplines, interdisciplinarity refers to a situation where two (or more) disciplines engage in dialogue and in complementary activities to the extent that they can transform not only those disciplines themselves but also the boundaries between them (Barry, Born, & Weszkalnys, 2008; Weingart & Stehr, 2000). There is a long-standing debate about whether interdisciplinarity questions the centrality of disciplines themselves, defined both as the cognitive and instrumental repertoires shared by research communities and as social organization patterns via which contemporary sciences develop and validate new knowledge. While some authors argue that interdisciplinarity is needed to counter the increasing domination of contemporary scientific specialization (Bonaccorsi, 2010; Lenoir, 1997) and to foster breakthrough innovations (Dogan & Pahre, 1991), others claim that the intellectual breadth of disciplines — as well as their internal differences — enables constant innovation (Jacobs, 2014).

Despite these debates, interdisciplinarity has become commonplace in science public policy over recent decades, with policy makers seeing it as a way to counter excessive academism in science. The political discourse on interdisciplinarity, which promotes logics of "accountability" and "innovation" in the public sciences (Barry et al., 2008), reached a climax in the 1990s,[5] with the call for a "Mode 2" of knowledge production, in which scientific research would be structured around problems to be solved in the real world (climate change, cancer, etc.) rather than around disciplines (Gibbons et al., 1994). This positive discourse about interdisciplinarity resulted in widespread efforts from research sponsors (funding agencies, local authorities, and firms) and university leaders to promote it. The rise of interdisciplinary initiatives has also led to the emergence of its own research field, especially with the publication of handbooks listing interdisciplinary actions taken by universities or in several scientific areas, and dealing with how to overcome obstacles to interdisciplinary research — see for instance, Frodeman, Klein, and Mitcham (2010). Some authors have also taken a critical stance toward interdisciplinary policies: they either show that the assumptions underlying the claims for their benefits are not being sufficiently questioned (Jacobs & Frickel, 2009), and that traditional disciplines also have a high innovation potential (Jacobs, 2014), or they observe a certain degree of decoupling between pro-interdisciplinary policies – emphasizing synergies between disciplines – and interdisciplinary practices – where certain disciplines still impose their working methods and their evaluation standards (Albert, Paradis, & Kuper, 2015; Louvel, 2015). Many analyses have been conducted addressing these issues in two settings.[6] First, the interdisciplinary university research centers that have multiplied in the last three decades in the United States – mostly with the support of the National Science Foundation and the National Institutes for Health (Etzkowitz & Kemelgor, 1998; Geiger, 1990; Stahler & Tash, 1994) – have been investigated in multiple dimensions: their effects on researchers' productivity (Sabharwal & Hu, 2013) and on scientists' collaborations (Boardman & Corley, 2008); their levels of institutionalization as assessed, for example, by resource allocation procedures, setting research agendas (Youtie et al., 2006), or effective knowledge management (Boardman & Ponomariov, 2014; Ponomariov & Boardman, 2010). Interdisciplinary research has also been investigated as a set of organizational and managerial challenges undertaken by numerous US universities. Scholars have analyzed how university leaders try to weaken the authority of disciplinary departments with the goal of "creating the future" (Brint, 2005, p. 38), rather than reaching excellence in traditional disciplines – for example, by creating interdisciplinary graduate programs (Newswander & Borrego, 2009) or by hiring faculty for interdisciplinary research reasons (Sá, 2008b). Those scholars who favor interdisciplinarity see the persistence of disciplinary departments as being anchored in institutional cultures and as principally serving established academic arrangements or political interests (Sá, 2008a). They argue that successful interdisciplinary university policies facilitate "transformational change," that is, change that is "pervasive, intentional, which occurs over a period of time, and has a strong influence on institutional culture" (Holley, 2009, p. 334). Critical scholars warn that "anti-disciplinary" university policies – for example, the organization of universities around flexible interdisciplinary arrangements – will increase the fragmentation of the sciences and focus research only on short-term objectives (Jacobs, 2014).

These numerous studies have shown the importance in the US context of two loci of organizational change (university research centers and university policies), and addressed issues of their articulation. However, one can wonder whether interdisciplinarity raises similar organizational and managerial problems in other contexts, particularly in European universities – which, indeed, also display several loci of organizational change. First, European universities are transforming themselves into "organizational actors" (Brunsson & Sahlin-Anderson, 2000) with strategic capacities to implement pro-interdisciplinary policies. As in US universities, these change strategies are often co-constructed between university leaders and departmental faculties (Gioia & Thomas, 1996; Jarzabkowski, 2008; Louvel, 2013; Townley, 1997) – in particular, deans (heads of departments) are often central actors in the elaboration of university strategies (De Boer & Goedegebuure, 2009). Moreover, European universities are fragmented or "pluralistic" organizations (Denis et al., 2007), composed of collectives (departments, research labs, research centers, etc.) each pursuing their own objectives, which may have conflicting views and expectations about and toward the university. These entities may also collaborate with – and seek funding from – commercial companies, local authorities, funding agencies, or foundations for interdisciplinary research. Their activities impact the universities' organizational structures in ways that are not directly addressed by university leadership teams, nor always explicitly integrated in their strategic plans, but are aligned with the notion of European universities as entrepreneurial actors (Clark, 1998).

How does the development of interdisciplinary research in European universities combine initiatives taken by university leaders, deans, and faculty members? What are the main loci of organizational change? How do interdisciplinary initiatives fit into universities' overall strategies? To address the specific organizational issues encountered by US universities, this paper compares the development of interdisciplinary nanomedicine at French and US universities.

METHOD

Nanomedicine as a Showcase for Interdisciplinary Research and Postgraduate Education

We focus our empirical study on research and postgraduate education in nanomedicine, which can be broadly defined as the application of nanotechnology to biomedical problems. Nanomedicine is often presented as an archetypal setting for scientific interdisciplinarity, associating – depending on the focus of the research project involved – cell and molecular biology with chemistry (synthesis and characterization of nanoparticles), pharmacology, applied physics (study of mechanical properties, with molecular and cell signaling), bioinformatics (simulation of molecular systems, design of molecules), electrical engineering (imaging technologies), material sciences (design of devices), etc. As in other interdisciplinary areas of the biomedical sciences, nanomedicine carries high expectations, both in clinical and economic terms, and so has been supported by massive efforts in many countries worldwide over recent years which have provided many opportunities to structure interdisciplinary research in the form of projects, networks, research centers, postgraduate programs, etc. Thus, considering nanomedicine opens a window to look more broadly at interdisciplinarity in the contemporary life sciences.

Some of these initiatives focus on nanomedicine as such, providing funding for interdisciplinary research labs and centers. The United States was probably the first country in the world to promote interdisciplinary nanomedicine centers as part of the *National Nanotechnology Initiative* (NNI), a federal policy launched in 2000 which benefited from a cumulative investment of $18 billion by 2013.[7] The National Institutes of Health (NIH) have contributed to the NNI by supporting the institution of eight *Nanomedicine Development Centers* (NDCs) since 2005; by initiating calls for tenders for research on *Nanoscience and Nanotechnology for Biology and Medicine*; and by launching sectorial initiatives, such as the *Alliance for Nanotechnology in Cancer* by the National Cancer Institute (NCI) in 2004. But nanomedicine has also benefited from funding from the Departments of Energy and of Defense, as well as from universities and local authorities. Subsequently, European countries have launched similar nanomedicine programs (e.g., the French national research agency's *Nano-Innov* initiative launched in 2009, and programs within the EU's Framework Programs 6 and 7). At the same time, nanomedicine has benefited from larger funding programs aiming at developing interfaces between biology and other disciplines, including chemistry, material sciences, physical sciences, and engineering sciences.

However, very few specific nanomedicine departments have been created at either US or French universities. Rather, nanomedicine research has been hosted by well-established departments (such as molecular and cellular biology, pharmacology, chemistry, material sciences) and/or by newly created interdisciplinary departments (in particular, biomedical engineering, which covers research areas combining biomedical and engineering sciences such as nanomedicine, but also areas such as synthetic biology).

A Case Study Approach in French and American Universities

We adopt a case study approach across several universities in order to
explore the organizational issues thrown up by interdisciplinary endeavors
and reveal the in-depth, situated knowledge about the organizational
choices taken by faculty, deans, and university leadership teams. For this
study, we chose universities from France and from the United States which
are regarded as leaders in the nanoscience area, and more specifically in
nanomedicine (considered in terms of research funding, publications, and
patents). We do not particularly question the reasons for this leadership —
rather this criterion ensures that the universities chosen as case studies have
critical mass in nanomedicine. Our case study universities also all have
interdisciplinarity in their mission statements — although they operationa-
lize this concept differently.

The material used in this paper mainly comes from an empirical study
of two French universities (Grenoble and Toulouse)[8] and three in the
United States (UC Berkeley, UC San Francisco, and UT Houston),
although we also include occasional examples from other universities
(e.g., UC Davis, UT Austin or Rice University) in our overall study. Our
source material comes from in-depth interviews conducted with academics
(vice presidents, heads of departments, heads of research centers, faculty
members), as well as relevant documents (reports, press releases, websites,
etc.). For the purposes of this paper, we use 50 interviews conducted
over a 4 year period (2009—2013),[9] and focus on those parts of the interview material that concern the organizational changes that accompanied
the rise of interdisciplinarity in those settings. Data coding was inductive
and guided by the following research questions: At which university levels
is interdisciplinarity gaining importance? To what extent does it alter
existing organizational structures, and in particular departmental boundaries? What are the respective roles of faculty and university managers in
its development? In which areas do actors involved in these interdisciplinary endeavors collaborate or conflict? Data analysis leads us to identify
three particular settings of organizational change (research teams, departments, and institutional structures) and to differentiate them according to
five dimensions: the promoters of interdisciplinarity; the objectives associated with it; the tools for its implementation; the organizational changes
involved; and the organizational issues (in terms of leadership, governance, and resource allocation) associated with those changes.[10]

RESULTS: SETTINGS OF ORGANIZATIONAL CHANGE; CHALLENGES AND ISSUES FOR UNIVERSITY POLICIES

Research Teams: Facilitating Bottom-up Dynamics

The development of interdisciplinary nanomedicine research and postgraduate education in US and French universities stems first from the actions of principal investigators (PIs) of research teams acting as "quasi-entrepreneurs" (Etzkowitz, 2003), applying for competitive grants and recruiting staff (mainly PhD students and post-docs). These actions are major driving forces behind the growth of interdisciplinarity, but that does not always imply that such growth enjoys strong institutional support from the universities concerned. However it explains the vitality of interdisciplinary research, even in universities where disciplinary departments are very powerful. Interdisciplinary research can be considered "science-driven," insofar as the central logic for creating such research teams is science oriented (in terms of the complementarity between the teams' different expertise; their expectations of making breakthrough innovations; and their hopes of overcoming competitors). Fluidity prevails over stability, as interdisciplinary cooperation is highly dependent on the availability of funding: indeed, most such interdisciplinary research teams are created and maintained via successful investigator-initiated grant applications. However, the conditions for awarding funding do not always seem to support interdisciplinary research — in particular, success rates for applications to major funding agencies have been decreasing in recent years, due to the growing number of applicants and (more recently) to funding cuts (e.g., NIH and NSF). For instance, success rates for applications to NIH were around 30% in the 1980s (Stephan, 2012), but had fallen to 8.6% by 2012 (for first submissions for R01 equivalent grants[11]) — and even lower in certain study sections. Success rates for French ANR grants have decreased more slowly (from 25.7% in 2005 to 21.3% in 2011), but vary a lot between different funding calls. Such competition for grant funding hinders these science-driven interdisciplinary dynamics in two ways. First, despite official support for interdisciplinary projects from funding agencies, principal investigators prefer to locate their research efforts within single disciplines. Indeed, they have learnt (from previous unsuccessful applications or from their own experience of reviewing grant applications) that reviewers try to minimize the chance of selecting risky proposals, and so tend to give multi-disciplinary applications – which are generally viewed as more risky than disciplinary ones, and about which there is usually greater disagreement between reviewers from different disciplinary backgrounds – lower scores (Lamont, Mallard, & Guetzkow, 2006):

> For the NIH, you almost have to be multidisciplinary now, you have to have a team, and you have to have more than one expertise at the same time. But when we have grant reviews, for example, many of the projects are so multidisciplinary that ... it is hard to get people who understand [them]. There are experts on every single topic .... And you can't satisfy everyone. (...) And so when I sit down [to report] on NIH study sections, there are always problems [with interdisciplinary proposals]. (Biomedical engineering PI, UCSF)

> It's absolutely certain that the lack of research funding forces people to stick to their discipline and to areas where they are not taking any risks. (French physicist, Toulouse)

Second, even though funding bodies present interdisciplinarity as the only way to "think outside the box" in emerging fields nowadays, nano-medicine PIs associate incentives for interdisciplinary research with a growing pressure to develop translational research and see funding agencies as becoming less interested in basic science, that is, investigations that are not directly linked to solving specific problems, but which can promote more general problem-solving approaches (Calvert, 2006). At the NIH, even though peer-reviewed, investigator-initiated grants may not respond directly to specific health considerations (Sampat, 2012), all grant applications for investigator-initiated research have been obliged (since January 2010) to include a section on "innovation." Although the submission guidelines describe "innovation" in very general terms,[12] PIs tend to interpret it as showing the potential of their research for clinical applications and as encouraging interdisciplinary collaborations between researchers and clinicians (toxicologists, pharmacologists, medical doctors, etc.). Furthermore, they feel pressured to practice translational research so as to bring basic science "from bench to bedside" when seeking alternative funding from foundations and local authorities. These translational objectives can seem to contradict the idea of interdisciplinarity research as fostering scientific discoveries for the long term (Albert et al., 2015).

University leaders and department deans may have little control over the development and directions of such interdisciplinary teams. As can also be the case in disciplinary research, project-based research funding tends to be subject to centrifugal dynamics (with PIs being essentially connected to networks outside their institutions), so hindering universities' abilities to set science policy priorities. While autonomy has been a characteristic of PIs since the rise of US research universities in the 19th century (Etzkowitz, 2003), it has gained importance in recent decades in French universities with the rise of project-based funding and the diversification of local, national, and European funding sources (Louvel, 2010). But universities can play roles in supporting such interdisciplinary endeavors without weakening their disciplinary departments (in particular, neither withdrawing resources from them nor transferring decision-making powers to university leaders). Both French and American universities facilitate the formation of interdisciplinary research teams by minimizing the risks involved (e.g., by distributing "seed grants" for which competition is less intense than for major grants from funding agencies). In France, national institutions also redirect a limited share of their resources toward interdisciplinary research.[13] For instance, the largest French national research organization – the CNRS (*Centre National de la Recherche Scientifique*) – supports a few large nanomedicine labs (*Unites Mixtes de Recherche*) in undertaking interdisciplinary research, which receive funding and funded posts (both academic and technical staff). The CNRS also supports positions for tenured researchers doing interdisciplinary research, thus opening (albeit only a few) opportunity spaces for interdisciplinary careers.[14]

Finally, universities facilitate interdisciplinary collaborations which emerge bottom-up by supporting transverse structures that strengthen linkages between departments, but preserve their autonomy. The most flexible of such organizations are university networks (e.g., the Berkeley Nanoscience Initiative (BNNI) and nanoscience research directories and websites at UC Davis and Grenoble), which both foster a sense of community among nanoscience researchers and increase the visibility of the field. Stimulated by a few academics, many universities (e.g., UT Austin, Grenoble) have also created shared nanoscience courses for PhD students, aiming both to deliver interdisciplinary training and to foster networking among students from very diverse backgrounds. The widespread practice of joint faculty appointments in American universities also integrates departments without affecting their separate resource allocations (with professors generally having "0% appointments" – neither getting paid by nor having any teaching duties – in departments outside their home disciplines). In some universities (e.g., UC Davis), departments associate in running interdisciplinary graduate groups (although some still organize their own disciplinary programs) in order to gather a critical mass of doctoral students. Other universities create umbrella organizations over departments, not replacing them but increasing students' opportunities to rotate between labs and their course choices (e.g., the Department of Biomedical Engineering which encompasses three Texan campuses).[15]

In a sense, interdisciplinary research teams form "liminal spaces" within universities where faculty can initiate interdisciplinary collaborations and interact over limited periods. University policies mainly aim at facilitating bottom-up dynamics rather than at institutionalizing interdisciplinary spaces. By contrast, a second type of interdisciplinary initiative aims at redrawing departmental boundaries − which are usually discipline-based.

Departments: Weakening the Links between Departments and Disciplines

Reforms of universities' departmental organizations are usually driven by several objectives − such as enhancing the university's capacity to innovate in interdisciplinary areas or orienting education and research toward priority business and societal areas − with the hope of generating revenues from partnerships with commercial/industrial organizations as well as from tuition fees. Such reforms are promoted and driven by deans and university leaders in alliance with "entrepreneurial academics." They can raise issues of governance when they are associated with centralized decision-making processes (in the hands of university presidential teams imposing reforms on departmental deans acting with or without the support of other departments) as well as of resource allocations between departments. Lastly, such projects benefit from external support − which helps them gain legitimacy to address organizational issues. In the US universities we studied, such support was provided by external sponsors (foundations, local authorities, and companies) funding interdisciplinary research and postgraduate education in the life sciences. In the French universities, organizational restructuring was facilitated by changes in the national higher education and research policy set by the French ministry, which increased universities' self-governing capabilities (Musselin, 2004).

Support from External Sponsors in US Universities
The *Health Sciences Initiative,* launched at UCB in 1999,[16] is an interesting example of entrepreneurial academics building on external support and allying with university leaders to fight against the organizational fragmentation of the university and to target emerging interdisciplinary research themes. First, in this case, interdisciplinarity aligns with the centralization of certain decisions and the setting of scientific priorities by university

leaders. This initiative took over interdisciplinary university policies from the 1980s when *"the campus reinvented the biological sciences by merging fields including anatomy, physiology, microbiology and zoology into three 'integrative' departments"* (UCB Chancellor Robert M. Berdahl, Press release, 10/6/1999). The creation of interdisciplinary life sciences departments relied on the lobbying efforts and proactivity of "institution builders" (Jong, 2008), such as Robert Tjian (a Professor in the Department of Cell and Molecular Biology) who convinced the university administration that the organizational fragmentation of biology was a major obstacle to the rise of biotechnology research, and Daniel Koshland (a Professor in the Biochemistry Department) who designed the outlines of the "integrated departments" in the early 1980s, and suggested giving universities' administrations more decision-making power over faculty recruitment so as to target appointments toward their priority areas. Both these "institution builders" encountered considerable opposition from several departments, but their strong links with the biotech industry gave their ideas legitimacy with the UCB university administration. Second, the UCB *Health Sciences Initiative* relied strongly on external sponsors. In particular, the Biomedical Engineering Department created in 1998 – which hosts part of nanomedicine research – was given $15 million from the Whitaker foundation in 2000.[17] These newly created departments gained legitimacy both from this external funding, and from their ability to attract students as well, so as to raise revenues from partnerships with biotechnology industry and pharmaceutical companies. These two characteristics, as well as the prospect of possible spillovers from and into other departments, are important for preserving biomedical engineering departments' legitimacy over the long term, as – after the initial impetus from the Whitaker Foundation's start-up finance – they have to compete with other engineering departments for university positions and funding:

> Traditionally-minded engineers may have visceral reactions about biology... [perhaps] they view [it] as a softer science [than] traditional engineering, they don't feel that it has a place in engineering schools certainly, at the level of legitimacy of a formal department. (Bioengineer, UC Berkeley)

In other universities, such interdisciplinary policies are not oriented so much toward breaking down perceived disciplinary "silos" as to raising the university's profile in a highly competitive research area. This is the case at UC San Francisco, which, over a few decades, has become a world-class health science campus by supporting interdisciplinarity (Bourne, 2011). New developments in the life sciences (such as nanomedicine) require extending the university's established disciplinary spectrum to disciplines such as physical sciences and computer sciences:

> We have no physics department, no engineering department. And so we need to be able to attract physicists and engineers, chemists, mathematicians, to look at USCF as a great place for them to work, for their careers, [but] there is no department, there is nothing that looks traditional to them. (Cell and molecular biologist, Vice-Chancellor for Research UCSF)

Creating specific interdisciplinary departments does not appear to be a suitable strategy as, by themselves, they do not attract enough students to open stand-alone undergraduate curricula. So the university leadership has strengthened interdisciplinarity between existing departments by enlarging their scientific boundaries and allocating faculty positions: for instance, the Department of Therapeutic Sciences has become the Department of Bioengineering and Therapeutic Sciences − the first joint department between UCSF schools of medicine and pharmacy − and now recruits both physicists and bioengineers. UCSF has also created transverse structures (such as inter-departmental or inter-school experimental platforms and doctoral programs) which have weakened the powers of traditional departments in terms of resource allocation and enabled researchers from minority disciplines to belong to inter-departmental groups. Lastly, UCSF has partnered with UCB to create a joint bioengineering graduate program.[18]

Pro-Interdisciplinary Policies Fostered by the "Institutional Empowerment" of French Universities

The French universities we studied have also both merged departments or grouped them into federal interdisciplinary structures. In these cases, fund-raising from entrepreneurial academics and university leaders has also played a role, even though the funds raised are much lower than in US universities. Moreover, such fund-raising for interdisciplinary reorganizations is developing as a result of the strengthening of French universities' "self-governing capabilities" (Musselin, 2004) and by the "institutional empowerment of French universities" (Musselin & Paradeise, 2009, p. 28) − an incremental process that began in the 1990s and accelerated after the adoption of the "*Loi sur la responsabilité et l'autonomie des universités*" (The Law on Liberties and Responsibilities of Universities) in 2007. In this context, French University leaders rely on multiple policy instruments to redraw departmental boundaries. Since as early as the 1980s and 1990s, they have received funding for interdisciplinary research and education when negotiating their university budgets with the higher education Ministry and the regional authorities.[19]

In the 2000s, some universities ended departments' monopolies on doctoral training by taking advantage of the French higher education Ministry's requirement to create interdisciplinary doctoral schools (which organize doctoral training, distribute doctoral funding, and award doctoral titles). More recently, under the impulse of the new legislation (2007) which gives them financial and operational autonomy, some universities have also designed global research strategies in which interdisciplinarity and collaborations between departments are a priority. In Grenoble, university leaders and departmental deans have used these various means to promote interdisciplinarity between physics and life sciences, and between physics and chemistry. This policy has also involved creating a large graduate school covering chemistry and biology, launching a major interdisciplinary program on "new physical approaches in the life sciences" (funded by the Ministry and the Region through a 2000–2006 State-Region plan worth €2.29 million), and funding new buildings to house these interdisciplinary research initiatives. Lastly, all university research activities in STEM (Science, Technology, Engineering and Mathematics) fields have been grouped since 2007 into four interdisciplinary "pôles" or clusters – umbrella organizations located above the 17 disciplinary departments – governed by boards composed of representatives from the pôles' research labs. The university research policy is defined by a board that brings together the four pôle leaders, has a dedicated budget for interdisciplinary projects (including nanoscience),[20] and sends its research priorities for new faculty positions to the academic senate. The University of Toulouse structure has undergone a similar reform, with the creation of four interdisciplinary research pôles – again above departments – in 2008. In both universities, these initiatives have been accompanied by strengthened managerial logics that emphasize formal objectives and performance indicators. In Grenoble, the establishment of these interdisciplinary research pôles has also allowed for the co-construction of science policy between some faculty members – in particular, the directors of large research labs – and university leaders, and thus has tended to reduce the authority of departmental deans and (to some extent) academic senates.

In France, interdisciplinary university policies are developing in a context in which the French ministry has moved away from the "faculty-focused character of university education steering" (Musselin, 2004, p. 67) and recognizes the legitimacy of university presidential teams for defining overall strategies. But French universities gain most of their financial room for manoeuver for developing such interdisciplinary policies from grants and contracts, and so – as in the United States – depend on fund-raising activities undertaken by faculty.

Lastly, the third type of organizational change involves the creation of large-scale interdisciplinary research organizations that are institutional structures (bringing together several universities and/or research institutions, and supported by funding agencies, local authorities and/or firms). These organizations include university-based research centers in the United States and large-scale university-based research projects in France. While US and French initiatives show high degrees of diversity in terms of organizational forms, governance structures, and funding models, many of them mobilize the same actors ("entrepreneurial" academics, deans, and university leaders from several universities), who build alliances between their institutions to leverage funds. While the French universities studied respond to demands from the French ministry of higher education and research, they are also motivated to form interdisciplinary alliances to represent themselves as world-class universities, encompassing all knowledge areas and having high international visibility (Musselin & Dif-Pradalier, 2014, p. 287).

Institutional Structures: Forming Large-Scale Interdisciplinary Research Organizations

These large interdisciplinary research organizations focus on research but include other components such as training, technological transfer, and, in the biomedical sciences, translation to clinical settings. They also imply some kind of geographical concentration on one campus, although not all the participating institutions may necessarily be colocated. They serve several interrelated policy objectives, such as attracting large amounts of funding but avoiding having to disperse it between large numbers of beneficiaries; reaching a critical mass for research in a given area; fostering the development of emerging and interdisciplinary sciences considered of high economic and social relevance. They usually distribute grants, facilitate interdisciplinary team-building, and/or give access to shared facilities.

Joint Fund-Raising Efforts from Faculty and University Leaders in French and US Universities

Large-scale interdisciplinary research organizations result from efforts to leverage funding for interdisciplinary research in particular areas and/or given territories (a campus, a city — or even a state in the United States). Such fund-raising efforts are generally cumulative, either in the sense that funding for such projects is too large to be provided by a single sponsor or that initial funds open opportunities for subsequent finance (e.g., a small grant from a funding agency or a university seed-grant enables researchers to prepare for a larger grant application). Nanomedicine research has developed from such initiatives in all the cases studied in France and the United States. For instance, the Texas Center for Cancer Nanomedicine,[21] a research center of the National Cancer Institute (NCI-NIH) which gathers five partner institutions, results from at least three fund-raising steps. First, the lobbying efforts of faculty members, deans, and university leaders from several Texan universities led to the constitution of the *Alliance for NanoHealth* (ANH) in Texas, which subsequently received major funding from the State of Texas and the U.S. Congress:[22]

> We worked closely with our politicians in the Houston area who helped us get Congress grants earmarked for this project. And we have been able to garner something like $27 million of federal support for the Alliance for NanoHealth [over its first four years]. (Chemist, co-PI for ANH, UT Houston)

During the same period, these entrepreneurial academics launched parallel fund-raising efforts aimed at foundations: for example, the *Gulf Coast consortia* (GCC), which gathers Texan universities around research conducted at the interface between the biomedical sciences and the hard physical sciences, is funded by the Keck and Dunn foundations. Finally, both the ANH and the GCC prepared applications to the NCI's competitive *Alliance for Nanotechnology in Cancer* call:[23]

> A NCI Centre grant often requires demonstration of continued funding, of funded research that can then be synergised by bringing together two or three different projects. The fact that we had multimillions of dollars to give small grants to catalyze research among people ... as well as to foster infrastructure and support was a very big factor [in the success of the Texas Center for Cancer Nanomedicine]. (Chemist, co-PI for ANH, UT Houston)

Fund-raising in California (and in Grenoble and Toulouse) was not directed toward creating a single large interdisciplinary nanomedicine research center: rather such efforts were multiple initiatives that either targeted nanomedicine, or wider biomedical research areas (such as cancer research), or life science approaches. This was the case for the *California Institute for Quantitative BioSciences* (QB3), which was created in 2000 by academics from UC Berkeley, UC Santa Cruz, and UCSF, and was mainly sponsored by the State of California and by biotechnology companies. Other similar initiatives in California include the *Synthetic Biology Institute* at UC Berkeley (SBI) created in 2011 between UC Berkeley and the Lawrence Berkeley National Laboratory with the aim of attracting industrial funding; and the *Synthetic Biology Engineering Research Center* (*Synberc*) founded by the National Science Foundation in 2006 in association with UC Berkeley, UCSF, MIT, Harvard, and Prairie View Agriculture and Mining.

In Grenoble, the *Nanobio* project, dedicated to fundamental research in the nano-biosciences, was sponsored by the university and CNRS, but also by regional authorities (which contributed €25 million between 2001 and 2004). The *Clinatec* project, launched in 2009 and aimed at developing translational research at the crossroads between nanotechnology and neurosciences, also gained significant finance (50% of its funding) from regional authorities and from research institutions (mostly CEA). Toulouse has three interdisciplinary research centers which include nanomedicine. The *InnaBioSanté* foundation (*Infotechnologies, Nanotechnologies, Biotechnologies, Santé*) was created in 2006 with national funding (€8 million from the French Ministry and the National Research Agency – ANR) as well as industrial funding from regional companies (€13.5 million from an oil company and from health companies). The *ITAV* initiative (*Institute for Advance Technologies in the Life sciences*) launched in 2011 by the CNRS, the INSA engineering school, and the University of Toulouse gathers technological platforms and projects. Lastly, the *Cluster on Cancer Research* (*Pôle de Compétitivité Cancer BioSanté*) gathers representatives from regional authorities, companies, research labs, and higher education institutions from the Toulouse region to fund interdisciplinary research projects.

These French and US interdisciplinary projects are all deeply rooted in the dynamics of local cooperation and actions, so their progress may largely depend on the will of partner institutions to join forces and to negotiate. Even if university departments and research labs benefit from them (e.g., by having access to shared research facilities financed through these large research centers), they may also consider them as competitors for certain university resources (principally for technical staff and faculty positions). In particular, such conflicts may develop over university leaders' choices of priority interdisciplinary areas, as most universities do not have enough resources to invest in several large interdisciplinary projects at the same time (Jacobs, 2014).

French Universities Complying with Ministerial Policies and Aiming to Achieve World-Class University Status
In France, interdisciplinary and institutional cooperation is also expanding in order to reduce the high level of fragmentation of higher education and

research efforts. Historically, many French campuses have been constituted by amalgamating autonomous institutions (universities, research institutions, *grandes écoles*, etc.). Cooperation between and/or integration of research and education structures are now central requirements of the French ministry for higher education and research. But French university leaders also believe in the value of cooperation and integration in helping them become world-class universities (Musselin & Dif-Pradalier, 2014). The rhetoric of interdisciplinarity facilitates the union or merging of the curricula of different institutions, which can then offer their students a wider range of complementary areas of study. In particular, joint interdisciplinary curricula have multiplied at the postgraduate level: for example, between 2007 and 2010, the University of Grenoble and the Grenoble Institute of Technology (an engineering school) jointly organized and delivered 42 masters' degrees.[24] Such instances of cooperation often stem from "bottom-up" initiatives led by faculty members and supported by university leaderships, which see them as ways to rationalize the provision of on-campus training. However, they are highly dependent on policies of cooperation between universities being in place − thus, the number of joint masters' degrees offered by these two Grenoble institutions fell from 42 to 16 during the 2011−2014 period, due to conflicts about how the institutions should share costs and revenues, as well as increasing competition for students.

Institutional cooperation around interdisciplinary projects has become almost mandatory since the Ministry of Higher Education and Research launched the *Investissements d'avenir* national science and innovation policy in 2010. The program is composed of several competitive calls for tender that oblige research groups, higher education and research institutions, and campuses to compete for funding. These funding mechanisms were designed to establish so-called "excellent" university campuses, which would then gain high ratings in international university rankings, an objective stressed clearly in a report designing this policy.[25]

> To support the transformation of a limited number (five to ten) groups of higher education and research institutions (...) into interdisciplinary institutions of global size and reputation, with the aim of getting them included in the top fifty universities in different world rankings. (p. 56)

> The projects submitted [for funding] (...) must involve groupings of several partners to form interdisciplinary ensembles characterized by their excellence. (p. 58)[26]

Interdisciplinarity and institutional cooperation (including mergers between several higher education and research institutions, as the term "groupings" above suggests) are presented as two interrelated requirements to reach such "excellence." So, even if these keywords are not presented as conditions of eligibility in the tender calls, they appear to operate as criteria for success. For example, the LABEX call (*Laboratoires d'Excellence*) launched in 2011 to fund scientific consortia stipulates that:

> ... research entities applying should gather, in their geographic areas, those organizations that are most active in their research topics and that thematic concentration, interdisciplinary openness and research at the borders of disciplines will be considered as important strengths. (p. 6)[27]

Calls for projects can pose very different governance problems, as they aim to structure scientific consortia (e.g., the LABEX and EQUIPEX – *Equipement d'Excellence* – project calls) or groups of universities and research institutions (e.g., the IDEX – *Initiative d'Excellence* – project call) in different ways. The LABEX and EQUIPEX calls often build on previous interdisciplinary collaborations. In Grenoble, the LABEX-funded project *ARCANE*,[28] set up to develop research at the interfaces between chemistry and biology, extends the partnerships built for the *Nanobio* program (see above). However, the LABEX and EQUIPEX projects differ from previous fund-raising actions in that they have to fit into the university's overall strategy – in fact, it is the university leadership (and not principal investigators) that submits the applications and can choose to support them more or less actively.

IDEX projects mobilize leaders of higher education and research institutions, relying differently (depending on the case) on university bodies, department deans, or ad-hoc project teams (Mignot-Gérard, 2009). Interdisciplinarity is central to the scientific dimension of IDEX projects and has to be organized at the institutional level. IDEX projects also include essential governance requirements, which again have to be institutional. This is not the first time that the French Ministry has encouraged higher education and research institutions to group (see the post-2006 creation of *PRES* or the higher education and research pôles). However the scale of the financial issues (funding for IDEX projects can reach €1 billion) may push universities to regroup – or even to merge – to comply with the institutional pressures involved.

The successful application by Toulouse higher education and research institutions to the 2012 IDEX call relied on a highly interdisciplinary project built on previous collaborations (interdisciplinary postgraduate training, and interdisciplinary "strategic thematic" or "transversal" actions), and on a radical reform of university governance (that resulted in the creation of the federal University of Toulouse-Midi-Pyrénées in October 2014, which gathered together all the region's higher education institutions). In contrast, Grenoble University's IDEX application failed twice (in 2010 and 2012), stressing the importance of governance issues in these very large interdisciplinary projects. While Grenoble's applications benefited from very rich interdisciplinary collaborations associating several institutions (joint research groups, joint masters, and the mergers of all the region's doctoral schools in 2009, and of several LABEX projects, etc.), both failed on governance issues (e.g., conflicts about whether institutions should merge or confederate, and institutional ambitions to preserve monopolies on particular disciplines).

CONCLUSION

This paper describes the diversity of the organizational arrangements under which interdisciplinarity is developing in French and American universities today. Using the example of nanomedicine, we show that interdisciplinary research and postgraduate education are being implemented at several levels (the research group, the department, the university, groups of higher education, and research institutions). So their development is not entirely in the hands of university leaderships, but also relies on complementary — and sometimes joint — initiatives between faculty, deans, and presidential teams who often negotiate interdisciplinary projects with funding bodies.

Our analysis first leads us to play down the significance of national differences, but rather to stress the similarities between the entrepreneurial efforts of academics and university leaders who support the development of interdisciplinarity in our two focal countries. This observation differs from the viewpoints of other authors who see American universities — and more generally, the American public science system in general — as being more highly favorable to interdisciplinarity than those in other countries, because of the flexibility of US public policies, which can quickly dedicate budgets to fields that emerge outside traditional disciplines (Bonaccorsi, 2007), and the high degrees of reputational competition and of intellectual pluralism (Whitley, 2003) that incentivize researchers to take more risks in their studies. Moreover, the institutional autonomy of American universities is generally seen as giving them great leeway to initiate very proactive interdisciplinary policies. In contrast, French academia is usually considered as less favorable to interdisciplinarity, in particular because of the lower degree of its universities' institutional autonomy, given the steering of their decisions by ministerial policies and their dependence on national institutions which favor established disciplines over interdisciplinary areas.[29]

However, interdisciplinary research in the life sciences has been strengthened in the last two decades in all French and US universities studied for this paper, which leads us to emphasize the similarity of the forces driving interdisciplinarity, and of the organizational changes that have accompanied the moves toward interdisciplinary research, in both countries. In particular, as research is increasingly funded via competitive calls that promote interdisciplinarity, we note the presence of multiple interdisciplinary teams, consortia, and research centers on all the French and US campuses we studied resulting from fund-raising efforts by entrepreneurial academics. University leaders have also made interdisciplinarity a priority, which has translated into incentives for interdisciplinary research, various attempts to weaken departmental boundaries, and joint fund-raising initiatives with entrepreneurial academics. Probably what differentiates interdisciplinary universities in the two countries most is the role played by the French ministry of Higher Education and Research in the development of pro-interdisciplinary university policies — rather than the level of interdisciplinarity. In the three American universities studied, interdisciplinarity mostly develops via fund-raising for interdisciplinary research projects (co-constructed by, and negotiated between, academics, university leaders, and funding bodies). The bargaining power of faculty members reflects both the strength of the academic profession in American universities (Cousin & Lamont, 2009), and its academics' ability to draw on external support to promote the interdisciplinary reorganization of the study of life sciences.

However, significant differences can be identified between the studied universities, which reflect the weight of disciplinary departments and their scientific perimeters, and the universities' strategies. At UCSF, faculty members and university leaders agree that disciplinary departments do not suit the university's scientific objectives (which are centered on biomedical research) or its strategic positioning vis-à-vis its competitors — which are large comprehensive universities. In contrast, at UCB, interdisciplinary life sciences have been implemented by a coalition of interests involving university leaders and entrepreneurial academics, which required the breaching of the disciplinary boundaries of departments that considered themselves threatened by interdisciplinary reorganizations.

Lastly, we should note that our case studies are not necessarily representative of all research universities in the United States. Indeed, universities' institutional autonomy and the strength of the academic professions in the United States mean that disciplinary departments remain very powerful, even if interdisciplinary research flourishes in some areas (Thoenig, 2015). In this case, faculties' interdisciplinary program initiatives are decoupled from university policies, which mostly remain disciplinary. The vitality of interdisciplinary research remains conditional on the availability of investigator-initiated grant funding. But on the contrary, some US universities have experienced a strengthening in their leadership, with university leaders introducing radical interdisciplinary reorganizations so as to leave their mark during their terms, so that *"interdisciplinarity seems likely to result in a shift of power away from faculty toward the central administration of the university"* (Jacobs, 2014, p. 210).

In the French universities we studied, we found that the organizational changes associated with the development of interdisciplinary research also come from the co-construction and negotiation of such projects between academics and university leaders. But the main difference from US universities is that pro-interdisciplinary university policies have been supported by considerable changes in the steering universities have received from the French Ministry of Higher Education and Research in recent decades. Indeed, the increased self-governance capabilities that the Ministry has granted French universities (Musselin, 2004) have enabled their leaders to initiate political moves toward interdisciplinary research and to bypass the resistance of departments. Also, since the 2000s, the Ministry has distributed competitive funding for large institutional and interdisciplinary research projects, with the aim of increasing both the societal and economic relevance and the international visibility of French universities.

This national policy has fostered the institutional restructuring of French universities around interdisciplinary projects, a political impetus that has created tensions. First, the resulting interdisciplinary reorganizations are not always aligned with the interdisciplinary scientific projects launched by local entrepreneurial academics, especially when they follow rationalization and cost reduction objectives. Second, there are sometimes contradictions between the governance objectives associated with this political stance — in particular, between strengthening the university's strategy and gathering several higher education and research institutions into more visible clusters with single governance structures — that hinder the integration of interdisciplinarity into a clearly defined institutional objective. Finally, it may be questioned whether this political impulse has really favored the development of interdisciplinarity in French universities. The overall answer for the two universities we studied is positive: local scientific communities and university leaderships have managed (after several years of conflicts and learning) to co-construct interdisciplinarity in ways that reconcile local scientific dynamics with the Ministry's governance and restructuration requirements.

NOTES

1. Faculty opinion on interdisciplinarity seems to be more nuanced, however. A survey indicates that 70% of college and university faculty in the United States value interdisciplinary more than disciplinary knowledge (Jacobs & Frickel, 2009, p. 46).

2. For a critical view on the relevance of pro-interdisciplinary university policies in liberal arts disciplines, see Jacobs (2014), especially chapter 10.

3. There are of course exceptions: US universities such as Arizona State University (see Jacobs, 2014, p. 214) or Stanford University have entirely restructured their organizations around interdisciplinary education and research areas.

4. The author – who collected the empirical data in California while a visiting scholar at UC Berkeley Center for Science, Technology, Medicine and Society – acknowledges support from the ANR: Nanoexpectation project (ANR-09-NANO-032; programme in Nanosciences, Nanotechnologies and Nanosystems P3N2009); Hybridtrajectories project (ANR 2010 Blanc - 1811 - 01).

5. One should however note that interdisciplinarity has a long history in disciplines as diverse as education, gerontology, feminist studies, organization studies, and public policy (Brint, Turk-Bicakci, Proctor, & Murphy, 2009, p. 156), areas in which it was meant to encourage both economic and social innovation.

6. American scholars have been remarkably active in the formation of the field of interdisciplinary studies, but European scholars have also taken an early interest in this topic (Boutier, Passeron, & Revel, 2006; Vinck, 2000).

7. *Source*: http://www.nano.gov/about-nni/what/funding. One hundred interdisciplinary education and research centers were created as part of the *National Nanotechnology Initiative*. Twenty-four of them are nanomedicine related: http://www.nano.gov/centers-networks

8. At the time of our study, there were three universities in each city – one for STEM (Science, Technology, Engineering and Mathematics), one for social sciences, and one for humanities. We conducted our empirical study at the two universities dedicated to STEM disciplines. For simplification's sake, we refer to them as "the University of Grenoble"/"University of Toulouse."

9. Interviews in French universities were conducted by the author and by research assistants (A. Gonthier, M. Libersa, and C. Mounet), and those in American universities by the author. All interviews were recorded, fully transcribed, and thematically coded using N-Vivo software.

10. See Table A1 in the appendix for a summary of the results.

11. R01 grants are non-targeted, investigator-initiated grants.

12. In January 2010, the NIH implemented a new format for its investigator-initiated grants. So far the grant applications had been 25 pages long and PIs wrote

a "research plan" divided into three sections: Background and Significance, Preliminary Studies and Progress Report, Research Design and Methodology. The new application is 12 pages long and the research plan is replaced by a section on "research strategy" divided into Significance, Innovation, and Approach. In the section on Innovation, applicants must: "*Explain how the application challenges and seeks to shift current research or clinical practice paradigms; describe any novel theoretical concepts, approaches or methodologies, instrumentation or intervention(s) to be developed or used, and any advantage over existing methodologies, instrumentation or intervention(s); Explain any refinements, improvements, or new applications of theoretical concepts, approaches or methodologies, instrumentation or interventions*" (U.S. Department of Health and Human Services, Public Health Service, Grant Application (PHS 398): Part I I-46).

13. These national institutions have traditionally supported the disciplinary organization of academia (Paradeise et al., 2015). For instance, the national body (*le Conseil National des Universités*) that allows French academics to apply for faculty positions (as assistant or full professors) is divided into 74 disciplinary sections.

14. Most tenured CNRS researchers are recruited by disciplinary committees. However the CNRS has created four interdisciplinary committees, two of them intersecting with nanomedicine (the committee for *Modélisation, et analyse des données et des systèmes biologiques:* the committee for *approches informatiques, mathématiques et physiques*).

15. The University of Texas at Austin, The University of Texas Health Sciences Center at Houston, and The University of Texas MD Anderson Cancer: http://www.utexas.edu/news/2006/05/17/engineering/

16. A $500 million initiative (which included $100 million in private gifts and $24 million of state support) aimed at "redefining health science research by uniting physical and biological scientists and engineers" (News release – 10/6/1999 – public affairs.

17. *Source*: Closing report of the Whitaker foundation, 2005. Approximately 30 such interdisciplinary departments were created in American universities in the 1990s and 2000s with financial support from the Whitaker foundation. In contrast, European universities have not benefitted from such outside patronage, and so have almost no biomedical engineering departments.

18. A similar association can be found in Texas with the graduate biomedical sciences program between UT Houston and MD Anderson.

19. Since 1984, universities have negotiated four- and five-year budgets with the Ministry and regional authorities via State-Region plan contracts (*Contrat de plan Etat-Région*).

20. In 2008, this budget amounted to €3 million (9.1% of the universities' total research budget): it had quadrupled since 2005 as a result of increases in universities' resources from grants and contracts (*source*: Report from the French National Evaluation Agency – AERES, 2010, p. 1).

21. The partner institutions are: the University of Texas Health Science Center; The University of Texas MD Anderson Cancer Center; Duke University; The Methodist Hospital Research Institute; Albert Einstein College of Medicine. *Source*: http://nano.cancer.gov/action/programs/uthsc/

354 SÉVERINE LOUVEL

22. The ANH is a consortium of six institutions: Baylor College of Medicine, the Methodist Hospital Research Institute, Rice University, Texas A&M Health Science Center, The University of Texas Health Science Center at Houston, The University of Texas MD Anderson Cancer Center, and The University of Texas Medical Branch at Galveston. *Source*: http://alliancefornanohealth.org/

23. The *Alliance for Nanotechnology in Cancer* centers are funded under NIH requests for applications (RFAs) which are "more political and more applied funding mechanisms" (Sampat, 2012, p. 1735) than other awards, such as RO1 grants.

24. Including Masters in nanoscience and nanotechnology.

25. Juppé and Rocard (2009).

26. Juppé and Rocard (2009), op. cit. – our translation.

27. Présentation 2011 de l'ANR sur l'objectif des LABEX.

28. https://www.labex-arcane.fr/fr/content/laboratoires-excellence-arcane

29. For instance, as explained above, French academic careers are partly managed by a national body (*Conseil national des universités*) which is structured in disciplines.

REFERENCES

AAU. (2005). *Report of the interdisciplinary task force*. Washington, DC: Association of American Universities.

Albert, M., Paradis, E., & Kuper, A. (2015). Interdisciplinary promises versus practices in medicine: The decoupled experiences of social sciences and humanities scholars. *Social Science & Medicine, 126*, 17–25.

Barry, A., Born, G., & Weszkalnys, G. (2008). Logics of interdisciplinarity. *Economy and Society, 37*(1), 20–49.

Boardman, C., & Ponomariov, B. (2014). Management knowledge and the organization of team science in university research centers. *The Journal of Technology Transfer, 39*(1), 75–92.

Boardman, P. C., & Corley, E. A. (2008). University research centers and the composition of research collaborations. *Research Policy, 37*(5), 900–913.

Bonaccorsi, A. (2007). Explaining poor performance of European science: Institutions versus policies. *Science and Public Policy, 34*(5), 303–316.

Bonaccorsi, A. (2010). New forms of complementarity in science. *Minerva, 48*(4), 355–387.

Bourne, H. R. (2011). *Paths to innovation: Discovering recombinant DNA, oncogenes, and prions in one medical school, over one decade*. San Francisco, CA: University of California Press Medical Humanities Consortium.

Boutier, J., Passeron, J.-C., & Revel, J. (Eds.). (2006). *Qu'est-ce qu'une discipline?* Paris: Éditions de l'EHESS.

Brint, S. (2005). Creating the future: 'New directions' in American research universities. *Minerva, 43*(1), 23–50.

Brint, S. G., Turk-Bicakci, L., Proctor, K., & Murphy, S. P. (2009). Expanding the social frame of knowledge: Interdisciplinary, degree-granting fields in American colleges and universities, 1975–2000. *The Review of Higher Education, 32*(2), 155–183.

Brunsson, N., & Sahlin-Anderson, K. (2000). Constructing organisations: The example of public reform sector. *Organisation Studies, 21*(4), 721−746.

Calvert, J. (2006). What's special about basic research? *Science, Technology and Human Values, 31*(2), 199−220.

Clark, B. R. (1998). *Creating entrepreneurial universities: Organizational pathways of transformation.* Guildford: Pergamon.

Cousin, B., & Lamont, M. (2009). Les conditions de l'évaluation universitaire. Quelques réflexions à partir du cas américain. *Mouvements, 60,* 113−117.

De Boer, H., & Goedegebuure, L. (2009). The changing nature of the academic deanship. *Leadership, 5*(3), 347−364.

Denis, J.-L., Langley, A., & Rouleau, L. (2007). Strategizing in pluralistic contexts: Rethinking theoretical frames. *Human Relations, 60*(1), 179−215.

Dogan, M., & Pahre, R. (1991). *L'innovation dans les sciences sociales: La marginalité créatrice.* Paris: Presses Universitaires de France.

Etzkowitz, H. (2003). Research groups as 'quasi-firms': The invention of the entrepreneurial university. *Research Policy, 32*(1), 109−121.

Etzkowitz, H., & Kemelgor, C. (1998). The role of research centres in the collectivisation of academic science. *Minerva: A Review of Science, Learning & Policy, 36*(3), 271−288.

EUA. (2015). *Trends 2015: Learning and teaching in European universities* (p. 133). Brussels, Belgium: European University Association.

Frodeman, R., Klein, J. T., & Mitcham, C. (2010). *The oxford handbook of interdisciplinarity.* Oxford: Oxford University Press.

Geiger, R. L. (1990). Organized research units − Their role in the development of university research. *The Journal of Higher Education, 61*(1), 1−19.

Gibbons, A., Limoges, C., Nowotny, H., Schwarzman, S., Scott, P., & Trow, M. (1994). *The new production of knowledge, The dynamics of science and research in contemporary societies.* London: Sage.

Gioia, D. A., & Thomas, J. B. (1996). Identity, issue and image interpretation: Sensemaking during strategic change in academia. *Administrative Science Quarterly, 41*(3), 370−403.

Global Research Council. (2013). *Statement of principles and actions for shaping the future: Supporting the next generation of researchers.* Retrieved from http://www.global-researchcouncil.org/statement-%20principles-research-integrity. Accessed on July 3, 2015.

Hackett, E. J. (2000). Interdisciplinary research initiatives at the US national science foundation. In P. Weingart & N. Stehr (Eds.), *Practising interdisciplinarity* (pp. 248−259). Toronto: The University of Toronto Press.

Holley, K. A. (2009). Interdisciplinary strategies as transformative change in higher education. *Innovative Higher Education, 34*(5), 331−344.

Hollingsworth, R., & Hollingsworth, E. J. (2000). Major discoveries and biomedical research organizations: Perspectives on interdisciplinarity, nurturing leadership, and integrated structure and cultures. In P. Weingart & N. Stehr (Eds.), *Practising Interdisciplinarity* (pp. 215−244). Toronto: University of Toronto Press.

Jacobs, J. A. (2014). *In defense of disciplines: Interdisciplinarity and specialization in the research university.* Chicago, IL: University of Chicago Press.

Jacobs, J. A., & Frickel, S. (2009). Interdisciplinarity: A critical assessment. *Annual Review of Sociology, 35,* 43−65.

Jarzabkowski, P. (2008). Shaping strategy as a structuration process. *Academy of Management Journal, 51*(4), 621−650.

Jong, S. (2008). Academic organizations and new industrial fields: Berkeley and Stanford after the rise of biotechnology. *Research Policy, 37*(8), 1267–1282.

Juppé, A., & Rocard, M. (2009). *Investir pour l'avenir. Priorités stratégiques d'investissement et emprunt national.* Report to the French Président, La Documentation Française, Novembre.

Lamont, M., Mallard, G., & Guetzkow, J. (2006). Beyond blind faith: Overcoming the obstacles to interdisciplinary evaluation. *Research Evaluation, 15*(1), 43–55.

Lenoir, T. (1997). *Instituting science: The cultural production of scientific disciplines.* Stanford, CA: Stanford University Press.

Louvel, S. (2010). Changing authority relations within French academic research units since the 1960s: From patronage to partnership. In R. Whitley, J. Gläser, & L. Engwall (Eds.), *Reconfiguring knowledge production: Changing authority relations in the sciences and their consequences for intellectual innovation* (pp. 184–210). Oxford: Oxford University Press.

Louvel, S. (2013). Understanding change in higher education as bricolage: How academics engage in curriculum change. *Higher Education, 66*(6), 669–691.

Louvel, S. (2015). Ce que l'interdisciplinarité fait aux disciplines: une enquête sur la nanomédecine en France et en Californie. *Revue Française De Sociologie, 56*(1), 69–97.

MESR. (2013). France Europe 2020: un agenda stratégique pour la recherche, le transfert et l'innovation (p. 96). Paris Ministère de l'Enseignement Supérieur et de la Recherche.

Mignot-Gérard, S. (2009). Le gouvernement d'une université face aux « initiatives d'excellence ». Réactivité et micro-résistances. *Politiques et management public, 29*(3), 519–539.

Musselin, C. (2004). *The long march of French Universities.* New York, NY: Routledge.

Musselin, C., & Dif-Pradalier, M. (2014). Quand la fusion s'impose: la (re) naissance de l'université de strasbourg. *Revue française de sociologie, 55*(2), 285–318.

Musselin, C., & Paradeise, C. (2009). France: From incremental transitions to institutional change. In C. Paradeise, E. Reale, E. Bleiklie, & E. Ferlie (Eds.), *University governance: Western European comparative perspectives* (pp. 21–49). Dordrecht: Springer.

Newswander, L. K., & Borrego, M. (2009). Engagement in two interdisciplinary graduate programs. *Higher Education, 58*(4), 551–562.

Paradeise, C., Noël, M., & Goastellec, G. (2015). Pression du marché, recomposition des alliances disciplinaires et impact épistémologique sur les disciplines. In A. Gorga & J.-P. Leresche (Eds.), *Transformations des disciplines académiques: Entre innovation et résistance.* Paris: Editions des archives contemporaines.

Ponomariov, B., & Boardman, P. C. (2010). Influencing scientists' collaboration and productivity patterns through new institutions: University research centers and scientific and technical human capital. *Research Policy, 39*(5), 613–624.

Sá, C. M. (2008a). Interdisciplinary strategies' in U.S. research universities. *Higher Education, 55*(5), 537–552.

Sá, C. M. (2008b). Strategic faculty hiring in two public research universities: Pursuing interdisciplinary connections. *Tertiary Education and Management, 14*(4), 285–301.

Sabharwal, M., & Hu, Q. (2013). Participation in university-based research centers: Is it helping or hurting researchers? *Research Policy, 42*(6), 1301–1311.

Sampat, B. N. (2012). Mission-oriented biomedical research at the NIH. *Research Policy, 41*(10), 1729–1741.

Stahler, G. J., & Tash, W. R. (1994). Centers and institutes in the research university: Issues, problems, and prospects. *The Journal of Higher Education, 65*(5), 540–554.

Stephan, P. E. (2012). *How economics shape science.* Cambridge, MA: Harvard University Press.

Thoenig, J.-C. (2015). Gouvernance organisationnelle et transformation des disciplines. In J.-P. Leresche & A. Gorga (Eds.), *Transformations des disciplines académiques: Entre innovation et résistance.* Paris: Editions des Archives Contemporaines.

Townley, B. (1997). The institutional logic of performance appraisal. *Organization Studies, 18*(2), 261–285.

Vinck, D. (2000). *Pratiques de l'interdisciplinarité: Mutations des sciences, de l'industrie et de l'enseignement.* Grenoble: PUG.

Weingart, P., & Stehr, N. (Eds.). (2000). *Practising Interdisciplinarity.* Toronto: University of Toronto Press.

Whitley, R. (2003). Competition and pluralism in the public sciences: the impact of institutional frameworks on the organisation of academic science. *Research Policy, 32*(6), 1015–1029.

Youtie, J., Libaers, D., & Bozeman, B. (2006). Institutionalization of university research centers: The case of the national cooperative program in infertility research. *Technovation, 26*(9), 1055–1063.

Zerhouni, E. (2003). The NIH roadmap. *Science, 302,* 63–72.

APPENDIX

Table A1. Synthesis of the Results.

Organizational Change Settings	Main Promoters	Main Objectives	Main Tools for Implementing Interdisciplinarity	Organizational Change Involved	Organizational Issues (Governance, Leadership, Resource Allocation)
Research teams	– Principal investigators of research teams	– "Creating the future" (Brint, 2005): innovation and breakthrough research for economic and societal needs	– Investigator-led grants provided by funding agencies – University leaders do not control these "centrifugal dynamics" – But they may facilitate the formation of ID research teams	– Research team formation and dissolution	– Resource allocation conflict at funding agencies between disciplinary and interdisciplinary projects – No major changes in resource allocation between departments
Departments	– "Entrepreneurial academics" (among faculty and department deans) and university leaders	– "Creating the future" (Brint, 2005) – Market positioning	– US universities: joint fund-raising efforts from universities and "entrepreneurial academics" – French universities: changes facilitated by a ministerial policy favoring their "institutional empowerment"	– Redrawing of departmental boundaries: Interdisciplinary departments – Inter-departmental structures, resources, and positions	– Shift of decision-making powers from department deans to university leaders and "entrepreneurial academics" – Resource allocation between departments

| Institutional structures | – "Entrepreneurial academics" (among faculty and department deans) and university leaders | – "Creating the future" Brint (2005)
– Market positioning
– French universities: joining world-class universities by merging | – Joint fund-raising efforts from universities and "entrepreneurial academics"
– French universities: ministerial policy favoring cooperation and/or merging between universities and research institutions | – Formation of large-scale team research centers or projects
– Alliances between several universities and research institutions | – Resource allocation between research centers and departments
– Competition between partnering universities and institutions
– French universities: shift of decision-making powers from department deans to university leaders and "entrepreneurial academics" |

DRAW ME A UNIVERSITY: ORGANIZATIONAL DESIGN PROCESSES IN UNIVERSITY MERGERS

Julien Barrier and Christine Musselin

ABSTRACT

Facing intense global competition and pressure from public authorities, several universities in Europe have engaged in merger and concentration processes. Drawing on two in-depth case studies, this paper considers university mergers as an opportunity to explore the processes involved in the creation of a new organizational structure. In line with recent scholarly calls to revisit the notion of organizational design, we combine insights from three different research streams to address the functional, political, and institutional dynamics that shaped the organizational architecture of the merged universities. Two main results are presented and discussed. First, although these mergers were initiated largely in response to the diffusion of new global institutional scripts, these scripts had little influence on organizational design: deeply institutionalized local scripts prevailed over global mimetic pressures. Second, while these institutional scripts provided many of the basic building blocks of the new universities,

The University under Pressure
Research in the Sociology of Organizations, Volume 46, 361–394
Copyright © 2016 by Emerald Group Publishing Limited
All rights of reproduction in any form reserved
ISSN: 0733-558X/doi:10.1108/S0733-558X20160000046012

in both cases their design was also heavily shaped by time pressures and power games. While a few powerful actors used the merger as an opportunity to promote their own reform agenda, some of the key features of the two merged universities stemmed from choices by exclusion, whose primary aim was the avoidance of conflicts.

Keywords: Decision-making processes; French universities; inhabited institutions; institutional scripts; organizational design; university mergers

INTRODUCTION

Mergers often provide an opportunity to design a new organization and rethink the formal structures, the functional interdependencies, the allocation of activities, and their relation to each other. But how is the new formal organization drawn? Who are the key players behind such processes, and what factors are taken into consideration? These are the question driving this paper, which aims to revisit the notion of organizational design to explain how the structure of a new organization is drawn.

We address this issue by examining university mergers in France. European institutions of higher education have felt increasing pressure to merge in order to strengthen their position in a competitive environment (Bennetot Pruvot, Estermann, & Mason, 2015). University mergers offer a key research opportunity to address the construction of a new organizational architecture, as the design of novel structures from pre-existing universities involves complex and often ambiguous decision-making processes (Eastman & Lang, 2001). This paper therefore considers university mergers as instances of extensive organizational design (or re-design) and analyzes the decision-making processes that contribute to the emergence of a new organizational form.

This study intends to contribute to the organizational literature — and reflections on organizational design in particular — to shed light on the mechanisms through which such processes occur. Beyond the empirical interest of this paper for higher education scholars interested in university mergers, our aim is to contribute to the study of organizational design processes and discuss different research streams that have addressed this issue. The first section of this paper contains a literature review comparing different perspectives on organizational design. Some scholars have a rather functionalist interpretation of the phenomenon, viewing it as a problem-solving process. Others interpret it as the result of power relations and conflicting interest. Still others argue that such a design reflects the diffusion of representations, schemes, and models considered as legitimate and rational by actors who reproduce them. We argue that none of these perspectives taken separately is sufficient to account for the cases we investigated, and therefore propose to combine them.

The movement to merge universities took hold in various countries in the 1990s. Although France might be considered a latecomer to the movement, plans to merge universities in that country have multiplied since January 2009, when the first such merger resulted in the University of Strasbourg. As of this writing (Spring 2015), four subsequent universities have been created out of the amalgamation of different institutions. They include the University of Lorraine and Aix-Marseille University, both in January 2012; the University of Bordeaux in 2014; and the University of Montpellier in January 2015. Several additional mergers have been proposed or are already underway.

Two elements must be noted in the context of French university mergers. First, all were voluntary mergers, decided by the universities themselves[1] (in contrast with the situation in countries like Norway in the 1990s (Skodvin, 1999)). Second, while the mergers were voluntary, they occurred in an environment that was increasingly favorable to such actions both institutionally and politically. Since the mid-2000s, successive policy initiatives have encouraged the development of inter-institutional cooperation at the local or regional level. The 2006 Act for Research (*Pacte pour la recherche*) first provided higher education institutions with the possibility to enhance their cooperation within meta-structures called PRES (*Pôles de Recherche et d'Enseignement Supérieur*, translated as Higher Education and Research Clusters). They aimed at mutualizing some university functions, increasing the international visibility of the institutions, and coordinating their teaching or research activities (Aust & Crespy, 2009). This trend went a step further with two large national initiatives: *Opération Campus* in 2008 and the *Initiative d'Excellence* program launched in 2010. Although they pursued slightly different goals, both initiatives provided universities with substantial incentives to consider a merger. Both were based on a national, competitive call for proposals that offered to fund large institutional development projects submitted by universities. And, most importantly, selection criteria in both cases favored projects involving a reinforcement of inter-institutional cooperation or a merger.[2] Last, the 2013 Act for Higher Education and

Research further promoted this process by setting new legal statutes to replace the existing PRES and tighten cooperation and coordination at the regional level.[3]

While these processes are particular to the French situation, the dynamics at play echo those of mergers occurring throughout Europe since the beginning of the 2000s. Further, these policy initiatives were built upon the premise that organizational restructuring was necessary to allow higher education institutions to deal with globalization and the intensification of competition. We observe the same objective of building large, comprehensive universities whose size, pluri-disciplinarity, and visibility better equip them to compete on the international scene (Aula & Tienari, 2011; Goedegebuure, 2012; Harman & Harman, 2008). Beyond the higher education sector, this evolution resonates with a larger trend in public management reforms throughout Europe that has favored mergers in order to restructure various administrations and public services (Bezes & Le Lidec, 2010). Some authors even speak of a *merger mania* (Kitchener & Gask, 2003).

At first glance, all of these elements seem to fit perfectly with the now classic institutionalist perspective inaugurated by Meyer and Rowan (1977), emphasizing how organizational structures are shaped by the diffusion and adoption of "rationalized myths," that is, discourses and scripts defining legitimate organizational models. Many recent studies have shown this perspective to be especially relevant in explaining institutional change in the field of higher education. The increasing globalization of academic competition goes hand in hand with the rise of global institutional scripts, promoting the new organizational ideal of a "rationalized university" (e.g., Krücken & Meier, 2006; Ramirez, 2009).

However, this paper proposes to refine this explanation by combining different analytical perspectives to understand the creation of a new organizational design in two university mergers. We draw on two in-depth case studies involving the creation of the University of Strasbourg in 2009 and the University of Lorraine in 2012.[4] We show that although both mergers were stimulated by the diffusion of rationalized myths in the field of higher education, the organizational design they developed resulted not from the transposition of external legitimate models but rather from a complex process mixing taken-for-granted assumptions, power struggles, and problem-solving strategies that was heavily shaped by time constraints. Following Bezes (2005), we emphasize the *material dimension* of the design process, as actors engage in power games to assert and defend their interests, as well as its *cognitive dimension*, referring to the ways of thinking of what an organization is or "should be." We also stress the key role of time pressures on these processes (specifically, how they limit the search for alternative solutions and therefore bound the rationality of actors, Simon, 1955).

We will first present the different theoretical frameworks related to organizational design processes and the limits of each one, followed by our combined approach. Next, we will discuss the two case studies and explain why their comparison is interesting and relevant. Finally, we will describe the different mechanisms and processes that shaped the making of a new organizational design.

REVISITING ORGANIZATIONAL DESIGN

The aim of this paper is to draw on cases of university mergers to contribute to the analysis of organizational design processes. Although much research has been dedicated to university mergers, this aspect is rarely stressed (or only incidentally so). Most scholars instead focus on three other themes. The first one addresses the *reasons* for the mergers; that is, the political, economic, or institutional factors that push universities to merge (e.g., Gamage, 1993; Kyvik, 2002). The second concerns the *consequences* of mergers, usually emphasizing their limitations such as conflicts persisting after the merger; limited − if any − economies of scale; or unexpected effects on academic activities (e.g., Mok, 2005; Norgård & Skodvin, 2002; Skodvin, 1999). A third stream of research is also interested in the merger process and thus partly addresses the issue of design, but mostly in the context of failures or shortcomings (Aula & Tienari, 2011; Eastman & Lang, 2001).

This relative lack of interest in the processes involved in the creation of a new organizational design echoes a larger trend in the sociology of organizations. While such processes figured prominently in foundational works − think of Simon's (1953) study of the creation of the economic cooperation administration, or Selznick's definition of the organizational leader as an "architect" (Selznick, 1957, p. 126) − the issue of organizational design has become increasingly less central for organizational scholars, according to Greenwood and Miller (2010). While not denying the richness of studies focusing on the invention, adoption, or abandonment of those practices or instruments that contribute to molding organizations (e.g., managerial methods, tools for control and reporting, techniques in resource management), Greenwood and Miller argue for a comprehensive approach rather than a compartmentalized one. In other words, rather than analyze the various instruments, processes, or practices separately, they view the organizational structure as a configuration, a global architecture, and a more or less coherent whole.

Greenwood and Miller adopt a rather macro perspective and take a generally functional approach that leads to some conclusions we don't completely share. However, their starting point is relevant to understanding the dynamics at work in university mergers. Their definition of organizational design suggests looking at the ways by which actors imagine, build, and negotiate the articulation of the various components of an organization and integrate them into a global architecture. From the extensive literature addressing the issue, three research streams can be schematically drawn. After successively presenting each one individually we will propose a model that combines them.

The Functional Perspective: Organizational Design as an Efficiency-Driven Adaptation to Internal or External Dynamics

The first approach was championed by Chandler (1977) at a macro-level in his seminal analysis of the emergence of the multi-divisional firm. This perspective conceives the architecture of organizations as a solution to the problems they face and regards the evolution of organizational forms as related to the transformation of the structure of markets, the rise of new technologies, or the evolution of consumer demand. Such "functional" approaches view organizational design as an adaptation to exogenous forces that may be linked to economic transformations, technological progress, or societal evolutions. Understanding organizational design as the result of a process of adequacy is an interpretation also favored by authors embracing the "structural contingency" approach, in order to explain why some firms succeed and other fail. For instance, Woodward (1965) stressed that each technology of production corresponds to a relevant organizational architecture, while Lawrence and Lorsch (1967) argue that the formal structure of a firm should fit with the type of environment (stable vs. perturbed) in which it evolves. Scholars of the Aston Group, such as Pugh (1988), further explored this conception of organizational design and tried to enrich it by taking multiple factors into account to arrive at a more efficient organizational solution. This stream of research also relies fundamentally on the postulate that the primary purpose of organizational architecture is problem-solving.

The limits of these approaches are well known. Most notably, they are ex post explanations that show relationships among the performance of a firm, its organizational design, and contextual factors, but they provide no insight into the intentions of those who first conceived this design or whether they indeed engaged in problem-solving attempts. The observed fit might well result from a succession of adjustments rather than a rational reflection undertaken at the beginning. Therefore, they fail to further our understanding of our area of interest regarding university mergers: the moment when a new organization is conceived and how it is concretely designed. These approaches do not closely analyze the actual work involved in the creation of a new organizational architecture. Also, they frequently make the assumption that actors are clear-sighted enough to identify the relevant problems and the structures that will solve them. However, as Herbert Simon showed in his 1953 analysis of the creation of a new adminis-tration dedicated to implementing the Marshall Plan, this rational scheme is not the one followed in the creation of an organization: conflicting goals and struggles for power also come into play (Simon, 1953).

The Power Approach: Organizational Design as Politics

A second stream of research disregards the functionalist approach and instead interprets the organizational design of firms as the result of power struggles between different competing groups. Fligstein (1985, 1990), for instance, revisited the longitudinal perspective of Chandler and studied the evolution of the relative importance of different functions within firms. He argues that, through this process, firms shape their market to a consider-ably larger degree than the reverse. He identifies four periods, each one cor-responding to a different form of control over the organizational field of firms (and thus over the market). These include direct control, control through production, control from the sales and marketing departments, and finally control by the finance division. Fligstein argues that a new con-ception of control emerges when powerful actors change their view of the relationship between their firm and its environment, and then succeed to promote their interests at the field level.

Similar mechanisms are addressed and observed in the literature on pub-lic administration that aims to explain the emergence of new structures (such as agencies, for instance) or new distribution of functions (such as the divide between strategic missions and implementation promoted by the tenants of New Public Management (Pollitt & Bouckaert, 2011). This line of research shows how top civil servants engage in "bureau shaping" (Dunleavy, 1991) and impose organizational models that serve their own interests (James, 2003), or propose solutions to problems they themselves contributed to defining (Besançon & Benamouzig, 2005).

In this perspective, an organization's architecture would be determined less by the challenges it faces and functions needed to address them than by power struggles and the pursuit of specific interests. Organizational design is thus viewed as the product of negotiations and conflicts among actors defending different conceptions and interpretations. Nevertheless, research focusing on struggles for power is also more interested in large principles of organizing than in the concrete conception of new design. In addition, studies centered on actors and their interests may overlook the role of dominant organizational templates and legitimate, institutionalized models.

The Institutional Perspective: Organizational Design as a Conformation to Legitimate Models

The third and last line of research discussed here is the neo-institutional approach. It stresses the role of organizational models, which gain power less through efficiency than because they are considered to be legitimate and confer legitimacy to those who adopt them (DiMaggio & Powell, 1983; Meyer & Rowan, 1977; Tolbert & Zucker, 1983). They work as rationalized myths.

In such a perspective, organizational designs are implemented to gain or to maintain legitimacy. According to DiMaggio and Powell (1983), actors implement the model adopted by other organizations that are considered efficient or successful (mimetic isomorphism); they adopt a design because it is imposed by powerful actors on which they depend for crucial resources (coercive isomorphism) or they adopt a design promoted by the members of a professional group sharing a distinctive set of norms (normative isomorphism). The adopted formal structure sort out organizations and signal their belonging to a specific institutional field. The organizational design is therefore also a marker: It is part of the representations and cognitive models taken for granted by actors, which they mobilize when they have to imagine a new organization chart and create a new structure in a specific field.

Another argument specifically developed by neo-institutionalists in the "world polity" perspective is that rationalized myths become increasingly global. Studies focusing on the field of higher education − for example, Ramirez (2006) and Meyer, Ramirez, Frank, and Schofer (2007) − described the global diffusion of the model of the "rationalized university." Nevertheless, if this myth provides legitimate representations of what universities should be − and therefore influences the cognitive dimension of designs − these studies do not address the concrete transcription of these representations into structures and organizational practices. This approach thus overlooks the role actors play in adopting, translating, interpreting, and implementing rationalized myths in organizations.

Arguably, the "world polity" perspective is probably the branch of institutional theory least interested in the concrete translation of myths into practices, structures, or devices. Scholars who subscribe to this perspective expect *loose coupling* between practice and myths to be the standard response of organizations to institutional pressures. But this tendency has been shared to a large extent by much of the institutional literature in organizational theory. Scholars in this tradition have been more concerned with how the structural characteristics of organizations might predict the adoption of a given practice or a managerial fad than with intra-organizational processes through which they are institutionalized and edited (Zbaracki, 1998). It is only over the last decade that studies in the institutionalist tradition have actually started to look at such micro-level processes (e.g., Bromley, Hwang, & Powell, 2012; Hallett, 2010; Tilcsik, 2010), in line with what has been labeled an "inhabited institutions" perspective by Hallett and Ventresca (2006). Still, these are only a few studies attempting to fully integrate the issue of power into an institutional theoretical framework, in order to understand how the translation or editing of myths might be shaped by divergent interests and power struggles.

Combining the Different Approaches

To understand the organizational designs of the two new universities in our study, we combine all three theoretical frameworks, taking into account the strengths and limitations of each one.

Following the neo-institutionalist perspective, we pay attention the role of legitimate models and institutional scripts in shaping the design of the merged universities. Data analysis led us to add a distinction between solutions that merely reproduce what is "naturally" associated with universities on the one hand and models that relate to globalized university models on the other. In addition, rather than exclude any functional explanation, we attempt to identify whether the organizational designers identified problems and tried to solve them by imagining novel solutions and assigning new functions to the structures they built. Likewise, we are also attentive to actors and their potential for agency – that is, how far they are able to detach themselves from the legitimate models and imagine new ones. We also pay attention to conflicts and power relationships between actors defending opposing interests. By so doing, we reflect upon the recent studies in institutional theory that revisit the interactions between institutions and agency and question the capacity of agents to think and act outside their institutional frames. One such example is the "inhabited institutions" perspective that considers organizations to be "replete with structure and agency at multiple levels of analysis" (Hallett & Ventresca, 2006, p. 204). By studying activity at the "shop-floor" level, looking closely at the actual practices and observing how a specific model will be utilized, these authors recognize the role of agency and question the over-determinant role of institutions. This is the perspective we will adopt in the next pages.

Finally, we consider one additional factor that played an important role in the choices and mechanisms that prevailed in both mergers, although it is rarely discussed in the three perspectives we presented above. That element is time pressure, in a context where actors experienced a feeling of urgency. For different reasons but in a similar context, the new organizational designs of the two universities were conceived and adopted under severe time constraints. We will see that this continuous pressure influenced the nature of relationships among actors, as well as the solutions they proposed.

INVESTIGATING ORGANIZATIONAL DESIGN PROCESSES IN TWO UNIVERSITY MERGERS

This section describes describe the empirical basis of this paper. This is a two-step process in which we first present the materials and methods we used to study the mergers, then we introduce our two cases, and describe the context in which the mergers occurred to understand the dynamics that shaped the design processes.

Materials and Methods

This paper draws on two in-depth qualitative case studies, focusing on the creation of the University of Strasbourg and the University of Lorraine.

For each case we investigated two factors: the reasons for the mergers (for results see Barrier, 2015; Musselin & Dif-Pradalier, 2015) and the management of the merger process itself. This paper focuses on the second dimension by examining the decision-making processes involved in the design of a new organization. Although we also collected some data on the aftermath of the merger, this paper focuses on a relatively short period of time (1–2 years) preceding the official launch of the two universities. The most important decisions concerning the design of the merged universities were taken during this period.

The Strasbourg case was selected because, as the first university merger in France, it allowed us to investigate a pioneering initiative of organizational re-design. The Lorraine case study was conceived as a replication of the first in order to gain a deeper understanding of university mergers and learn which aspects of the first case could be generalized. The analysis of empirical materials showed that although the two cases differed in terms of substance, similar social mechanisms and processes were at play. Thus, rather than contrast the two cases to assess differences, this paper stresses the commonalities across the two cases in order to increase the robustness of our argument.

The research method consisted of about 40 interviews for each institution with persons involved in the preparation of the merger. These included faculty members, academic leaders, university administrators, representatives of the unions, local political or administrative actors, and management consultants. Each interviewee was asked to recount in as much detail as possible the decision-making processes that resulted in the merger. For example, they were asked which options were discussed, what arguments were made, and how and by whom decisions were taken. We also collected and analyzed several documents (e.g., minutes of the university boards, minutes of special working group meetings, press articles, press releases, and communications) in order to precisely reconstruct the discussions and negotiations that occurred around each merger and its implementation. To control for retrospective bias, interviews were carefully prepared and triangulated with available documents.

The Organization of the Two Merged Universities at a Glance

The University of Strasbourg (created in 2009) resulted from the merger of three universities established in the city of Strasbourg but located on different campus sites across the city. Each specialized in a distinct set of disciplines, with no redundancy. The University of Lorraine (created in 2012) is a slightly more complex case, involving the merger of four institutions located in two different cities in the Lorraine Region: Nancy and Metz, which are about 60 kilometers (37 miles) apart from each other. In contrast with Strasbourg, the contours of the institutions did not exactly follow disciplinary boundaries, as many disciplines were present in two or more of the four institutions. Further, one of the merged institutions – the *Institut National Polytechnique de Lorraine* (INPL) – was a federation of engineering schools with a specific legal statute. Although INPL was legally assimilated as a university, the schools composing this institution had considerably more strategic autonomy than is usual for standard faculties in French universities (Table 1).

Due to these differences in disciplinary composition, geographical scope and timing, the two mergers led to slightly different organizational forms. The Strasbourg merger mainly concerned the restructuring of the central administrative offices of the three universities into one. The perimeter of each of the 39 schools and faculties that composed the three universities remained unchanged: They were merely put under the same organizational umbrella. An intermediary organizational level was nevertheless added to regroup schools and faculties into broadly defined disciplinary domains, with the creation of nine structures called *collegiums*.

Table 1. Comparison of the Two Mergers.

University of Strasbourg 46,000 Students, Created in 2009	University of Lorraine 53,000 Students, Created in 2012
Merger of three institutions located in the city of Strasbourg (population 270,000):	Merger of four institutions located in the two main cities of the Lorraine region: Nancy and Metz:
– Université Strasbourg 1 – Louis Pasteur (Science, Engineering, Mathematics, and Medicine) – Université Strasbourg 2 – Marc Bloch (Arts, Humanities, and Social Sciences) – Université Strasbourg 3 – Robert Schuman (Management, Political Science, and Law)	– Université Nancy 1 – Henri Poincaré (Science, Engineering, Mathematics, and Medicine) – Université Nancy 2 (Arts, Humanities, Social Sciences, and Law) – Institut National Polytechnique de Lorraine, based in Nancy (Engineering and Technology) – Université de Metz – Paul Verlaine (Multidisciplinary)

The mission of each collegium is to promote coordination between its constituent units and build synergy. However, the academic leader in charge of a collegium has no budget, no staff, and no decision-making power.

A slightly different model was developed at the University of Lorraine. First, negotiations during the merger process concentrated on the reorganization of teaching and research structures rather than on central administrative offices. In addition to various institutional innovations that will be addressed later, the main difference lies in the organization of intermediary structures. The 55 schools, institutes, and faculties composing the merged institutions were also regrouped into collegiums. But, while collegiums in Strasbourg included both teaching departments and research units, the eight collegiums in Lorraine regrouped teaching structures only: Research units were gathered in 10 "*pôles scientifiques*" (scientific clusters). As a result, the organization of the university was presented as a "matrix structure" based on the separation of teaching and research: Each faculty member simultaneously belonged to a *pôle scientifique* in charge of research and a *collegium* in charge of teaching activities. Last, these intermediary organizational layers had more decision-making power than those in Strasbourg (Box 1).

Box 1. The Organization of French Universities.

Without going into too much detail about the intricacies of French universities, it is important to recall some of their basic features at the time the mergers occurred. Each of the institutions that merged in Strasbourg and in Lorraine was headed by a president − a faculty member elected to a five-year term. The presidents were assisted by a team of vice presidents and advisors in charge of specific missions. We will refer to them collectively as the "presidential team." At the time of the mergers each institution had three central university councils headed by VPs. These were the *Conseil scientifique*, in charge of research; the *Conseil des études et de la vie universitaire*, responsible for teaching and student affairs and the *Conseil d'administration*, an executive governing board. As in all French universities, the support staff and administrative service offices were put under the supervision of a professional administrator (*directeur général des services*). For ease of translation, we will refer to them as "heads of university administration" or "registrars."

Two Merger Processes with Similar Characteristics

Despite some differences and variations across the two cases, they share two common characteristics that make the comparison relevant. First, both mergers led to substantial organizational innovations due to the fact that both were voluntary mergers with no pre-existing model imposed on the new institutions by public authorities. When the universities in Strasbourg decided to merge, there was no precedent of a university merger in France and therefore no point of reference. The merger in Lorraine occurred three years later, but was nevertheless an unprecedented adventure in itself. Given the long-time political and economic rivalries between the cities of Metz and Nancy, as well as between their universities, the idea to merge was often described as a revolution. Even more to the point, the organizational design of the merged university included several institutional innovations at odds with common university regulations, pushing the university to apply for a special *"grand établissement"* statute. This statute is granted by the Ministry of Higher Education to only a few institutions as an exemption to common regulations, and the decision to apply was not trivial. In addition, neither of these two cases could be considered a merger by absorption, where the model of one institution would be merely transposed to the others, thereby limiting organizational innovation. In both cases, the merger process was initiated by a university specializing in science and medicine (Université Louis Pasteur in Strasbourg and Université Henri Poincaré in Lorraine). Both of these institutions were considered the most prestigious and powerful at the local level. However, despite their influence in the design process, they did not merely impose a model. In our two cases, the merging universities took the opportunity to imagine a new institution, rather than merely replicating one of them.

Second, both mergers occurred in a context marked by a sense of urgency in France's higher education sector and both were initiated by university presidents. They were concerned about their institutions losing out to the globalization of higher education and the intensification of academic competition. The presidents not only initiated the mergers but they also tightly managed the whole process with their close advisors and vice presidents. Although all key decisions concerning the mergers had to be voted upon by the university councils, the presidents were clearly in charge of the process. We will therefore refer to them as the "reformers." In both cases, these individuals argued that inaction would be dramatic. They repeatedly insisted that in order to survive, French universities had to become more visible and adopt what they presented as international norms. This perception was further reinforced by the pace and the scope of the reforms led by the Sarkozy government between 2007 and 2012. In a relatively short period of time, universities were urged to compete for several major multi-million Euro grants allocated by national programs such as *Opération Campus* in 2008 or the *Initiative d'Excellence* in 2010). Meanwhile, legislation was also enacted requiring universities to implement a new policy with far reaching consequences for their governance: the 2007 Act on university autonomy, known as the *Libertés et Responsabilités des Universités* (translated as "freedoms and responsibilities of universities.") Basically, this reform aimed at increasing the institutional autonomy of universities vis-à-vis national state authorities, by granting them more discretion over the management of their budget, staff and resources. This reform represented another challenge for French universities, as they had to completely restructure their internal management processes to meet the requirements of the new law before the end of 2012.

Thus, in both cases, the mergers had to fit within a tight schedule along-side the preparation of institutional projects needed to comply with national initiatives and implement a governance reform. In Strasbourg, preliminary negotiations started eight years before the merger. However, actual reflection on the architecture of the future university did not begin until early 2008, after the university councils from the three institutions voted in favor of the merger. January 1, 2009, was the date set for the merger, less than 10 months after the vote, in order to make the new insti-tution among the first to implement the 2007 act on university governance. A feeling of urgency also prevailed in Lorraine, where the merger schedule was influenced by the timing of the *Opération Campus* initiative. Because this initiative favored university mergers, the presidents stated in early 2008 that they had plans for a merger in 2020. But, by the end of 2008, they had completely revised their plans and proposed to implement the merger in 2012 to show their commitment to national authorities. The first reflections on the merger and the design of the new institution officially started in Spring of 2009, and the merger was approved by vote in January 2011. On January 1, 2012, the University of Lorraine was born.

INVENTING A NEW ORGANIZATIONAL DESIGN: REPRODUCING LEGITIMATE MODELS AND DEFENDING SPECIFIC INTERESTS

Two elements of these merger processes are especially noteworthy. First, references to an international model of universities were often used to justify the mergers. However, these references disappeared from the actual discussions on designing the future university. Instead of global rationalized myths, the most influential models were deeply institutionalized local conceptions of universities.

Second, although some functional considerations were expressed and potential alternatives were ready to develop, the time pressure lead to the acceptance of solutions whose primary aim was the avoidance of conflicts.

From the Myth of the Global University to Locally Taken-for-Granted Assumptions

The Weakness of Global Institutional Scripts

The arguments justifying university mergers in France frequently invoke the rise of global competition and international norms while claiming that France's higher education system lags behind those of other developed countries with regard to performance. However, we did not observe processes of mimetic isomorphism. In neither of our two cases did the reformers try to transpose the formal structure of institutions considered as models — or top-performing universities — at the international level. The absence of an obvious international model to emulate is further reinforced by the fact that the two universities chose rather different models and none of the reformers pushed for a specific design.

First, in some of the discussions transcribed in university board minutes or presented in the interviews, the actors involved in the merger process sometimes made references to organizational models from foreign universities. Yet, when schemes or practices from other institutions in France or abroad were mentioned in the discussions about the mergers, it was in a rather superficial and piecemeal fashion. Thus, we did not find any evidence of the adoption or even the adaptation of an external, pre-existing model as a whole. For instance, while a few cases of university mergers in Europe were used to justify the idea of a merger, actors did not engage in a systematic benchmark or a study of the structures of merged universities in order to build a new organizational design. In this same vein, the non-use of the Aghion report[5] (2010) is revealing. Although the report was available while the merger in Lorraine was still under discussion, we did not find evidence in interviews or documents that it played any significant role, either as a model or a counter-model.

Second, although management consultants often act as the vehicles for the diffusion of organizational models and managerial fads, they had a limited role in both mergers. In Strasbourg, members of the management consulting firm that were asked to help with the reorganization of the university central administrative office stated that they studied the organizational charts of some foreign universities, big firms, or local civil services, but none of these models were actually used. A management consulting firm was also hired in Lorraine to assist with the reorganization of the central administrative services, but it intervened very late in the merger process and it did not have much impact on organizational design. The idea to utilize consultants was pushed by the heads of university administrations. However, they sought their services mainly to convince the presidents to pay more attention to technical and administrative issues in the merger, rather than to develop specific recommendations based on managerial models.

Third, when the structure design was debated, nobody mentioned the models available in management handbooks. Nor was any reference made to ideal-typical university models, such as the Humboldtian model that put the professors at the center of universities; the collegial model relying on collective decision-making and shared values (Goodman, 1962; Millett, 1962); or the entrepreneurial model (Clark, 1998). In discussions, actors mobilized notions such as collegiality, efficiency in decision-making, and the need for universities to develop links with society. But, again, these notions were invoked as generic, legitimate values, rather than as the basis of specific blueprints that would set the foundations of the new organization.

Therefore, we cannot speak of the diffusion of some identified models that would have informed the reflection of the reformers, although they justified the merger with the argument that French universities should align themselves on international standards. One must admit that there are no equivalents in higher education to the legitimate standards described by Greenwood and Miller (2010) or Greenwood and Suddaby (2006) for the global service firms. The top-ranked universities follow different forms of organizing (compare Oxford and Berkeley, for instance), thereby creating ambiguity on the definition of THE model to follow and imitate. In addition, as one of the leading reformers in Lorraine stated in an interview, the coexistence of several different — and sometimes "irreconcilable" — visions of the aims of higher education among academics precluded attempts at building a model based on an idealized, abstract definition of the university.

Reactivating Local Institutional Scripts
Nevertheless, this does not mean that institutionalized categories and assumptions did not intervene in the process — quite the contrary. But

instead of strong mimetic processes happening, a set of loosely defined ideas and rationalized myths about university mergers was overlaid onto unquestioned assumptions about universities. This led to the reproduction of already well-established ideas that provoked little debate, as they belong to the usual repertoire of standards in higher education institutions and conform to traditional representations. This is not to say that the design process was devoid of conflicts about the merger or the definition of new structures − our intent here is simply to stress that several design options were validated without much debate and with no alternative solutions explored. In their reflections, the reformers never abandoned these "evident" representations and conceptions but relied on these familiar forms when designing the new universities.

First, in the two cases, the reformers shared a political rather than a managerial view of the merger. They felt a merger was necessary to make their institution visible on the global scene and thus avoid a gloomy destiny. They also asserted that bringing together institutions covering different disciplines would more communication across disciplines and benefit research and teaching. By contrast, they did not argue that merging would allow economies of scale or facilitate the pooling of resources. This raises the question of whether the actors were genuinely concerned with improving academic standards, or if their silence about managerial objectives could be aimed at avoiding resistance. This is impossible to say, but the overall process appeared to be dominated by the academic missions of the future university rather than by concerns over managerial and economic efficiency. In the same vein, the mergers were dominated by the distinction between what is described in France as the "political" dimension of university governance on the one hand (i.e., the decision-making processes involving academics elected for leadership positions such as presidents, vice presidents or deans as well as the elected deliberative bodies such as the university council), and the "administrative" dimension of university management on the other hand (i.e., the matters pertaining to the "execution" of "political" decisions by support staff and professional administrators). Although the respective tasks and roles of academic leaders and professional administrators are interdependent (at least in the sense that the latter are supposed to implement the decisions taken by the former), this distinction is prominent and strongly institutionalized in discourses about the governance of French universities. This often leads to tensions stemming from the divergence between administrative and academic logics (Mignot-Gérard, 2006). This familiar distinction was reproduced in both merger processes, where the reorganization of the central administration of the new university was disconnected in the reflection process from issues such as the size and composition of the future deliberative bodies, the rules for electing the vice presidents, and so on. Two distinct processes developed in parallel, each one involving different actors (the university presidents and their vice presidents on the one hand, and the registrars on the other). This decoupling was rooted in institutionalized categories but further fueled by the management of the merger process by the university presidents. Specifically, their attention was heavily focused on the containment of potential conflicts on sensitive issues, such as the representation of the different university stakeholders (students, faculty members, external stakeholders, etc.). In Strasbourg as in Lorraine, the distinction between administrative and political matters is so entrenched that it never occurred to the actors to examine the issues jointly.

The decoupling of the two processes inevitably led to tensions between the presidents and the registrars. For instance, in Strasbourg, when the registrars suggested the creation of a new position of assistant registrars, the presidents rejected the proposal out of fear that this supplementary hierarchical level would lower their influence on the administrative staff. In Lorraine, the registrars believed the presidents did not pay enough attention to administrative issues and feared that the new central administrative office would not be in good working order on the date of the merger. The registrars finally decided to hire a management consulting firm to convince the presidents to take action. Although most of the consultants' suggestions were not followed according to interviews, they nevertheless helped to legitimize the registrars' claims regarding the importance of administrative issues in the merger.

Second, the categories and scripts taken for granted by the reformers, as well as the organizational structures that embodied them, not only resulted in inertia or mere reproductions of existing patterns; it also contributed to intensifying ongoing institutional trends. For instance, in both cases, the action of the reformers tended to intensify the processes of administrative centralization and strengthen the executive leadership — a trend that has prevailed in French universities since the 1990s. While French universities were long dominated by the deans and faculty members who embodied the power of discipline-based structures, the growing institutional autonomy of universities has empowered university presidents at the expense of the deans, who have become less influential in defining policy and strategy within their institution (Mignot-Gérard, 2006). This was observed to be the case in both Lorraine and Strasbourg. This trend has been supported by the gradual rise of institutional scripts and policy discourses at the national level, tying the performance of universities to strong strategic and leader-ship capabilities at the presidential level. Unsurprisingly, as university pre-sidents, the reformers strongly adhered to these ideas and did little to involve the deans in the merger process. There was almost no specific reflec-tion on their role in the new structure or any additional responsibilities or competencies they might take on, which could only further marginalize them. The presidents were also convinced that the mergers should provide an opportunity to follow, if not reinforce, the process initiated by the 2007 Act on University Autonomy that strengthened the central administration of universities. They therefore accentuated this trend during the merger.

Likewise, because institutionalized categories tend to be embedded in the design of existing organizational structures, the fact that the reformers had to build upon pre-existing structures led in some instances to the repro-duction of established organizational patterns and categories. This is exem-plified by the case of the organizational divide between teaching and research — one of the key features of French universities — that was further institutionalized by the creation of a formal "matrix organization" in Lorraine. Although the basic organizational units composing French universities are called Teaching and Research Units (UFR — *Unités de Formation et de Recherche*), they are actually weakly involved in the man-agement of research activities. Since the 1960s, the management of research has been increasingly taken over by "research units" or "research centers," which are usually affiliated simultaneously with one or more universities and one or more national public research organizations (such as CNRS). In this context, when the reformers started to think about the organization of research and teaching structures, they realized that the presidential team of the merged university would have to deal with a larger number of UFRs and research units. In order to keep the future university manageable, they felt it necessary to create some sort of intermediary layer between the between the presidency and the many UFRs and research units. The ratio-nale was primarily functional: An intermediary layer would facilitate coor-dination and communication. But the implementation of this rather simple idea was constrained by the contours of existing structures. In brief, the complexity of the academic landscape in Lorraine (four institutions located in two different cities, with research units sometimes simultaneously affiliated with more than one university), made it impossible to regroup both research units and UFRs in the same type of structure. As a conse-quence, the decision was made to create collegiums for the coordination of teaching activities, and scientific clusters for the coordination of research. In order to enable coordination between teaching and research, a further decision was made to create a special board at the university level including the heads of all collegiums and scientific clusters. In symbolic terms, the image of a matrix organization conveyed of the idea that the coordination between research and teaching would be increased. Yet, several intervie- wees noted that the actual design of collegiums and scientific clusters was more prone to build two different decision-making circuits, thereby further institutionalizing the divide between research and teaching structures. This divide was less severe in Strasbourg. The collegiums regrouped both UFRs and research units, but they did not actually improve coordination between them: They were simply put together in the same overarching structure. But the perimeters of the nine collegiums did not match the three scientific domains organizing research at the University of Strasbourg.

Therefore, we clearly observed that deeply institutionalized local scripts – as opposed to global myths – played a key role in shaping the design of the merged universities. Yet, this could only account for a part of this process, which was also influenced by power games and time constraints.

Keeping the Merger under Control: Power and Time Constraints in the Organizational Design Process

Some actors regarded the merger as a high-stakes situation that could potentially threaten their interests and positions in the new university. The design process might therefore be understood as a bargaining process involving power relations between different actors. However, this process was heavily shaped by a powerful specific factor: time pressure. As men- tioned, there was relatively little time between the merger decision and its completion in both cases. This was both a constraint and an opportunity for the reformers. On the one hand, they engaged in various tactics – ranging from avoidance of tricky issues to bargaining with actors with veto power – to avoid delays in the process. This resulted in an organizational design that largely stemmed from choices by exclusion. On the other hand, the time pressure gave the reformers a key advantage by placing them in a position of strength to shape the organizational design according to their own interests.

Choice by Exclusion: How the Presidents' Willingness to Prevent the Emergence of Conflicts Shaped the Design Process
In both Lorraine and Strasbourg, several organizational design choices were made *by exclusion*. In other words, reformers adopted certain

solutions not because these were their preferred options, but in order to avoid the emergence of conflicts. It was crucial not to weaken the process, as each step had to be approved by the different parties and the councils. A negative vote could have delayed if not stopped the entire merger process. There were four distinct ways in which the organizational design of the new institution was shaped by the exclusion of potentially contentious options.

First, in both cases, the reformers dismissed a few options out of hand with no real discussion due to anticipated conflicts. For example, it was crucial for the reformers to prevent labor disputes with administrative staff members as this would have paralyzed the process. Thus, they decided in both cases not to reduce staff or lower their qualifications, thereby reinforcing the idea that the mergers were not driven by cost-efficiency concerns. In addition, in Strasbourg, the reformers made a commitment concerning the harmonization of work conditions and regulations across the three merged universities: They promised that, in each case where the former institutions had different rules, the rule most advantageous for staff members would be applied throughout the new university. In Lorraine, while the reformers did not have to make a commitment to such an upward harmonization of work conditions, they had to make a concession on what was locally a very sensitive issue because the cities of Metz and Nancy are 60 kilometers apart, many staff members were concerned about their jobs being relocated to another city. Accordingly, the presidents clarified early in the process that no such relocation would be imposed on administrative staff members. This had an important consequence later on because it meant that support staff offices could not be totally centralized.

Second, time constraints coupled with the need to prevent conflicts forced the reformers to concentrate on the most pressing issues while postponing decisions on complex or difficult matters after the official date of the merger. In Strasbourg, for instance, agreeing on the reorganization of teaching and research seemed impossible. Because the three institutions involved in that merger each specialized in a different disciplinary area, it was easy to simply put them next to each other in the same structure, without making any attempts to actually combine them (an arrangement which still persists today). The first negotiations about the future organization of the UFRs stumbled, and the reformers shifted their attention to the implementation of the 2007 Act on university autonomy. This led them to focus on merging and reorganizing the three central administrations. Any thoughts about changing the teaching and research structures were put on hold. As mentioned, the reformers simply created structures with few prerogatives – the collegiums – with each UFR being allowed to join the collegium of its choice. In Lorraine, by contrast, the reorganization of teaching and research structures was prioritized over the merger of central administrative offices. Indeed, as several disciplines were simultaneously present in different institutions, it was crucial to reach an agreement on the organization of intermediary structures for teaching and research. Moreover, given the fact that the existing administrative offices were located in two distant cities, their reorganization seemed considerably more problematic than was the case in Strasbourg. As a result, the reorganization of the central university administration was not fully completed on the date of the merger. The basic administrative functions were in place, but much remained to be done in terms of administrative routines and procedures.

Third, the reformers' attempts to prevent conflict had another important consequence besides the avoidance or postponement of tough decisions. It also led them to pay close attention to the preferences of actors who could act as veto players in the process: It was less costly to seek solutions acceptable to critical actors than to risk turning them into full antagonists. That meant that some of the actors who were the most skeptical about the conditions of the merger had a decisive role in shaping some of the features of the new organization. This is well illustrated by a decision concerning the composition of the central governing council of the new Strasbourg University. The relevant councils from each merging institution had to vote on this issue. Members from one of the universities were unable to agree on the right number of council members or the repartition of members by statutes: Several council members thought that the provisions of the 2007 Act on University Autonomy allocated too few seats to representatives of the student body and the support staff as compared to external stakeholders. The project of a council that would include 30 members was rejected. This created a sense of crisis: Without agreement many feared the council size would be reduced to 20 members,[6] a solution no one wanted. The university president decided to convoke an extraordinary session of his university council, proposing a new solution that would be presented to the other two universities. The terms were as follows: There would be 30 members, the number of external stakeholders would not be changed but one of them would be an alumnus selected by the student representatives and another one by the representatives of the administrative staff. This solution was largely adopted.

In Lorraine, the organizational design of the new university was significantly shaped by the reluctance of the *Institut National Polytechnique de*

Lorraine (INPL), which had reservations about the merger. Here, we must recall that INPL was a federation of engineering schools that benefited from a specific administrative statute granting more strategic autonomy than the three other universities in Lorraine. Many faculty members and representatives from INPL feared that merging would mean a loss of autonomy. Therefore, a key issue for the reformers was to make the conditions of the merger acceptable to INPL. Given the prestigious status of INPL and its weight within the regional higher education landscape, its defection would probably have led to the abortion of the whole merger. This allowed INPL to gain substantial bargaining power over the process. INPL pushed forward options that aimed at securing its position and autonomy within the future merged university. INPL was, for instance, supportive of the creation of collegiums because this intermediary structure was seen as a way to "reproduce" the pre-existing perimeter of INPL within the new institution.[7] But in order to secure its influence and autonomy, INPL also advocated that collegiums should have a significant role in decision-making and resource allocation processes (in contrast with Strasbourg, where collegiums have limited prerogatives). For legal and administrative reasons that we will not detail here, it was not possible to create the type of collegium promoted by INPL under usual university statutes. This was one of the key reasons the reformers opted for a special *grand établissement* statute for the new university.[8] As a result, the specific demands of INPL contributed to setting the standards of what a collegium would be for the university as a whole.

Fourth, in line with the latter example, some of the choices initially made by exclusion triggered a domino effect by further enabling or constraining the range of organizational design options. This is evidenced by the case of Lorraine, where the creation of a collegium of engineering had indirect consequences on how the contours of other collegiums could be defined. Three of the universities in Lorraine hosted several *Instituts Universitaires de Technologie* (IUTs), which are vocational-oriented colleges delivering two-year undergraduate degrees. Although IUTs are legally part of a parent university, they have a special statute which grants them more autonomy than other equivalent university sub-units (such as the UFRs). The creation of a collegium of engineering opened a window of opportunity for IUTs, which also asked for their own collegium in order to collectively secure their autonomy in the new institution. In addition, because many IUTs covered several disciplines (e.g., there could be both a chemistry and a management department in the same IUT), they feared that the creation of collegiums based on academic disciplines would jeopardize their internal cohesion. Because the reformers wanted to avoid conflicts, IUTs successfully emulated engineering schools in their efforts to create a collegium based on the amalgamation of entities with similar statutes, rather than on a disciplinary basis. Thus, early in the process, it was clear that, at the very least, one collegium would be dedicated to engineering (regrouping engineering schools) and another to technology (regrouping IUTs). This significantly constrained the combinations available for the creation of the other collegiums; for example, it was no longer possible to build a collegium for chemistry because this discipline was already scattered in those two collegiums. The organizational design process therefore resulted from the successive arrangements of different bricks used to build the size, format, and composition of the future structure, but also created irreversibility by pre-empting further choices.

The Visible Hand of University Presidents: Building upon the Merger as a Momentum to Advocate Specific Organizational Options
In the preceding section, we have mostly stressed the defensive dimension of the discussions on the new organizational design by focusing on mechanisms of choice by exclusion. But the process also opened a window of opportunity for some actors — especially the presidents — to actively promote their own reform agenda on issues that were not directly linked to the merger.

In both cases, the time pressure reinforced the central role of the presidents vis-à-vis other university actors because the pace of the process made it difficult for faculty members not belonging to the presidential teams to get actively involved in the discussion and elaborate alternative proposals. While all key decisions had to be debated and voted on by university councils, they were carefully prepared beforehand by the presidents in order to accelerate the process. Further, in contrast with the presidents — who devoted considerable time resources to the merger — the vast majority of faculty and support staff members lacked the time and motivation to grasp all the technicalities of the process. Although consultative working groups were created in both cases to widen and enrich reflections on the merger (they dealt with issues such as governance, human resource management, etc.), they did not facilitate the emergence of alternative proposals. At Strasbourg, for instance, the sheer number and specialization of these groups (at one point there were more than 40 committees working in parallel) meant that no group was able to have an overview of the process. In Lorraine, there were far fewer working groups, but their actual input was limited anyway; a close advisor to the presidents explained that the groups functioned mostly as forums where the presidents and their teams tested and refined their ideas, rather than as places fostering the bottom-up emergence of new ideas.

In this context, the presidents were the only actors able to figure out how to piece together the various elements of a complex institutional puzzle. In fact, few alternatives were developed to amend the propositions already pushed forward by the presidents. They mostly occurred in specific cases where it was immediately evident to actors that the merger could negatively affect their interests (as exemplified by the case of INPL in Lorraine). In other words, while the presidents had to make concessions, they generally had a wide open path to assert their vision of how the new university should be organized and governed.

The central position of the presidents in the design process enabled them to promote design options that secured the prerogatives and power of the presidential team in the future university. For instance, projecting themselves into the position of the merged university's president, they were wary not to give too much decision-making power or administrative capacity to intermediary structures (such as collegiums) within the new institution. Even in Lorraine, where collegiums in principle had greater decision-making capacities compared with their counterparts at Strasbourg, the presidents insisted that the directors of collegiums should not have a large support staff. The idea was to keep the management of the structure as light as possible, in order to push the directors of collegiums to act merely as go-betweens between the presidential team and university sub-units rather than as managers of a structure in their own right. Essentially, they wanted to minimize the strength of the layers between the presidential team and basic university organizational units. Likewise, in some instances, the presidents pushed for very specific changes. In Strasbourg, representatives of Henri Poincaré University referred to national evaluation reports criticizing the governance of the two other universities to promote their own governance model based on a stronger presidential leadership. They would have rejected, for example, a statute not allowing the president from controlling the choice of the vice presidents. In Lorraine, one of the presidents had been involved in the debates on the preparation of the 2007 Act on university autonomy. He regretted that his proposal to create a large academic Senate, in addition to existing university boards, was not included in the new legislation. Seeing the merger as an opportunity to bring new life to his proposal, the adoption of a *grand établissement* statute enabled him to successfully argue for the creation of an academic Senate in Lorraine. The proposals pushed forward by the presidents were all the more legitimate as they resonated with institutional scripts about university governance and leadership circulating at the national level. Nevertheless, if the presidents had less control over the process, it would probably have been more difficult to shape the new organization according to their specific vision.

Thus, in both cases, the presidents appeared to view the merger as a window of opportunity to promote their own vision and interests. Yet, amidst the vast number of reorganization initiatives undertaken during the merger, a few other actors also managed to advance their causes. In comparison with the presidents — who were the main institutional entrepreneurs of the design process — these others may be described as "entrepreneurs of the second circle." Their closeness to the presidents provided them with an attentive ear to advocate specific proposals — provided they did not contradict the vision of presidents. In Strasbourg, for instance, during the reflection on the merger of the three central administrations, the three former registrars were responsible for the process with a consultancy firm they commissioned, while the presidents were mobilized by the "political" dimension of the merger. Sharing the same views about the need to transform the management of universities, the registrars used the opportunity of the merger to envision the creation of an office in charge of indicators and internal auditing. The presidents accepted this, as it did not conflict with their own vision. We encountered similar examples in Lorraine. One instance concerned a proposal pushed by a student representative which was welcomed by the presidents and became a distinctive feature of the merged university. The student representative sought to promote a reorganization of the council in charge of teaching and student affairs. Along with other faculty members, he observed that the agenda of the existing councils was mostly dominated by discussions about teaching and the organization of the curriculum, usually leaving little time to discuss student affairs such as housing and campus life. To give more weight and attention to student affairs, he argued that the council should be split in two, with a council specifically created to deal with this issue. Nobody really opposed this idea (all felt there was no harm in trying), and the presidents even considered it with a keen eye: It would add another institutional innovation in the Lorraine model. It appealed to the presidents for another reason as well because this council could not be created under common university statutes, it represented a supplementary argument to convince skeptics of the relevance to apply for the *grand établissement* statute they advocated for the merged university.

CONCLUSION

In this paper, we proposed to consider university mergers as revealing empirical cases for the analysis of organizational design processes by drawing on two case studies of university mergers in France. Although it is clear that organizational (re)design processes happen under diverse circumstances in universities, mergers arguably provide a strategic research opportunity to analyze these processes as the scope and pace of organizational change are magnified in such situations. By combining insights from three streams of literature that have addressed the functional, political and institutional dimensions of organizational design, we have sought to show how the two new organizations that resulted from the mergers were simultaneously shaped by several factors interacting with each other.

Although the elaboration of a new design was clearly driven by the will of the president-reformers to solve what they considered as governance and organizational problems, their definitions of problems and solutions were shaped by institutionalized categories. Yet, we found little evidence for the influence of global institutional scripts in this process: Global mimetic pressures were less significant than locally institutionalized representations. In other words, reformers strongly believed that the globalization and intensification of competition in higher education should lead to the adoption of international norms (Musselin & Dif-Pradalier, 2015), but at the same time they remained embedded in their local (national) institutional settings. In both cases, we barely observed mimetic isomorphism or institutional transfers. In this situation − and in a context of time pressure − legitimate and deeply institutionalized conceptions of what a French university is (and should be) were naturally reproduced in the new structure.

Building on these "institutional bricks," the actors involved in the mergers engaged in the definition of various design options, gradually elaborating what looked more like a patchwork of specific solutions than the translation of a global model. We have shown that the university presidents, who were the initiators and main proponents of the merger in both cases, had a decisive role in shaping the new universities according to their own interests. Their position in the process gave them leverage over the discussion of design options. Yet, they did not unilaterally impose a model. This is due in no small part to the fact that they had no well-defined, comprehensive model in mind when they embarked on the merger process. This also led them to integrate proposals elaborated by actors who seized the merger as an opportunity to promote their own reform agenda, like the registrars in Strasbourg or a student representative in Lorraine. Last, and perhaps most importantly, the presidents had to anticipate and address potential conflicts. Facing severe pressure to meet the deadlines set for the mergers, they had to make choices by exclusion. Several design options were adopted not because they were preferred by the reformers, but because they allowed for the reduction or complete avoidance of conflicts, which was especially important when dealing with actors who could act as veto players and delay or challenge achievement of the merger.

Thus, in both cases, the construction of a new organizational design can be described as a "muddling through" process (Lindblom, 1959). We did not observe a victory of one model over another. Despite their key role in the process, the university presidents were at least as concerned (if not more so) with downplaying undesirable options than promoting those they found relevant. The resemblance of the design to a patchwork is reinforced by the fact that the different bricks constituting the new architecture were most often borrowing from different models. Legitimate, textbook-like models were, of course, a source of inspiration. The reorganization of administrative service offices in Strasbourg drew on ideas typical of New Public Management (Pollitt & Bouckaert, 2011) that strategic and operational functions should be carefully separated, with the presidents on one side and the registrars on the other. Likewise, the model of a matrix organization that prevailed in Lorraine was – at least nominally – inspired by principles of corporate management. But it is clear that neither of the two models was directly imported into the new design: They were edited and overlaid on existing structures. The patchwork-like quality of the new design also resulted from the characteristics of the process, where the participation of several actors was rather punctual and fluctuant. While INPL was quite active in the discussion about collegiums in Lorraine, it was more passive on other issues. Likewise, in Strasbourg, once it was decided there would be no assistant registrars, university presidents and registrars were able to collaborate and cooperate on other issues. Tensions were limited, circumscribed to specific issues and actors, and weakened once they were able to agree on a solution.

The processes at play should not be interpreted in exclusive terms: They do not result exclusively from either problem-solving initiatives, power games, or global institutional pressures. They should rather be interpreted as contingent processes of negotiation, adjunction, and combination of organizational elements, strongly influenced by institutionalized categories and ideas. Using the image invoked by Lascoumes (1993) in his book on French environmental policy, the new organizational design is comparable to a Tinguely machine, in which old elements are recycled and combined with new ones.[9]

This process of invention and combination is all the more ambiguous because it did not fully stop with the official completion of the merger: not all elements were fully stabilized on the date of either merger. They continued to evolve in the following years. To make another, supplementary metaphor, one could represent the design of the new universities as a map. Then, at the date of merger, it would be a map representing mostly the broad outlines of large territories, with some regions drawn in a finely grained fashion and others left nearly blank.

Last, our results suggest further research questions concerning the role of global institutional scripts in the transformation of higher education, but also perhaps of organizations in general. In both cases, the model of a global rationalized university (Krücken & Meier, 2006; Ramirez, 2009) worked as a trigger for the mergers. However, local/national categories and structures soon resurfaced and dominated the processes. This echoes similar observations in studies of Europeanization processes, where some authors speak of "renationalization" of policies (Musselin, 2009; Palier & Surel, 2006). But it is also common to observe that external models might be translated and adapted to the local situation: the transfer of the Humboldtian model to US universities by the late 19th century being probably one of the better known cases of transfer, adaptation, and recycling in higher education. Models and representations travel globally, but their transfer depends on local translation and implementation. This might have been reinforced, in our cases, by the fact that global institutional scripts prompted university presidents to advocate a merger but offered no blueprint on how to proceed. It has long been acknowledged that decoupling institutional scripts from practices generally occurs because coupling would create intractable tensions (Meyer & Rowan, 1977). In the cases we studied, the main reason for the relatively low influence of global scripts might be that there was no clear model to imitate nor were there available methods or influential professionals to assist in the process, thereby pushing actors to reinvent a local model. In this view, our results contribute to the growing body of research interested in the "incarnation" of institutional myths in organizations (e.g., Hallett, 2010), by looking at how institutional scripts come to be inhabited by actors.

NOTES

1. Revealingly, in the case of Strasbourg, the Ministry of Higher Education was actually reluctant to support the merger advocated by the university presidents (Musselin & Dif-Pradalier, 2015) when initially proposed.

2. The goal of *Opération Campus* was to create a dozen top university clusters in France by providing large investments dedicated to renovating campus facilities or building new ones. Although it was not a requirement, universities were strongly encouraged to submit proposals for projects based on consortiums of institutions. The incentive to strengthen inter-institutional cooperation was even greater with the *Initiative d'Excellence* in 2010, which sought to devote special grants worth millions of Euros to a few academic clusters of excellence. This funding was available only for projects proposed by consortiums and the jury responsible for the selection of proposals favored projects submitted by merged universities or by consortiums claiming they were going to merge.

3. PRES are to be replaced by a new organizational form, the *Communautés d'Universités et d'Etablissements* (COMUE – Communities of Universities and Higher Education Institutions).

4. Fieldwork was conducted in Strasbourg in 2009 and 2010 by Mael Dif-Pradalier with Christine Musselin, and in Lorraine by Julien Barrier in 2011 and 2012.

5. This report was commissioned to the well-known Harvard economist by the Minister of Higher Education and Research to draw on the experience of foreign "universities of excellence" to outline governance principles and schemes that could be emulated by French universities.

6. According to the 2007 Act, the central governing bodies could count between 20 and 30 members. The council members voting on the composition of the future council of the new universities feared the ministry would impose an undesirable composition and allow them the smallest number of members if they were not able to come to a decision.

7. There would be a collegium of engineering consisting of all the former engineering schools of INPL, plus three engineering schools that were formerly members of Louis Poincaré University.

8. The choice of this exceptional legal statute related to the demands of INPL, but it also resonated with – and enabled – other proposals that were not possible under default regulations. It allowed, for instance, the creation of two new university councils with a new board exclusively devoted to student affairs, as well as an academic senate.

9. Tinguely machines refer to some of the most well-known creations of the Swiss contemporary artist Jean Tinguely (1925–1991), who assembled spare mechanical parts to create intriguing, complex machines that had no apparent functional purpose.

ACKNOWLEDGMENTS

This paper draws on MUTORG-ADMI, a research project funded by the Agence Nationale de la Recherche and coordinated by Philippe Bezes and Patrick Le Lidec. We are greatly indebted to them for having suggested the very idea of a research on mergers in the public sector. We also thank the editors of this volume, Elizabeth Popp Berman and Catherine Paradeise, and an anonymous reviewer for their valuable comments and suggestions. We would also like to thank the participants to seminars held at the Centre de Sociologie des Organisations, Sciences Po, and the University of Bordeaux, as well as the participants to a conference organized at Boston College "The Phenomenology of Organizations: A SCANCOR Celebration of the Work of John Meyer," whose questions and remarks were helpful in the development of this paper. The usual caveat apply.

REFERENCES

Aghion, P. (2010). *L'excellence universitaire: leçons des expériences internationales.* Intermediary report to Valérie Pécresse, Ministre de l'enseignement supérieur et de recherche. Retrieved from http://media.enseignementsup-recherche.gouv.fr/file/2010/61/5/Mission_Aghion_Rapport-etape_135615.pdf. Accessed on September 20, 2014.

Aula, H.-M., & Tienari, J. (2011). Becoming "world-class"? Reputation-building in a university merger. *Critical Perspectives on International Business, 7,* 7−29.

Aust, J., & Crespy, C. (2009). Napoléon renversé? Institutionnalisation des pôles de recherche et d'enseignement supérieur et réforme du système académique français. *Revue Française de Science Politique, 59,* 915−938.

Barrier, J. (2015). Fusionner les universités pour revitaliser la Lorraine? La genèse de l'Université de Lorraine, entre concurrence nationale, rivalités universitaires et convergences territoriales (2005−2009). *Annales de la Recherche Urbaine, 109,* 44−59.

Bennetot Pruvot, E., Estermann, T., & Mason, P. (2015). *University mergers in Europe: Define thematic report.* European University Association. Retrieved from http://eua.be/Libraries/Publications_homepage_list/DEFINE_Thematic_Report_2_University_Mergers_in_Europe_final.sflb.ashx. Accessed on July 10, 2015.

Besançon, J., & Benamouzig, D. (2005). Administrer un monde incertain: les nouvelles bureaucraties techniques: Le cas des agences sanitaires en France. *Sociologie du travail, 47,* 301−322.

Bezes, P. (2005). Le modèle de l'Etat-Stratège: genèse d'une forme organisationnelle dans l'administration française. *Sociologie du travail, 4,* 431−450.

Bezes, P., & Le Lidec, P. (2010). L'hybridation du modèle territorial français. RGPP et réorganisations de l'Etat territorial. *Revue française d'administration publique, 136,* 919−942.

Bromley, P., Hwang, H., & Powell, W. W. (2012). Decoupling revisited: Common pressures, divergent strategies in the U.S. nonprofit sector. *Management, 15,* 468−501.

Chandler, A. (1977). *The visible hand: The managerial revolution in American business.* Cambridge, MA: Belknap Press.

Clark, B. R. (1998). *Creating entrepreneurial universities.* Oxford: IAU and Elsevier Science.

DiMaggio, P., & Powell, W. (1983). The iron cage revisited: Institutional isomorphism and collective rationality in organizational fields. *American Sociological Review, 48,* 147−160.

Dunleavy, P. (1991). *Democracy, bureaucracy and public choice.* London: Harvester Wheatsheaf.

Eastman, J., & Lang, D. (2001). *Mergers in higher education: Lessons from theory and experience.* Toronto: University of Toronto Press.

Fligstein, N. (1985). The spread of the multidivisional form among large firms: 1919—1979. *American Sociological Review, 50*, 377—391.

Fligstein, N. (1990). *The transformation of corporate control.* Cambridge, MA: Harvard University Press.

Gamage, D. T. (1993). The reorganisation of the Australian higher educational institutions towards a unified national system. *Studies in Higher Education, 18*, 81—94.

Goedegebuure, L. C. (2012). *Mergers and more: The changing tertiary education landscape in the 21st century.* HEIK Working Paper No. 2012/01. University of Oslo, Faculty of Educational Sciences.

Goodman, P. (1962). *The community of scholars.* New York, NY: Random House.

Greenwood, R., & Miller, D. (2010). Tackling design anew: Getting back to the heart of organizational theory. *Academy of Management Perspective, 24*, 78—88.

Greenwood, R., & Suddaby, R. (2006). Institutional entrepreneurship in mature fields: The big five accounting firms. *Academy of Management Journal, 49*, 27—48.

Hallett, T. (2010). The myth incarnate: Recoupling processes, turmoil, and inhabited institutions in an urban elementary school. *American Sociological Review, 75*, 52—74.

Hallett, T., & Ventresca, M. (2006). Inhabited institutions: Social interactions and organizational forms in Gouldner's patterns of industrial bureaucracy. *Theory and Society, 35*, 213—236.

Harman, G., & Harman, K. (2008). Strategic mergers of strong institutions to enhance competitive advantage. *Higher Education Policy, 21*, 99—121.

James, O. (2003). *The executive agency revolution in Whitehall: Public interest versus bureaushaping perspectives.* London: Palgrave Macmillan.

Kitchener, M., & Gask, L. (2003). NPM merger mania. *Public Management Review, 5*, 19—44.

Krücken, G., & Meier, F. (2006). Turning the university into an organizational actor. In G. Drori, J. Meyer, & H. Hwang (Eds.), *Globalization and organization: World society and organizational change* (pp. 241—257). Oxford: Oxford University Press.

Kyvik, S. (2002). The merger of non-university colleges in Norway. *Higher Education, 44*, 53—72.

Lascoumes, P. (1993). *L'Eco-pouvoir: Environnements et politiques.* Paris: Editions la Découverte.

Lawrence, P., & Lorsch, J. (1967). Differentiation and integration in complex organizations. *Administrative Science Quarterly, 12*, 1—30.

Lindblom, C. (1959). The science of "muddling through". *Public Administration Review, 19*, 79—88.

Meyer, J., Ramirez, F., Frank, D., & Schofer, E. (2007). Higher education as an institution. In P. Gumport (Ed.), *The sociology of higher education* (pp. 187—221). Baltimore, MD: The Johns Hopkins University Press.

Meyer, J., & Rowan, B. (1977). Institutionalized organizations: Formal structure as myth and ceremony. *American Journal of Sociology, 83*, 340—363.

Mignot-Gérard, S. (2006). *Echanger et argumenter. Les dimensions politiques du gouvernement des universités françaises.* PhD dissertation, Institut d'Etudes Politiques de Paris, Paris.

Millett, J. D. (1962). *Academic community: An essay on organization.* New York, NY: McGraw-Hill.

Mok, K. (2005). Globalization and educational restructuring: University merging and changing governance in China. *Higher Education, 50*, 57—88.

Musselin, C. (2009). The side effects of the Bologna process on national institutional settings: The case of France. In A. Amaral, G. Neave, C. Musselin, & P. Maassen (Eds.), *European integration and the governance of higher education and research* (pp. 181—206). Dordrecht: Springer.

Musselin, C., & Dif-Pradalier, M. (2015). When merging appears the thing to do: The (re)birth of the university of Strasbourg, English version of «Quand la fusion s'impose: la (re) naissance de l'université de Strasbourg». *Revue Française de Sociologie, 55*, 285–318.

Norgård, J. D., & Skodvin, O.-J. (2002). The importance of geography and culture in mergers: A Norwegian institutional case study. *Higher Education, 44*, 73–90.

Palier, B., & Surel, Y. (2006). *L'Europe en action: L'européanisation dans une perspective comparée*. Paris: L'Harmattan.

Pollitt, C., & Bouckaert, G. (2011). *Public management reform: A comparative analysis of new public management, governance, and The Neo-Weberian state*. Oxford: Oxford University Press.

Pugh, D. (1988). The Aston research programme. In A. Bryman (Ed.), *Doing research in organizations* (p. 124). London: Routledge.

Ramirez, F. (2006). The rationalization of universities. In M.-L. Djelic & K. Sahlin-Andersson (Eds.), *Transnational governance: Institutional dynamics of regulation* (pp. 224–245). Cambridge: Cambridge University Press.

Ramirez, F. (2009). World society and the socially embedded university. *Social Science Review, 40*, 1–30.

Selznick, P. (1957). *Leadership in administration: A sociological interpretation*. New York, NY: Harper & Row.

Simon, H. (1953). Birth of an organization: The economic cooperation administration. *Public Administration Review, 13*, 227–236.

Simon, H. (1955). A behavioral model of rational choice. *Quarterly Journal of Economics, 69*, 99–118.

Skodvin, O.-J. (1999). Mergers in higher education: Success or failure? *Tertiary Education and Management, 5*, 65–80.

Tilcsik, A. (2010). From ritual to reality: Demography, ideology, and decoupling in a post-communist government agency. *Academy of Management Journal, 53*, 1474–1498.

Tolbert, P. S., & Zucker, L. G. (1983). Institutional sources of change in the formal structure of organizations: The diffusion of civil service reform. *Administrative Science Quarterly, 28*, 22–39.

Woodward, J. (1965). *Industrial organization: Theory and practice*. Oxford: Oxford University Press.

Zbaracki, M. J. (1998). The rhetoric and reality of total quality management. *Administrative Science Quarterly, 43*, 602–636.

SELLING STUDENTS: THE RISE OF CORPORATE PARTNERSHIP PROGRAMS IN UNIVERSITY CAREER CENTERS

Daniel Davis and Amy Binder

ABSTRACT

This study documents a new case of the further commercialization of the university, the rapid adoption of corporate partnership programs (CPPs) within centralized university career services departments. CPPs function as a type of headhunting agency. For an annual fee they facilitate a corporate hiring department's direct access to student talent, allowing the company to outsource much of its hiring tasks to the university career center. CPPs are a feature found predominantly, though not exclusively, on campuses where there is a highly rationalized logic around the economic benefits of academic science. Further, CPPs represent a commercialization of practice that is in tension with the student-development mission of traditional career counselors. Using an inhabited institutionalist approach, we show how the models differ and how staff on each side attempt to negotiate their competing roles in the multiversity environment. We also discuss some of the potential impact

The University under Pressure
Research in the Sociology of Organizations, Volume 46, 395–422
Copyright © 2016 by Emerald Group Publishing Limited
All rights of reproduction in any form reserved
ISSN: 0733-558X/doi:10.1108/S0733-558X20160000046013

on students, on the career services profession, and on college-to-work pathways.

Keywords: Corporate partnership programs; commercialization of higher education; student career formation; campus corporate recruiting; career services centers; occupational stratification

Over the past several years, scholars have documented the unmistakable shift toward commercialization in colleges and universities (Bok, 2003; Morphew & Eckel, 2009; Slaughter & Rhoades, 2009). This adoption of a more corporatized logic — in the sense of coming to see parts of the university in terms of their contribution to the bottom line, rather than to some non-financial mission of the university — has occurred on multiple fronts. Campuses sell academic research to companies, curriculum to students, as well as a variety of other products and services originating from units across campus.

A new and growing formulation, which we explore in this paper, is universities' increasingly common view of students as a product for sale to prospective employers. Such is the case with corporate partnership programs, or CPPs. Since the early 2000s, CPPs have proliferated in university career centers, particularly on campuses with significant academic science profiles. Sharing several features of the Industrial Affiliates Programs first studied by Berman (2012), CPPs are an organizational form that serve as a type of headhunting agency, selling access to students to corporate hiring departments that are willing to pay universities' set annual fees. This creates semi-exclusive hiring arrangements between a university and its corporate partners — a new model that is at odds with the decades-long professional orientation of career centers. Whereas career centers have traditionally been student-focused, providing career counseling and job search skills for students to lead their own job searches, CPPs attempt to directly deliver students to a small portfolio of companies willing to pay rents to the career center. This commercialization of practice is in tension with the student-development model of traditional career counselors.

In this study we use a mix of methods. First, by searching the internet and contacting career centers, we track the spread of CPPs nationwide.

Then, using an inhabited institutionalism approach, we employ field observations and interviews to show how the two career services models differ and how career services staff on each side attempt to negotiate their competing roles in the multiversity environment – particularly as the CPP model continues to expand.

CPPs bring benefits to their host campuses (e.g., revenue, social capital with firms, streamlined hiring processes), but if left unchecked, CPPs also have the potential to increase inequality across campuses by fixing hiring opportunities reflective of campus/firm agreements. Students from campuses lacking such an arrangement may find their job applications locked out of preferred candidate pools. CPPs may also create additional hurdles for startups, non-profits, and smaller firms by providing a small handful of elite companies – willing to pay CPP fees – with privileged access to top student talent.

LITERATURE

Higher Education's Evolving Commercialization

In her book *Creating the Market University*, Berman (2012) charts the multi-decades process by which research university administrators and faculty increasingly have treated academic science as a product for economic gain. This change in orientation toward science has been accomplished largely through deregulation via the Bayh-Dole Act of 1980, which allowed universities to patent inventions made through federal funding. In her account, Berman notes that faculty entrepreneurship quickly exploded, aided by the creation of tech-transfer offices on university campuses, as well as through university industry research centers. Colyvas and Powell (2007) show the growing institutionalization of scientific entrepreneurism among faculty at Stanford University over many decades – a sort of ground zero for the phenomenon. They quote a faculty member stating that to be considered a successful faculty member at Stanford today, it is an unwritten rule that one must start a company (p. 255). Rhoten and Powell (2010) map the shift of the U.S. university from being centrally land grant institutions, to federal grant-dependent, to being fundamentally patent-granting institutions.

Commercialization processes have taken place by somewhat different strategies on teaching-centered campuses. Brint and Karabel (1989)

illustrate how community college leaders, over several decades, have voca-
tionalized their curriculum to serve the needs of the local labor force.
Kraatz and Zajac's (1996) survey of 600 four-year private liberal arts
colleges shows how students, beginning in the 1970s, gradually replaced
a largely humanistic set of values with utilitarian drives for financial
success. They also demonstrate how colleges reacted: Nearly all of the
colleges in Kraatz and Zajac's sample professionalized their curricula in
response to student consumers – in large part, through the creation of
new majors more clearly linked to vocational pathways than to the liberal
arts and sciences. In a later paper, Kraatz, Ventresca, and Deng (2010)
map the emergence of the enrollment management office, which unites
admissions and financial aid into the same unit. Although this is a
seemingly prosaic organizational form, tying admissions and financial aid
to one another changes the logic of admissions from a need-blind search
for academic potential, to one that makes admissions decisions with the
additional motive of ensuring that each new cohort can afford rising
tuition rates. Davis (2016) and Kezar (2010, 2012) summarize the
literature on the shift toward the use of contingent faculty labor, a
practice that is more pronounced on teaching campuses and which erodes
the power of faculty to resist various types of commercialization.

What is more, the trend toward the commercialization of higher education is not confined to the United States; international examples abound
(see collection by Brown, 2011). For example, studies range from animating
students' expectations on the career return from their degree in the United
Kingdom (Molesworth, Nixon, & Scullion, 2009) to undergirding administrators' bottom-line conscious practices in Kenya (Munene, 2007). One text
(Brown & Carasso, 2013) has the telling title, "*Everything for Sale?*" Even
business scholars have identified the trend as amounting to an international
"ethical crisis" (Natale & Doran, 2011). While we are agnostic on the mor-
ality of the shift, what is clear is that this growing commercialized logic is
not just a local phenomenon.

Commercialization of the university takes place in multiple forms.
Slaughter and Rhoades (2009) illustrate this well, from the patents and
copyrights discussed above, to interlocking boards between campuses
and firms, to sports contracts and trademarks, to educational markets, and
more. Corporate partnership programs represent yet another evolution in
the spreading commercialization across units of the university. Table 1
gives examples of these logics and the organizational features that typify
them. As seen on the table, selling students to corporations is the logic
embodied by CPPs.

Table 1. Example Formations of University Commercialization Logics.

Logic	Product	Consumer	Organizational Examples	Example Scholarship
I.	Scientific research	Corporations	Tech-transfer offices; industry affiliate programs	Berman (2012)
II.	Curriculum	Students	Vocational and professional programs; enrollment management departments	Brint and Karabel (1989), Kraatz et al. (2010)
III.	Services	Community	Event ticket sales	Kahn (2007)
IV.	Curriculum	Corporations	Corporate universities	Rademakers (2014)
V.	Students	Corporations	Corporate partnership Programs	*Present Study*

Multiversities: Home to Multiple (and Competing) Organizational Logics and Forms

While the move toward a logic of greater commercialization in higher education has taken root as an organizational realignment in a range of college and university settings, its emergence does not mean that it has simply replaced all other possible organizational logics. Faculty continue to create knowledge for knowledge's sake and for the social good, and students continue to be educated in areas designed to both create more beauty and lead them to become better citizens. Indeed, no formal organizational system is home to one all-encompassing organizational logic. Most – perhaps all – large organizational settings contain competing ideologies, values, interests, and mythologies (Hallett & Ventresca, 2006). While early statements of new institutional theory – the dominant contemporary approach to organizational theory – generally favored a picture of a single hegemonic cultural script dominating action within an institutional field, today's scholars working in the tradition acknowledge multiplicity in organizational ideologies (Scott, 2015). Some logics may be dominant in an organizational setting while others are submerged (Binder & Wood, 2013; Bok, 2013; Eliasoph & Lichterman, 2003), but each of these logics has the potential to drive action. Different units within universities, and stakeholders both on and off campus, emphasize various missions differently. More than 50 years ago, Clark Kerr famously coined the term *multiversity* to refer to the varied and conflicting interests in this "inconsistent institution" (2001 [1963], p. 14).

Scholars often have viewed such competing ideologies to be a net negative, since the presence of multiple logics threatens to lead to fragmentation (Hallett, 2010; Kraatz et al., 2010). Yet inasmuch as competing ideologies may have harmful effects, some scholars have come to recognize their potential positive consequences. Kraatz and Block (2008) show that "institutional pluralism," or the situation in which competing logics or missions/mythologies co-exist, may improve an organization's legitimacy claims and, therefore, survival. Organizations that successfully embody multiple values to a varied set of stakeholders may appear to be more legitimate than are organizations that embody only one logic. A university that is successful at both teaching and research, for example, may obtain greater legitimacy among its varied stakeholders. Or, in the case of this paper, a career center that can pursue multiple types of activities and goals – delivering students to corporate portfolios *and*, more traditionally, helping them craft their own career goals – may have improved results.

Yet while many logics may exist on a given campus or in a given unit (and the claim of greater survivability is an empirical question), we should not expect organizational actors to hold each cultural logic equally or statically (Binder, 2007; Hallett & Ventresca, 2006). Scott (2015) describes universities as "layered and multiplex affairs, containing both dominant forms and challenging actors, shared and contested values" (p. 38). Organizational actors do not embrace new forms seamlessly, without contestation. When deinstitutionalization of logics occurs – when the legitimacy of one organizational practice erodes, and another stands to gain (Oliver, 1992) – actors experience considerable turmoil (Hallett, 2010). Oliver outlines the conditions under which such a process is likely to take place – from increased external scrutiny, to shifting sources of funding, to changing consumer preferences. These are precisely the conditions that traditional career services offices have faced in the past decade. Out of such conditions, CPPs have arisen.

Rise and Spread of Corporate Partnership Programs

The corporate partnership programs we study in this paper are one of the newest organizational features in the rapidly commercializing American higher education system. In initial interviews for this project, we discovered that CPPs were created just a decade ago, with the first of them established at Stanford in 2003. These programs do not share uniform nomenclature across campuses: Multiple titles exist, usually starting with "corporate" or "industry," and they also include terms such as partnerships, alliance, ventures, engagement, outreach, and networks. CPPs are located in centralized university career centers at both private and public universities, and function to connect corporate clients to a campus's students and recent graduates by creating structured recruitment networks. Whereas the field of career services traditionally has been oriented to helping students develop their individual pathways through college and beyond (Rayman, 1999), today, an increasing segment of career service units on campus are oriented to forging partnerships with corporate firms. This is not wholly unlike structured recruitment processes that have existed for the past three decades on Ivy League campuses geared toward finance and consulting sectors (Ho, 2009; Rivera, 2011), but CPPs introduce practices that are more routinized and widespread than what has previously been documented for a small number of professions.

The existing campus feature that CPPs most closely resemble are Industrial Affiliate Programs (IAPs), found almost exclusively in engineering and applied science departments at research universities, and which sprang up on campuses shortly after World War II. As Berman (2012) illustrates, university staff in IAPs charge fees to corporations in exchange for a collection of services in return – chiefly, various access points to faculty research. IAPs – such as those at Stanford, MIT, Caltech, and the University of Pennsylvania – are able to consistently draw large annual fees (regularly in the tens-of-thousands of dollars annually per client) from their industry affiliates, while many of these schools' competitors have a much more difficult time making connections with corporate firms. After their initial emergence, IAPs subsequently plateaued, but thanks to the increased corporate investment in research following the Bayh-Dole Act, the prominence of IAPs grew once again, well into the 1990s when Berman's historical account ends. IAPs are alive and well today, still almost exclusively found in STEM disciplines, and at institutions with strong tech-transfer practices.

CPPs adopt many features of the IAP model; indeed, the services are so similar that specialists in both areas share a single professional organization, the Network of Academic Corporate Relations Officers, or NACRO, founded in 2006. But whereas IAPs have a research-based focus in specific applied academic departments, CPPs direct their activity to a hiring-based focus in centralized university career centers – predominantly, though not exclusively, trying to place undergraduates.

CPP staff members are tasked with coming up with as many ways as possible to turn functions of the university into products or services. These bundles of services typically come with a "menu," complete with a tiered set of purchase plans available to firms. Most of the menus offer one-to-two dozen services, with streamlined access to student hiring as the chief service. For lesser-known companies, the services include strategies to establish greater brand presence on campus, in hopes of making the company a highly prized work destination for students from that school. This could include simple things such as preferential placement at career fairs or various logo-placements around campus, to more complex strategies such as hosted events or companies' direct access to specific student clubs. Other firms may be more interested in introductions to faculty and researchers which CPP staff can help facilitate, or access to campus facilities or equipment they may find useful.

While surveying the offerings of a single CPP is fairly simple (since most programs have an online presence), information concerning their origin, spread, and potential contestation within career services offices is not as readily available. What does the adoption pattern of this organizational form look like, and to which campuses have CPPs spread? How do career services staff members understand and navigate this new organizational form? Do multiple internal logics compete within career services units that have CPPs, and if so, which logic dominates under current conditions of the commercializing university? As commercialization processes are met with evolving forms of rationalization across various organizational subunits, what happens to staff who do not embrace the "new normal": How do they negotiate and make meaning out of potentially conflicting tasks? In the sections below, we address these questions in turn.

DATA AND METHODS

To map the origins and adoption patterns of CPPs in universities across the country, we initially inventoried the 60 U.S. campuses in the prestigious, invitation-only Association of American Universities (AAU). The AAU represents a clearly defined sample of leading higher education institutions across the United States, all of which fit the multiversity model.[1] In most cases, an in-depth review of the career services website of AAU members was enough to determine whether a campus had a CPP or not. If it did, the website often included a copy of the "menu" of buy-in options and, frequently, a list of current corporate partners. In a few cases, we could not verify the presence of a CPP on a given campus, and we sent emails to the career centers to inquire.

As shown in Table 2, we found that of the 60 AAU campuses in the United States, 33, or 55 percent, have a CPP. Of the 33 campuses across the country with a CPP, 23 of them list their corporate partners publicly.

Table 2. AAU Campuses with CPPs in Their Career Centers, 2014.

Region	Campuses	Number (%) with CPP	Campuses with CPPs	Campuses without CPPs
West	13	11 (85%)	Stanford, USC, U of Arizona, U of Colorado-Boulder, U of Washington, U of Oregon, UC Berkeley, UCSB, UCLA, UCI, UCSD	UC Davis, Caltech
Midwest	16	6 (38%)	U of Kansas, U of Iowa, Washington U-St. Louis, Purdue, Northwestern, Case Western Reserve	U of Minnesota-Twin Cities, Iowa State, U of Missouri-Columbia, U of Chicago, U of Illinois-Urbana Champaign, U of Wisconsin-Madison, Indiana U, Ohio State, Michigan State, U of Michigan
South	13	8 (62%)	Texas A&M, U of Florida, Tulane, Georgia IT, Emory, U of North Carolina-Chapel Hill, U of Maryland-College Park, U of Virginia	U of Texas-Austin, Rice, Vanderbilt, Duke, Johns Hopkins
Northeast	18	8 (44%)	Carnegie Mellon, U of Pittsburgh, U of Rochester, Rutgers, New York U, Stonybrook U SUNY, MIT, Brandeis	U of Buffalo SUNY, Cornell, Pennsylvania State, U of Pennsylvania, Princeton, Columbia, Yale, Brown, Harvard, Boston

Fig. 1 is a network visualization of these campuses and their corporate partners. As depicted in this figure, low network density is due to the fact that most of the companies have only one or two campus partners, indicating semi-exclusive arrangements. Very few companies have a strategy of partnering with multiple campuses across the country. Most firms appear to have hiring needs that can be satisfied via structured relationships with only one or a few core campuses.

Table 2 indicates that the concentration of CPPs is densest in California, with all but two of the state's AAU-affiliated universities having already

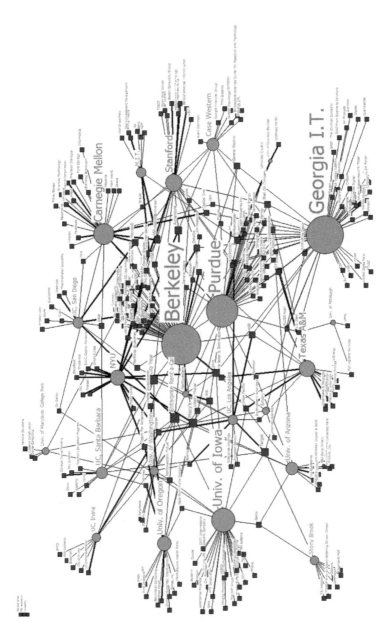

Fig. 1. AAU Campuses (Circles) and Their Corporate Partners (Squares); Top Tier Partnerships (Thick Lines), Lower Tier Partners (Thin Lines).

established a program. Due to this density and the fact that our initial research revealed that the first CPP emerged at Stanford, we decided to make California the focus of this study. We were interested to find out whether CPPs are located predominantly in Research 1 universities (such as those included in the AAU) or if they had spread to lower tier campuses across the state, as well.

To minimize variation in institution types, we focused exclusively on four-year non-profit colleges in California, both public and private, which offer comprehensive undergraduate programs. Thus, we excluded campuses with more narrow offerings, such as UC San Francisco (a medical campus) and the California Institute of Technology (a highly specialized science and engineering campus). Each of the campuses falls into one of three mutually exclusive groups: the public, highly selective University of California system (such as UC Berkeley and UC Santa Barbara); the public, less selective California State University system (such as Cal State Long Beach and San Francisco State), or the private Association of Independent California Colleges and Universities (AICCU) which represents both highly selective and less selective private institutions. Use of the AICCU allowed us to exclude the hundreds of vocational academies in the state, which often bill themselves as colleges. All AICCU campuses are regionally accredited, non-profit, and degree granting.

Of the private AICCU campuses that met our criteria, two are clear multiversities (Stanford and the University of Southern California), 21 are non-sectarian liberal arts campuses (for example, Claremont McKenna and Soka), and 30 are religiously affiliated liberal arts campuses (such as the University of San Francisco and Pepperdine). This left us with four categories to examine for organizational density of CPPs: 10 multiversities (the eight comprehensive UCs, plus USC and Stanford), all 23 CSUs, 21 liberal-arts campuses, and 30 religiously affiliated campuses. Fig. 2 shows the percent of campuses that have CPPs for each of these institutional types.

As seen in Fig. 2, 9 of the 10 top-tier research universities in California that include comprehensive undergraduate programs have built a CPP. UC Davis is the sole University of California campus without one. In an email exchange to understand the reasoning for not having a program at UC Davis, we learned from a staff member that the career center is currently in the process of planning for the launch of a program. Thus the UC Davis campus is more a late adopter than a negative case. But even if campus leaders do not establish a CPP at Davis, there is still a 90 percent saturation of CPPs among the top-tier multiversities in California.

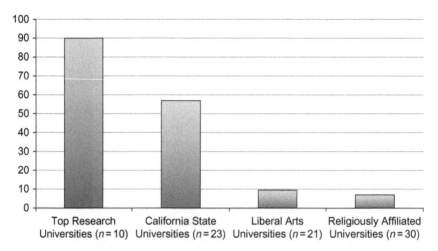

Fig. 2.   Organizational Density of CPPs in CA: From "Multiversities" to Liberal
Arts Campuses, Number and Percentage.

Private liberal arts campuses show an equally strong – albeit opposite –
pattern. Among the 30 religiously affiliated liberal arts campuses in the
AICCU, only two campuses (6.7 percent) have a CPP. Among the 21 non-
sectarian private liberal arts colleges, again, only two campuses (9.5 percent)
have a CPP. Of the 23 California State University campuses the outcome
was split, with 13 campuses (56.5 percent) having CPPs.

As these findings show, CPPs are not being adopted uniformly across
regions of the country, nor by type of institution. They have a greater organizational density in the West, and are most common in large, decentralized, research-oriented multiversities. As Table 2 indicates, many of the
Northeast Ivies do not have CPPs, perhaps because their historically structured recruiting practices have functioned in parallel ways without the
more explicit programing. Thus the greater isomorphic density of the
feature in the West, driven by Stanford's lead and the near-uniformity of
the UC system, makes California an ideal target region for understanding
this phenomenon at a qualitative level.

Fieldwork in Career Services Offices

In addition to exploring where and in what types of institutions CPPs
have een adopted, we wanted to understand how ground-level staff and

Table 3. Summary of Interviews and Field Observation at Each Site.

	Interviews – CPP Staff and Related Administrators	Interviews – Career Counselors/ Advisors	Interviews – Students and Alumni[a]	Field Observations
UC Public University	5	3	3	Approx. 50 hours
Elite Private University	7	4	29	Approx. 5 hours
Campuses without a CPP	0	4	0	0
Total	12	11	32	Approx. 55 hours

[a]Alumni are all within two years post-graduation.

administrators make sense of these programs and negotiate between the traditional logic of career services and the rationalized commercial logic of corporate partnerships. We selected two California campuses as case study sites, both of which are members of the AAU and are among the universities with the most highly established CPPs. Our two campuses – with pseudonyms – are UC Public University and Elite Private University. We conducted a total of 23 university staff interviews at these two universities, including traditional career counseling staff, staff affiliated with the CPPs, and with administrators having oversight of student career-guidance functions. The data from the two case study campuses come from a mix of interviewing and field observations. However, more extensive field observations were made at UC Public University in the Career Services Center office and at career-related student events, which gave us insights to guide more streamlined data collection at Elite Private University, where we also conducted additional student interviews. See Table 3 for a breakdown of interviews and field observations across each site.

At UC Public University, during Spring and Summer 2014, we conducted more than 50 hours of field observations and unstructured interviews in the career center office, at career center activities (such as career fairs and workshops), and with student recipients of career counseling. We then conducted eight additional semi-structured interviews, split between traditional career counselors and CPP staff. We also conducted three very recent alumni interviews. Observations of the CPP staff included listening to sales calls to prospective companies, a review of "pitch materials" (including slide shows and printed items to give to potential corporate clients), observing "brag boards" (where staff progress in recruiting companies is charted), attending a monthly team meeting, review of new staff training materials, discussion of logarithms used to pick prospective companies to go after, and so on. We typed up field notes immediately after leaving the field. We recorded most interviews, but when recording permission was not granted, we relied on hand-written note-taking.

At Elite Private University, during Summer and Fall 2014, we conducted 11 semi-structured interviews with relevant staff, faculty, and administrators in and out of the career center. These interviews were conducted in both face-to-face settings and over the phone. We conducted another 20 student and 9 recent alumni/ae interviews at Elite Private University as part of a larger project, which included information regarding the use of the career center and other career advising services. While the scope of this paper is focused more on campus staff than on students, the student perspectives were useful to confirm the impact of the various programming efforts discussed in this paper on the development of their career choices. All interviews were recorded, transcribed, and reviewed for patterns.

Our two case study campuses have many features in common, especially their Carnegie Classification as RU/VH, or Research Universities with Very High annual research output. Both engage in significant tech-transfer activities and both have industry affiliate programs. Both have comprehensive undergraduate programs with many thousand students. For the purposes of this study, their similarities are more pronounced than their differences. However, the status of one campus as private and the other as public shows that the logic of the CPP has diffused across the private/public divide in highly selective universities in similar ways.

Finally, we purposively selected four interviews at universities without CPPs (two public, two private), to better understand why some career centers have chosen not to build a CPP. These interviews were also useful for getting counter perspectives on the CPP model. This was particularly important since the non-CPP career center staff in our two primary cases — mostly career counselors — were reluctant to talk freely about their views of the CPPs that had sprung up on their campuses, and access to additional interviews was limited. This was understandable, as interviews with career center directors revealed that previous staff had been replaced when they resisted the CPP model inside the career center. We will cover this finding in a later section.

FINDINGS

We discuss our field observations in two major thrusts. First is how CPPs further advance a commercialized logic in higher education. We discuss this, initially, as a feature of their isomorphic similarities to IAPs, and then in the way they bundle services and students to sell to their corporate partners in hopes of becoming "core" campuses to those corporations. Next, we show how CPP staff and more traditional career counselors co-inhabit career services centers and must navigate the professional tensions that exist between them.

Isomorphic IAP and CPP Features

Organizational innovation does not take place in a cultural vacuum but, rather, reassembles existing cultural resources in new ways (Becker & Knudsen, 2009; Sewell, 1992). As gleaned from our interviews, staff in CPPs draw on organizational logics from other campus departments, such as modes of recruitment from human resources departments, multi-tiered buy-in levels from advancement offices, and alumni tracking in targeted prospective companies from alumni associations. This was highlighted by the fact that many of our interviewees working in CPPs had professional backgrounds in one or more of these fields. Others had sales backgrounds outside of academia.

But the organizational form that CPPs most closely resemble is that of Industry Affiliate Programs (IAPs), which exist primarily on campuses engaged in large amounts of tech-transfer activities around academic science. At institutions best positioned to capitalize on academic science, tech-transfer offices are of central importance (Berman, 2012). Between 1980 and 2000, alone, the number of patents assigned to American universities increased "more than 850 percent" (Powell & Owen-Smith, 2002, p. 109) and have continued to proliferate. Both of our case study campuses are highly engaged in the economics of academic science. During a field observation at a science-geared career event hosted by an IAP at UC Public University, an executive-level administrator told a group of students that undergraduate education was only 11 percent of the university's overall budget, dwarfed by the amount spent on research, which is "the real business of the university" (Sal, Administrator, UC Public University). Elite Private University's engineering department alone boasts over

30 separate IAPs. One of its most popular IAPs, which we have given the pseudonym Technology Agora, lists nearly 115 corporate partners in Fall 2014. Each corporate partner pays more than $20,000 annually to partici- pate, a sum nearing $2.5 million – going to a single academic department.

We identify a link between these two features. Where a significant amount of tech transfer has taken place, competition can be fierce for access to university patents. IAPs create strategic advantages for client companies. Where IAPs exist, their cousin feature, CPPs, are less culturally anomalous to the campus as a whole. IAPs act as a precedent-setting orga- nizational form, perhaps explaining why CPPs originated in, and dominate on, RU/VH campuses. Furthermore, the career center-based corporate relations officers who work in CPPs have jobs that are similar to the corpo- rate relations officers who work in IAPs.

The half-dozen CPP staff at UC Public are organized by industry sectors and related majors, such as biotechnology, computer science, finance, and non-profit sectors. At Elite Private, five staff have explicit roles dedicated to building corporate relationships around the corporate partnership pro- gram, and multiple others have indirect roles at cultivating networks with employers and alumni. The designated team members are also broken into broad industry areas: entertainment, startups, business and consulting, STEM, and healthcare professions. Within the industry area to which designated staff members are assigned, they must target and attempt to recruit partner companies in their sector. These staff must be knowledge- able about various faculty, programs, clubs, and research on campus relevant to their sector, since a major part of their service is to offer introductions and access to resources that corporate clients may be inter- ested in. Having first access to university patents is a privilege with signifi- cant consequences in quickly evolving fields like high tech and bio-tech. One CPP staff member at UC Public, named Kenton, whom we were able to shadow at the career center said, "If [our corporate partner] gets first access to a new technology, they have market advantage, and that can mean so much more [than the cost of paying our fee]."

In addition, on both campuses, CPP staff are well aware of the work going on in the multiple IAPs around campus. While individual IAPs are designed to focus on specific departments, the CPP program as a whole attempts to represent the entire student body. CPP staff sometimes call meetings with various IAP staff members to coordinate which corporate entities each unit is actively soliciting, as they can easily find themselves try- ing to seek annual fees from the same companies. One CPP staff member at UC Public University said, "If [Company X] wants to go with [IAP Y] that's fine; it may be better for them if they just want that one type of student. But I am trying to help [Company X] understand that I am the gateway for hiring access to *all* of our students of *all* kinds. And I can just offer them more" (Ricky, UC Public, Corporate Relations Officer).

Conflict apparently does occasionally break out over IAP and CPP juris-diction, as illustrated by a phone call we made to a Midwestern university to ask why its career center no longer has a CPP. This interviewee told us that there had been tension between corporate relations staff in the CPP and corporate relations staff in a high-grossing IAP, both soliciting some of the same companies. When the career center director subsequently left, for reasons our interviewee did not state, the CPP was suspended until the new director could determine how to negotiate the impasse.

While there is an overarching logic governing CPP practice, there is variability in how staff members get the job done, depending on their assigned industry sector. A notable difference in role existed for one CPP staff member at UC Public who was tasked with developing the non-profit and public sector network. The majors she most commonly tries to place hail from departments that do not have IAPs. As a result, she reported that she enjoys some advantages because "I don't have to worry about any red tape" — meaning she does not have to worry about negotiating with IAPs for prerogative, unlike her colleagues working with bio-tech and computer science companies. But at the same time, she said, "It cuts both ways, because it can be a challenge to decide who to go after. It's wide open, [since] there's not always obvious employers to link up with who need another psychology student" (Lauren, UC Public). Thus, while CPPs are similar to IAPs in many ways, borrowing from their repertoire of activities, the broader focus of CPPs on getting students of *all types* placed is a key distinguishing feature.

Becoming Core and Bundling "Non-Specialty" Students

In much the same way that Rivera's study of elite law, banking, and consulting firms reveals preferential hiring from "core" and "target" uni-versities (Rivera, 2011, 2015), CPP staff also distinguish between different types of relationships with employers. These labels are so well recognized, in fact, that one staff member corrected his interviewer's use of the terms by saying, "No, we are not trying to make Microsoft a core company *to us*. We are trying to become a core university *to them*" (Kenton, UC Public). Staff like Kenton described a "target" university as one where a company has an existing relationship with the university, and/or maybe a lower tier corporate partnership with the career center. But typically, that company is only looking for "specialties," or a certain type of student on campus, for example, chemical engineering majors. When a university is a target university for a particular corporation, there is typically a history of hiring by that corporation, and several well-placed alumni advocates within the corporation. Being a target is good, however the real goal is to become a core university.

Core status is achieved when the company not only hires specialties, or students with specific technical expertise (which may have drawn the corporation to the campus in the first place), but when the company also agrees to hire "talent" (students) whom CPP staff refer to as "non-specialty." Non-specialty students work in the units of the company requiring less scientific expertise, such as business development, management, accounting, human resources, or marketing and advertising. Employers can seek such employees elsewhere, of course, but because of the university's achieved core status, the company focuses its hiring – for all majors, in all of the firm's divisions – on the partner campus. Kenton, of UC Public University, continued his earlier thought and said, "When they hire non-specialty, it shows their loyalty to our campus."

This bundling of students is an important way to increase student recruitment beyond just specific niche areas. It is also seen as a good way to increase hiring of the harder-to-place humanities and social science students. Teri, from Elite Private University, said that her school's CPP was "lending a helping hand to the humanities" by "increasing the employment chances of philosophers and artists" (Teri, Elite Private). Although CPP staff on both campuses say they celebrate students who pursue less obviously employable majors, they also are faced with a more daunting task to place them. They believe that such students enjoy better opportunities because of their office's cultivation of strong alumni networks with key companies. Jane, responsible for recruiting companies that will hire social science students at UC Public said, "Even the psychology majors get preferential hiring at say, [Company Y]" because those students "happen to be from one of the core universities where [Company Y] goes for their electrical engineers" (Jane, UC Public).

Granting access to student clubs to CPP corporate clients is an additional common form of bundling students for companies. In one section of a PowerPoint slideshow designed for potential corporate clients, CPP staff demonstrated how their office can help companies strategize the best way to reach students in clubs, such as through visits, hosted events, guest speaking, and résumé drops. The slideshow − customized to each company − includes a slide listing the number of clubs that could be relevant to the employer. In one case we observed, the potential client was a bank, and CPP staff had identified 48 out of the more than 500 campus clubs that the bank might be interested in. Not only were economics and finance-related clubs under consideration, as might be expected, but also ethnic and gender based clubs − none directly related to finance. The UC Public staff member presenting the slides explained that companies sometimes have a hard time balancing their diversity ratios. To help, he was offering the bank access to clubs such as the Society of Women Engineers (SWE), the Society of Black Engineers (SBE), and the Society of Hispanic Professional Engineers (SHPE). Though the students in these clubs were probably engineering majors, Kenton told the bank it would likely be successful at attracting some of them to his sector if it offered junior-year paid internships that could be converted to job offers early in students' senior year.

Additionally, when we posed the question of why companies are willing to pay annual fees for customized and streamlined recruiting services when they might just hire through their own HR offices, one team member opened the PowerPoint slide used to pitch clients who asked the same question. The slide contained data from the 2012 Recruiting Benchmarks Survey, by NACE (National Association of Colleges and Employers). It showed how much the average company spends to recruit one person, by size-of-company, ranging from $7,645.28 (for a company with fewer than 500 employees) to $2,885.68 (for a company with 20,000 + employees). The slide, titled "ROI on Partnership," was the part of the pitch presentation used by CPP staff to explain why it was cheaper for companies to do the majority of their hiring from the university rather than through other channels. Because they were a "one-stop recruiting shop," they could lower firms' cost per hire, effectively "paying back" the company in savings, the costs of the annual partnership fee (James, UC Public). The more they hired from the campus, the higher their annual savings by outsourcing many features of their hiring process to the university career center. Several of our interviewees explained that this was just the tip of the iceberg, because if their efforts and connections also helped a company get first access to cutting-edge research, it could mean untold amounts in gains with a new product to market, plus the prestige of being associated with the university.

In short, CPP staff are committed to helping corporate clients get whatever potential hires, or introductions across campus, they need. This bundle of services then provides an incentive to the corporate partner to hire a bundle of students – specialty and non-specialty alike – thereby making the university a core campus. This effort to become core, which is the chief work of CPP staff, is significantly different than the role of the career counselors who also work in the career center.

Career Services Mission Contested: Tension between CPP Staff and Career Counselors

In addition to support staff, events coordinators, and administrators, career centers on our case study campuses are divided into two main groups of staff: CPP staff and career counselors. Professionally and ideologically, there are divisions between these two groups of staff members. At UC Public, where we conducted field observations, even the architecture of the building reflects the separation of these two groups. The first floor houses the career counselors, a workshop room, a student resource library, and peer counselors (students on work-study, well-versed in career center resources). The second floor houses the CPP staff, corporate-sponsored interview rooms with prominent corporate logos, and the brag-board where news of progress on key metrics is posted (such as new companies that have joined the CPP, or existing partners making a significant batch of recent hires). The administrative offices for the career center and alumni outreach office are also on the second floor, as well as a large digital screen rotating the logos of unit's corporate partners. Various support staff and event staff are distributed between both floors. Each floor also includes a separate front desk and reception area. This physical separation creates a sense of distance between the two groups, with the salutary effect of minimizing tensions as staff operate with largely different logics and reward structures in day-to-day practice, but with the potentially negative effect of prioritizing one group over the other. The first floor is the domain of students and counselors; the second floor, the domain of administrators, fundraisers, and corporate relations officers (i.e., the CPP staff). Both campuses have a greater number of career counselors than corporate relations officers, but the number is nearing parity with additional hires on the horizon, according to our interviewees.

When asked to describe the activities of his CPP staff, the director of the career center at UC Public University expressed great enthusiasm:

> What's different and innovative about this place is that we've now taken that whole function of alumni outreach, taken that model, and brought it into the employee

relations realm where, instead of being a career services center that's just reactionary to the employers that are coming in − which is the place that we've been probably since the center was founded − we are now staffing to the place where we're dictating who our portfolio companies are going to be. Who do we want recruiting our students? And equipping an outbound team to go get those companies to come in. (James, UC Public University)

As can be seen in this quote, the career services director draws a bright line between what is new and exciting in his world on campus (creating more entrepreneurial ties to the local, regional, and national labor market) versus what is old school and passé (traditional logics governing career services).

Elite Private University administrators show similar pride in their sense of innovation, relative to traditional career services practices. The director of the career services center named a handful of campuses making similar changes, and shared his desire to inspire still more universities to adopt the model:

[Private Elite] is really on the cusp of just completely changing the field. I care deeply about our field of career services being elevated to a newer level .... We're no longer in a straight-out counseling model, and many universities still have that .... Maybe it will give them the wakeup call that they have to change. Otherwise they're going to be a dinosaur, if they're not already. (Pierre, Elite Private)

To this administrator, a campus that does not embrace the CPP model is outdated. Several lower level CPP staff at both institutions expressed similar ideas. They see their work as creatively responding to various needs the campus faces. One CPP staff member at UC Public University added that her work helped assuage parents' concerns around high unemployment rates in the wake of the recent recession, because "if a parent calls, we can point them to our list of [employer] partners who have made a real commitment to hiring students just like their kid" (Jane, UC Public). CPP staff point to one other benefit of their model. Fiscally, they say, the CPP adds additional revenue annually, but it is also an act of cultivation of *future* potential alumni donors. James (UC Public) explained that when students get jobs under the old model, they feel that they landed it personally, "despite" the university. But if the university largely lands it for them through its network of CPP partner firms, students feel that their professional success was launched "because" of the university − inspiring longer-lasting positive regard for the campus.

Not all career center staff view the CPP model with equally positive lenses. The career centers at both of our case study schools house career counselors who remain committed to the traditional mission of developing students to conduct their own job searches. These staff members − whose numbers are decreasing on each of our campuses — are not convinced by the new emphasis on corporate clients, and they worry that the CPP model is connected to an economic development philosophy that favors market-place rewards, rather than the holistic student-development model into which they were professionalized.

This distinction is real on both of our case study campuses. One counselor at UC Public emphasized, "We are not just trying to help them find jobs when they graduate, but to know themselves and uncover their own passions and strengths so they can investigate multiple careers over their lifespan" (Kim, Career Counselor, UC Public). Kim went on to say that while innovations are needed, they would be better focused on new delivery models of student advising — such as more group counseling. At Elite Private, Nancy, a long-term career counselor shared innovative ideas she thought would be useful, among them an expanded mentoring program so that students can try out a series of different fields early on. Another is the use of automated technologies to help the career center send individualized communications to students, in hopes of staying in better contact with them through their time on campus. She reported that she is pleased that her office had begun a program to meet with students in their residence halls. Each of her ideas for career center changes clearly center on student development, rather than corporate cultivation.

In keeping with these quotes, staff who hold to the more traditional model of career counseling on our case study campuses expressed skepticism about developing more structured corporate ties, but were careful not to overtly criticize CPPs. This is in contrast with far more derisive staff on other campuses without CPPs, who charged that the CPP model turns career services into "wind-up, coin-operated vending machines" (Kelley, Career Services Director, liberal arts Catholic University). Kelley believes that the reward structure of CPPs on other campuses lead career centers to place too much emphasis on large companies that can afford the fees, to the detriment to student career opportunities at smaller firms. Another career center staff member at a public university without a CPP echoed the sentiment, saying her university would not want to "give unfair advantage to some companies over others" (Cameron, East Coast State University).

Despite the more careful tone of the counselors at our case study sites, this conflict has created considerable turmoil at both UC Public and Elite Private universities. Such conflict, though, seems to be subsiding as the CPP logic has largely won the day, thanks to administrator support. The career center directors acknowledge that the shift in organizational priorities threatens staff who continue to focus on the traditional student-development/counseling model. The director at UC Public University mentioned conversations he has had with other career center directors who realize that, "Trenches are being dug because there's fear of what will happen one way or the other" (James, UC Public). According to Elite Private University's career center director, these fears are not unfounded. He recounted:

> There are clearly some characters who are very resistant because they philosophically don't agree with the direction. And if that's the case, I mean if you can't convert them, then often what happens is they have to find another opportunity elsewhere where they can find that – philosophical alignment .... They are not bad people, but this model that we're creating is not for everyone .... (Pierre, Elite Private)

Pierre, himself, has fired multiple staff in the shake-up.

Career services professionals have been skeptical of the logic upon which the CPP model is based since the 1990s, when they warned in professional journals of the coming trend. Leaders cautioned that the model would tempt universities to both solicit corporate support to generate external funding (Rayman, 1999) and create programs that focus more attention on facilitating corporate recruitment of students than on preparing students to lead their own job searches (Wessel, 1998). Both of these practices were seen to detract from providing high quality, student-focused career services. Yet when packaged specifically as CPPs in the 2000s, echoing the cultural organizational form of IAPs, and driven by administrator support – especially after the recession – the model has been able to swiftly sweep into the field in the past 15 years. Nevertheless, it represents a point of contention between those who seek to conserve a focus on cultivating students' self-awareness of their strengths and professional desires, vocational curiosities, and job search skills, on the one side; and those who see a brighter future in cultivating networks of employer relationships. The second option entails becoming a target school for employers, or even better, a core university.

CONCLUSION

CPPs address multiple challenges faced by universities, chief among them to increase the employability of graduates and to subsidize the cost of career services through its own revenue generation. Secondarily, CPP staff see their programs as potentially increasing the confidence of parents when helping their children choose between schools, and potentially cultivating future alumni donors who as student job seekers may have benefited from CPP networks. At a day-to-day level, CPP staff are focused on tracking alumni leads to determine which companies to pursue and solicit, in hopes of becoming a core campus to them, with annual high-volume student recruitment. While this type of core-campus preferential hiring is nothing new to elite Ivy League schools and their peers, the CPP makes the process more explicit and rationalized in an attempt to bring the patterns of hiring preference down from the handful of most selective institutions to the next tier of elite school selectivity. There are advantages to the CPP model – including for students who are not in STEM fields – but dysfunctional consequences may arise from these arrangements as well.

Future scholarship on higher education will gain from investigating the ways that these commercially oriented CPPs are transforming the cultural understandings of the career services profession. Career services has long had a student-development emphasis, whereby staff use one-on-one counseling, assessment instruments, job fairs, and skills workshops to develop student self-awareness and ability to conduct their own job searches. The new corporatized model places the emphasis less on cultivating the student and more on cultivating university-company networks of alumni and hiring professionals. The old model is seen to fail students in times of higher unemployment or to reach students too late in their college careers to be of much help. The new model is still unproven in its effects, both manifest and latent. Both models have their strengths and weaknesses, but whether they ultimately prove to be contradictory philosophies or complementary supplements will be seen as the campus realignments continue to play out. While the two cases in our study are home to staff devoted to both models, the CPP model currently appears to be the dominant logic, in large part driven by the directors at each career center, with the explicit blessing of their respective campus presidents.

At UC Public University, career counselors are physically separated from CPP staff in the building where they worked; thus, most of the day-to-day negotiations over how to achieve their disparate goals are insulated from one other. At Elite Private University, multiple counselors resistant to the new model have been fired; simultaneously, a dozen new staff members at the time of this writing are in the process of being hired to further develop the CPP and employment networks.[2] While it is unlikely that the traditional career counselor job will disappear completely from either campus, professionals working under this model no longer enjoy the dominant perspective in the career services center unit in our two case studies. An inhabited institutionalist lens (Binder, 2007; Hallett & Ventresca, 2006) is useful for understanding these negotiations. Once top administrator support began to drive the change of the career center model, traditional career counselor opposition was largely tempered. As our data indicate, the remaining resistance appears more as ambivalence and faint praise of the changes. Some counselors show light subversion by trying to brainstorm new initiatives to show they are not out of date, but their changes focus on alternative delivery methods of counseling services to students and do not include links with corporate partners.

Further research could uncover if middle-tier institutions that adopt CPPs – such as the California State University campuses depicted in Fig. 2 – reap much reward, or if there is a carrying capacity that is exhausted by the leading universities, such as Berman (2012) found with IAPs. Are middle-tier university CPPs equally effective, even if perhaps more focused on localized markets, or is the adoption of the CPP feature primarily the result of mimetic isomorphism, imitating career centers perceived as more prestigious (DiMaggio & Powell, 1983), but achieving few actual results for students?

Researchers could also try to understand the effectiveness of CPPs at leading universities in terms of increasing actual rates of student employment. Do the corporate partnerships and semi-exclusive hiring pathways really shrink the percentage of students who graduate and cannot find work, all else being equal? Or alternately, does it result in restricting the number of companies students end up in, with more students funneled to corporate partners? In a similar vein, do CPPs significantly alter the type and size of employers the university most often engages with? CPP staff have clear incentives to go after larger firms with both the resources to pay annual fees and the likelihood of needing to make several hires per year. If CPP programs continue to grow and spread, they will need intentional efforts to attract smaller firms, startups, and non-profit organizations, or else they risk further privileging the already most resourced firms. For example, Elite Private University is attempting interventions such as a specialized startup career fair, a new nonprofit career fair, and has plans to pro-rate CPP fees by firm size. Further research should evaluate if such efforts effectively offset the risk of CPPs exacerbating unequal access to student talent in favor of a few elite companies. If so, similar best practices might be adopted by CPPs at other campuses.

Our research also has implications for college to work pathways. Sharone (2014) shows that U.S. job seekers, more than in other countries, tend to rely on characteristics outside of simple skill qualifications when seeking employment. CPPs potentially exacerbate this for right-out-of-college job placements. Elite firms in such fields as finance and consulting have long had semi-exclusive recruitment practices with the most elite colleges (Ho, 2009; Roose, 2014). Rivera (2011) shows that elite firms develop a short list of target and core schools, and that any who come from outside campuses are not considered as seriously, if they are considered at all. CPPs also appear to create semi-exclusive arrangements, as highlighted in Fig. 1, which may have the unfortunate effect of extending Rivera's findings to the next tier of campuses and companies. This has implications for reifying inequality if students who attend smaller liberal arts colleges or mid-tier state schools that lack CPPs cannot get their applications taken seriously by prospective employers of choice, for jobs for which they are otherwise well qualified.

NOTES

1. There are 62 AAU members, two of them in Canada. We included only member institutions in the United States.
2. This information is contained on the university's organizational chart.

ACKNOWLEDGMENTS

We are grateful to the Kauffman Foundation, the Spencer Foundation, and the University of California, San Diego for their generous support of this project. We would also like to thank John Skrentny and the participants of the UCSD Department of Sociology Practicum II class.

REFERENCES

Becker, M. C., & Knudsen, T. (2009). Schumpeter and the organization of entrepreneurship. In P. Adler *The Oxford handbook of sociology and organization studies: Classical foundations*. Oxford: Oxford University Press. doi:10.1093/oxfordhb/9780199535231.003.0014

Berman, E. P. (2012). *Creating the market university: How academic science became an economic engine*. Princeton, NJ: Princeton University Press.

Binder, A. (2007). For love and money: Organizations' creative responses to multiple environmental logics. *Theory and Society, 36*(6), 547–571.

Binder, A., & Wood, K. (2013). *Becoming right: How campuses shape young conservatives*. Princeton, NJ: Princeton University Press.

Bok, D. (2003). *Universities in the marketplace: The commercialization of higher education.* Princeton, NJ: Princeton University Press.

Bok, D. (2013). *Higher education in America.* Princeton, NJ: Princeton University Press.

Brint, S., & Karabel, J. (1989). *The diverted dream: Community colleges and the promise of educational opportunity in America, 1900–1985.* Oxford: Oxford University Press.

Brown, R. (Ed.). (2011). *Higher education and the market.* New York, NY: Routledge.

Brown, R., & Carasso, H. (2013). *Everything for sale? The marketisation of UK higher education.* New York, NY: Routledge.

Colyvas, J. A., & Powell, W. W. (2007). From vulnerable to venerated: The institutionalization of academic entrepreneurship in the life sciences. In M. Ruef & M. Lounsbury (Eds.), *The sociology of entrepreneurship* (Vol. 25, pp. 219–259). Research in the Sociology of Organizations. Bingley, UK: Emerald Group Publishing Limited.

Davis, D. (2016). *The adjunct dilemma.* Sterling, VA: Stylus.

DiMaggio, P. J., & Powell, W. W. (1983). The iron cage revisited: Institutional isomorphism and collective rationality in organizational fields. *American Sociological Review, 48*(2), 147–160.

Eliasoph, N., & Lichterman, P. (2003). Culture in interaction. *American Journal of Sociology, 108*, 735–794.

Hallett, T. (2010). The myth incarnate: Recoupling processes, turmoil, and inhabited institutions in an urban elementary school. *American Sociological Review, 75*(1), 52–74.

Hallett, T., & Ventresca, M. J. (2006). Inhabited institutions: Social interactions and organizational forms in Gouldner's patterns of industrial bureaucracy. *Theory and Society, 35*(2), 213–236.

Ho, K. (2009). *Liquidated: An ethnography of wall street.* Durham, NC: Duke University Press.

Kahn, L. M. (2007). Markets: Cartel behavior and amateurism in college sports. *The Journal of Economic Perspectives, 21*(1), 209–226.

Kerr, C. (2001 [1963]). *The uses of the university* (5th ed.). Cambridge, MA: Harvard University Press.

Kezar, A. (2012). *Embracing non-tenure track faculty: Changing campuses for the new faculty majority.* New York, NY: Routledge.

Kraatz, M., & Block, E. (2008). Organizational implications of institutional pluralism. In R. Greenwood, C. Oliver, R. Suddaby, & K. Sahlin (Eds.), *The SAGE handbook of organizational institutionalism* (pp. 243–276). London: Sage Publications.

Kraatz, M., Ventresca, M., & Deng, L. (2010). Precarious values and mundane innovations: Enrollment management in American liberal arts colleges. *Academy of Management Journal, 53*, 1521–1545.

Kraatz, M., & Zajac, E. J. (1996). Exploring the limits of the new institutionalism: The causes and consequences of illegitimate organizational change. *American Sociological Review, 61*(5), 812–836.

Molesworth, M., Nixon, E., & Scullion, R. (2009). Having, being and higher education: The marketisation of the university and the transformation of the student into consumer. *Teaching in Higher Education, 14*(3), 277–287.

Morphew, C. C., & Eckel, P. D. (Eds.). (2009). *Privatizing the public university: Perspectives from across the academy.* Baltimore, MD: Johns Hopkins University Press.

Munene, I. I. (2007). Privatising the public: Marketisation as a strategy in public university transformation. *Research in Post-Compulsory Education, 13*(1), 1–17.

Natale, S. M., & Doran, C. (2011). Marketization of education: An ethical dilemma. *Journal of Business Ethics*, *105*(2), 187–196.

Oliver, C. (1992). The antecedents of deinstitutionalization. *Organization Studies*, *13*(4), 563–588.

Powell, W. W., & Owen-Smith, J. (2002). The new world of knowledge production in the life sciences. In S. Brint (Ed.), *The future of the city of intellect: The changing American university* (pp. 107–130). Stanford, CA: Stanford University Press.

Rademakers, M. F. (2014). *Corporate universities: Drivers of the learning organization*. New York, NY: Routledge.

Rayman, J. R. (1999). Career services imperatives for the next millennium. *The Career Development Quarterly*, *48*(December), 175–184.

Rhoten, D. R., & Powell, W. W. (2010). Public research universities: From land grant to federal grant to patent grant institutions. In D. Rhoten & C. Calhoun (Eds.), *Knowledge matters* (pp. 319–345). New York, NY: Columbia University Press.

Rivera, L. (2011). Ivies, extracurriculars, and exclusion: Elite employers' use of educational credentials. *Research in Social Stratification and Mobility*, *29*, 71–90.

Rivera, L. (2015). *Pedigree: How elite students get elite jobs*. Princeton, NJ: Princeton University Press.

Roose, K. (2014). *Young money: Inside the hidden world of Wall Street's post-crash recruits*. New York, NY: Grand Central Publishing.

Scott, W. R. (2015). Higher education in America: Multiple field perspectives. In M. W. Kirst & M. L. Stevens (Eds.), *Remaking college: The changing ecology of higher education* (pp. 19–38). Stanford, CA: Stanford University Press.

Sewell, W. H. (1992). A theory of structure: Duality, agency, and transformation. *American Journal of Sociology*, *98*(1), 1–29.

Sharone, O. (2014). *Flawed system, flawed self: Job searching and unemployment experiences*. Chicago, IL: University of Chicago Press.

Slaughter, S., & Rhoades, G. (2009). *Academic capitalism and the new economy: Markets, state, and higher education*. Baltimore, MA: Johns Hopkins University Press.

Wessel, R. (1998). Career centers and career development professionals of the 1990s. *Journal of Career Development*, *24*(3), 163–177.

PART IV
WHAT FUTURE FOR THE
UNIVERSITY?

UC BERKELEY'S ADAPTATIONS TO THE CRISIS OF PUBLIC HIGHER EDUCATION IN THE U.S.: PRIVATIZATION? COMMERCIALIZATION? OR HYBRIDIZATION?

George W. Breslauer

ABSTRACT

The University of California at Berkeley now delivers more to the public of California than it ever has, and it does this on the basis of proportionally less funding by the State government than it has ever received. This claim may come as a surprise, since it is often said that Berkeley is in the process of privatizing, becoming less of a public university and more in the service of private interests. To the contrary, as the State's commitment to higher education and social-welfare programs has declined, UC Berkeley has struggled to preserve and even expand its public role, while struggling simultaneously to retain its competitive excellence as a research university. This paper delineates how UC Berkeley has striven

The University under Pressure
Research in the Sociology of Organizations, Volume 46, 425–452
Copyright © 2016 by Emerald Group Publishing Limited
All rights of reproduction in any form reserved
ISSN: 0733-558X/doi:10.1108/S0733-558X20160000046014

to retain its public character in the face of severe financial pressures. A summary of the indicators invoked can be found in the Table near the end of the text. This paper then addresses the sustainability and generalizability of the Berkeley strategy.

Keywords: Public education; privatization; competitive excellence; access

INTRODUCTION: THE IDEAL OF PUBLIC HIGHER EDUCATION

The University of California was founded in 1868 as a public institution and by early in the twentieth century was one of a handful of public universities that were competitive with the great private institutions of the east in the quality of the research and doctoral training being delivered. The political and economic leaders of the state were proud of UC's high standing, and supported it very generously with tax dollars, even as UC expanded to multiple campuses beyond Berkeley during the mid-century decades. This tradition of strong public support culminated in the 1960s with the "Master Plan for Higher Education," which provided a clear division of labor among (1) the UC System itself; (2) a system of four-year state colleges, later universities, oriented more toward teaching and vocational training; and (3) a system of two-year community colleges from which a large number of high-achieving students could then transfer to the one of the four-year systems.

Because of generous State funding, the systems also shared another trait – affordability – for the fees charged to students were nominal. Very few parents were unable to afford to send their children to these colleges and universities because of the fee or "tuition" levels. (The cost of room and board for students residing on campus, however, was not trivial.) The deal between public higher education and the State of California was clear: the campuses would enroll and educate huge numbers of students and the State would pay almost the entirety of the operating budget.

The tacit, de facto definition of UC Berkeley's status as a "public" research university was based on four features: (1) the very large number of California-resident students it enrolled and taught; (2) the very nominal fees those students were charged; (3) the fact that the State of California provided most of the revenues required to pay the bills; and (4) accountability to a governing board ("Board of Regents") that was appointed by the State. At the time, this "deal" was based on a broad acceptance, by both the population of California and the legislators, that higher education was a public good, providing both social mobility for the residents of California and research-and-teaching contributions that helped to fuel the State's economy, culture, and civic life.[1]

Much has changed since the 1960s. The State has disinvested very substantially from higher education institutions, and without much complaint from the mass public. UC Berkeley, in response, has sought to adapt in ways that are driven by a determination to maintain and enhance the breadth and depth of UC Berkeley's excellence as a research-and-teaching university.

These adaptations have led some observers to argue that UC Berkeley has effectively "privatized," that is, departed from the de facto ideal of a public university. In this paper, I argue otherwise. UC Berkeley's necessary adaptations to changes in its environment have led to a hybrid form that is better thought of as a different type of public university, but one that serves the public interest as much, if not more, than was the case in the 1960s.[2]

DISINVESTMENT BY THE STATE OF CALIFORNIA

Some basic facts about UC Berkeley illustrate the changes that have transpired. Before the wave of budget cuts in the mid-1970s, the State had been contributing about 70% of the total annual expenditures of UC Berkeley. By the late-1990s, this was down to about 30%.[3] By 2015, it had dropped to about 13%. To be sure, this exaggerates the extent of State divestment, because the denominator (total expenditures) has risen greatly over time as a result of the search for alternative sources of income: principally, rising tuition, private fund-raising, and a growing portfolio of research grants and contracts. So let me put it differently. Fifteen years ago, the State was contributing about $500 million per year to UC Berkeley's operating budget; in 2015, the State is contributing about $300 million in nominal dollars. In real dollars (adjusted for inflation), this represents about a 60% reduction in purchasing power. And from a different angle: the State's contribution of ~$500 million 15 years ago covered the salaries of all regular faculty and almost all career staff; today, the State's contribution barely covers only the salaries and benefits of the faculty.

How did this come to be? The State of California's disinvestment from public higher education was a response to severe and cyclical economic shocks of the 1970s (post-Vietnam War and OPEC-induced stagflation), the early 1990s (recession), the early 2000s (the bursting of the IT bubble), and the late 2000s (the collapse of the financial system and the so-called Great Recession) — compounded by voter-adopted restrictions on property and income taxes and by a vast, voter-induced expansion of the prison system. Just as the promise of the Master Plan was born of the prosperous 1950s and 1960s, at which time anything seemed possible, so the fraying of the Master Plan was a product of the State's eventual inability or unwillingness to afford it. Instead, and with the support of the voters, the State gave priority to public safety, investing huge sums in the construction and operations of prisons, at the expense of public higher education.

ADAPTATIONS TO DISINVESTMENT

So how has UC Berkeley coped in response to these cuts? Surely, the fact that total expenditures continued to increase in both nominal and real dollars signals that the university generated alternative sources of revenue. The principal alternative source has been student tuition. In the 1980s, this was raised from a truly nominal sum that everyone could afford to a slightly more challenging $1,500 a year. But then, as cuts continued during the past quarter century, tuition was increased significantly and today stands at about $13,000 a year for California residents (plus another ~$2,000 a year in the so-called "mandatory fees"). In addition, the University turned to private fund-raising. This began in earnest only about 30 years ago, in the early 1980s, when the campus administration geared up for, and launched, the first "capital campaign" in its history. That campaign, over an eight-year period, yielded a total of about $440 million in endowed and expendable funds. Since then, two additional campaigns were conducted: the first (1990–2000) yielded $1.44 billion and the second (2005–2013) yielded more than $3.1 billion by the end of 2013. Ongoing fund-raising yields $300–400 million per year — and all this without a medical school, which, elsewhere, typically raises about 50% of the total raised by leading private and public universities that have medical schools.

UC Berkeley's fund-raising for competitive research grants and contracts has also intensified and, from governmental, foundation, not-for-profit, and corporate sources, currently brings in $600–700 million per year.[4] In all, during the past decade, the State of California has dropped from first place to fourth place in the hierarchy of the four sources of UC Berkeley's major

funding, led now by student tuition, research grants and contracts, and philanthropy (including yield on endowment).

Of these four, State funds and student tuition (minus about one-third
that is used for financial aid), constitute discretionary resources that can be
deployed for any purpose. Except for overhead (technically called "indirect
cost recovery"), the hundreds of millions of dollars in grants and contracts
can only be used for the direct research costs for which they were raised –
while the overhead on those grants is used to pay for maintenance of the
research infrastructure, and even then only constitutes partial reimburse-
ment of these costs. Similarly, the large majority of philanthropy is tied to
purposes specified in a gift agreement. Thus, the flexible use of student tuition has made it possible to substitute partially for the loss of discretionary
State funds, and probably accounts for the fact that UC Berkeley was able
to navigate this latest storm without a ship-wreck.

But revenue-generation from these "Big Four" remains inadequate to
cope with rising cost pressures in a variety of areas: (1) faculty and staff
wages, health-care, and pensions; (2) faculty recruitment and retention
packages, especially in the sciences – in the face of stiff competition from
peer, especially private, universities – and increasingly from universities in
Europe and Asia; (3) information-technology maintenance and renewal; (4)
capital renewal (new construction and renovation of existing plant); (5) the
cost of growing numbers of student services to meet the needs of an
increasingly diversified student body; and (6) the growing administrative
costs of remaining in compliance with an increasingly dense web of local,
state, and federal regulatory rules.

To cope with these cost pressures, UC Berkeley, among other things,
instituted processes of administrative rationalization that promise eventually to reduce recurring costs by some \$75–100 million per year. This
required a large-scale reduction in administrative staffing, far more than
could be accomplished through attrition alone. But it also entailed reconfiguration of administrative staffing, based on "shared services," in order to
avoid repeated, across-the-board staff reductions that, to be sure, save
money, but that also could reduce many units to dysfunction from insufficient levels of staffing. In addition to personnel reductions, the university
will also save tens of millions of dollars per year by having changed its
approach to procurement of supplies. Here it teamed up with UC San
Francisco and UC Davis to force down the unit price of bulk purchases.

Still another component of the strategy was to increase (from 10% to
23%) the percentage of the undergraduate student body that comes from
outside of California (domestic and abroad). Because nonresidents of

California pay tuition that is almost three times that of Californians (~$35,000 per year vs. ~$13,000 per year), this more-than-doubling of the number of nonresidents nets the university almost $80 million per year in additional, discretionary tuition dollars.

Student tuition, philanthropy, research contracts/grants/gifts, and large cuts in costs are the main drivers of UC Berkeley's strategy. But in addition, the administration envisages generating significant new revenues from what is called "unit-level entrepreneurialism." On this score, all units − both academic and nonacademic − are encouraged to seek opportunities to use their expertise and other assets to generate new revenue streams for their departments, schools, or administrative units. This can take many, many forms: from rental of rooms in athletics facilities for weddings and other celebrations; to professionalizing the sale of tickets to athletic and arts performances; to academic units' offering "executive education" programs (and certificates) to domestic and foreign audiences; to the exploitation of online technologies to offer courses, programs, certificates, or degrees for a fee to audiences throughout the world. There are almost as many such opportunities for revenue-generation as there are distinct units on campus, some of which may raise small sums, others of which may raise very large sums. But the hoped-for outcome is that perhaps 10−20 million additional dollars per year may eventually flow into the campus.

ADAPTATIONS AS PRIVATIZATION?

Let me now argue, however, that despite all these adaptations to fiscal austerity, UC Berkeley has not, in fact, "privatized." The accusation of privatization is based on a stylized depiction of the private sources of many funds. Yet, as Carla Hesse, UC Berkeley's current dean of social sciences has argued (personal communication), the definition of "public" versus "private" should be based, not on where the money comes from (students, philanthropists, research-funding agencies, and nonmatriculated "customers," rather than the State) but on how it is spent.

Consider the question: "who benefits" from a UC education? One could argue that, with respect to the population it serves, UC Berkeley is vastly more "public" today than it was in the 1960s. At that time, the undergraduate student body was overwhelmingly Caucasian (~90%), predominantly male (64%), and very largely middle or upper class. By contrast, in Fall 2014, the California-resident undergraduates were 54% female, 30%

Caucasian, 43% Asian-American, 17% Hispanic, 4% African-American (the remaining 6% declined to state their ethnicity or race). In addition, almost 40% of in-state students are from low-income households making less than $45,000 per year. In all, this constitutes a revolutionary transformation in the demographics of the undergraduate student body – and one that would have been impossible to realize had UC Berkeley adopted the strategy of "legacy admissions" (i.e., priority admission for children of alumni and donors) that is so common at leading private universities. The level of gender, ethnoracial, and socio-economic diversity of the in-state, undergraduate student body has never been higher – though the absolute and percentage numbers of African Americans is both striking and disturbing.[5]

This stark socio-economic diversity is the direct product of a highly redistributive financial aid policy, which ensures that students coming from low-income households have all their tuition and more than half their living expenses covered by grants, with the remainder of their living expenses – currently about $8,600 per year – covered through low-interest loans and on campus, part-time employment. Middle-class students coming from households earning less than $80,000 pay no tuition, though they must cover a larger proportion of their living costs than do low-income students. And students coming from households earning between $80,000 and $140,000 have a corresponding portion of their tuition defrayed. This strategy of inter-class cross-subsidization did not just happen. It was the product of a commitment on the part of the campus leadership to craft a student body recruited from the best and brightest among all strata of California's population. The campus returns about one-third of resident tuition dollars to financial aid for low-income and middle-income students.[6] In this respect, the University remains very much a public good, the "good" in this case being broad access to UC Berkeley, regardless of ability to pay.

Put differently, the ~25% of ~20,000 California-resident undergraduates who come from wealthy families, and the 23% of undergraduates (~6,000 students) who are non-Californians and who pay nonresident tuition, make it possible for students from less financially fortunate, primarily Californian households to accept UC Berkeley's offer of admission. This is an explicit strategy of inter-class cross-subsidization ("soak the rich," some might say), but it remains noteworthy that California students from wealthy households pay far less for a UC Berkeley education than they would pay at an equally prestigious private university. The great irony – which is difficult to "sell" politically – is that a freeze on tuition is a subsidy for the upper classes at the expense of low-income students − for it would not generate additional revenues to transfer to low-income students to protect them from inflationary increases in living costs.

The University's financial aid policy is only part of the equation. The U.S. federal government also spends tens of billions of dollars a year on so-called Pell Grants, which currently provide ~$6,000 per low-income student to help cover their living expenses. And the State of California spends billions of dollars a year on so-called Cal Grants, which provide ~$13,000 a year to cover the tuition of low-income students. Note that both Pell Grants and Cal Grants come from *public* sources: the federal and state governments.[7] Note also that, despite its disinvestment from the operating costs of the University, the State has *not* disinvested from the financial aid that it provides directly to the individual, low-income student. Were the federal or state governments to abandon their commitments to Pell and Cal Grants, UC Berkeley would become much less "public," as measured by social access, for it would not have the resources to subsidize the tuition and living costs of low-income, not to mention middle-income students. Fortunately, politics at the federal and state levels do not appear to constitute an imminent threat of such a cut-off.

The result of this tripartite (University, State, Federal) coverage of financial aid is that the debt-load of UC Berkeley's graduating students is low by national standards. According to the most-recent data (2013−2014), 39% of in-state UC Berkeley undergraduates borrowed money to help finance their education. And the average debt-load for graduating seniors who had taken out loans was $17,584, compared to a national average of about $25,000.[8]

Thus, the current model of a public university, as represented by UC Berkeley, retains one important feature of the 1960s model: the enrollment of very large numbers of students, including transfer students from community colleges. What has been lost from that model is the State's funding of most costs (and the full cost of faculty and staff salaries and benefits), and all students' receipt of a tuition-free education. And yet, the student body today is far more diverse − socio-economically and by race, ethnicity, and gender − than it was in the 1960s, which can only add to the "public" character and definition of the university. Thus, the ideal of an *affordable* education has been retained, while a much broader swath of the "public," in terms of demographic groups, has gained access to the university as students.[9]

Perhaps the university is less public, and more private, because of the emphasis on *private* fund-raising that has sought funds to substitute for lost public funds. This is a more formidable argument that the University has privatized, if only because it seems true by definition: private funds replace lost public funds. But if we again invoke Dean Carla Hesse's dictum about the uses, rather than just the sources, of funds, we paint a different picture. For what have funds been raised? The bulk of the $3.1 billion raised in the recent capital campaign (as also in the earlier campaigns) has gone to fund endowed chairs for faculty, the construction of new buildings, academic research or teaching programs, scholarships for undergraduate students, and fellowships for graduate students. There are strict rules in place to guard against conflicts of interest or donor skewing of research priorities or institutional values or the student-admissions process. While it is always true, even in funding from governmental and foundation sources, that some (perhaps many) researchers will adjust their research agendas to the thematic priorities of funders, there is no evidence to suggest that this phenomenon is greater at UC Berkeley as a result of the need for increased private fund-raising and vigorous efforts to expand the grants and contracts portfolio. Even in the 1960s model, the research priorities of faculty members who sought funding from governmental agencies and foundations were subject to some shaping by the changing thematic priorities of those public sources.

The debate over whether the University is privatizing contains an additional dimension. The more than doubling of high-tuition-paying nonresidents of California (roughly, from ~2,500 to ~6,000 out of ~26,000 undergraduates) has elicited criticism from those who invoke "California patriotism." Taxes paid by citizens of the State of California helped to build the University of California and to support it to greater or lesser degrees throughout its history. Hence, the University is said to owe a special allegiance to the *California public* to ensure their access to a Berkeley education. This is surely a legitimate argument, though only if taken in isolation and framed categorically. By contrast, if one asks how those incremental $80 million from nonresident tuition are spent, one can argue that the 77% of the undergraduate student body who hail from California benefit from a superior education and credential (because the funds are used to maintain UC Berkeley's excellence and competitiveness) as well as from enhanced access for low-income students among the ~77% (because some of the funds are also used to support financial aid for Californians). The only categorical "losers" are those ~2,500 Californians who will have been displaced from admissions to UC Berkeley by the additional national and international students — assuming one does not consciously admit a student body that is much larger than can be serviced adequately.[10]

UC Berkeley also remains as "public" as ever in its *governance structure*. Unusually, the University of California is constitutionally autonomous from formal State intrusion into the academic enterprise. This was written into the State constitution already in the 1800s. Formally at least, the State legislative and executive branches cannot dictate policy to the University. That right resides with the Board of Regents of the UC system, composed of some 20 individuals who meet 6 times a year. And yet, political influence, though not formal control, is always an ominous presence. For one thing, the Governor appoints the Regents and the State legislature must confirm the appointments; for another, the Governor is an ex officio member of the Board of Regents, and has the ability to influence the proceedings of Regental meetings. In addition, because the UC *system* remains dependent on the State for about ~\$2.5 billion per year in discretionary dollars (out of total expenditures throughout the system of ~\$22.5 billion), UC leaders cannot turn their backs on the State. Were they openly to defy the Governor's demand that tuition remain frozen for four years, he could reduce the State's direct allocation to the University commensurately — as the Governor has "blue-pencil" veto authority over line items within the State budget. Finally, there remains the ever-present threat that the leaders of the executive and legislative branches could sponsor a referendum to amend the State Constitution — for example, to revoke UC's constitutional autonomy or to freeze tuition or to limit the number of non-Californians in the UC student body. In recent years, State leaders have variously threatened to do precisely these things, and the California referendum process has historically been receptive to retributive populist initiatives.

In short, rather than reinvesting very greatly in the University, California politicians have sought to increase their public-political control to prevent the University from adapting to budget cuts by means that violate the politicians' definitions of the University's public mission and responsibilities. This may be undesirable — indeed, I have co-authored a proposal for formally reducing Regental and State control of the university (Birgeneau, Breslauer, King, Wilton, & Yeary, 2012) — but recent trends actually constitute an affirmation and intensification of the university's formal accountability to the "public."

The University is often referred to as a "public good," by which is meant that it serves the broad, public interest. That concept extends beyond matters of access, the quality of research and education, and political accountability, to the "public service" functions performed by the university. In this realm, the university is more public than ever before. About 8,000 UC Berkeley students annually engage in community service of some kind.

Several heavily enrolled programs send students overseas to help alleviate global poverty. More UCB graduates participate in "Teach for America" (teaching in primary and secondary schools in disadvantaged neighborhoods) than does any other university in the country. More than 3,600 UCB graduates have entered the Peace Corps since its inception, the largest number of any university in the country. Moreover, public discourse, campus literature, and leaders' speeches continuously celebrate grass-roots public service of these kinds. "Public service" is widely viewed as integral to the UC Berkeley ethic of responsibility of students, faculty, and staff. The latest emphasis is "service learning," community engagement, and "engaged scholarship." None of these themes have changed as a result of the financial crunch of the past decade. And the sheer quantity of "public service" is likely far greater than had been the case in the 1960s.

The University also contributes to the public good through the large number of companies that its graduates found, and the economic impact of its inventions and discoveries. The University of California as a whole is often referred to as both an engine of social mobility and a locomotive of economic growth in the State. On this score as well, UC Berkeley, it is safe to assume, is significantly more of a contributor to the public good than it was in the 1960s, before the emergence of Silicon Valley and Emeryville as loci of the information-technology and bio-technology revolutions – though systematic data for the 1960s are not available.

But some things are changing as a result of recent, determined efforts to increase revenues and cut costs. Traditionally, the ideal of the public university (never realized fully in practice) invoked a sharp division between the sphere of education and the sphere of commerce. That ideal was easier to invoke when the State underwrote most of the costs of public higher education. As that support faded, the sphere of commerce intruded increasingly into the sphere of education, which made it easy for critics to claim that the university was privatizing.

However, rather than call these changes "privatization," I see them as side-effects of commercialization practices, efficiency imperatives, and the corporate discourse embraced to justify these. They are also products of changes in the technological environment of higher education. Thus, as the demand for high-quality services increases, and the complexity of the systems and staffing required to deliver those services does too, more of the work has to be done by well-paid specialists both within and outside the university. This leads to an inevitable encroachment on the ideal of the university as a cottage industry. UC Berkeley now recruits high-priced staff in administration and finance from the private sector (some of them on short-term contracts), and asks them to design programs that will cut costs, improve strategic planning, and rationalize finances. The campus administration never could have hoped to launch large-scale programs of administrative rationalization (which are collectively called "Operational Excellence") without the assistance of these outside consultants. At the same time, their efforts, and the rhetoric that justifies those efforts, are replacing or corroding the practices and ethos that had been characteristic of the university in the 1960s. These trends have to be watched carefully. Some elements are necessary and desirable; others are neither, and need to be contained or reversed.

Thus, when campus officials incorporate into their public discourse the language that is prevalent in the corporate sector — for example, calling education an "industry" (better: "enterprise"); or referring to faculty and students as "customers" (better: "users" or "members of our community"); or referring to UC Berkeley's "brand" (better: "reputation"), it is jarring to the academic ear and legitimately triggers fears that those who are steering the university are not prioritizing either academic values or the image of a university as an intellectual community that seeks to advance many values, not all of which are consistent with a financial "bottom line."

Or when the urge to generate new revenues led Samsung and Macy's to briefly set up stalls on central campus to sell their wares to students, staff, and faculty, it triggered legitimate fears that the university was unnecessarily and visibly endorsing consumerism as a core value. Similarly, when all academic departments are asked to think of ways that their professors might generate revenues for the department through ancillary private pursuits like executive education, some faculty members legitimately wonder what has become of the ideal of the university as a place in which faculty concentrate on their research, teaching, and public service, confident that the university is taking care of their basic infrastructural needs. They also wonder where all this is headed: will some proportion of academic freedom be sacrificed to the demands of commerce?

When the naming of new buildings no longer honors past presidents and academic luminaries of the university's history, but now instead honors present-day philanthropists, this too alters the ethos of the campus. Similarly, when departments within the College of Letters and Science begin to be named after donors who gave large sums for the right, this too raises legitimate concerns among some faculty members about ethos and organizational "character."[11]

The next frontier in this regard may be UC Berkeley's long-standing prohibition on naming of departments, colleges, schools, or buildings after corporations. The Chancellor recently turned down two prospective gifts — each in the $20–30 million range — that were being solicited from corporations, because the *quid pro quo* was that the building be named after the corporation. This restriction may be relaxed or abolished within the next decade, but only if the State's unwillingness to help pay for most new buildings requires the University to search for large corporate sponsors of much-needed new construction. Will the necessary replacement of a crumbling building, currently named after an academic luminary in the history of chemical research, lead to a new building named for Dow Chemical? And what would be the impact of such a change on the perception of prospective restrictions on academic freedom? Here the tension between maintaining academic excellence and maintaining a sharp boundary between the sphere of public education and the sphere of commerce comes into sharpest relief.

When the desperate need for new revenues leads to the re-construction of the football stadium to provide high-priced, luxury, shaded seats for large donors, directly across from masses of students in less comfortable seats located directly in the sun, this creates an understandable sense among critics that stratification within what was once a fairly egalitarian university community is proceeding inexorably in the pursuit of dollars to substitute for lost State funding.[12]

The need to cut administrative costs has also led to accusations of corporatization or privatization with respect to the terms of employment for staff. With respect to staff, a situation obtained for decades that was common to most state universities: perverse incentives, balkanization of information flows, and over-staffing. These features often blunted the best efforts of thousands of highly talented and dedicated employees. But rather than fix the situation, the campus for decades allowed administrative drift to prevail. An ethos developed that made a virtue of the situation: it was said that work at public universities, ostensibly for lesser pay than one could receive in the private sector, should be rewarded with excellent pensions and few lay-offs. Hence, when UC Berkeley began to lay off large numbers of staff after losing the State funding required to pay them, it was accused of taking a ruthlessly "corporate" approach and of violating a tacit social compact — that it was sacrificing community to efficiency considerations. This is a valid indicator of "privatization" only if one assumes that the more-lax model of the "public university" required that the university sacrifice efficiency to community.

An interesting attempted redefinition of the University's obligations to the public has arisen in the context of the international "Occupy" movement. This political movement has sought to occupy public spaces (squares, parks) and unused private spaces (boarded-up buildings; unoccupied houses and land) as a means of dramatizing growing levels of inequality in U.S. society (and elsewhere). At UC Berkeley, the movement attempted to set up tent cities on the main plazas of the central campus and also to occupy farmland owned by the University. The justification for the occupations was that the University is a public good and the land on which it sits is therefore owned by, or owed to, "the public." The debate is basically about property rights: does the University have the right to expel occupiers from the land it owns? Or does its obligation as a public entity require it to share property rights with squatters? UC Berkeley leaders chose to defend the university's property rights on behalf of its educational and research missions, but this is no different from the 1960s model of the public university, which also sought to defend its property rights against occupiers.[13]

At some universities, such as those in Texas, where politicians have flexed their muscles and the universities enjoy less constitutional autonomy, measures have been adopted by university administrations that appease the politicians at the expense of academic values. Thus, at one university in Texas, individual faculty "performance" is measured by the amount of money professors bring into the university in grants, contracts, and philanthropy. Not surprisingly, humanities faculty members are the greatest victims of this evaluation system. In most states, this type of politically imposed commercialization is an ever-present danger, though it has not yet happened within the UC system.

To sum up (see Table 1), Berkeley in the 1960s educated large numbers of students for nominal fees and was largely funded by the State government. The student body was highly homogeneous by race and socio-economic status, and the male-female ratio was 3:2. Faculty members spent their time on research, teaching, and personal pursuits. Deans and most administrators, when not dealing with student protests (Berkeley in the 1960s was not a quiet place), were involved largely in desk work at a relaxed pace — and were paid accordingly. Staff employees worked in fairly relaxed work environments and could hope to spend decades at the institution, assuming their performance was not manifestly poor.

Berkeley today retains many features in common with the public university model that Berkeley represented in the 1960s. It still educates very large numbers of students, raises large amounts of research funds from public agencies and foundations while receiving only a small proportion (11–12%) of its research funding from corporations,[14] and remains more

Table 1. Two Versions of UC Berkeley as a Public University.

Indicators	Mid-Late 1960s Public Model	2014 Hybrid Model
Points of continuity		
# of California UG students	Large (~17,000)	Large (~20,000)
Level of corporate funding of research	Low (% unknown)	Low (11–12%)
Naming of schools and buildings by corporations?	No	No
Governance structure	Regental/state	Regental/state
Transfer students as % of UG student body	~33%	~33%
Defense of University's property rights?	Yes, with exceptions	Yes, with exceptions
Points of discontinuity		
Drivers of revenues and costs		
Level of State funding	~70% of expenditures	~13% of expenditures
Intensity of competition for faculty and grad students by peer institutions	Low/medium	Very high
Private fund-raising (philanthropy)	Very low	Very high
% of UGs nonresident	<10%	~23%
Unit-level commercialization and entrepreneurialism	Low	Medium and growing
Cost-cutting as priority	Low	High
Level of Cal student tuition	<$300/year	~$13,000/year
Level of nonresident tuition	~$1,200/year	~$35,000/year
UCB financial aid allocated	Low	High
State and federal financial aid allocated	Medium	High
Impact on students, staff, campus ethos, and public good		
Level of student debt on graduation	Very low	Moderate (~$17,584)
Demographics of Cal UGs	64% male (1962)	46% male
	90% white (1966)	30% white
	5.2% Asian-American (1966)	43% Asian-American
	1.3% Hispanic (1968)	17% Hispanic
	2.8% African-American (1968)	4% African-American
	Largely middle-class and above	Largely middle-class and below
Public service as ideal and practice	Medium	Very high
Corporate discourse	Low	Medium and growing
Staff work environment	Relaxed	Apprehensive
Contribution to State's economy	(Unmeasured)	Very high

true than ever to a commitment to community public service. It has managed to do this without sacrificing its commitment to recruiting top-quality faculty and students.

But other things have changed. Today, tuition is high and State funding is low. The student body is now highly heterogeneous by race, gender, and socio-economic origins. Faculty members are now encouraged to work with deans and administrators to seek opportunities for private fundraising and revenue-generation. Deans and administrators are required to be energetic entrepreneurs who both raise new revenues and cut administrative costs. Staff members now work in tense environments ("will I lose my job in the next budget cut or performance review?"), with metrics for success and annual performance evaluations informed by a declarative commitment to "continuous improvement." Commercialization and entrepreneurialism better describe the new directions of practice and discourse than does "privatization." And yet, those processes could alter the ethos of the campus and challenge the traditional boundary between the sphere of education and the sphere of commerce, with potential implications for academic freedom and the ideal of dispassionate inquiry. Some of these alterations are containable or reversible through changes in discourse and vigilant attention to the boundaries of the permissible. Others are likely to remain, given the financial pressures. UC Berkeley remains very much a public university, though new features suggest movement toward a hybrid form (Table 1).

HOW SUSTAINABLE IS THE BERKELEY STRATEGY?

Whether all this proves sufficient to maintain both competitive excellence and social access will likely depend on the State of California. Although the State has (for now) stopped cutting the UC budget, and, in 2013, began restoring some sums, such that it now contributes about 13% of total expenditures, the executive and legislative branches have announced intentions that, if pursued, threaten to throw UC Berkeley back into deep deficit. The Governor has declared that he will pull back on direct funding to the University if it raises tuition anytime in the coming years. He has also stated that the State will no longer liberally issue bonds to help pay for new buildings or for the retrofitting of existing, earthquake-vulnerable buildings.[15] Additionally, until recently the State had made no commitment to contributing reliably to the UC pension system, as it does to the CSU system, which could soon require the employer (UC campuses) to contribute 16% of both faculty and career-staff payroll to that retirement system. And the Governor had stipulated that, in exchange for freezing tuition, annual increases in the State's contribution to UC will be limited in coming years to an average of 4.5% of the base allocation.[16]

The combination of these four constraints would rapidly wipe out the positive results of recent efforts to adapt. And the impact of this combination is too great to offset through current revenue-generation and cost-cutting efforts. The best financial modeling at UC Berkeley projects a structural deficit of some $50 million in 2015–2016, which will grow to over $125 million by 2020 (Wilton, 2013). Notably, the coming fiscal cliff, and the size of growing deficits, are almost entirely a product of the rise in the required employer contribution to the retirement fund (pensions + health benefits), and assume no resumption of State contributions to that fund. The UC system is a rare case of a "defined benefit" pension plan, at a time when almost the entire corporate sector, and most universities, offer "defined contribution" plans. Efforts were made in the late 2000s to gradually transition the system to a defined contribution plan, but the effort was largely aborted by pressure on the UC president from the system wide Academic Senate and from staff unions. Securing State support for a stressed "defined benefit" retirement fund, however, may prove especially difficult at a time when the State and municipal pension funds are approaching insolvency and the Governor is seeking to redefine the terms of those plans.

Hence, the main task has been political: to persuade the State, and in particular the Governor and leaders of the Legislature, to allow regular, but modest, increases in tuition, to continue funding capital needs, and to increase the State allocation well in excess of 4.5% of the base, so as to cover as well the escalating cost of maintaining the pension fund. This will be a continuing and difficult political challenge. Indeed, during 2015, some State legislators threatened to introduce bills to cap or roll back the numbers of nonresident enrollments at UC campuses and to forbid further tuition increases. Formally, the legislature does not have the power to enforce such prohibitions, given the UC system's constitutional autonomy. But the threat of further deep cuts to the State allocation to UC, combined with the ever-present threat of a constitutional amendment through a ballot initiative, add credibility to these populist forces.

The appointment in 2013 of a former governor (Janet Napolitano of Arizona), rather than an educator, as president of the UC system held out hope of a successful renegotiation of the State's financial relationship to its premier system of higher education. Recently, President Napolitano and Governor Brown struck a deal that committed the State, among other things, to contribute more than $400 million over three years to the UC pension fund and to continue annual base-allocation increases of 4% a year for four years, in exchange for a continuing, two-year freeze in resident tuition and a commitment not to raise tuition thereafter in excess of the rate of inflation.[17] From personal conversations, I have heard differing opinions as to whether this agreement is likely to exacerbate or, alternatively, significantly alleviate UC Berkeley's budgetary distress.

HOW GENERALIZABLE IS THE BERKELEY STRATEGY?

As shown in this paper, UC Berkeley has adapted rather deftly to the withdrawal of State support, even though a financial cliff continues to challenge the university in the not-distant future. But in addition to the nominalist question, "has the university compromised its public character?" – the question that largely drives this essay – one might ask whether there are lessons here to be learned that are transferrable to other public universities. Almost all public universities are struggling with a secular decline in the level of budgetary support for operations that comes from the state in which they are located. Many of them have, in response, raised tuition and enrolled increasing numbers of nonresident applicants. Many of them have sought means of reducing administrative costs – either through greater operational efficiency (which typically means lay-offs of staff or increased reliance on online instruction) or through a reduction in the size of their intellectual portfolio by disestablishing some academic departments and/or reducing the total size of the ladder faculty in favor of increased numbers of itinerant lecturers. The question is whether the Berkeley strategy of increased tuition, increased enrollments of nonresidents, capital campaigns, unit-level entrepreneurialism, intensified grantsmanship, and reduction in the cost of operations – but without reducing the university's intellectual portfolio or greatly increasing the proportion of courses taught by nonladder faculty – is a strategy that other public universities could adopt.

The answer to this question might depend on which cohort of public universities is the comparator. Let me begin by distinguishing between AAU and non-AAU publics. Forty-seven public universities are members of the Association of American Universities (AAU), which, along with 15 privates encompass those 62 universities that, by AAU standards of academic coverage and accomplishment, constitute the "elite" universities in the country.[18] A trait that these "elites" have in common is heavy competition among themselves to recruit, and then retain, outstanding faculty and graduate students. This competition proves extremely costly and has a serious impact on the campus budget. Yet campus leaders are loath to consider reducing costs by abstaining from the competition or by reducing the campus's intellectual portfolio.

Cost-Cutting Options

One thing that has been treated as a binding constraint on UC Berkeley decision-makers' choices has been a commitment to retaining the breadth of academic coverage that currently exists on the campus. In addition to Letters and Science, UC Berkeley boasts 13 professional schools and colleges. Given that most of these 13, as well as all departmentally based divisions within Letters and Science (Arts and Humanities; Biological Sciences, Mathematical and Physical Sciences; and Social Sciences) are very highly ranked relative to their AAU and international comparators (so-called "peers"), administrators have defined Berkeley's breadth, depth, and excellence of scholarship as a great comparative advantage, both intellectually and competitively. Hence, they have never seriously countenanced a strategy of eliminating major academic units in order to save money. This is likely a wise stance to adopt. Such a move would only save money in the long term, since tenured faculty would have to be placed elsewhere in the faculty. In the near term, the effect would be to demoralize the campus faculty and graduate students ("who is next?"), and reduce Berkeley's competitiveness (headline: "UC Berkeley eliminates academic departments!") by discouraging prospective recruits and leading existing faculty and graduate students to look elsewhere. In sum, UC Berkeley's commitment to so-called "comprehensive excellence" narrows the parameters within which choices about cost-control are made.[19]

Other AAU public universities probably adhere to some variant of this strategy, since almost all of them have suffered steep reductions in State support, yet have not eliminated entire academic divisions in response.

A corollary of "don't fire the faculty!" is found in the approach to defining the breadth of the intellectual and curricular portfolio. A cost driver in all comprehensive research-and-teaching universities is the fact that accretions of new areas of knowledge are not instituted at the expense of eliminating "old" areas of knowledge. And yet, new areas of knowledge are continuously appearing. When one adds, say, a Department of Cognitive Sciences, one does not condition the addition on the subtraction of an existing department of comparable size. Or, when student interests shift and enrollments increase in new areas (e.g., Bioengineering), while declining in other areas (e.g., medieval history), one can shift resources to accommodate student demand for courses, but one does not seriously consider eliminating low-demand areas of inquiry. What is low-demand today may be of higher demand tomorrow. "Old" knowledge is not necessarily obsolete knowledge. Hence, it is not surprising that both the total size of the faculty and the total number of teaching and research areas represented within the university will rise steadily over time. This is not unique to Berkeley; it is a common cost pressure at comprehensive research-and-teaching universities.

Many other AAU publics have striven to reduce costs by paring administrative staffing, though, more often than not, this takes the form of mandatory budget cuts on all units, which leads to widespread lay-offs of staff. Some public universities have pursued more systematic administrative reorganizations, along the lines of Berkeley's "operational excellence" campaign (e.g., Cornell, Indiana, Michigan), though few of them have set as ambitious a savings target as has Berkeley. Presumably, other publics could do more along these lines. Yet some administrative areas are both hugely costly and in very high demand. Information-technology departments in all research-and-teaching universities are the prime example. Forty years ago, the internal communications department was responsible largely for keeping the telephones in good order. Since the IT revolution, both students and faculty expect to avail themselves continuously of the latest hardware, software, and technical support. Computers are widely deemed to become obsolete within three years; software upgrades become available more frequently still. Privacy laws demand the continuous upgrading of the campus's firewalls and computer-security efforts; failures in this area incur expensive "clean-up" efforts and, at times, large regulatory fines. All this means that IT departments must be both heavily subsidized and heavily staffed by high-priced specialists. UC Berkeley has not found significant cost-savings in this area; it is likely that few major universities have, either.

Student services are another area in which costs have risen continuously over the decades at all AAU public universities. Compared to the 1960s, the breadth of advising and other services available to students has skyrocketed. To some extent this is a predictable product of diversification of the ethnoracial, gender, and sexual-orientation composition of undergraduate student bodies, which is a nationwide trend. For better or for worse, universities have responded by providing differentiated services (both academic and social) for the various segments of the student body. These cost money, especially in staff salaries.

Still another cost driver that is largely common to major universities has been the regulatory environment. Compared to the 1960s and 1970s, the number of regulatory requirements – local, state, and federal – has exploded. Failure to abide by these regulations incurs significant financial penalties. Compliance requires costly staffing to monitor and regulate the campus environment. The addition of new regulations is rarely accompanied by the elimination or attenuation of existing regulations. Hence, it is rare for universities to be able to contain costs by shifting current personnel into new areas. Dealing with regulatory compliance accounts for a significant portion of growing administrative costs over time. Obviously, this is not unique to UC Berkeley.

Let me address a cost-cutting canard that appears frequently in the press and in politicians' speeches: the compensation of top-level administrators. Those who bemoan tuition increases often call for paring the salaries of high-level administrators. Yet reducing the salaries of the top 50 administrators on a campus by, say, 20%, might save $1–1.5 million dollars a year, but this would not do much, if anything, to reduce the need for tuition increases or State support to make ends meet. In fact, with a few exceptions (Penn State, Michigan, Ohio State), the average salary and compensation of AAU public university presidents are far below those of AAU private university presidents. And the average compensation of the chancellors of the ten UC campuses was, until recently, in the bottom half of the AAU *publics*.[20] Sometimes the argument is made in radical-egalitarian and moral terms, be this California Governor Brown's call for a philosophy of "servant leadership" (which, by his standard, would reduce UC chancellors' current salaries by more than 50%) or be this labor unions decrying the disparity between the salaries of leading administrators and the salaries of unskilled workers within the university. One might put this latter argument in broader perspective. In the early 1980s, the ratio of the average compensation of corporate CEOs to the average salaries of their workers was about 30:1; this ratio ballooned to 383.4:1 (including realized options) in the year 2000 before dipping to 231:1 in 2010 (as a result of the financial crash) (Mishel, 2012; also, Mishel, 2015). Notably, today the ratio of the average salary of UC chancellors to the average salary of nonspecialist workers within the system is about 10:1, or perhaps 12:1 (depending on how one categorizes the nonspecialist workers). From a radical-egalitarian perspective, a ratio of 10:1 (e.g., \$450,000:\$45,000) may appear obscene. From a different perspective – be it comparison with AAU private universities (and some publics) or with the corporate sector – it is arresting and perhaps even impressive.

Revenue-Generation Options

With respect to revenue-generation, Berkeley's strategy has been to increase tuition from both State residents and nonresident enrollments, increase private fund-raising, intensify grantsmanship, and incentivize entrepreneurial activities by academic and nonacademic units. Many other AAU public universities have also raised tuition and increased nonresident enrollments, with Michigan and Virginia having gone even farther than UC Berkeley. The University of California, however, has increased tuition to higher levels than have most AAU publics. UC Berkeley's prestige may make it easier for this university to attract highly qualified nonresident students, but the pool of qualified international students – especially from East Asia – appears almost limitless. Hence, though the politics of each state (including California) may determine a given university's ability to raise tuition and enroll nonresidents, there is no reason that this element of Berkeley's strategy cannot be generalized.

Private fund-raising and grantsmanship may be an area of comparative advantage for UC Berkeley. In only the third capital campaign in its history, raising \$3.1 billion in private funds, and having done so without a medical school, may be testimony to the prestige and intellectual vigor of the institution, not to the fact that there are some 450,000 living alumni of UCB. (Most AAU publics have several hundred thousand living alumni – and only about 70,000 of UCB's alumni contributed in this latest campaign.) Berkeley's level of prestige and intellectual vigor may not be generalizable, but all AAU publics have the capacity to raise funds privately. That said, it is important to bear in mind that most funds raised privately are not fungible; they cannot be used to relieve pressure on the operating budget through diversion from their stated purpose (e.g., endowed chairs; student scholarships and fellowships; the creation of new research centers; construction of new buildings and facilities). Hence, private fund-raising, while a boon to the intellectual enterprise and to the morale and productivity of faculty and students who benefit from it, cannot be expected to substitute for increased tuition and State support – fungible resources that pay basic operating expenses, salaries, and benefits.

Successful grantsmanship is a boost to the morale and intellectual productivity of the faculty, but the "overhead" from those grants is insufficient to cover even the costs of housing and conducting the research. Hence, rising levels of "indirect cost recovery" (i.e., overhead) cannot greatly offset the cost pressures facing AAU publics.

"Unit-level entrepreneurialism" is something that other AAU publics can undertake — and are undertaking. At Rutgers University, for example, one department has generated large new revenues by offering online reaccreditation courses to mid-career specialists throughout the region. This approach is generalizable to many professional schools within research universities. Units with the potential to generate fungible monies can thus offset cuts to their operating budgets in hard times. This is certainly a generalizable feature of UC Berkeley's strategy. But notably, there is one area of unit-level entrepreneurialism in which Berkeley is at a comparative *dis*advantage. Most AAU public universities have medical schools and medical centers; Berkeley does not. The cash flow to those medical centers is typically very high, and often allows them to subsidize the general campus to some limited extent.[21]

Online education is often cited as both a potential cost-saver and revenue-generator for strapped universities of all kinds, AAU or not. Those who tout it as a cost-saver argue that it can reduce the size (and therefore cost) of the professoriate by having students taught online for many introductory courses, especially those in the STEM fields (Science, Technology, Engineering, and Mathematics). At the extreme, this strategy would go one step beyond the current national trend toward replacing professors with itinerant lecturers. Online instruction would thus lower the cost of instruction even more. In principle, universities could go this route, but such a move would be based upon assumptions about the student learning experience that, as yet, are not proven. The potential pedagogical "downside" would be ignored in favor of cost-cutting.

UC Berkeley has experimented with online education. In 2012, it joined the consortium created by Harvard and MIT, called "edX," which develops MOOCs ("Massive Open Online Courses") for use both within campuses and for "educating the world."[22] UCB then set up an office, the Berkeley Resource Center for Online Education (BRCOE),[23] which is charged with coordinating and encouraging experimentation with online teaching in its many forms. The emphasis of BRCOE is not cost-cutting, for the university administration has discovered that high-quality online courses cost a lot of money to create and field (and then to revise continuously). Rather, the two main emphases are (1) pedagogical innovation, using online as an adjunct to, not replacement for, in-person professorial instruction, and thus hopefully enhancing the learning experience[24] and (2) revenue-generation, directing online courses toward audiences that are willing and able to pay for the education or training they receive from afar or in a hybrid model that entails their spending some portion of the term in residence on campus. The hybrid model is currently being deployed by several professional schools at Berkeley and promises to become a reliable revenue stream for several of those schools.

From the standpoint of generating fungible revenues that are controlled by the campus leadership and can alleviate some budgetary stress, the most promising avenue could prove to be "University Education" (UNEX), an off-campus adult-education enterprise that most AAU, and many non-AAU, universities possess. At Berkeley, UNEX has fielded over 150 profit-able, online courses. The audience for such courses is enormous, and could turn UNEX, and its counterparts at other reputable institutions, into "cash-cows" for a strapped university. Some of that audience is simply intellectually curious; some need accreditation or reaccreditation training; others seek training in a field into which they would like to move. There is no competitive admissions process to enter these courses and certificate-generating programs. Indeed, to link these observations to the primary con-cern of this paper, UNEX thus performs a public service function that is consistent with the university's public mission. Fortunately, it has the potential, at Berkeley and elsewhere, to relieve financial stress on the gen-eral campus. Were it otherwise — were UNEX to operate at a deficit — a hard choice would have to be made as to whether to subsidize this particu-lar form of public service at the expense of the general campus.

In all, though, while unit-level entrepreneurialism may alleviate some of the local deprivations caused by budget cuts, not even a highly profitable UNEX could generate sufficient funds for the campus as a whole to obviate increases in tuition (resident and nonresident) and State support. The forms of unit-level entrepreneurialism I have mentioned or outlined above are avail-able to all AAU public universities, and to many non-AAU publics as well. But they are no panacea for offsetting austerity.

In sum, most of UC Berkeley's strategies of cost-cutting and revenue-generation are capable of being emulated by the AAU publics, though with results that are likely to vary. Some universities may prove better able to achieve results than others. And some universities may not be able to over-come political pressures to hold down tuition and nonresident enroll-ments.[25] Those that are least able to cut costs, raise revenues, and resist populist political pressures may ultimately be forced to contract their intellectual portfolios, eliminate academic departments, selectively abandon efforts to compete for outstanding faculty and graduate students, and ultimately redefine themselves largely as teaching, no longer "teaching and research" universities.

NOTES

1. By UC being a "public good," I mean that it was an institution viewed as a valued contributor to the broader "public interest." I do not use the term in the technical sense employed in the discipline of economics, where a public good is an entity that is freely open to the public and the use of which by some citizens does not diminish the opportunity for other citizens to access the good (e.g., a park).

2. On tensions among public access, research excellence, contributions to citizenship development and growth of the economy, see Kerr (2001b); on challenges specific to UC Berkeley in the 1960s, see Kerr (2001a).

I should add that public higher education throughout the United States has been subject to financial stresses often as large as those in California. And many public universities have also adopted strategies of adaptation that have raised accusations of "privatization." This paper deals principally with the strategies adopted at UC Berkeley, though I will speculate later in the paper on the generalizability of the Berkeley strategy.

3. Here we are discussing State contributions to the operating budget of the university, not to the large sums the State of California allocates annually to low-income students in colleges and universities, public and private, throughout the State (so-called "Cal Grants").

4. See http://coeus.spo.berkeley.edu/faction.aspx for the precise breakdown; sort by "budget period."

5. Many of the data about the current demographics of the student body, tuition levels, and student debt can be found at http://opa.berkeley.edu/campus-data/common-data-set. Data on composition of the student body in the 1960s come from several sources: on the male-female ratio in 1962, see Nerad (1999, p. 133); on ethnoracial and class composition in the 1960s, see Karabel et al. (1989). This Report also notes that, in 1966, 5.2% of undergraduates were of Asian ancestry (Chinese and Japanese), while, in 1968, 2.8% were "Black" and 1.3% Hispanic.

6. In 2011, and despite budgetary pressures, UC Berkeley introduced a "Middle-Class Access Plan" (MCAP), to shield such students from the impact of further increases in tuition. The Plan was devised and adopted to alleviate some of the financial pressures on students who were not eligible for Cal Grants (<$45,000 household income), Pell Grants (<$45,000), and the system's Blue & Gold program (<$80,000), but who were not wealthy enough to easily afford the ~$34,000/year cost of tuition and living expenses. Two years later, and inspired by UC Berkeley's MCAP, the State of California introduced a middle-class aid plan that uses State resources to alleviate tuition pressures on families earning $80,000–$150,000 in annual household income.

7. Students at private universities are also eligible for Pell Grants from the federal government, if they come from low-income households. But UC Berkeley enrolls almost as many Pell Grant recipients as all eight Ivy League (private) universities combined.

8. This figure pertains to those undergraduates who entered as freshmen. A larger percentage of transfer students (almost half) borrow money, but they also enter as juniors and therefore graduate with a lower UC debt-load than do their classmates who entered as freshmen (see http://opa.berkeley.edu/campus-data/common-data-set).

9. Let me qualify this strong claim by noting that the demographic composition of the State of California has changed dramatically since the 1960s, becoming far more diversified, racially and socio-economically. Similarly, a much larger proportion of young women now seek college admission. This diversification of the applicant pool has been a "driver" of diversification of the student body. Nonetheless, the University's admissions strategy has made it possible for the Statewide demographic changes to be reflected in the composition of the student body, albeit not to the point of a quota-driven "match" of proportions. Compared to their proportion of the State population, and also to their proportion of high school graduates, African Americans, Hispanics, and Caucasians are greatly underrepresented in the in-state undergraduate body, while Asian Americans (East Asia + South Asia) are greatly overrepresented.

10. Also, a significant percentage of those nonresident students will likely settle in California after graduation, contributing to the State as producers, consumers, tax-payers, and citizens. Finally, it is noteworthy that the average academic quality of the nonresidents is actually greater than that of the average California enrollees; so "sacrifice of quality" is not a convincing argument against nonresident enrollments.

11. Full disclosure: when serving as dean, I advocated forcefully for accepting the gift that was conditioned on naming the department (Political Science) after the donors.

12. In fairness, I should note that those students are seated in sections that enjoy the best views of the football game; the seats are also priced far below what they could have been sold for on an open market.

13. Not always successfully, though. So-called "People's Park," a small parcel of land that is owned by the University, was occupied in 1969 and has largely been left as an open space ever since. No Chancellor has wanted to do battle with community activists who would mobilize to thwart any effort to develop the property for other uses.

14. See http://coeus.spo.berkeley.edu/faction.aspx; sort by "budget period."

15. In 2014, however, the State was persuaded to pay 50% of the cost of replacing a large academic building on the Berkeley campus, housing both the Department of Psychology and the Graduate School of Education, which was deemed too-great an earthquake risk to be occupied for the long term.

16. Recall that the State allocation is now (2015) ~13% of total UCB expenditures; so a 4.5% increase in that allocation is less than 1 percent of total expenditures. Even this assumes that the UC systemwide Office of the President does not distribute that 4.5% increment inequitably among the ten campuses. In fact, during

the past 15 years, Berkeley's percentage of the systemwide allocation has been cut more than that of any other UC campus (*Source*: Office of the Vice Chancellor for Administration and Finance, UC Berkeley).

17. For further details of the agreement, see University of California, Office of the President (2015).

18. For a list of all current members, see https://www.aau.edu/about/article.aspx?id=5476

19. "Comprehensive excellence" is a slogan that is not truly descriptive of the intellectual portfolio of the campus, though it performs a useful mythical function on campus. That portfolio is not comprehensive: UCB has no medical school, for example. And the excellence of that portfolio is widespread but not comprehensive; many units are stronger than others. Given the rankings of UC Berkeley's departments and programs, however, it would be accurate to say that, compared with its AAU comparators, UC Berkeley enjoys an unusually high breadth and depth of excellence.

20. In September 2014, the Regents of the University of California decided to correct this situation by raising the salaries of chancellors significantly, such that they now average about $450,000 per year (in a range from ~$386,000 to an anomalous $750,000 on the medical campus [UCSF]). This brings the average up to approximately the average of AAU publics' presidents/chancellors.

21. John Wilton, UC Berkeley's Vice Chancellor for Administration and Finance, notes that, within the UC system, campuses with medical centers have been better able to cushion the impact of budget cuts and tuition freezes than campuses without medical centers (John Wilton, personal communication, February 18, 2015).

22. See www.edX.org for full details of their efforts.

23. See www.online.berkeley.edu for details.

24. An example is the so-called "flipped classroom," where students watch the professor's lecture online before class at their leisure and then come to the lecture hall for collective discussion, group learning, and professorial facilitation and prompting. It remains to be seen whether this will be an improvement on the traditional model.

25. An important constraint on generalizability may be the fact that few public universities enjoy the constitutional autonomy that the UC system possesses. Hence, it is easier elsewhere for the state legislature to micro-manage its leading public universities.

ACKNOWLEDGMENTS

The author served as dean of social sciences at UC Berkeley from 1999 to 2006 and as the campus's executive vice chancellor and provost from 2006 to 2014. An earlier version of this paper was presented at the conference "From Prestige to Excellence: The fabrication of academic excellence," University of Paris, Paris, France, September 12–13, 2013. For comments on earlier drafts, I am grateful to Elizabeth Berman, Elizabeth Berry,

Arthur Bienenstock, Helen Breslauer, Ken Breslauer, Janet Broughton, Catherine Cole, John Douglass, Carla Hesse, David Hollinger, Martin Jay, Thomas Laqueur, Daniel Melia, Catherine Paradeise, Robert Price, Andrew Szeri, Gaye Tuchman, John Wilton, Mark Yudof, and an anonymous reviewer for the press. I alone am responsible for the claims and conclusions in this paper.

REFERENCES

Birgeneau, R., Breslauer, G., King, J., Wilton, J., & Yeary, F. (2012). *Modernizing governance at the University of California: A proposal that the regents create and delegate some responsibilities to campus boards.* Berkeley, CA: Center for Studies in Higher Education, UC Berkeley. Retrieved from http://www.cshe.berkeley.edu/publications/modernizing-governance-university-california-proposal-regents-create-and-delegate-some

Karabel, J., Bailey, R., Koenigsberg, E., Lin, D., Mei, K., Miller, L., ... Wilkerson, M. (1989). *Freshman admissions at Berkeley: A policy for the 1990s and beyond.* Report by the Committee on Admissions and Enrollment, Berkeley Division, Academic Senate, University of California, Professor Jerome Karabel, Chair. Retrieved from http://academic-senate.berkeley.edu/committees/aepe/freshman-admissions-berkeley-policy-1990s-and-beyond

Kerr, C. (2001a). *The gold and the blue: A personal memoir of the University of California, 1949–1967* (Vol. 2). Berkeley, CA: University of California Press.

Kerr, C. (2001b). *The uses of the university* (5th ed.). Cambridge, MA: Harvard University Press.

Mishel, L. (2012, May 3). *CEO pay 231 times greater than the average worker.* Economic Snapshot. Economic Policy Institute, Washington, DC. Retrieved from http://www.epi.org/publication/ceo-pay-231-times-greater-average-worker/

Mishel, L. (2015, July 1). *CEO pay has grown 90 times faster than typical worker pay since 1978.* Economic Policy Institute, Washington, DC. Retrieved from http://www.epi.org/publication/ceo-pay-has-grown-90-times-faster-than-typical-worker-pay-since-1978/

Nerad, M. (1999). *The academic kitchen: A social history of gender stratification at the University of California, Berkeley.* Albany, NY: SUNY Press.

University of California, Office of the President. (2015). *University of California framework for long-term funding.* Retrieved from www.budget.universityofcalifornia.edu

Wilton, J. (2013). *Time is not on our side, Parts 1 and 2.* Retrieved from www.vcaf.berkeley.edu

THIS TIME IT REALLY MAY BE DIFFERENT

Irwin Feller

ABSTRACT

Since at least the 1970s, the American research university system has experienced episodic periods of austerity, frequently accompanied by expressions of concern about the threats that these conditions pose to U.S. scientific and technological leadership. In general, austerity has been tied to fluctuations in Federal Government funding of academic research and macroeconomic fluctuations that have shrunk state government budget revenues. Even amidst these episodes, the system has continued to expand and decentralize. The issue at present is whether this historic resiliency, of being a marvelous invalid, will overcome adverse contemporary trends in Federal and state government funding, as well as political trends that eat away at the societal bonds between universities and their broader publics. The paper juxtaposes examinations of the organizational and political influences that have given rise to the American research university system, trends in research revenues and research costs, and contemporary efforts by universities to balance the two. It singles out the secular decline in state government's support of public universities as the principal reason why this period of contraction is different from those of the past. Rather though then these trends

The University under Pressure
Research in the Sociology of Organizations, Volume 46, 453–488
Copyright © 2016 by Emerald Group Publishing Limited
All rights of reproduction in any form reserved
ISSN: 0733-558X/doi:10.1108/S0733-558X20160000046015

portending a market shakeout, as some at times have predicted, the pro-
jection here is that the academic research system will continue to be
characterized by excess capacity and recurrent downward pressures on
research costs. Because the adverse impacts are concentrated in the pub-
lic university sector, they may also spill over into political threats to the
current system of awarding academic research grants primarily via com-
petitive, merit review arrangements.

Keywords: Academic research; state government disinvestment;
market shakeout; research revenues; research costs

INTRODUCTION

"Our basic message is simple. We have been here before." This sentence
taken from *This Time Is Different*, Reinhart and Rogoff's highly influential
if controversial study of the 2008 financial crisis (Reinhart & Rogoff, 2009,
p. xxv) sets the historical and analytical context for this paper. It accepts as
factually accurate contemporary descriptions of the parlous state of
research universities in the United States, while also viewing the rhetoric in
which they are cast as at time designed at times more to impact upon
national or state government policies than as evidence directed at stated
hypotheses. It too begins by asking the questions, is this time different, and
if so, why? Rather though than stopping with answers to these questions, it
ventures on to consider the implications of its offered explanations for why
or why not.

Generically, many of the pressures described below being felt by U.S.
universities are also being experienced by counterpart institutions in several
OECD countries (Higher Education Funding Council for England, 2013;
Krull, 2009; Vincent-Lancrin, 2009; Whitley, 2011). The effort though to
contextualize empirical and institutional arrangements within a chapter's
prescribed space limits leads to treatment of the U.S. setting alone.
Compensation for this tight focus is hopefully provided for by attention to
the acknowledged international leader in academic research and graduate
education. U.S. universities dominate various global rankings of the world's
best universities. It is the home of 7 of the top 10 and 15 of the top 20 "best
global universities" in 2014—2015, as gauged by the Times Higher World
University Rankings.[1] Despite increased international competition, both

quantitatively and qualitatively, in research inputs and research outputs (National Academies, 2007, pp. 70–82; National Science Board, 2014, pp. 5-35–5-38), the United States remains the established model for other national higher education systems and individual institutions as they seek to attain or retain research distinction.

Relatedly, the paper focuses primarily on the pressures of universities as performers of research, treating only in passing their historic, larger missions as providers of education, principally to undergraduates. This choice is purposive. With few exceptions (e.g., Clotfelter, 1996; Ehrenberg, Rizzo, & Jakubson, 2007), examination of the problems besetting U.S. universities has tended to deal with one or the other of a university's core mission or teaching and research, not both.[2] Indeed, as noted by Nicholas Dirks, chancellor of the University of California – Berkeley, "The near absence of discussions of research in the spate of publications about college over the past decades is perhaps the most astonishing lacuna in the higher education literature" (Dirks, 2015, p. B9).

ORGANIZATION

The paper is organized as follows. The section "Problem Statement: Is This Time Different?" arrays and parses previous accounts of the pressures on U.S. research universities. The section "Framing the Baseline Setting" splices two analytical approaches rooted in different disciplinary perspectives to recount the post-World War II development of the U.S. research university system in order to establish a baseline to better understand contemporary pressures on the system, in whole and in its parts. One approach consists of considering alternative scenarios about the future size and structure of the U.S. academic research system; the approach is akin to treating higher education as a multi-product, multi-firm industry entering on to an uncertain long-term growth path. The framework and language underlying this approach is an economic one, albeit reflecting what Winston (1999) termed the "awkward economics of higher education."

The second approach draws on narratives and analyses found in the writings of Jencks and Riesman (1969), Geiger (1993), Gumport (1993), Clark (1995), Thelin (2004), Paradeise and Thoenig (2013), among several others. Its underpinnings are the history of higher education and organizational sociology, with their analyses of the ascendency of research performance and PhD production as the criteria by which both faculty and institutions have come to define and measure academic excellence and prestige, as well as the strategies universities have adopted or considered to survive (and prosper) as research institutions amidst changing external environments.[3]

The section "Problem Statement: Is This Time Different?" addresses the "is this time different" question. It compares various contemporary pressures on the system to those that have appeared in the past. To anticipate, it views the current pressures as largely a repeat of past episodes. As tellingly highlighted in recent analysis of the "systemic flaws" besetting the U.S. academic biomedical community (Alberts, Kirschner, Tilghman, & Varmus, 2014), the recurrence of these pressures arises from dynamic imbalances between research revenues and research costs in highly competitive markets (for resources and prestige) in which entry or expansion as a research-oriented institution has been relatively easy but from which exit is hard. Where this time is different though is the accumulating effects of state disinvestments in public higher education. Section "Show Me the Money" traces the implications of this line of analysis. In a seemingly contradictory but nevertheless internally consistent weaving together of its several strands, after stating that this time is different, it offers an assessment that the future may not be too different from the present. It concludes with a projection of the consequences of this contradiction for the performance of the U.S. academic research system.

PROBLEM STATEMENT: IS THIS TIME DIFFERENT?

Accounts of the pressures on American research universities have been so frequently stated for so long in some many settings and by so many esteemed university leaders and scholars as to themselves constitute a subfield of research interest. Starting here with the deceleration in growth of federal support of academic research in the 1970s that followed the halcyon, oft-termed golden age of academic science of the 1960s, spurred by America's shocked and hurried reaction to the 1957 launch of Sputnik and Cold War threats (Hart, 1998), at least a five-foot book shelf can be constructed of the plight/challenges/discontents of the America's research university. To cite only a few of these works selected for their pithy titles and phrasing, in 1971 Cheit (1971) titled his study of financial conditions at 41 colleges and universities, *The New Depression in Higher Education*; in 1979, Mortimer and Tierney wrote about the *3 "R"s of the Eighties: Reduction,*

Reallocation and Retrenchment; Rosenzweig and Turlington called attention to the eroding research base within universities, highlighting in particular the "severe threat to the quality of scientific research and advanced training due to a serious deterioration in the quality of the tools necessary for the research and of the facilities where the research is done" (Rosenzweig & Turlington, 1982, p. 84); Kerr in 1994 wrote of *Troubled Times for American Higher Education*; toward the end of the decade, Vest, President of MIT, in a contribution to an edited volume entitled, *The American University: National Treasure or Endangered Species*, described research universities as overextended, under focused, overstressed, and underfunded (Vest, 1997); and in 2004 Thelin described American higher education between 1970 and 2000 as "a Troubled Giant" (Thelin, 2004, p. 317).

To bring these lamentations to the present, after describing America's research universities as a "major national asset, perhaps even its most potent one," a 2012 NRC report sounded though the tocsin that "Despite their current global leadership, American research universities are facing critical challenges." Paramount among these challenges was current threats to their financial health "as each of their major sources of revenue has been undermined or contested" (National Academies-National Research Council, 2012b, p. 3). In the same year, these concerns reached a crescendo in the report, *The Current Health and Future Well-Being of the American Research University*, prepared by the Research Universities Futures Consortium, an ad hoc assemblage of leading research universities: "Today the future of the American research university is more uncertain than it has been in the last 50 years." Noting that there had been periods during this half-century "when public funding of academic research paused in its growth," the report continued in stark terms: "However, never before have research universities faced combined pressures of: declining federal funding, record reductions in state funding, erosion of endowments, soaring tuition, costs reaching unaffordable limits, intensifying, internal as well as global competition, increasing compliance and reporting requirements, as well as the loss of political and public confidence in the value of university-based research" (Research Universities Futures Consortium, 2012, p. 9).

Bypassing here any effort to calibrate the comparative severity of the current situation — "never before"? — the very fact that the U.S. academic research system has so often experienced periods of "boom and bust" (Teitelbaum, 2014) makes it difficult at present to differentiate between a cyclical downturn and secular stagnation or decline. The use here of

concepts from the economic growth/business cycle literature is deliberate
because it highlights the underlying question of whether and the extent to
which the contemporary setting (as could have been asked of similar ones
in the past) is caused by specific historically bounded events; by systemic
features such that periods of prosperity contain the seeds of ensuing down-
turns[4] that in turn set the conditions for an upswing, and so on; or whether
the concatenation of contemporary adverse events and trends do indeed
mark a structural, long enduring erosion of the foundations upon which
the U.S. research university system is built.

The consistent theme across episodes of retrenchment, crisis, or pressure
is that their primary causes are the instability and shortfall in external
funding for academic research. To address only the current situation, contemporary accounts center its etiology in the putatively stagnant level in
real terms of Federal funding for academic research.[5] The financial stresses
afflicting public research universities have been further aggravated by the
slow, only partial restoration of levels of state government appropriations
to state universities following the 2008 downturn. Yet additional pressures
have arisen recently (2015) in the form of draconian cuts in appropriations
being proposed in several states. In combination, these events have drained
the revenue streams needed by universities to cover (in the form of indirect
cost recovery and charges against funded research projects) the costs
they incurred in expanding plant and facilities and faculty complements
in response to earlier increases in federal funding for academic R&D,
most notably the doubling of NIH funding that occurred between 1998
and 2004.

Difficult to disagree with in its particulars, this interpretation explains
too much, too simply. Normatively (and politically), it places responsibility for the challenges that universities confront in maintaining, enhancing, or enlarging their research programs on the actions of external
actors, thereby minimizing or eschewing examination of the internal
dynamics of the behaviors of single universities and of the aggregation of
research-oriented institutions as contributing factors to the current state
of affairs.

More substantively, aggregating the several forms of stress upon research
universities into Job-like lamentations conflates and indeed confounds different pressures stemming from different causes on different components of the
U.S. system of research universities. Nested within these lamentations are
concerns about the health of undergraduate education (being conducted by
research-intensive, PhD granting institutions); the respective and relative roles
and prospects of private and public universities as research institutions;

declining proposal success rates and thus the current and future well-being of the scientists, especially "younger" scientists in biomedical fields who are recent products of these institutions; the longer terms consequences of current distress in the academic research system on the willingness of prospective future cohorts of students (undergraduate and graduate) to invest time and resources into the increasingly risky and stress-ridden career of a faculty member at a research-oriented institution; the implications of the above stresses, singly and collectively, on the aggregate performance of America's scientific and technological enterprise − its ability to "stay on top" (Mervis, 2013) in an increasingly competitive global environment; and, perhaps most importantly, the contribution of America's research universities to a portfolio of national objectives.

Here, reflexive attribution of the U.S.'s global leadership in academic research and graduate education to its seamless integration of properties that is more than a simple summation of its parts − a gestalt − gets in the way of a finer grain analysis (and prediction). A standard listing of these properties begins of course with the co-production in a single organization of undergraduate instruction, graduate education, research, and, for public universities, outreach, alongside increasing commitments for all universities to "third mission" outputs such as technology transfer, incubators, start-ups, and the like. The existence of both public and private institutions has provided both an historic as well as contemporary foundation for high degrees of institutional autonomy, diverse revenue streams, mission portfolios, modes of governance, and more compared to universities in other countries. These properties nest within a post-War War II political consensus to outsource sizeable portions of Federal government investments in both basic research and mission-relevant research to academic institutions, in part because of the coupling of research and graduate education, a pattern substantially different from those of other OECD countries where national laboratories and public research organizations occupy relatively larger places within national science and technology systems (Laredo & Mustar, 2009). Yet another consensus has been to allocate these funds in the main on the basis of competitively awarded, peer reviewed researcher initiated project/center grants rather than on the basis of population, political jurisdiction, or as commonplace in other countries via block grants to institutions. Finally, all these pieces come together and rest within a national setting based upon and repeatedly extolling, if not always implementing, open competition for research inputs, valorization of research output, and institutional standing (Feller, 2000).

For present purposes it is necessary to separate these pressures, asking in turn in what ways they affect the competitive performance of single institutions, classes of universities, and the academic research system, writ large. Consider, for example, Clark's statement that for reasons of legitimacy, public support, imagery, income from tuition, and state appropriations (as well as alumni contributions), "[N]o institution, public or private, could afford to let go of the undergraduate tier" (Clark, 1987, p. 10). However authoritative this assessment may be, thus adding further saliency to issues surrounding access, affordability, student indebtedness, and productivity to an understanding the general malaise pervading discourse on the conditions of American universities, attention to them does not necessarily provide diagnostic or curative insights about *The Current Health and Future Well-Being of the American Research University*, to cite the title of the Research Consortium report.

FRAMING THE BASELINE SETTING

To examine the systemic pressure on research universities, the paper makes use of the framework of alternative scenarios related to the size and structure of the American research university system developed in 1992 by the Government-University-Industry Research Roundtable (GUIRR) in its report, *Fateful Choices*. The framework contains three scenarios of the size of the academic research system: expansion, steady state, downsizing; and three for its structure: more concentrated, current configuration, more diversified. The nine alternative scenarios produced by this 3×3 matrix are presented in Fig. 1.

Taking the setting of the 1960s as the (status quo) starting point, the general direction of change as measured by every mainstream measure has been toward an expanded, less centralized system, even allowing for the years of austerity and angst summarized above (Graham & Diamond, 1997). A brief review highlights the magnitude of these trends. In 1969, commenting on the U.S. academic research system, Kaysen spoke of some 30 universities that really mattered (alluding presumably to the institutions listed in Geiger's narratives on the rise of the U.S. system of research universities (Geiger, 1986, p. 232, 1993, p. 209)). At the time, this number seemed to constitute an adequate number, as suggested by the observation in the Carnegie Commission's 1971 report, New Students and New Places, "We find no need whatsoever in the foreseeable future for any more

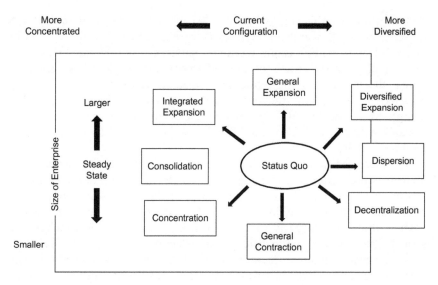

Fig. 1. Framework of Alternative Scenarios. *Source*: Government-University-Industry Research Roundtable (1992, p. 34).

research-type universities granting the PhD" (as quoted in McCormick & Zhao, 2005, p. 52). The 1991 U.S. Office of Technology Assessment's report, *Federally Funded Research: Decisions for a Decade*, speaks of 50−100 research universities, plus "hundreds of universities that also compete for Federal research funding" (U.S. Office of Technology Assessment, 1991, p. 198). By 1992, the President's Council of Advisors on Science and Technology put the number at between 175 and 200, cautioning though against "programs that would increase the net capacity of the system of research-intensive universities" (President's Council of Advisors on Science and Technology, 1992, p. 12).

Contrary to these expectations and concerns, the pattern since the early 1990s has been for continued expansion and decentralization. The Carnegie Foundation's 1994 classification of colleges and universities reported that the number of doctorate granting institutions had increased from 173 to 236 between 1970 and 1994, with the number of institutions in the Research University I category increasing by 52−88, or 69% (Carnegie Foundation for the Advancement of Teaching, 1994, Tables XIB, XIV). In 1998, Noll, building atop and slightly modifying the 1994 Carnegie Commission criteria, estimated the number of research universities at around 125 (Noll, 1998; p. 10). Jumping to the present, the latest Carnegie classification in 2010, employing its 2005 revised typology, described 108 universities as "Research universities (very high research activity)," 98 as "Research universities (high research activity)," and 89 as "Doctoral/ research universities," for a total of 295 research institutions.[6] As generally noted, the increase in the number of research active universities largely reflected the growth of the public university sector.[7] Public universities comprised 73 of the 108 universities classified as having a very high research activity, and 73 of the 98 universities classified as having a high research activity.

The increased number of public research universities also contributed to an increased geographic dispersion, or spatial decentralization. PhD granting institutions exist in all 50 states. In FY2012, 41 states had at least one higher education institution within the top 125 performers of academic R&D; beyond the usual suspects (e.g., California, New York, Massachusetts), some had two or more universities in this category.[8]

A somewhat different picture of the U.S. university research system emerges when considered in terms of academic R&D expenditures. For even as the number of research activities universities has increased, academic R&D expenditures have historically remained concentrated among a small, essentially unchanging set of institutions (Geiger & Feller, 1995). In FY2012, among the 907 colleges and universities in NSF surveys reporting R&D expenditures above a threshold level of $150,000, 20 institutions accounted for 31% of total academic science and engineering research and development expenditures and 100 institutions accounting for 79% of the total (Geiger & Feller, 1995; NSB, 2014, pp. 5–17). Also, allowing for small movements in ordinal place, there has been little turnover in the institutions that comprise the top 10 or 20 institutions.

A related pattern of concentration exists in the distribution of these funds among states. In FY2012, five states (California, New York, Maryland, Pennsylvania, and Texas) received a total of $15.5 billion in federal academic research awards, or 38.7%, of the federal total of $40.1 billion. By way of contrast, the 10 states with the lowest levels of these awards received in the aggregate $925 million, or 2.3% of the total. Not surprisingly, the former set of states includes the nation's most populous, those in which premier private universities are located, and those which have large public universities. Conversely, the states at the bottom of the distribution tend to have the opposite characteristics.[9]

Tensions between distributing funds on the basis of the "best science" – "efficiency" – and on the basis of distributive criteria (e.g., population; political jurisdiction; institution) – "equity" – are recognized factors in the shaping of national policies toward support of academic research (GUIRR, 1992, p. 28; Hicks & Katz, 2011; Kleinman, 1995). Geographic concentration, even if sanctioned as the outcome of competitive, merit review processes, butts up against widely shared social and politically bipartisan adherence to the proposition that "The talent necessary to succeed in science and engineering resides in all states" (National Academies-National Research Council, 2012b, p. 5). It also butts up against pragmatic acknowledgment that the distribution of political power in the U.S. Congress is considerably more geographically dispersed than is the distribution of Federal academic R&D awards. As noted in *Fateful Choices*, "The notion that each state or region should possess a world-class institution of higher education has enormous political appeal."

The resultant of the contending forces of equity and efficiency has been a de factor compromise, involving obeisance to each criterion. The mechanism of competitive, merit based review is repeatedly extolled by academic researchers and science agency administrators, especially those working within the penumbra of NIH and NSF, as the gold standard by which academic research awards are to be allocated − the most important scientific questions being addressed by the best scientists, as determined by peers. Indeed, adoption and adherence to this allocation system is often cited as a critical contributor to U.S. global leadership in science (the contrasting mechanisms being those of block grants to institutions or chairs).

Departures from this mechanism in the name of (institutional/geographic) equity are longstanding, though (Chubin & Hackett, 1990; Feller, 2013). One form of departure is congressional designation (earmarking) of funds for capital facilities and research programs to specific institutions, or as a functional equivalent, by legislative language to so narrowly define specific research topics that only one or a pre-selected set of institutions (located in specific states) could qualify (De Figueiredo & Silverman, 2007; Hedge & Mowery, 2008; Payne, 2006; Savage, 1999). Another is the creation of set aside, capacity-building programs that provide sheltered competitions for states (and their constituent higher education universities) with low percentages of competitively awarded grants.[10]

More than numbers though are measured in the above data. They are but external manifestations of the internal cultural, institutional, and aspirational changes that have led to the rise (and ascendancy), of the U.S. research-intensive, PhD granting university. Also well known are several chapter titles in this narrative: redefinition, and more importantly, reprioritization of institutional missions; new standards for faculty recruitment, promotion, and tenure; expectations that faculty will maintain ongoing research program, financed by external grants; articulation and fleshing out of supportive physical and administrative infrastructures. In brief, the "academic revolution" involving the "graduate imperium" that Jencks and Riesman wrote about in 1969 is today's status quo; it is the position toward which the system seeks to return whenever beset by external shocks.

Even as the U.S. system has evolved seemingly inexorably in the direction of an expanded, increasingly decentralized direction, recurrent concerns have been expressed about whether it could "afford to continue expanding the university research system" (Cordes, 1990). Likewise, fervid expressions that the academic scientific house is falling for lack of funds have been countered by trenchant responses of the form, "What do you mean there's not enough money?" (Noonan, 1993). Or as more recently phrased by Stephan, "Many of the problems that confront the funding of science are scale related. A system that worked relatively well when the research community was small does not work nearly as well when the enterprise grows by a factor of 12, as the U.S. enterprise has done in the past fifty years" (Stephan, 2012, pp. 149−150).[11]

This perspective also highlights the ambiguity or purposeful fuzziness that exists in phrases such as Kaysen's earlier cited reference to "really matter" or Cole's assessment that of an estimated 260 universities classified as research universities, "only about 125 contribute in meaningful ways to the growth of knowledge" (Cole, 2009, p. 6). "Really matter" and "meaningful ways" have both quantitative and qualitative dimensions. The former relates to absolute or relative measures of the inputs and outputs of the research-intensive, doctoral granting university of the type that undergird Carnegie-like classification systems. The latter relates the assessments of relevant scientific communities and users about the novelty, relevance, and impacts of knowledge and human capital outputs that follow upon the utilization of these research and educational inputs. As phrased by S. Stigler, the competition that occurs among universities is "primarily in the currency of ideas .... What makes the intellectual gain from teaching and research unusual is that it requires competition for its recognition and award: it is only through the competitions itself that we can tell when we are successful" (Stigler, 1994, p. 133). It is these assessments that bestow prestige upon a faculty and their university.

Issues of what is being measured, or deemed important, and of distinctions between the roles and prospects of public universities and private universities enter here. In terms of academic R&D expenditures, public research universities are the larger performers. Six of the top 10 performing institutions of academic R&D, and 12 of the top 20, are public universities.[12]

In terms though of international prestige rankings, the U.S.'s leadership position is attributable in the main to the performance of its private universities. As noted above, 7 U.S. universities ranked among the world's top 10: 6 of these are private universities, the University of California – Berkeley being the sole public institution represented. And of the 14 U.S. universities in the top 20, 11 are private universities (being joined by 2 additional public universities: University of California – Los Angeles and University of Michigan).

The quantity/quality dichotomy between public and private universities also appears in bibliometric data. Brint's analysis of publication counts between 1995 and 2005 indicates that "Of the 20 most prolific research faculties during this period, two-thirds (13) were located at public universities." This leading role though is attributed to research faculty size, "the key advantage of public universities" (Brint, 2007, p. 105).[13] A different picture about threats to U.S. preeminence emerges if citations rather than publication counts are used as the metric of excellence or prestige. Treated here as reflecting the scientific community's assessments of the "contribution" embodied in publications, private research universities occupy the dominant position. As an illustration, Table 1, calculated from the CWTS Leiden Ranking 2014 (Appendix), employs the PP (top 10%) measure to position the United States in global rankings of scientific output.[14] U.S. universities held the top 18 places in this ranking, 19 of the top 25, and 39 of the top 50 places. This dominance was attributable in large part to the performance of private research universities, which held 10 of the first 25 places and 13 of the next 25.[15] Relatedly, in terms of geographic dispersion, also strikingly evident in these data is the concentrated location of these universities in a few states: California is the home of 9 (including 5 in the top 10); Massachusetts, 6; and New York, 6; or 21 of the U.S. total of 39. Five other states have two universities in the top 50.

Table 1. U.S. Share of PP (Top 10%), 2014.

Rank	Public	Private	Total
1–25	9	10	19
26–50	7	13	20
	16	23	39

Source: Calculated from data compiled by Leiden University – Center for Science and Technology Studies (CWTS). Retrieved from http://www.leidenranking.com/ranking/2014

SHOW ME THE MONEY

Consideration about whether contemporary pressures are but another episode of financial hardship, subject to amelioration, as in the movie, Jerry
McGuire, by infusions of external research funds, or something more fundamental, requiring substantial changes in the size and structure of the current system, requires a fresh look at the crossroads at which the pace of
scientific inquiry, commitments of universities to a research ethos, research
costs, and research revenues intersect.

A detailed mapping of each of the features in this landscape warrants a
more substantive treatment than is possible here. Thus, treated here as unlikely to undergo significant change in the foreseeable future are acceptance
of the proposition that science constitutes an endless frontier with ever present new opportunities and challenges relevant to a panoply of societal
needs and aspirations; continuation of broad-based political support for
the Federal government's role as a patron of scientific and technological
research, especially in the functional areas of defense, space, health, and
basic research; and reliance on universities to conduct substantial portions
of this research.

A final given, essential to propelling the dynamics outlined below, is the
continuing internalization within existing research-intensive universities
and those aspiring to such status of the proposition advanced in 1871 by
James Angell in his inaugural address as president of the University of
Michigan, that "the institution which is not steadily advancing is certainly
falling behind."[16] For even amidst a contemporary setting frequently
described in terms of pressures and stresses and replete with challenges to
their performance as suppliers of undergraduate education, scans of recent
statements and actions by a number of public universities indicates that
several continue to pronounce their commitments to enlarging and enhancing their research profiles (Kerr, 1991). In 2013, the University of South
Florida announced with considerable pride its surge up to No. 43 in federal
rankings of academic R&D expenditures — a 10-place upward move
(University of South Florida News, 2013) — while more recently the
University of Connecticut (ranked #80 in R&D expenditures in FY2012)
announced new research initiatives buttressed by the hiring of new faculty in
a full page ad in the Chronicle of Higher Education (on January 23, 2015).

Far fewer is the number of universities purposefully proposing a substantial contraction or withdrawal from research, akin to the University of
Alabama — Birmingham's decision, however momentary, to drop Division

I football because of what were deemed to be unsustainable costs. Syracuse University, a private university, is perhaps a singular example, as its competitive research position and national rankings have fallen, leading it to exit the Association of American Universities, all to the displeasure of its faculty, who faulted its former chancellor for unduly emphasizing research related to the city of Syracuse and channeling resources toward broadening the demographic composition of its undergraduate student body (Wilson, 2011; see also, Roop, 2010). The more frequently observed event is the flaming out of aspirations voiced by incoming governors or university chancellors/presidents to have the state's public universities rise rapidly in prestige league tables, earning standing as a top 10 public/research-intensive/AAU-worthy institution.[17]

Accepting these givens leaves projected research costs and revenues as the proximate determinants of future scenarios about size and structure. For it is at this point, that the generic pressures on the university research system both resemble and differ from past periods of austerity.

Treating costs first, participation in the competitive contests for external support necessary to conduct the cutting edge, frontier research that produces the significant discoveries that lead to publications in highly regarded and widely cited journals, thereby bringing prestige, reputation, and future revenues streams both to faculty and institution requires substantial upfront and life cycle costs. These costs are only partially recouped by indirect cost recovery (Ehrenberg, 1999, p. 105). Stephan, for example, has estimated the costs of acquiring equipment for an individual laboratory at between $250,000 and $1 million, with the costs of more expensive equipment, such as an NMR, shared by several laboratories (Stephan, 2012, p. 86). Relatedly, start-up packages to acquire equipment and support research personnel for an initial period are staple items in competitions to recruit prospective faculty, both established "stars" and the most promising future researchers. The average amount of these packages was estimated in 2003 to be $489,000 for an assistant professor in chemistry and $983,929 for a senior faculty member, with roughly comparable sums needed in biology (Stephan, 2012, p. 84).

The revenue side of the ledger is presented in Table 2. The trends in relative shares are clear. The Federal government is by far the largest single source of funds for academic R&D, providing approximately 60% of the total in recent decades (62% in FY2012), down though from the peak period circa 1970–1980 when its share was in the 67–70% range. State and local government's share (for directly identified R&D activities) has declined steadily since the 1960s, and now constitutes between 5% and 6% of the total. Business support rose from 2.6% in 1970 to 3.9% in 1970,

Table 2.   Higher Education R&D Expenditures, Science and Engineering
by Source of Fund, Selected Years (Dollars in Millions).

Year	All R&D	Source of Funds				
		Federal government	State and local government	Institutional funds	Business	All other sources
2012	62,266	38,935	3,440	12,086	3,201	4,603
2010	58,360	36,510	3,605	10,674	3,117	4,454
2000	30,084	17,548	2,200	5,925	2,156	2,255
1990	16,290	9,640	1,324	3,006	1,127	1,191
1980	6,063	4,098	491	835	236	403
1970	2,335	1,647	219	243	61	165
1960	696	408	85	64	40	52
		Percentage distribution				
2012	100	62.5	5.5	19.4	5.1	7.4
2010	100	62.5	6.1	17.3	5.3	7.6
2000	100	58.3	7.3	19.7	7.2	7.5
1990	100	59.1	8.1	18.5	6.9	7.3
1980	100	67.6	8.1	13.8	3.9	6.6
1970	100	70.5	9.7	10.7	2.6	7.1
1960	100	62.7	13.2	9.9	6.2	8.0

Source: National Science Foundation National Center for Science and Engineering Statistics,
Higher Education Research Development Survey.

surged in the years between 1980 and 2000, the take-off period of the era of
university—industry R&D partnerships, but has declined since then to
slightly over 5%. All other sources have remained relatively constant at
about 7%.

The most striking change in the magnitude of relative shares has been in
Institutional Funds. This share rose from 10% to 18.5% between 1960
and1980 and slightly thereafter to 19%, its current level. This increase
reflects several trends: increases in cost-sharing requirements in selected
Federal research awards; unreimbursed research costs linked to caps on
allowable institutional expenses under OMB or agency policies; and
upfront, anticipatory investments in research facilities and recruitment and
start-up packages to be better positioned to compete for Federal awards.
Implicitly too, they reflect intensified commitments by established and new-
comer universities toward a research orientation. Differences in sources of
funds between public and private institutions loom large here. Public universities received about 7% of their research funds from state and local
governments, compared with about 2% for private universities, but public

universities financed about 22% of their expenditures from internal sources as compared with 13% for private institutions.

In effect, the upward trend over recent decades in the share contributed by Institutional Funds highlights the realities that standing, much less relative advancement, as a research active university has become a pay to play game. It also suggests that the pile of chips needed for an ante and to play enough hands until becoming a winner has increased over time.

Abstracting from the known unknowns of future macroeconomics events, the above data have special bearing on future scenarios of size and structure. Skipping over contemporary (and perennial) budgetary battles over the level of appropriations to the agencies that fund academic R&D, and for the objectives toward which these funds are to be directed (Mervis & Cho, 2015), the most significant trends at the Federal level are those that relate to the share of the federal budget allocated to nondefense, discretionary expenditures. It is in the apportionment of this share that both academic and non-academic nondefense R&D competes with other national objectives, programs, stakeholder communities, and political interests. Over the period covered here, the portion of the Federal budget allocated to mandatory expenditures (e.g., interest on the national debt; Social Security payments) has increased, while that allocated to nondefense, discretionary expenditures has decreased. The portion has fallen from slightly under 50% in 1980 to about 39% at present, and could drop to 24% under the terms of existing budgetary control legislation (Hourihan & Parkes, 2015, p. 11). The share of R&D within the discretionary budget has fluctuated between 11% and 13% in recent decades, currently being at 12.6%. Viewed in yet broader terms, since reaching a peak in 1964 in its share of total U.S. R&D expenditures (69%) and in its ratio to gross domestic product (1.92%), the relative role of the Federal government as the funder of the nation's R&D activities has declined (to 31% and 0.89%, respectively, in 2009) (Jankowski, 2013).

Decisions about the size and composition of the Federal budget, including obviously the level and structure of taxes used to generate revenues, are inherently political ones. Any projection of future trends in Federal funding of academic R&D thus requires predicting the outcome of future elections, especially the presidential and congressional elections of 2016. Eschewing any such attempt, the safest proposition to advance at the present time is that future levels of Federal support of academic R&D will be dependent on higher order political agreements about the size and share of the nondefense discretionary budget, with academic R&D neither receiving preferential treatment or being singled out for disproportionate reductions if the nondefense discretionary budget is cut.[18]

If this assessment is correct, then in Reinhardt and Rogoff's terms, we have indeed been here before, for the causes of the present distress are similar to those present in previous boom and bust cycles in Federal funding of academic R&D. Additionally, as pointed to by the predominance of references in contemporary accounts of the pressures on U.S. research universities to the financial and professional austerity besetting the field of biomedical research attendant on the stagnant state of NIH funding, if stasis and volatility in Federal funding is the larger single cause of these pressures, it follows that the most impacted parts of the total system (e.g., fields of research, institutions, locus of governance, states) will be those most dependent on federal funding, both in the aggregate and by specific agency.

Where this time truly does seem to be different, however, is in state government financing of public higher education. Well known is the financial plight of public universities consequent upon a secular decline since 1987 in the percentage of state budgets allocated to higher education (from 12.3% in 1987 to 10.3% in 2011; National Association of State Budget Officers, 2013) and as a percentage of institutional revenues, with these trends aggravated by the steep drop in state funding between 2007 and 2010 from which recovery is still underway and incomplete. The consequence of these relative and absolute budget reductions has been a long-term decline in average state appropriations per student and a rise in net tuition for individual students and their families (U.S. General Accounting Office, 2014).[19]

Reductions in state appropriations eat away at the ability of public universities to self-finance the expenditures necessary to maintain and/or enhance research infrastructure and thus competitiveness for external research funding from all sources. The reductions are widely cited as the proximate cause of faculty layoffs, the closing of laboratories, and the termination of programs at a number of institutions. The larger, longer term impact of the erosion of state government support on the research competitiveness of public universities may yet be forthcoming. Latent in the concatenation of pressures for increasing student access, reduced levels of appropriations per student and de facto caps on tuition is the prospect of incremental but cumulative withdrawal of the subsidy of faculty salary and time, the latter, according to Clark, being "the most basic of all research subsidies" (Clark, 1995, p. 135).[20]

Especially worrisome for the public university sector is the evolving rationales behind these budget developments. The conventional story is that beginning sometime in the 1980s other demands on state government budgets – prisons, Medicaid, K-12 education – essentially squeezed out incremental support for public universities, leading them to raise tuition to maintain/enhance the quantity and quality of their composite services. From the perspective of state officials, this policy shift could be justified on the basis of estimates of high private rates of return from higher education. Continued though as it was for an extended period, this policy led universities to substantial increase tuition and fees, generating widespread concerns noted above about affordability and access in public higher education, as well as the substantive and symbolic content of what was meant by a public university (Duderstadt & Womack, 2003, Chapter 6). Atop and reinforcing these cost-shifting trends came the impact of the macroeconomic contraction of 2008, followed by dramatic reductions and rescissions in state appropriations to public universities from which recovery is still in progress.

More portentous for the future performance of public universities, encompassing their educational and outreach missions as well as their research competitiveness, is that contemporary, 2015, budget proposals in a number of states — Wisconsin, Kansas, and Louisiana being highly visible examples in early 2015 — effectively provide for a permanent reduction in the state's commitment to public higher education. The direct cause of these proposed reductions are recently adopted tax policies that permanently reduce state tax bases in the belief that these fiscal policies will stimulate economic growth. The immediate consequence of the failure to date of such "supply side" policies to produce the projected rates of growth policies (not unexpected given their shaky theoretical and empirical underpinnings) has been substantial state budget shortfalls that in turn has led to gubernatorial proposals for draconian cuts in higher education appropriations. Portentously, the longer term implication of such policies is a reduction in the revenue pool from which appropriations to public higher education could be allocated, even if the share of the state budget allocated to public universities fell no further.

Equally of concern looking into the future are state policies, as intimated by the imbroglio caused by Wisconsin's governor's attempt to fundamentally alter the mission statement of the University of Wisconsin that would have hollowed out the statutory basis for the Wisconsin Idea, and comparable legislative proposals elsewhere on faculty working conditions and institutional tenure policies, recent initiatives in several states cannot but be viewed as anything other than antipathy to the research/public servicemissions of universities (and their faculties), or indeed to any activities other than those that train workers for the state's workforce. In effect, these events point to a de facto renegotiation — or more precisely imposition by one party to the transaction – of more stringent terms to the "fragile (social) contract" (Guston & Keniston, 1994) held to exist between research universities and the societies from which they have drawn resources.[21]

IMPLICATIONS

In 1992, reviewing trends in revenues and costs along the lines of this paper, Donald Langenberg, Chancellor of the University of Maryland System, predicted a market shakeout.[22] Shakeout, as the term is conventionally used in economics, refers to a reduction in the number of suppliers or firms in an industry, usually caused by competitive processes. Such a shakeout in the number of research-intensive universities obviously has not occurred. Indeed, the academic research system has continued to expand as well as to decentralize. If anything, returning to Teitelbaum's account of five cycles, the U.S. academic research system has exhibited ratchet-like properties: it evidences an ability to grow when receiving infusions of funding; it is resistant to contraction when funding is static or declines.

Why is this so? Why indeed have so many predictions about the future size and structure of the U.S. academic research system proven wrong? The questions take on special import here because shifting the trends reported above yields the prediction that its most likely future is for little if any expansion, and indeed for a possible contraction, accompanied by increased concentration. But this prediction, like similar ones before it, is likely to be wrong. The low likelihood of a sizeable downsizing of the research commitment by any significant number of universities, especially among those whose aggregate expenditures represent more than a negligible share of the total, is itself a prediction, and indeed the one assigned the highest probability being offered here. Such a prediction has its own consequences. If there is no downsizing, the absence of any sizeable and sustained increase in the level of funding provided by the federal government or state governments implies a continuing state of financial pressure and chronic jeremiads.

Assessing the prospects for stasis, expansion, or contraction perforce entails authoring and assigning probabilities to various federal and state government budget scenarios. No Boltzmann constant as in chemistry, for example, constrains the share of Federal discretionary appropriations to the recent 11–13% range cited above. Continuing concern, for example, about a competitively debilitating U.S. deficit innovation (Massachusetts Institute of Technology, 2015) and the increasingly importance of academic medical centers as regional economic pillars have the potential to weld together otherwise divergent political interests to upwardly torque currently projected Federal appropriations.

In a contrary manner though, it is not difficult to envision a situation in which academic R&D becomes the sacrificial lamb that releases funds under rigid budget ceilings so that other national objectives and/or political interests may be saved, with its share driven to the low end of its historic range (11%), or even lower. Possible also in these out year dynamics are ever harsher trade-offs across and within agencies and fields of research, such that gains or reduced losses for one come more manifestly at the expense of another. Relatedly, the pace of improvement of state budgets remains slow and uneven. Additionally, few signs exist as yet that the priority attached to buttressing core university functions in either education or research has changed much for the better. Instead, the tenor of contemporary expert commentary has been that the "recent funding troubles at public institutions will not go away" (Morson & Schapiro, 2015, p. B4).[23]

An implication of less than robust increases in federal support of academic R&D and of anemic state government appropriations is a slowdown and possible contraction in the role of public universities as sources of research output and graduate education. By default, these changes would lead to relatively increased roles (quantitatively and qualitatively) for the private sector and a Spencerian subset of existing public universities (Feller, 2007).[24] This latter cohort of institutions has the internal resources to both sustain their research infrastructures in austere times, to invest in emerging research areas, including raising graduate stipends and fellowships to attract premier graduate students, thereby retaining or further increasing their first mover advantages when federal agencies are again in a financial position to fund new initiatives. Additionally, as described by Paradeise and Thoenig, these institutions have the "homeostatic properties that help them reproduce themselves while adapting to their changing environment" that exhibits itself in "a remarkably swift capacity to redesign new and more competitive frameworks for regenerating sub-disciplines, research agendas, educational offers, and collaboration with outside third parties such as business firms" (Paradeise & Thoenig, 2013, p. 212).

But this prediction is as likely to be wrong as were earlier ones. For like them, it fails to fully consider the resiliency of the academic research system. This resiliency is the product of the awkward economics of higher

education, political influence, and internalized values both on the part of
faculty and institutions.

Two metaphors play a large role in what follows. The first, taken from
the experience of the Broadway musical theater, is "marvelous invalid";
the second, taken from the economics of industrial organization, is "sick
industry." Each subsumes the same immediate responses by universities to
fiscal austerity but diverge at the point if and when the responses prove
adequate.

The marvelous invalid metaphor refers to a system's ability to withstand
debilitating influences for extended periods, relying on a combination of its
own curative properties and hoped for new cures to return to full health.
As applied to Broadway, it is akin to suffering through a series of shows
that close soon after opening night but hanging on awaiting one or more
smash hits − Les Mis; The Lion King. The Wiz − that (re)fill theater seats
and box office revenues and provide sustained employment for performers
(and returns on investments for backers).

For universities, the curative properties and new cures involve first tapping into or enlarging alternative sources of revenue and then reorganizing
how research is performed in order to reduce costs to levels commensurate
with projected revenues. The two approaches are means of maintaining a
research presence as close as possible to one's performance peak until such
time as events at the national and state levels generate raise revenues to
levels commensurate with full capacity costs. Adoption and increased attention to these approaches also implicitly reflects acceptance (resignation?) of
permanent changes in relationships with state government − the much discussed trend toward the "privatization" of public universities.

And indeed universities are adopting both approaches. In their search
for additional revenues they are setting ever higher capital campaign goals;
intensifying efforts to garner intellectual property revenues, ventures in
MOOCs, participation in multi-institutional research programs, recruiting
full fare foreign and out-of-state students, and the like, all in the effort
to support both their general operations and to upgrade their research
infrastructures to competitive levels. As best as can be gauged by news
accounts, organizational reports such as AUTM surveys, and university
press releases, these efforts have indeed produced both localized institutional successes and general increases in university revenues. Whether they
either compensate for deceleration in federal R&D expenditures, reductions in state government appropriations or are commensurate with
the rising costs of academic research remains of course the unanswered
question.

Also underway are efforts to reduce both general institutional expenses and those related to research.[25] Prominent among these cost reducing efforts are factor substitution, exerting downward pressure on input costs to bring them in line with revenue flows, and pruning of "unprofitable" lines of (research) business. Factor substitution involves the replacement of lower cost for higher cost inputs to the extent that the firm's production processes permit this to occur. The substitution of full-time and part-time non-tenure-track ("contingent") faculty for tenure-track faculty, a well-known practice that shows no sign of abating, is a classic example of this adjustment strategy. It is a technique for supplying the increased quantity of instructional hours commensurate with the increased numbers of under-graduate student enrollments without requiring, on average, tenure-track research-oriented faculty to reallocate their efforts between teaching and research. Thus, according to Stephan and Ehrenberg, "Large start-up packages are one of several factors that lead universities to substitute non-tenure-track faculty for tenure-track faculty" (Stephan & Ehrenberg, 2009, p. 259). The strategy of keeping input costs down also is visible in the low rate of increase in faculty salaries in recent years, especially at public universities, a strategy constrained mainly by concerns about adverse selection in faculty mobility. Pruning is simply another way of expressing the strategic planning mantra of recent years that one cannot be all things to all people, leading to increased attention to prioritizing institutional research investments in selected fields, terminating others or allowing them to fend for themselves.

There is considerable logic to the strategies above. Historically, universities have struggled through and succeeded in maintaining and even expanding their research capacities in past periods of financial austerity. Organizationally, it is difficult to comprehend how any sizeable diminishment in a commitment to research for institutions whose rise to such standing has taken some 50 years or so to develop would not rend it asunder. The basic elements of a research orientation — 3/6 hour teaching loads, graduate student RA's supported by external grants, expectations to publish in high impact journals, possible only through securing external grants — constitute the life's experience of today's complement of faculty and administrators. Resilience and patience until the current period of austerity shall pass, as have similar ones in the past, is a defensible strategy against a bruited Darwinian shakeout (Lohmann, 2004).

The above strategies though are institution-based. More difficult to organize but also part of a longer term systemwide adjustment is achieving balance in the growth in the number of researchers in a field dependent on external funding with the growth of these funds. This is not a new phenomenon in the history of labor market conditions in many occupations, academic or otherwise. In terms of recent pressures on U.S. research universities its most visible manifestation, as explicitly stated in several of the laments cited above and implicit in many others, is the plight of "younger" biomedical scientists who are unable to land tenure-track positions or to secure independent funding for their own research because of the retardation in rates of growth of NIH funding (Basken & Voosen, 2014; Daniels, 2015). Attending to this field thus holds considerable potential for lessening systemwide pressures.

In a significant departure from the mainstream prescription that the etiology and thus cure for this situation lies in the size of NIH's budget, Alberts et al. have recently offered a different diagnosis and thus a different remedy. Cited by them as the cause of the biomedical research system's malaise is its "Malthusian" propensity to repeatedly expand beyond its resource base, thereby "generating an ever-increasing supply of scientists vying for a finite set of research resources and employment opportunities" (Alberts et al. 2014, p. 5774). Strikingly though, finessing the Fateful Choices outlined above, most of their specific recommendations are directed toward the terms and procedures by which federal grants are awarded. And those that relate to university policies, such as increasing the ratio of permanent staff positions to trainee positions carry with them the caveat that the likely consequences of these changes "will be an increase in research and a reduction in the average size of laboratories."

For present purposes, the reference to Malthus is both apt and incomplete. It is apt in that the austere labor market and career settings for biomedical researchers correspond to what Malthus termed "positive checks" on population growth: hunger and death. It is incomplete in that it stops short of analyzing and recommending forms of "preventive checks," the academic counterparts of abstinence and other forms of birth control.

Acknowledging the palliative qualities of revenue enhancing and cost reducing strategies, again at both the institutional and system level now being implemented or considered, what if things in fact do not get better? In such a scenario, resilience and resistant produce what is termed a "sick industry" (Kahn, 1988, pp. 173–178). Such an industry is characterized by high fixed relative to variable costs, low profit margins or losses, intermittent plant closings (read, departments/colleges/centers) on the part of multi-plant, multi-divisional firms, and, above all, continuing excess capacity. As applied to universities, high fixed costs have both monetary and non-monetary dimensions. The monetary dimensions mean carrying costs on building and facilities that can no longer be financed by indirect costs on federal grants and a salary structure for tenured faculty predicated on the proposition that these faculty would be self-supporting in part via research grants, thereby generating salary savings that could be used to finance other general operating expenses. The non-monetary fixed charge is the above referred to value system, behaviors, and expectations of faculties hired and tenured during recent decades whose worldview is geared to research and professional communities and who would now be required to return to the classrooms.

In a sick industry scenario, there is no shakeout but rather slow, incremental contraction in the size of the system and movement toward a more concentrated structure. Retrospectively, a contemporary current period of pressure is but the dimly perceived onset of a climacteric.

Indeed, it is this concern about the long-term vitality of America's global performance in science that underlies what is perhaps the most plangent concern of recent studies of the well-being of the research university system, namely the threats to its ability to attract "talented young people into careers in science and engineering" and to then provide "opportunities for them to become researchers on their own merits" (Stephan & Ehrenberg, 2009, p. 261). For whatever staying power a sick industry may have for those currently involved with it, it is ill-equipped to attract new investments of either financial or intellectual capital.

The implications do not end here, however. Yet further system level consequences are possible. For exit along the lines of a firm leaving an industry is not the only option available, especially for the public university sector if salving relief from current financial stresses upon the academic research system proves not to be forthcoming or effective. To employ Hirschman's (1970) classic choice paradigm of "exit or voice," voice is an alternative to exit. Voice here has a special meaning. Circling back to the above accounts of the institutional and geographic concentration of competitively awarded Federal academic R&D awards, it implies challenges to the predominant reliance on competitive, merit review procedures to allocate federal academic research awards. Drawing upon the ever present populist ethos in American culture that is prone to depicting private universities as elitist as well as the ever present influence of distributive politics manifestly evident in the existence of set aside programs, it is not unreasonable to expect that events moving the system toward increased concentration, by institution and/or state, would be countered by calls for increased use of earmarks, set asides, or formula based funding systems. In effect, to preserve the role of public research universities, the Federal government would be called upon to fill the gap caused by state government disinvestment in public higher education, altering thereby the allocation mechanism that is held to have contributed to its global preeminence. This truly would be different.

NOTES

1. The respective numbers are 8 of the top 10 and 16 of the top 20 in the Shanghai Jiao Tong University 2014 rankings.

2. Blumenstyk's (2014) overview of pressures upon U.S. universities, for example, is limited to examination of undergraduate instruction only. The research mission of universities receives scant mention. Christensen and Eyring's (2011) treatise on disruptive innovation provides even less coverage. Other attempts to deal concurrently with the pressures on the undergraduate and research missions of universities, as in the 2012 National Research Council (NRC) study of the meanings of productivity in higher education have encountered formidable conceptual issues and limitations of data, and have therefore concentrated on the undergraduate instructional mission only (National Academies-National Research Council, 2012a). Crow and Dabars' (2015) call for a new model for American research universities contains an extensive summary of the contribution of research universities to national and regional economic growth, but discussion of research funding is limited to the experiences of Arizona State University, with little said about the overall pressures on the research university system. Relatedly, the current vogue among American state governments to employ performance-based budget formulae in appropriating funds for the undergraduate instruction role of public universities has little to do with state support of academic research programs targeted at high tech economic growth (Hillman, Tandberg, & Fryar, 2013).

3. To cite but one of numerous such characterizations of the American research university, "Research is a 'good' because it opens the ways for new solutions and opportunities, and the prize, media recognition, and extra income simply reflect its value. Prestige brings the institution comparative advantage in the competitive market for faculty as well as intrinsic pride in accomplishment and recognition .... Institutions compete for prestige, and over time the quest becomes self-fulfilling and regenerating" (Massy, 1994, p. 31; also Brewer, Gates, & Goldman, 2002).

4. Teitelbaum (2014) describes five rounds or clusters of events underlying the boom and bust character of Federal support of higher education and research between 1948 and 2008, as well as the cyclical dynamics by which the doubling of the NIH budget contributed after several years to an increase in number of biomedical researchers requiring continuing external support if they were to secure stable employment in universities and to sustain their research programs. Stephan (2012, pp. 228–235) offers a similar analysis.

5. Nondefense R&D in real terms increased by 134% between 1983 and 2004. Since then, "regular appropriations for nondefense R&D have generally either ticked down or remained flat, with increases in some years offset by reductions and inflation in others" (Hourihan & Parkes, 2015, p. 14).

6. This number measures the number of institutions that satisfy the Carnegie criteria; it is not a measure of the "host of intangibles that constitute institutional identity" (McCormick & Zhao, 2005, p. 55), including upwardly aspiring strivings of universities that have yet to satisfy the criteria. Earlier research based on interviews with senior officials in several upwardly mobile universities reported that they saw themselves not as "wannabe's," but as here to stay as major performers of research. They were both confident and comfortable with the expressed view, "why not '400' research universities" (as quoted in Feller, 2001, p. 205).

7. "In general, the four decades since the end of World War II have witnessed a growing prominence of the state research universities. Not that private universities did not prosper. A small group of them continued to serve as national pacesetters .... But the state universities, as a general group have prospered even more. Considerably larger in size on the average, they have developed huge embedded resources in the form of regular state allocations based on student numbers that may be many times larger than their private counterparts" (Clark, 1995, p. 133).

8. Florida, for example, has 5: University of Florida (#23), University of South Florida (#43), University of Miami (#61), Florida State University (#93), and University of Central Florida (#136).

9. A different picture of the state level distribution of Federal academic R&D awards emerges when computed on a per capita basis. North Dakota and Vermont move from the bottom tier of 10 states to 6th and 7th place at the top, while California drops from #1 to #21 and Texas drops from #5 to #34 (National Academies, 2013, Table 1-1).

10. The National Science Foundation's Experimental Program to Stimulate Competitive Research (EPSCoR), established as an "experimental program" in 1979, with an expected duration of five years, is the exemplar of this approach. An initial set of awards designed to "catalyze" increased research competitiveness, that is improve the ability of researchers at these institutions and the institutions themselves to perform better under competitive, merit-based review procedures was made in 1980 to five states. By 2012, relaxation of the program's eligibility criteria and the establishment of counterpart, if somewhat different, programs in six other federal agencies increased the number of participating jurisdictions to 32 (29 states and 3 territories), serving likewise to produce a more than doubling of the funds set aside for these programs from $225 million in 2001 to $484 million in 2012 (IDA-Science & Technology Policy Institute, 2014; National Academies, 2013; NSB, 2014, p. 5–14).

11. Pointedly, several of these reservations start from the proposition that the goal underlying Federal support of academic R&D is the health of U.S. science and engineering, not necessarily the health of its performers or of the institutions in which they are located. Again to cite Noonan, "There will *never* be enough money to fund every good project and every good researcher. There may not even be enough to fund all the *excellent* projects and researchers .... The federal government's responsibility is for the health of *science and engineering*, not the health of *scientists and engineers*" (Noonan, 1993, p. 254, italics in original).

12. The relative role of the public university sector is even greater for the production of doctorate degrees. In 2013, public universities occupied the 9 of the top 10 places – Stanford, at #4, being the sole private university represented – and 16 of top 20 places (NSF, 2013). Overall, in FY2012, of the $65.8 billion spent by higher

education institutions on research and development, public institutions were responsible for 68% of this total ($44.2 billion) compared with 32% for private institutions
($21.6 billion) (National Science Board, 2014, Tables 5-2). The relative roles are
somewhat closer in terms of the $40.1 billion in higher education R&D funded by
Federal sources, with a ratio of roughly 62–37% ($25.1 billion compared with 15.1
billion).

13. This advantage may be slipping away, though. Adams' attributes a pending
erosion in U.S. pre-eminence in higher education to a relative slowdown in its publication output, "with much of the slowdown located ... in public universities"
(Adams, 2009, p. 28).

14. The PP (top 10%) measures, "The proportion of the publications of a university that, compared with other publications in the same field and in the same year,
belong to the top 10% most frequently cited" http://www.leidenranking.com/
methodology/indicators. Accessed on February 3, 2015.

15. The top 10 research universities in terms of citation impact per paper also are
reported as being the "less expensive producers of citations" (Adams & Griliches,
1996). Eight of these 10 universities are private institutions.

16. Lest this emphasis on upwardly aspiring behavior of university faculty and
administrators appear pejorative, it is helpful to view this behavior as a deeply
ingrained and much lauded American trait, for as expressed by Thoreau in 1854,
"In the long run, men hit only what they aim at. Therefore, they had better aim at
something high."

17. North Dakota presents such a recent example. Fueled by the recent energy
boom, North Dakota experienced rising state government revenues that in part
were targeted for a quantitative and qualitative enhancement of its public research
universities. Led by a newly appointed chancellor whose stated aspirations were to
move these institutions to the top tier of public universities, the state's universities
seemed to be at the cusp of major advancements. The chancellor however soon ran
afoul of state politics and left within two years; the 2014–2015 crash in oil prices
will likely dampen any sustained infusion of state funds, likewise dampening the
university system's brief Camelot like moment (Kiley, 2013).

18. Teich's comment in 1998 on an earlier period of budget austerity for federal
support of academic research still holds: "With only a couple of exceptions in areas
of significant political controversy, the projected reductions in R&D are not the
result of any antipathy political leaders of either party have toward science and
technology, R&D, or universities. Indeed the broad-based bipartisan support for
the nation's R&D (especially basic research) remains largely intact, despite the end
of the cold war. Rather, the reductions in R&D programs are the fallout from
efforts to balance the federal budget by reducing discretionary spending" (Teich,
1998, pp. 102–103).

19. For The Pennsylvania State University, as an example, the percent of its
General Funds Budget provided by a state appropriation fell from 62% in
1970–1971 to 13.2% in 2014–2015, while the share provided by tuition and fees
over this period rose from 32% to 79.4%, in the process producing the second highest tuition costs among U.S. public universities.

20. "[W]ithin the bounds of the state and institutional subsidy of faculty time, in
any university seriously invested in research, the time spent on teaching is held to

such a level that a third or a half of more of professional time is available for research" (Clark, 1995, p. 135).

21. Only passing treatment is possible here of the often vaunted shift in state government economic development strategies circa 1980 toward fostering the birth and recruitment of science and technology-based industries relative to an historic foci on resource-based growth and "smokestack" chasing incentives (e.g., tax abatements). A component of that shift was increased emphasis on the research prowess of state-based universities, leading to a portfolio of initiatives, such as university-based centers of excellence in selected research areas and support for endowed chairs (Eisinger, 1988; Feldman, Lanahan, & Lendel, 2014). The substantive impact of these university-centered programs remains open to question. With limited exception, as in California, New York, and Georgia, the programs were of modest size, short-lived, susceptible to policy fads, and turnover in gubernatorial and economic development offices. Over time too, state policies shifted towards increased emphasis on public-private partnerships involving subsidies to the private sector. Of primary relevance here though is that the shift towards viewing universities as engines of economic growth had little positive effect on general appropriations for the larger, core research and instructional programs of a state's public universities. Rather, state governments are held to have followed "an implicit strategy of seeking to skim the cream or to highly leverage federal, and to a lesser extent, industrial investment in academic R&D by modest investments in selected technology programs and selected areas of technology, leaving the larger institutional educational and research infrastructures to fend for themselves" (Feller, 2004, p. 147).

22. "Is a market shakeout for research and education in the cards?" His answer was unequivocal: "Absolutely" (Langenberg, 1993, p. 209).

23. As candidly expressed in a recent Council of State Government report, after first noting that States with strong research ecosystems are able to attract, grow, and retain large, innovative companies and high-wage jobs, it continues on, "Given budget constraints, investing more money in research is not necessarily the most practical option for many states .... [I]t is important for states and universities to do more with less" (2015, p. 10).

24. Presidents of leading public universities have called attention to this prospect for several years. See Feller (2009, pp. 72–75) for relevant quotes.

25. These efforts in part are the product of the post-1980 "management revolution in higher education" with its accoutrements of strategic planning, revenue centered management, and disruptive innovation. See Keller (1983), Priest, Becker, Hossler, and St. John (2002), Shattock (2010), Christensen and Eyring (2011), Nature (2012), Birnbaum (2000), and Kirp (2003).

ACKNOWLEDGMENTS

I am indebted to Diana Hicks, John Jankowski, and Jon Nelson for their guidance through the data sources and literatures cited in this paper. Responsibility for the analysis and conclusions are mine, alone.

REFERENCES

Adams, J. (2009). *Is the U.S. losing its preeminence in higher education?* National Bureau of Economic Research (NBER) Working Paper No. 15233. National Bureau of Economic Research, Cambridge, MA.

Adams, J., & Griliches, Z. (1996). *Research productivity in a system of universities.* NBER Working Paper No. 5833. National Bureau of Economic Research, Cambridge, MA. Reprinted in D. Encaoua (Ed.). (2000). *Economics and econometrics of innovation* (pp. 105–140). Berlin: Springer.

Alberts, B., Kirschner, M., Tilghman, S., & Varmus, H. (2014). Rescuing US biomedical research from its systematic flaws. *Proceedings of the National Academy of Sciences, 111,* 5773–5777.

Basken, P., & Voosen, P. (2014). Strapped: University scientists abandon studies and students as funds dry up. *Chronicle of Higher Education,* February 28.

Birnbaum, R. (2000). *Management fads in higher education.* San Francisco, CA: Jossey-Bass.

Blumenstyk, G. (2014). *American higher education in crisis?* New York, NY: Oxford University Press.

Brewer, D., Gates, S., & Goldman, C. (2002). *In pursuit of prestige.* New Brunswick, NJ: Transaction Publisher.

Brint, S. (2007). Can public universities compete? In R. Geiger, C. Colbeck, R. Williams, & C. Anderson (Eds.), *Future of the American public research university* (pp. 91–118). Rotterdam: Sense.

Carnegie Foundation for the Advancement of Teaching. (1994). *A classification of institutions of higher education.* New York, NY.

Cheit, E. (1971). *The new depression in higher education, a study of financial conditions at 41 colleges and universities, a general report to the Carnegie commission on higher education.* New York, NY: McGraw-Hill.

Christensen, C., & Eyring, H. (2011). *The innovative university: Changing the DNA of higher education from the inside out.* San Francisco, CA: Jossey-Bass.

Chubin, D., & Hackett, E. (1990). *Peerless science: Peer review in US science policy.* Albany, NY: State University of New York Press.

Clark, B. (1987). *The academic life.* Princeton, NJ: Carnegie Foundation for the Advancement of Learning.

Clark, B. (1995). *Places of inquiry.* Berkeley, CA: University of California Press.

Clotfelter, C. (1996). *Buying the best.* Princeton, NJ: Princeton University Press.

Cole, J. (2009). *The great American University.* New York, NY: Public Affairs.

Cordes, C. (1990). Policy experts ask a heretical question: Has academic science grown too big? *Chronicle of Higher Education,* November 21.

Crow, M., & Dabars, W. (2015). *A new model for the American research university.* Baltimore, MD: Johns Hopkins Press.

Daniels, R. (2015). A generation at risk: Young investigators and the future of the biomedical workforce. *Proceedings of the National Academy of Sciences of the United States, 112,* 313–318.

De Figueiredo, J., & Silverman, B. (2007). How does the government (Want to) fund science? Politics, lobbying and academic earmarking. In P. Stephan & R. Ehrenberg (Eds.), *Science and the university* (pp. 36–51). Madison, WI: University of Wisconsin Press.

Dirks, N. (2015). Rebirth of the research university. *The Chronicle Review,* May 1.

Duderstadt, J., & Womack, F. (2003). *The future of the public university in America*. Baltimore, MD: Johns Hopkins Press.

Ehrenberg, R. (1999). Adam Smith goes to college: An economist becomes an academic administrator. *Journal of Economic Perspectives, 13*, 99–116.

Ehrenberg, R., Rizzo, M., & Jakubson, G. (2007). Who bears the growing cost of science at universities. In P. Stephan & R. Ehrenberg (Eds.), *Science and the university* (pp. 19–35). Madison, WI: University of Wisconsin Press.

Eisinger, P. (1988). *The rise of the entrepreneurial state*. Madison, WI: University of Wisconsin Press.

Feldman, M., Lanahan, L., & Lendel, I. (2014). Experiments in the laboratories of democracy: State scientific capacity building. *Economic Development Quarterly, 28*, 103–106.

Feller, I. (2000). Strategic options to enhance the research competitiveness of EPSCoR universities. In A. H. Link, S. D. Nelson, C. McEnaney, & L. L. Stephen (Eds.), *AAAS science and technology policy yearbook* (pp. 341–363). Washington, DC: American Association for the Advancement of Science.

Feller, I. (2001). Elite and/or distributed science. In M. Feldman & A. Link (Eds.), *Innovation policy in the knowledge-based economy* (pp. 189–212). Boston, MA: Kluwer Academic Publishers.

Feller, I. (2004). Virtuous and vicious cycles in state government funding of research universities. *Economic Development Quarterly, 18*, 138–150.

Feller, I. (2007). Who races with whom; who is likely to win (or survive); why. In R. Geiger, C. Colbeck, R. Williams, & C. Anderson (Eds.), *Future of the American public research university* (pp. 71–90). Rotterdam: Sense Publishers.

Feller, I. (2009). Size, share, and structure: The changing role of America's public research universities. In J. Douglass, C. J. King, & I. Feller (Eds.), *Globalization's muse, university of California-Berkeley* (pp. 67–80). Berkeley, CA: Berkeley Public Policy Press.

Feller, I. (2013). Peer review and expert panels as techniques for evaluating the quality of academic research. In *Handbook on the theory and practice of program evaluation* (pp. 115–142). Cheltenham: Edgar Elgar.

Geiger, R. (1986). *To advance knowledge*. New York, NY: Oxford University Press.

Geiger, R. (1993). *Research and relevant knowledge*. New York, NY: Oxford University Press.

Geiger, R., & Feller, I. (1995). The dispersion of academic research in the 1980s. *Journal of Higher Education, 66*, 336–360.

Government-University-Industry Research Roundtable. (1992). *Fate choices*. Washington, DC: National Academy Press.

Graham, H., & Diamond, N. (1997). *The rise of American research universities*. Baltimore, MD: Johns Hopkins University Press.

Gumport, P. (1993). Graduate education and organized research in the United States. In B. Clark (Ed.), *The research foundations of graduate education* (pp. 225–260). Berkeley, CA: University of California Press.

Guston, D., & Keniston, K. (1994). Introduction: The social contract for science. In D. Guston & K. Keniston (Eds.), *The fragile contract* (pp. 1–41). Cambridge, MA: MIT Press.

Hart, D. (1998). *Forged consensus*. Princeton, NJ: Princeton University Press.

Hedge, D., & Mowery, D. (2008). Politics and funding in the U.S. public biomedical R and D system. *Science, 322*, 1797–1798.

Hicks, D., & Katz, J. (2011). Equity and excellence in research funding. *Minerva, 49*, 137–151.

Higher Education Funding Council for England. (2013). Financial Health of the Higher Education Sector, March 2013/2014, Issues Paper.

Hillman, N., Tandberg, D., & Fryar, A. (2013). Evaluating the impacts of 'New' performance funding in higher education. *Educational Evaluation and Policy Analysis, 20*, 1–19.

Hirschman, A. (1970). *Exit, voice, and loyalty.* Cambridge, MA: Harvard University Press.

Hourihan, M., & Parkes, D. (2015). *The president's R&D Budget in recent and historical context* (pp. 11–24). In AAAS report XL – Research & Development FY2016. Washington, DC: American Association for the Advancement of Science.

IDA-Science & Technology Policy Institute. (2014). *Evaluation of the National Science Foundation's Experimental Program to Stimulate Competitive Research (EPSCoR): Final Report.* IDA Paper No. P-5221. IDA-Science & Technology Policy Institute, Washington, DC.

Jankowski, J. (2013). Federal R&D – Sixty years advancing the frontier. In *The state of science policy* (pp. 1–28). Washington, DC: American Association for the Advancement of Science.

Jencks, C., & Riesman, R. (1969). *The academic revolution.* New York, NY: Doubleday Anchor Book.

Kahn, A. (1988). *The economics of regulation.* Cambridge, MA: MIT Press.

Kaysen, C. (1969). *Higher learning: The universities, and the public.* Princeton, NJ: Princeton University Press.

Keller, G. (1983). *Academic strategy.* Baltimore, MD: Johns Hopkins Press.

Kerr, C. (1991). The new race to be Harvard or Berkeley or Stanford. *Change, 23*, 8–15.

Kerr, C. (1994). *Troubled times for American higher education.* Albany, NY: State University of New York Press.

Kiley, K. (2013). Tapping into the well. *Inside Education*, January 9. Retrieved from http://www.insidehighered.com/news/2013/01/09/oil-boom.

Kirp, D. (2003). *Shakespeare, Einstein, and the bottom line.* Cambridge, MA: Harvard University Press.

Kleinman, D. (1995). *Politics on the endless frontier.* London: Duke University Press.

Krull, W. (2009). Fostering creativity and competition in German higher education. In J. Douglass, C. J. King, & I. Feller (Eds.), *Globalization's muse* (pp. 195–204). Berkeley, CA: Berkeley Public Policy Press.

Langenberg, D. (1993). Academic institutions in a market shakeout. In S. Nelson, K. Gramp, & A. Teich (Eds.), *Science and technology policy yearbook, 1992* (pp. 209–213). Washington, DC: American Association for the Advancement of Science.

Laredo, P., & Mustar, P. (2009). General conclusion: Three major trends in research and innovation policies. In P. Laredo & P. Mustar (Eds.), *Research and innovation policies in the new global economy* (pp. 497–509). Cheltenham: Edward Elgar.

Lohmann, S. (2004). Darwinian medicine for the university. In *Governing academia* (pp. 71–90). Ithaca, NY: Cornell University Press.

Massachusetts Institute of Technology. (2015). *The future postponed, report by the MIT committee to evaluate the innovation deficit.* Cambridge, MA: MIT.

Massy, W. (1994). Measuring performance: How colleges and universities can set meaningful goals and be accountable. In J. Meyerson & W. Massy (Eds.), *Measuring institutional performance in higher education* (pp. 29–54). Princeton, NJ: Peterson's.

McCormick, A., & Zhao, C.-M. (2005). Rethinking and reframing the Carnegie classification. *Change, September–October*, 51–57.

Mervis, J. (2013). How long can the U.S. stay on top? *Science, 340*(21), 1394–1399.

Mervis, J., & Cho, A. (2015). House science chief unveils contentious vision of science. *Science, 348*, 24.

Morson, G., & Schapiro, M. (2015). Bullish on 2040. *Chronicle of Higher Education*, May 26.

Mortimer, K., & Tierney, M. (1979). *The three "Rs" of the eighties: Reduction, reallocation and retrenchment.* AAHE-ERIC/Higher Education Research Report No. 4. American Association for Higher Education, Washington, DC.

National Academies. (2007). *Rising above the gathering storm.* Washington, DC: National Academies Press.

National Academies. (2013). *The experimental program to stimulate competitive research.* Washington, DC: National Academy Press.

National Academies-National Research Council. (2012a). *Improving measurement of productivity in higher education.* Washington, DC: National Academies Press.

National Academies-National Research Council. (2012b). *Research universities and the future of America.* Washington, DC: National Academies Press.

National Association of State Budget Officers. (2013). State Expenditure Reports, FY1987–FY2011.

National Science Board. (2014). *Science and engineering indicators.* Arlington, VA: National Science Board.

National Science Foundation (NSF). (2013). *NCSES Academic institute Profiles-Rankings by Total R&D Expenditures.* Retrieved from https://ncesdata.nsf.gov/profiles

Nature. (2012). *Creative tensions.* Editorial, 484:5–6 (April 5, 2012).

Noll, R. (1998). The American research university: An introduction. In R. Noll (Ed.), *Challenges to research universities* (pp. 1–30). Washington, DC: Brookings Institution.

Noonan, N. (1993). What do you, there isn't enough money. In M. Meredith, S. Nelson, & A. Teich (Eds.), *AAAS science and technology policy yearbook, 1991* (pp. 251–254). Washington, DC: American Association for the Advancement of Science.

Paradeise, C., & Thoenig, J.-C. (2013). Academic institutions in search of quality: Local orders and global standards. *Organization Studies, 34*, 189–218.

Payne, A. (2006). Earmarks and EPSCoR. In D. Guston & D. Sarewitz (Eds.), *Shaping science and technology policy* (pp. 149–172). Madison, WI: University of Wisconsin Press.

President's Council of Advisors on Science and Technology. (1992). *Renewing the promise: Research-intensive universities and the nation.* Washington, DC.

Priest, D., Becker, W., Hossler, D., & St. John, E. (2002). *Incentive-based budgeting systems in public universities.* Cheltenham: Edward Elgar.

Reinhart, C., & Rogoff, K. (2009). *This time is different.* Princeton, NJ: Princeton University Press.

Research Universities Futures Consortium. (2012). The current health and future well-being of the American Research University.

Roop, L. (2010). Debate continues over future direction of UAH. *Huntsville Times*, May 23.

Rosenzweig, R., & Turlington, B. (1982). *The research universities and their patrons.* Berkeley, CA: University of California Press.

Savage, J. (1999). *Funding science in America.* Cambridge: Cambridge University Press.

Shattock, M. (2010). *Managing successful universities* (2nd Ed.). England: Open University Press.

Stephan, P. (2012). *How economics shapes science.* Cambridge, MA: Harvard University Press.

Stephan, P., & Ehrenberg, R. (2009). *Looking to the future.* In P. Stephan & R. Ehrenberg (Eds.), Science and the university (pp. 259–261). Madison, WI: University of Wisconsin Press.

Stigler, S. (1994). *Competition and the research universities.* In J. Cole, E. Barber, & S. Graubard (Eds.), The research university in a time of discontent (pp. 131–152). Baltimore, MD: Johns Hopkins Press.

Teich, A. (1998). *The outlook for federal support of university research.* In R. Noll (Ed.), Challenges to research universities (pp. 87-104). Washington, DC: Brookings Institution.

Teitelbaum, M. (2014). *Falling behind?* Princeton, NJ: Princeton University Press.

Thelin, J. (2004). *A history of American higher education.* Baltimore, MD: Johns Hopkins University Press.

University of South Florida News. (2013). University of South Florida Surges in National Rankings to No. 43. *USF News*, December 2.

U.S. General Accounting Office. (2014). *State funding trends and policies on affordability.* Report No. GAO-15–151. U.S. General Accounting Office, Washington, DC.

U.S. Office of Technology Assessment. (1991). *Federally funded research: Decisions for a decade.* Washington, DC: U.S. Government Printing Office.

Vest, C. (1997). Research universities: Overextended, underfocused, overstressed, and underfunded. In R. Ehrenberg (Ed.), *The American university: National treasure or endangered species* (pp. 43–57). Ithaca, NY: Cornell University Press.

Vincent-Lancrin, S. (2009). *An OECD scan of public and private higher education.* In J. Douglass, C. J. King, & I. Feller (Eds.), Globalization's muse (pp. 15–44). Berkeley, CA: Berkeley Public Policy Press.

Whitley, R. (2011). Changing governance and authority relations in the public sciences. *Minerva, 49*, 359–385.

Wilson, R. (2011). Syracuse's slide. *Chronicle of Higher Education*, October 2, W2011.

Winston, G. (1999). Subsidies, hierarchy and peers: The awkward economics of higher education. *Journal of Economic Perspectives, 13*, 13–36.

APPENDIX

Table A1. CWTS Leiden Ranking 2014.

Rank	University	PP (Top 10%)
1	Rockefeller University	29.1%
2	Massachusetts Institute of Technology	25.2%
3	Harvard University	23.0%
4	University of California – Berkeley	22.5%
5	Stanford University	22.3%
6	California Institute of Technology	22.2%
7	Princeton University	21.9%
8	University of California – Santa Barbara	21.2%
9	University of California – San Francisco	20.2%
10	Yale University	20.0%
11	Rice University	19.2%
12	University of California – Santa Cruz	18.9%
13	Northwestern University	18.8%
14	University of California – San Diego	18.7%
15	University of Colorado – Boulder	18.6%
16	University of Texas – Southwestern Medical Center	18.4%
17	University of Pennsylvania	18.4%
18	University of Chicago	18.4%
19	University of Cambridge	18.4%
20	University of California – Los Angeles	18.1%
21	Ecole Polytechnique Federale de Lausanne	17.7%
22	Weizmann Institute of Science	17.7%
23	London School of Hygiene and Tropical Medicine	17.6%
24	University of Oxford	17.6%
25	ETH (Swiss Institute of Technology) Zurich	17.5%
26	Columbia University	17.4%
27	Johns Hopkins University	17.4%
28	Washington University – St Louis	17.3%
29	Duke University	17.2%
30	University of Massachusetts Medical School	17.2%
31	University of Washington – Seattle	17.1%
32	Cornell University	16.9%
33	Imperial College London	16.8%
34	University of North Carolina – Chapel Hill	16.5%
35	New York University	16.4%
36	Icahn School of Medicine – Mt Sinai	16.3%
37	Boston University	16.1%
38	University of Michigan	16.1%
39	University of St Andrews	16.1%
40	Boston College	16.0%
41	University College London	16.0%

Table A1.   (*Continued*)

Rank	University	PP (Top 10%)
42	Dartmouth College	15.9%
43	University of Texas – Austin	15.8%
44	Emory University	15.5%
45	King's College London	15.4%
46	Carnegie Mellon University	15.3%
47	University of California – Irvine	15.3%
48	University of Massachusetts – Amherst	15.2%
49	University of Bristol	15.1%
50	Georgia Institute of Technology	15.1%

TWO CONTINENTS DIVIDED BY THE SAME TRENDS? REFLECTIONS ABOUT MARKETIZATION, COMPETITION, AND INEQUALITY IN EUROPEAN HIGHER EDUCATION

Pedro Teixeira

ABSTRACT

It is not rare to read positive comments about North American higher education from higher education stakeholders in Europe, particularly policy-makers and institutional managers. The aspects of the system which are most often praised are the degree of institutional competition and the benefits this brings in terms of institutional flexibility, responsiveness, and adaptability. Moreover, those voices also enhance the resourcefulness of North American higher education institutions in finding alternative sources of funding to cope with the steady decline in public funding. In recent decades European higher education has felt the impact of the aforementioned trends and the effects have been not altogether

The University under Pressure
Research in the Sociology of Organizations, Volume 46, 489–508
Copyright © 2016 by Emerald Group Publishing Limited
All rights of reproduction in any form reserved
ISSN: 0733-558X/doi:10.1108/S0733-558X20160000046016

dissimilar from the ones identified in North American higher education. Moreover, the growing integration of European higher education systems has also contributed to enhance some convergence with some of the trends identified in the American case. In this paper, we reflect on the impact of the increasing marketization of funding and governance mechanisms on the European higher education landscape and compare it with the impact of those trends discussed in the papers by Irwin Feller and George W. Breslauer.

Keywords: Higher education; markets; competition; inequality; Europe; funding

INTRODUCTION

It is not rare to read positive comments about North American higher education from higher education stakeholders in Europe, particularly policy-makers and institutional managers. The aspects of the system that are most often praised are the degree of institutional competition and the benefits this brings in terms of institutional flexibility, responsiveness, and adaptability. Moreover, those voices also enhance the resourcefulness of North American higher education institutions in finding alternative sources of funding to cope with the steady decline in public funding.

The papers written by Irwin Feller and George W. Breslauer offer two very insightful accounts of those trends toward greater marketization and inter-institutional competition faced by American universities, especially those that are more research oriented. Feller focuses on the pressures that declining, unstable levels of external funding impose on American universities and how they affect competition between institutions and research activities. Feller notes that the impact of the adverse funding climate has been variable and that some institutions (or groups of institutions) have been more affected than others. He also considers those trends in the context of the expansion of higher education and geographical diversification of the research base that took place over the last quarter of the twentieth century. In particular, he reflects on the conflict between research effectiveness and geographical and institutional equity and discusses various scenarios in which research potential increasingly becomes concentrated in a small number of institutions or regions.

Breslauer focuses instead on revenue diversification and the decline in public funding for research universities. He points out that the efforts of many institutions to compensate that decline through other sources may be facing a threshold, besides being associated with variable levels of discretion that may affect research universities' capacity to sustain an autonomous, fruitful research agenda that is not driven by short-term financial concerns. This concern with market-biases in research is particularly enhanced by the fact that the growing reliance on private revenue among many American research universities has been followed by similar trends in the governance and decision-making processes of many public research universities, and this has affected the range their activities.

In recent decades European higher education has experienced in funding and governance several of the trends that have affected U.S. higher education (Amaral, Jones, & Karseth, 2002; Middlehurst & Teixeira, 2012; Shattock, 2008). Moreover, the growing integration of European higher education systems has enhanced the parallels with the American case. In this paper, therefore, we reflect on the growing marketization of funding and governance mechanisms and how this has affected the European higher education landscape, comparing the impact of marketization in Europe with some of the effects on the American system discussed by Fellner and Breslauer. In the section "Marketization in European Higher Education" we present briefly the main trends toward greater marketization and privatization in European universities. Then we focus on the impact of marketization and privatization on funding, with particular emphasis on inter-institutional competition for public and non-public funds. In the section "Integration and Competition in European Higher Education" we reflect on the extent to which the trend to greater European integration has enhanced competition between institutions and increased revenue diversification and thence how competition and revenue diversification might affect institutional stratification and the geographical distribution of resources in European higher education. We end this paper by comparing possible future scenarios for European higher education with those presented by our American colleagues.

MARKETIZATION IN EUROPEAN HIGHER EDUCATION

Over the last couple of decades European higher education has faced a wave of significant change that threatens several of the features that have characterized it in modern times. As in other public sector domains, there has been increasing debate about the public mission, funding, and provision of higher education. This debate takes places in the context of higher education systems that have been dominantly public funding for most of the last century. At the same time political discourse on higher education has shifted noticeably toward market regulation and to issues such as competition, privatization, and efficiency (Regini, 2011; Teixeira, Jongbloed, Dill, & Amaral, 2004). The U.S. higher education system has traditionally been more lightly regulated than the European system when it comes to funding and other instruments. European higher education has traditionally felt the strong arm of the government, especially after successive waves of legislation bringing higher education within the remit of the state. Thus, throughout most of the twentieth century, particularly after the Second World War, a regulatory model dominated European higher education systems that some aptly termed "rational planning and control" (Neave & Van Vught, 1991).

Changes to the strong governmental regulation of European higher education began in the last two decades of the twentieth century; they were especially visible in Continental Europe where previous state dominance had been more complete. Thus, from the 1980s onward we have seen a wave of reforms to European higher education systems that has strengthened (in some cases one might almost say created or recreated) institutional autonomy.[1]

However, the move toward greater autonomy in European higher education came with strings attached, as it was linked with an insistence on universities becoming more response to external needs and to "the market." European governments wanted not only to make universities more autonomous and more flexible, but also to make them work more closely with economic and social actors and adapt to their demands and needs. Policy reforms in several parts of Europe have encouraged higher education institutions (HEIs) to adopt private sector-like rules and practices intended to deliver greater flexibility and efficiency (Morphew & Eckel, 2009). Public HEIs have been encouraged to behave as if they were private, quasi-commercial organizations and to change their governance and management structures in order to become more responsive to external demands (Huisman, 2009). These changes have been particular controversial and complex in Europe, since in the postwar period their prevailing attitude was that higher education should be part of the public sphere (Bache, 2006).[2]

In modern times European higher education has been dominated by public provision and government regulation; however, recent developments have changed this, and over the last two decades — as in many other parts of the world (Altbach & Levy, 2005) — private institutions have begun to play a greater role in many European systems (Teixeira, 2009). The collapse of the communist regimes at the end of the twentieth century paved the way for private higher education to become a particularly significant component of the higher education systems in many Central and Eastern European countries (Wells, Sadlak, & Vlăsceanu, 2007). To this growth of private higher education in Central and Easter Europe should be added those private sectors that have developed in recent years in Southern European countries such as Portugal, Spain, France, and Italy.[3]

The increasing marketization of European higher education is also associated with a change in perceptions of the purposes and nature of public institutions. As in North America, European societies and governments have altered their views about the social role of higher education, with significant implications for the identity of universities and the organization of the whole sector (Amaral et al., 2002; Teixeira et al., 2004). Educational decisions have increasingly been motivated by economic factors and educational institutions were more and more seen as commercial institutions (Bok, 2003). Moreover, the social contribution of educational and scientific organizations has increasingly been measured against their economic relevance (Weisbrod, Pallou, & Asch, 2008). Hence, policy-makers and institutional managers have been exploring ways of using economic incentives to influence behavior at individual and institutional level, in accordance with the general trend to apply ideas derived from economics and management to higher education and research (Amaral et al., 2002; Middlehurst & Teixeira, 2012).

The changes in the political perspective on higher education and how the sector should manage its resources have had a significant impact on the academic reward structure and the incentives used to attract and retain highly qualified staff in many European systems (Huisman, de Weert, & Bartelse, 2002). One of the main effects of marketization has been the increasing differentiation of academic positions. There are indications that Europe is starting to reflect a trend observed for some time in North America, more specifically there is evidence that the proportion of temporary and un-tenured positions is increasing (Ehrenberg, 2002b). This may foreshadow increasing segmentation of teaching and research labor markets, in line with trends in the labor market at large.

As in other areas of social and public policy, the introduction of market regulation was backed by rhetoric about the potential benefits. Markets have been presented as a powerful mechanism for enhancing social choice that, through the rational, utility-maximizing behavior of individuals would – as if an invisible hand were at work – distribute goods in such a way that, when an optimal situation would be reached, no-one could be better off without making anyone else worse off (Wolf, 1993). Marketization has resulted in greater competition for funding, students, and staff, and the development of private higher education in several parts of Europe (Regini, 2011; Wells et al., 2007).

However, this trend toward greater marketization was not easily accepted; there has been strong political, social, and cultural resistance. Moreover, economic analysis also notes that some markets do not always produce the optimal outcome from a society's point of view, which raises a question about the self-regulating capacity of markets, that is, their ability to regulate supply and demand. This situation is a case of *market failure*. The main market failures, identified have been in regard to public goods, the existence of externalities (spillovers), information asymmetry and monopoly power. All except the first example are potentially relevant to higher education (Johnes, 1993).

Hence, in recent years we have seen growing debate about the implications and the effects of the increasing market regulation of higher education (Regini, 2011; Teixeira & Dill, 2011). The social benefits associated with higher education are an important issue, as self-interested individuals may not take into account the fact that their decision about investment in higher education will affect the well-being of others. The same holds for firms investing in research or development. In both cases reliance on market regulation may increase the risk, from society's point of view, of underinvestment in higher education and research. There are also important information-related problems in the higher education sector when it comes to assessing the performance (including the quality) of academics and students (Dill & Soo, 2004). The effects of imperfect information are also visible in the student loans market, where there is an asymmetry in the information available to students taking up loans and the banks (or government agencies) that supply the loans (Callender, 2006). Finally, there is the case of market failures associated with market power. Whilst there are unlikely to be natural monopolies in higher education (i.e., very large economies of scale that would facilitate the concentration of supply in the hands of a very small number of providers), market power may be concentrated in the hands of a selected number of providers, causing them to behave as a cartel and to erect barriers to entry to deter potential new providers. It is also possible that some universities would be at an advantage when it comes to attracting resources (pecuniary or other), thereby distorting the competition. This seems to be the case with respect to some expensive activities such as research, but we will come back to this issue in the later sections of this paper.

This growing reliance of many governments on market regulation has led, especially in Europe, to what have been labeled publicly funded "quasi-markets" (Le Grand, 2006). In a *quasi-market* situation decisions about supply and demand are reached using market-like mechanisms, but only some of the elements of a market are introduced, often gradually. Government regulation and government funding remain important tools for influencing supply and demand, but other market mechanisms, such as competition, user charges, and freedom of choice, are gradually introduced. Many have argued that applying market forces to higher education is inappropriate because higher education is a "public good." Moreover, in many − mainly European − countries this argument is used to condemn both private provision of higher education and the requirement for students and their families to contribute directly to the cost of higher education. Many of these critics, however, use the term "public good" synonymously with "public benefits" and seem to assume that the latter benefits must be publicly provided; however, this way of defining "public good" conflicts with the economic definition. In economics a pure public good is a good or service that will not be provided by the market because of the inability of private providers to exclude those who do not pay for it (Barr, 2004). Education can be provided by the private sector, although not necessarily in the quantity or form demanded by society. Moreover, the argument is more complex when we consider research, as research activities often have a strong public dimension and require a significant financial contribution from public sources. It is therefore common to refer to higher education as a "merit good" rather than a strictly public good.

After many decades of heavy government intervention, in recent years European higher education has moved toward a mixed model of regulation in which market mechanisms play a greater role. This process, which has been implemented to varying degrees in different European higher education systems, is still controversial. The example of higher education on the other side of the Atlantic has provided important evidence for and against the move to a mixed regulatory model, because U.S. higher education has been dealing with the multiple demands of the state and the market for a longer period. Thus, the concerns expressed by Breslauer and Feller should prompt deeper reflection about the impact that further marketization may have on European higher education. As Breslauer and Feller outline in their papers, the key elements in marketization have been funding mechanisms and funding sources, so we now turn our attention to those matters.

COMPETITION FOR FUNDING AND REVENUE DIVERSIFICATION IN EUROPEAN HIGHER EDUCATION SYSTEMS

The growing marketization of higher education has meant that today European HEIs face a much more demanding and complex financial situation (Barr & Crawford, 2005). Arguably the area in which market mechanisms have played the largest role in Europe is that of funding mechanisms and funding sources (Teixeira, 2009) and so in this section we discuss some of the major trends in higher education funding, outlining how they have been shaped by growing application of market principles, namely greater institutional competition, more emphasis on certain types of efficiency and the increasing importance of non-public sources of funding. We also reflect on some of the major effects of those funding trends, notably their contribution to the growing financial differentiation of European HEIs.

Following several decades of expansion, European societies and governments are currently more reluctant to put additional public resources into the higher education system for a variety of reasons not dissimilar to those identified by our American colleagues, for example, the rising cost of higher education (Archibald & Feldman, 2010), financial austerity (Johnstone & Marcucci, 2010) and changes to the orthodox view of the role of the state and the nature of public services (Pollitt & Bouckaert, 2011). The increasing emphasis on efficiency has had a clear impact on the sources and mechanisms of funding of higher education in Europe. The system for allocation of funding now specifies output criteria, and performance-based funding and contract funding are becoming more popular (Herbst, 2006). The adoption of these funding models has been associated with the creation of so-called funding formulae. Although in many countries an institution's funding is still determined mainly by the number of students and by the kind of courses they are following there is an increasing willingness to adopt an outcome-oriented approach to allocation of funding based on criteria such as number of graduates and their success in entering the job market.

This tendency is also reflected in the development of another funding model that is essentially based on outputs, namely performance-based funding. Under this model governments specify performance objectives and funds are distributed on the basis of how effective institutions are at meeting these objectives. The majority of European countries have adopted some sort of performance-based mechanism for allocating higher education funding, and these mechanisms have been used to disguise reductions in overall funding (Orr, Jaeger, & Schwarzenberger, 2007). Because funds are distributed in a differentiated mode it is more difficult for HEIs to react collectively. This differentiation tends to penalize the weaker institutions in the system; in the context of higher education the penalty is not forced exit from the system (as it would be in a pure market system) but deterioration in the institution's financial position and status and in the quality of its activities.

This trend toward greater inter-institutional competition for funding is also reflected in the revenue structure of many HEIs, where there is grow-ing emphasis on revenue diversification (Teixeira & Koryakina, 2010). Tuition fees have been a major source of revenue in some European coun-tries, although the amount charged varies considerably across Europe and fees are still lower than in public HEIs in the United States (let alone pri-vate HEIs). The vast majority of European countries now charge tuition fees for public HEIs, even the traditionally free Nordic higher education systems have started experimenting with the concept by charging non-EU students tuition fees (Denmark, Sweden, and Finland had a pilot project over the 2010−2014 period for some Masters degrees). The fees paid by international students are an increasingly important revenue, especially in countries that charge foreign students higher tuition fees.

Philanthropy is another potential source of funding that has started to figure in the calculations of many European HEIs. There is a long history of philanthropic support for U.S. higher education and in recent years European countries have also started to tap this source of support for higher education. This is one instance in which many European HEIs are encouraged to make emulating American success a strategic priority. Thus, we have increasingly seen the spread of American-style endowment campaigns. In a more general way, an increasing number of universities have turned toward the segment of the private sector personified by their alumni. Many HEIs have set up development offices and created extended alumni databases, although very few come close to the average American university in the organizational effectiveness or capacity to fundraise from alumni.

The trend toward revenue diversification has been documented in several recent studies (see Estermann & Pruvot, 2011; Teixeira & Koryakina, 2010). Taken together these studies confirm that revenue diversification is becoming an institutional priority across the entirety of the European higher education landscape. Most institutions still obtain most of their income from public funds, but in proportional terms public funding has declined to around 2/3 of the overall budget in a large number of countries. The second main source of funding is student contributions, followed by funding streams such as contracts with the business sector, philanthropic donations, international funding, and commercialization of research and teaching services. Although the latter sources continue to play a minor role, several studies have confirmed that most European HEIs are presently managing a number of funding sources.[4]

A similar trend toward diversification is observable in the case of research funding (Geuna, 2001; Lepori, Benninghoff, Jongbloed, & Salerno, 2007). National governments are still by far the largest source of funding although there is considerable variation among European countries. The evidence also seems to introduce some doubts about the reality dominated by a discourse of public financial retrenchment, since most institutions included in these studies presented a picture of stability regarding the contribution of governmental funds. There is much greater institutional and national diversity in the contribution made by other sources, such as national contracts, business and private research contracts and European and international funds, although the overall trend seems to be toward an increase in non-public funding.

Non-governmental funding sources still represent a small proportion of total funding and in several systems there are no indications that they are becoming more significant. Nonetheless, an analysis of grants and contracts with external partners reveals that these tend to be concentrated in a few institutions to a much greater extent than government funding. A similar situation prevails with respect to private contracts; these appear to be becoming a significant source of income for a minority of institutions although the evidence on this is still very limited. This apparent paradox illustrates two important issues. On the one hand, the importance of those additional revenues may be understood not so much in absolute value, but *vis-à-vis* their relative importance. The marginal contribution these less traditional sources make to HEIs' budgets may nevertheless justify the effort required to secure them, especially in systems where public funding is scarce or comes with increasing restrictions attached. There is, however, much more uncertainty surrounding the likelihood of securing such revenue and success in doing so seems to be unevenly distributed.

These recent trends in funding have caused considerable controversy. Firstly, there are concerns that these emerging funding structures will make the income of HEIs more unstable. There are related concerns about the impact that the greater instability in alternative types of research funding may have on the quantity, quality, and regularity of research output. Secondly, there are concerns about the extent to which the emerging model of funding will foster institutional inequalities. Not all HEIs will be equally successful in their attempt to diversify their income streams and attract non-public funding and institutional factors will play a role in this (see Ali, Partha, & Olejniczak, 2010; Geuna, 2001). Overall, the limited evidence available suggests that the current trends will lead to an increased concentration of resources and exacerbate or reinforce effects already emerging in other dimensions of academic production. Finally, there is concern that the pressure to secure funding — often short-term — from a multitude of small sources could skew institutional activities toward short-term results, eroding the commitment to basic, long-term — and more risky — educational and research activities (Middlehurst & Teixeira, 2012; Teixeira & Koryakina, 2010).

INTEGRATION AND COMPETITION IN EUROPEAN HIGHER EDUCATION

Several of the changes noted in the previous section are also being exacerbated by important developments at European level. Important recent developments such as the Sorbonne Declaration (1998) and Bologna Declaration (1999) paved the way for a series of reforms and contributed significantly to the emergence of European Higher Education and Research Areas (Amaral, Neave, Maassen, & Musselin, 2009). This trend toward growing integration across European higher education systems raises another interesting comparison with U.S. higher education. A couple of decades ago the comparison between European and American higher education would have been complicated by the specificity of factors affecting the former, but several decades of European integration have left their mark on the higher education landscape, notwithstanding the fact that this is a domain in which political and social attitudes have tended to be strongly influenced by national history and traditions.

After a couple of decades of marketization at national level, we now observe a growing willingness for greater integration at European level. The supra-national discourse on higher education is being shaped significantly by market forces and by a discourse that focuses on the advantages of competition, autonomy, and managerial approaches (see Aghion, Dewatripont, Hoxby, Mas-Colell, & Sapir, 2010; Ritzen, 2010). Competition and institutional autonomy are seen as important mechanisms for strengthening HEIs and enhancing their contribution to Europe's competitiveness and economic strength, often dominating other purposes in the process of integration in European higher education. With the emergence of a large European higher education area increasingly shaped by marketization it is important discuss to whether that will result in European higher education systems sharing some of the characteristics of the more competitive, market-oriented American higher education system.

It is particularly important to consider the effects on students of further integration within the European higher education area, not the least because one of the main objectives of the Bologna process was the promotion of greater student mobility within Europe. The U.S. experience is very relevant, as its system has witnessed the concentration of its higher education sector – especially the research-oriented sub-sector – in a smaller number of areas and sites. Using data on elite U.S. HEIs Cook and Frank (1993) analyzed trends in the distribution of the most highly qualified students and noticed that although the reputational hierarchy of colleges and universities has remained rather stable over most of the latter part of the twentieth century, in recent years reputation had become an increasingly important factor in the competition for the top students. Cook and Frank noted that a large and growing proportion of the country's top students is concentrated in a relatively small number of very highly ranked institutions. Given that over the same period there has also been a steep increase in the cost of attending an elite institution (Archibald & Feldman, 2010) this trend appears even more significant.

It should be noted that this concentration process has been intensified by the strong competition for students, especially among the best institutions. This has led to what some authors have called an "arms race" in U.S. higher education: affluence, elite institutions have competed fiercely in multiple arenas, including attraction of the best candidates at undergraduate and graduate level (Clotfelter, 1996; McPherson & Schapiro, 2006). This process was enhanced by an apparent rise in the importance attached by students and families to universities' ranking and "brand" when deciding to which institutions they should apply (Ehrenberg, 2002a). It will be interesting to see whether similar trends emerge in European higher education in the near future.

As we have discussed above, the pressure to diversify revenue is felt across the system; however, many HEIs are not in a position to attract alternative resources. Some insight into the factors at play can be obtained by considering the distribution of the generous research grants awarded by the European Research Council (ERC) to outstanding scholars at various stages of their careers. Competition for these grants is intense and the available data indicate that to date certain countries have been much more successful in obtaining these grants than others. According to the data referring to first years of these grants, the United Kingdom is clearly in the lead, followed by Germany and France. The size of the country or its higher education sector and research system do not seem to be critical; some smaller countries capture a significant proportion of these grants, notably the Netherlands, Switzerland, Belgium, and Israel. Some parts of Europe have been much less successful in the competition for these attractive grants. The 11 Central and Eastern European countries (Austria, Czech Republic, Slovakia, Slovenia, Hungary, Poland, Latvia, Lithuania, Estonia, Bulgaria, and Romania) have not been particularly successful in this respect. The South of Europe has also not performed very well, particularly if one takes into account that this region includes two large countries with many HEIs (Italy and Spain), plus two other smaller countries with less reputation for scientific excellence (Portugal and Greece). Even the five Northern European countries have shown less than impressive performance in this respect; together Sweden, Denmark, Norway, Finland, and Ireland hold less than 10% of these grants.

Although these ERC grants represent only a small portion of European research funding, they are quite significant for various reasons. The competition for them is intense and thus highlights the relative success of countries in the context of European competition. Moreover, the grants are awarded to individuals and were designed to give successful applicants considerable freedom to move between institutions and countries. This freedom at individual level has generated further competition among European institutions, because the grant holders can move to another country to take up their award or during the lifetime of the grant. The distribution and dynamics involved in this grant system thus highlight how growing institutional and national competition within Europe influences the allocation of research funding and provide some evidence on the movement of elite academic and research staff within Europe. If the ERC anticipates future scenarios, then we should expect a significant concentration of research funding and elite research staff in a small number of countries and of institutions.

The overall picture presented by major rankings in higher education corroborates the process of geographical and institutional concentration of resources and elite institutions. Ranking systems tend to be controversial, because they provide only a superficial picture of an institution and can over-simplify and over-homogenize (see Kehm & Stensaker, 2009). They have also been justly criticized for their bias toward research activities and elite institutions. However, these data are relevant to point out to a raising awareness about the institutional and national positions in a European and international context. In particular, ranking and league tables have made visible the growing competition for places in the most highly ranked institutions in Europe and elsewhere (see Altbach & Balán, 2004; Salmi, 2009).[5]

The overall picture with regard to the relative status and success of different European higher education systems and HEIs is that British institutions are prominent and two rather small higher education systems – those of the Netherlands and Switzerland – also perform strongly. Large countries like France and Germany perform less well in relative terms, especially at the highest level. When we look at groups of less preponderant countries, we see that Southern and Central-Eastern European higher education systems perform very poorly (totally absent from those high positions), whereas Northern European higher education systems do rather well. In terms of the ranking systems, the distribution of elite European research institutions is very uneven; moreover the ranking system appears to promote further polarization at national and supra-national level (Brown, Lauder, & Ashton, 2011).

CONCLUDING REMARKS

Several important trends, which have emerged in European higher education in recent decades, are not altogether dissimilar from those seen in U.S. higher education. The most significant of them is the shift from government to market regulation of higher education; this started earlier in the United States but has since extended to Europe. Until the 1970s the governments in many Western countries coordinated their higher education systems through rather centralized control systems; however, over the last quarter of the twentieth century there was a move toward less direct regulation and more market-based approaches in many countries. Thus, the focus of debate is now the identification of frameworks of institutional rules and incentives that produce welfare-maximizing competition among increasingly autonomous albeit – mainly – publicly subsidized academic institutions. This shift has been underpinned by rhetoric to the effect that competition delivers better outcomes in terms of the quality and quantity of education and research.

Discussion of the decline in public involvement in higher education systems has in recent years often centered on funding issues, particularly the mechanisms for allocating public funds and the revenue structure of public universities. These have been major themes on both sides of the Atlantic, although in Europe the impact of changes in funding patterns probably has more to do with its novelty and the resistance it has faced rather than the actual extent of the changes. Underpinning those trends has been not only a pragmatic financial motive, namely the need to manage resources and balance income and expenditure, but also the argument that financial mechanisms can be used to strengthen the relationship between HEIs and society and the responsiveness of the former to the latter. Although revenue diversification in Europe still falls short of the levels seen in most American universities there has been a marked change in the political climate; it remains to be seen whether this will be sufficient to bring European higher education significantly closer to the North American model.

As in the United States, the changes to funding mechanisms have brought significant inter- and intra-institutional competition. Institutions have come under increasing pressure to reassess and rationalize their priorities and the breadth of their educational and research portfolios. They have also been incentivized to reward individual members of staff and departments for demonstrating commitment to revenue diversification and responsiveness to economic and social needs. This environment creates tensions because not all institutions, departments, and individuals are able to respond in the same way to this kind of competitive pressure. At the institutional level, many European HEIs realize that they will not be able to compete effectively in all areas and thus prioritize certain research areas, often according to their visibility and competitive financial advantage. It is likely that this is prompting inter-institutional cooperation, as groups of HEIs seek to combine their resources and expertise to achieve critical mass, especially in the more expensive areas of research.

Moreover, the growing integration of European higher education systems has also enhanced its resemblance to the American system in certain respects. That process of European integration has helped to strengthen the structural change occurring in many European higher education systems and in European higher education as a whole, namely the move toward greater stratification and differentiation (Palfreyman & Tapper, 2009). Under the pressure of competition for resources and prestige, many systems seem to be evolving toward greater structural and functional differentiation and stratification (see Vaira, 2009). In many European systems this has resulted in attempts to concentrate resources in a small number of institutions, either by selective treatment or by encouraging mergers and the formation of institutional consortia that will be better placed to compete for top rankings.[6] European integration thus seems to be accompanied by a significant concentrating of resources and prestige, driven by European competition and national policies. This may bring European higher education closer to the stratified and differentiated model that our American colleagues have analyzed in their papers.[7]

Some of these trends are still in the early phase, so one needs to be careful when drawing conclusions. One caveats is that in the case of Europe we are still talking about 28 different national higher education systems and regulatory frameworks (further complicated in the case of federal or quasi-federal countries such as Germany and Spain) that may modulate integration processes and the trends seen at European level.[8] Moreover, there are several forces hindering further integration and there remains significant national variation in higher education (e.g., Teixeira, 2014), not the least in terms of the degree of stratification. There is considerable national variation in willingness to promote greater competition and stratification, and in the political and economic resources needed to do so. It is unlikely that systems which still reflect very important political and cultural traditions will converge to such an extent in the near future as to constitute a homogeneous bloc. Finally, political and economic trends are neither inexorable, nor permanent, as has been painfully illustrated with respect to other aspects of European integration in recent times.

Like their American counterparts, European HEIs feel the need to reflect on how the increasing competition may affect internal cohesion at the institutional, national, and supra-national levels (see, Geiger, 2011; Slaughter & Leslie, 1997). Although there remain important differences between higher education systems on the two sides of the Atlantic, the apparent similarity in recent trends should encourage comparative research and analysis into the challenges faced by higher education in Europe and in the United States and the changes occurring in both systems. In this paper, we have only scratched the surface of some of the most important trends, namely the increasing marketization of higher education, the increasing use of competition, and the impact of austerity. It would be valuable to continue the dialogue with colleagues across the pond about how these trends may influence future developments in higher education.

NOTES

1. The changes were slightly different in Britain where the state, although it played a significant role in the second half of the twentieth century, did not

dominate higher education in the same way as its Continental counterparts and there was a stronger tradition of institutional autonomy (see Becher & Kogan, 1992). Nevertheless, from the 1980s onward the growing influence of New Public Management has led to a more centralized a system, in a landscape where higher education institutions traditionally enjoyed greater institutional autonomy in funding, quality assessment, or access policies. Thus, although it has become increasingly marketized, the British system has also become much more tightly regulated by the state and institutions are much more publicly accountable (see, for instance, Kogan & Hanney, 2000; Williams, 2004).

2. For a complementary analysis of the effects of these changes at the institutional level, see the paper by Otto Hüther and Georg Krücken in this volume.

3. In these countries the private sector includes both for-profit and not-for-profit HEIs, though the boundary between the two groups may be less pronounced than anticipated by regulators and policy-makers (see, among others, Slantcheva & Levy, 2007; Teixeira, Rocha, Biscaia, & Cardoso, 2014a, 2014b).

4. This poses a considerable challenge as the studies indicate that although the additional revenue is often fairly small, the effort required to secure it is non-trivial. This simply emphasizes that even revenue streams that are small in absolute terms play a critical, if minor, role in the budgets of cash-strapped HEIs.

5. On the effects of rankings see Kehm and Stensaker (2009). Catherine Paradeise and Ghislaine Filliatreau's paper in this volume also discusses how the development of rankings and metrics has fostered the extension of a whole industry.

6. For discussion of the relevance of mergers in current trends in European higher education see also the paper in this volume by Julien Barrier and Christine Musselin.

7. This trend toward stratification is not altogether incompatible with the trend to stronger institutional isomorphism presented in the paper by Hüther and Krücken in this volume. It is possible to have a system that is more stratified in terms of the allocation of academic and financial resources and the distribution of prestige, alongside strong institutional isomorphism with respect to several organizational dimensions. In this scenario, weaker institutions become second or third rate imitations of more prestigious ones and cater to demand that is unfulfilled by them.

8. A good illustration may be the variation in how the "Bologna process'" has been implemented at national level and the multiple ways in which it has been influenced by national issues and policy agendas (see Amaral et al., 2009).

ACKNOWLEDGMENT

This research has been funded by FCT — Foundation for Science and Technology (Portugal) through Projects PEST-OE/CED/UI0757/2013 and UID/CED/00757/2013.

REFERENCES

Aghion, P., Dewatripont, M., Hoxby, C., Mas-Colell, A., & Sapir, A. (2010). The governance and performance of universities: Evidence from Europe and the US. *Economic Policy*, *25*, 7−59.

Ali, M. M., Partha, B., & Olejniczak, A. J. (2010). The effects of scholarly productivity and institutional characteristics on the distribution of federal research grants. *Journal of Higher Education*, *81*, 164−178.

Altbach, P., & Balán, J. (2004). *World class worldwide: Transforming research universities in Asia and Latin America*. Baltimore, MD: The John Hopkins University Press.

Altbach, P., & Levy, D. (Eds.). (2005). *Private higher education: A global revolution*. Rotterdam: Sense Publishers.

Amaral, A., Jones, G., & Karseth, B. (Eds.). (2002). *Governing higher education: National perspectives on institutional governance* (Vol. 2). London: Kluwer Academic Publishers.

Amaral, A., Neave, G., Maassen, P., & Musselin, C. (2009). *European integration and governance of higher education and research*. Dordrecht: Springer.

Archibald, R. B., & Feldman, D. H. (2010). *Why does college cost so much?* New York, NY: Oxford University Press.

Bache, I. (2006). The Europeanization of higher education: Markets, politics or learning? *Journal of Common Market Studies*, *44*, 231−248.

Barr, N. (2004). *Economics of the welfare state* (4th ed.). Oxford: Oxford University Press.

Barr, N., & Crawford, I. (2005). *Financing higher education − Answers from the UK*. Abingdon: Routledge.

Becher, T., & Kogan, M. (1992). *Process and structure in higher education*. London: Routledge.

Bok, D. (2003). *Universities in the market place. The commercialization of higher education*. Princeton, NJ: Princeton University Press.

Brown, P., Lauder, H., & Ashton, D. (2011). *The global auction − The broken promises of education, jobs, and incomes*. Oxford: Oxford University Press.

Callender, C. (2006). Access to higher education in Britain: The impact of tuition fees and financial assistance. In P. Teixeira, D. B. Johnstone, M. J. Rosa, & J. J. Vossensteyn (Eds.), A fairer deal? Cost-sharing and accessibility in Western higher education. Dordrecht: Springer-Kluwer.

Clotfelter, C. (1996). *Buying the best − Cost escalation in higher education*. Princeton, NJ: Princeton University Press.

Cook, P. J., & Frank, R. H. (1993). The growing concentration of top students in elite higher education. In C. Clotfelter & M. Rotschild (Eds.), *Studies of supply and demand in higher education* (pp. 121−140). Chicago, IL: Chicago University Press and NBER.

Dill, D. D., & Soo, M. (2004). Transparency and quality in higher education markets. In P. Teixeira, B. Jongbloed, D. Dill, & A. Amaral (Eds.), *Markets in higher education. Rhetoric or reality?* (pp. 61−86). London: Kluwer Academic Publishers.

Ehrenberg, R. (2002a). *Tuition rising − Why college costs so much*. Cambridge, MA: Harvard University Press.

Ehrenberg, R. (2002b). Studying ourselves: The academic labor market. *Journal of Labor Economics*, *21*(2), 267−287.

Estermann, T., & Pruvot, E. (2011). *Financially sustainable universities II − European universities diversifying income streams*. Brussels: European University Association.

Geuna, A. (2001). The changing rationale for European university research funding: Are there negative unintended consequences? *Journal of Economic Issues, 35,* 607–632.

Herbst, M. (2006). *Performance based funding.* Dordrecht: Springer.

Huisman, J. (Ed.). (2009). *International perspectives on the governance of higher education.* London: Routledge.

Huisman, J., de Weert, E., & Bartelse, J. (2002). Academic careers from a European perspective: The declining desirability of the faculty position. *The Journal of Higher Education, 73*(1), 141–160.

Johnes, G. (1993). *The economics of education.* London: MacMillan Press.

Johnstone, B., & Marcucci, P. (2010). *Financing higher education worldwide: Who pays? Who should pay?* Baltimore, MD: The John Hopkins University Press.

Kehm, B., & Stensaker, B. (Eds.). (2009). *University rankings, diversity, and the new landscape of higher education.* Rotterdam: Sense Publishers.

Kogan, M., & Hanney, S. (2000). *Reforming higher education.* London: Jessica Kingsley.

Le Grand, J. (2006). *Motivation, agency, and public policy: Of knights and knaves, pawns and queens.* Oxford: Oxford University Press.

Lepori, B., Benninghoff, M., Jongbloed, B., & Salerno, C. (2007). Changing models and patterns of higher education funding: Some empirical evidence. In A. Bonaccorsi & C. Daraio (Eds.), *Universities and strategic knowledge creation* (pp. 85–111). Cheltenham: Edward Elgar.

McPherson, M., & Schapiro, M. (2006). US higher education finance. In E. Hanushek & F. Welch (Eds.), *Handbook of the economics of education* (Vol. 2, pp. 1403–1434). North-Holland: Elsevier.

Middlehurst, R., & Teixeira, P. (2012). Governance within the EHEA: Dynamic trends, common challenges, and national particularities. In P. Scott, A. Curaj, L. Vlasceanu, & L. Wilson (Eds.), *European higher education at the crossroads: Between the Bologna process and national reforms* (Vol. 2, 527–551). Berlin: Springer.

Morphew, C., & Eckel, P. (Eds.). (2009). *Privatizing the public university – Perspectives from across the academy.* Baltimore, MD: John Hopkins Press.

Neave, G., & Van Vught, F. (Eds.). (1991). *Prometheus bound: The changing relationship between government and higher education in Western Europe.* London: Pergamon Press.

Orr, D., Jaeger, M., & Schwarzenberger, A. (2007). Performance-based funding as an instrument of competition in German higher education. *Journal of Higher Education Policy and Management, 29*(1), 3–23.

Palfreyman, D., & Tapper, T. (Eds.). (2009). *Structuring Mass higher education: The role of elite institutions.* New York, NY: Routledge.

Pollitt, C., & Bouckaert, G. (2011). *Public management reform.* Oxford: Oxford University Press.

Regini, M. (2011). *European universities and the challenge of the market: A comparative analysis.* Aldershot: Edward Elgar.

Ritzen, J. (2010). *A chance for universities in Europe.* Amsterdam: Amsterdam University Press.

Salmi, J. (2009). *The challenge of establishing world-class universities.* Washington, DC: World Bank.

Shattock, M. (Ed.). (2008). *Entrepreneurialism in universities and the knowledge economy: Diversification and organizational change in European higher education.* Oxford: Oxford University Press.

Slantcheva, S., & Levy, D. (Eds.). (2007). *Private higher education in post-communist Europe − In search for legitimacy*. New York, NY: Palgrave/MacMillan.

Slaughter, S., & Leslie, L. (1997). *Academic capitalism*. Baltimore, MD: The Johns Hopkins University Press.

Teixeira, P. (2009). Economic imperialism and the Ivory tower: Economic issues and policy challenges in the funding of higher education in the EHEA (2010−2020). In J. Huisman, B. Stensaker, & B. M. Kehm (Eds.), *The European higher education area: Perspectives on a moving target* (pp. 43−60). Rotterdam: Sense Publishers.

Teixeira, P. (2014). Market integration in European higher education: Reflecting about drivers and barriers. *Journal of the European Higher Education Area, 4*, 1−14.

Teixeira, P., & Dill, D. (Eds.). (2011). *Public vices, private virtues − Assessing the effects of marketization in higher education*. Rotterdam: Sense Publishers.

Teixeira, P., Jongbloed, B., Dill, D., & Amaral, A. (Eds.). (2004). *Markets in higher education. Rhetoric or reality?* London: Kluwer Academic Publishers.

Teixeira, P., & Koryakina, T. (2010). Funding diversification in the EHEA − Patterns, challenges and risks. In *Handbook on leadership and governance in higher education*. Berlin: RAABE Academic Publishers.

Teixeira, P., Rocha, V., Biscaia, R., & Cardoso, M. F. (2014a). Public and private higher education in Europe: Competition vs. complementarity. In A. Bonaccorsi (Ed.), *Knowledge, diversity and performance in European higher education − A changing landscape*. Cheltenham: Edward Elgar.

Teixeira, P., Rocha, V., Biscaia, R., & Cardoso, M. F. (2014b). Policy changes, marketization trends and spatial dispersion in European higher education: Comparing public and private sectors. *Cambridge Journal of Regions, Economy and Society*. doi:10.1093/cjres/rst027

Vaira, M. (2009). Towards unified and stratified systems of higher education? Systems convergence and organizational stratified differentiation in Europe. In B. Khem & B. Stensaker (Eds.), *University rankings, diversity, and the new landscape of higher education*. Rotterdam: Sense Publisher.

Weisbrod, B., Pallou, J., & Asch, E. (2008). *Mission and money − Understanding the university*. Cambridge: Cambridge University Press.

Wells, P. J., Sadlak, J., & Vlăsceanu, L. (Eds.). (2007). *The rising role and relevance of private higher education in Europe*. Bucharest: UNESCO − CEPES.

Williams, G. (2004). The higher education market in the United Kingdom. In P. Teixeira, B. Jongbloed, D. Dill, & A. Amaral (Eds.), Markets in higher education. Rhetoric or reality? London: Kluwer Academic Publishers.

Wolf, C. (1993). *Markets or governments: Choosing between imperfect alternatives*. Cambridge, MA: MIT Press.

ABOUT THE AUTHORS

Mikaila Mariel Lemonik Arthur is Associate Professor of Sociology at Rhode Island College. She holds a BA from Mount Holyoke College and a PhD from New York University. She is the author of *Student Activism and Curricular Change in Higher Education* (Ashgate, 2011) and is currently working on a project about educational outcomes in the comprehensive college as well as several projects related to social science pedagogy.

Julien Barrier is Assistant Professor of Sociology at Ecole Normale Supérieure de Lyon and the French Institute of Education. He is a member of "Triangle," a multidisciplinary research center affiliated with CNRS. His research focuses on academic work, university governance, and university—industry relations.

Sondra N. Barringer is Postdoctoral Research and Teaching Associate at the Institute of Higher Education at the University of Georgia. She received her Ph.D. in Sociology from the University of Arizona. Her research looks at the ties and dependencies between and within higher education organizations (HEOs) and how changes in these affect college and university behaviors. Her current projects use organizational and nonprofit theory to understand the effect of stakeholder influence on HEO financial behaviors; the establishment and consequences of foundations, endowments, and other nonprofits on the HEOs they are affiliated with; and the precursors and consequences of university investments in interdisciplinary research.

Elizabeth Popp Berman is Associate Professor of Sociology at the University at Albany, SUNY. Her book *Creating the Market University: How Academic Science Became an Economic Engine* was published by Princeton University Press in 2012, and a second, *Thinking Like an Economist: How Economics Became the Language of U.S. Public Policy*, is under contract. Her research interests include organizational, economic, and political sociology, and the sociology of knowledge.

Manuelito Biag is Senior Researcher at the John W. Gardner Center for Youth and their Communities at the Graduate School of Education at

Stanford University. His research interests include postsecondary education, education policy, and urban school reform.

Amy Binder is Professor of Sociology at the University of California, San Diego. In 2014–2015, she served as Chair of the American Sociological Association's section on the Sociology of Education, and is a deputy editor of the leading journal *Sociology of Education*. She is the author of multiple articles and two books, including *Becoming Right: How Campuses Shape Young Conservatives* (2013) with Kate Wood. Her research centers on the intersection of small group cultures and organizational structures in education institutions and other organizations.

George W. Breslauer has been Professor of Political Science at the University of California, Berkeley, since 1971. He served as UC Berkeley's Dean of the Division of Social Sciences (1999–2006) and Executive Vice Chancellor and Provost (2006–2014) before retiring in 2014 into the *emeritus* status of professor of the graduate school. He has published several articles about the administration of higher education during his service as provost. His research specialty is Russian politics.

Daniel Davis is a PhD candidate in Sociology at the University of California, San Diego. He was previously a research fellow with CREATE (the Center for Research on Educational Equity, Assessment and Teaching Excellence) at UC San Diego and is the author of *The Adjunct Dilemma* (2016), a monograph exploring the labor conditions of adjunct faculty members at teaching institutions. His research interests are in the areas of higher education, student career formation, and organizational culture.

James A. Evans is Associate Professor of Sociology, Director of the Computational Social Science program, and Director of Knowledge Lab at the University of Chicago. His research focuses on the collective system of thinking and knowing, ranging from the distribution of attention and intuition, the origin of ideas and shared habits of reasoning to processes of agreement, accumulation of certainty, and the shape of human understanding. He is especially interested in innovation – how new ideas and practices emerge – and the role that social and technical institutions (e.g., scientific teams, the Internet, markets) play in collective cognition and discovery. His work has been published in *Science, Proceedings of the National Academy of Sciences, American Journal of Sociology, American Sociological Review, Social Studies of Science,* and many other outlets.

Irwin Feller is Emeritus Professor of Economics at The Pennsylvania State University, and Visiting Scientist, American Association for the Advancement of Science. He has published extensively on the organization and assessment of government research and technology programs, the economics of research and development, the performance of research-intensive universities, and evaluation methodology. He has a BBA in economics from the City University of New York and a PhD in economics from the University of Minnesota.

Ghislaine Filliatreau, Director of Research at Inserm, is Director of the *Observatoire des Sciences et des Techniques* of French HCERES. The OST is dedicated to the conception and delivery of analyses for Higher Education and Research policies, based on quantitative indicators. As a practitioner, she is involved in the U-Multirank project and in the development of a French multidimensional ranking, CERES. She also deals with studies about indicators, their methodological limits and use in policy-making. See for instance Graphical comparison of world university rankings. *Higher Education Evaluation and Development, 8*(1), 1−14 (2014); New perspectives and challenges for the design and production of S&T indicators. *Research Evaluation, 17*(1), 33−44 (2008); and *Big is (made) beautiful: some comments about the Shanghai ranking of world universities.* In The world-class university and ranking: Aiming beyond status. UNESCO-CEPES and Shanghai Jiao Tong University, pp. 141−160 (2008).

Joseph C. Hermanowicz is Professor of Sociology and Adjunct Professor in the Institute of Higher Education at the University of Georgia. His work, covering students, faculty, and institutions, has sought to develop a sociology of higher education. He is the author of *Lives in Science: How Institutions Affect Academic Careers* (Chicago, 2009), *The Stars Are Not Enough: Scientists—Their Passions and Professions* (Chicago, 1998), *College Attrition at American Research Universities: Comparative Case Studies* (Agathon, 2003), and editor of *The American Academic Profession: Transformation in Contemporary Higher Education* (Johns Hopkins, 2011).

Otto Hüther is a postdoctoral Research Assistant for Sociology at the Department for Social Sciences at the University of Kassel (Germany). He is also a member of INCHER-Kassel, the International Centre for Higher Education Research at the University of Kassel. His main research interests include higher education research, governance studies, and organizational studies.

Daniel Lee Kleinman is Associate Dean in the Graduate School at the University of Wisconsin-Madison, where he is also a Professor in the Department of Community and Environmental Sociology. He is the inaugural editor of *Engaging Science, Technology, and Society*, the open access journal of the Society for the Social Studies of Science. His book, *Vanishing Bees: The Science and the Politics*, with Sainath Suryanarayanan, will be published by Rutgers University Press.

Georg Krücken is Professor of Higher Education Research and Director of INCHER-Kassel, the International Centre for Higher Education Research, both at the University of Kassel (Germany). He received his Ph.D. in sociology from Bielefeld University in 1996. From 2006 to 2011 he was a full professor at the German University of Administrative Sciences. From 1999 to 2001 and in 2011 he was a visiting scholar at Stanford University (Department of Sociology and School of Education). He taught as a guest professor at the Institute for Science Studies, University of Vienna, and at the Centre de Sociologie des Organisations, Sciences Po, Paris. His research interests include higher education research, science studies, organizational studies, and neo-institutional theory.

Séverine Louvel is Associate Professor in the Sociology of Science at Sciences Po Grenoble (PACTE). She is the Director of the Master's program 'Technology, Science and Decisions' (Sciences Po Grenoble and Grenoble Institute of Technology), and a researcher at the PACTE research lab (CNRS and University of Grenoble). Her most recent research explores the organizational and professional dimensions of the development of interdisciplinary nanomedicine in French and US universities.

Christine Musselin is the Vice President for Research at Sciences Po and a member of the Centre de Sociologie des Organisations, a Sciences Po and CNRS research unit. She leads comparative studies on university governance, public policies in higher education and research, and academic labour markets.

Robert Osley-Thomas is a PhD candidate in Sociology at the University of Wisconsin-Madison. His work sits in conversation with the sociology of science, the sociology of education, and the sociology of organizations. His current research assesses prominent discourses put forth by conservatives and liberals about the ability of universities to respond to market changes and to students' civic and economic needs. He has also studied the organization of industrial science.

Catherine Paradeise is Professor Emeritus at University Paris-Est and member of the LISIS (Interdisciplinary Research Group on Science, Innovation and Society). She has been involved in several expert groups and scientific boards dealing with indicators-issues in France and abroad. In the field of higher education, she recently published with Jean-Claude Thoenig *In Search of Academic Quality*, London, Palgrave-McMillan, 2015. She co-edited in 2009 *Global Science and National Sovereignty. Studies in Historical Sociology of Science*, New York, Routledge with G. Mallard and A. Peerbaye and *University Governance: Western European Comparative Perspectives*, Dordrecht, Springer, with E. Reale, I. Bleiklie and E. Ferlie.

W. Richard Scott is Professor of Sociology Emeritus at Stanford University with courtesy appointments in the Schools of Business, Education, Engineering, and Medicine. He is a long-term student of professional organizations and of the interaction between organizations and institutions.

Abby Stivers is a doctoral candidate in sociology at the University at Albany, SUNY. She is currently working on her dissertation, which explores the relationship between identity, meaning and various kinds of monetary debts.

Pedro Teixeira is Associate Professor in Economics and Vice Rector for Academic Affairs at the University of Porto and Director of CIPES – Centre of Research on Higher Education Policy. His research focuses on the economics of higher education and the history of economic thought. His work has been published in leading scientific journals, including: *Applied Economics; Applied Economic Letters; Cambridge Journal of Regions, Economy and Society; European Journal of Education; European Journal of History of Economic Thought; European Journal of Operational Research; Higher Education; Higher Education Policy; Higher Education Quarterly; History of Political Economy, History of Economic Ideas; Journal of Economic Methodology; Journal of Economic Issues; Minerva; Public Administration Review; Research Policy; and Studies in Higher Education*.

Craig Tutterow recently graduated with a PhD in Organizations and Markets from the University of Chicago, Booth School of Business. His dissertation research looks at the emergence of central intermediaries in financial markets and higher education, and models their system-level impact on the distribution of resources across and within firms as both sides of the market react to new information.